GEORGE III AND
WILLIAM PITT, 1783-1806

GEORGE III AND WILLIAM PITT, 1783–1806

A NEW INTERPRETATION BASED UPON A STUDY OF THEIR UNPUBLISHED CORRESPONDENCE

By

DONALD GROVE BARNES

OCTAGON BOOKS

A DIVISION OF FARRAR, STRAUS AND GIROUX

New York   1973

Reprinted 1965
by special arrangement with Stanford University Press

Second Octagon printing

OCTAGON BOOKS

A DIVISION OF FARRAR, STRAUS & GIROUX, INC.

19 Union Square West

New York, N. Y. 10003

Library of Congress Catalog Card Number: 65-25873
ISBN 0-374-90399-9

Printed in U.S.A. by
NOBLE OFFSET PRINTERS, INC.
New York, N.Y. 10003

To three mellow scholars in three universities:

ELBERT J. BENTON
EDWARD McMAHON
HENRY D. SHELDON

PREFACE

W HEN I first started my research on the relations of George III and William Pitt I had in mind a very different study from the one which is here presented. At that time I accepted the conventional thesis that George III had won a Pyrrhic victory over the Whigs from 1782 to 1784 but that the fruits of victory had passed to Pitt, who in his great ministry from 1783 to 1801 had established or re-established the principles of modern cabinet government on the ruins of the King's personal government. This point of view, expressed with varying degrees of emphasis, may be found in the quotations from the conclusions of some of the best-known writers on this period of English history which are brought together in the Appendix. The original purpose of my study then was to trace in detail and step by step how the control slipped away from George III and passed into the hands of the Prime Minister and the cabinet. The conclusions in textbooks and in biographies of George III and Charles James Fox published in 1936 and 1937 adhere in the main to those expounded in works of a half-century ago. This point of view is well expressed by the opening sentence in a review of Mr. C. E. Vulliamy's *Royal George: A Study of King George III,* published in May 1937: "The last attempt to foist a dictatorship on Britain has never been more forcefully presented than in Mr. Vulliamy's latest biography, which is as brilliantly written as it is historically convincing."

After a careful examination of thousands of letters and memoranda written by George III and Pitt, I came to the conclusion that the commonly accepted thesis of the loss of power by the King and of the rise of Pitt to the position of a modern prime minister and the headship of the Tory Party was in accord neither with the facts nor with the opinions then held by the ruler and his Minister. The evidence at my disposal seemed to establish beyond a reasonable doubt that the political principles of the King were the same in 1760, in 1783, and in 1806, and those of Pitt the same in 1783, in 1801, and in 1804. The most significant change, it appeared, came in 1785, when Pitt discovered that the position which he held did not insure him the influence in legislation that he had expected an all-powerful minister to have; he did not, however, change his fundamental principles as a result, but merely scaled down the field of his activities.

vii

The plan which I follow in this monograph is to give: first, a brief outline of the constitutional background and of the clash between George III and the Whigs from 1760 to 1783; second, character sketches of the King and Pitt in 1783 at the time their alliance was formed; and, third, a detailed account of the clashes between the two on constitutional principles and on the significant and crucial issues of the years 1783 to 1801 and 1804 to 1806. This third section is based primarily on an intensive study of the Pitt Manuscripts of the Chatham Papers in the Record Office in London and on the unpublished correspondence of George III for the years following 1783. Unfortunately for scholars working in this field, the six-volume edition of the *Correspondence of King George the Third* ends with December 1783, and it is possible to work on this all-important source after that date only by going over the originals in the Windsor Castle Library or by making use of the transcripts for the years 1783 to 1810 which are now in the W. L. Clements Library in Ann Arbor, Michigan. These transcripts contain the most important documents which Sir John Fortescue hoped to publish for these twenty-seven years.

In addition, I have, to the best of my knowledge, used all important printed sources and secondary works covering the reign of George III. I have not, however, attempted to write the entire history of Great Britain covering the years 1783 to 1806 from source material. I have drawn heavily on definitive works covering certain phases of these years and have then merely worked out the relation of the King and Pitt to these movements and events. Thus I have built on the firm foundation provided by such historians as Dr. J. H. Rose, Sir John Fortescue, Professor G. S. Veitch, and the authors of *The Cambridge History of British Foreign Policy*. With the exception, however, of Sir John Fortescue, who had access to the papers of George III from 1912 until his death, none of the standard histories and recent biographies appear to have taken into account the correspondence of the King after 1783. I feel that it is only by placing together the letters and answers written by George III and by Pitt, and by those with whom they corresponded, that a complete picture can be secured. In many instances before the discovery of the papers of George III in 1912 historians were forced to form a conclusion with only one side of the exchange of letters available.

No bibliography appears at the end of the volume, because, as I have explained, this work is based primarily on a careful study of largely unpublished letters and papers of George III and Pitt and because the works from which I have quoted or from which I have taken material that is summarized in the narrative will be found cited in the footnotes.

I fear that in view of the more or less justifiable antipathy displayed toward George III by Americans and by British Whigs and Liberals I may be accused of whitewashing or rehabilitating George III. I hope I have made clear in the course of my narrative that such is by no means the case; and that I believe his policies toward the American Colonies, the French Revolution, and Catholic Emancipation were fundamentally wrong and unsound. Such an interpretation, however, does not preclude the point of view that George had a well-formulated set of constitutional principles, to which he adhered consistently, and that he fought for these principles and for his policies with both sincerity and skill. During the last week of December 1937 at the meetings of the American Historical Association I had the good fortune to listen to many brilliant papers expounding various political, social, and economic theories for the years preceding 1789. My chief regret was that George III could not listen to them. His own principles and theories were so concrete and fixed that I fear he would have failed to appreciate the brilliance of some of these twentieth-century cobweb-like creations. Paraphrasing two quotations from him in my narrative, probably he would have said either: "None of your American metaphysics"; or, "You would think those gentlemen could compress their thoughts into a smaller space." The reading of thousands of his letters and memoranda has convinced me that he was suspicious of metaphysics and that he was capable of compressing his own principles and theories.

Since Pitt is as popular with the great mass of historians, past and present, as George III is unpopular, I am liable to be charged not with whitewashing but with blackening him. I have the greatest admiration for Pitt as an orator, as a "House of Commons man," and as a finance minister; but I have no admiration at all for him as a war minister. Also, I feel that his constitutional principles did not have the flexibility of those of either George III or the Rockingham-Portland Whigs, but, like those of his father, the great Chatham, were determined too much by his own personality and outstanding ability to serve as a model for other statesmen under a constitutional monarchy.

I am heavily indebted to six persons for inspiration and ideas gained from reading their works, although of this group I have met only Professor L. B. Namier personally. In reading Lord Passfield's and Mrs. Beatrice Webb's monumental *English Local Government,* I first appreciated that many of the principles which they laid down for the local government in eighteenth-century England were equally applicable to the national government. My debt to Sir John Fortescue and to Dr. J. H. Rose will be evident to anyone who reads the narrative. It was from Professor L. B. Namier's three volumes from 1754 to 1763 and from personal conversations with him that I gained my knowledge of the structure of the British government at the beginning of the reign of George III which I used as a basis of comparison with the twenty-three years from 1783 to 1806. Also I found Mr. C. S. Emden's *The People and the Constitution* most stimulating.

I wish to express my appreciation to certain publishers and their authors, as indicated in the footnotes, for their courtesy in permitting me to quote in the narrative and in the Appendix: to Cambridge University Press; Oxford University Press; G. Bell & Sons, Ltd.; Constable and Company, Ltd.; Geoffrey Bles, Ltd.; William Blackwood & Sons, Ltd.; J. W. Arrowsmith, Ltd.; Jonathan Cape; Hodder & Stoughton, Ltd.; Duckworth & Co.; and Herbert Jenkins, Ltd., all of London, England; to Manchester University Press, Manchester, England; to The Macmillan Company, The Vanguard Press, Henry Holt and Company, Harper and Brothers, D. Appleton-Century Company, and Harcourt, Brace and Company, all of New York, N.Y.; to Houghton Mifflin Company and to Ginn and Company, of Boston, Mass.; to The Johns Hopkins Press, Baltimore, Md.; and to The Bobbs-Merrill Company, Indianapolis, Ind.

I have received financial assistance from several sources. The John Simon Guggenheim Memorial Foundation, which awarded me a fellowship in 1928–29 to gather material for a life of Henry Pelham, after I had fulfilled the eleven months' requirement on the Pelham project gave me permission to devote several weeks to an examination of the Pitt Manuscripts and to the unpublished correspondence of George III. The Research Committee of the University of Oregon generously granted me money to have copied important letters and documents in the British Museum and the Public Record Office. The Social Science Research Council gave me a grant-in-aid which made it possible for me to devote the summer of 1932 to the Transcripts of the Corre-

spondence of George III in the W. L. Clements Library at Ann
Arbor, Michigan. This grant not only saved me a trip to London
but gave me an opportunity of becoming familiar with that para-
dise for research scholars, the W. L. Clements Library. I am
indebted to Mr. Randolph G. Adams and his staff for a most
profitable and pleasant sojourn.

My colleagues at Western Reserve University were most helpful in the final stages: Professor Finley M. K. Foster read and
criticized all of the manuscript except the two final chapters and
Professor John Hall Stewart the entire manuscript. Lastly my
wife generously spent an enormous amount of time in criticizing
the manuscript and checking the footnotes.

DONALD GROVE BARNES

WESTERN RESERVE UNIVERSITY
February 1, 1938

POSTSCRIPT TO THE PREFACE

The fact that circumstances forced me to read proof on this
work in London gave me the opportunity to check the quotations
from the Transcripts of the Correspondence of George III in the
W. L. Clements Library with the originals in Windsor Castle.
I have to acknowledge the gracious permission of His Majesty
the King to make use of material from the Royal Archives, Windsor Castle.

I regret that I was unable to make use of Mr. Keith G. Feiling's *The Second Tory Party, 1714-1832*, which was published
recently. Although I am unable to agree with Mr. Feiling's interpretation of the relationship of Pitt to the Tory Party, I should
have found the parts of his book before 1783 very helpful in
writing the first chapter of my work.

D. G. B.

BRITISH MUSEUM
September 1, 1938

TABLE OF CONTENTS

I. GEORGE III AND THE CONSTITUTION, 1760 TO 1783

The Constitution with which George III was supposed to have tampered successfully during the first twenty-three years of his reign was regarded by eighteenth-century statesmen, politicians, and students in a manner different from that of twentieth-century writers of textbooks. Although the significance of tradition, precedent, and steady growth were not entirely disregarded in the eighteenth century, emphasis was then placed on the Revolution Settlement of 1689 and on the acts of the years immediately following. Englishmen of the years from 1689 to 1832 seem to have regarded their Constitution more as Americans of the last two or three generations look upon theirs, namely, as a finished masterpiece which should be reverenced and jealously guarded but changed only under most unusual circumstances. The phrase "Our blessed Constitution in Church and State" might be found on the lips of practically anybody in eighteenth-century England except a political radical or a religious dissenter.

The "Constitution in Church" was based not only on the Elizabethan Settlement but also on the Clarendon Code, 1661–1665, the Test Acts of 1673 and 1678, and the Toleration Act of 1689. On the "State" side it was believed that the Bill of Rights and the necessity for an annual meeting of Parliament to vote supplies and to pass the Mutiny Bill had revived the union of King-in-Parliament,[1] which had been lost under the Stuarts, and had divided the government between a limited king and a limited parliament. Neither the two-party system nor the cabinet solidarity and joint responsibility of the nineteenth century was dreamed of in 1689; and William III clearly believed in the departmental idea of a cabinet and ministry rather than in that of joint responsibility. Practically all evidence points to the conclusion that neither the framers of the Revolution Settlement nor the first three rulers after 1689—William, Mary, and Anne—anticipated the constitutional developments of the next three-quarters of a century. Parliament, it was held, might either initiate policies or endorse those proposed by the King and his ministers; but the King and his ministers were to execute these policies. On more than one occasion

[1] I. D. Jones, *The English Revolution* (London, 1931), p. 4.

1

William III was forced by Parliament to act contrary to his wishes and judgment; but, whether he acted according to his own ideas or according to those of Parliament, he administered the government himself.

In the reigns of George I and George II two important constitutional developments took place: first, the evolution of a principal or prime minister; and, second, the organization of Parliament by the King's ministers for the purpose of securing a majority. Neither development was entirely new. For centuries English rulers had often tended to rely on the advice of a single individual, and Charles II and James II usually had one minister who occupied an outstanding position. The development of the prime minister under George I, however, was due in part at least to the fact that because of his linguistic shortcomings the King no longer attended the cabinet meetings. If the interpretation of the parallel development of a committee of the Privy Council without the King and of the cabinet with the King from the later years of the reign of Charles II to the accession of George I is accepted, then either the committee or the cabinet was discontinued soon after 1714 and the other went on without the presence of the King. Thus the absence of the sovereign from these deliberations after 1714 would tend to give one minister an outstanding position as the presiding officer.

The second important development—the organization of the House of Commons in such a way as to secure a majority for the King and his ministers—was likewise in no sense new. This practice dated back at least to the time of Danby and the Cavalier or Pension Parliament of Charles II. The Septennial Act of 1716, by making the life of a parliament seven years instead of three, enormously increased the advantage of securing a majority. Thus, if the King and his ministers were, by a variety of practices, able to make certain that a majority of both houses of Parliament would support their measures, they would be able to set aside the theory of the Revolution Settlement. All that was now necessary to enable the ruler and his chief ministers to control the government was to avoid initiating policies which would receive too violent opposition from that intangible thing known as public opinion. The relative degree of influence wielded, respectively, by the ruler and the chief minister came to depend largely upon the ability and personality of each and upon circumstances which were often of a temporary nature.

The Prime Minister after 1714 usually occupied the post of First Lord of the Treasury, for after that date the older office of Lord Treasurer was put in commission and the head of the treasury came to be known as the First Lord. If he were a member of the House of Commons he usually combined the headship of the treasury with the office of Chancellor of the Exchequer. The other important posts in the government which almost invariably insured a place in the cabinet were those of Secretary of State for the Northern Department, Secretary of State for the Southern Department, Lord President, Lord Privy Seal, Lord Chancellor, First Lord of Admiralty, and Lord-Lieutenant of Ireland. Because practically every First Lord of the Treasury since Walpole is listed as the Prime Minister, there has been a tendency to assume that this superior position was as universally recognized before 1832 as after. Rather, in the first part of the eighteenth century at least, there was a tendency on the part of other important ministers to consider themselves as holding office from the King on an equal footing with the First Lord of the Treasury. This attitude was apt to be especially marked in the case of a Lord Chancellor or of a leading Secretary of State. The Chancellor had a vague claim as keeper of the King's conscience which might be ruthlessly exploited by an able and ambitious man or by one who was very close to his sovereign. Since the two Secretaries of State, in the main, performed joint duties, except in the sphere of communicating with different foreign countries, and since one foreign policy had to be pursued in any case, unity of action was necessary for the two. This unity was usually secured by the fact that one of the secretaries dominated the other. The system worked best with an outstanding statesman in one of the two positions and either a young protégé of his or an elderly figurehead in the other. This leading Secretary of State often felt that his position in the government was just as important and influential as that of the First Lord of the Treasury. The attitude taken by Lord Townshend, the Duke of Newcastle, and Charles James Fox brings out this point very clearly.

Obviously the relations of the King with his ministers varied considerably. The First Lord of the Treasury might be easily first in influence, or he might share this favor with a Secretary of State, a Lord Chancellor, or a group of ministers. Consequently the policies pursued in Parliament would naturally, in the case of differences of opinion, be the result of the usual compromises

reached under such circumstances. Since the King and his ministers initiated the policies during the eighteenth century, it is
important to understand the make-up of both houses of Parliament from which the government had to secure its majority.

From the beginning of the century until 1780 the actual
number of lords showed comparatively little variation. Turberville states it thus:

In 1707, just before the Union, there were 21 dukes, 67 earls,
8 viscounts, 65 barons, 2 archbishops, and 24 bishops, making a total
of 187 . . . . In 1728, at the commencement of the reign of
George II, there were 4 royal dukes, 24 dukes, 1 marquis, 71 earls,
15 viscounts, 64 barons, making with the episcopal bench and the
Scots peers a total of 221. In 1750 there were 2 royal dukes, 20 other
dukes, 1 marquis, 81 earls, 10 viscounts, 58 barons, a decrease of 7
from the figures of 1728. The year 1780 showed a slight increase,
there being 3 royal dukes, 21 other dukes, 1 marquis, 78 earls, 14 viscounts, and 65 barons, i.e., the total was 224. Thus, taking the period
as a whole, the average membership of the House was about 220.[2]

The long and uninterrupted line of Whig ministries from 1714
to 1760 found it comparatively easy to secure a majority from
this 220. An important division could be counted on to attract
from a half to two-thirds of the members of the House of Lords,
and the government could almost invariably rely on a comfortable
majority from that number. Any ministry could expect, under
normal circumstances, the support of the sixteen Scots peers and
of the twenty-six members of the episcopal bench. In addition
there were a great many placemen or officeholders upon whom
the government could depend. For example, in 1774 there were
86 in the House of Lords. Summons from the proper authority
would ensure the presence at a division of the great majority of
the Scots peers, of the bishops, and of the placemen;[3] and almost
without exception both before 1760 and from 1760 to 1780 their
votes were decisive.

Between the Union with Scotland in 1707 and the Union with
Ireland in 1801 no real change took place in the representation
of the British House of Commons. According to the classification popularized by Porritt,[4] there were 513 members from
England and Wales and 45 from Scotland. The 513 were appor-

[2] A. S. Turberville, *The House of Lords in the XVIIIth Century* (Oxford:
Clarendon Press, 1927), pp. 4–5.   [3] *Ibid.*, p. 493.
[4] E. Porritt, *The Unreformed House of Commons* (Cambridge, 1903), Vol.
I, chapter iii.

tioned: 92 members from 52 shires; 417 from 216 cities, boroughs, and Cinque Ports; and 4 from the Universities of Oxford and Cambridge. By the Act of 1430 the right to vote in the English counties was vested in the forty-shilling freeholders; and by the Act of 1535–36 this franchise was extended to the Welsh ones. No such uniform qualification' for voting prevailed in the English boroughs, but for the sake of clarity the 204 which sent representatives to Parliament in the eighteenth century are classified as "scot and lot," "burgage," "corporation," and "freemen." The numbers of these four kinds were 59, 39, 43, and 63, respectively. Because so much depended on local customs and usages, there was, with the exception of the six months' residential qualification for voting in the scot and lot boroughs, little uniformity in the conditions regulating the right to vote.[5] Professor L. B. Namier, on the other hand, has divided the boroughs according to the number of voters: those with over a thousand; those with from five hundred to a thousand; those with about five hundred; and those with a small number, the "narrow" constituencies.[6] During the eighteenth century the first three under this last classification were usually distinguished from the fourth by the terms "open" and "close" boroughs. The narrow constituencies or "close" boroughs are, however, more generally distinguished from those with more numerous voters by the labels "rotten" and "pocket" or "nomination." In a "rotten" borough the voters were few and were susceptible to bribery; and in a "pocket" borough the voters were under the control of a patron who nominated the candidates whom he wished to have elected.

During the reigns of the first three Georges the House of Commons was made up roughly of three main groups: first, the placemen or officeholders; second, the representatives of pocket and rotten boroughs; and, third, the independents. These groups often overlapped, since either a placeman or an independent might sit for any borough or shire.

Although it is unsatisfactory, a classification of this kind throws some light on the methods employed by the ministers to secure a majority in the eighteenth century. From the three groups listed above, the King's ministers from 1714 to 1760 worked to secure a majority of the 558 votes of the House of

[5] *Ibid.*, I, 30.

[6] L. B. Namier, *The Structure of Politics at the Accession of George III* (London: Macmillan & Co., Ltd., 1929), Vol. I, chapter ii.

Commons. It has been estimated that during the reigns of George I and George II there were on the average about 120 placemen in Parliament,[7] and one estimate placed the number as high as 257[8] in the first Parliament of George I. With the placemen as a nucleus, the ministry had to secure enough votes from the other two groups to carry ministerial measures. The two chief means employed were patronage and oratory. If speeches by members of the opposition to the ministry were taken at their face value, both of these methods would be subordinated to a third method—bribery and corruption. The recent researches, however, of Professor L. B. Namier on the period from 1754 to 1763, which deal with the amount of money actually devoted to the Secret Service fund in the reigns of George I and George II, indicate that the effect of outright bribery has been greatly exaggerated.[9] Patronage included sinecures and pensions and places in the Army, the Navy, the Civil Service, and the Church. Oratory was very important, because the party whip system was not so effective as later and because many members of Parliament, particularly the so-called independents, were greatly influenced by the arguments of well-known statesmen; the number of really effective speakers during the eighteenth century was so limited that their services were in great demand by the government.

So far little has been said about the Whig and Tory parties. Without doubt there were Whigs and Tories in the third quarter of the eighteenth century, but they were groups of men who held certain ideas on religion and politics rather than well-organized political parties. As Professor L. B. Namier has expressed it:

There was a Whig and Tory mentality; each was expressed in certain conceptions of State and Church, had its own ideology and idealism, and responded to certain sentimental appeals and traditional watchwords; the same types are with us even now . . . . In the absence of clearly defined issues, these types, which, like everything organic, fail to reproduce the straight (imaginary) lines of human thought, cannot yield clear divisions. Moreover, the disturbing element of personal connexions is always present in politics; the game is played by groups, and human ties continually cross and confound the logic of social and political alinements.[10]

[7] R. Muir, *A Short History of the British Commonwealth* (Yonkers-on-Hudson: World Book Company, 1922), I, 658.

[8] Porritt, *op. cit.*, I, 221.   [9] Namier, *op. cit.*, Vol. I, chapter iv.

[10] L. B. Namier, *England in the Age of the American Revolution* (London: Macmillan & Company, Ltd., 1930), p. 212. Quoted by permission of the Mac-

Within the Whig Party at the end of the reign of George II and in the first years of the reign of George III there were at least four divisions.[11] First in importance for the years covered by this chapter were the Newcastle Whigs, or, as they came to be called after the leadership passed to the Marquis of Rockingham, the old Whigs. A second group were the friends of Pitt, later known as the Chatham Whigs, who represented the commercial interests of London and the other great seaports. Its best-known members were Lord Temple, Pitt's brother-in-law; Lord Shelburne; and Beckford, the great London merchant. Closely allied to the Pitt Whigs was a third group called the Grenville Whigs. Their acknowledged leader was George Grenville, the younger brother of Lord Temple and the brother-in-law of Pitt. The fourth group was called the Bedford Whigs or the Bloomsbury Gang. Its best-known members were Lord Egremont, Lord Sandwich, and Rigby; as the title implies, they acknowledged the leadership of the Duke of Bedford. The Tories, in the early years of the reign of George III, were led first by the Earl of Bute and then by Lord North. The absence of strict party organization and the existence of so many groups of Whigs was to have a profound influence on the policy pursued by George III throughout his reign.

The description given in the preceding pages of the Revolution Settlement, the Crown, the two houses of Parliament, and the parties indicates roughly the state of politics at the accession of George III. Some years have elapsed since historians really believed that George intended to make himself an absolute ruler and to overthrow the liberties of the English people. Actually what the new King planned was a return to the letter if not to the spirit of the Revolution Settlement of 1689 and 1701; for he intended to allow the majority of Parliament to give its approval or disapproval of the policies of his government. He did not, however, plan to restore the relationship which had existed between William III and the parliaments of the years 1697–1701, since the evolution of a chief or prime minister and the control of the House of Commons through patronage, oratory, and

millan Company. The best accounts of what the Whigs and Tories represented during the years from the middle of the eighteenth century to the Reform Bill of 1832 are to be found in pp. 206–33 of this work and in chapters ii and vii of H. W. C. Davis, *The Age of Grey and Peel* (Oxford, 1929).

[11] R. W. Postgate, *That Devil Wilkes* (New York: The Vanguard Press, 1929), pp. 12–15.

bribery by the Whig ministries from 1714 to 1760 had shown George III a better line of action. If the King did not discard the practices which had grown up since the beginning of the reign of William III, the use which he might make of them was quite obvious: first, he could secure a majority of the House of Commons by the very methods which the Whig ministries had used; and, second, he could find a chief minister who was capable of controlling Parliament and who was willing to carry out his policies. Of the two tasks George III seems to have found the first by all odds the easier. In the years following 1761 George succeeded the Duke of Newcastle as the distributor of patronage and the supervisor of general elections; and at no such election did he ever find himself on the losing side. On several occasions the King was obliged to accept chief ministers whom he hated and distrusted, but never as the result of losing a general election. The task of finding a satisfactory prime minister turned out to be a very difficult one indeed; it took George III nearly ten years to find such a man. The fact that he had six chief ministers— Newcastle, Bute, Grenville, Chatham, Grafton, and North—from 1760 to 1770 brings out forcibly the inability of the King to find a man who could combine the two requirements. Some possessed the ability to lead Parliament and others the willingness to "co-operate" with the King; but it was not until North became First Lord of the Treasury that both qualifications appeared in one man.

The influence of his mother, of Lord Bute, of Blackstone, and of Bolingbroke in forming George III's ideas as to what a king should do are related in every history treating the early years of his reign. But although George seems to have known his formula even before he became king, it took him several years to acquire the political *savoir faire* to carry out his plans. It is impossible to fix the date when he mastered the art of government; probably the ministry of Grafton after Chatham's retirement in 1767 is as satisfactory as any. The passing of the preliminaries of the Peace of Paris in December 1762 was justly considered a great triumph for the King. This victory in the House of Commons by a vote of 319 to 65, which was followed by a wholesale dismissal of the Whigs and of friends and dependents of the Duke of Newcastle in high and low offices, should be considered a dramatic proclamation of the King's future policies rather than the realization of an ideal.

Nevertheless, the 319 to 65 vote in the House of Commons,

the shouts of triumph from the King's Friends, and the wails of anguish from the dispossessed followers of Newcastle were sufficient to convince the public that control of the government had passed into the hands of George III and Lord Bute. Immediately a reaction set in which made the young King far more unpopular during the next few years than at any other time during his life; for the feeling became widespread that he had captured the House of Commons through "influence" and was in a position to rule practically as he chose. The result was that George III was faced with a formidable opposition both in Parliament and outside during the years 1762 to 1782. This opposition may be treated under three heads: first, "Wilkes and Liberty," 1763–1780; second, the Whigs in Parliament, 1762–1778; and, third, the reform movement in and out of Parliament, 1778–1782. The nature of the opposition to the new King was of course strongly influenced by the political structure of the nation which at the time, according to Professor L. B. Namier, could be divided into five groups: "the territorial magnates, the country gentry, the official class, the trading community, and the lower classes in the towns." The freeholders were excluded from this classification because they "were declining in numbers and importance," and the village laborers because they "had neither votes nor facilities for effective rioting."[12]

The Wilkite Movement was the result of the feeling outside Parliament that the King had captured the House of Commons and might menace the liberties of Englishmen; and it centered around the personality and career of the colorful John Wilkes. The prosecution of Wilkes for writing Number 45 of the *North Briton* in 1763 began a period of opposition to the King's prerogative which ended with the Gordon Riots of 1780. The strength of Wilkism depended upon two somewhat different elements: the wealthy merchants of London and the lower middle and working classes of Greater London.[13] Vigorous attempts were made after 1768 to add the support of different classes, particularly the smaller freeholders, in the provinces. The Society of the Bill of Rights, founded in February of 1769 to "maintain and defend the legal, constitutional liberty of the subject" and to pay the debts of Wilkes, discovered both objects to be difficult of fulfillment.

In the course of the years 1763 to 1771 Wilkes engaged in

[12] Namier, *England in the Age of the American Revolution*, p. 207.
[13] Postgate, *op. cit.*, p. 197.

three great constitutional struggles and emerged triumphant in all of them: he helped to destroy general warrants, to vindicate the rights of the electors against Parliament, and to secure the liberty of the press.[14] His victory on the question of the legality of general warrants, which resulted from his arrest for writing Number 45 of the *North Briton,* cost him four years of exile and an imprisonment of twenty-two months; and it led to the great controversy over the Middlesex elections of 1768–69. Four times Wilkes was elected to represent Middlesex in the House of Commons. After each of the first three elections he was expelled; and after the third he was declared incapable of sitting in the House. When the fourth election also resulted in the choice of Wilkes, his unsuccessful opponent was declared to be the duly elected representative of Middlesex. If this principle had been established, the House of Commons would have had the power to seat the opponent of every successful minority candidate. In 1771, less than a year after his release from prison, Wilkes' third triumph took place. It was as alderman of the City of London that he deliberately brought on the clash between the House of Commons and the privileges of the City over the right to publish debates in Parliament. As a result of the affair, the House of Commons made no serious effort in the future to prevent the publication of its debates.

From 1774 to 1780 Wilkes continued to be a figure of national importance as a member for Middlesex in the House of Commons and as alderman, Lord Mayor, and Chamberlain successively in London. His career as the most dangerous opponent to the King's system of influence came to an end with stunning unexpectedness in the Gordon Riots of 1780. When the Protestant petitioners, headed by Lord George Gordon, presented a protest to Parliament on June 2, no one was prepared for the riots which followed. For nearly two weeks London was held in the grip of what can best be described as a "pogrom" directed against the Catholics. Attacks first centered on Catholic chapels, homes, and businesses; but soon they were extended to prisons and eventually to the Bank of England. Wilkes as alderman viewed the first days of the riots with considerable misgivings, and when the attacks reached the Bank he became one of the leaders against the rioters. This abruptly terminated his active career, because it split the

---

[14] See the accounts in Postgate; in O. A. Sherrard, *A Life of John Wilkes* (London, 1930); and in Horace Bleackley, *Life of John Wilkes* (London, 1917).

two groups which had made possible the Wilkite Movement: "The two political horses which he drove had parted company. The merchants were not for many months likely to take up popular agitation again. The people, who had been Wilkes' chief support, cared nothing for religious scruples; they knew only that he had shot down Wilkites in defense of Lord Mansfield and in the name of the king."[15] George III profited most by the destruction of the Wilkite Movement, but he did not come into the greater part of his legacy until the general election of 1784. It is true that he acted like the adroit politician which he had become by dissolving Parliament on September 1, 1780, and by securing a favorable House of Commons in the election while the memory of his firm conduct during the riots and the excesses of the rioters were still fresh in the minds of the voters. Even a new and favorable House of Commons, however, was not sufficient to offset the disasters of the American Revolution and the precarious state of the British Empire from 1780 to 1782.

The second phase of the opposition to George III, that of the Whigs in Parliament from 1762 to 1778, is a story very different from that of the Wilkite Movement. On the whole it marks a succession of disheartening defeats and lost opportunities. The failure of the Newcastle-Rockingham, the Bedford, the Grenville, and the Pitt (after 1766, Chatham) Whigs to unite or agree upon a common policy from 1760 to 1771 enabled the King during those years to escape from many predicaments. Opportunities presented themselves for united action by these Whig groups not only on several occasions when George III wished to rid himself of the unsatisfactory prime ministers but also upon such vital issues as Wilkes and general warrants in 1763–64, the Middlesex elections, the Corsican and Falkland Islands affairs, and the American problems. The same opportunities for successful cooperation were not presented during the years following 1770, because Lord North showed great ability in coping with the Whig groups and because the events of the first years of his ministry added to, rather than detracted from, the strength of the government.

On first thought it may occasion some amazement that one or more of the four main groups of Whigs did not exploit, from 1763 to 1771, so obvious an asset as the Wilkite Movement.

---

[15] Postgate, *op. cit.*, p. 235.

Probably the fundamental reason for this failure is to be found in the attitude of the Whig leaders toward a man who was so popular with the common people. The Whigs of the first years of the reign of George III must not be confused with nineteenth-century Liberals, for their point of view was decidedly an aristocratic one. Consequently the enthusiastic support given Wilkes by the working class in London and elsewhere made him an object of suspicion in the eyes of many prominent Whigs. Although the Rockingham and Chatham Whigs were not averse to exploiting the principle involved in the Middlesex elections of 1768–69, there was no warmth in the relation of either group toward Wilkes. The latter did not make a *rapprochement* easy; for he seems never to have been on particularly good terms with any prominent Whigs except Pitt and Temple. His friendship with Pitt ended when the latter, in "defending" him in the House of Commons for having written Number 45 of the *North Briton* and the *Essay on Women,* stated that Wilkes "did not deserve to be ranked among the human species—he was the blasphemer of his God and the libeller of his King";[16] likewise his friendship with Temple, who was for years his financial and political backer, when, during his imprisonment in the King's Bench Prison from 1768 to 1770, he refused that lord's request to drop the question of the legality of his past treatment by the government. Wilkes was allowed to take his seat in the House of Commons in 1774, after being chosen as the representative of the county of Middlesex in the general election, and like the Whig leaders he vigorously opposed the coercive measures taken against the American Colonies and later the war itself. Neither the Rockingham nor the Chatham Whigs made any real effort to co-operate with him, even though his point of view on the war and the ministry of Lord North was practically identical with their own. Thus upper-class suspicion on the part of the Whigs toward Wilkes and his unwillingness to forget their failure to support him in the great crises of his career prevented a union of forces against the King and North at a time when a united attack, particularly from 1778 to 1780, would have proved most effective.

The years 1778–1782 mark a new phase in the struggle of the Whigs against the "influence" of the King. Since the death in 1770 of Grenville and in 1771 of Bedford, the Whig opposition

---

[16] *Anecdotes of the Life of the Earl of Chatham* (London, 1810), I, 397.

had been, in the main, composed of the Rockingham and Chatham groups rather than of the four described in the period of the seventeen-sixties. From the point of view of effective action against the government the death of Chatham in 1778 was important, for the Rockingham Whigs found Lord Shelburne, who succeeded to the leadership of the Chatham group, much easier to work with than his imperious and arrogant predecessor. Also the good fortune and support of public opinion which George III and Lord North enjoyed from 1770 to 1777 began to decline after the news arrived of the disaster at Saratoga. When this defeat was followed by the Franco-American alliance and the entrance of France, Spain, and Holland into the war against England, even the House of Commons began to falter in its support of the King and his minister. The opposition found it much easier to convince members of Parliament of the mismanagement and expensiveness of the war than of its wickedness. Thus the strength of the two Whig groups and the unpopularity of the war made possible the gradual whittling down of the majority of the ministry.

The program of the Opposition was admirably summed up in the famous Dunning Resolution, which passed the House of Commons on April 6, 1780, "That the influence of the Crown has increased, is increasing, and ought to be diminished." The Gordon Riots which followed less than two months after the passing of this resolution did not deal a death blow to the hopes of the Whigs, as they did to the Wilkite Movement, because both groups, and particularly the Rockinghams, were too aristocratic in their sympathies to be associated with the excesses of the mob. When the disasters of the war with the American Colonies and with European powers continued, the gains which the King had secured as a result of the Gordon Riots began to melt away. Consequently, despite the absence of joint action with Wilkes, the Whigs, through the support which they secured both in Parliament and outside, were able from 1778 to 1782 to carry on an ingenious agitation. The dislike or aversion which they had for lower-class support has been noted; and hence the Whigs tended to avoid agitation which concentrated on manhood suffrage, equal electoral districts, annual parliaments, and abolition of rotten and pocket boroughs. They were no more anxious than was the King to introduce real democracy or to infringe upon property rights by the abolition of borough representation in places where they controlled the voters. For these reasons the so-called economical reform of the years from 1778 to 1782 suited the Whig purposes. If only the sources of influence which the Crown alone could use were swept away and those which the King and the Whigs could both use were retained, the latter would enjoy the enviable position of being ardent reformers without sacrificing their own interests.

The Whigs were doubly fortunate in obtaining the support of a movement outside Parliament headed by Christopher Wyvill, which had for its objects the securing of both economical and Parliamentary reform. Thus they gained the necessary impetus outside Parliament to help force economical reform through a reluctant House of Commons and at the same time the Whigs felt strong enough to ignore the demands for Parliamentary reform. Wyvill, the leader of this popular movement outside the House of Commons, was a clergyman who had married his wealthy cousin and moved to Burton Hall, the fine country home of the Wyvills in the North Riding of Yorkshire, where he led the life of a country squire and of a political reformer. Yorkshire made a suitable county in which to begin the agitation for economical reform because: first, Wyvill himself lived in the county; second, Lord Rockingham, the acknowledged leader of the group of Whigs most active in sponsoring economical reform in Parliament, was one of the most influential landowners in Yorkshire; third, Sir George Savile, a Rockingham Whig and one of the representatives of the county, had an unusually high reputation for political honesty and hence made a fine leader for the movement; and, fourth, the Yorkshire freeholder believed that the land tax pressed upon him with unusual severity because the assessment was a century old and he argued that land values had advanced more rapidly in the south of England.[17]

Wyvill evidently made use of the machinery which the Archbishop of York had revived during the uprising of 1745, that of a meeting of the freeholders to vote a loyal address to the King, and employed it to carry a petition for economical reform. This gathering, which was called on the authority of 209 gentlemen, was made up of "the Nobility, Gentlemen, Clergy and Freeholders of the County" of York. Despite certain vigorous objections by a small minority, a petition to Parliament asking for economical reform was passed unanimously and when circulated for signatures secured between eight and nine thousand. The petition was

[17] G. S. Veitch, *The Genesis of Parliamentary Reform* (London: Constable & Company, Ltd., 1913), pp. 56–57.

presented in the House of Commons by Sir George Savile on February 8, 1870; and twenty-eight other counties and at least eleven
cities followed the example of Yorkshire. As these petitioners
wished to form some sort of association, Wyvill, on March 11,
1780, succeeded in arranging a conference of representatives from
eighteen counties and cities at the St. Albans Tavern in London.
Here the delegates advised local committees to agitate for Parliamentary as well as economical reform. By the term Parliamentary
reform the conference meant shorter parliaments and more knights
of the shire from each county, and by economical reform the
remedying of a definite set of abuses. But Parliamentary reform
suffered from the fact that it meant not only several different
reforms but also that each reform was subject to several interpretations. For example, shorter parliaments might mean annual,
triennial, or quinquennial ones; abolition of rotten boroughs
might mean with or without compensation to the "owners"; and
the right to return members in the place of these rotten boroughs
might be given to the county or even to the hundred in which
these boroughs were located, or to the growing cities in the mid-
lands and north. It was this very uncertainty in matters of detail
which made any progress in the direction of Parliamentary reform
practically impossible at this time. Most of the followers of Rockingham were unwilling to go beyond economical reform; and it
was upon measures of this type that his wing of the party concentrated in Parliament. Thus the real achievement of the movement headed by Wyvill was to furnish the impetus outside Parliament which helped make possible the victory over the King in
economical reform.[18]

The attacks on the influence exerted by the King through
wasteful and corrupt expenditure in order to maintain his Parliamentary majority began nearly two years before Wyvill called
the meeting of December 30, 1779. On April 13, 1778, Sir Philip
Jennings Clerke, member for Totnes, asked leave to introduce a
bill to exclude from membership in the House of Commons any
person holding a government contract or for whom one was held
in trust unless the contract were obtained at a public bidding under
circumstances which made influence or corruption impossible.[19]
This bill reached the third reading before it was defeated by a

[18] *Ibid.*, pp. 80–82.

[19] *The Parliamentary History of England, 1066–1803* (London, 1806–1820),
XIX, 1090. Hereafter cited as *Parliamentary History.*

postponement. A similar bill shared the same fate on the second reading in 1779. On December 15, 1779, a few days before Wyvill's meeting, Burke[20] gave notice in the House of Commons of a comprehensive plan which would save the exchequer two hundred thousand pounds and cut off influence equivalent to fifty seats in the House of Commons. Burke seems to have had little hope that anything would come of his proposal, but the efforts of Wyvill's followers outside Parliament and the introduction of the Yorkshire petition in the House of Commons by Savile paved the way for a vigorous campaign. On February 11, 1780, Burke[21] obtained permission of the Commons to introduce a bill for economical reform. It provided for a reorganization of the royal household by abolishing numerous unnecessary offices, an improved method of supplying the royal table, and a better method of managing the royal parks. The mint was to be reformed, the Crown lands sold; such subordinate jurisdictions as Lancaster, Wales, Chester, and Cornwall were to be abolished; and the Pension List, subject to such reservations as the Secret Service made necessary, was to be published. The measure even struck at certain departments in the government, for it included the abolition of the office and department of the Third Secretary of State and of the Board of Trade and Plantations. The bill was defeated, evidently in committee,[22] on June 23; and it is not unlikely that the Gordon Riots had something to do with its failure. Other measures striking at the influence of the Crown followed Burke's success of February 11. The bill, which had been introduced as far back as February of 1770, to disfranchise revenue officers was now revived; another bill to exclude placemen from the House of Commons was lost on the second reading; and Clerke's bill to exclude contractors from the Commons actually passed the lower house only to be beaten in the House of Lords. As far as this session of Parliament was concerned the reformers had to be satisfied with the passing of three resolutions in committee: the first, and most famous of the three, was Dunning's Resolution, already cited; the second affirmed the right of the House of Commons to inquire into all branches of public expenditure; and the third declared for a redress of the abuses listed in the petitions demanding economical reform. Thus the economical reformers

---

[20] *Parliamentary History*, XX, 1293–1301.
[21] *Ibid.*, XXI, 72–73.
[22] *Ibid.*, p. 714.

had only moral victories to show for their strenuous efforts from February to June, 1780.

The interest shown in economical reform and the bright prospects of success in the next session of Parliament seem to have encouraged the Parliamentary reformers to take more decided action to secure their objectives. In April of 1780 the Society for Promoting Constitutional Information was founded. It was decidedly a "respectable" as opposed to a radical organization; for among the members were Sir Cecil Wray, first president, Major John Cartwright, Capell Lofft, John Jebb, the Duke of Richmond, Sawbridge, Sir John Sinclair, and Sir Joseph Mawbey.[23] Members of the society on the whole seem to have believed that mere economical reform was inadequate. Without doubt this society occupies an honorable and important place in the history of ·Parliamentary reform, but the immediate effect of its organization and first activities evidently caused divisions to appear in the ranks of the reformers. Although Lord Shelburne, who had succeeded to the leadership of the Chatham Whigs, professed to believe in shorter parliaments and more equal representation, few of the Rockingham Whigs desired, for the present at least, to go beyond economical reform.

Unfortunately this difference of opinion was not the only factor which prevented the reformers in Parliament from carrying to a successful conclusion the promising beginning of the 1779–80 session. In June occurred the Gordon Riots, with the result that the King suddenly dissolved Parliament and called for a new election in the autumn of 1780. Thus when the new Parliament assembled, the members were not so enthusiastic for economical reform as the previous Parliament had been a year earlier. On February 15, 1781, Burke's bill[24] for economical reform was beaten on the second reading, 233 to 190; and on March 21 Clerke's bill[25] for excluding government contractors from the House of Commons and Crewe's bill for disfranchising revenue officers were lost. It is doubtful whether or not the reformers would have been able to accomplish anything at this time if the continued ill success of the war in America had not once more turned public opinion against the King's policy. The news of Yorktown was decisive. A cry for economy went up, particu-

[23] Veitch, *op. cit.*, pp. 71–73.
[24] *Parliamentary History*, XXI, 1292.
[25] *Ibid.*, pp. 1398–99.

larly from the big commercial cities, and the surge of public opinion outside Parliament either influenced or coincided with that in the two houses. All the political acumen of George III could not save him from the results of Yorktown. On February 27, 1782, a motion[26] to address the King to discontinue the war was passed, on March 20 Lord North resigned, and on March 27 Lord Rockingham became First Lord of the Treasury.

The new government, which George III accepted with the greatest reluctance, was not composed entirely of his enemies. It is true that only Thurlow, the Lord Chancellor, could be classed as one of the King's Friends; but George III felt himself to be much closer to Lord Shelburne and his followers than to the Rockingham group. Thus the ideal of a united ministry held by the Rockingham Whigs was not realized. Although for the time being the King seemed helpless, as the next two years were to show, he had not exhausted his resources. The Rockingham Whigs, however, were now in a position to carry out their program of economical reform. A royal message, which must have cost the King considerable anguish, recommended that the Commons consider economy in all branches of public expenditure. Thus the way was paved for the passage of the three bills which had been the platform of the reformers in the House of Commons during recent years.

Clerke's bill to exclude contractors from the House of Commons and Crewe's bill to disfranchise revenue officers passed both Houses and received the royal assent on May 17[27] and June 3,[28] respectively. Burke next introduced for the third time his bill for economical reform. The act as passed attempted to remedy two sets of abuses: abolition of unnecessary officers, and a stricter regulation of the Pension List. The third Secretaryship of State, that for the Colonies, was abolished; the work done by the Board of Trade was transferred to a committee of the Privy Council; and many offices in the King's household were swept away. No grant of more than £300 a year was to be made to any one individual until the Pensions List was reduced to £90,000. The entire amount granted for a single year was not to exceed £600 and a list of these pensions was to be given to Parliament. The Secret Service fund was protected, but the First Lord of the Treasury

26 *Parliamentary History*, XXIII, 1101.
27 Veitch, *op. cit.*, p. 78.
28 *Ibid.*

was compelled to take oath that no money paid out of this fund was used to corrupt either members of Parliament or voters in Parliamentary elections. Burke next abolished the practice of allowing the Pay-Master of Forces to make enormous profits by keeping large sums of money belonging to the government in his hands. Since Burke was holding this office at the time the reform was passed, it shows the sincerity of his belief in economical reform. Apparently the big measure for economical reform passed the House of Commons without opposition on any reading. That reform was practically inevitable seems to have been recognized by all groups in Parliament.

The ease with which economical reform finally passed has naturally caused some speculation as to the reasons for the failure of Parliamentary reform. At the time the more advanced reformers felt that the same pressure exerted by the Whigs in the direction of Parliamentary reform might have resulted in the same degree of success. It is unlikely, however, that the death of Rockingham on July 1, 1782, and the subsequent split in the Whig ranks when Shelburne succeeded to the office of First Lord of the Treasury had any decisive influence in bringing about this failure. The attitude of Rockingham, Fox, Sheridan, and other well-known Rockingham Whigs ranged from lukewarm support of Parliamentary reform to outright hostility. To Burke, who played the most prominent part in securing economical reform, there was all the difference in the world between the two reforms: economical reform cut away the corruption which threatened the magnificent English Constitution; whereas Parliamentary reform suggested an actual change in a perfect structure. Burke, in taking this stand, was consistent with his later position on the French Revolution. Thus to expect that the Rockingham Whigs would carry on a vigorous campaign for Parliamentary reform as they had for economical reform is to misunderstand their fundamental political principles. Economical reform took from the King certain of the liquid assets which he used to control Parliament and did not take anything from the Whigs. With the government contractors barred from the Commons, revenue officers disfranchised, and the King's Pension List sliced, the Whigs with their share of the rotten and pocket boroughs and of able parliamentarians might hope to compete with the King on a more equal footing than they had since the general election of 1761. It is true that Lord Shelburne had often expressed himself as friendly to more frequent parliaments and more equal representation, but he would have had no chance to carry Parliamentary reform even had he so desired, because the King and the Tories under North were strongly opposed and the Rockingham Whigs would not have supported any such proposal. The Parliamentary reformers pinned their hopes more and more on William Pitt, one of the Shelburne Whigs; but for the present the movement gave way, within Parliament at least, to more pressing matters.

The events after the death of Lord Rockingham show that the King was as successful in repelling the Whig attacks as he had been from 1762 to 1771. This success was due to dissension between the Rockingham and the Shelburne Whigs, to the errors in tactics and the increasing unpopularity of Charles James Fox, to the ability of George III to take advantage of both dissension and errors, and to the growing popularity of the King and William Pitt. The weight which should be given to each item depends largely upon whether the astuteness of the King or the mistakes of Fox be considered the more important factor.

If the Whigs hoped to triumph over the "influence" of the King, it was essential that they keep their ranks united. They failed because personal jealousy and the lure of holding office were stronger than the desire to diminish this influence. Shelburne and Pitt both preferred holding office under the King to continuing the struggle; and Fox preferred to go into opposition to Shelburne rather than to serve under him—not because of real difference in policies but because he disliked and distrusted him. Yet Fox was willing to form a coalition with North for the sake of holding office. It might be argued that Fox was willing to go to any lengths to strike a blow at the King's influence, and that in refusing to serve under Shelburne and in forming the coalition with North he was acting true to this principle. To this it may be answered that Fox served with Shelburne under Rockingham and was unable, when pressed in the House of Commons, to show wherein their principles differed materially; and that, in view of North's record from 1767 to 1782, he could not hope for warm support in an attack on the King's prerogative. Whether the failure of the Whigs to present a united front against the King was due to the actions of Fox or to those of Shelburne and Pitt is certainly open to dispute.

Fox appears to have been sincere in his fundamental object of striking additional blows at the King's influence and in his willingness to be associated with practically anybody except Lord Shelburne in dealing such blows. Nevertheless the refusal of Fox to become a member of Lord Shelburne's ministry in July of 1782 certainly played into the hands of the King, since a combination of the King's Friends, the Shelburne Whigs, and some of the followers of Rockingham who refused to follow Fox into opposition made possible the formation of a Coalition ministry which was at least acceptable to George III. Although he might not have the same approbation for the ministry of Shelburne which he had had for that of Lord North, the King appreciated that it was infinitely superior to that of Lord Rockingham or to one headed by Charles James Fox. Of the 558 members of the House of Commons it was estimated that approximately 140 acknowledged the leadership of Shelburne, 120 that of Lord North, and 90 that of Charles James Fox.[29] Shelburne's 140 supporters were made up of his own Whig followers and of King's Friends. Thus about two hundred members were unattached and subject to the influence of oratory in the House of Commons and to changes in public opinion outside. It was obvious at the time that a combination of any two of the groups could control the House of Commons.

Up to the present, historical research has not shown conclusively why George III and Shelburne did not make a greater effort to secure an alliance with Lord North. Perhaps both felt that the chance of the alliance of North with Fox was too remote to occasion concern. Nevertheless, this does not explain why a greater effort was not made to consolidate the forces in opposition to Fox. It is likely that during the preceding fifteen years George III had been given so much evidence of Lord North's reluctance to oppose the will of his sovereign that he did not expect so independent a stand. When overtures were finally made to North by Shelburne and the King, they were too late. On the other hand, from the point of view of what both Fox and North wished to accomplish *immediately,* a coalition was an admirable arrangement. Fox would be able to overthrow Shelburne and, by returning to office, to strike additional blows at the King's prerogatives. At first sight the stand taken by North is puzzling. Why should he refuse a chance to return to office, either under Shelburne or at the head of a ministry? Certainly it would have

[29] J. H. Rose, *Life of William Pitt* (London: G. Bell & Sons, Ltd., 1923), I, 115.

been in the nature of a vindication and should have afforded North some satisfaction. The explanation seems to lie in North's fear of Fox's threat to impeach him and in his entire unwillingness to take orders again from George III. By a coalition, North might accomplish two things: first, make it impossible for Fox to impeach him for the loss of the American Colonies; and, second, make it unlikely that George III would ever again appoint him First Lord of the Treasury. Thus in February of 1783 Fox rejected overtures from Shelburne presented by William Pitt, and Lord North rejected similar ones from Shelburne offered by Henry Dundas. A few days later the forces of Fox and North by a vote of 207 to 190 passed a vote of censure on the Shelburne ministry because of the peace terms made with the Bourbon powers and the American Colonies. Shelburne resigned at once.[30]

Although George III seems to have had no great liking for or confidence in Shelburne, the latter's resignation came as a great blow. Alternatives to accepting the Fox-North Coalition were a return of North or a continuation of the elements making up the Shelburne ministry under a new leader. For thirty-seven days the King tried every possibility. Upon the recommendation of Shelburne he offered the position of First Lord of the Treasury to Pitt, and when Pitt declined he made every effort to induce Lord North to desert Fox and accept the post. With the failure of this attempt as well as that of negotiating with the Coalition, the King once more, but without success, offered the place to Pitt.[31] The despair of George III was so great that on two occasions he considered abdicating and retiring to Hanover.[32] In the end, however, he accepted the Coalition under the nominal leadership of the Duke of Portland. The Duke became First Lord of the Treasury; Fox, Foreign Secretary; and North, Home Secretary. It is unlikely that the King thought seriously of abdicating. He may have been sincere in his threat at the time he made it, but he had faced similar crises more than once and was too astute a politician not to realize the weaknesses of the Coalition ministry. The attitude of the King is probably better expressed by the

[30] *Life of William Pitt,* I, 123.

[31] Pitt MSS, in the Public Record Office, London, 103. These manuscripts are now classified in the Public Record Office as "Chatham Papers (G.D. 8)." Letters of March 25–26, 1783.

[32] Sir John Fortescue (ed.), *Correspondence of King George the Third* (London: Macmillan & Company, Ltd., 1928), VI, 314–17, No. 4259 and No. 4260.

well-known story of his expression at the time Fox and North kissed hands upon receiving the seals of office; a bystander remarked that George III turned back his ears and eyes "just like the horse at Astley's when the tailor he had determined to throw was getting on him."[33]

Looking back over the struggle between George III and the Whigs from 1760 to 1783 it is obvious that the King had triumphed consistently over his opponents. Whether or not this long series of victories had come to an end as a result of the Fox-North Coalition was a question which would be answered during the remaining months of 1783. The Whigs had only temporary gains to show for the long struggle of nearly twenty-three years, and hence the success or failure of the Coalition was of vital concern to them.

The King, with the exception of certain setbacks, had been fairly successful in carrying out his two fundamental plans of securing both majorities in the two houses of Parliament and satisfactory prime ministers. The success of George III in the first of these plans—securing Parliamentary majorities—was due largely to the fact that he took over the elaborate edifice which the Whigs had built up in the reign of his predecessor with most of its "residents";[34] and to the fact that he had shown unusual skill in handling patronage and in taking advantage of the divisions and mistakes of his opponents.

The attempts of George III to secure a first minister who would and could carry out the royal policies fall logically, as was pointed out earlier in the chapter, into three divisions: from 1760 to 1770; from 1770 to 1782; and from 1782 to 1783. It was necessary for the King to select his chief minister from the small group of Tories, the King's Friends, or from one of the groups of Whigs. Of the prime ministers from 1760 to 1783, Newcastle, Grenville, Rockingham, Chatham, Grafton, Shelburne, and Portland were Whigs and only Bute and North were Tories. It was because the Whigs did not stand together that the King had any success in securing ministers who were able to carry on the government. A united stand by Newcastle and by Pitt in 1761–62 would have made impossible the triumph of Lord Bute; and the support of Pitt would have saved the Rockingham ministry in 1766. This point of view, however, assumes a state of mind on

33 Rose, *op. cit.*, I, 128.
34 Namier, *England in the Age of the American Revolution*, p. 219.

the part of the Whigs which is a product of the century since the Reform Bill of 1832 and which was foreign to their political ideas in the third quarter of the eighteenth century. Further, when the formation of the ministry of William Pitt in December 1783 is dealt with in the next chapter it will be seen that this ministry did not mark any innovation; for Pitt was merely one more Whig who was willing to become First Lord of the Treasury for George III. This ministry, like practically every one between 1760 and 1783, was a coalition, since it was composed of Pitt's Whig followers, the King's Friends, and Tories.

What then had the Whigs, during the first twenty-three years of the reign of George III, done to offset the King's control of Parliament and his policy of keeping their groups of factions divided? In the main their efforts consisted of spasmodic assaults on the King's ministers; of intermittent attempts to combine the various groups of their party or even to coalesce with the Tories, as in the case of the Fox-North Coalition; and of attacks on the Crown's flagrant use of certain forms of patronage without interfering with the "close" borough system. Because of their lack of unity and application, the willingness of their prominent leaders to act as chief minister to the King, and their failure to exploit either the Wilkite Movement or Parliamentary reform, it is small wonder that the Whigs experienced so little success. The King possessed not only the advantages of the Crown but unity of command and tenacity of purpose. Under these circumstances it is difficult to see how the Whigs could have expected any greater success than they actually experienced.

If, then, George III did not attempt to stage a constitutional revolution in 1760 and the years following but merely took over the Whig's elaborate machinery for controlling both houses of Parliament, what was either significant or unique in the constitutional history of the years from 1760 to 1783? In the opinion of the present writer two points which are usually given little consideration should be accorded this distinction: first, the absence of an adult heir to the throne; and, second, the reconstruction of the House of Lords, which began in 1776 and was carried out during the long ministry of Pitt from 1783 to 1801.

From 1689 until the regency of 1810 there was, with the exception of the years between the birth of Prince George in 1762 and his political "coming out" in about 1783, no period in which the heir to the throne did not offer a bright future to statesmen and officeholders who were excluded by the reigning monarch. Under William III it was the Princess Anne; under Anne, the Electress Sophia; under George I, his son Prince George; and under George II, first, his son Frederick, and, second, his grandson Prince George. Soon after the eldest son of George III reached the age of twenty-one he became, as later chapters will show in detail, the chief hope of the Foxite Whigs securing office. After the Reform Bill of 1832 the two-party system offered His Majesty's Opposition the chance of holding office, while under conditions prevailing in the eighteenth century the opportunity so often could come only with the death of the reigning monarch. It was during this period alone, when Prince George was a minor and without the benefit of a court such as George III had enjoyed at Leicester House from 1751 to 1760, that the dissatisfied statesmen and would-be officeholders could not rally around "The King to Come." Also it is not without significance that it was during these very years that the Rockingham Whigs evolved, somewhat vaguely and incompletely it is true, the ideas of a government based on a Parliamentary majority and headed by a cabinet whose members were jointly responsible for policies and who took office and resigned as a group.

One of the most amazing parts of George III's taking over the Whig edifice in 1760 was the case with which he captured the House of Lords. It might have been expected that the long supremacy of the Whigs before the accession of George III would have insured them a majority in the upper house for some time. This point of view, however, would fail to take into account three important factors.: first, that the bishops, sixteen Scots peers, and placemen were among the residents taken over with the edifice; second, that after 1760 the great lawyers such as Mansfield and Thurlow, who so strongly influenced the House of Lords, were King's Friends and not Whigs; and, third, that conservatism and patriotism caused many lords to support the government as a matter of course.[85] George III seems to have been so confident of having nothing to fear from the Lords that he not only did not watch them as he did the Commons but during the first sixteen years of his reign did not even attempt to "pack" the upper chamber with men who would swamp the

[85] Turberville, *op. cit.*, pp. 493–94.

Whigs. Until 1776 the King was most niggardly in creating new peers, and it was not until he came to realize that the normal majority of the government in the House of Lords was waning that he consented to bolster it by ten new creations in that year. Only when the large majorities which George III had secured in the House of Commons by the general elections of 1774 and 1780 began to dwindle in the face of the disasters of the war with the American Colonies does he seem to have considered the House of Lords as a second line of defense for the Crown.

From April to December 1783 the Constitution was still to George III "our blessed Constitution in Church and State," and it needed no change. The trouble was, from his point of view, that a group of unprincipled men had forced their way into his cabinet in a most unconstitutional manner.

II. GEORGE III AND WILLIAM PITT IN 1783

In this study an attempt will be made to trace the results of the clash of the personalities and political principles of George III and William Pitt with respect to the policies of the English government and the development of the English Constitution from 1783 to 1806. In the preceding chapter the clash between George III and the Whigs was traced briefly; in this chapter brief sketches of the personalities of the King and of Pitt and a short account of their lives to 1783 will be given.

GEORGE III

George III was born on June 4, 1738, and hence was nearly forty-five years old at the time the Fox-North Coalition took office. Until recently it has not been the fashion to spend much time on the childhood and teens of the subjects of biographical studies; for, it has been argued, little profit can be derived from a study of these years and the "bib and porringer" period is less likely to attract than to repel.[1] But in recent years it has become customary to seek the explanations for conduct later in life in the bib-and-porringer and youthful periods.

Prince George William Frederick, as George III was christened, was the son of Frederick, eldest son of George II, and Augusta, daughter of a Duke of Saxe-Gotha. Frederick, in the tradition of the House of Hanover, was usually on hostile terms with his father, George II. This coldness, which at times became downright hatred, was not without its effect on Prince George, because his mother carried on the feud after the death of his father in 1751. Prince Frederick appears to have left no permanent mark on the ideas or personality of his son, who was nearly thirteen years old when his father died. When he was six years old, his education was entrusted to Dr. Francis Ayscough, the brother-in-law of Lord Lyttelton. Either the Doctor was a poor instructor or the Prince was unusually stupid, for when the latter was eleven years old his mother found that he could not read English.[2] Probably the greatest influence upon him was that exerted between the years 1751 and 1760 by his mother and Lord Bute. During those ten years his education was

[1] Lord Rosebery, *Pitt* (London, 1923), p. 5.
[2] Lewis Melville, *Farmer George* (London, 1907), I, 36.

27

subject to continual intrigues. The King, the Prince's mother, and the ministry were all interested in having a representative near George as his governor, sub-governor, preceptor, or sub-preceptor. Constant bickerings and resignations, such as that of Lord Harcourt, prevented any real continuity of educational policy. It has been suggested that Lord Harcourt refused to discuss his resignation with anyone except the King because he felt that the Prince of Wales was being taught objectionable doctrines by Lord Bute.[3]

The part played by Lord Bute in the early training of George was very great even before the latter was given a separate establishment in 1756. Bute owed his prominent position to rather unusual circumstances. It is true that he became third Earl of Bute at a comparatively early age, inherited the Wortley estates by marrying the only daughter of Lady Mary Wortley Montagu, and became a representative peer for Scotland in 1737. Despite these advantages he played only an unimportant part in British political life until in 1747 he met Frederick, Prince of Wales, at a cricket match played in Richmond. Bute, who greatly impressed the Prince, soon became an influential member of Frederick's Leicester House court. Even after the death of the Prince in 1751, Bute's influence continued undiminished. In fact the unpleasant notoriety which he gained came as a result of his relations with the Dowager Princess of Wales after that date. His influence which Bute exerted over the Princess has been explained on the grounds that it was a mere continuation of the confidence which her husband had in Bute's ability, that she believed in the political principles which Bute could inculcate into her eldest son, or that, as Horace Walpole stated, there was an "amorus connexion" between the two. Certainly English public opinion held strongly to the third of these explanations, probably without justification, and both Bute and the Dowager Princess were subjected to an almost unbelievable number of slurs and insults during the twelve years from 1751 to 1763. At least the Princess found a man in Bute who held the same ideas as her own on kingship and the same suspicions of the life led in the court of George II.

Out of all the conflicting accounts of the boyhood of George III certain conclusions appear certain: he was lazy, indolent, and

[3] Melville, *Farmer George*, I, 39–40.

ignorant; he was brought up in seclusion; and he was taught to suspect George II and the loose moral life of the royal court.

We are fortunate in having valuable testimony on the development of George's character and personality in the years immediately before 1760. In the character sketch of the future king given in 1758 by his governor, Lord Waldegrave, available for over a century, it is interesting to trace through his later life the traits so shrewdly pointed out before his accession to the throne:

The Prince of Wales is entering into his 21st year, and it would be unfair to decide upon his character in the early stages of life, when there is so much time for improvement.

His parts, though not excellent, will be found very tolerable, if ever they are properly exercised.

He is strictly honest, but wants that frank and open behaviour which makes honesty appear amiable.

When he had a very scanty allowance, it was one of his favorite maxims that men should be just before they are generous: his income is now very considerably augmented, but his generosity has not increased in equal proportion.

His religion is free from all hypocrisy, but is not of the most charitable sort; he has rather too much attention to the sins of his neighbour.

He has spirit, but not of the active kind; and does not want resolution, but it is mixed with too much obstinacy.

He has great command of his passions, and will seldom do wrong, except when he mistakes wrong for right; but as often as this shall happen, it will be difficult to undeceive him, because he is uncommonly indolent, and has strong prejudices.

His want of application and aversion to business would be far less dangerous, was he eager in the pursuit of pleasure; for the transition from pleasure to business is both shorter and easier than from a state of total inaction.

He has a kind of unhappiness in his temper, which, if it be not conquered before it has taken too deep a root, will be a source of frequent anxiety. Whenever he is displeased, his anger does not break out with heat and violence; but he becomes sullen and silent, and retires to his closet; not to compose his mind by study or contemplation, but merely to indulge the melancholy enjoyment of his own ill humor. Even when the fit is ended, unfavorable symptoms very frequently return, which indicate that on certain occasions his Royal Highness has too correct a memory.

Though I have mentioned his good and bad qualities, without flattery, and without aggravation, allowances should still be made, on account of his youth, and his bad education: for though the Bishop of Peterborough, now Bishop of Salisbury, the preceptor; Mr. Stone, the sub-governor; and Mr. Scott, the sub-preceptor, were men of sense, men of learning, and worthy, good men, they had but little weight and influence. The mother and the nursery always prevailed.

During the course of the last year, there has, indeed, been some alteration; the authority of the nursery has gradually declined, and the Earl of Bute, by the assistance of the mother, has now the intire confidence. But whether this change will be greatly to his Royal Highness's advantage, is a nice question, which cannot hitherto be determined with an certainty.[4]

Additional evidence on conditions under which George was reared has been unearthed in the Bute Papers by Professor L. B. Namier, who concludes that,

so far from being taught doctrines of prerogative, he was nurtured on constitutional platitudes which he duly copied, adorning them with the current verbiage about virtue and liberty. . . . .

No doubt he was continually reminded by his guardians and teachers of the high station to which fate had predestined him—what prince is not? Still, he was brought up not so much in particularly high notions of royalty as in an atmosphere of dynastic opposition, both his mother and Lord Bute confirming him in his hatred and contempt of the King, his grandfather. He was encouraged to hate before he could think, and a cleavage developed in his feelings which made him see himself surrounded by devils and angels, all the devils at St. James's and all the angels at Leicester House; the neurotic boy, bitter in soul and mentally underdeveloped, concentrated on the King the hostility of the heir and rival, while his love went out to Lord Bute, to him the incarnation of a tutelary paternal spirit.[5]

Perhaps most significant of this new material in the Bute Papers is a series of letters from George to Bute. One written in June of 1756 is, as Professor Namier remarks, "a pathetic human document, which circumstances endow with high historic importance." This letter was written when George II contemplated settling the Prince at Kensington Palace and St. James's in order to withdraw him from the influences of Leicester House:

    [4] James Earl Waldegrave, *Memoirs from 1754 to 1758* (London, 1821), pp. 8–10.
    [5] L. B. Namier, *England in the Age of the American Revolution* (London: Macmillan & Company, Ltd., 1930), pp. 94–96. By permission of The Macmillan Company, publishers.

My dear Lord—I have had the pleasure of your friendship during the space of a year, by which I have reap'd great advantage, but not the improvement I should if I had follow'd your advice; but you shall find me make such a progress in this summer, that shall give you hopes, that with the continuation of your advice, I may turn out as you wish.

It is very true that the Ministers have done everything they can to provoke me, that they have call'd me a harmless boy, and have not even deign'd to give me an answer when I so earnestly wish to see my friend about me. They have also treated my Mother in a cruel manner (which I will neither forget nor forgive to the day of my death) because she is so good as to come forward and to preserve her son, from the many snares that surround him. My Friend is also attack'd in the most cruel manner, not for anything he has done against them, but because he is my Friend, and wants to see me come to the Throne with honor and not with disgrace and because he is, a friend to the bless'd liberties of his country and not to arbitrary notions. I look upon myself as engaged in honor and justice to defend these my two Friends as long as I draw breath.

I do therefore here in the presence of Our Almighty Lord promiss, that I will ever remember the insults done to my Mother, and never will forgive anyone who shall offer to speak disrespectfully of her.

I do in the same solemn manner declare, that I will defend my Friend and will never use evasive answers, but will always tell him whatsoever is said against him, and will more and more show to the world the great friendship I have for him, and all the malice that can be invented against him shall only bind me the stronger to him.

I do further promise, that all the allurements my enemies can think of, or the threats that they may make pour out upon me, shall never make me in the least change from what I so solemnly promiss in this paper.

I will take upon me the man in every thing, and will not shew that indifference which I have as yet too often done.

As I have chosen the vigorous part, I will throw off that indolence which if I don't soon get the better of will be my ruin, and will never grow weary of this, tho' - - - - - - - [George II] should live many years.

I hope my dear Lord you will conduct me through this difficult road and will bring me to the gole. I will exactly follow your advice, without which I shall inevitably sink.

I am young and unexperienc'd and want advice. I trust in your friendship which will assist me in all difficulties.

I know few things I ought to be more thankfull for to the Great Power above, than for its having pleas'd Him to send you to help and advise me in these difficult times.

I do hope you will from this instant banish all thoughts of leaving me, and will resolve, if not for my sake for the good of your country to remain with me. I have often heard you say, that you don't think I shall have the same friendship for you when I am married as I now have. I shall never change in that, nor will I bear to be in the least depriv'd of your company. And I shall expect that all my relations shall show you that regard which is due to the Friend of the whole family.

I sign my name with the greatest pleasure to what I have here written which is my firm and unalterable resolution.[6]

Over and over again George wrote to Bute pouring out the agony and mortification he suffered from his own failure to carry out certain resolutions and promises. Bute's upbraidings evidently seared his soul, for letter after letter attempts to explain past failures which the youth could not account for in conversation with his tutor. After beginning with a paragraph acknowledging how hurt he was by the last conversation with Bute and admitting the truth of all charges made about his indolence and negligence, George would immediately plunge into good resolutions:

I will apply all my time upon business, and will be able for the future to give you an account of everything I read.

As to what you mention'd in your note of last night concerning F-x it has made me strictly examine myself; and I do now here tell you that I am resolv'd in myself to take the resolute part, to act the man in everything, to repeat whatever I am to say with spirit and not blushing and afraid as I have hitherto, I will also never shew the least irresolution, and will not from being warm on any subject, by degrees grow quite indifferent about it, in short my conduct shall convince you that I am mortified at what I have done, and that I despise myself as everybody else must, that knows how I have acted; I hope that by altering now, I shall be able to regain your opinion which I vallue above everything in this world.[7]

A short time later, after admitting how often he had broken promises of reformation, he renewed his resolutions to put aside indolence and negligence:

All I beg is that you would have a little patience and judge by my actions whether my words are not my firm and unalterable resolutions.

I mean from the present hour to apply with the greatest assiduity

---

[6] Namier, *England in the Age of the American Revolution*, pp. 96–97.
[7] *Ibid.*, p. 100.

to attempt if it is possible to regain the many years I have fruitlessly spent; I will engage that you shall find a very visible alteration in me, the thoughts of what I ought to be shall ever be in my mind, and that added to my desire of making a good figure in the station it has pleased Almighty Providence to place me in, will make me spare no pains to accomplish this, though I own I am of such an unhappy nature that if I cannot in a good measure alter that, let me be ever so learned in what is necessary for a King to know, I shall make but a very poor and despicable figure. My dearest friend the only small return I can make you for your unwearied pains for my future quiet and honour, and the happiness of this my dear country is the making it appear that the many things you have said in my favour are not entirely void of truth.

I therefore desire that we may regulate my studies, and that you would at least once a week examine what I have done.[8]

It is interesting to compare Lord Waldegrave's rather serene estimate of the character of Prince George in 1758 with Professor Namier's recapitulation after examining the letters in the Bute Papers:

What mental diagnosis can be drawn from these letters for one who finally had to be diagnosed as hopelessly insane? Sensitive and brought up under abnormal conditions; imbued with high moral principles and paralyzed by an overwhelming consciousness of guilt; and yet all the time reminded of the high place he would some day have to fill; a youth who had never been allowed to be young and who had not managed to grow up; not diverted from serious work by passions and pleasures, but sinking helplessly into sad indolence; perceiving such a distance between what he felt himself to be and what he wanted to become, that he was bound to seek refuge in dissimulation; ready to resign his will completely to the man in whom he believed to have found his ideal; and yet, in that self-imposed bondage, yearning after great achievements.[9]

The characteristics so vividly described by Waldegrave and Professor Namier can be traced with both ease and profit during the fifty years of the King's life from his accession to the throne in 1760 until he became insane in 1810. Waldegrave's prophecy "that his parts, though not excellent, will be found very tolerable if ever they are properly exercised" turned out to be a very accurate one. His letters to Bute indicate the self-imposed discipline by which George compelled himself to use what ability

[8] *Ibid.*, p. 101.
[9] *Ibid.*. p. 102.

he possessed. Also his honesty, which Waldegrave acknowledged but criticized as lacking the frankness and openness which makes that trait appear amiable, continued to lack attractive features.

Three other characteristics which Waldegrave mentioned deserve even closer attention because they continued to influence fundamentally the King's relations with other people, particularly his ministers and political opponents. First, was absence of hypocrisy from his religion but the presence of too great attention to the "sins of his neighbour." George III certainly objected to excesses in the private life of his most prominent opponents although he seems to have ignored them in the cases of indispensable ministers. Second, his inability to distinguish right from wrong; it was difficult for him to change his mind because of his indolence and strong prejudices. It is true that his indolence vanished soon, but his strong prejudices did not diminish. Third, was the unhappy temper which, instead of breaking out in heat and violence, took refuge in a sullen retirement to the closet not to compose his mind but to "indulge the melancholy enjoyment of his own ill humor"; even a long sulk in the closet did not end the incident, because, both as Prince and as King, George retained too vivid a recollection of the wrongs which he felt had been done to him.

What can account for the transformation of the poor creature, whose shortcomings have been catalogued, into the shrewd, self-reliant King who, during the twenty-three years from 1760 to 1783, defeated the Whigs at practically every turn? Probably the most reasonable explanation of this transformation is that George did apply himself with the fervor which he had promised Lord Bute to the task of making a good figure in the station in which it had "pleased Almighty Providence" to place him. By the time he came to the throne he was able to make public appearances with dignity and poise. His first speech from the throne was spoken with such precision and calmness that he made an unusually favorable impression. Interest and participation in amateur theatricals have been suggested as a possible explanation for this improvement. In any case he had made good his promise to Bute "to repeat whatever I am to say with spirit and not blushing and afraid as I have hitherto." The influence of his mother had evidently declined before George became king; but that of Bute appears to have lasted until the resignation of Grenville in 1765.

It is unfortunate that we do not possess a real record of the history of George III's change in attitude toward Lord Bute. It would be interesting indeed to learn when the King first began to suspect that his "dearest friend" was not the superman he had imagined; or that he might have exaggerated when at the age of twenty he told Bute: "As to honesty, I have already lived long enough to know you are the only man I shall ever meet with, who possesses that quality." There is contemporary testimony to indicate that the King was quite relieved to be rid of Bute as Prime Minister in 1763. Perhaps he had already tired of the tutor-pupil relationship or even then may have recognized Bute's limitations. Such speculations, however, will probably remain unsatisfied because in later life the King's sense of loyalty appears to have prevented him from speaking, as he did of so many of his ministers, his honest opinion of Bute. George Grenville, despite George III's assurance to the contrary, believed that he owed his fall to the influence of Bute. When Rockingham took office in 1765, one of the conditions which he and his colleagues insisted upon was that Bute should have no influence, directly or indirectly, upon the affairs of state. There is good reason to believe that the King and Lord Bute did not see one another in private after 1765.

As already suggested in chapter one, it is difficult to say exactly when the political apprenticeship of George III came to an end. Bute and the King used Newcastle to manage the general election of 1761 and Henry Fox to pilot through the peace treaties of 1762–63, and to break the political machine of the Duke of Newcastle in December of 1762 by a wholesale dismissal of the Duke's followers and dependents from places in the ministry and from lord lieutenancies down to the lowest officials in the Customs and Excise Service. Thus, because it marked not only the victory of the King in the peace preliminaries on the 9th, and "the massacre of the Pelhamite Innocents" at Christmas time, but also the origin of a party believing in Parliamentary opposition in the nineteenth-century sense of the word, December 1762 is an epoch-making month in English constitutional history. Acting on his own initiative after parting with Bute in 1763, George made several bad blunders. He believed that the right of an English sovereign to appoint his own ministers was a most fundamental one. When, however, George Grenville, his First Lord of the Treasury, annoyed and humiliated him, he was unable to find a competent man who was willing to take office. Both in 1763 and in 1765

George made tactical errors which he would, in all probability, not have committed later in life. In 1763, desiring to be rid of Grenville, the King approached William Pitt concerning the formation of a ministry but in the end refused to allow the Whigs to come in as a group under Pitt. This afforded Grenville an opportunity to dictate the conditions under which he would remain in office. Again in 1765, angered by the manner in which the Grenville ministry had handled the Regency question, George III, on May 18, informed his chief minister that he contemplated a change in the government. The King commissioned his uncle, the Duke of Cumberland, to make overtures to Pitt. Success appeared to be in sight. But Lord Temple, brother of Grenville and brother-in-law of Pitt, refused to join in a ministry to displace his brother; and on May 22 Temple and Grenville, who had been on bad terms for several years, became reconciled. Pitt, unwisely it would seem, declined to serve in a ministry unless Temple were included. The Duke of Cumberland, after failing with Pitt, tried unsuccessfully to induce first Lord Lyttelton and then Charles Townshend to form a ministry, and after the failure advised his nephew to call back Grenville. The ministers now demanded humiliating concessions from the King, and were unmoved even by his tears. A few weeks of suffering under Grenville caused the King to request the Duke of Cumberland to renew his offer to Pitt. But once more Pitt, with great reluctance, refused, because Lord Temple would not join him. After two years and three months of Grenville, George decided that even the Whigs *en bloc* could not be worse than Grenville, and so sent the Duke of Cumberland to ask the Marquis of Rockingham to form a ministry.[10] The King used the Rockingham ministry merely as a breathing spell in which to come to terms with Pitt. In August of 1766 the latter finally succumbed to the insistent pleas of his sovereign and consented to form a ministry. Pitt's elevation to the peerage as Lord Chatham and his subsequent mysterious illness really removed him from the political scene as a serious menace to the King. When Chatham retired the Duke of Grafton, who was First Lord of the Treasury in this ministry, became the actual head of the government. Since George III was able to control both Grafton and North during the fifteen years following 1767, this phase of his political apprenticeship may be said to have ended during the Chatham-Grafton ministry.

10 Melville, *op. cit.*, I, 295.

Another phase, that of managing the House of Commons by influencing the choice of its members during elections and then their votes, lasted about the same length of time as that of dealing with chief ministers. This aspect of public affairs seems to have exercised the same fascination on George III that it did on the Duke of Newcastle. Evidently Thackeray did not intend to be complimentary when he wrote:

He knew all about the family histories and genealogies of his gentry, and pretty histories he must have known. He knew the whole ARMY LIST, and all the facings and the exact number of the buttons, and all the tags and laces, and the cut of all the cocked hats, pigtails and gaiters in his army. He knew the PERSONNEL of the Universities; what doctors were inclined to Socinianism, and who were sound Churchmen; he knew the etiquette of his own and his grandfather's Courts to a nicety, and the smallest particulars regarding the routine of ministers, secretaries, embassies, audiences; the smallest page in the ante-room or the meanest helper in the kitchen or stables. These parts of the Royal business he was capable of learning, and he learned.[11]

This description may be true; but it is misleading. George III was no mere antiquarian and his mind was not filled with unimportant knowledge. Many of the facts mentioned by Thackeray were the King's stock in trade; and he knew how to use these apparently insignificant details in a most effective fashion. But even more important in controlling the House of Commons, George III knew conditions in the English boroughs and counties, as well as the Welsh and Scottish ones, represented in the House of Commons; he knew the approximate amount of financial assistance that candidates who wished to represent these boroughs and counties would need to carry their elections; and he knew the patrons who controlled the rotten and pocket boroughs and the kind of influence to which they were most susceptible. The King evidently developed the same affection for details of this kind which Newcastle had possessed; and, apparently, this was one form of mental activity to which he did not have to drive himself. Although, as already noted, George and Bute used Newcastle to supervise the election of 1761, by 1768 the King felt quite capable of assuming control himself. Thus we may conclude that this phase of his political apprenticeship was also complete by 1768.

---

[11] W. M. Thackeray, *The Four Georges* (London, 1924, Everyman's ed.), pp. 373–74.

Probably the essay of George III on authority and government, which his secretary Lieutenant-General Sir Herbert Taylor preserved, is a result of his experiences during these years of apprenticeship. At least Taylor states that it was written during the early period of the long reign. The following excerpts from this essay make an interesting addition to the testimony given in the Waldegrave and Bute Papers:

The nature of man is the same in all places, and in all times, but varied, like their statures, complexions, and features, by the influence of the several climates where they are born, and by the education and manners they adopt; these produce generally the same forms of Government in the same sort of countries. . . . .

For there seems to be but two general kinds of Government; the one exercised according to the arbitrary command of a single person; the other according to certain laws introduced by custom or agreement, and not to be changed without the consent of many; but under these may be classed the various distinctions that are, by the authors who treat on this subject, so fully expatiated upon.

All Government is a restraint upon liberty, and under all, the dominion is equally absolute where it is the last resort.

So that when men seem to be contending for liberty, they are in reality only attempting to change those that rule, or to regain the forms of Government they formerly had been accustomed to; though when they enjoyed them it was not without some pressure and complaint.

Authority arises from opinion of wisdom, goodness, and valour, in the persons who possess it.

Wisdom enables men to judge what are the best ends, and what the best means of attaining them.

Goodness obliges men to prefer their duty and their promise before their passions or their interests, and is properly the object of trust, and consequently best expressed by the name of honesty.

Valour ensures respect, and promises protection.

Eloquence, beauty, and nobility have also some effect on the opinions of the vulgar; to which may be added another source from which usually springs greater authority than from all the rest, which is the opinion of Divine favour or designation of the persons or of the races that govern.

Piety, prosperity, and splendour in palaces also beget authority yet authority is confirmed and strengthened by nothing so much as by custom.

Power follows authority in civil bodies, as in natural (bodies) the motions of the body follow those of the mind. . . . .

Governments founded on contract may have succeeded those built on authority; but they seem rather to have been agreements between princes and subjects, than between men of equal rank and power.

It is needless to enter into the arguments or comparisons of the several forms of government that have been, or are in the world; that cause seems best that is supported by the ablest advocates; they have all their advantages and disadvantages; and that form suits best a nation that has been longest by use and custom established there. And in general those are the best Governments where the best men govern; and the difference is not so great in the forms of Magistracy, as in the persons of the Magistrates.[12]

If the conclusions reached in the preceding pages are correct, before Pitt became his Prime Minister in 1783, George III had had about fifteen years in which to enjoy his life as a political master craftsman and to polish off the rough corners of his technique after completing his apprenticeship. This advantage is one that is often overlooked in studying the relations of the two men.

Another factor which must be reckoned with is the King's private life down to 1783. On September 7, 1761, he married the Princess Charlotte of Mecklenburg-Strelitz and settled down to the quiet life of a country gentleman. For years he lived at Buckingham or Queen's House, Richmond Lodge, Kew, and Windsor Castle. Socially both George and his queen turned out to be a great disappointment to the upper classes in England. He frowned on gambling, racy conversation, expensive parties, and the pleasures of the table and bottle; opposition to the last two mentioned, as he readily admitted, came from the fear that he would in time become as corpulent as his uncle, the Duke of Cumberland. His admirers, however, are fond of pointing out that if he were averse to leading the life of the rake, he did lead that of the typical English gentleman of the time; not "the finicking, frivolous, heartless, three-bottle townman of quality, but the pleasant, God-fearing, self-respecting, amiable country squire," who enjoyed reading, music, outdoor sports, and a "friendly" game of cards.

The King's fundamental interest in private life was his rapidly growing family. Beginning with Prince George in 1762 and ending with the Princess Amelia in 1783, Queen Charlotte bore him fifteen children. He seems to have combined a genuine and in-

[12] Ernest Taylor, *The Taylor Papers: Being a Record of Certain Reminiscences, Letters, and Journals in the Life of Lieut.-Gen. Sir Herbert Taylor* (London: Longmans, Green & Company, 1913), pp. 62–64.

tense affection for all these children with a decided satisfaction in instructing them in what he considered to be correct principles. The pains which he took in their education he justified on the ground that the twig must be bent when young. He contended that "it is chiefly owing to the parents, if the children are devoid of proper principles." If the good King still believed in this thesis after the conduct of so many of his children showed that "proper principles" had not taken root, he must have suffered untold agonies. Since many of them turned out to be such bitter disappointments, it must have been doubly galling if he adhered to the belief that the conduct was due to his own failure to train them properly. George appears to have enjoyed his family most in the years before 1783. Until that time the King probably experienced greater pleasure in instructing his many children in correct principles than pain from their childish errors. The amours of his eldest son, which scandalized or delighted practically all classes in England, seem to have started in 1781. It is decidedly questionable whether the pain was not greater than the pleasure after that year. Thus the comparative calm of the King's family life during the years before the younger Pitt became Prime Minister in 1783 and the stormy time which His Majesty had with his sons during the long ministry from 1783 to 1801 are of primary importance in the constitutional history of the reign. George III had domestic problems which occupied more of his time during the 1780's than earlier. This in turn meant that he might leave to a Prime Minister, whom he felt he could trust, certain details which earlier in his reign he might have believed he should look after himself.

To sum up, we find George III, when Fox and North took office in April 1783, a man nearly forty-five years old, a father with a family of fifteen children, and a ripe politician with over twenty-two years of experience. The misfortunes of the two previous years had been harrowing. He had been forced to recognize the independence of the American Colonies, to grant legislative independence to Ireland, and to negotiate unfavorable peace treaties with both France and Spain. In addition, against his will, he had been compelled to submit to economical reform and to accept the Rockingham and Portland ministries. To offset partially these losses and humiliations he had within a short time rid himself of the obnoxious Rockingham ministry, and from his point of view, best of all, he had not been forced to surrender a single principle harmful to his prerogative.

WILLIAM PITT

The young man of twenty-four who in December 1783 became First Lord of the Treasury was in many respects in marked contrast to his sovereign. In no respects was this contrast more apparent than in the childhood and early precocity of Pitt. "The bib and porringer" study of the latter has received greater attention from recent biographers than Lord Rosebery deemed necessary; but so far as the background of the Pitt ancestry is concerned no one has done more to popularize it than Lord Rosebery himself in *Chatham, His Early Life and Connections*.

The swashbuckling career of "Diamond" Pitt, William's great-grandfather, and the brilliant record as War Minister of William Pitt, the first Earl of Chatham, should be well known to every student of the eighteenth century. On his mother's side the younger Pitt had illustrious relatives of a different caliber from those on his father's side. His mother, Hester Grenville, was the sister of Lord Temple and George Grenville. From the time Lord Temple, at that time Richard Grenville, succeeded to the estates of his uncle, Lord Cobham, until well into the nineteenth century the Grenvilles played an important part as one of the hereditary ruling families of England. Thus young Pitt had a double inheritance: from his father that of a man who raised his country and himself to glorious heights through sheer ability and personality; and from his mother that of being a member of the small group of ruling families. His father's career and abilities undoubtedly served as a model for him, but he seems to have inherited more of the personality and personal appearance of the Grenvilles. The starchy, half-sulky aloofness of his early Parliamentary conduct is certainly most typically Grenville.

Even the time of his birth gave him a marked advantage over his royal master. George III came into the world at a time when his parents were on bad terms with George II, and he suffered from the effect of the suspicion with which his father and grandfather regarded one another. Pitt was born on May 28, 1759, the year of the most amazing of the tremendous victories which England won during the years from 1757 to 1761, at a time when his father was Secretary of State and virtual war dictator.

But the childhood and early manhood of the King and of William Pitt varied even more than the conditions at the time when they were born. The early life of George III was characterized by indolence, ignorance, and backwardness. Pitt, on the other hand, was an infant prodigy. His health from earliest days was delicate, but it seems never to have impaired his intellect. The early years of his life were spent at Hayes, his father's estate in Kent, some twelve miles from London. The great War Minister seems to have devoted considerable time to the early training of his second son. A recent writer has speculated upon the impression which the conversations at Hayes, on such subjects as the war, the East India Company, members of Parliament, and the American Colonies, made on the active mind of the little boy. The very topics discussed were the ones which were to hold the interest of the boy during his entire life. This writer has gone so far as to say that "the feebleness of body became rather a help than a hindrance: it kept him indoors, within touch of events, when many a lad might have been playing games at the other end of the park."[13] Without discounting the value of listening in on the conversation of distinguished elders, it might not be inappropriate to remark that in later life Pitt on many occasions, such as the Westminster survey of 1784, showed that he lacked something which he might have learned had he played games with other lads in the park.

At the age of six William was placed under the care of a tutor; but at times his health was so bad that he was able to do little studying. Taken as a whole, however, the next eight years were profitably employed in the improvement of his mind; and these are the years in which he gained a reputation as an infant prodigy. Perhaps the best-known story is the one ascribed to Lady Caroline Holland, the mother of Charles James Fox. It was, apparently, genuine admiration for young Pitt, as well as misgivings about the training her own sons were receiving, which caused her to say: "I have been this morning with Lady Hester Pitt, and there is little William Pitt, *not eight years old,* and really the cleverest child I ever saw, and *brought up so strictly and so proper in his behaviour,* that, *mark my words,* that little boy will be a thorn in Charles' side as long as he lives."[14] He studied Greek, Latin, and mathematics under his tutor, and in addition received valuable assistance from his father whenever the health of that now very erratic man permitted. According to tradition Chatham read aloud to him and selected the best English and classical poets and

---

[13] E. Keble Chatterton, *England's Greatest Statesman: A Life of William Pitt, 1759–1806* (Indianapolis: The Bobbs-Merrill Company, 1930), p. 100. Used by special permission of the publishers.

[14] Lord John Russell, *Memorials and Correspondence of Charles James Fox* (London, 1853–1857), I, 25.

orators for him to read. Of even greater significance for the future was the training in oratory which he lavished upon William, for Chatham gave the youth the benefits of his own vast ability and experience in speaking in the House of Commons. This training included both ordinary extempore talks, and smooth translations of famous speeches of Greek and Roman orators. Since William was the younger son and would inherit little property, his father planned to have him take up law as a profession.[15] The training he received fitted him for the law as well as for politics, and the transition from the career of a barrister to a politician was not a difficult one.

At the age of fourteen William was sent to Pembroke Hall, Cambridge. The choice seems to have been determined by the fact that Pembroke was the college of his tutor, Wilson. His three years as an undergraduate, from 1773 to 1776, were spent in hard study. In fact too serious application to intellectual work impaired his already delicate health, and during his first term he became seriously ill. Dr. Addington, whose son was to succeed Pitt as Prime Minister, prescribed long hours of rest, open-air exercise, and a diet in which port wine played an important part. Six months at his home worked such improvement that Pitt was able to return to Cambridge.[16]

After his return Pitt seems to have resumed his serious life and hard studying. He appears to have had neither the time nor the inclination to sow wild oats. His tastes were obviously intellectual rather than convivial, and there is no reason to believe that it was a great sacrifice on his part to avoid disgracing the name of Pitt by refraining from gambling and carousing. The man who had the greatest influence on Pitt during his years in Cambridge was, from all accounts, George Pretyman. Although the latter was only about eight years older than Pitt, and hence not one of the mature dons, the two seem to have formed a relationship pleasing to Pitt and profitable to Pretyman. Later Pitt was able to reward Pretyman as George III rewarded his tutor Bute. The relaxation and vacation which Pitt enjoyed most was a trip to London to hear his father make his famous speeches in the House of Lords.

After taking his degree in 1776—without an examination, since as the son of a peer he was privileged to do so—Pitt re-

[15] Chatterton, *op. cit.*, p. 104.
[16] *Ibid.*, p. 111.

mained at Cambridge and resumed his studies. He continued to study classics and mathematics; but he also spent much time reading Locke and Adam Smith, practicing public speaking, and attending lectures on law to fit him for his career as a barrister.[17] The death of his father in May 1778, a few days before Pitt was nineteen years of age, made it necessary at once for him to consider the question of his profession. Chatham had left the estate in a bad tangle financially, and Pitt, as a younger son, could count on an income of only about three hundred pounds a year. His wealthy uncle, Lord Temple, helped him to purchase chambers at Lincoln's Inn for what Pitt called "a frightful sum" of £1,100.[18] A recent biographer of Pitt has speculated upon the effects which a few additional years as a barrister might have had in breaking down Pitt's proud reserve. As a barrister he would have been dependent on solicitors for his briefs, on juries for his verdicts, and on judges for his points of law.[19]

But his career at the bar was merely a passing phase because his real interest was in a Parliamentary career. When barely twenty years old Pitt had definitely decided to attempt to secure one of the two Cambridge University seats at the next general election. His reasons for selecting the University were because "It is the seat of all others the most desirable, as being free from expense, perfectly independent, and I think in every respect extremely honourable."[20] Perhaps this decision was reached as a result of Lord Rockingham's refusal, on August 7, 1779, to find Pitt a constituency; but it is likely that the latter actually preferred to represent the University for the reasons assigned. Rockingham's letter is of interest both because of its actual wording and because of the effect that it may have had on Pitt's relationship to the followers of that nobleman. It read: "I am so circumstanced from the knowledge I have of several persons who may be candidates, and who indeed are expected to be so, that it makes it impossible for me, in this instance, to show the attention to your wishes which your own, as well as the great merits of your family entitle you to."[21] This letter evidently caused Pitt to redouble his efforts

---

[17] Chatterton, *op. cit.,* p. 114.

[18] P. W. Wilson, *William Pitt the Younger* (New York: Doubleday, Doran & Company, 1930), p. 33.

[19] *Ibid.,* pp. 33–34.

[20] Lord Stanhope, *Life of William Pitt* (London, 1861–62), I, 31.

[21] Lord Albemarle, *Memoirs of the Marquis of Rockingham and His Contemporaries* (London, 1852), II, 423.

in Cambridge, because a week later he wrote to his friend the Duke of Rutland, thanking him for letters written to influential persons in the University. Plans to contest a University seat before reaching the age of twenty-one showed considerable assurance on the part of a young man even with the Pitt and Grenville background.

The result at Cambridge University in the general election of 1780 was the first disappointment Pitt was to suffer in his political life. He found himself at the bottom of the poll, despite the assets of the names of Pitt, Grenville, and Manners upon which he had counted so strongly. The Duke of Rutland, however, was able to use his influence in another direction with greater success. He introduced Pitt to Sir James Lowther and paved the way for the unsuccessful Cambridge candidate to enter the House of Commons as a representative of the pocket borough of Appleby. It is one of the ironies of history that William Pitt, whose private and political life were so spotless as to give him the title of the "immaculate boy," and whose first few years in Parliament were spent as an ardent advocate of both economical and Parliamentary reform, should have been able to enter the House of Commons only through the influence of the most notorious borough patron of the generation. In any list of a half-dozen of the most prominent borough patrons, Sir James's name was certain to be found; for, in addition to being noted for his arrogant and unpleasant personality, he had the reputation of controlling nine seats in the House of Commons. The fact that William Lowther, Esq., had been elected on September 18 for both Carlisle and Appleby and chose to sit for Carlisle, thus creating a vacancy, made it possible for Sir John to confer on Pitt the constituency of Appleby. Pitt was chosen on January 8, 1781, without appearing before the electors; and on January 23 he took his place in the House of Commons. It is a coincidence, seldom omitted in any work on Pitt, that he died on the twenty-fifth anniversary of this date.

Thus a period of less than three years elapsed from the time Pitt entered the House of Commons until he became First Lord of the Treasury. These years fall logically into three divisions: January 1781 to July 1782; July 1782 to March 31, 1783; and March 31 to December 19, 1783. In the first, Pitt was a private member; in the second, Chancellor of the Exchequer under Lord Shelburne; and in the third, one of the recognized leaders of the opposition to the Portland ministry. Such a remarkable rise certainly requires an explanation.

Two factors paved the way for a cordial reception of the new-comer in the House of Commons: the amazing reputation of his father's oratory in both houses; and his own reputation as an infant prodigy. Neither, however, would have insured young Pitt the permanent respect of the Commons had he failed in his first speech and continued to be unimpressive. Much has been made of the excellence of his first speech; and with justice. Speaking in the House of Commons requires a particular type of courage; and many a man who has been a successful speaker outside Parliament, either as a barrister or public lecturer, has failed within the House of Commons. Occasionally a man will make a brilliant first speech but will be disappointing in his later efforts. Such outstanding initial performances are often the result of long and careful preparation and come under the classification of set speeches; but the history of Parliament shows clearly that no man can make and keep a reputation merely by delivering carefully prepared speeches.

Pitt, it will be remembered, entered Parliament after the election of 1780, and as a result found himself in a House of Commons less friendly to economical and Parliamentary reform than the one dissolved the previous year. The attitude of the new House and the influence of the Gordon Riots had rendered the chances of reform measures unlikely in this session. It was on February 26, 1781, on the second reading of Burke's bill for the better regulation of His Majesty's Civil List revenue, and for abolishing several useless, expensive, and inconvenient places, that Pitt made his first speech. He had been urged by Byng, the member for Middlesex, to speak on this measure, but he appears to have decided against so doing. Whether or not the cries "Mr. Pitt! Mr. Pitt!" which arose when Lord Nugent sat down came unexpectedly and forced Pitt to speak, prepared or unprepared, there was no doubt as to the success of this initial effort. According to the editor of his speeches, "he displayed great and astonishing powers of eloquence. With a voice rich and harmonious; an easy and elegant manner; and language beautiful and luxuriant, he exhibited, in this first essay, a specimen of oratory worthy the son of the immortal Chatham."[22] Speaking strongly in support of Burke's bill, he stressed the necessity of retrenchment because of the critical financial condition of the country. In view of the fact that Pitt was speaking against abuses which vitally affected the King and

---

[22] *Speeches of the Right Honourable William Pitt* (London, 1808, 2d ed.), I, 1.

that the latter offered him the post of First Lord of the Treasury a little more than two years later, the references made to His Majesty are not without interest. After insisting that the King's ministers should have taken up this reform without having it forced on them, Pitt asked:

But if ministers failed to do this; if they interfered between the benignity of the sovereign and the distresses of his people, and stopped the tide of royal sympathy; was that a reason why the House of Commons, his Majesty's public counsellors, should desist from a measure so congenial to the paternal feelings of the sovereign, so applicable to the wants and miseries of the people?[23]

Later in the speech he pointed out that the Civil List revenue was granted by Parliament to His Majesty

for other purposes than those of personal gratification. It was granted to support the power and the interests of the empire, to maintain its grandeur, to pay the judges and the foreign ministers, to maintain justice and support respect; to pay the great officers that were necessary to the lustre of the crown; and it was proportioned to the dignity and the opulence of the people.—The people who granted that revenue, under the circumstances of the occasion, were justified in resuming a part of it, under the pressing demand of an altered situation. They clearly felt their right; but they exercised it with pain and regret. They approached the throne with bleeding hearts, afflicted at the necessity of applying for retrenchment of the royal gratifications; but the request was at once loyal and submissive. It was justified by policy, and his Majesty's compliance with the request was inculcated by prudence, as well as by affection.[24]

At the conclusion of the speech Pitt was showered with congratulations by North, Fox, and Burke. The accounts of the excellence of this initial effort were widely spread and gave the young man a great parliamentary reputation at the very beginning of his career.

Pitt's second speech, delivered May 31, 1781, is significant because of the clear statement of his views of the English Constitution. It was given in the course of a debate which followed the motion by Colonel Barré that the committee on the bill for paying into the exchequer the balances in the hands of public accountants should be instructed that they have power to make provision in the bill for removing the commissioners named by the said act, and for substituting other commissioners in their stead, who are mem-

---

[23] *Ibid.*, p. 2.
[24] *Ibid.*, pp. 6–7.

bers of the House of Commons. Lord North opposed the motion
and in answering his objections Pitt declared:

The noble lord had said, that the present commissioners of accounts were merely to enquire, examine, and report, and that it was
reserved for parliament to judge, to determine, and to act; that the
final deliberation was reserved to them, and they had the power to
reject such measures, proposed by the commissioners, as they might
deem inconsistent with the public welfare. How humiliating, how
miserable a picture of parliamentary power was this! So then, all
the power of parliament, with respect to the alleviation of national
burthens, the redress of grievances, the reform of expense, the
economy, the system, the elucidation of office, was sunk into a disgraceful negative! One positive power, indeed, an odious power,
remained—the power of taxing the people, whenever the noble lord
thought proper; the power of making them pay for the noble lord's
wild schemes and lavish corruption. If any plan was formed and suggested, by which thousands might be saved, by which the expenditure might be simplified, the influence of the crown diminished, and
the responsibility of ministers be more clearly established; by which
the engine of government might be relieved from that load of
machinery which rendered its movements so slow, so intricate,
and so confused; then the House of Commons possessed only the
power of putting a negative upon every such proposition. The power
of oppressing and burthening the people, therefore, was the only
parliamentary power that remained positive and active, while the
power of doing good, and of relieving the distresses of the subject,
was merely negative. He had often heard that the crown had a
constitutional power of putting a negative on the acts of the commons, but he had never before heard that the commons had the
power to put a negative on the wishes of the people, when those
wishes tended towards the establishment of a plan of reformation.
He was almost going to say, he could hardly have imagined that the
noble lord would have ventured to assert as much: perfectly sure
he was that no man else would have dared to have suggested even
an opinion that approached toward such a position.[25]

The phrase "the influence of the crown diminished, and the responsibility of the ministers be more clearly established" certainly
could leave no doubt in the mind of the King as to the constitutional position of Chatham's son at this time.

Pitt's stand on the American Revolution was, in view of his
father's stand, quite comprehensible. Nevertheless, the vehemence

[25] *Parliamentary History* (London, 1806–1820), XXII, 363–64.

with which he referred to the struggle in his third and fourth speeches marked him as a bitter opponent of the cause so dear to the King. Speaking on June 12, less than two weeks after the speech quoted in the preceding paragraph, Pitt declared that

He was persuaded, and would affirm, that it was a most accursed, wicked, barbarous, cruel, unnatural, unjust, and diabolical war! It was conceived in injustice; it was nurtured and brought forth in folly; its footsteps were marked with blood, slaughter, persecution and devastation; in truth, everything which went to constitute moral depravity and human turpitude were to be found in it . . . . The nation was drained of its best blood, and of its vital resources of men and money. The expense of it was enormous, much beyond any former experience and yet, what had the British nation received in return? Nothing but a series of ineffective victories, or severe defeats.[26]

Speaking again on November 28 after news of Yorktown had reached England he insisted that he must

give vent to those sentiments of indignation which, in the present disastrous situation of our affairs, he found it impossible for him to suppress; they rendered his situation too distressing to be borne in silence; the duty he owed to his sovereign and to his country would not permit him to remain in silence when he saw ministers running headlong into measures which could end only in the ruin of the state: he wished to shew his attachment to the sovereign and his family, by holding to him a language which would shew him that he had been deceived by those to whom he looked for advice: he wished to discharge his duty to his country, by endeavouring to prevent parliament from precipitately voting an Address, which pledged the House in the most direct manner to prosecute the American war, and support the continuance of that fatal system which had led this country, step by step, to the most calamitous and disgraceful situation that ever a once flourishing and glorious empire could possibly be driven to! A situation that threatened the final dissolution of the empire, if not prevented by timely, wise, and vigorous efforts![27]

The opponents of the American war had secured a valuable recruit.

The effect of these speeches was to make Pitt acknowledged as one of the outstanding men in the House of Commons; and clearly he regarded himself as such or he would have been incapable of making the two astounding declarations of January and March,

[26] *Ibid.*, XXII, 488–89.
[27] *Ibid.*, XXII, 731–32.

1782. The first came when in joining the attack on the Earl of Sandwich as First Lord of the Admiralty he made the significant statement of principle that

he was too young to be supposed capable of entertaining any personal enmity against the Earl of Sandwich; and he trusted that when he should be less young it would appear, that he had early determined in the most solemn manner, never to suffer any private and personal consideration whatever to influence his public conduct at any one moment of his life.[28]

The second and better-known declaration came on March 8, at the time the North ministry was tottering:

That he could not expect to take any share in a new administration; and were his doing so more within his reach, he never would accept of a subordinate situation.[29]

Some question arose at the time and has continued to the present as to whether Pitt did not speak on the impulse of the moment and immediately regret so arrogant an avowal of his own importance. Since he remained true to this principle when offered a subordinate, though lucrative, position in the Rockingham ministry, the weight of evidence seems to indicate that this declaration did not represent an impulse. It has been argued that Pitt would have been willing to accept a subordinate post if it had not meant swallowing his pride. Naturally such a question cannot be settled with mathematical accuracy, but the actions of Pitt both before and after the declaration and the refusal would seem to tilt the balance in the direction of the consistent policy rather than of the impulsive statement.

The failure to include Pitt in the Rockingham ministry was merely another of the many Whig mistakes in judgment which made possible the continuous triumphs of George III. Without doubt it was the highest presumption on the part of Pitt to expect to be taken into the cabinet at the age of twenty-two after being a member of Parliament for only fourteen months. Yet it was the consistent failure of the Whigs from 1760 to 1807 to retain in their ranks promising recruits that made it possible for the King to secure first-class parliamentarians to carry on his government. When negotiations through Lord Shelburne were going on between the Whigs and George III after the resignation of Lord

---

[28] George Tomline, *Memoirs of the Life of Pitt* (London, 1821), I, 52–53.
[29] *Parliamentary History,* XXII, 1149.

North in March of 1782, there seemed a strong probability of Pitt's being offered a place in the cabinet. Lord Shelburne evidently urged it and believed that success was assured, since he received a letter from Lady Chatham dated March 28 in which she expressed her satisfaction both with the honor done to her son and with the recent change in the administration.[30]

Doubtless, Lord Rockingham and prominent members of his division of the party felt justified in excluding Pitt from the cabinet both because of his extreme youth and inexperience and because of the treatment which the young man's father had given them on various occasions from 1762 to 1778. At the same time it must have tended to increase Pitt's grievance against the Rockingham Whigs, who had refused to help find him a Parliamentary seat in 1779, and to make him willing to associate more closely with a group who were not so vigorous in their attacks on the King's prerogatives.

Despite the fact that the actions of the Rockingham Whigs tended in the long run to throw him into such associations, Pitt showed the greatest interest during the brief ministry of Rockingham in the question of Parliamentary reform. During the next three years the Parliamentary reformers found in Pitt their ablest leader. The Rockingham Whigs had proved a disappointment after securing economical reform; and the reformers came more and more to pin their hopes on the Shelburne Whigs, and particularly on Pitt. It is true that

advocates of reform were also to be found amongst the Rockinghams: Savile, a slow convert, but no weathercock, and an earnest reformer throughout the short remainder of his life; Charles Fox, rapidly converted and as rapidly discouraged, frequently lukewarm, but readily redeemed by his gift of easy penitence; and Richmond, whose outright advocacy of sweeping reform may help to explain the cessation, a few months later, of his association with the Rockingham party.[31]

Pitt has been criticized for bringing up the question of Parliamentary reform as a private member instead of waiting for the Rockingham ministry to do so after it had had the opportunity of grappling with more pressing problems. It seems, however, more

[30] Lord Fitzmaurice, *Life of William Earl of Shelburne* (London, 1912, 2d ed.), II, 91.

[31] G. S. Veitch, *The Genesis of Parliamentary Reform* (London: Constable & Company, Ltd., 1913). p. 83.

than doubtful whether the ministry was interested in going beyond economical reform. Pitt's speech of May 7, 1782,[32] appears to have been one of his best. He merely proposed that a committee be appointed to inquire into the best means of carrying out a "moderate and substantial reform." He attacked with impartial vigor the Treasury, the pocket, and the rotten boroughs and claimed that the interests of the people and the rights of the electors were sacrificed to interests of the Treasury and of the great man, whether lord or commoner, who had a connection with the borough. His case was summed up in the passage:

It was of the essence of the constitution, that the people should have a share in the government by the means of representation; and its excellence and permanency was calculated to consist in this representation having been designed to be equal, easy, practicable and complete. When it ceased to be so; when the representative ceased to have connection with the constituent, and was either dependent on the crown or the aristocracy, there was a defect in the frame work of representation, and it was not innovation, but recovery of constitution to repair it.[33]

Although the Rockingham Whigs might be displeased with the vigor of this independent reformer, George III was certain to be even less pleased.

Despite the defeat of his motion, Pitt continued to support reform in and out of Parliament. On May 17 he spoke in support of Alderman Sawbridge's motion to reduce the duration of parliaments below the existing seven-year limit. On May 18 he attended a meeting of the friends of Parliamentary reform at the Thatched House Tavern, which was held, apparently, under the auspices of the Society for Promoting Constitutional Information.[34] The minutes of the meeting, which are in Pitt's handwriting, contain a motion passed to petition Parliament for "a substantial reform of the Commons House of Parliament." In 1793–94 Pitt was to find his conduct at this time a source of embarrassment.

Soon after, the death of Rockingham on July 1 resulted in the elevation of Shelburne to the place of First Lord of the Treasury and of Pitt to that of Chancellor of the Exchequer. Thus the young man attained an office which was, in all probability, better than the one he had been denied in March. The first few months

---

[32] *Parliamentary History*, XXII, 1416–22.   [33] *Ibid.*, p. 417.

[34] J. H. Rose, *Life of William Pitt* (London: G. Bell & Sons, Ltd., 1923), I, 109.

in office were taken up largely with the duties of his new office and with cabinet meetings to pass on negotiations with the American Colonies and the Bourbon powers. The session of Parliament ended July 11, and the next one did not open until December 5. Without doubt these months were of great importance in furnishing Pitt an apprenticeship as an administrator and a member of a cabinet; but since the important issue was peace with America, Spain, Holland, and France, which was to be finally settled before Pitt became Prime Minister in December 1783, the details need not concern us at this point. The breakup of the Shelburne ministry as a result of the Fox-North Coalition has been described in chapter one. Internal dissension before the coalition was formed seems to have paved the way for the overthrow of the government; but even Pitt's opponents admit that he remained loyal to Lord Shelburne during the last weeks in which the ministry tottered toward its fall.

From the point of view of the future of William Pitt and Charles James Fox, the fall of Shelburne was not so important as the results of the interview between the two men which preceded the formation of the Fox-North Coalition. The King, Shelburne, and other ministers realized that the ministry must be reinforced by the addition of either Fox or North. But the fact that Fox refused Pitt's, and North refused Dundas' offer, is less important than the results of Fox's refusal on his own future and that of Pitt. The latter, in an interview on February 11, proposed to Fox that he should join the government. Fox then asked whether or not Shelburne was to remain as the First Lord of the Treasury; and when Pitt replied in the affirmative, he ended the matter by declaring that he was unwilling to enter any administration in which Lord Shelburne was Prime Minister. Pitt is alleged to have said: "I did not come here to betray Lord Shelburne."[35] Such an attitude was bound to seem offensive to Fox. The breach between the two men was irreparable.[36]

The results of this interview were a most important factor in bringing years of political happiness to the King, Pitt, and Dundas, and exclusion from office to Charles James Fox. The interview not only widened the differences between Pitt and Fox but it also brought the former closer to the King's Friends.[37] The King was

[35] Tomline, *op. cit.*, I, 89.
[36] Rose, *op. cit.*, p. 117.
[37] Lord Fitzmaurice, *op. cit.*, II, 233.

the chief gainer, since it meant that the two important leaders of the Whigs who, united, might have forced their will and policies upon him were now practically irreconcilable. Pitt and Dundas, who soon became Pitt's right-hand man, were after December able to look forward to years of office. Fox, on the other hand, with Shelburne and North, absorbed the loss; but whereas they retired from active competition, Fox was to face more than twenty-two years in opposition as a result of this and other blunders.

The bitterness aroused by the failure of the negotiations of Pitt and Dundas with Fox and North and the subsequent coalition of the latter is shown in the debates which followed on the preliminary articles of peace. On February 17, only six days after his famous interview with Fox, Pitt showed his feelings in answering a witty speech by Sheridan:

No man *admired* more than he did the abilities of that hon. gentleman, the elegant sallies of his thought, the gay effusions of his fancy, his dramatic turns, and his epigrammatic points; and if they were reserved for the proper stage, they would no doubt receive, what the honourable gentleman's abilities always did receive, the plaudits of the audience; and it would be his fortune, *Sui plausu gaudere theatri.* But this was not the proper scene for the exhibition of these elegancies; and he therefore must beg leave to call the attention of the House to the serious consideration of the very important question then before them.[38]

This tendency to deprecate flippancies is a common one in Pitt's early speeches. His admirers claim that he was very witty outside the House of Commons but felt that his youth disqualified him from indulging in pleasantries and witticisms in speaking in the Commons. In this instance, however, he laid himself open to a retort by Sheridan which touched two points upon which he was most sensitive: his good taste and his extreme youth. In replying, Sheridan

took notice of that particular sort of personality which the right honourable gentleman had thought proper to introduce. He need not, comment on it. The propriety, the taste, the gentlemanly point of it, must have been obvious to the House. But, said Mr. Sheridan, let me assure the right hon. gentleman, that I do now, and will at any time when he chooses to repeat this sort of allusion, meet it with the most sincere good humour. Nay, I will say more—flattered and encouraged by the right honourable gentleman's panegyric on

[38] *Parliamentary History,* XXIII, 489–90.

my talents, if ever I again engage in the compositions he alludes to, I may be tempted to an act of presumption, to attempt an improvement on one of Ben Jonson's best characters, the character of the Angry Boy in the Alchymist.[39]

Four days later Pitt spoke at far greater length in his defense of the peace preliminaries. His feeling ran even higher against the Coalition, for after a point-to-point discussion of the treaties he declared:

I repeat then, Sir, that it is not this treaty, it is the Earl of Shelburne alone whom the movers of this question are desirous to wound. This is the object which has raised the storm of faction; this is the aim of the unnatural coalition to which I have alluded. If, however, the baneful alliance is not already formed, if this ill-omened marriage is not already solemnized, I know a just and lawful impediment, and, in the name of the public safety, I HERE FORBID THE BANNS.[40]

Then follows the most remarkable part of this heated speech. Pitt gives what is practically a defense and apologia of his brief tenure in office. It is studded with such jewels as:

My own share in the censure, pointed by the motion before the house against his Majesty's ministers, I will bear with fortitude, because my own heart tells me I have not acted wrong.[41]

It has been the great object of my short official existence to do the duties of my station with all the ability and address in my power, and with a fidelity and honour which should bear me up, and give me confidence, under every possible contingency or disappointment.[42]

High situation, and great influence, are desirable objects to most men, and objects which I am not ashamed to pursue, which I am even solicitous to possess, whenever they can be acquired with honour, and retained with dignity. But even these objects I am not beneath relinquishing, the moment my duty to my country, my character, and my friends, renders such a sacrifice indispensable.[43]

Although these selected passages certainly sound priggish and self-righteous when printed, the testimony of listeners makes clear that the speech when spoken had a tremendous effect on members of the House of Commons. But despite the thrill which the members may have enjoyed, the eloquence was not sufficient to save Lord Shelburne. By a majority of 17 the vote of censure proposed by

[39] *Ibid.*, p. 491.   [40] *Ibid.*, p. 552.   [41] *Loc. cit.*

[42] *Ibid.*, p. 553.   [43] *Loc. cit.*

Lord John Cavendish was passed,[44] and on February 24 Lord Shelburne resigned.

THE RAPPROCHEMENT OF GEORGE III AND WILLIAM PITT, FEBRUARY TO DECEMBER, 1783

During the thirty-seven-day interval from February to April 1783, in which George III tried desperately to avoid accepting Portland, Fox, and North as his ministers, Pitt was twice offered the position of First Lord of the Treasury. The first offer came immediately after Lord Shelburne's resignation; and the weight of evidence indicates that the suggestion came from Shelburne and not from Dundas, as the latter claimed at a later date. According to the King Pitt on the 27th declined because of the uncertainty of obtaining a majority in the House of Commons.[45] The King offered the place to Lord North, then to Lord Gower, and, finally, with significant reservations, to the Duke of Portland. The real difference between Portland and the King, and indeed between the fundamental political philosophy of the Whigs and that of the King, was summed up by George III in describing a conversation with the Duke:

He, to my astonishment, said this was want of confidence in him for that the Cabinet once laid before Me, he expected that on his coming to the head of the Treasury, I should rely on his making no propositions but such as He thought necessary for my affairs and consequently that I should acquiesce in them. This unexpected idea, I fortunately did not treat with the warmth it deserved, but on finding that [the] Duke would not see the singularity of the proposition and that on discussing it he began to grow warm, said I must have time to consider of a proposition I thought so novel.[46]

The King expected Portland to send him what he called "the whole Plan of Arrangements" to examine before giving any opinion on particular parts; but Portland expected to hand to the King a list of the names of seven men who were to make up the cabinet. The King expected a government which would exclude no party; and the Duke of Portland wanted one based on the principle of cabinet solidarity and joint responsibility.

[44] *Parliamentary History,* XXIII, 571.

[45] Sir John Fortescue (ed.), *Correspondence of King George the Third* (London: Macmillan & Company, Lt., 1928), VI, 322. Hereafter cited as *Correspondence of King George the Third.*

[46] *Ibid.,* p. 325.

The King's second offer to Pitt came as a result of the failure to come to an understanding with Portland. Pitt's letter of refusal, although couched in words of conventional respect, shows a determination to make the refusal final.

Mr. Pitt received this Morning the Honour of Your Majesty's Gracious Commands. With Infinite Pain he feels himself under the Necessity of humbly expressing to Your Majesty that with every sentiment of dutiful Attachment to Your Majesty and of zealous desire to contribute to the Public Service, It is utterly impossible for Him after the fullest consideration of the situation in which things stand, and of what passed yesterday in the House of Commons, to think of undertaking under such circumstances the Situation which Your Majesty has had the condescension and Goodness to propose to Him. As what Mr. Pitt now presumes to write, is the final Result of his best Reflection, He should think Himself inexcusable· if by delaying till tomorrow humbly to lay it before Your Majesty, ... he should be the cause of Your Majesty's not immediately turning your Royal Mind to such a Plan of Arrangement as the Exigency of all the present circumstances may in Your Majesty's Wisdom, seem to require.[47]

The King clearly expected this refusal, as in a letter written to Lord Weymouth a few hours before he received Pitt's reply he wrote that he was certain Pitt meant to play false, and wanted him to resume negotiations with the Coalition.[48] His lack of hope, however, did not prevent him from expressing deep disappointment in his answer to Pitt. The latter's letter had been dated "March 25th, 1783. m.30 pt. One p.m." and the King's reply, "m.35 pt. 4 p.m." on the same date. The King wrote: "I am much hurt you are determined to decline at an hour when those who have any regard for the Constitution as established by Law ought to stand forth against the most daring unprincipled faction that the Annals of this Kingdom ever produced."[49] This stiff reply indicated that Pitt might have paid dearly for this refusal had the King been able to find anybody else of ability to fill the position of First Lord of the Treasury. During this period of mortification George III appears to have felt closest to Jenkinson, Thomas Pitt, William Grenville, and Lord Temple. A memorandum drawn up by the King brings out that he offered the place of first minister to

[47] Pitt MSS, 101, March 25, 1783.
[48] *Correspondence of King George the Third,* VI, 310.
[49] *Ibid.,* pp. 311–12. By permission of the Macmillan Company, publishers.

Thomas Pitt; and the correspondence between George III and Lord Temple indicates that the latter would in all probability have received a similar offer had he not been in Dublin. Very soon, however, the King was speaking of Pitt in high terms to William Grenville and Lord Temple. That Pitt did not earn a permanent place on the King's blacklist seems to have been due to the fact that George III had fewer counts against him than against Fox, North, and Shelburne. In the King's estimation, Fox was the lowest of politicians, North an ingrate and a deserter, and Shelburne a broken reed. George III's attitude when forced to accept the Coalition is summed up in a paragraph of his letter of April 1 to Lord Temple:

A Ministry which I have avowedly attempted to avoid by calling on every other description of Men, cannot be supposed to have either My favour or confidence and as such I shall most certainly refuse any honours that may be asked by them; I trust the eyes of the Nation will soon be opened as my sorrow may prove fatal to my health if I remain long in this thraldom; I trust You will be steady in Your attachment to Me and ready to join other honest Men in watching the conduct of this unnatural Combination, and I hope many months will not elapse before the Grenvilles, the Pitts and other men of abilities and character will relieve Me from a Situation that nothing but the supposition that no other means remained of preventing the public finances from being materially affected would have compelled me to submit to.[50]

During the days between Pitt's refusal and this communication the King drew up two letters of abdication;[51] but it is extremely doubtful if either represented more than a passing mood. The reasons why the King did not abdicate are in all probability contained in a memorandum by Thomas Pitt.[52] Whether or not they were original with Thomas Pitt the ideas appear to be the ones which caused the King to accept the Coalition and which determined his policy during the next nine months. After elaborating on the difficulties of the new ministry—the popular odium, their discordant principles, the disappointments of interested individuals, and the problems of state—the memorandum concluded:

Under such circumstances left to themselves and to the course of things, they would become contemptible in the eyes of the public, insignificant as leaders of party and would in a short time give way to

---

[50] *Correspondence of King George the Third*, VI, 330.
[51] *Ibid.*, pp. 314–17.   [52] *Ibid.*, pp. 318–19.

what must be the wish of every honest Man, an administration which could at once establish itself in the confidence of H.My. and in the hearts of his People.[53]

When, "left to themselves and to the course of things," the Coalition did not fall, George III took measures of his own. He did not believe that all things come to him who waits.

Pitt did not spend his time between March and November in attempting to conciliate George III or in paving the way for the events of December 18–19. Although perfectly aware of the King's attitude toward Parliamentary reform, he moved three resolutions on May 7 : the first to prevent bribery and expenses at elections ; the second to disfranchise a borough when the majority of the voters were found guilty by a select committee of the House of gross and notorious corruption ; and the third to give the shires and the metropolis additional representatives.[54] One section of Pitt's speech made in support of these resolutions could not but give offense to the King, since he insisted that :

The house itself had discovered, that a secret influence of the crown was sapping the very foundation of liberty by corruption : the influence of the crown had been felt within those walls, and had often been found strong enough to stifle the sense of duty, and to over-rule the propositions made to satisfy the wishes and desires of the people ; the House of Commons [in former parliaments] had been base enough to feed the influence that enslaved its members : and thus was at one time the parent and the offspring of corruption. This influence, however, had risen to such a height, that men were ashamed any longer to deny its existence, and the house had at length been driven to the necessity of voting that it ought to be diminished. Various were the expedients that had been thought of, in order to affect so salutary a purpose, as was that of guarding against this influence ; of shutting against it the doors of that house, where, if it once got footing, after the resolution alluded to, liberty could no longer find an asylum. The House of Commons, which, according to the true spirit of the constitution, should be the guardian of the people's freedom, the constitutional check and control over the executive power, would, through this influence, degenerate into a mere engine of tyranny and oppression, to destroy the constitution in effect, though it should, in its outward form, still remain.[55]

Pitt then dealt with three commonly expressed expedients to bar the entrance of this influence into the Commons and gave his

---

[53] *Ibid.*, p. 319.   [54] *Parliamentary History*, XXIII, 834.   [55] *Ibid.*, p. 830.

opinion of all three. First, manhood suffrage, which assumed that an individual should be governed only by the laws to which he had given his consent in person or by his representative, Pitt rejected because it meant that the persons who voted for the defeated candidate were unrepresented and hence were slaves. His idea of representation was that the members once chosen represented not only those who had voted for them but also those who had not voted for them and those who were not entitled to vote. He concluded his arguments against manhood suffrage with the expressed hope "that no one would ever attempt to introduce it into the laws of England, or treat it in any other light than as a mere speculative proposition, that may be good in theory, but which it would be absurd and chimerical to endeavour to reduce to practice."[56] The second expedient suggested was to abolish the franchise of rotten boroughs. While admitting that borough members were more susceptible to influence than county members, Pitt felt that cutting the roots of this influence was using a remedy that might be worse than the disease. He was, therefore, unwilling to disfranchise such boroughs but believed undue influence could be kept down by a counterbalance. The third expedient was to add members to the House of Commons who should be returned by the metropolis and the counties. This plan was endorsed by Pitt on the ground that it was the least objectionable of the three. Certainly there was nothing subtle in the appeal which he made to the country gentlemen. "It was unnecessary," Pitt pointed out,

for him to say, that the county members in general were almost necessarily taken from that class and description of gentlemen the least liable to the seduction of corrupt influence, the most deeply interested in the liberty and prosperity of the country, and, consequently, the most likely to pursue such measures as appeared to them the most salutary to their country: in the hands of such men the liberties of their constituents would be safe, because the interests of such representatives, and the represented must necessarily be the same.[57]

Even the increase in the number of representatives did not appear to Mr. Pitt to be a great evil, because he felt that after disputed elections in the future the select Committee of the House of Commons would disqualify certain boroughs from sending representa-

---

[56] *Parliamentary History*, XXIII, 831.
[57] *Ibid.*, pp. 832–33.

tives to Parliament. In this manner the number of members in the House of Commons would be reduced down to nearly the existing number.

Despite Pitt's effective speech the resolutions were rejected 293 to 149.[58] The size of the majority against him may be ascribed to the opposition of Lord North and the King's Friends and to the indifference of Fox and other Rockingham Whigs. The King's answer to Fox's account of the debate gives an indication of his feelings toward both Fox and Parliamentary reform; for it merely stated that Fox's list of the speakers in the debate had been received.[59] Certainly Pitt did nothing to further a *rapprochement* with the King by his vigorous denunciation of the growing influence of the Crown and his demand for even so mild a kind of Parliamentary reform as additional members for the metropolis and counties.

Pitt, likewise, introduced a measure on June 17 to provide for retrenchment in the offices of the Treasury, Admiralty, Ordnance, Excise, and Stamps.[60] Since this measure failed to become a law and because reforms of this kind were carried out by Pitt when he became Prime Minister, it is unnecessary to devote further time to them at this point. Its only significance in June of 1783 was that it further deepened the King's impression of Pitt as a reformer and, in all probability, was one of the reasons why George III did not overthrow the Coalition on the question of the allowance for the Prince of Wales. Partly owing to the influence of Charles James Fox, the Prince's tastes in pleasure and in politics ran directly contrary to those of his father. As a result of exploiting these tastes the Prince, to the dismay of George III, had fallen deeply in debt. The Duke of Portland in writing to the King on June 15 suggested a hundred thousand pounds for the Prince's establishment. This amount had been agreed to rather reluctantly by Lord North and Lord Stormont, as later correspondence with George III was to show. When the King found that his son was to receive so large an allowance and that the ministry expected him to pay his son's outstanding debts, which Portland estimated at 29,000 pounds, his indignation reached new heights. In a letter to the Duke written on June 16 he poured out all the suppressed fury of recent months:

[58] *Ibid.,* p. 875.

[59] *Correspondence of King George the Third,* VI, 379.

[60] *The Speeches of William Pitt in the House of Commons,* I, 52.

It is impossible for me to find words expressive enough of my utter indignation and astonishment at the letter I have just received from the D. of Portland; these words are certainly strong and would be inexcusable if not authorised by the following facts. When the D. of Portland desired I would turn my thoughts to fixing on a sum for the Separate Establishment of the P. of Wales, when He arrives at the age of twenty one years, I desir'd he would with the rest of the efficient Ministers consider what proposal should be made to Me on that subject; about a fortnight since He acquainted Me that it was their unanimous opinion, that a sum of one hundred thousand pounds, including the Revenue of the Dutchy of Cornwall should be obtained from Parliament; I instantly shewed my surprise at so lavish an idea and the more so when my subjects are so much loaded with Taxes, and said I thought fifty thousand pounds in Addition to the Revenue of Cornwall which would nearly exceed Twenty seven thousand per annum of what the late King thought sufficient for Me in a similar Situation was all that could with any reason be granted; and consequently desired that Duke to acquaint the Ministers with my opinion and of my wish that they should reconsider this business, on the 6th of this month the D. of Portland told Me they continued to think it right to propose that sum to Parliament from whom they meant the whole sum should come; that the reasons of putting it so high arose from a knowledge that the P. of Wales had debts which must be paid out of his Annual Income, besides the Expence of fitting himself out; and that they meant to acquaint Him of this and that no addition could be made whenever he married: I did not deny that I still thought the Sum too large though I acknowledged if no encrease was made whenever He married that I would make no further Objection.

I therefore was surprised on the 13th to find the D. of Portland had not the Drafts of the Messages, but that they would soon be sent to me, from which time I have been in expectation of them; but this suspence is now fully explained, for the whole proposition is changed, I am to be saddled with the whole Odium of this measure, and the expence at the same time ultimately to fall entirely on Me who am not from my numerous progeny in a Situation to bear it; though I had been assured no part was to be paid by Me, and in addition I am pressed to take twenty nine thousand pounds of debts on myself which I have not incurred, that the Public May blame me and the P. of Wales with so unreasonable an income not be subject to this sum which can alone arise from shameful extravagance.

I therefore must declare that unless the proposal is brought back to the mode in which the D. of Portland first stated it to Me and that all expences are thrown on the P. of Wales, I cannot proceed in this business, and shall think myself obliged to let the Public know the cause of the delay and my opinion of the whole transaction. I cannot conclude without saying that when the D. of Portland came into Office I had at least hoped he would have thought himself obliged to have my interest and that of the Public at heart, and not have neglected both to gratify the passions of an ill advised Young Man.[61]

Members of the ministry evidently expected the King to follow so vigorous a letter with a real attempt to secure new ministers;[62] since his concluding sentence gave the impression that he would never "forget or forgive" the actions so angrily denounced. Some ministers believed that such language meant the King had "settled with the enemy." Although he had his way in the Prince of Wales's settlement, since Parliament agreed to vote £60,000 for the debts of the Prince and £50,000 a year out of the Civil List, the fear that the King would turn out the ministry did not materialize. Writing a month later to Lord Northington,[63] Fox ascribed the escape to the fact that no understanding existed between the King and Lord Temple to form an administration because otherwise it was inconceivable that so skillful a tactician as George would allow this wonderful opportunity to be lost. Had the King demanded the resignation of the ministry, dissolved Parliament, and appealed to the country, Fox admitted that the King and Temple "would have had on their side the various cries of Paternal Authority, Economy, Moderate Establishment, Mischiefmaking between Father and Son, and many other plausible topics."[64] Since the ministry had survived this ordeal, Fox felt that its position was fairly strong. The King, he believed, was neither pleased nor displeased, and had in mind no other administration. Admitting that he might be a bit sanguine, he based his confidence on the strength of the ministry in the House of Commons, the acknowledgment even by the enemy that there was no hope of dissension between the two parts of the Coalition, and the difficulty of Shelburne, Pitt, Temple, and Thurlow arranging a satisfactory agreement. Since he claimed to have definite knowledge that these four were having scarcely any communication with one another Fox felt the danger of being "overturned in Parliament quite chimerical." With a foresight too often lacking, Fox

[61] *Correspondence of King George the Third,* VI, 399–401 (London: Macmillan & Company, Ltd., 1928). By permission of the publishers.

[62] Lord John Russell, *op. cit.,* II, 112–13.

[63] *Ibid.,* pp. 115–21.

[64] *Ibid.,* p. 115.

conceded that the India Bill which he planned to introduce in the next session would be the issue upon which the Opposition would be likely to be formidable. Had he but known that within less than a week Thurlow sounded Pitt on the question of forming an administration, Fox might have been less confident. The account of his interview with Thurlow is contained in a letter from Pitt to Temple.[65] Thurlow insisted that the King would never forgive his present ministers and he attempted to discover Pitt's attitude on Parliamentary reform and on the influence of the Crown. In the light of his acceptance of the position of First Lord of the Treasury in December, Pitt's attitude at this time is significant. Since he felt that Thurlow was evasive on many points and was attempting to create the impression that the King did not feel the need for a new ministry, Pitt wrote to Temple:

I stated in general that if the King's feelings did not point strongly to a change, it was not what we sought. But if they did, and we could form a permanent system, consistent with our principles, and on public grounds, we should not decline it. I reminded him how much I was pledged to Parliamentary reform on the principles I had publicly explained, which I should support on every reasonable occasion. I treated as out of the question any idea of measures being taken to extend influence, though such means as are fairly in the hands of Ministers would undoubtedly be to be exerted. And I said that I wished those with whom I might act, and the King (if he called upon me) to be fully apprized of the grounds on which I should necessarily proceed.[66]

In his answer Lord Temple[67] graciously commended Pitt for the manner in which he had conducted himself in the interview with Thurlow. Admitting that Pitt was pledged to Parliamentary reform, "whenever there is a reasonable prospect of success," Temple deplored the fact that "the other reform" had missed its great objects. The most significant passage in the answer, however, comes when he gives Pitt his idea of the conditions under which a ministry should be formed:

But, whatever we may think upon time or mode I am most clearly and decisively of opinion that we cannot be too explicit in our refusal to engage in government upon the avowed or implied system of re-

[65] Historical Manuscripts Commission, *The Manuscripts of J. B. Fortescue, Esq., Preserved at Dropmore* (London, 1892–1927), I, 215–16.

[66] *Ibid.*, p. 216.

[67] *Ibid.*, pp. 216–18.

placing in the hands of the Crown that influence which has been already taken from it; excepting in any instance (if such there be) where an improper new arrangement may make a change necessary, not for influence but for proper administration of each department; and even this last exception should be kept out of sight in order that no superstructure may be built by Lord Thurlow upon it.[68]

Since the King was unwilling to continue the existing ministry, to recall Lord North, or to depend upon Lord Gower alone, his only hope, Lord Temple concluded, was to bring in a Temple-Pitt government under conditions as favorable as he could extract.

Why did George III not reach some agreement with Pitt and Temple in June or July instead of waiting until December? The answer may be that either the King or Pitt was willing to make concessions at the end of the five months. The most likely explanation, however, is the one which Lord Temple claims to have impressed upon His Majesty:

I thought it my duty to offer to him my humble advice to go on with his Ministers, if possible, in order to throw upon them the ratification of the Peace, which they professed to intend to ameliorate, and to give them scope for those mountains of reform, which would inevitably come very short of the expectations of the public.[69]

Whether or not he was indebted to Temple for these ideas, George III appears to have acted in accordance with them and for the time being to have given up the thought of ridding himself of the Coalition. Pitt also seems to have felt that no action was to be taken in the direction of a change in ministry because he took advantage of the recess between sessions to visit the Continent.

The ministry handled the peace treaties and reform as Temple prophesied that it would. The ministers were unable to secure any better terms in the definite treaties of peace which were signed in September; and there was no prospect of Parliamentary or even additional economical reform, as the vote on Pitt's motion of the previous May and June had shown. The issue upon which the ministry was overthrown was, as Charles James Fox had feared in July, the India Bill.

The merits of this India Bill, which in most respects were high, are not so important in this connection as the part which it played in the struggle between George III and the Whigs. The handling

[68] *Ibid.*, p. 217.
[69] The Duke of Buckingham, *Memoirs of the Court and Cabinets of George III* (London, 1853), I, 304.

of the measure was merely another of the many blunders which the Whigs, and particularly Fox, made in this struggle. The feature of the bill which caused the greatest protest was that which provided for the appointment of a commission to deal with Indian affairs for the next four years. The members of the commission could not be removed during this four-year period and were to be appointed by the ministry. Even though after the first appointments this power was to pass to the Crown, the provision brought about the vigorous opposition of the King, the East India Company, and the Parliamentary reformers. The King had no desire to see friends of Fox put in charge of India for four years or to see so important a power taken from the Crown. The East India Company was alarmed at the prospect of having so great a part of the administration of its own affairs transferred to the hands of an irremovable commission. The reformers were indignant at the danger of a new source of patronage being built up in India on the order of that wiped out by the economical reform of 1782.

On November 18 Fox asked permission of the House of Commons to introduce a bill for the better government of India. North, who had less fervor but considerably more political judgment than Fox, saw the danger. Either he did not care sufficiently to oppose Fox or he found his opposition useless. The bill was hurried through the House of Commons where it passed the third reading by 208 to 102.[70] Outside Parliament, however, the bill was not so popular. A caricature by Sayer appears to have summed up public opinion admirably. It portrayed Fox as an Oriental potentate, entering Leadenhall Street on the back of an elephant, which was led by Burke and had a face like Lord North. Popular fury outside Parliament could not affect the votes in either house to any great extent, but the King had devised another method of checkmating the ministry. Using Lord Temple as his messenger, George III let it be known that any lord who voted for the India Bill might expect to feel the weight of the royal disapprobation.[71] The hint was effective, and the bill was beaten in the Lords by 95 to 76.[72] Although this was not a vote of no confidence in the ministry, the King felt sufficiently certain of his power to demand that the ministers resign; but under the circumstances they refused to do so. The King, however, was not to be thwarted and sent a mes-

[70] Parliamentary History, XXIV, 61.
[71] The Duke of Buckingham, op. cit., I, 285.
[72] Parliamentary History, XXIV, 196.

senger demanding the return of the seals of office.[73] In this manner the Coalition ministry came to an end on December 18, 1783.

Within twelve hours of the forced resignation of the Portland
ministry, William Pitt had accepted the office of First Lord of the
Treasury. It is inconceivable that the King had taken his action of
the preceding day without first assuring himself of the support of
Pitt. Certainly George III would not have run the risk of repeating his dreadful experience of February, March, and April of the
same year when he had tried for thirty-seven days to find an alternative to Fox and North; for another hunt of this sort would have
been doubly humiliating. When the King sent an under-secretary
to secure the seals, Fox is alleged to have exclaimed: "the King
would not dare do it." It is unlikely that he would have dared had
he not made arrangements with William Pitt in advance.

The question naturally arises as to why Pitt accepted the position of First Lord of the Treasury in December when he had twice
refused it in March and had been cool to Thurlow's proposals in
July. Formerly the explanation offered was that Pitt fought in
the face of fearful odds during the first months of his administration for the sake of his country and his King. Researches by Professor Laprade show that other explanations less to the credit of
his idealism but more to that of his political sagacity were in all
probability the decisive factor. The King had employed John
Robinson, who had been one of his campaign managers in the
elections of 1774 and 1780, to make an estimate of the probable
attitude of the members of the House of Commons under the Fox-
North ministry and of the composition of a new house in case a
general election were held. The results of this investigation, made
evidently during the second week of December, were enough to
convince Pitt that he would be more than reasonably safe in accepting the position which he had refused in March. Robinson divided members of the existing House of Commons and those of a
new house which would result from a general election into four
classifications—pro, hopeful, doubtful, and con. The estimate of
the present membership showed 149 pro, 104 hopeful, 74 doubtful,
and 231 con. The estimate of a new house after the general election showed 253 pro, 116 hopeful, 66 doubtful, and 123 con.[74]

[73] Henry B. Wheatley (ed.), *Memoirs of Sir Nathaniel William Wraxall*
(London, 1884), III, 198.

[74] W. T. Laprade (ed.), *Parliamentary Papers of John Robinson, 1774–
1784* (London, 1922), pp. 65–105.

Thus if the hopefuls and doubtfuls ran true to estimate, the Coalition could count on 305 members as against 253 for Pitt; but in case of an election the Coalition could count on only 189 as opposed to Pitt's 369. That the estimate of the probable membership was approximately accurate is shown by the fact that Pitt had a majority of 168[75] when he met the new House of Commons after the general election.

Thus far the history of the negotiations between the King and Pitt before December 19 has not come to light. The correspondence of George III, Pitt, Lord Temple, W. W. Grenville, and Charles James Fox throws no light on the subject. In all probability the arrangements were made through Lord Temple. That the arrangements for other places in the ministry were not made in advance after the fashion of Robinson's is shown by the fact that Pitt took several days after December 19 to form his government. Considering the "feelers" put out in July by Thurlow, it would be most interesting to know the terms under which Pitt became First Lord of the Treasury. It is true that the King could now remove Pitt's fears of lack of support in the House of Commons by showing him Robinson's estimates; but the question of the King's influence and of Pitt's stand on reform, which interested Thurlow most in the July conversations, had to be settled. There appears to be no documentary evidence available on the manner in which these two points were settled. Pitt, it is safe to assume, would not take the place of Lord North as the first servant of the King's prerogative and would not abandon reform. On December 23 the King began a letter to Pitt with the words: "To one on the edge of a precipice every ray of hope must be pleasing."[76] This certainly indicates no surrender on the part of Pitt. Evidently the King agreed either outright or tacitly that his new First Lord of the Treasury could avow that he was not merely the first servant of George III; at least Pitt publicly repudiated such a rating. Of far greater importance in this study, however, was the decision reached on issues upon which the King and Pitt differed, especially that of Parliamentary reform. Judged by the manner in which controversial issues of this sort were handled during the next few years, Pitt was allowed to take independent action on such questions but not to make government measures

[75] *Parliamentary History,* XXIV, 843.

[76] Sir John Fortescue, "Correspondence of King George III," Transcripts in William L. Clements Library, I, 8.

of them. This safeguard may have been the chief factor in preserving the King's prerogative during Pitt's administration.

COMPARISON OF GEORGE III AND WILLIAM PITT
ON DECEMBER 19, 1783

These two men who were to begin a strange partnership of over seventeen consecutive years had many similar and dissimilar characteristics. Each had missed a normal boyhood and lacked the give and take which comes from years of healthy play. Each had been greatly influenced by a tutor: Bute in the case of George III, and Pretyman in that of Pitt. Both were proud, stubborn, and sulky. Neither was interested in ordinary dissipation. The King was abstemious in eating and drinking in order to avoid corpulency, while Pitt was forced by a weak constitution to eat with care and to drink port wine for medicinal purposes. Each had a high opinion of the post he was called upon to fill and endeavored to fill it with dignity. George III was impressed with the enormity of the responsibility he owed to God and to the British Constitution; and Pitt was equally impressed with what he owed to the name of Pitt and to the British people.

The points of difference between the two men were equally significant. Pitt was an intellectual prodigy, while George III had developed very slowly. At twenty-four Pitt was Prime Minister through his own abilities, and the King at the same age was relying upon Bute and Henry Fox to put through the peace preliminaries of 1762. Pitt's abilities were clearly those of a financier and "House of Commons man"; George III's were those of a politician who pulls strings behind the scenes. Pitt's speeches and letters are very clear, but the letters of the King are often so vague in phraseology that they resemble the utterances of the Delphic oracle. Pitt's strength lay in his command of the House of Commons and of the cabinet and in his grip on the people outside Parliament; the King's strength lay in his enormous knowledge of, and real insight into, the manipulation of the unreformed House of Commons, in his uncanny ability to keep the Whig leaders separated, and in his grip on the people outside Parliament. One of the greatest assets which both had in 1783 and in the years which followed was Charles James Fox. In fact it is impossible to separate the popularity of George III and William Pitt from the popular hostility to Fox. This popularity, which the King and Pitt shared, was partly based on a belief in the purity of their morals, partly on the growing admiration for George III dating from the Gordon Riots, and partly on the name of Pitt and the belief that he was immaculate from a political as well as a moral point of view.

On December 19, 1783, the position of Pitt was apparently superior to that of the King; for George III admitted being on the edge of a precipice. If Pitt failed he would merely slip back into the class with other ministers who had attempted tasks too great for their strength. At his age and with his abilities it was certain to be a temporary setback without great loss of prestige. To the King, Pitt's failure would bring about a mortifying surrender to the Coalition similar to the one to which he had been forced to submit in 1763 and 1765 at the hands of George Grenville. On the other hand, in case Pitt was successful, as there was every reason to believe he would be in view of the statistics of John Robinson, the King ran the risk of Pitt's retaining the spoils of victory. The usual interpretation of the seventeen years following 1783 is that Pitt did retain the spoils. In making Pitt First Lord of the Treasury George III was forced to take a man whose principles concerning the King's prerogative and Parliamentary reform were distasteful to him. Perhaps the most valuable concession which George III secured was that issues upon which the ruler and minister did not agree should not be governmental measures but that ministers and members of Parliament should be free to follow their own judgment. In addition, George III counted on his political experience and knowledge of statesmen and politicians, and on the hope that Pitt might in time become less hostile to the principles which the King held so dear. The history of the relations of George III and William Pitt from 1783 to 1806 will make clear whether his hopes or fears were fulfilled.

III. THE VICTORY OF THE KING AND PITT, 1783 TO 1784

The weeks from December 19, 1783, to the dissolution of Parliament on March 25, 1784, are significant ones in Pitt's political career despite the fact that we now know how John Robinson paved the way for his triumph in the general election; for had Pitt failed before the Parliamentary eloquence and attacks of the Coalition, half of the triumph in the general election would have been lost for George III and in all likelihood the majority would not have been so great. The period falls into two divisions: the formation of the new ministry and the recess; and the fierce struggle in the two houses after Parliament reassembled on January 12.

Despite his advantages over the King upon assuming office, Pitt was certain to find the formation of a government a difficult one. It is true that during his three years as a member of the House of Commons he had made a brilliant record; but many prominent Whigs, especially if they did not know the results of the activities of John Robinson, were skeptical of his ability to make a successful stand against the experience and votes of the Coalition. Pitt could not blame them for taking this attitude, since it was the very one which he himself had taken in February and March of the same year.

Although no mention is made of the fact in the Memorials of C. J. Fox, the Fortescue Papers, the Buckingham Memoirs, or in the works of Tomline, Stanhope, and Dr. J. H. Rose, Pitt apparently attempted a coalition with Fox as his initial step. This seems clear in a letter from Lord Temple to the King on December 21,[1] the very date, according to Tomline,[2] upon which that nobleman decided to resign. Temple reported that Pitt had taken advantage of the permission extended by His Majesty to discuss with Lord Spencer that morning the "general idea of an accommodation." After a few hours of consideration the reply came in the following words:

---

[1] Sir John Fortescue, "Correspondence of King George III," Transcripts in William L. Clements Library, I, 5. Hereafter referred to as Clements Transcripts.

[2] George Tomline, *Memoirs of the Life of William Pitt* (London, 1821), I, 233.

71

Mr. Fox, the D. of Portland, & L. John Cavendish have determined that they cannot consider this as a proper moment for a negotiation in general; besides the particular objections there might be to a negotiation such as was proposed one of them in particular (viz., that relating to L. North) would from their present situation with respect to him be absolutely insuperable.[3]

Apparently Pitt and Temple hoped for a Whig ministry which would unite what had been the Rockingham and Shelburne groups and from which Lord North would be excluded. Such an arrangement would have been perfectly consistent with the professed political principles of both Pitt and Temple. The King, judged by his answer to Temple, must have consented with considerable reluctance to these negotiations and in all probability did so because he felt certain that Fox would not accept. There is a note of relief in his statement that "Lord Temple's note is only a confirmation of what He must remember I suspected when He the last night first broached the idea of a willingness in Mr. Fox to negotiate."[4] No wonder George III wrote to Pitt two days later that "To one on the edge of a Precipice every ray of hope must be pleasing."[5] What might be urged as corroborative evidence of this offer on the part of Pitt to negotiate with Fox is given in a letter which the latter wrote to Charles Townshend on December 30 agreeing that Townshend was certainly right in wishing him not to join Pitt.[6]

Pitt suffered an additional rebuff the next day, December 22, when Lord Temple suddenly resigned as Secretary of State. Various reasons for this unexpected action were suggested at the time and since. Certainly the letter written to the King on December 21 breathes no hint of resignation.[7] The reason assigned publicly for this action was that he wished to answer in a private capacity and not to handicap the ministry by any charges which might be brought against him for his conduct in influencing the votes of peers on Fox's India Bill.[8] Another explanation offered was that Temple wished an immediate dissolution of Parliament but that Pitt insisted upon waiting; and thus that the resignation came as a result of real difference in policy.[9] Fox somewhat ungenerously

[3] Clements Transcripts, I, 5.   [4] *Ibid.*, I, 6.

[5] Pitt MSS, 103, December 23, 1783.

[6] Lord John Russell, *Memorials and Correspondence of C. J. Fox* (London, 1853–1857), II, 223.

[7] Clements Transcripts, I, 5.   [8] Tomline, *op. cit.*, I, 231.

[9] Lord Stanhope, *Life of William Pitt* (London, 1861–62), I, 161–63.

ascribed Temple's action to cowardice.[10] On the whole, the most likely explanation is that Lord Temple resigned in a huff when he was not given some honor—perhaps a dukedom—which he expected as a reward for services rendered as Lord Lieutenant of Ireland and in the affair of Fox's India Bill.

The sudden resignation of Temple was evidently a bad shock to both the King and Pitt. Tomline testifies that it gave Pitt a sleepless night[11] and, as has already been noted, it helped give the King the "edge of a precipice" feeling. The question naturally arises as to why some effort was not made to conciliate Temple even if it cost a dukedom. Dr. J. Holland Rose explains it on the ground that Pitt found out for the first time the use which Temple had made of the King's name when the India Bill was beaten and that as a result of the indignation experienced he refused to press Temple's claims.[12] In view of the close relationship of Pitt and Temple this seems unlikely. When this lord's well-known pride and sensitiveness are taken into consideration, it is more probable that his "flareup" and resignation aroused the stubborn pride of both Pitt and the King and that they refused to plead with him to return even though they felt his loss keenly. Pitt wrote two very friendly letters to Temple on December 23 which gave no evidence of hard feelings, but the Earl's reply of December 29 overflowed with ill-suppressed grievances.[13] He complained that no approbation of his conduct in Ireland had been given by the King and that he considered it "as the strongest disavowal of my Government in Ireland, and·(not to use harsh expressions) as the most personal offence to me." Temple's feelings toward Pitt were indicated by the formal nature of the letter which began "Dear Sir" and ended, "I am, with very sincere regrets, and with the deepest sensations of pain for what has passed, and for what is yet to come . . . ."

Regardless of the reasons for Temple's resignation, the King and Pitt redoubled their efforts to secure recruits for a ministry. The day after this resignation Pitt wrote to the King that the Duke of Richmond, Lord Gower, Lord Thurlow, and he would wait on His Majesty at any convenient hour and that they would

[10] Lord John Russell, op. cit., II, 224.

[11] Tomline, op. cit., I, 233.

[12] J. H. Rose, Life of William Pitt (London: G. Bell & Sons, Ltd., 1923), I, 153.

[13] The Duke of Buckingham, Memoirs of the Court and Cabinets of George III (London, 1853), I, 291-93.

attempt in the interval to fill some of the vacancies in the government. The King in reply expressed the fervent hope that the four might be able to "fill up an arrangement which if they cannot they already know my determination."[14] This ambiguous utterance probably means that George III was again threatening abdication. During the next few days the King and Pitt exchanged many letters pertaining to appointments below cabinet rank. As finally formed the cabinet was made up of the following seven members: First Lord of the Treasury and Chancellor of the Exchequer, William Pitt; Foreign Secretary, Marquis of Carmarthen; Home Secretary, Lord Sydney; Lord President, Earl Gower; Lord Chancellor, Lord Thurlow; Lord Privy Seal, Duke of Rutland; Admiralty, Viscount Hood. To these seven on January 13, 1784, the Duke of Richmond, Master-General of Ordnance, was added.

Every member except Pitt was in the House of Lords, and thus he was forced to bear the brunt of the Coalition attack in the House of Commons. Most of them, however, would have been of little assistance to him in debate, since, "apart from Pitt and Thurlow, not one of the Ministers could make a tolerable speech, or possessed the strength of character which makes up for oratorical deficiencies."[15] Members of the ministry below cabinet rank were: Henry Dundas, Treasurer of the Navy; Sir George Yonge, Secretary at War; George Rose and Thomas Steele, Secretaries of the Treasury; William Grenville and Lord Mulgrave, Paymasters of the Forces; Thomas Orde, Secretary to the Lord-Lieutenant of Ireland; Lloyd Kenyon, Attorney-General; and Pepper Arden, Solicitor-General. This ministry was made up of Rockingham and Shelburne Whigs, Tories, King's Friends, and personal friends of Pitt from Cambridge University.

When we consider the tremendous amount of criticism which the Fox-North Coalition had evoked, and the large number of capable men who did not follow either Fox or North and yet were not included in the new ministry, the weakness of the cabinet and ministry is puzzling. The explanation seems to lie largely in lack of confidence in the ability of the head of the ministry to maintain himself against the Coalition attacks. Pitt appears to have made no effort to include Shelburne in his new arrangement, in spite of the fact that he was personally friendly to his former chief, because he felt that the presence of that nobleman in the

[14] Pitt MSS, 103, December 23, 1783.
[15] J. H. Rose, op. cit., I, 156.

cabinet would be a greater liability than an asset. Shelburne appears to have realized that his own unpopularity excluded him, and he seems to have made no effort to hamper Pitt. But in practically all other instances Pitt received decided rebuffs, even when he wrote obsequious letters, since places in his ministry were refused by his brother-in-law, Lord Mahon, and by Lord Camden, the Duke of Grafton, Earl Cornwallis, and Lord Sackville. As solicitations of this sort were distasteful to a man of Pitt's stiff pride, it is easy to see that he deemed unusual steps necessary at this time. Nothing shows Pitt's desperation more clearly than the letter of December 29 to Lord Sackville, whose record at Minden and during the American Revolutionary War would naturally have caused Pitt to shun him, in which the latter's support is humbly requested:

In the arduous situation in which His Majesty has condescended to command my services at this important juncture, I am necessarily anxious to obtain the honor of a support and assistance so important as your Lordship's. I flatter myself Mr. Herbert will have had the goodness to express my sense of the honor your Lordship did me by your obliging expressions towards me. Permit me to add how much mortification I received in being disappointed of his assistance at the Board of the Admiralty, which I took the liberty of proposing to him, in consequence of the conversation Lord Temple had had with your Lordship. I should sincerely lament if any change of arrangements produced by Lord Temple's resignation should deprive the King and country in any degree of a support which the present crisis renders so highly material to both. If your Lordship would still allow us to hope that you might be induced to mark by Herbert's acceptance your disposition in favour of the King's government, the opening may be made with the greatest ease at any moment, and Your Lordship's commands on the subject would give me particular satisfaction.[16]

The spirit of levity with which the followers of Fox and North treated Pitt was probably more painful to him than outright abuse would have been. Loud laughter in the House of Commons greeted the announcement of Pitt's appointment, and comments in letters of this period show the lack of seriousness with which contemporaries regarded the new ministry. The prevailing spirit was the oft-quoted line from *The Rolliad,* "A kingdom trusted to a schoolboy's care."[17]

[16] *Ibid.,* p. 155; see also Pitt MSS, 102.
[17] *The Rolliad* (London, 1812), 22d ed., p. 27.

The significance of the gallant fight made by Pitt in the House of Commons from January 12, when Parliament reassembled after the Christmas recess, until it was dissolved on March 25 has been somewhat impaired by the researches of Professor Laprade into the activities of John Robinson.[18] Nevertheless it would be a mistake to discount the skill and leadership which Pitt displayed in these few weeks. The King could be practically certain of a majority in any general election, as all such contests before and after this time showed, but he could not be certain of securing a minister who could carry on in the face of the superior ability and debating powers of the Coalition. The manner in which Pitt bore the brunt of this able and experienced attack showed the nation and the King that he was capable of holding his own against the best the House of Commons could offer. While Pitt may have been encouraged by the knowledge of how Robinson's negotiations were progressing, this knowledge in itself is not sufficient to account for his success. Probably the most uneasy person was the King. He had found a man who was capable of controlling the House of Commons, but he was not certain that this man would take instructions from him. At the time he accepted the office of Prime Minister, Pitt, without doubt, made it clear that he did not intend to be another Lord North; and he gave further evidence of this feeling in attempting to reach an understanding with Fox as soon as he had accepted the seals of office. This independent attitude was continued even after Parliament reassembled on January 12 and torrid conflicts began with the followers of Fox and North. Probably the King was greatly relieved when Parliament was eventually dissolved without Pitt and Fox reaching an understanding. By 1784 he was a sufficiently good judge of men to realize that he must make allowances for Pitt's pride and political principles; and while he must have been annoyed at the expression of these principles both in private and in the House of Commons, he knew that the alternative to Pitt's stiff-necked attitude was the return of the Coalition.

At the first meeting of Parliament after the recess, in the course of a debate on Fox's motion for the House to go into committee on the state of the nation, Pitt took an opportunity to declared that

18 W. T. Laprade (ed.), *Parliamentary Papers of John Robinson* (London, 1922).

. . . . He came up no backstairs; that when he was sent for by his sovereign to know whether he would accept of office, he necessarily went to the royal closet; that he knew of no secret influence, and that his own integrity would be his guardian against that danger: but the house might rest assured whenever he discovered any, he would not stay a moment longer in office. I will neither have the meanness, said Mr. Pitt, to act upon the advice of others, nor the hypocrisy to pretend, when the measures of an administration in which I have a share are deserving of censure, that they were measures not of my advising. If any former ministers take these charges to themselves, to them be the sting. Little did I think to be ever charged in this house with being the tool and abettor of secret influence. The novelty of the imputation only renders it the more contemptible. This is the only answer I shall ever deign to make on the subject, and I wish the house to bear it in their mind, and judge of my future conduct by my present declaration: the integrity of my own heart, and the probity of all my public, as well as my private principles, shall always be my sources of action. I will never condescend to be the instrument of any secret advisers whatever, nor in any one instance, while I have the honour to act as minister of the crown in this house, will I be responsible for measures not my own, or at least in which my heart and judgment do not cordially acquiesce.[19]

Doubtless the King hoped that the acrimonious debates which followed this declaration of principle on January 12 and succeeding days would eliminate any chance of Pitt's seeking to renew the understanding with Fox. George III expressed far greater indignation in his letters commenting on the defeats which the government suffered in the House of Commons than did Pitt himself. After Pitt made the statement quoted above, the House of Commons by a vote of 232 to 193 passed Fox's motion to go into committee to consider the state of the nation.[20] Next several resolutions were passed condemning as unconstitutional the appointment and continuance in office of the present ministry on the grounds that it did not possess the confidence of either the House or the people.[21] These resolutions filled the King with alarm, and he wrote at once:

Mr. Pitt cannot but suppose that I received this communication of the two divisions in the long debate which ended this morning with

[19] *Parliamentary History* (London, 1806–1820), XXIV, 294.
[20] *Ibid.*, p. 299.
[21] *Ibid.*, p. 317.

much uneasiness, as it shows the House of Commons much more willing to enter into any intemperate resolutions of desperate men than I could have imagined, as to myself I am perfectly composed as I have the self satisfaction of feeling I have done my duty ; . . . . At all events I am ready to take any step that may be proposed to oppose this faction, and to struggle to the last period of my life; but I can never submit to throw myself into its power; if they in the end succeed my line is a clear one, and to which I have fortitude enough to submit.[22]

Clearly the King was suggesting the likelihood of his abdication in the hope of impressing Pitt; but the latter does not seem to have been particularly susceptible to this sort of persuasion.

The King found some consolation in the fact that permission was given to Pitt on January 14 to bring in his India Bill and that two days later the majority against the government had fallen to 21. These favorable omens caused him to express the hope that "a few days will shew that the majority is in favour of decorum instead of siding with anarchy."[23] On January 23, when the India Bill was beaten on the second reading by a vote of 222 to 214,[24] Pitt was pressed by the House to give some information on the rumored dissolution of Parliament. He remained silent despite "a loud and violent call" from every side of the House, and only when General Conway charged him with standing against the voice of the representatives of the people "by means of bribery and by other dark and intricate arts" did he rise to answer. After calling Conway to order and stating that the charges could not be proved, he declared that he would not answer questions which gentlemen had no right to ask, and concluded in "a tone of high and elevated sentiments, and a classical text."[25] The King believed the time ripe for a dissolution of Parliament and could scarcely restrain his impatience. The very day the India Bill was beaten he wrote to Lord Gower conveying the information that there appeared to be no instance of a dissolution of Parliament since the Revolution of 1689 without a previous prorogation, and suggested that the Chancellor be asked whether such a ceremony was absolutely necessary.[26] The next day the King in high

[22] Pitt MSS, 103, January 13, 1784.
[23] *Ibid.*, January 17, 1784.
[24] *Parliamentary History*, XXIV, 412.
[25] *Ibid.*, p. 424.
[26] Clements Transcripts, I, 60.

excitement wrote to Pitt at nine in the morning and again at six in the afternoon. In the first letter he stated: "I own I cannot see any reason, if the thing is practicable, that a Dissolution should not be effected; if not, I fear the Constitution of this country cannot subsist."[27] In the second letter he asked Pitt to get the opinion of the confidential ministers on the question of dissolution, but he made it clear that he himself could see no reason why Parliament should not be dissolved on Monday.[28] The following day he wrote to Pitt in an even stronger vein:

Though indecision is the most painful of all situations to a firm mind, I by no means wish Mr. Pitt should come to me till he has, with his brother Ministers, gone through the various objects the present crisis affords. I should hope by half an hour past nine he may be able to lay before me the result of their deliberations. The Opposition will certainly throw every difficulty in our way, but we must be men; and if we mean to save the country, we must cut those threads that cannot be unravelled. Half-measures are ever puerile, and often destructive.[29]

What explanation can be offered for the failure to "cut those threads," that is, to dissolve Parliament, when the King was so anxious to do so? The obvious one is that Pitt was unwilling at this time to break definitely with the Rockingham Whigs and to rely on the King's Friends for so large a portion of his Parliamentary strength. The report of John Robinson, showing the pros, cons, hopefuls, and doubtfuls of both the existing House of Commons and of one in case a general election were held, was certainly familiar to Pitt. Furthermore, he had a chance to check the accuracy of this estimate in the rapidly decreasing size of his own minority. At this time Pitt was a young man of high ideals, a firm believer in strong Whig traditions and in Parliamentary reform, and an opponent of the increasing influence of the Crown. He saw in Fox, Portland, Burke, Sheridan, and their followers his natural allies exactly as he still saw in Lord North his enemy. Thus at the end of March Pitt was finally driven to take a course which at the end of January he had refused to adopt. In no other manner can the failure to dissolve Parliament after the defeat of Pitt's India Bill on January 23 be satisfactorily explained. The King was more than anxious for the dissolution and the arrange-

[27] Pitt MSS, 103, January 24, 1784.
[28] *Ibid.*, second letter of January 24, 1784.
[29] *Ibid.*, January 25, 1784.

ments for the general election appear to have been completed or at least to have reached a satisfactory stage. Pitt, evidently, still believed that a union with the Whigs was possible and necessary.

An easy and honorable means of seeking this union was at hand. The "independents," as Pitt styled them (in a letter to the Duke of Rutland), or "the gentlemen at the St. Albans Tavern," as the King called them, afforded this channel of communication. On January 26 fifty-three members of Parliament met at this tavern with the avowed intention of negotiating a peace between Fox and Pitt.[30] After making Mr. Thomas Grosvenor chairman, an address was voted requesting Mr. Pitt and the Duke of Portland to communicate in an effort to iron out the differences between the two groups of Whigs. Pitt agreed at once to confer with the Duke; but Portland, after interviewing Fox, refused to negotiate until the Prime Minister resigned. The King, naturally, was decidedly uneasy at the prospect of an understanding between Pitt and the Portland Whigs. With obvious lack of enthusiasm he gave Pitt permission to continue negotiations or, as he phrased it, to make "himself master if possible of what the D. of Portland means though I cannot suggest the mode."[31] George III, however, could not refrain from expressing the opinion that the gentlemen at the St. Albans Tavern might better spend their time "co-operating in preventing a desperate faction from compleating the ruin of the most perfect of all human formations, the British Constitution."[32]

The answer of Portland was exactly what might have been expected, since Fox expressed identical views in the House of Commons on the same day.[33] Pitt showed considerable forbearance in his answers when one considers the flood of denunciation with which his opponents showered him. Although it must be conceded that a too prominent vein of self-righteousness and priggishness runs through his speeches, nevertheless his replies to Fox and other Whigs were sufficiently moderate to keep the door open for further negotiations. Three days after Portland's initial refusal of January 26, Fox inveighed against the ministers for holding office in direct opposition to the expressed sense of the House.[34] In reply Pitt declared that he was conscious that no

30 Tomline, op. cit., I, 318.
31 Pitt MSS, 103, January 30, 1784.
32 Ibid.
33 Tomline, op. cit., I, 319.   34 Parliamentary History, XIV, 437–41.

public or official action of his required an apology. His present situation admittedly was delicate and required discretion in handling; but the course he was pursuing was the result of deliberation and he hoped that he would make no palpable mistakes. If the present ministers were so criminal as the gentlemen in opposition insisted, why did not the latter impeach them or petition the King to remove them? In conclusion Pitt finished with a burst of self-righteousness: "Nothing could be imputed to him for which he had any reasons to be ashamed. His heart, his principles, his hands were pure; and while he enjoyed the conscious satisfaction of his own mind, no language of the right honourable gentleman, no clamour, no artifice of party, no unfounded imputations, should affect him."[35] After making allowances for the serene smugness of this defense, it must be admitted that Pitt still did not by justifiable vituperation close the door to an understanding with Fox and that he did not weaken the strength of his position.

The contest was renewed on February 2, when Grosvenor, chairman of the St. Albans Tavern group, moved that the state of the country called for a united and extended ministry.[36] Fox insisted that the had no personal objection to Pitt but that the first step toward such a united and extended ministry must be the resignation of the present ministry. Pitt likewise held that he had no personal objection to Fox and expressed a willingness to unite on public principles. On the strength of the apparent unanimity on this point the resolution of Grosvenor was passed without a single negative. Immediately Coke of Norfolk, one of Fox's closest friends, moved another resolution that the continuance of the present ministry in office was an obstacle which prevented the formation of an administration in which the House of Commons would have confidence. Fox then insisted that Pitt must resign before the followers of Fox and Portland would even hold a conference with him.[37] After having made what appeared to him to be all the concessions in the affair, Pitt expressed his indignation at such a stand.

With what regard to personal honour or public principle could it be expected that he should consent to march out of it with a halter about his neck, change his armour, and meanly beg to be re-admitted and considered as a volunteer in the army of the enemy? . . . . The

35 *Ibid.*, XXIV, 443.
36 Tomline, *op. cit.*, I, 322.
37 *Ibid.*, pp. 322–23.

sacrifice of the sentiments of men of honour was no light matter, and when it was considered how much was to be given up to open a negociation for union, when it was considered what insulting attacks had been made, and what clamours had been excited, he conceived that some regard ought to be paid to his being willing to meet the wishes of those respectable gentlemen, who had called for an union of parties.[38]

The indignation of Pitt, under the circumstances, appears to have considerable justification; but despite his fine defense Coke's motion was passed by a majority of 19.[39]

When the news of the results of these two divisions reached him, George III did not remain satisfied with the defense offered. Early the next morning he wrote to Pitt that in view of the passing of the two motions there was a likelihood of the Commons carrying an address that very day, and that consequently he felt that it would "highly become the House of Lords to throw off their lethargy, and also vote an address that shall show they feel each branch of the legislature has its fixed bounds and that the executive power is vested in the Crown and not to be infringed by the Commons."[40] In order to make certain that the Lords would throw off their lethargy he wrote that evening to Lord Sydney expressing the same sentiments. His Majesty warned Sydney that, although it may have been prudent for the Lords to remain quiet while the Commons confined themselves to resolutions, it would be dangerous for the upper house to continue such a policy when these resolutions became measures. To make certain that Sydney and the other lords might not be assailed with doubts as to the proper procedure for them to adopt, he called attention to the fact that a faction in a most shameless fashion was attempting to grasp the executive power, and he suggested the sentiments which an address from the Lords should take.[41] A memorandum in the King's handwriting, of which he seems to have sent a copy to Sydney, states:

That from experience that House has had of His Majesty's uniform attachment to the Constitution, it will most cordially support such an Administration as He may in his Wisdom think fit to form in every Measure that may appear conducive to the Public Good, and trust

---

[38] *Parliamentary History,* XXIV, 483.
[39] *Ibid.,* XXIV, 484.
[40] Pitt MSS, 103, February 3, 1784.
[41] Clements Transcripts, I, 76.

there will not be wanting that Public Spirit and sense of Duty in those who shall be honoured by His Majesty's Nomination, that may incline them to exert themselves in the Public Service.[42]

The King's suggestions were based on the unconstitutionality of the actions and the unwillingness of the Coalition to co-operate with Pitt and on exposing real or alleged opposition to the policy pursued by the opposition.

Because George III was striving "tooth and nail" to prevent Pitt from reaching an agreement with Fox and Portland, and because he realized that Pitt was at this time a conscientious constitutionalist, we find the clearest exposition of the royal constitutional views during February of 1784. His letter to Pitt of February 4 is couched in language which he felt would have the greatest appeal to the young man.

I trust the House of Lords will this day feel that the hour is come for which the wisdom of our ancestors established that respectable corps in the state, to prevent either the Crown or the Commons from encroaching on the rights of each other. Indeed should not the Lords stand boldly forth this constitution must soon be changed, for if the two only remaining privileges of the Crown are infringed that of negativing Bills that have passed both houses of Parliament, or that of naming the ministers to be employed, I cannot but feel as far as regards my Person that I can be no longer of utility to this country, nor can with honor continue in this stand.[43]

Both Pitt's resolution and George III's adaptability are very much in evidence during the days which followed. Pitt showed his attachment to his views by resisting the royal pleas, arguments, and threats to abdicate; and the King showed his tactical ability by fighting an effective rear-guard action instead of either making a last-ditch stand or beating a precipitate retreat. On February 7 His Majesty consented to give his approval "for effecting the formation of an administration on the widest basis,"[44] which indicates that Pitt must have made him see clearly the necessity of not giving up the negotiations for a union of the Whig groups. Again on February 11 the King expressed a willingness to listen to any such proposition, but not to one "formed out of only a part of my subjects."[45]

[42] *Ibid.*, I, 77.
[43] Pitt MSS, 103, February 4, 1784.
[44] *Ibid.*, February 7, 1784.
[45] *Ibid.*, February 11, 1784.

On that same day Fox, in the House of Commons, professed to be willing to serve with Pitt and even to compromise on the terms of a new India Bill on condition that the latter should comply with the terms of the Constitution.[46] At this point Pitt showed clearly that while he was more than willing to reach an understanding with Portland and Fox he was not willing to include Lord North in the arrangement.[47] That urbane and charming gentleman at once offered to stand aside if his presence in the government prevented a strong ministry from being formed.[48] The spirit expressed by all three of these important men indicated that a union of parties was likely if the matter of Pitt's temporary resignation and of the division of places in the cabinet and ministry could be arranged in a satisfactory fashion. No single document testifies more eloquently to the resolute stand of Pitt and the reluctant consent of the King to carry on these negotiations than the letter which George III wrote to his chief minister on February 15:

Mr. Pitt is so well apprized of the mortification I feel at any possibility of ever again seeing the heads of the Opposition in public employments, and more particularly Mr. Fox, whose conduct has not been more marked against my station in the Empire than against my person, that he must attribute my want of perspicuity in my conversation last night to that foundation; yet I should imagine it must be an ease to his mind, in conferring with the other confidential Ministers this morning, to have on paper my sentiments, which are the result of unremitted consideration since he left me last night, and which he has my consent to communicate, if he judges right, to the above persons.

My present situation is perhaps the most singular that ever occurred, either in the annals of this or any other country; for the House of Lords, by not a less majority than near two to one, have declared in my favour; and my subjects at large, in a much more considerable proportion, are not less decided; to combat which, Opposition have only a majority of twenty or at most thirty in the House of Commons, who, I am sorry to add, seem as yet willing to prevent the public supplies. Though I certainly have never much valued popularity, yet I do not think it is to be despised when arising from a rectitude of conduct, and when it is to be retained by following the same respectable path which conviction makes me esteem that of duty,

[46] Tomline, op. cit., I, 354–58; Parliamentary History, XXIV, 588.
[47] Parliamentary History, XXIV, 589–90.
[48] Ibid., p. 591.

as calculated to prevent one branch of the legislature from annihilating the other two, and seizing also the executive power to which it has no claim.[49]

In the remainder of the letter the King, although stressing his lack of confidence in the leaders of the Opposition and their willingness to form a government on a broad basis, consented to write to the Duke of Portland and express a desire that the latter meet Pitt to discuss the possibility of a ministry on this basis. George III was frank in his reluctance to act in such a manner and freely expressed how distasteful such a step was to him. On the other hand, he felt that since the Opposition had so far refused even an interview with Pitt the chances of success in such a conference would be more than doubtful. Thus the King, apparently, gave his consent because he feared to offend Pitt at this point and because he felt reasonably certain that no agreement would be reached; but, doubtless, he continually stressed his reluctance both because it was real and because it placed Pitt under obligations to make concessions as well. He may have had this point in mind when, after suggesting Lord Sydney as the proper person to convey a message from him to Portland, he added: "but should the Duke of Portland, when required by me, refuse to meet Mr. Pitt, more especially upon the strange plea he has as yet held forth, I must declare that I shall not deem it right for me ever to address myself again to him."[50]

The King immediately sent a message to Portland by Lord Sydney indicating that he wished to have the Duke and Pitt meet to confer on the formation of a new administration "on a wide basis, and on a fair and equal footing."[51] The Duke of Portland answered Lord Sydney on the same day and raised exactly the objections which the King, no doubt, hoped that he would. First, the Duke insisted Pitt must resign, or, as he phrased it:

But your Lordship is too well apprized of my unalterable opinion, that the confidence of the House of Commons is indispensibly necessary to any arrangement which can promise quiet to the Country or energy to His Majesty's Government, not to perceive the impossibility of my conferring with Mr. Pitt on any Plan of Ministerial Settlement until he shall have signified to them in some way or other, his Inclination to comply with their Wishes.[52]

---

[49] Pitt MSS, 103, February 15, 1784.   [50] Ibid.
[51] Clements Transcripts, I, 95.   [52] Ibid., I, 98.

The King must have been elated when he read this passage because he felt certain that Pitt, because of his public declarations and pride, would never submit. The second objection raised by Portland was one which from both its nature and from its phraseology must have been very offensive to George III. The Duke stated:

I must beg leave to add that before I can take any steps towards any Arrangement, it will be indispensibly necessary for His Majesty's Service that I should receive the same proofs of His Majesty's Confidence as Your Lordship will remember I thought necessary on a former Occasion, and which I then obtained.[53]

It is obvious that Portland referred to the prolonged negotiations in the thirty-seven days which followed the resignation of Shelburne on February 24 of the previous year. At that time the King had attempted to secure a list of the proposed ministers through a third person exactly as he made use of Lord Sydney at this time. Portland had insisted on the King seeing him and making the arrangements personally. The fact that George III had been forced to yield in the previous year had not convinced him that he was wrong, and this almost malicious reminder of the episode must have further stiffened the King's resistance. In short, it seemed to George III that the Whigs were asking him to pass under the yoke as he had in April of 1783. It is impossible to deny the insolence of the Whigs in this connection; but whether it was due to personal malice or high constitutional principles or was caused by confidence in immediate triumph or premonition of impending defeat it is difficult to say.

The King could scarcely conceal his elation when Portland's letter to Sydney was sent to him; and as a keen politician he could not refrain from calling attention to the tactical errors involved. In his answer to Sydney George III stated:

Though I did not doubt his Sentiments were to have everything in his own, and in reality by that means in the hands of Mr. Fox, yet I thought his advisers would have been more wise than thus openly on the outset to have avowed it. The Ministers could not be five minutes in deliberating on the impropriety of the Sentiments of such a proceeding, and that it forever closes any attempt from Me on that party, unless time should bring it to more moderate ideas; indeed such as will ever be found in those who really love this Country and do not center their Affections with the narrow limits of a party.[54]

[53] Clements Transcripts, I, 98.   [54] *Ibid.*, I, 100.

George III then set about acting on the premises of this letter. Two days later he is urging Pitt not to come to court that day but to "better employ part of the time" in consulting the cabinet as to necessary measures and pressing members of the House of Commons to take part in the debates in case the Coalition decided to propose another address to the Crown.[55]

The point of view of the Opposition is best portrayed in the letters of Fox's *Memorials and Correspondence*. The King used the Duke of Richmond, uncle of Fox, and Lord Sydney to convey his ideas to Portland and Fox. On February 16, the day after the many letters exchanged by the King, Sydney, and Portland, the Duke of Richmond through Mr. Ogilvie gave the views of George III. These sentiments were conveyed to Fox by the Duke of Portland. The King made clear his willingness to have a union of parties but only on condition that Thurlow, Richmond, Gower, and Pitt should be in the administration even though all of them were not included in the cabinet; that he considered it unreasonable to expect all of or any part of the present administration to resign for purposes of negotiation, since that would be a direct acknowledgment that they had acted in an unconstitutional manner; and that, if the House of Commons were rash or wicked enough to refuse or postpone supplies, the present ministry would resign and with his support defeat every measure which the new government might send up to the House of Lords. There seems to be no reason to doubt that this is exactly the line of attack and defense planned by the King and that he considered it good generalship to let the enemy know in advance what his plan of campaign was to be.[56]

The reference above to the refusal or postponement of supplies suggests, along with the refusal to pass a new mutiny bill, the tactics which Fox and Portland expected to adopt. By the admission of the King, Parliament could not be dissolved and a new one elected in time to pass a mutiny bill before the present one expired on March 25. Fox evidently counted on holding back the supplies or mutiny bill in order to force the existing ministry to a humiliating resignation. For this reason Fox's stand on February 18 is an interesting one. Whether or not his moderation was due to the warning which the King had sent through the Duke of Richmond it is impossible to say, but he merely proposed

[55] Pitt MSS, 103, February 18, 1784.
[56] Lord John Russell, *op. cit.*, II, 236-38.

that the report of the Committee on Supply should be postponed for three days. The reason he advanced for such a delay was to give the Commons more leisure to consider the anomalous position of the government, and at the same time he denied an intention of obstructing the public business. Pitt insisted upon treating the motion as a refusal of supply and in the division which followed it was carried by a majority of twelve.[57]

Although the failure of the negotiations of February 15 and 16 had convinced the King and the Coalition that a further union of the parties was impossible unless one side was willing to capitulate, the independent members of the House of Commons still believed that an agreement could be reached between Pitt and the Opposition. Accordingly, Powys, immediately after the division on the refusal of supply, moved "that this House, impressed with the most dutiful sense of his Majesty's paternal regard for the welfare of his people, relies on his Majesty's royal wisdom to take such measures as may tend to give effect to the wishes of his faithful Commons, which have already been most humbly represented to his Majesty, and which his Majesty has been graciously pleased to assure this House, that he will take into his consideration."[58] He was induced to withdraw this motion almost at once, but he moved it again on February 20. On the 19th Powys had felt moved to explain that he had voted to postpone considering supply not because he believed in permanently withholding it from the government but because he was of the opinion that the problem of the union of parties should receive first consideration. After a long debate on February 20 the Powys resolution was passed by a vote of 197 to 177.[59] Fox then followed up this apparent advantage by moving

That an humble Address be presented to his Majesty, most humbly to represent to his Majesty, that this House, impressed with the most dutiful sense of his Majesty's paternal regard for the welfare of his people, relies on his Majesty's royal wisdom, that he will take such measures as, by removing any obstacle to the formation of such an administration as this House has declared to be requisite in the pres-

[57] *Parliamentary History*, XXIV, 617.

[58] *Ibid.*

[59] *Parliamentary History*, XXIV, 667. An amendment moved by Eden was passed earlier in the debate which inserted after the words "measures as": "by removing any obstacle to the formation of such an administration as this House has declared to be requisite in the present critical and arduous situation of public affairs" (*ibid.*, p. 629).

ent critical and arduous situation of public affairs, may tend to give effect to the wishes of his faithful Commons, which have already been most humbly represented to his Majesty.[60]

After another long debate Fox's motion was passed by 177 to 156.[61] Considering the fact that it was 5:30 A.M. when the House adjourned, the size of the vote cast is remarkable. In order to make this address more impressive it was decided to have the whole House present it.

The King's opinion of this procedure is shown by his pungent letter to Pitt when news of the stormy session reached him. He admitted that at any other period of his reign he would have been astonished at such proceedings, but that he felt none at present; and he ended his letter with the shrewd comment that, "As the Opposition seem so fond of bringing King William forward on all occasions, I should think his exact words in 1701, with such additional ones as the peculiar moment may call for, would not be improper to be uttered from the Chair of State when the whole House bring up this strange, and I may add as an ungrounded position, this unconstitutional address."[62] Pitt asked the King's consent to delay receiving the address of the Commons until Wednesday, February 25, in order that the ministers might have an opportunity of drawing up an appropriate answer. The King consented, but expressed the desire that the answer, though civil, would contain a clear support of his own rights.[63] The answer, drawn up by the ministers, seems to have met with George III's approbation if not with that of the majority of the House of Commons:

GENTLEMEN:

I am deeply sensible how highly it concerns the honour of my Crown, and the welfare of my people, which is the object always nearest my heart, that the public affairs should be conducted by a firm, efficient, united, and extended administration, entitled to the confidence of my people, and such as may have a tendency to put an end to the unhappy divisions and distractions in this country. Very recent endeavours have already been employed, on my part, to unite in the public service, on a fair and equal footing, those whose joint efforts appear to me most capable of producing that happy effect; these endeavours have not had the success I wished. I shall be always

[60] *Ibid.*, p. 668.
[61] *Ibid.*, p. 672.
[62] Pitt MSS, 103, February 21, 1784.   [63] *Ibid.*, February 22, 1784.

desirous of taking every step most conducive to such an object; but I cannot see that it would, in any degree, be advanced, by the dismission of those at present in my service.

I observe, at the same time, that there is no charge, or complaint, suggested against my present ministers, nor is any one or more of them specifically objected to; and numbers of my subjects have expressed to me, in the warmest manner, their satisfaction in the late changes I have made in my councils. Under these circumstances, I trust, my faithful Commons will not wish that the essential offices of executive government should be vacated, until I see a prospect that such a plan of union as I have called for, and they have pointed out, may be carried into effect.[64]

Despite this firm and almost defiant answer to Fox's resolution, Pitt showed a willingness to continue the negotiations with the St. Albans Tavern group. If the King, Pitt, and the other ministers agreed on this stiff reply to the address, Pitt, at least, indicated that he was still interested in Powys' motion which was passed the same night as the address. On February 26 Pitt wrote to the King that as a result of consulting with the other ministers it had been decided to submit to him the advisability of bringing the matter of a union of parties to an issue by having George III see Pitt and the Duke of Portland together. Pitt then quoted from a document evidently familiar to both of them, which may have been taken from a communication of Powys himself or the St. Albans Tavern gentlemen as a group or, what is more likely, from the letter which Pitt would send to Portland, that having brought Pitt and the Duke together it would be possible to lay commands on them "to assist Your Majesty in giving effect to the unanimous vote of the House of Commons and to confer together on a Plan for the formation of a new Administration on a wide basis, and on a fair and equal footing, to be laid before Your Majesty."[65] Pitt argued that it might play into the hands of the Opposition if this offer from Powys was ignored.

The King's attitude at this time shows his skill as a practical politician. He was anxious to have these negotiations fail, and made no attempt to conceal the fact. On the other hand, he seems to have diagnosed Pitt's character in a way that the Opposition had failed to do. An abrupt refusal might have driven Pitt into the arms of Portland and Fox or, what is more likely, into an im-

---

[64] *Parliamentary History*, XXIV, 677–78.
[65] Clements Transcripts, I, 111.

mediate resignation. Every time that the King made a concession
of this sort he showed Pitt how much more willing he was to
co-operate than was Portland or Fox; thus he attempted to place
Pitt under greater obligations to him. In short, George III's
technique was to impress upon Pitt how distasteful such concessions were to him and to place such reservations on the negotiations as would meet with Pitt's approval and which might make
the terms unpalatable to the Coalition. His letter in answer to
Pitt is a masterpiece:

I should not deal with that openness towards Mr. Pitt which his
conduct deserves, if I did not state my hopes that the D. of Portland
will not come into what I may deem reasonable; a subject requiring
from his Sovereign exact words agreeable to which he can alone enter
into negotiation, is very revolting; but as the other Ministers seem
to advise that this last trial should be made, I will not object to it,
provided, in addition to the words proposed, Mr. Powys shall explain
specifically to that Duke that his being called upon is to give him no
right to anything above an equal share to others in the new Administration, not to be the head of it, whatever employment he may hold.[66]

Knowing Portland's insistence both in 1783 and earlier in February that he be called into the King's presence and offered the
place of First Lord of the Treasury, George III, doubtless, expected that the Duke's pride would cause him to take offense at
this last reservation.

The negotiations between Pitt and Portland failed exactly as
the King had hoped. The message which Pitt sent to Powys
contained the significant passage: the object for which His
Majesty calls on the Duke of Portland and Mr. Pitt to confer
is the formation of a new administration on a wide basis, and
on "a fair and equal footing."[67] The Duke, however, insisted
that the word "equal" be defined before he would hold the conference, and explained that he had no objection to the word "fair,"
which was a general term, but that the word "equal" was a limited
and specific term and he wished to know in advance how it was
to be applied. Further, Portland complained that the idea of each
party having an equal number in the cabinet seemed to promise
small hopes of a real union, and he indicated clearly that he
believed the basis of a new arrangement should be "mutual confidence and unity of principles."[68] Pitt felt that the definition of

[66] *Ibid.*, I, 112.
[67] Lord John Russell, *op. cit.*, II, 241–42.   [68] Tomline, *op. cit.*, I, 399–400.

words might well be left to the conference. The Duke of Portland then made two proposals, but since they embodied the two fundamental points upon which previous attempts at conciliation had broken his action was equivalent to breaking off negotiations. The first proposal was that he should construe Pitt's message as a virtual resignation. Pitt's "halter" speech earlier in the month had showed the light in which he viewed such an action. The second proposal was that Portland should "receive his Majesty's commands" on the conference with Pitt from the King in person.[69] This was asking George III to pass under the yoke again. In short, the Duke demanded from both Pitt and the King the concession which each was least likely to make. Unconditional surrender was virtually what the Coalition insisted upon, and neither the King nor Pitt was in so desperate a position as to make such action necessary. The disappointment which the gentlemen of the St. Albans Tavern felt was admirably expressed by their closing declaration:

That they heard with infinite concern, that all further progress towards a union was prevented by a doubt respecting a single word; and that they were unanimously of opinion, that it would be no dishonourable step in either of the gentlemen to give way, and might be highly advantageous to the public welfare.[70]

It is questionable, however, whether the result would have been any different had the doubt respecting the single word been settled and the conference held. The Coalition was bent upon forcing Pitt to resign as Shelburne had resigned, and upon making the King summon Portland again as he had summoned him after the thirty-seven-day strike in 1783. Since it is unlikely that Portland would have surrendered to Pitt's arguments or Pitt to Portland's, it is doubtful if the failure to hold the conference affected the outcome of this constitutional struggle.

The bitterness which resulted from the failure of these negotiations was further accentuated by the attack on Pitt opposite Brooks's Club, the virtual headquarters of the Whigs, upon his return from the City on the evening of February 28. On that day amidst great ceremonies Pitt had been conducted from his home in Berkeley Square—where he had been presented by the

---

[69] The point of view of Portland is expressed in two letters to Fox, in Lord John Russell, *op. cit.*, II, 238–41.

[70] Tomline, *op. cit.*, I, 400.

representatives of the Corporation of London with a vote of thanks and a gold box containing the paper giving him freedom of the City—to the Grocers' Hall in Poultry. It was upon his return late in the evening that the carriage in which he was riding with his brother and Lord Mahon was attacked by men armed with bludgeons and broken chair-poles. It was only natural that the Whigs should be blamed for this outrage. The King seems to have looked upon the attack in this light and hastened to assure Pitt that he trusted every means would be "employed to find out the abettors of this, which I should hope may be got at."[71] Even though the Whig leaders may have had nothing whatever to do with the attack and Pitt, in his heart, may not have actually believed they did, nevertheless it was certain to make the relations between the Coalition and Pitt more strained and to make the possibility of a union of parties even more remote.

The feeling that a chance for an understanding had passed was evident on March 1 when Fox, by a vote of 201 to 189, carried a second address to the King, asking that the ministers be dismissed.[72] This address to the King coming so soon after the first one was an unmistakable declaration of war. It concluded: "and do therefore find themselves obliged again to beseech his Majesty, that he would be graciously pleased to lay the foundation of a strong and stable government, by the previous removal of his present ministers."[73] The King insisted that he was more sorry than surprised that the Coalition could still command a majority. He took consolation, however, from what he termed the "pleasant part of the debate, the declaration that all negotiation is broken off," and he could not resist adding that it was most fortunate that no union of parties had taken place, because it would have been a bad thing for the country and inconvenient for those men who took part in the new arrangement.[74] Three days after the second address passed the Commons, the King answered in much the same language which he had used in the first one. The burden of his reply was that, although his sentiments on the matter of removing his ministers remained unchanged, he was always glad to have his faithful Commons exercise their right of offering him advice.[75]

[71] Pitt MSS, 103, February 29, 1784.
[72] *Parliamentary History*, XXIV, 713.   [73] *Ibid.*, p. 700.
[74] Pitt MSS, 103, March 2, 1784.
[75] *Parliamentary History*, XXIV, 717–18.

Since every attempt to make Pitt resign as a preliminary to the formation of a new government and to force the King to dismiss the ministry had failed, the last resort of the Opposition was to refuse to grant supply or to pass the Mutiny Bill. On the day after the King's answer to the second address was received, Fox moved that consideration of the motion to go into committee on the Mutiny Bill be postponed until the following Monday. This amendment was passed by only 171 to 162,[76] a majority which gave little hope to the Opposition leaders that they would be able to refuse supply or defeat the Mutiny Bill.

The last real blow struck by the Coalition came on March 8, when Fox moved for a Representation to the King on the state of public affairs. The Representation was a statement of the case of the majority of the House of Commons against the King and ministry, and covers three and a half columns in the *Parliamentary History*.[77] At the end of his speech Fox stated that the suggested union of parties had become a total impossibility because Pitt had proved to be averse to it. This aversion he ascribed to "immoderate ambition." In the course of the debate, Powys, who had taken the lead in the attempt of the country gentlemen to bring about a union of parties, lamented that Pitt had not been willing to accept the terms offered by the Coalition. Wilberforce argued shrewdly that Pitt could not trust himself in an administration upon unequal terms because Fox emphasized the importance of unity of principles and such unity could be secured only by the party of the latter being the stronger. In the end the Representation was passed by 191 to 190.[78] It marked the last serious attack by the Coalition on the Pitt ministry.

No letter written by George III in his entire reign showed greater elation than the one he wrote to Pitt upon receiving news of the events of March 8:

Mr. Pitt's letter is undoubtedly the most satisfactory I have received for many months, an avowal on the outset that the proposition held forth is not intended to go farther lengths than a kind of manifesto; and then carrying it by the majority of only one, and the day concluding with an avowal that all negotiation is at an end, gives me every reason to hope that by a firm and proper conduct this faction will by degrees be deserted by many, and at length be forgot. I shall ever with pleasure consider that by the prudence as well as rectitude

---

[76] *Parliamentary History*, XXIV, 732–33.
[77] *Ibid.*, pp. 736–39.   [78] *Ibid.*, p. 744.

of one person in the House of Commons this great change has been affected, and that he will be ever able to reflect with satisfaction that in having supported me he has saved the Constitution, the most perfect of human formations.[79]

Pitt's reactions were not so joyous. In a letter of March 10 to his friend the Duke of Rutland he stated: "I write now in great haste, and tired to death, even with victory, for I think our present state is entitled to that name."[80] The reason why Pitt did not get the tremendous satisfaction out of the triumph which the King enjoyed is fairly obvious. The failure of the negotiations for a union of parties seems to have been a genuine disappointment to him. He was faced with three possible lines of action, and the acceptance of no one of them could give him complete satisfaction: first, to submit to the mortification of resignation and re-admission to the ministry as Portland suggested; second, to resign and become a free lance once more; and, third, to remain as the minister of the King backed by the almost inevitable majority that he could secure by the approaching general election. He chose the third as the least unsatisfactory of the three; but no one who has followed his attempts to reach an understanding with Fox and Portland will believe that he considered this choice, in the light which the King obviously regarded it, namely, as the best of all possible endings.

In many respects the most interesting of all debates during the period of this constitutional crisis came on March 9. No opposition was offered to the motion of the Secretary at War that the blank in the Mutiny Bill be filled in with the words "from the 25th of March 1784, to the 25th of March 1785."[81] The discussion then turned on the causes for the triumph of Pitt and the King over the majority of the House of Commons. It had all the earmarks of a political post-mortem, since admissions of defeat were common. Sir M. W. Ridley stressed the importance which the people outside Parliament had played in the victory of the Crown and ministry:

He had embarked on that test with the purest motives, and had concurred with the majority of the House, as long as he had any hopes that the House could fight with effect the battles of the consti-

[79] Pitt MSS, March 9, 1784.

[80] *Correspondence between William Pitt and Charles Duke of Rutland, 1781–1787* (London, 1842), p. 8.

[81] *Parliamentary History*, XXIV, 745.

tution. But with regret he was now forced to say, that the House was defeated, and defeated by those who ought to be its natural supporters and defenders—the people. Ministers and their adherents had so misrepresented the nature of the contest, that the people, for whom alone the Commons had entered the lists, had not only abandoned them, but turned against them: with such auxiliaries, ministers had triumphed; they had taken from the Commons their heavy artillery (their constituents) and turned it upon themselves. No wonder that with such auxiliaries prerogative should triumph over the privileges of the Commons. But whether it was wonderful or not, it was a melancholy truth that the House of Commons had been defeated, and that prerogative now reigned triumphant. A misguided people had been taught to desert their natural guardians, and fly for protection to the crown: he made no doubt but the day would come when they would have cause to repent that they had lent a hand to degrade their own representatives: their repentance he feared would come too late.[82]

From general testimony on the causes for the victory of the Crown and ministry the discussion turned on the reasons for the failure of the negotiations for a union of parties. Here Powys, who had been the unquestioned leader in the attempt to bring the ministry and Opposition into agreement, came out flatly on the side of Portland and Fox; and he conceded that "The House was indeed conquered; for though a vote of the Commons could once bestow a crown, it could not now procure the dismission of a minister." Next he gave an ironical description of the forces that were led by Pitt:

The first might be called his body-guard, composed of light young troops, who shot their little arrows with amazing dexterity against those who refused to swear allegiance to their chief. The second might be called the corps of royal volunteers, staunch champions for prerogative, every ready to fall with determined valour upon those who should dare to oppose privilege to prerogative, or arraign the conduct of their chief. The third was a legion composed of deserters, attached to their leader by no other principle than that of interest; and who after having deserted to him from that principle would desert from him on the same grounds, when they saw their interest would suffer if they should stand by him.[83]

In his conclusion Powys insisted that the Opposition had made concessions on all three points requested by Pitt, but that Pitt

[82] *Parliamentary History*, XXIV, 745-46.
[83] *Ibid.*, p. 749.

had made no concession on any of the three asked by his opponents. The first three were the exclusion of Lord North, changes in the India Bill, and interview with Portland on fair and equal terms; and the second three were that Sydney's letter asking the Duke and his friends to participate in a new administration should be construed as a virtual resignation by Pitt, that Portland should see the King personally to propose a plan for the new arrangement, and that the word "equal" should be explained.

Pitt's reply to Powys was not one of his happiest efforts. Certainly there appears to have been nothing in the latter's conduct or speech to justify Pitt's sneer that "the honourable gentleman had an opportunity of knowing the secrets of the army; for having served on both sides, and having undertaken the task of negociating, he was able to do his friends signal service, by the information he might collect as a spy, while he enjoyed the privileges and immunities of an ambassador."[84] When Powys entered a vigorous protest, Pitt insisted that he had not meant to insinuate dishonorable conduct in the course of the negotiations. In defending himself against the charge of receiving but making no concessions, he declared that he had not asked Lord North to stand aside; that the offer on the India Bill was valueless until the actual terms were written in the bill; that he was certainly unwilling, as he had often indicated, to have any action considered as a virtual resignation; and that the words "fair and equal" were so obvious that if anyone took exception to them it was evident that such a person was not willing to meet upon such conditions as the words implied.[85]

From the time of this bitter debate on March 9 through the speech of the King which put an end to the session on March 24 little of interest took place in Parliament; for the opposition, true to their statements of March 9, made no attempt to stop supplies or to pass the Mutiny Bill for a shorter time than a year.

During these slack days, however, a debate on a phase of Parliamentary reform took place which was prophetic of the fate that movement was to suffer at the hands of Pitt. This debate took place on March 13 over Alderman Sawbridge's motion for a reform of Parliament. But even before this acrimonious dispute Pitt had given an indication that his enthusiasm for Parliamentary reform, which it is impossible to doubt, had been somewhat

[84] *Ibid.*, p. 751.
[85] *Ibid.*, pp. 751–52.

tempered by his responsibilities as Prime Minister. On January 16 Duncombe had presented a petition from the freeholders of the county of York asking the House to take into consideration the present inadequate state of representation and to apply such a remedy as the House deemed necessary. Pitt in a brief speech endorsed the object of the petition and stated that the best argument for the necessity of a reform lay in the recent conduct in the House of Commons. But he would not, he insisted, "be understood to be an advocate for every species of reform which might appear necessary to other men; but a temperate and moderate reform, temperately and moderately pursued, he would at all times, and in all situations, be ready to promote to the utmost of his power."[86] When the petition was brought in and Mr. Duncombe moved that it should lie upon the table, Pitt seconded the motion. The Earl of Surrey then upbraided him for barely seconding so important a measure, and declared that the freeholders of York expected something more. "They," he pointed out, "reposed the greatest confidence in his abilities, which were certainly of the first rate; and as they had formed an opinion that he would not consent to make any part of a cabinet in which there was a man hostile to a parliamentary reform, so they presumed that success would attend this application." Pitt answered with a note of exasperation that he:

. . . . was surprised to hear the noble lord censure him for not doing something more than second a motion that the petition should lie upon the table. He might have expected a censure indeed if he had gone any further as he might have afforded the gentlemen on the other side an opportunity to cry out that he had presumed, with defiled hands, to pollute the fair petition of the people; that he, the creature of secret influence, had dared to interfere when there was question of a measure which was to root influence out of that House. He was ready to return the noble lord his thanks for the flattering opinion he entertained of his abilities, if by other parts of his speech he was not convinced that this was overbalanced by a bad opinion of his political conduct in other respects; he was, however, thankful to the freeholders of York for the favourable sentiments they entertained of him; but he was at a loss to conceive where they learned that he never would make part of a cabinet, any one member of which should be hostile to a parliamentary reform; perhaps it would be absolutely impossible to form such a cabinet; the proposition was a point on which there were so many different opinions, that he believed if the country was to remain without a cabinet until one could be formed that should be unanimous on this subject, England would never see an administration. To him, on the other hand, it appeared not a little singular, that the noble lord and his friends, who were such determined enemies to influence, should expect that a measure relating simply to the Commons, such as a reformation in the representation of the people, should in any degree originate in the cabinet, or come forward under their influence and protection. All he would add was, that individually he would exert the utmost of his ability to support the measure of a reform in parliament, whenever that subject should be brought before the House.[87]

So explicit a statement of his stand in January may have been repeated in private conversations with various reformers after that date. In any case it appears that Pitt reiterated these views to Alderman Sawbridge, since the latter openly charged the minister with refusal to take an active part in sponsoring such a measure in the Commons. Sawbridge, in moving on March 13 that a committee be appointed to inquire into the present state of representation in the House of Commons, referred to Pitt in language which showed only too clearly the fears and feelings of the reformers. He had hoped, Sawbridge stated, that Pitt would not only introduce a motion for Parliamentary reform but also use his weight and influence to insure the success of the measure.

In consequence of those hopes it was that he called upon the right honourable gentleman before he gave notice that he would move any proposition on the subject, in order to know whether he intended to take up the matter or not; from the right honourable gentleman's having declined it, and from the tenor of his proposition of the last year, which met with general disapprobation of the friends of parliamentary reform, he was led to apprehend that the right hon. gentleman had abandoned the idea in his heart as completely as he was supposed, and had been stated to have abandoned other principles that he had formerly professed.[88]

Pitt in reply inferred that his opposition came from the belief that it was neither a fit nor favorable time for bringing forward such a measure, and that "it would have looked more like candour and sincerity, had the worthy alderman forborne to allude to him, and to talk of his conduct, in language the most invidious, the

[87] *Ibid.*, pp. 350–51.
[88] *Ibid.*, pp. 757–58.

most false, the most malicious, and the most slanderous."[89] At this point he was called to order by Fox. Pitt, after apologizing, declared that he naturally felt resentment at being accused of abandoning all idea of Parliamentary reform and his other principles; and he defied Sawbridge to prove that he had abandoned any principle that he had professed or that he was not as firm a supporter of Parliamentary reform as ever. Sawbridge in reply stated that since Pitt's language concerning him had been declared unparliamentary he would not answer it "otherwise than retorting the same expressions on the right honourable gentleman."[90] After Sawbridge's motion had been beaten by 141 to 93,[91] the Earl of Surrey asked Pitt if he intended to bring forward any specific motion on Parliamentary reform, since, if Pitt did not do so, he intended doing so himself. Pitt declined to give a specific answer, on the grounds that so much depended upon time and situation.

George III must have read the account of this debate with a relish second only to that experienced upon reading those of March 9, in which the victory of the King and Pitt had been freely conceded. Even the fact that Pitt had reiterated his zeal for reform could not seriously perturb the King. Two things in the debates of January 16 and March 13 were certain to give him great satisfaction: Pitt's statement that he could give reform only his individual support and could not, considering the personnel of the ministry, be expected to make it a government measure; and the obvious cleavage between the reformers and Pitt which resulted in mutual suspicion and harsh language. The King had prevented Pitt from joining with the enemies of prerogative in the formation of a ministry, and now without much exertion on his own part he saw Pitt separating himself from the reformers.

With the exception of the debate on Sawbridge's motion, on the bill to regulate expenses at elections, and on the passing of measures granting supply and the Mutiny Bill, the period from March 9 to March 24 was comparatively uneventful. Parliament was prorogued on March 24 and dissolved on March 25. The details of the highly significant election which followed have been worked out by Professor Laprade.[92] The conventional explana-

---

[89] *Parliamentary History,* XXIV, 763.
[90] *Ibid.,* p. 764.
[91] *Loc. cit.*
[92] *Parliamentary Papers of John Robinson,* pp. 65–132.

tion for the overwhelming victory which the King and Pitt won is that public opinion, outraged by the infamous coalition of Fox and North and charmed by the gallant fight waged by Pitt, decided the election. Although public opinion may have been as over-whelmingly on the side of the King and Pitt as the contemporary diarists and speakers in Parliament stated, it could not because of the state of representation under the unreformed House of Commons be decisive. In addition to the estimates made by John Robinson, probably in the second week of December 1783, two other significant memoranda in his papers throw additional light on the decisive factors in the election. The first paper already referred to contained a list of the members of the House of Commons rated pro, hopeful, doubtful, and con, and a parallel list showing the probable number under each of these four classi-fications in case a general election were held. The results of these two estimates, as has been stated, undoubtedly influenced Pitt in his determination to accept the place of First Lord of the Treas-ury. The first of the two additional memoranda was, probably, prepared by Robinson between December 15 and December 31. It divides into six groups the seats in the greater part of the English boroughs: friends, close or under decisive influence, 39; for communication, those partly accessible in one way and part in another, 65; money, 51; no money, 27; adverse, 20; and open boroughs where seats may probably be obtained with expense, 17.[93] The second memorandum was drawn up at some time be-tween February 14 and the dissolution of Parliament on March 25. The paper was endorsed: "Places where may be contests in open boroughs and Cinque Ports." Then followed a list of boroughs and candidates, and a statement opposite suggesting the tactics which the government should adopt in each instance.[94] These memoranda, combined with the actual results of the election, show beyond a reasonable doubt the methods employed to win the election of 1784 by so great a majority. When the new Parlia-ment met on May 18, Pitt had a majority of 168, which closely approximated the various estimates made by Robinson in the different memoranda referred to in this paragraph.

Only the results, and not the details, of the election of 1784 are of concern in this monograph. In view of the significance in English constitutional history of the events in 1783–84, some

[93] *Ibid.*, pp. 106–13.
[94] *Ibid.*, pp. 113–18.

explanation must be offered for the fact that Pitt allowed over three months to elapse after he became First Lord of the Treasury before he dissolved Parliament. The old explanation is that he waited for public opinion to veer around to his side; the new one suggested by the researches of Professor Laprade is that time was needed to arrange the details of the proper influence to be used in each borough. Yet Robinson had completed his survey of the pros, hopefuls, doubtfuls, and cons in the existing House of Commons and of the same classifications in case of a general election during the second week in December, as well as the memoranda on the Parliamentary state of boroughs, which Professor Laprade believes was drawn up between December 15 and December 31, 1783. Clearly it was possible to dissolve Parliament soon after Pitt became First Lord of the Treasury on December 19 and to secure practically the same results as those which followed the general election of 1784. The Coalition feared a dissolution, and was not reassured until the King's declaration before the Christmas recess that he contemplated no such action. Thus the suggestion that time was needed to make arrangements for the general election with prospective candidates is not convincing. If, then, the three months were not needed to win over public opinion or to make the undercover arrangements, what explanation can be offered for the delay?

Obviously the one who held back was Pitt; but the reasons why he held back are not so clear. Apparently only one of two explanations can account for his stand. Both are based on the supposition that Pitt was a sincere young man who still believed in Parliamentary reform and opposed the influence of the Crown as he did at the time of his interviews with Thurlow in July of 1783.

The first explanation is that Pitt suddenly yielded to the King's pleas and arguments based on the actions of the Coalition and the statistics of Robinson and then refused to carry his action to the logical conclusion by consenting to an immediate general election. The reasons why he refused might be a genuine desire to find out if he could hold his own with the debating powers of the Coalition, an added precaution to take more time to make certain of the support of "hopefuls and doubtfuls," or a firm conviction that he should reach an understanding with Portland and Fox to form a new government. Any one of these three reasons assumes that Pitt accepted the place of First Lord of the Treasury without having made up his mind definitely as to the course he would pursue.

The second explanation is that Pitt had come to a very definite conclusion on the course that he would pursue before he accepted the task of heading the government on December 19. He had ambitions and ideals which, as his speeches indicate, he hoped to realize. The ideal arrangement, from his point of view, would have been a union with the Whigs in which he retained his position at the head of the government and would be in a position to carry out the reform measures in which he believed. Delay in holding the general election would assist in two objects: it would make possible, if necessary, prolonged negotiations with the Whigs; and, in case he proved his ability to cope with the orators of the Coalition, it would enhance the chance of the success of these negotiations and of the relative strength of Pitt in a new government. But if the negotiations with the Whigs failed, Pitt could at least retain his position as First Lord of the Treasury. Perhaps the second of these alternatives, remaining at the head of the government without a union with the Whigs, became more alluring as the weeks went by. Pitt certainly gained even greater self-confidence as his successes in debate became more frequent, and he became less eager for the union when the demands of Portland and Fox seemed so arrogant. In contrast with this harsh and unyielding attitude of the Whig leaders, the conduct of George III was characterized by tact and consideration and by an understanding of the personality and point of view of Pitt which contributed in no small measure to the outcome of this constitutional struggle. Even the decided approbation of public opinion to which so many contemporaries refer, but which Professor Laprade has shown did not materially affect the outcome of the general election, must have influenced Pitt in his decision to remain as head of the ministry in case the union of parties failed.

The present writer is convinced that the second of the two explanations for Pitt's conduct between December of 1783 and March of 1784, which was described in the preceding paragraph, is the correct one. It is inconceivable that Pitt, whose conduct from March to December of 1783 showed such extreme caution, should have acted impulsively by yielding to the pleas of the King as the first explanation suggests. The second explanation can be reconciled with all the important facts for these months. In short, Pitt, by accepting the King's offer on December 19, did not discard either his political principles or his ambitions. He hoped to reach an understanding with the Whigs and to be able to oppose "influence" and to further reform. It may be objected that he could have reached an understanding with the Whigs without antagonizing them by assisting in the overthrow of the Portland ministry as he did. The obvious answer is that Pitt did not want North in the new arrangement and that he wished his own place to be a higher one than he could secure by entering the Whig ranks as an apprentice. In case he failed to reach an understanding with the Whigs, he could remain as the King's chief minister, without loss of prestige or honor if he adhered to his political principles. He became reconciled to this alternative as a result of the success he attained as a debater, of the arrogant demands of Fox and Portland, of the widespread expression of public opinion in his favor, and of the skillful manner in which George III handled him.

The real hero of the constitutional crisis from December 1783 to March 1784 was George III. He appears to have diagnosed the strength and weakness of Pitt with uncanny accuracy. Pitt was particularly sensitive on the subject of his youth and of his political idealism. Members of the Opposition were continually making hilarious references to the angry boy and the immaculate youth both in and out of the House of Commons. The King, on the other hand, treated Pitt with a dignified formality which seems to have been exactly what the young man yearned for at the time. There is, during these years, nothing of that note of personal affection which is so evident in the letters which George III wrote earlier to Lord North and later to Addington. The King also showed the greatest consideration for Pitt's political principles. It was, of course, the only way he could hold Pitt; but the manner in which he carried it out showed that he was gifted with the highest political acumen. By respecting Pitt's principles he could insist upon respect and consideration for his own. This enabled George III to follow successfully the line of action which meant eventual triumph for him: where he, and his friends in the cabinet, differed from Pitt on the advisability of a measure, such as Parliamentary reform, each group was left free to speak and vote as it saw fit; but the measure was not to be made a governmental one. The significance of such an arrangement will become more obvious later. The King's judgment, however, reached its height in the patient and skillful manner in which he permitted Pitt to carry on the negotiations with the Whigs for a union of parties. Over and over again he expressed his extreme repugnance toward such a policy. Each time he yielded he stressed the fact that it was against his better judgment that he did so, and he allowed Pitt to feel that it was only to please the latter that he consented. Doubtless the King would have refused to make important concessions had the possibility of a union of parties materialized; but he was in the position to profit by the blunders of his enemies and to appear to be making concessions that would make possible the union which Pitt desired. Thus when the terms of Portland and Fox were fixed so rigidly, the King was comparatively safe in his ostentatious and reluctant consent to further negotiations. In addition George III could emphasize to Pitt the contrast between the royal flexibility and the Whig inflexibility. As a result of his own adroit handling of the situation and the blunders of his opponents, the King had secured the objects for which he fought. The contest had terminated exactly as he had hoped, and his only fear lay in the reform principles of Pitt. To checkmate these he had the innocuous arrangement that Pitt could advocate his reforms as his individual but not as government measures, and the possibility that the minister might tire of being a reformer under such circumstances.

Next to George III, Lord North stands out in the crisis of 1783–84. He had entered the Coalition a year earlier for reasons already described, and he seems to have been perfectly aware of the dangers of Fox's India Bill of November of 1783. Even his enemies, both contemporary and later, concede that his offer to retire from the Coalition, if he stood in the way of a union between the Whigs and Pitt, was extremely generous. His willingness to sacrifice personal ambition and position in order to make possible the kind of government which the country needed was certainly superior to the attitude of either Pitt or Fox. They were willing to hold office for their country, and North was willing to renounce the hope of a return to office. Of course, North had served in a high office almost continuously since 1767, whereas both Fox and Pitt had barely tasted the joys of a place of cabinet rank. But, in the case of Sir Robert Walpole earlier and of Pitt himself later, a long period in office made the holder that much more reluctant to surrender the place. Whether or not such an offer meant a great sacrifice to him, North defended his position with dignity and straightforwardness. To Pitt's scornful statement that there was one individual (North) with whom he would not serve, North made the obvious retort that the opinion of one person meant nothing to him but that the interests of his country mattered a great deal. In the course of his long and over-censured public career North did or said nothing which he could look back upon with more pride than his stand at this time.

The losers—and they deserved to lose by the tactics they employed—were Fox and Portland. Fundamentally they were fighting for the modern principle of ministerial responsibility to a majority of the House of Commons and of cabinet solidarity against those of the right of the King to appoint his own ministers regardless of party or political differences. Yet the underlying principles were so interwoven with personalities and inconsistencies that the issue was seriously befogged. The ousted Coalition made its fight against Pitt after December 19 on the ground that he did not command a majority of the House of Commons. In view of the fact that two groups with such different fundamental political principles as the followers of Fox and North had coalesced, it was difficult for them to stress the modern principle of the cabinet members professing unanimity in public. Instead, the Coalition was forced to take the stand which the King and Pitt adopted, namely, that upon issues in which the two groups failed to agree each should speak and vote in Parliament as its members saw fit. The coalition of Fox and North seems to have functioned only because the latter allowed the former to have his way and to take the initiative in most measures, and that the ones upon which their followers could not agree, such as Parliamentary reform, were not made serious issues during the short Portland ministry. Despite the fundamental inconsistency in a coalition with North, the Whigs stood for a ministry based on measures and not on men; whereas George III, as he stated over and over again, held that he had the right to select as he saw fit his own ministers from any group or party. Pitt's views coincided fairly closely with those of Fox and Portland. In fact, where a difference was evident, as on reform, Pitt was likely to be more at odds with the King than were the Whig leaders. The memoranda which George III drew up of his conversations with Portland leaves little doubt that Fox and Portland had in mind a cabinet based on political solidarity which should act as the real executive.

The Whigs had worked out the plan of cabinet solidarity based on the majority of the House of Commons, and Portland stuck tenaciously to it in his negotiations with George III and Pitt. The points upon which he insisted, as will be remembered, were that Pitt should resign and that George III should summon him personally to form an administration. Why then have the Whigs not received greater credit as the upholders of the great constitutional principle of the nineteenth century? Probably the explanation lies, as was suggested in the preceding paragraph, in the inconsistencies and personalities which confused the fundamental issue. By forming a coalition with North, Fox and Portland made it very difficult to secure for themselves a reasonable hearing on the question of a government based on political solidarity. It was difficult to make converts to such a doctrine in view of the fact that Fox joined with North after refusing to serve with Shelburne. Fully as damaging as this inconsistency were the obvious clashes of personality. Fox, unfortunately, showed that personal animosity to Lord Shelburne and to George III outweighed the principle of a government based on common principles; and after December 19 Fox and Portland insisted upon the resignation of Pitt as a prerequisite to negotiations in a manner which indicated all too clearly a personal bias. In short, although the Whigs adhered faithfully to a very important constitutional issue, they rendered this adherence almost worthless by placing even greater emphasis on personal dislikes and by such enormous inconsistencies as the refusal of Fox to serve with Shelburne but his willingness to do so with North.

The most serious error made by Fox and Portland, however, was in their treatment of Pitt. This young man was obviously the key to the situation in the years 1783–1784, and the failure of the Whig leaders to recognize this fact proved costly to themselves, the country, and perhaps even Pitt himself. George III was the chief residuary legatee of the errors of the Whig leaders. The King could be practically certain of securing a majority in any House of Commons as a result of a general election, but he experienced great difficulty in securing an able man who would satisfy him and could control the majority of the Commons. The Whig mistakes in handling Pitt began with Rockingham's refusal to find him a seat in the Commons during the election of 1780 and continued through the failure to reach an understanding over the union of parties in 1784. They kept him out of the cabinet in the Rockingham ministry of 1782 and further widened the breach by the bitterness aroused over the refusal of Fox and his followers to serve under Shelburne and by the Fox-North Coalition. Nevertheless, the door to reconciliation was not closed by Pitt until the negotiations described at length in this chapter had failed. If the Whig leaders did not appreciate the strength and unusual position of Pitt during the Shelburne and Portland ministries, there was no excuse for pleading such ignorance after Pitt had held his position as First Lord of the Treasury for a few weeks. If Fox and Portland could not see clearly, at least George III could.

To believers in the constitutional principles of cabinet solidarity and responsibility to the majority in the House of Commons, which were generally accepted after the Reform Bill of 1832, the almost incredible number of mistakes made by the Whigs during the years from 1780 to 1784 is decidedly disheartening. One is tempted to quote Junius' statement to the Duke of Grafton: "It is not that you do wrong by design, but that you should never do right by mistake."[95] How the Whigs hoped to win a victory over George III, when they threw away every advantage with almost incredible recklessness, it is difficult to say. With the tremendous advantage of patronage, the prestige of the Crown, and the growing personal popularity of George III after the Gordon Riots it should have been clear to the Whigs that they could not win a general election.

The obvious superiority of the King at election time needed to be offset by every means which the Whigs could muster. Yet failing to profit by the Wilkes lesson they had not affiliated themselves with the movements for Parliamentary reform, had made no attempt to work with the followers first of Shelburne and then of Pitt, had offended the wealthy commercial interests by the India Bill of 1783, and had alienated certain middle-class and liberal support by the coalition with Lord North. Some of these mistakes could be rectified in the future: it was still possible to secure the backing of the reformers, and to win the support of the commercial classes if Pitt offended them as he did in 1785 with his Irish Resolutions. The chances of a real union with Pitt were never good after the early months of 1784. When coalitions were proposed at later dates, Pitt had changed his point of view, and consequently a union would have been one of expediency and not of spirit. The chances of winning over the section of middle-class

[95] George Woodfall (ed.), *Junius Letters* (London, n.d.), p. 158, May 30, 1769.

opinion which had been alienated as a result of the coalition with North was not good; for this element became more and more attached to the King on grounds of private morality and less and less friendly to Fox and his followers because of the belief that the personal and political morals of the latter were on the same level. Thus the Whigs lost a great opportunity in the years 1780–1784 and did not have another to compare with it until 1830.

Although the general election of 1784 decided that the Whigs were not to realize the constitutional principles which the Duke of Portland had explained to George III and which the latter found so novel, it did not decide the relationship between the King and Pitt. It took the sessions of 1784 and 1785 to settle the question whether George III or his First Lord of the Treasury was to be the senior partner in the firm.

IV. THE BEST YEARS OF WILLIAM PITT, 1784 TO 1785

When the new Parliament met on May 18, 1784, Pitt had the large majority to which the efforts of Robinson, the errors of the Whigs, the skill of the King, and his own clever leadership entitled him. In this chapter his efforts to control this majority, particularly on reform measures which his allies the King and the commercial interests would oppose, will be traced.

In 1784 Pitt was successful in passing an India Bill and some beneficial changes in the budget of the year. He found success on the former comparatively easy because of his large majority in the House of Commons and because with the King's knowledge he had come to an agreement with the East India Company over the terms of the proposed measure. Thus no great difference of opinion between the King and Pitt need detain us at this point. The second bill naturally received harsh treatment from the Opposition speeches, but was not seriously threatened on any reading in either house. The fundamental principles upon which the bill was based were an emphasis on the development of peaceful commerce and the avoidance as much as possible of alliances or policies which might lead to war. Although the Company saved itself from the loss of powers of which Fox's bill of 1783 would have deprived it, yet the governments in India were subjected to the control of a committee of the Privy Council. This committee was entrusted with general control over Indian policy, with preparing legislation for India, and with recalling the officers of the Company. Some complaints were made in the debates about the losses suffered, but at least some control over patronage and the more strictly commercial phases were left to the Company.

Since it is in the direction of financial and budgetary problems that Pitt's reputation is highest, his first efforts are naturally of some interest. As a result of the wars ending in 1783 and of the failure of the many ministries since North's resignation to deal effectively with the problems, he found the finances of the Kingdom in a low and involved state. Pitt's great achievements during the 1784 session are: first, the funding of part of the floating debt at a high rate of interest, five per cent, and issuing it at 93; second, a blow at abuse of the privilege of "franking" letters; and third, the crippling of the widespread practice of smuggling tea into the country by reducing the duty on the cheaper kinds from an average of 119 to 12½ per cent.[1] Although even Pitt's admirers admit that his financial abilities developed slowly, the achievements of his first year as a finance minister are decidedly creditable. In his Indian and fiscal measures Pitt had the support of the King, and hence no clash of personalities or of constitutional principles was at stake. The letters which George III wrote to Pitt during the session of 1784 continued to show an understanding of the stiff pride of the youthful minister, and all the suggestions he offered were made in a courteous tone and cordial manner. Treatment of this kind seems to have been increasingly effective and was in marked contrast to the attacks which Pitt had to bear from the Coalition and to the slights from impatient reformers.

The longer the King could delay any of Pitt's reform measures the more difficult it became for Pitt to break with him and the greater became the exasperation and suspicion of the reformers. The smouldering ill-feeling between Pitt and Alderman Sawbridge which had burst into flames in the famous clash of March 13, 1784, threatened to break out a second time in the session from May to August of the same year. Pitt had attempted to reassure Wyvill two days before this clash when he had written:

I consider myself greatly obliged to you for the favour of your letter, which I received upon the 6th instant. I beg leave to assure you that my zeal for Reform in Parliament is by no means abated, and that I will ever exert my best endeavours to accomplish that important object.[2]

This attempt to prevent Sawbridge from making his annual motion had proved futile in March, and similar attempts to dissuade him in the next session were equally unsuccessful. Despite Pitt's promise to bring up the question of Parliamentary reform in 1785, Alderman Sawbridge refused to postpone consideration of the subject in this session. When Sawbridge pressed for a division on the question, his measure was beaten by a majority of 74.[3] The difference in the treatment accorded Pitt by George III and by the reformers was striking: the King's attitude was that he appreciated the high abilities and ideals of his minister and that differences between them must be settled on the understanding that both were honorable men and each must respect the opinions of the other; while that of the reformers and the Whigs was that Pitt

[1] J. H. Rose, *Life of William Pitt* (London: G. Bell & Sons, Ltd., 1923), I, 184.　　　　　　　　　　[2] *Ibid.*, p. 197.
[3] *Parliamentary History* (London, 1806–1820), XXIV, 1006.

had abandoned his principles and was guilty of moral turpitude. In the long run these parallel treatments unquestionably influenced the proud, sensitive, and conceited young man to a considerable extent. The King having written to Pitt, "It is impossible to frame a more proper letter than Mr. Pitt has in answer to the Duke of Rutland, as it in a masterly manner contains all difficulties in the present stage of the business of forming a decided opinion,"[4] it was only natural that the young minister should prefer such sentiments to those Alderman Sawbridge expressed.

The year 1785 is the decisive one in the history of Pitt's career. During the brief session of 1784 he had made a satisfactory showing in his financial measure and India Bill; now he was to grapple with several problems which were fully as dear to his heart as fiscal and Indian measures but upon which he was to meet disheartening opposition. In the course of this session he was defeated decisively on four measures: the Westminster election scrutiny; the Irish commercial resolutions; the fortification of Plymouth and Portsmouth; and Parliamentary reform. These defeats, as subsequent events were to show, ended Pitt's career as a real reformer. According to one biographer: "After the severe disappointments of the session of 1785, the signs of friskiness vanish from the life of Pitt."[5]

These four measures will be considered in the order listed in the preceding paragraph, which is the order in which they were brought before Parliament. The first of these four, the scrutiny into the Westminster election of 1784, had been dealt with in the session of 1784 but no decision had been reached. It arose from the attempt of Pitt to prevent Fox's sitting for Westminster. After an exciting election of forty days, about which many legends flourish, Fox finished ahead of the second of the two court and government candidates, Sir Cecil Wray. At the close of the election Fox stood 460 votes below Lord Hood but 236 above Sir Cecil. There were charges of irregularity from both sides, and Sir Cecil demanded a scrutiny. The High Bailiff of Westminster not only granted the scrutiny but refused to make any returns for the election. Thus both Fox and Hood were prevented from taking their seats as members for Westminster when the new Parliament met in May. Fox was not excluded from the House of Commons, because he had been returned for the Orkney and Shetland

4 Pitt MSS, 103, July 28, 1784.
5 J. H. Rose, *op. cit.*, I, 270.

Islands. Pitt's attitude on the question is nowhere more clearly shown than in his letter of May 24, 1784, to the Duke of Rutland:

Our first battle was previous to the address, on the subject of the return for Westminster. The enemy chose to put themselves on bad ground, by moving that two members ought to have been returned, without first hearing the High Bailiff to explain the reasons of his conduct. We beat them on this, by 283 to 136. The High Bailiff is to attend to-day, and it will depend upon the circumstances stated whether he will be ordered to proceed in the scrutiny, or immediately to make a double return, which will bring the question before a committee. In either case I have no doubt of Fox being thrown out, though in either there may be great delay, inconvenience, and expense, and the choice of the alternative is delicate.[6]

The second half of this last sentence was more prophetic than the first. Pitt was able to hold his large majority when he insisted upon a scrutiny. At the end of months of inquiry into the legality of the votes cast, however, the results of the election were not changed appreciably. Thus when the 1785 session of Parliament was opened on January 25 practically everybody except Pitt seems to have been thoroughly tired of the scrutiny. Yet he persisted, and even his greatest admirers find difficulty in justifying his actions. Lord Stanhope says that it was because Pitt had "a sense of consistency and a regard to the course he had formerly pursued";[7] while Dr. J. Holland Rose explains that "it is likely that he acted, not from rancour, not from a desire to ban his enemy, least of all under any dictation from Windsor (of this I found no sign), but rather from the dictates of political morality."[8] It may be added that many of his followers did not hold so exalted a view of Pitt's conduct, for they deserted him in great numbers when he attempted to continue the fight in the session of 1785. His majority of 147, which he boasted of to the Duke of Rutland, and of 168 on the address to the King at the opening of the session of 1784, dwindled rapidly. Three successive motions on March 3, 1785, requiring the High Bailiff to make an immediate return showed the turn of the tide. The first was beaten by 39, the second by 9, and the third, after a motion to adjourn had been lost by 162 to 124, was passed without a division.[9]

[6] *Correspondence between William Pitt and Charles Duke of Rutland* (London, 1842), pp. 13–14.

[7] Lord Stanhope, *Life of William Pitt* (London, 1861–62), I, 254.

[8] J. H. Rose, *op. cit.*, I, 271.

[9] *Parliamentary History*, XXV, 74, 103, 105.

The effect of Pitt's defeat so early in the session of 1785 is significant. It was galling to see majorities of 147 and 168 at the opening of one session fall to a minority early in the next, since this decline reflected upon his ability to hold together the heterogeneous groups under his command. Even worse was the charge which his friends at the time and his admirers since have been unable to answer successfully, namely, one of an ungenerous attitude and a violation of the spirit of fair play. The defense which Stanhope offers for this charge of vindictive rancor toward a rival is the rather feeble affirmation that it was unfounded. No pro-Pitt historian seems to have made a defense of the Prime Minister on tactical grounds; for it is the almost unanimous verdict of historians that Pitt made a very bad blunder. Neither the defense of Pitt's admirers nor the charges of unfriendly critics appear entirely satisfactory. The publication of the Robinson Papers has shown that Pitt was not quite the noble and idealistic youth that Stanhope and Dr. J. H. Rose have painted, but rather a very shrewd young man who knew his way about politically. On the other hand, this very shrewdness would have prevented Pitt from continuing so costly a fight if only personal vindictiveness had been back of his actions. The most plausible explanation is the one offered by Professor Laprade: that Pitt, sensing that the struggle for popular leadership would lie between Fox and himself, was anxious to prevent his opponent from securing so strong a claim to such leadership by being chosen the "people's tribune." This bitter struggle between the government and the Whigs for the two seats at Westminster did not close with Pitt's defeat in 1785 but was continued in later elections. Because of this fact it seems clear that Pitt did not desist because the disapprobation of his followers convinced him that his conduct toward Fox was unworthy of an English gentleman. The real significance of the scrutiny from the point of view of this work, however, is the effect which it had on Pitt's measures dealing with the Irish commercial resolutions, the fortification of Plymouth and Portsmouth, and Parliamentary reform. Without doubt the desertion of his followers on a question where he had felt supremely certain of victory shook his confidence when the important reform measures came up for consideration. Still, had Pitt succeeded in keeping Fox from sitting for Westminster merely by means of his majority it would have been too close a duplication of the principle at stake in the Middlesex election of 1768–69. In addition it would have handicapped Pitt as a reformer of the House of Commons had he barred his foremost rival from so significant a seat merely because the government possessed a large majority at that time.

Before considering his Irish resolutions, a brief account of the background of the Irish problem is necessary for an appreciation of what Pitt attempted in 1785.[10] As a result of the centuries of unsatisfactory relations between the two countries, notably from the massacre of 1641 through the reign of William III, it might be said that three main sets of grievances against Great Britain had grown up in Ireland: political, religious, and economic. These grievances against the British government are so closely inter-woven with those of the great mass of the Catholic peasantry against the Anglican oligarchy that it is difficult to separate them. In all three instances the interests of the three main groups of people—the Anglican ruling class, the Catholic peasants, and the Presbyterian Ulsterites—must be kept in mind. All three of these social-religious groups had opposed the control exerted down to 1782 by the British government. Various laws passed in England from the reign of Henry VII to George I gave the English Parliament and, after 1707, the British Parliament the right to pass laws governing Ireland. In addition, the British Privy Council had by law been given the right to veto bills passed by the Irish Parliament. Both of these rights had been abandoned in 1782 when the Rockingham ministry granted legislative independence to Ireland. But the right of the King to veto bills had not been abandoned. Thus the chief political grievance upon which Anglican landlords, Catholic peasants, and the Ulster commercial interests had been united was removed in 1782. The redress of grievances, however, did not mean that Catholics and Dissenters were any better satis-fied with either the unreformed Irish Parliament, which was if anything more unrepresentative than the British, or the religious disabilities for holding office and for voting.

The penal code, which in modern times has been generally con-ceded to have been the worst feature of the English rule in Ire-land, was in the main the result of laws passed by the Anglican Irish Parliament against Irish Catholics. Hence the religious grievances which Catholics and Dissenters suffered under were due more to the Anglican minority in Ireland than to the British people and Parliament.

[10] A full account of Pitt's Irish policy for 1784–85 is given in chapters ii to iv of Lord Ashbourne's *Pitt*.

Even though the various groups in Ireland had bitter grievances against one another, all three could agree on the economic
discrimination of Great Britain as they could agree on the unde-
sirability of having the British Parliament or Privy Council interfere in Irish affairs. This economic discrimination lay in shutting
out of England the Irish agricultural and industrial products and
in preventing Ireland from sharing in the trade of the British Empire. The critical position of the North ministry during the War
of the American Revolution had resulted in substantial concessions
being made to Ireland during the four years before legislative
independence was granted. These concessions came largely as a
result of the efforts of the Volunteers, an organization composed
of Protestants formed for the ostensible purpose of defending the
country against French attacks. Once organized, these Volunteers
took advantage of their own strength and the distress of Great
Britain after 1778 to extract concessions along religious, commercial, and political lines. Being Protestant, they wrung from
the Irish Parliament in 1780 a repeal of the sacramental test for
holding local and civil offices. It was not until 1828 that English
Dissenters received the same concession. North's attempts to
throw open the trade with the British Colonies to Ireland aroused
such opposition in commercial centers in England that he was
forced to abandon nearly all proposed concessions. But so great
was the growing influence of the Volunteers that early in 1780 the
British Parliament gave way and admitted Ireland to a share in
the trade of the Empire and withdrew the prohibition on the ex-
portation of woolen goods from Ireland.

Thus by 1782 the Volunteers had secured a removal of the civil
disabilities for Dissenters, important commercial concessions, and
legislative independence. These were indeed notable achievements;
but the organization decided to go forward rather than stop to
consolidate its gains. The Volunteers now began to enroll Catholics and to plan to reform the Irish Parliament and to protect Irish
industrial products from English competition. The situation in
1784 was critical, and certainly constituted one of the major problems for Pitt in the session of 1785. His interest in the Irish problem is shown by the fact that one of his closest friends, the Duke
of Rutland, had been sent to Ireland as Lord Lieutenant. The correspondence[11] between the Prime Minister on the one hand and

[11] Lord Ashbourne, *Pitt,* chapter iv.

the Lord Lieutenant and his chief secretary, Mr. Thomas Orde, on the other has been treated fully by Lord Ashbourne. It is clear that Pitt investigated the Irish problem thoroughly before formulating his Irish resolutions of 1785. His long letter to Orde on September 19, 1784, is evidence of what careful preparation was made before the resolutions were introduced in the session of 1785.

So far as the relations of George III and Pitt are concerned the Irish question is of little significance. A cabinet minute of January 5, 1785, in the handwriting of Lord Sydney gave the King a full account of the proposed resolutions. In a reply dated the following day George III stated:

The minute of Cabinet on the means of putting a final close to the Restrictions on the Trade of Ireland, and the advantages to be acquired for the defence of the whole Empire from the Revenue that may be raised by it is so conformable to the rough Plan shewn last week to Me by Mr. Pitt, that with a very cursory reading I am able to give my Assent to it and to authorize Lord Sydney to write to the Lord Lieutenant a letter agreeable to it, which cannot be too soon dispatched to Ireland.[12]

The ministers made it clear in a second cabinet minute to the King that the question of Parliamentary reform in Ireland was to be shelved if possible by the Lord Lieutenant until the same question was settled in England and until the commercial arrangements for Ireland were complete.[13] Apparently George III made no objection to this procedure since he approved of the commercial resolutions and had high hopes that the matter of Parliamentary reform in England would not be settled to the satisfaction of Pitt and the reformers.

The failure of Pitt to secure the consent of the English and Irish parliaments to his admirable proposals merely shows the weakness of the position of a reformer who comes into power as Pitt did in 1783. Fox and the Whigs now turned the tables on Pitt and used against him the very tactics which he had successfully employed against them. The personal animus of Fox was so great as a result of the events since the death of Rockingham and especially of the Westminster Scrutiny that Pitt could count on bitter opposition on practically any proposal, good or bad, which

[12] Sir John Fortescue, "Correspondence of King George III," Transcripts in William L. Clements Library, I, 298. Hereafter cited as Clements Transcripts.

[13] *Ibid.*, I, 301.

was suggested by the ministers. Because of the novelty of the measures Pitt knew they were certain to be attacked from both England and Ireland. He had the option of introducing the resolutions in the English or Irish Parliament, and chose, perhaps erroneously, the latter. Subsequent events, however, showed that he would have encountered difficulties regardless of where the propositions were first introduced. On February 7 ten propositions were introduced into the Irish Parliament the purpose of which was to improve the regulation of foreign and colonial commerce, to equalize the duties on the goods and products of the two islands, and, with a few exceptions, to sweep away prohibitions on inter-insular trade. These concessions were accepted by the Irish Parliament, but Pitt's plan of having Ireland contribute to the maintenance of the British Navy when the so-called "hereditary revenue" exceeded a certain sum aroused instant and widespread opposition in Ireland. The best terms which Rutland and Orde could secure were the addition of a further proposition to the original ten stating that when the hereditary revenue, which was at that time £652,000 annually, should exceed £656,000 in time of peace, the surplus should be used to support the imperial Navy, but only in such a manner as the Irish Parliament should direct.[14]

Pitt refused to accept the condition in the new resolution and instead decided to bring the entire question before the British Parliament. Despite the merits of his case, he could count on opposition from several directions. Fox and his followers were practically certain to oppose anything he suggested; the British commercial and industrial interests were equally certain to look with suspicion on any concessions which they feared might do them any immediate damage; and other members of Parliament representing a considerable element in the population without any personal grievance or economic interest were indifferent or hostile to change or to anything which might benefit Ireland. Pitt's speech of February 22 was one of his best.[15] After the eleven resolutions passed by the Irish Parliament were read he made a clear and to the modern ear a convincing case for revising the commercial relations between the two islands. Pitt concluded by moving a resolution:

That it is the opinion of this committee, that it is highly important to the general interest of the empire, that the commercial intercourse

14 J. H. Rose, *op. cit.,* I, 252–53.   15 *Parliamentary History,* XXV, 314–28.

between Great-Britain and Ireland shall be finally adjusted; and that Ireland should be admitted to a permanent and irrevocable participation of the commercial advantages of this country, when the parliament of Ireland shall permanently and irrevocably secure an aid out of the surplus of the hereditary revenue of that kingdom, towards defraying the expense of protecting the general commerce of the empire in time of peace.[16]

That Pitt expected any other treatment than that which he received from Fox and the threatened interests is a bit astonishing. He apparently labored under the delusion that his popularity in 1783 and 1784 was due to the principles which he advocated; whereas it was due, to a far greater extent, to the animosity directed against Fox and North, to the favor of the King, and to a widespread belief in the purity of his (Pitt's) motives. Pitt seems to have been certain that the expression of confidence in him and the actual merits of his proposals would be more than sufficient to offset personal opposition. When Fox and the other Whigs played politics and stirred up popular prejudice against these really meritorious resolutions, Pitt was aggrieved.

Opposition came in the form of vigorous petitions against the proposed measures from all commercial and industrial groups which felt their interests threatened. Silk manufacturers and the planters and merchants of the West Indies, Manchester, Lancaster, Dudley, Glasgow, Paisley, and Bristol, all sent in vigorous petitions against some of the eleven resolutions. It was estimated that sixty-four petitions in all were drawn up against the proposals. One of the most interesting forms of opposition came in the organization of the manufacturers, who formed a Great Chamber under the chairmanship of Wedgwood for the avowed purpose of defeating these Irish propositions. At first Pitt was undaunted and believed that if the subject could be freely discussed the true principles would triumph. He felt, evidently, that the opposition of the threatened interests, unlike the personal attitude of the Whigs, was due to ignorance and that if the fallacies could only be explained to these business men they would be converted to his point of view. Not until he realized that the petitioners were selfish rather than ignorant was Pitt thoroughly disillusioned.

Although he was convinced of the merits of his proposals, Pitt decided that he could make no headway against the gale of protests from the threatened interests; and as a result on May 12 he

16 *Ibid.*, pp. 327–28.

introduced twenty new resolutions, which made substantial concessions to those interested in trade with India and the West Indies
and in industry. He still insisted, however, that Ireland's contribution to the imperial Navy must be a perpetual one. Fox and his
Whig followers had now accomplished what they had set out to
do : they had forced Pitt to make concessions along the lines of
their criticism and incidentally managed to ruin the best features
of the proposed reforms. But Pitt's opponents did not stop at this
point. The debates on the new resolutions[17] of May 12 gave them
the opportunity of inflaming Ireland in a way that would make it
impossible for the Irish Parliament to accept the changes, and thus
of striking an effective blow against Pitt. The chance for the
latter was especially good in view of the recent failure of Pitt to
prevent Fox from sitting for Westminster and of the new connection which Charles Jenkinson, the former subordinate of North
and the man generally recognized as the leader of the King's
Friends, had formed with the government. The Board of Trade,
which had been abolished in 1782, was now brought back under
the title of a "committee of council for the superintendence of
commerce." The fact that Jenkinson was placed at its head gave
the Opposition too good an opportunity to miss. Fox, who was on
the alert to call attention to any hint of Pitt's bowing to "influence"
and "prerogative," could not refrain from contrasting the attitude
of the Prime Minister at this time with that of the months before
the general election of 1784. According to Wraxall, Fox declared :

Until of late he has affected to disclaim any connection with certain
obnoxious characters. In a high tone he disavowed and reprobated
all friendship with the individual who has long been suspected of
exercising an unconstitutional influence over the government of this
country. Such was his language at the time when a momentary popularity, founded on delusion, placed him, as he conceived, above the
degradation of such an alliance. The case is now altered. He has involved himself, by his temerity, his confidence in his own ability, and
his presumption, in a dilemma relative to Ireland from which he
knows not how to extricate himself. Misery makes us acquainted
with strange companions. Now that he begins to feel his weakness
and insecurity, his expressions are less inflated and his proud rejection of obnoxious associates is heard no more . . . . He is now
reduced to invoke assistance on any terms and from any quarter. The
Irish propositions, ill digested, and framed for the surrender of every

[17] *Parliamentary History,* XXV, 575–778.

object dear to the people of Great Britain, have excited universal alarm. He is fallen from his elevation. Hence it arises that the light of influence has condescended to shine down upon him with unusual lustre. He has been openly comforted and caressed.[18]

Certainly Pitt's failure to answer this charge, which until this time he had been so quick to resent, is one of the strongest reasons for suspecting its truth. Wraxall, in describing the incident, declared:

It might have been supposed that a Minister accustomed to meet and to repel every accusation which the ingenuity of party could fabricate, and little disposed to give quarter when misrepresented or attacked, would have risen to efface the impression made by Fox's speech. I own I anticipated it with a sort of certainty. He nevertheless sat silent. His conduct had been different on the 12th of January, 1784 when, under a similar imputation he instantly denied his knowledge of any secret influence. But he was not then supported by a majority.[19]

Pitt was content to remain silent through many of the debates and to rely upon his majority to follow him blindly now that the objectionable features of his Irish resolutions had been removed. They passed the House on May 30[20] and the third reading in the House of Lords on July 18.[21] These efforts, however, were entirely wasted because the debates in the English House of Commons and the concessions which the Opposition had forced Pitt to make in his revised resolutions made the measure as it finally passed the House of Lords unpalatable to the Irish nation and Parliament. When the Irish government could muster a majority of only nineteen in the House of Commons for permission to introduce a bill based on the resolutions which had passed the English Parliament, Pitt decided to give up this attempt to regulate the commerce between the two countries. Although he did not suffer actual defeat in the sense of being beaten on a division in either Parliament, Pitt recognized clearly that he had experienced a serious reverse.

The joy of the Opposition in Pitt's defeat despite his recent understanding with Jenkinson is well expressed in "Probationary Ode Number XX, Irregular Ode for the King's Birth-Day." The last two sections of the ode especially reflect this feeling:

---

[18] H. B. Wheatley (ed.), *Memoirs of Sir Nathaniel William Wraxall* (London, 1884), IV, 128–29.   [19] *Ibid.*, p. 129.

[20] *Parliamentary History*, XXV, 707–78.   [21] *Ibid.*, XXV, 885–86.

Now, heavenly Muse, the choicest song prepare;
Let loftier strains the glorious subject suit;
Lo! hand in hand, advance th' enamoured pair,
This Chatham's son, and that the drudge of Bute;
Proud of their mutual love,
Like Nisus and Euryalus they move,
To Glory's steepest heights together tend,
Each careless for himself, each anxious for his friend!
Hail! associate Politicians!
Hail! sublime Arithmeticians!
Hail! vast exhaustless source of Irish Propositions!
Sooner our gravious King
From heel to heel shall cease to swing;
Sooner that brilliant eye shall leave its socket;
Sooner that hand desert the breeches-pocket,
Than constant George consent his friends to quit,
And break his plighted faith for Jenkinson and Pitt!

CHORUS.

O deep unfathomable Pitt!
To thee Ierne owes her happiest days!
Wait a bit,
And all her sons shall loudly sing thy praise!
Ierne, happy, happy Maid!
Mistress of the Poplin trade!
Old Europa's fav'rite daughter,
Whom first emerging from the water,
In days of yore,
Europa bore
To the celestial Bull!
Behold thy vows are heard, behold thy joys are full!
Thy fav'rite Resolutions greet,
They're not much chang'd, there's no deceit!
Pray be convinc'd, they're still the true ones,
Though sprung from thy prolific head,
Each resolution hath begotten new ones,
And, like their sires, all Irish born and bred!
Then haste, Ierne, haste to sing,
God save great George! God save the King!
May thy sons' sons to him their voices tune,
And each revolving year bring back the fourth of June![22]

The third of the four measures upon which Pitt suffered defeat
was the proposal to fortify Portsmouth and Plymouth. Although

[22] *The Rolliad* (London, 1812), 22d edition, pp. 349–51.

the plan was originally introduced on March 14, 1785, the final debate and vote did not take place until the night of February 27–28, 1786. The plan for the fortifications was that of the Duke of Richmond, the Master of Ordnance; and sympathetic historians have found in the unpopularity of the Duke a possible explanation for the defeat of the measure. On the night the motion was lost, however, Pitt himself introduced the business and made a long and powerful speech in favor of the plan. At 7:00 A.M. the House divided 169 to 169; and the speaker then cast the deciding vote in the negative.[23] Pitt seems to have received this defeat with considerably less agitation than he did those on the Westminster Scrutiny, the Irish commercial resolutions, and Parliamentary reform.

George III sent a gracious note to Pitt depreciating the significance of this particular defeat. The King, seemingly, was neither elated, as in the case of the rejection of Pitt's request to introduce a measure for Parliamentary reform, nor downcast at this fourth defeat which his prime minister had suffered. His object in writing appears to have been to reassure Pitt and explain away any uneasiness which the latter might suffer. The communication read:

Mr. Pitt's moving an approbation of the Plan of Fortifications previous to the Speaker's leaving the Chair was undoubtedly the most likely method of gaining consent to the Measure; but the postponing the consideration from last session to this, though it arose from candour it had the appearance of avoiding the decision and certainly gave time to the enemies of the fortifications to gain more strength; I do not in the least look on the event as any want of confidence in Mr. Pitt from members of the House of Commons, but their attachment to old prejudices and some disinclination to the projector of the fortifications.[24]

The defeat of Pitt's fourth measure, that on Parliamentary reform, was more significant than the other three because of its influence on his career as a reformer and his relations with the King. When Pitt accepted the position of First Lord of the Treasury in December 1783 the chief points of difference between the two were on "influence" and reform. In the account of the debates of May 12 on the Irish resolutions it has been pointed out already how he had reached a working agreement with Jenkinson, the chief advocate of "influence." This action and his stand after the defeat of his motion for Parliamentary reform made on April 18

---

[23] *Parliamentary History*, XXV, 1156–57.
[24] Stanhope, *op. cit.*, I, xviii–xix, February 28, 1786.

mark the definite triumph of the King on both points of difference. Both George III and Pitt appear to have looked forward to the issue with some misgivings.

Pitt made it clear to Wyvill and the Yorkshire Association that he intended to carry on the movement for Parliamentary reform. On March 11, 1784, he had written Wyvill: "I beg leave to assure you that my zeal for Reform in Parliament is by no means abated, and that I will ever exert my best endeavours to accomplish that important object.[25] Again on December 27 he assured Wyvill that he intended to bring forward a reform bill as early as possible in the session of 1785 and that he would "exert his whole power and credit *as a man, and as a minister, honestly and boldly,* to carry such a meliorated system of representation as may place the constitution on a footing of permanent security."[26] Wyvill then gave this announcement wide publicity in the form of a circular letter to the friends of reform throughout Great Britain. Despite his suggestion that caution be used to see that this promise was not published, it reached the newspapers and resulted in "malevolent paragraphs" appearing on the subject. Pitt may have been annoyed at this announcement becoming public property at the time it did, but when the question of the authenticity of the circular letter was raised he openly declared that it expressed accurately his sentiments on the question of reform. Wyvill seems to have been correct in stating that "the sincerity of his attachment to the cause of Reformation, *at this time,* seems to be unquestionable."[27]

The King was decidedly alarmed at the account of this circular letter which he read in the newspapers. He thus unburdened his mind to Lord Sydney in a letter of January 4, 1785:

I cannot conclude without confidentially acquainting Lord Sydney for his own information *alone*; that I have been much hurt at reading a *certain letter* in the public papers, I had flattered myself that a certain person though unhappily engaged to propose if He can produce a *rational* plan of Reformation, yet I did not think He would have enabled a known Demagogue to take advantage of a conversation to heat men's minds, allarm the well disposed and consequently lay the foundation of ill humour for this session, when it must be the wish of all wise Men that it should pass with as little heat as possible that Government may by degrees get the confidence at Home and abroad

25 J. H. Rose, *op. cit.,* I, 197.
26 *Parliamentary History,* XXIV, 1396. Italics Wyvill's.
27 *Wyvill's Political Papers* (London, 1794–1804), IV, 16. Italics Wyvill's.

without which this nation must remain in a despicable situation in the opinion of all other countries.[28]

The alarm experienced as a result of this letter by Wyvill may have been one of the factors which kept a reference to reform from being made in the King's speech at the opening of the session of 1785. On the other hand, Pitt may not have been able to "produce a rational plan" which would satisfy George III.

It was March 19 before Pitt sent the King a sketch of his proposed Parliamentary reforms. Whether nervousness, difficulty in drawing up a plan which would satisfy reformers and King, or preoccupation with other things such as the Irish commercial resolutions accounts for the delay from early January to March 19 is not clear. The tense feeling which existed between Pitt and the King is well brought out by the letter in which the former enclosed the heads of his proposal for reforming representation:

Mr. Pitt humbly presumes to submit to Your Majesty's gracious consideration the enclosed Papers which contain the Heads of what Mr. Pitt conceives it may be his duty to open to the House of Commons on Wednesday next previous to moving for leave to bring in a Bill for amending the Representation. Mr. Pitt flatters Himself that these propositions will at least appear free from the objections against undefined Innovations, and that they may be proved strictly consonant to the principles on which our Constitution has in fact been framed, and in truth a strong confirmation of those Principles.

As the Motion on Wednesday is proposed to be only for Leave to bring in a Bill, the detail of the necessary Regulations, may be explained and adjusted in the farther Progress, if the first Motion is carried. Mr. Pitt humbly hopes to be honored with Your Majesty's Commands, and to be permitted to add such explanations as Your Majesty may judge necessary, when He pays His duty to Your Majesty on Monday. He trusts in the meantime to Your Majesty's Indulgence to excuse his trespassing so far on your time at present as to add that He most firmly believes the success of the measure by no means improbable, and the event of it of the last importance to the credit and stability of the Administration which Your Majesty has been pleased to honour with so many marks of Your Majesty's favour and confidence. It is from the extreme solicitude to discharge His duty to Your Majesty in representing the real trend of this business that He begs leave further to state that there is but one issue of the business to which He could look as fatal; and which he trusts is of all others most improbable; that is the possibility of the Measure being

[28] Clements Transcripts, I, 292. Italics as in the original.

rejected by the weight of those who are supposed to be connected
with Government. Such an event, if it were to take Place, might
weaken and dissolve the Public confidence, and in doing so would
render every future effort in Your Majesty's service but too probably
fruitless and ineffectual. Mr. Pitt was detained so late yesterday in
the House of Commons by a tedious examination as to make it impossible for Him sooner to lay his thoughts before Your Majesty.
And Your Majesty will He trusts pardon the liberty He takes in thus
submitting them on so important an occasion.[29]

Without question Pitt is pointing out to the King the inadvis-
ability of the King's Friends openly opposing this reform measure,
because it would be equivalent to proclaiming to the world that a
breach had been made between the followers of George III and
those of his chief minister. The point of view of the King is more
accurately expressed in his letter written the same day, March 19,
to Lord Sydney than in his better-known communication of March
20 to Pitt. To Sydney George III wrote:

Undoubtedly I am not obliged to take any notice of it till I see
Him on Monday; but there are some expressions which seem to require being properly understood between us; I have therefore drawn
up the enclosed answer which if Lord Sydney sees no objection to, I
mean either to night or early in the morning to send to Mr. Pitt, for
though out of attention to Mr. Pitt I carefully avoid expressing my
unalterable Sentiments in any change in the Constitution, yet more
must not be expected from me.[30]

In reply Lord Sydney made it clear why, in his opinion, Pitt persisted in bringing forward the measure at this time:

Lamenting extremely that the subject of a Parliamentary Reform
should come into Discussion at this time in particular, when so many
circumstances tend to make it detrimental to His Majesty's Service,
he is however persuaded that Mr. Pitt's own opinion of the necessity
of his bringing it forward is the only motive of his conduct, and that
Mr. Pitt conceives, that a dereliction of that measure at present
would put him in a situation to be of much less use to His Majesty,
than his persisting in it.[31]

The King's answer to Pitt shows all too clearly the results of
twenty-five years of experience as a successful politician. It is
amazing how much George III managed to put in the following
short letter:

[29] Clements Transcripts, I, 326
[30] *Ibid.*, I, 333.   [31] *Ibid.*, I, 334.

I have received Mr. Pitt's Paper containing the Heads of His Plan for a Parliamentary Reform, which I look on as a mark of attention. I should have delayed acknowledging the receipt of it till I saw him on Monday, had not his letter expressed that there is but one issue of the Business He could look upon as fatal that is the possibility of the Measure being rejected by the weight of those who are supposed to be connected with *Government*. Mr. Pitt must recollect that though I have ever thought it unfortunate that He had early engaged himself in this measure, yet that I have ever said that as He was clear of the propriety of the measure He ought to lay his thoughts before the House; that out of personal regard to Him I would avoid giving any opinion to any one on the opening of the door to Parliamentary Reform except to Him; therefore I am certain Mr. Pitt cannot suspect my having influenced anyone on the occasion; if others choose for base ends to impute such a conduct to Me I must bear it as former false suggestions. Indeed on a question of such Magnitude I should think very ill of any Man who took a part on either side without the maturist consideration, and who would suffer his civility to any one to make him vote contrary to his own opinion. The conduct of some of Mr. Pitt's most intimate friends on the Westminster Scrutiny show there are questions Men will not by friendship be biased to adopt.[32]

The King showed careful consideration for Pitt's feelings and pride, but he made absolutely no worth-while concession. He was careful to point out that he had always felt it to be unfortunate that Pitt had engaged himself so early to Parliamentary reform, but also that out of personal regard for his minister he was willing to avoid giving an opinion on the matter to anyone else. The King was confident that Pitt would not suspect him of having influenced anyone on this question. But the master stroke of all came at the end of the letter. The King stated that he would think ill of any man who voted contrary to his opinions; and to clinch his arguments he pointed out that some of Pitt's most intimate friends had voted against him on the Westminster Scrutiny. This last was both a reproof and a warning, and was the only part of the letter from which Pitt could possibly take offense.

This letter of the King to Pitt has been interpreted by many historians, notably Dr. J. Holland Rose,[33] as an answer to a threat by the chief minister to resign in case George III attempted to influence the vote in the House of Commons. Now that Pitt's let-

---

[32] Pitt MSS, 103, March 20, 1785.
[33] J. H. Rose, *op. cit.*, I, 204.

ter which brought the King's reply is available, another interpretation seems more likely. The problem for Pitt, in the light of his attitude toward Parliamentary reform after this session, seems to have been to find a way to save his face. Although the full realization of his limitations as the chief minister of the King, under existing conditions, may not have struck Pitt until he experienced defeat on Parliamentary reform, the Irish resolutions, and the fortifications of Plymouth and Portsmouth, nevertheless his defeat on the Westminster Scrutiny and the difficulties he was experiencing with these three measures, upon which later he suffered defeat, must have given him an inkling of their probable fate. In reality the King's letter to Pitt appears to point subtly to the way out of the difficulties. Pitt had committed himself to use his utmost efforts as a man and a minister to put through some measure of Parliamentary reform. The King believed this promise to be an error in tactics, as he believed any reform of Parliament wrong in principle. George III's assertion of the lofty principle that he would think ill of any man who should vote contrary to his own opinion is really amusing when his action on such an occasion as the vote on Fox's India Bill in the House of Lords in December 1783 is taken into consideration. Once Pitt allowed himself to be maneuvered into such a position, he was lost. His only chance of putting through reforms which the King disliked was to force the latter to give his reluctant support. When Pitt demanded the neutrality of George III, he made defeat almost inevitable; and the eagerness with which the King guaranteed neutrality shows that he appreciated its significance. Because the royal disapproval of Parliamentary reform was common knowledge, and hence George III's promise not to give "any opinion to any one on the opening of the door to Parliamentary Reform"[34] except to Pitt was no real concession. Thus the well-known attitude of the King on this question and the fact that no statement had been issued indicating that he had changed his opinion, when combined with the absence of any mention of the question in the speech at the opening of Parliament in the session of 1785 and with hints on the order of the one given to Lord Sydney in the letter of March 19, made the royal opposition as effective as though it had been open and public.

Pitt was far too astute a young man not to realize that the King's silence would be equivalent to opposition. Two interpreta-

---

[34] Pitt MSS, 103, March 20, 1785.

tions of his conduct at this time, both plausible, are possible: first, that he believed he could force through Parliament a reform measure if the King maintained the promised neutrality and did not bully members who were favorable to the measure; and, second, that he had no real hope of seeing his reform pass but felt that he must put forth his best efforts, since he had pledged himself as a man and minister. If the first interpretation is accepted Pitt's disappointment when the measure was beaten on April 18 was a real one, for it made clear that the majority of the House of Commons elected in 1784 would not support him on what he considered to be his most significant reform. If the second interpretation is preferred it merely means that Pitt realized before April 18 what he was compelled to acknowledge after that date. In short, both interpretations lead to the same result. The chief difference appears to lie in the effect of each upon Pitt. If the first alternative is the correct one, then Pitt had a very exalted opinion of what his name, reputation, and oratory could accomplish and the shock of April 18 must have been very great indeed. If the second alternative is accepted, then Pitt must have been grateful to the King for the tactful way in which the King had treated him.

Although no copy of Pitt's proposals for Parliamentary reform are to be found in the papers of George III along with the correspondence of March 19–20, without doubt they followed very closely the ones submitted to Wyvill in March or April.[35] When after considerable delay Pitt finally brought the question before the House of Commons on April 18, he did not introduce these resolutions but at the end of a long and able speech merely moved "that leave be given to bring in a Bill to amend the Representation of the People of England in Parliament."[36] At the beginning of his speech Pitt admitted the difficulties that confronted him but justified his third attempt to effect a reform of Parliament on the ground that his two previous attempts had been before the last general election. He divided those who opposed reform into several groups:

Those, who, with a sort of superstitious awe, reverence the constitution so much as to be fearful of touching even its defects, had always reprobated every attempt to purify the representation. They acknowledged its inequality and corruption, but in their enthusiasm

[35] *Wyvill's Political Papers*, IV, 103–109.
[36] *Parliamentary History*, XXV, 432–50.

for the grand fabric, they would not suffer a reformer, with un-
hallowed hands, to repair the injuries which it suffered from time.
Others, who, perceiving the deficiencies that had arisen from circumstances, were solicitous of their amendment yet resisted the attempt
under the argument, that when once we had presumed to touch the
constitution in one point, the awe which had heretofore kept us back
from the daring enterprise of innovation might abate, and there was
no foreseeing to what alarming lengths we might progressively go,
under the mask of reformation. . . . . The fabric of the house of
commons was an ancient pile, on which they had been taught to look
with reverence and awe: from their cradles they had been accustomed
to view it as a pattern of perfection; their ancestors had enjoyed freedom and prosperity under it; and therefore an attempt to make any
alterations in it would be deemed, by some enthusiastic admirers of
antiquity, as impious and sacrilegious. No one reverenced the vener-
able fabric more than he did; but all mankind knew that the best institutions, like human bodies, carried in themselves the seeds of decay
and corruption, and therefore he thought himself justifiable in proposing remedies against this corruption, which the frame of the constitution must necessarily experience in the lapse of years, if not
prevented by wise and judicious regulations.[37]

Pitt laid down as his fundamental principles that the number
of the House of Commons should remain the same and that no
change should come by disfranchising boroughs. His plan he explained consisted of two parts: the first to bring about an early if
not immediate change of borough representation, and the second
to establish a rule by which representation should change with
changes in the country. He assumed that the House would agree
with him that about thirty-six boroughs were so decayed as to
come under the operation of his scheme; and he proposed that the
seventy-two members from these boroughs should be added to
those of the counties in such proportion as Parliament should deem
wise. The change would not be immediate because the thirty-six
boroughs would be disfranchised only after their own voluntary
application to Parliament. When such an application was made
an adequate consideration was to be paid to bodies or individuals
who thus parted with valuable property rights. The second part
of the plan provided that, after the thirty-six boroughs had been
extinguished and their members transferred to the counties, any
other decayed boroughs might, after due compensation had been
paid, surrender their franchises and have their members trans-

[37] *Parliamentary History,* XXV, 432–33.

ferred to such populous boroughs as were anxious to enjoy the rights of representation. This rule was to apply to all future time.[38]

Despite the dislike which modern reformers instinctively have for payment to disfranchised boroughs and individuals, the plan offered by Pitt was a statesmanlike one and England might have been much better off in the long run had she accepted it. The most telling speech made against the motion was that by Lord North. The witty lord heaped up evidence to show that the country displayed no real interest in the question of reform, and declared that the attempt to interest the provinces might be summed up in the line from the *Rehearsal:* "What horrid sound of *silence* doth assail mine ear?"[39] Some of Pitt's friends and supporters of reform, notably Bankes, criticized certain points in his proposals. When the division on Pitt's motion took place it was lost by a vote of 248 to 174, or a majority of 74.[40]

The defeat of this motion merely to bring in a bill based on the principles enumerated was a turning point in the career of Pitt and a very significant day in English constitutional history. Whereas the defeats which Pitt experienced later on the Irish resolutions and on the proposals to fortify Plymouth and Portsmouth were merely severe blows to him as a reformer, the defeat on Parliamentary reform was a blow to him both as a reformer and as a constitutional minister. George III was on his side on the Irish and fortification questions but was his most important opponent on that of Parliamentary reform. Thus Pitt's disappointment must have been intense: he had failed as a reformer, as the defeats on the Irish propositions and Parliamentary reform showed; he had failed to retain the exalted position which had been his in 1784; he had failed to oust Fox from the Westminster seat; and he had lost to the King on the two disputed points of "influence" and reform.

The events from the resignation of Lord North in March 1782 through the defeat of Pitt's motion on Parliamentary reform in April 1785 make up one of the most important constitutional periods in modern English history. If the interpretation offered in this chapter is the correct one, however, these years do not mark a change or transition to modern constitutional practices as so many modern historians of this period claim, but rather the triumph of George III over the united cabinet principle of the

---

[38] *Ibid.*, p. 439.   [39] *Ibid.*, p. 458.   [40] *Ibid.*, p. 475.

Whigs and the all-powerful minister plan of Pitt. The fundamental reason for the triumph of George III was the failure of the
Whigs and Pitt to unite. Had a union been accomplished on the
basis of Pitt's heading the ministry and recognizing the Whig
principles of cabinet solidarity which George III found so novel
when they were expounded to him by the Duke of Portland in
1783, it is possible the King would have lost. If the test, however, applied to the outcome of this significant struggle is political
judgment and acumen, George III, and not the Whigs or William
Pitt, deserves the victory. The Whig errors in tactics have been
already fully discussed. They consisted, first, in failure to appreciate the value of Pitt and to secure his adherence to their party
and principles during the years from the general election of 1780
when Rockingham had refused to find him a seat in the House of
Commons, until March 1784; and, second, in the failure to associate themselves with the popular movement opposing George III
before the Gordon Riots and with those movements to reform
Parliament before and after the riots. Pitt's errors in judgment
came as a result of overrating the importance of his name, his
reputation, and his abilities. Perhaps he used good judgment in
accepting the position of First Lord of the Treasury in December
1783 in order to prove to the Whigs that he had more to offer
in the negotiation which followed than they would otherwise
have believed. But if he considered that the alternative policy of
remaining First Lord of the Treasury without coming to an understanding with the Whigs stood an equal chance of success, as he
must inevitably have done, then Pitt made a great mistake in not
securing better terms from the King. When George III was, in
his own words, on the edge of a precipice in December 1783, Pitt
had his best chance to extort valuable concessions. This was his
glorious opportunity to compel the King to consent to Parliamentary reform exactly as he had secured the reluctant consent of
the sovereign to negotiate with the Whigs for a union of parties.
After the general election of 1784 George III was never again on
the edge of a precipice and Pitt was never again in a position to
make such a demand. Moreover, after he broke off negotiations
with the Whigs in March of 1784 it was impossible for Pitt to go
over to the Whigs except by passing under the yoke. This his
proud spirit made unlikely and left him with no alternative between adherence to the King and retirement. He seems to have
been confident up to the defeat of his motion on Parliamentary re-

form of April 18, 1785, that his name, reputation, and abilities would be sufficient to carry through the reform measures in which he sincerely believed and which he was justifiably confident were good ones. He enormously underestimated three factors: first, the inert conservatism of the great mass of the upper and middle classes and especially of the members of Parliament; second, the influence of the King even though it were expressed by silence and not by active opposition; and, third, the bitter fight which the remnants of the Fox-North Coalition would make against any measure which he sponsored. Pitt felt that the praise showered upon him during 1783–84 by members of Parliament and important individuals outside meant approbation for his principles, whereas in reality it rather represented disapprobation of the Coalition. It is difficult to say whether or not Pitt believed by 1785 that the silence of the King on Parliamentary reform was all that was necessary; but at least it was all that he could ask at the time. Pitt really seems to have been truly astonished at the fierce opposition to his reform measures on the part of the members of the Coalition who were liberal in their point of view; for evidently he failed to realize that his actions in accepting the office of First Lord of the Treasury in December 1783 at the expense of North, Fox, and Portland, his conduct at the time of the election of 1784, and his stand on the Westminster Scrutiny in 1784–85 would be certain to influence these men when they came to consider his really statesmanlike proposals. Pitt was so confident of the purity of his own motives, which he constantly referred to in the House of Commons amid the cheers of the country gentlemen, that he found it difficult to understand how his opponents looked on his conduct from the time he became First Lord of the Treasury until he was defeated on the Westminster Scrutiny. He expected his three favorite measures of 1785 to be considered on their merits; but his enemies were seeking revenge.

After his defeats in 1785 Pitt had a choice of one of three policies: first, to retire from office; second, to form a working agreement with the Coalition; or, third, to remain chief minister for George III. He chose the third. The first choice would have taken the most important interest out of his life; the second would have been too humiliating to bear; the third entailed neither humiliation nor retirement, only disappointment. He could count on George III's treating him with that exquisite consideration which twenty-five years of experience had taught the crafty monarch; he could demand and receive from his colleagues in the cabinet the recognition of his superior position; he could give his best efforts to improving the finances of the government and to foreign affairs; and he could share with the King the distribution of patronage. What, then, did Pitt lack which a modern Prime Minister has? He could not hope to force through Parliament any measures of which the King did not approve; and he ran the risk of being discharged as Newcastle, Grenville, Rockingham, Grafton, and Portland had been before him and Lord Grenville after him.

Because of his unfortunate experiences with both of them, Pitt probably gave up his hopes for a coalition with the Whigs and his alliance with reformers with less reluctance than he would have felt earlier. The Whigs, so it appeared to Pitt, had been positively vindictive during the session of 1785; and the reformers had in the main shown a lack of consideration for the difficulties which he had encountered with his King and colleagues. Small wonder that Pitt found an understanding with George III more satisfactory than the stony path of reform with Wyvill. The *Rolliad* sums up this point of view admirably:

> K---. When heedless of your birth and name,
>   For pow'r you barter'd future fame,
>   On that auspicious day,
>   Of K--gs I reign'd supremely blest:
>   Not Hastings rul'd the plunder'd East
>   With more despotic sway.

> P-tt. When only on my favour'd head
>   Your smiles their royal influence shed
>   Then was the son of Ch-th-m
>   The nation's pride, the public care,
>   P-tt and Prerogative their pray'r,
>   While we, Sir, both laugh'd at 'em.

> K---. Jenky, I own divides my heart,
>   Skill'd in each deep and secret art
>   To keep my C-mm-ns down;
>   His views, his principles are mine;
>   For these I'd willingly resign
>   My Kingdom and my Crown.

> P-tt. As much as for the public weal,
>   My anxious bosom burns with zeal
>   For pious Parson Wyv-ll;

> For him I'll fret, and fume, and spout,
> Go ev'ry length—except go out,
> For that's to me the devil!

> K---. What if, our sinking cause to save,
> We both our jealous strife should wave,
> And act our former farce on:
> If I to Jenky were more stern,
> Would you, then, generously turn
> Your back upon the Parson?

> P-tt. Though, to support his patriot plan,
> I'm pledg'd as *Minister* and *Man,*
> This storm I hope to weather;
> And since your Royal will is so,
> *Reforms,* and the *Reformers* too,
> May all be damn'd together![41]

Thus in the session of 1785 George III won his greatest triumph. The danger in which he had found himself between the resignation of Lord North in 1782 and the general election of 1784 had vanished. The combination which might have triumphed, the Whigs and Pitt, was made impossible by Pitt's acceptance of the place of First Lord of the Treasury, by the clever manner in which the King took advantage of the differences between the Whigs and Pitt, and by the results of the election of 1784.

George III's next problem was to exploit Pitt's popularity and ability but at the same time to prevent him from carrying through undesirable reforms and from otherwise disregarding the wishes of his sovereign. The King had the rare good fortune to solve this problem in the session of 1785. Owing to the defeats he suffered, Pitt was driven into a position most satisfactory to the King. It is significant that the minister wrote only one more letter to Parson Wyvill, and that early in 1786, to assure the reformer that his father had not been taken off the pension roll. Pitt thus definitely broke with the Parliamentary reformers either because he felt discouraged over the prospect of success or because he decided that it was expedient to bow to the royal will. Since there is no letter from Pitt to the King on the division of April 18 and no comment by the latter on the result, it is necessary to conjecture what decision was reached by the two in private conversation.

It is highly probable that the King pointed out, courteously, that

[41] *The Rolliad,* pp. 442–43.

Pitt had fulfilled his promise to back reform as a man and a minister, and that if he were wise he would let the question drop; it is possible that Pitt reached this conclusion himself without the King's dropping a hint; and it is possible, though not probable, that the King delivered an ultimatum to Pitt. The first of these three possible explanations appears most likely when considered in the light of the methods which George III had employed in handling Pitt since 1783. The result in any case, however, was the same; for the King had his way and Pitt abandoned reform. The year 1785 also witnessed Pitt's capitulation to "influence." Not only did he associate himself from this time more closely with the King's Friends, but he tended to draw away from his reforming friends, notably his closest friend, Wilberforce. This capitulation also took the form of using methods of influencing members of Parliament similar to those employed by other chief ministers who had little political idealism or had lost what they possessed.

George III believed that the most important constitutional rights of the sovereign were to appoint his own ministers and to veto bills of which he disapproved. These rights meant refusing permission to his ministers to introduce bills of which he disapproved and ousting them if they persisted. Only in periods when he was unable to replace the offending ministers did he suspend these principles. In 1785 he felt himself to be on safe ground. He did not wish to part with Pitt, and he was willing to treat him with the greatest courtesy and to make many minor concessions in order to hold him; but in view of his letter to Sydney written March 19 and of his actions over Catholic emancipation in 1801, it is practically certain that he would have accepted Pitt's resignation had his minister insisted on making Parliamentary reform a government measure. The King was too astute to insist upon Pitt's giving up his opinions on Parliamentary reform or on other reforms in which the latter believed. George III secured what he desired by letting it be known either positively or negatively that he disapproved of such measures.

With Pitt effectively harnessed by prerogative and influence, George III could look forward to his happiest years from the constitutional if not from the personal point of view. He had secured his most desirable first minister; for if he did not like Pitt personally in the sense that he did Bute, North, and Addington, there were other compensations. Pitt was the ablest finance minister of his reign and second to none in control of the House of Commons.

By inducing Pitt to co-operate with his "Friends" and to stop any undesirable reforms and measures at their source, George III secured the results he wished with less effort and worry to himself than in any other period of his reign. What appears to be a slackening of his interest in the affairs of government after 1785 was merely the relaxation which an administrator takes in any walk of life after he has the machinery properly functioning. George III was to reap the rewards of twenty-five years of experience, and particularly of a judicious handling of the situation during the years 1782–1785.

This endorsement of the King's technique does not imply an endorsement of his principles. In the light of history George III was wrong far oftener than he was right on the big issues of the day, both before 1785 and after. But it is not necessary to approve of his principles in order to recognize that George III won a notable victory by defeating the Whigs who championed the doctrine of the subordination of the sovereign to the ministry which controlled a majority of the House of Commons and by making use of the most important political figure of the time. If skill in playing political cards is the criterion, George III richly deserved his victory.

V. THE BEST YEARS OF GEORGE III, 1785 TO 1789

In view of the great increase in the domestic difficulties of George III during these years and of the terrible experience he underwent at the end of 1788 and the beginning of 1789 the title of this chapter may seem a bit ironical. The term refers, however, not to the King's domestic happiness or to his personal health, but to his political eminence. By the election of 1784 he had secured an enormous majority and, as a result of the events of the years from 1783 to 1785, a minister who had the ability and willingness to carry out his wishes. The only years which, from the point of view of George III, could compare with those from 1785 until he was stricken in the autumn of 1788 were the first years of the ministry of Lord North. But even the period from 1770 to 1775 was scarcely as satisfactory as that from 1785 to 1788 because of the troubles over the American Colonies and the unpopularity of the ruler and the chief minister. After 1785 the King had the satisfactions of having the country enjoy a period of great prosperity —a fact which was the most important cause of the success of Pitt's fiscal measures—of seeing the prestige of the nation restored as a result of an effective foreign policy, of realizing that the reforms which he feared and disliked would not be made ministerial measures, and of enjoying the tremendous popularity which attended him and his chief minister.

So far as Pitt was concerned, the years are certainly his most successful ones, even though they followed his defeat by George III on the two important issues of reform and "influence." Probably the main reason for the success of Pitt during these years was the great economic recovery; but this fact does not detract from his outstanding achievements in fiscal and foreign policies. In addition Pitt certainly handled a difficult situation in the Regency Crisis of 1788–89 in a most skillful and successful manner.

The history of Pitt's fiscal measures and foreign policy during these years has been carefully described at great length in many histories and hence only a short summary of each is necessary here. Yet since our interest in all policies formulated and carried out in this period lies not so much in their success or failure as in the attitude taken and the influence exerted, respectively, by the King and Pitt, this chapter will treat in succession, first, fiscal measures and reforms; second, foreign policy; third, the trial of

Warren Hastings; fourth, proposals for Parliamentary reform, the abolition of the slave trade, and the repeal of the Test and Corporation acts; and, fifth, the Regency question of 1788–89.

An indication of the relations of the King and Pitt at the opening of the session of 1786 is given in an exchange of letters dealing with the speech from the throne. The minister wrote:

Mr. Pitt humbly presumes to trouble Your Majesty with a draft of the Speech, in which some alterations have been proposed since Mr. Pitt had the honour of submitting it to Your Majesty's perusal, but which make little change in the general tenor of it.[1]

In reply the King stated:

The draft of the Speech which I have just received from Mr. Pitt is undoubtedly but little changed in the general tenour of it, from the one he shewed me on Wednesday, but at the same time, the corrections of particular parts are very judicious and remove any objections that seemed to occur in its former state; as for instance the first paragraph, and also the one on the propriety of adopting a fixed plan for the Reduction of the National Debt; I therefore think Mr. Pitt may now be thoroughly satisfied with it.[2]

The speech from the throne on January 24 emphasized the friendly attitude of Continental powers, the improvement of the revenue, and the advisability of a gradual reduction of the national debt. On all points the King and minister appear to have been in substantial agreement.

In treating Pitt's fiscal measures and reforms, first consideration must be given to his sinking fund plan. On March 29, following the suggestion made in the King's speech of January 24, Pitt explained at considerable length his plan for reducing the national debt. Without doubt he owed a great deal to the pamphlets and personal suggestions of a nonconformist minister, Dr. Price.[3] After carefully showing that his plan did not require any increase in taxation but merely the setting aside of a million pounds of surplus from existing revenues, he came to the fundamental idea underlying the sinking fund plan:

If this million, to be so applied, is laid out, with its growing interest, it will amount to a very great sum in a period that is not very

[1] Clements Transcripts, II, 506.

[2] Ibid., II, 507.

[3] J. H. Rose, *Life of William Pitt* (London: G. Bell & Sons, Ltd., 1923), I, 188–95.

long in the life of the individual, and but an hour in the existence of a great nation: and this will diminish the debt of this country so much as to prevent the exigencies of war from raising it to the enormous height it has hitherto done. In the period of twenty-eight years the sum of a million, annually improved, would amount to four millions per annum.[4]

Recalling the fate of an earlier sinking fund, Pitt insisted that the fund must not be broken in upon; and to prevent this he suggested "that this sum be vested in certain commissioners, to be by them applied quarterly to buy up stock; by this means, no sum so great will ever lie ready to be seized upon on any occasion, and the fund will go on without interruption."[5] Pitt expressed the belief that the Speaker of the House, the Chancellor of the Exchequer, the Master of the Rolls, the Governor and the Deputy-Governor of the Bank of England, and the Accountant-General of the High Court of Chancery should be members of the commission.[6] Although criticisms were offered as to certain details of the motion, it was agreed to without opposition. A bill based on this motion became a law on May 26.

Until after the outbreak of the great war with France the sinking fund plan seems to have fulfilled expectations. So long as the million pounds diverted to the fund came from a surplus of revenue over expenditures, the original plan was a success. Later, during the French Revolutionary and Napoleonic wars, however, money was borrowed at a higher rate of interest in order to maintain the sinking fund. It was this fallacy, so obvious to posterity, which later gave the entire plan such a bad name; nevertheless the later abuse of the system does not detract from the achievements of Pitt during the years covered by this chapter.

The King and Pitt were in full agreement on the matter of the sinking fund. George III's letter of March 30, the day following Pitt's speech on this subject, shows not only this complete agreement but also the technique of the King in combining praise of his Minister with a clear expression of his own views on public questions as well:

Mr. Pitt's laying before the House of Commons a plan for raising the national credit by paying off a million of debt at least annually, and at the same time putting it out of the power of a minister by an

[4] *Parliamentary History* (London, 1806–1820), XXV, 1309.
[5] *Ibid.*
[6] *Ibid.*, p. 1310.

hasty vote to turn such sum to defraying the expenses of the year by securing it by an Act of Parliament must have given such general satisfaction that there is no wonder that the observations made by Sir Guy (?) Cooper, Mr. Sheridan and Mr. Fox had not the effect of diminishing so pleasing sensations; considering Mr. Pitt has had the unpleasant office of providing for the expenses incurred by the last war it is but just He should have the full merit he deserves of having the public know and feel that he has now proposed a measure that will render the nation again respectable if she has the sense to remain quiet some years, and not by wanting to take a shewy part in the transactions of Europe again become the dupe of other Powers and from ideas of greatness draw herself into lasting distress. The old English saying is applicable to our situation. England must cut her coat according to her cloth.[7]

Clearly when the King and his minister held views so nearly identical on the necessity of improving the finances of the country, there could be no serious clash or any question of one of them having to give way to the other as had been necessary more than once during the years 1783 to 1785.

In the session of 1787 Pitt succeeded in putting through Parliament another reform which won the applause even of the Opposition. On February 26 he introduced in the House of Commons his project for simplifying the collection of revenue in the departments of customs, excise, and stamps and for consolidating the existing customs duties. According to the plan offered, one general duty was to be substituted for the many imposts collected in the department of excise and one duty for the many collected in that of customs. According to Gifford,

Some idea of the magnitude of this project, for simplifying the collection of duties, may be collected from the number of resolutions which it was necessary for the House to adopt, in order to carry it into effect; this was no less than *three thousand*.[8]

For once there appears to have been unanimity on the part of the King, Pitt, and the leaders of the Opposition; for Burke,

with a frankness highly honourable to his character, rose immediately after him, and declared, that the plan proposed was in itself so obviously necessary, beneficial, and desirable, and Mr. Pitt had opened it with such extraordinary clearness, and perspicuity, that he thought

---

[7] Pitt MSS, 103, March 30, 1786.

[8] John Gifford, *A History of the Political Life of William Pitt* (London, 1809), I, 372. (*Parliamentary History* gives 2,537.)

it did not become him, or those who, like him, unfortunately felt it to be their duty frequently to oppose the measures of government, to content themselves with a sullen acquiescence; but to do justice to the Minister's merit, and to return him thanks on behalf of themselves and the country.[9]

On March 7 Pitt moved that a bill based on these resolutions should be introduced.[10] In view of the unanimity described the bill passed both houses of Parliament without difficulty.

When we turn to the conduct of foreign affairs during these four years, we see how closely connected the financial and foreign policies of the government actually were. This was true not only because both the King and Pitt were convinced that England must put her finances in order before, in the words of the former, she could "take a shewy part in the transactions of Europe" but also because both financial and foreign policies were involved in the Eden commercial treaty with France. England had emerged from the wars with the American Colonies and the Continental powers weakened in prestige and financial strength. To Pitt at least, playing a "shewy part" did not mean revenge on either France or America. "But if he did not desire for his country revenge, he desired honour, weight in the counsels of Europe 'respectability,' as the word was understood in the eighteenth century. These were the things which money, well used, could buy."[11] Pitt, however, was not interested, as an isolated account of the sinking fund project might indicate, in improving the financial position of England merely to pay off the national debt. From the first he was interested in building up the Navy and each year spent considerable sums in carrying out this policy. As a result he was ready to risk war.[12] Clearly, so far as Pitt was concerned, improved national finances meant a stronger Navy, which in turn meant increased prestige in the eyes of the Continental nations.

Unquestionably the most significant events in the field of foreign affairs during the years 1785 to 1789 were the Eden Treaty with France and the problem of the United Provinces which culminated in the Triple Alliance of 1788. Although the commercial treaty with France in 1786 fitted in with Pitt's plans for rehabili-

[9] Gifford, *op. cit.*, pp. 372–73.

[10] *Parliamentary History*, XXVI, 733.

[11] Sir A. W. Ward and G. P. Gooch (eds.), *The Cambridge History of British Foreign Policy* (New York: Macmillan, 1922), I, 146–47. By permission of The Macmillan Company.

[12] *Ibid.*, p. 147.

tation in the spheres of finance and foreign politics, the credit for securing this desirable arrangement does not primarily lie with him.

According to the eighteenth article of the Treaty of 1783 England and France were to nominate commissioners to draw up a commercial treaty based on reciprocity. These commissioners were to be nominated at once, and by January 1, 1786, the treaty was to be completed. The credit not only for the original article but also for the insistence on its being carried out appears to lie with the French minister, Vergennes.[13] Although he had deliberately taken advantage of the revolt of the American Colonies to improve the position of France at the expense of England, Vergennes did not consider Great Britain as a natural enemy. The point of view which he took seems to coincide with that of Pitt and Shelburne, since both held what was then the comparatively novel point of view that both nations might profit by trading with one another. In view of Pitt's able financial policy it is difficult to understand why he delayed carrying out the terms of article eighteen. The probable explanation lies in his anxiety to carry through the Irish commercial resolutions of 1785 before negotiating with France.[14] This delay might have proved costly, since Pitt failed in his attempt to settle the problem of the Anglo-Irish commercial relations and Vergennes took advantage of the delay to extend French influence in the Low Countries. In 1785 Vergennes gave his approval to the re-establishment of a French East India Company; and British statesmen feared that this Company might exploit the new relationship with Holland.[15] Efforts made by Vergennes in 1784 and 1785 to induce Pitt to take some action toward carrying out article eighteen failed. As a result he took the position that if a new treaty were not completed by January 1, 1786, the existing commercial relations between England and France must lapse on that date. In order to give weight to this point of view he had issued a series of edicts interfering with English exports to France. The most important of these forbade the importation of foreign cottons, muslins, linens, iron, steel and cutlery. A British protest against the edict on textiles resulted in Vergennes agreeing to suspend its operation on condition that negotiations should be actually opened between the two countries.[16]

Whether because of the failure of his Irish commercial policy or because he felt that it was not safe to procrastinate any longer

---

[13] *Ibid.*, p. 164.   [14] *Ibid.*, pp. 165–66.
[15] *Ibid.*, p. 165.

[16] *Ibid.*, p. 166.

Pitt, after securing an extension of six months and eventually of twelve months beyond January 1, 1786, appointed a competent agent, William Eden, later Lord Auckland, to carry on the negotiations.[17] After working hard to secure evidence from December 1785 until March 1786, Eden crossed to France to open actual negotiations. Partly because of his opposition to Pitt's Irish resolutions his appointment had been a popular one with the British manufacturers, who gave him considerable information. After several months of negotiations with the French representatives a treaty was signed on September 26, 1786.

The chief central clauses, first, reduced the duty on French wines to the level of that on the wines of Portugal, and adjusted, favourably to France, duties on vinegar, brandy and oil; secondly, fixed a maximum duty of 10 per cent. *ad valorem,* in either country, on hardware, cutlery, and miscellaneous metal wares; thirdly, fixed a similar maximum duty of 12 per cent. on cottons, woollens, porcelain, earthenware and glass. Silk and all goods mixed with silk remained mutually prohibited.[18]

If he had comparatively little to do either with initiation or the negotiation of the treaty, Pitt made an unusually fine defense of its terms in the House of Commons on February 12, 1787. The Whigs, who had employed the tactics of stirring up opposition in the industrial and commercial classes during the discussion of the Irish commercial resolutions in 1785, now attempted, but without success, to repeat this performance. The reason for their failure is fairly obvious: the interests which felt threatened in 1785 were more than gratified by the terms of the Eden Treaty. In defending the Treaty against the charges that he was making concessions to the natural enemy of Great Britain, Pitt denied both that France was a natural enemy and that he had given as great concessions as he had received.

Considering the treaty in its political view, he should not hesitate to contend against the too-frequently advanced doctrine, that France was, and must be, the unalterable enemy of Britain. His mind revolted from this position, as monstrous and impossible. To suppose that any nation could be unalterably the enemy of another, was weak and childish.[19]

[17] Ward and Gooch, *The Cambridge History of British Foreign Policy,* I, 166-67.

[18] *Ibid.,* p. 170.

[19] *Parliamentary History,* XXVI, 392.

In answering the objection that the treaty would be as beneficial to France as to England, he maintained that

It was ridiculous to imagine that the French would consent to yield advantages without an idea of return: the treaty would be of benefit to them; but he did not hesitate to pronounce his firm opinion, even in the eyes of France, and pending the business that though advantageous to her, it would be more so to us. The proof of this assertion was short and indubitable. She gained for her wines and other produce a great and opulent market; we did the same, and to a much greater degree. She procured a market of eight millions of people, we a market of twenty-four millions. France gained this market for her produce, which employed in preparation but few hands, gave little encouragement to its navigation, and produced but little to the state. We gained this market for our manufactures, which employed many hundreds of thousands, and which, in collecting the materials from every corner of the world, advanced our maritime strength, and which, in all its combinations, and in every article and stage of its progress, contributed largely to the state. France could not gain the accession of £100,000 to her revenue by the Treaty; but England must necessarily gain a million. . . . . It was in the nature and essence of an agreement between a manufacturing country and a country blessed with peculiar productions, that the advantage must terminate in favour of the former: but it was particularly disposed and fitted for both the connexions. Thus France was, by the peculiar dispensation of Providence, gifted, perhaps, more than any other country upon earth, with what made life desirable, in point of soil, climate, and natural productions. It had the most fertile vineyards, and the richest harvests; the greatest luxuries of man were produced in it with little cost, and with moderate labour. Britain was not thus blest by nature; but, on the contrary, it possessed, through the happy freedom of its constitution, and the equal security of its laws, an energy in its enterprise, and a stability in its exertion, which had gradually raised it to a state of commercial grandeur; and not being so bountifully gifted by Heaven, it had recourse to labour and art, by which it had acquired the ability of supplying its neighbour with all the necessary embellishments of life in exchange for her natural luxuries.[20]

It has been suggested that Pitt was indiscreet in arguing that the treaty was more advantageous to England than to France.[21] In his defense it must be pointed out that the memory of the three defeats which he had suffered at the hands of the Whig Opposi-

[20] *Ibid.,* XXIX, 394–95.
[21] Ward and Gooch, *The Cambridge History of British Foreign Policy,* I, 169.

tion in 1785 and 1786 was still fresh in his mind. Doubtless he felt that it was better to embarrass Vergennes than to risk a repetition of his defeat on the Irish commercial resolutions of 1785. The comparative ease with which Pitt pushed his resolutions through Parliament may indicate that so vigorous a statement of British advantages was unnecessary; but evidently he felt that he could not afford to make a more cautious one at the time.

The evidence as to the King's attitude toward the treaty with France is somewhat scanty. There appear to be no letters from George III to Pitt on this subject in the correspondence of either of the two. The King during these years, however, so frequently expressed his opinion on the necessity of improving the revenue and avoiding trouble with Continental nations that his hearty approval was a foregone conclusion. In a letter dated October 6, 1786, the Duke of Dorset congratulated Eden on the success of his treaty and added: "I never saw the King in such spirits— they rise in proportion to the stocks, which are beyond the sanguine expectations of everybody."[22] But the fact that George III favored the Eden Treaty did not mean that he believed in the advantages of a better understanding with France in the spirit of Shelburne or of Pitt. Seemingly he favored it because he felt that it would strengthen the financial position of his government. On April 27, 1787, he wrote to Pitt that

one cannot but with comfort reflect that this country is now annually paying off one million of its debts whilst France exceeds its Peace Establishment near six millions and seems not likely soon to adopt any plan either for diminishing its Debts or even reducing its expenses to within the bounds of its income.[23]

Thus while George III may have been as keenly interested in the Eden Treaty as Pitt, it was not because of the mutual advantage to the two countries, but because it gave evidence of further strengthening England's financial position without improving that of France. The King took considerable satisfaction in the French financial predicament because of the fact that part of the difficulty came from the assistance rendered the American Colonies during the Revolution and because the situation made it less likely that France would upset the peace of Europe in the immediate future.

[22] *Correspondence of William, First Lord Auckland,* I, 393.
[23] Pitt MSS, 103, April 27, 1787.

The fundamental points of view of the King and Pitt can be best studied during these years in England's relations with the Dutch.

Nothing seemed more shocking to British diplomatic opinion than the decline of British influence at Amsterdam and the Hague during the War of American Independence. For four years (1783–7), the struggle to recover that influence is the master-thread of British policy in Europe. For rather less than four years more (1787–91), the recovery of it is the keystone in the rather ill-cemented structure of the Triple Alliance of Great Britain, Holland, and Prussia.[24]

From 1689 to the end of the War of the Austrian Succession in 1748 the combination of Great Britain, Austria, and the United Provinces had been, with the exception of a few brief intervals, the main check on the Bourbon powers. Although the relative importance of the United Provinces declined even before 1748, and Austria in 1756 sought the French alliance in place of this traditional friendship, still the long tradition of friendship with these powers lingered on in England. Even the continuation of the Austro-French alliance after 1756 and the fact that the United Provinces had in 1780 joined the Bourbon powers and the American Colonies in the war on Great Britain did not entirely wipe out this tradition. Close relationship between the two countries, however, was not limited to sentiment based on former alliances. Because of her geographical location and her Navy, England was in a position to do greater harm to Holland than was any other nation. The Stadholder at this time, William V of Orange, was weak and incompetent; and he was unpopular because of his lack of ability, the belief that he was too much influenced by his Prussian wife, and the suspicion that he had acquired alien sympathies from his English mother.[25]

The French eagerness to control the Netherlands rested on the desire not only for diplomatic prestige and the advantages of closer relationship with a country occupying so strategic a geographical position but also for the opportunities in the colonial field as well. Without doubt certain interests in France hoped that closer relations with Holland and the other six provinces might lead to French domination of the Dutch East India Company and the Dutch East Indies, and make possible a reversal of

[24] Ward and Gooch, *The Cambridge History of British Foreign Policy* (New York: Macmillan, 1922), I, 159. By permission of The Macmillan Company.
[25] *Ibid.*, p. 160.

the British victory over the French in India during the Seven Years' War.

Had the struggle between the English and the French for the control of the Netherlands been unconnected with the main threads of European diplomacy, it would be much easier to fit it into the scheme of this chapter. It is impossible, however, to treat the Dutch crisis even from the English point of view without an understanding of the policies of the two most daring rulers of Europe, Joseph II of Austria and Catherine II of Russia. Joseph II, in addition to being elective head of the Holy Roman Empire, was ruler over a heterogeneous group of states extending from the English Channel and northern Italy in the west to the Carpathian Mountains on the east. As a good example of the so-called enlightened despots of the eighteenth century he undertook to solidify these scattered possessions, to centralize the administration in Vienna, and to carry out various reforms. Although in the main these proposed reforms were enlightened, they almost inevitably aroused the opposition of local sentiment or vested interests. The particular plan of Joseph which concerned Great Britain was the proposal made first in 1778 and revived in 1785 to exchange the Austrian Netherlands for Bavaria. If the Bavarian royal family were transferred to these Belgian provinces the arrangement made by the Treaty of Utrecht in 1713 would be upset. By the terms of this treaty no change could be made in the status of these provinces without the consent of the signatory powers; and by those of the Barrier Treaty of 1715 the Dutch troops were to garrison certain fortresses in the Austrian Netherlands which lay close to the French border. Joseph II now aroused great uneasiness in England and Holland when he ordered out these Dutch troops and demanded, first, that the navigation of the Scheldt below Antwerp, which had been closed to outside commerce since 1648, should be free from Dutch control; and, second, that the Dutch cede Maestricht to him.[26] The high-handed actions of the Austrian ruler were made possible by the agreement which he had reached in 1781 with Catherine II whereby Joseph had agreed to help the empress against the Turks and in return she had guaranteed the integrity of his widely scattered possessions.

Since the parts of Europe in which England was most concerned, the Dutch and Austrian Netherlands, seemed about to

[26] J. H. Rose, *Life of William Pitt,* pp. 297–98.

come under the control of hostile powers, the years from 1783 to
1786 were, from the British point of view, a continuation of the
black years of the war from 1778 to 1783. Under the circumstances England naturally attempted to come to terms with Russia, Austria, and Prussia. All her overtures were rejected. Attempts to appeal to Russia on the grounds of common commercial interests, to Austria on those of old friendships, and to Prussia on those of common interests and enemies and of the alliance
during the Seven Years' War all failed. Russia and Austria evidently felt strong enough to spurn any overtures, especially since
England appeared to be so weak that neither power desired her as
a friend or feared her as an enemy. The attitude of Prussia
seems to have been the result of the personal bias of that elderly
genius, Frederick II, rather than of any fundamental state policy,
for the interests of both Prussia and England would have been
served by some sort of alliance. Many arguments could be cited
in favor of such an agreement; whereas the only one of force
which could be urged against it was the possibility that it might
result in the drawing closer together of France, Austria, and
Russia. That Frederick was as much opposed to the proposed exchange of Bavaria for the Austrian Netherlands as was England
is evidenced by the fact that he formed a League of German
Princes to oppose the plan. His repulse of England in 1785 is the
more remarkable because George III as Elector of Hanover acceded to this League.

George III was careful to keep the foreign policy of Hanover
entirely separate from that of England. On numerous occasions
he had signified these intentions in no uncertain words. Catherine II and Joseph II were indignant when George III as elector
of Hanover acceded to the League; and on August 5, 1785, Count
Woronzow, the Russian Ambassador at London, sent a vigorous
protest to the English government. In this letter Woronzow suggested that Russia might find it necessary to form alliances disagreeable to England unless George III as elector withdrew from
the League. The episode is interesting because it shows how Pitt
and the King handled a matter which from many points of view
was very ticklish. Pitt, on the day after the arrival of the protest,
sent Woronzow's letter to George III accompanied by a communication in which he suggested that

The influence which Your Majesty's engagements respecting your
Electoral Dominions may have on the general state of the continent,

and on Your Majesty's relative situation with Foreign Powers, must also eventually affect the interests of this country. In this point of view, Your Majesty's heart will pardon me the presumption of adding that if you should think proper to direct any more particular information to be given with respect to the Treaty in question, it would be of essential advantage in enabling Your Confidential Servants to submit to Your Majesty's wisdom any opinion, either as to the line to be pursued, or the language to be held on the part of Great Britain, with the different powers of Europe at this important crisis.[27]

In his reply to Pitt the King made perfectly clear both his opinion of the Russian protest and his attitude on the part which the English ministers should play in the foreign policy of Hanover:

I have this instant received Mr. Pitt's letter enclosing the one brought him by Count Woronzow's secretary and the paper that accompanied it which is a copy of the one given on friday to Lord Carmarthen. Count Woronzow also visited Lord Sydney and insisted a council was to be held next day to give him an answer whether I could break the treaty I have in my Electoral Capacity finally concluded with the King of Prussia and the Elector of Saxony to prevent all measures contrary to the Germanick Constitution. If no one has such dangerous views this association cannot give umbrage; but the times certainly required this precaution. My only difficulty in giving any answer to the Empress of Russia is that Her Declaration was so strongly the shape of a command that it requires a strong one. The having succeeded in that kind of conduct with the Court of Denmark, has encouraged Her adopting it on this occasion; but as what I owe in my Electoral capacity to the future stability of the Empire has alone actuated my conduct, and makes me feel that Russia has no right to interfere. An experience of twenty years has taught Me not to expect any return for the great assistance she has received from this Country. Mr. Pitt shall receive from Me when prepared copies of the answer, that has been given to the Imperial Minister and the Russian at Hamburgh which will fully apprise him of the business and it is but natural that to so improper a declaration I should propose time taken before any answer is returned.[28]

Thus in 1785 British interests in the Dutch Netherlands appeared to be threatened by the policy of France and in the Austrian Netherlands by that of Joseph II. Before the year was over, however, the Austrian danger had been minimized and the French

[27] Clements Transcripts, I, 441–42.
[28] Pitt MSS, 103, August 7, 1785.

menace accentuated. When Joseph II continued to press the Dutch to cede to him Maestricht and to open the Scheldt to navigation below Antwerp, the situation became acute. At this point Vergennes won one of his greatest diplomatic victories, for by the Treaty of Fontaincblcau, November 8, 1785, he induced the Emperor to abandon these two demands in return for a payment of fifteen million florins. The French minister secured the agreement of the Dutch by making his own government responsible for half the amount. Thus in saving the Dutch from the possibility of having to cede Maestricht and of opening up the Scheldt, Vergennes paved the way for the Franco-Dutch alliance which was signed on November 10. By the terms of this treaty France guaranteed the integrity of the Netherlands and each country agreed to assist the other in case of attack. It is largely because the results of this diplomatic triumph lasted so short a time that greater emphasis is not given to it in so many histories covering this period. The victory of 1785 has been overshadowed by the diplomatic defeat of 1788 and the French Revolution. But at this time it was clear that

France now held a most commanding position in Europe. By the new compacts she influenced Hapsburg policy, she forced Frederick the Great into almost abject deference, she allured Catharine, and she controlled the Dutch Netherlands. This last triumph crowned the life-work of Vergennes. The recent treaties relieved him from the disagreeable alternatives of choosing between Austria and the United Provinces in case of a rupture. They emphasized the isolation of England. Above all, they prepared the way for joint action of the French and Dutch East India Companies which might prove to be fatal to British ascendency in India.[29]

J. Holland Rose admits that the nonchalance of the Prime Minister was astounding, but explains and partly excuses it on the ground that here as so often he was handicapped by the King. This handicap, the explanation continues, resulted from George III's insistence on avoiding foreign entanglements as King of England but not as elector of Hanover; and from his reluctance to acquiesce in demands on the Civil List when the expenses of his growing family were already a matter of grave concern.[30] But in view of George III's letter to Pitt after the debate on the speech from the throne of January 24, 1786, and other communications

[29] J. H. Rose, op. cit., I, 317.
[30] Ibid., pp. 317–18.

of like tenor, the charge that the King handicapped his minister must be dismissed.

In this speech from the throne attention was called to the friendly attitude of foreign powers and to the improvement in revenue. Fox, with the memory of the three defeats inflicted on Pitt in 1785, was not likely to overlook so vulnerable a point as the French diplomatic victory of the past November; he censured the ministry for neglecting the formation of Continental alliances and blamed its criminal misconduct for the successes of the French. Fox recommended a closer connection with Russia and Austria and insisted that the Austro-French agreement had been reached because Joseph II became "imprudently disgusted" by the conduct of George III as elector of Hanover.[31] Pitt in replying "complimented Mr. Fox on the instinctive dexterity with which he was accustomed to leave out of his speeches such parts of the subject as were unfavourable to him," and defended the King's actions as elector of Hanover. This reply gave Fox a chance to express, in a manner which he was quite confident would be offensive to George III, his opinions on the misfortune under which England labored of having a ruler who was also the elector of Hanover.[32] But in his letter to Pitt, alluded to in the preceding paragraph, the King did not take exception to the debates in the Commons so much as to Lord Stormont's criticisms in the House of Lords:

The Opposition choosing to avoid the subjects touched on in the speech is the strongest encomiums on the measures of the Government; Lord Stormont giving a dish of foreign politicks on the occasion as not a subject before the House is certainly highly irregular and not becoming the dignity of the Upper though a common though not respectable conduct in the Lower House. The taking advantage of the blessings of Peace by improving the Revenue and making treaties of commerce seem the wise measure. No system of Foreign Alliance can be devised that will not perhaps within a year bring us into a War which I am certain no man of sense can wish, and the other line of conduct will in a few years put us in a situation to be courted. Now I fear if we move it must be by courting.[33]

In the light of these three last sentences written on January 26, 1786, it is difficult to see how the King can be accused of handi-

[31] Gifford, *op. cit.*, I, 283.
[32] *Ibid.*, pp. 285–87.
[33] Clements Transcripts, II, 515.

capping Pitt. The policies suggested were: improving the revenue, making commercial treaties such as the one soon to be made with France, and avoiding war until the country was in a position to act effectively and possessed something which other countries sought. These are almost exactly the policies pursued by Pitt with great success from 1786 to 1788. Either Pitt agreed with them from the start or he came to adopt them voluntarily or by necessity. No matter which of the three possibilities is chosen, no case can be made against the King.

If one may judge by the despair expressed by Sir James Harris, the British envoy at The Hague, Pitt during the first half of 1786 did not give any indications of pursuing an aggressive policy in the Netherlands. Even though in a private conversation with the King he may have expressed a desire to take vigorous action as a result of the Franco-Dutch alliance of 1785, it is evident that Pitt relinquished such a plan either willingly or reluctantly. Although Harris continued his almost frenzied efforts to save the British position in the Netherlands, no ray of hope appeared until August 1786. The Patriots of Holland, whose strength lay in the commercial aristocracy, became increasingly bold after November 1785, since the alliance with France was a distinct triumph for them. The apparent indifference of Pitt, the opposition of George III, and the refusal of Frederick the Great to co-operate with the English made the task of Harris seem a hopeless one. The tide turned with the death of Frederick on August 17, 1786, and that of Vergennes on February 13, 1787. The Patriots suggested first limiting the powers of the Stadholderate, next removing the unpopular Stadholder in favor of his son, and eventually abolishing the office entirely.[34] Harris was continually asking for money to carry on propaganda in favor of the Stadholder; and it was the demand for financial and diplomatic backing which George III steadily opposed. On September 22, 1786, in his letter to Pitt, George III showed clearly that he had not changed his opinions on the Dutch problem since January:

The accounts from Holland yesterday have much affected Me as the great activity of Sir James Harris and his inclination to commit this country, must draw us into difficulties if great caution and sane temper is not shown in the answer to Him. I therefore wish to see

[34] Ward and Gooch, *The Cambridge History of British Foreign Policy,* I, 172.

Mr. Pitt at St. James's a little before one this .... for it would be unjustifiable when this country if she remains some years in Peace will regain former wealth and consideration by being too meddling should be drawn into a fresh War which must bring on ruin be it ever so prosperous.[35]

As the year 1786 advanced Pitt seems to have given more consideration to Harris' strong representations. Several reasons may be advanced for this increased interest: the chance of support from Prussia now that the brother of the Princess of Orange had succeeded Frederick the Great; improvement in the financial position of England; less pressing internal problems; a growing conviction that the attitude of Harris was the correct one; and the increasingly critical condition of French finance. The King's objections to the campaign of Harris seem to have rested, first, on a fear that it might involve England prematurely in a war and, second, that the plan to finance the Orange party in Holland might cause the royal family inconvenience by making inroads on the Civil List. George III expressed this latter fear quite freely in a letter to Pitt written on January 8, 1787:

Sir James sets the annual money that must at present be issued for encouraging the Party in the United States at twelve thousand per annum, and keeps a door open to demand further sums. Where is this sum to be obtained if the hazard it may occasion of involving us in a war is risqued? Certainly it cannot come from the Civil List. I have two of my Younger Sons already of age who must be maintained at a much larger expence when they return to England; a third within two years of manhood, and my daughters growing up; these considerations must I think make Mr. Pitt think twice before he enters into a plan which the Foreign Secretary of State seems very eagerly to encourage.[36]

In this instance the pacific policy of the King and Pitt prevailed over the more spirited measures suggested by Harris and supported by Carmarthen. Thus Pitt either agreed with George III or was converted to his point of view; and so Harris was obliged to continue his "Sisyphus toil"[37] for five months more. On May 23, 1787, a cabinet meeting was held in the home of Thurlow at which Harris was present and stated his arguments in favor of active intervention and even of going to war with

[35] Pitt MSS, 103, September 22, 1786.
[36] Clements Transcripts, II, 641.
[37] J. H. Rose, *op. cit.*, I, 358.

France. According to J. Holland Rose, "so far as we can judge, Pitt alone was for complete neutrality. Nevertheless, his view prevailed. An interview which Harris had with him on the morrow did not change his sentiments."[38] But in spite of Pitt's reluctance to intervene the cabinet agreed on May 26 to allow Harris twenty thousand pounds to assist the provinces loyal to the Orange cause. On June 10 an additional sum of seventy thousand pounds for the same purpose was advanced.[39] Pitt, in his letter of May 26 to the King, explained his reasons at great length for adopting such a position:

Mr. Pitt feels in common with the rest of Your Majesty's Servants that although it would be imprudent to commit this Country in the present moment to an unforeseen extent, even for so interesting an object as the independence of the Provinces yet on the other Hand, with the prospect which appears to exist at present of effective exertions being made with only *Pecuniary Assistance,* it would be unwise to relinquish altogether the hopes of defeating the dangerous views of France and of restoring the United Provinces to their ancient connection with this Country. The measures now proposed seems attended with no inconveniences but in point of expence ; and as far as this may exceed the sum provided for in the estimate of the Civil List, Mr. Pitt ventures to submit it to Your Majesty as his confident Persuasion that there can exist no difficulty in obtaining from Parliament a vote to make it good at the beginning of next session. The circumstances of the French finance make it highly improbable that they should embark in hostile operations ; and unless they should march an army to the support of Holland, there seems at least an equal chance of a favourable issue to the present struggle. If France should take any more violent resolution the question would become infinitely more serious to this Country. Tho' upon a nearer view of the question Mr. Pitt must confess that he entertains doubts of the possibility of this country remaining totally inactive in that contingency (however painful the alternative) yet all He wishes to submit to Your Majesty at present is that the step now proposed necessarily leads to no determination on that question. It must require the fullest and most anxious consideration if it should occur.[40]

It is clear from the King's reply to Lord Carmarthen, also written on May 26, that the only argument which he appreciated was the offer of Pitt to see that Parliament reimbursed him if he advanced money from the Civil List. The communication

[38] *Ibid.,* p. 360.   [39] *Ibid.,* p. 360.
[40] Clements Transcripts, II, 669–70.

expressing this attitude is one of the most pungent in all the King's correspondence:

Had Lord Carmarthen's letter accompanied by a Minute of the Cabinet not been also by Mr. Pitt's letter, I should certainly have declined consenting to risking the advancing £70,000 to the Stadholderian Party in the United Provinces; and though I now reluctantly consent to it from fatal experience of having fed the Corsican cause and Ministry never having, as they had promised, found means of its being refunded to Me, which made me conveniently appear afterwards in an extravagant light to Parliament; yet I trust to Mr. Pitt's honour that He will take such arrangements on this occasion as shall prevent postponing the regular payments of the Civil List, and that Parliament shall make good the payment of the next winter, without supposing that the demand arises from any extravagance on My Part.[41]

From this time events moved rapidly. Both the Orange faction and the Patriots armed, the latter relying on their Free Companies. The climax came at the end of June when the Princess of Orange, who with her husband had retired to Nymwegen, decided on June 28 to return to The Hague in order to make a personal appeal to the States-General. She was stopped by the Free Companies, and after being a prisoner for one night was permitted to return to Nymwegen. When her brother, King Frederick William, heard exaggerated reports of the insults offered her, she seems to have made no serious effort to enlighten him. In fact, it seems more likely that she was intent on deliberately exploiting this error on the part of the Patriots. Although the Prussian king vacillated over the question of armed intervention, Carmarthen at least went on the assumption that such a policy was inevitable.[42] Pitt, who had pursued a cautious policy down to this point, seems to have decided that the time for action had come if he could count on the support of the Prussian Army. On August 2 he wrote to Cornwallis to seize Trincomalee from the Dutch as soon as hostilities broke out in order to prevent the French from using it as a base for attacks on England in the Far East.[43]

At this juncture everything broke favorably for the English and the Prussians and unfavorably for the French. The latter

[41] Clements Transcripts, II, 671
[42] Ward and Gooch, *The Cambridge History of British Foreign Policy*, I, 173.
[43] *Ibid.*

could, in all probability, have saved themselves by a more astute course. A more diplomatic treatment of the vacillating and uncertain Prussian king might have prevented military intervention; and this result might have been secured by inducing the Patriots to offer some kind of satisfaction which would not have been humiliating. The action of the British government in preparing to hire Hessians and to place ammunition at the disposal of the Orange party, combined with news that Turkey had decided to declare war on Russia and that as a result Joseph II would be in no position to act in the west, made it easy for the Prussian monarch to take decisive action. Having failed to secure satisfaction from the States of Holland, Frederick William sent the Prussian Army under the command of the Duke of Brunswick across the frontier on September 21. The States of Holland first issued an appeal to France for aid and then withdrew it. On October 10 Amsterdam surrendered to Brunswick, and the triumph of Prussia was complete.

Perhaps the best explanation for the paralysis of France is the irresolution displayed by Montmorin, who had succeeded Vergennes in February. Before Prussian intervention and until France made the humiliating Declaration on October 27 that she had not intended to intervene and held no hostile views toward any party concerned,[44] Montmorin seems to have had no clearly defined policy. The rapidity with which events moved and the precarious state of French finance may well account for the indecision displayed.

Pitt had, it would seem, decided on a vigorous policy from the time the Princess of Orange was stopped by the Free Companies. It is interesting to note when and why George III acquiesced in a show of force. On September 16, three days after Brunswick crossed the frontier, he wrote to Pitt:

On returning to the Secretary of State's office the dispatch from Mr. Eden of the 13th, I cannot help accompanying it with a few lines to Mr. Pitt, though the language of M. de Montmorin is so very *offensive* that I can scarcely mention it with *Temper*. I dissaprove of such language and consequently cannot recommend its being *retorted*. We have held a fair conduct during the whole business, and France has been double to the greatest excess. I think they feel they cannot do much, and therefore from spleen, indulge themselves in this unjustifiable language which any one but Mr. Eden would have declined

---

[44] *Ibid.,* p. 175.

hearing and still more, reporting. I trust temper may still bring things into the line of negotiation, and while we are desirous that France should with politeness be told that we shall be obliged to stand by the United States against the faction in the Province of Holland if France persists in the idea now communicated of supporting it with Arms. I suppose Our Ships if M. Barthelemey's language shews France means to act without hearing further from Us, ought to appear off the Dutch Coast for a few days, which might decide measures previous to the arrival of any material force from France. Ought not some one instantly to go to France who may know better how to talk with M. de Mont Morin than Mr. Eden.[45]

Pitt in reply expressed "his entire conviction that the line Your Majesty is pleased to point out is the only one which can be adopted with propriety."[46] He added his opinion that it would be best to take immediate steps to arm the fleet and also suggested "that it may be of great utility if Your Majesty should think proper to direct as large a corps as possible of Hanoverians to be put into readiness to march at the shortest warning, if eventually Your Majesty should approve of their being taken into the Pay of this Country."[47] The King answered that he had already sent provisional orders to find out what force could be collected in Hanover on short notice, but that he could go no further until he received this information and was assured that England would take such a force into pay.[48]

All through this crisis George III showed clearly that he kept his finger on the progress of events, and his support of Pitt's suddenly vigorous and daring policy undoubtedly contributed to its success. The King was as willing as Pitt to change from a policy of comparative inaction when so bright an opportunity presented itself. Giving Pitt due credit for foresight, tact, and determination,[49] it is a one-sided presentation which ignores the attitude of the King.

The declaration and counter-declaration signed by Eden and Dorset for England and by Montmorin for France on October 27 was merely the first of three triumphs for England which emerged from the Dutch crisis. The statement that the French king never had any intention of intervening in Dutch affairs, that he held no hostile views toward any country as a result of the affair, and

---

[45] Clements Transcripts, II, 722.
[46] *Ibid.*, II, 723.   [47] *Ibid.*, II, 723.   [48] *Ibid.*, II, 725.
[49] J. H. Rose, *Life of William Pitt*, I, 381.

that he would disarm, while highly satisfactory to Pitt, Carmarthen, Harris, and George III, did not cause them to stop at this point. An Anglo-Dutch treaty and the Triple Alliance of England, Prussia, and the United Provinces were to follow. It was only natural that an Anglo-Dutch alliance should result from the diplomatic defeat of France. Pitt, however, showed that he was not interested in the Netherlands merely from the point of view of diplomatic prestige and victories, for his fundamental interest before and after this triumph was in naval and colonial spheres. French domination of the fleet, colonies, and East India Company of the United Provinces would be a distinct menace to England; hence, since his interest was in this direction, Pitt refused to return Negapatam to the Dutch either as the price of the alliance or to insure greater cordiality between the two countries. Eventually the Dutch government assented to an alliance in which each country agreed to guarantee the possessions of the other and to assist in case of an attack. This treaty, which was signed April 15, 1788, gave Pitt exactly what he wanted; but the Dutch, because they felt that they had given more than they received, do not appear to have regarded it with the same enthusiasm.

The third of Pitt's diplomatic triumphs in the years 1787–88 was the alliance with Prussia, which completed what is usually called the Triple Alliance of England, Prussia, and the United Provinces. As far back as September 1787 the Prussian king had expressed an eagerness to conclude such an alliance, and this desire was no doubt enhanced by the decision of Austria to join Russia in the war on Turkey. Pitt, however, was reluctant to join such an alliance because he did not wish to become committed to Prussia's Eastern expansion. Since England's interests were in maintaining the peace of Europe and Prussia's in securing an ally to offset the dangers of the entente of Joseph II and Catherine II, there were some delays in the realization of this alliance. In fact, the instructions drawn up for Sir James Harris in his conference with Frederick William at Loo in June of 1788 stressed the desirability of the alliance in order "to contribute to the general tranquillity."[50] Thus the provisional treaty agreed to between Harris and the Prussian king on June 13 was a great disappointment to those Prussians who were looking for an ally to aid in Eastern expansion. The permanent treaty, signed in

[50] *Ibid.*, p. 388.

Berlin on August 13, 1788, was defensive in character. In addition to each state's agreeing to help the other, with certain exceptions noted, both pledged themselves to defend the United Provinces and to uphold the existing Dutch constitution.[51]

In the twelve months following 1787 the position of England in the world of diplomacy was wonderfully improved. Several factors account for this change: the events in eastern Europe, the state of French finance, the death of Vergennes, the enormous improvement which Pitt had brought about in both national finances and the Navy, and the clever manner in which he had handled the situation during the trying months. At the same time it is absurd to overlook the part played by George III both before and after Pitt undertook his vigorous foreign policy. The King was consistently for peace in order that the country might put its finances in order and once more play an important role in European affairs. It is unfair to ascribe his pacificism entirely to his interest in saving the money for his growing family. Perhaps he did not show the same interest as Pitt in building up the Navy; but in the general principles of foreign policy and in the steps taken to carry out specific decisions he seems to have been in substantial agreement with his Prime Minister. That Pitt consulted the King before decisions were reached even after his great triumphs of 1787 and 1788 is shown by Pitt's letter of October 19, 1788, after the King had been stricken with that illness which was soon to produce the Regency Crisis. The letter began:

Mr. Pitt has had the honour of receiving Your Majesty's commands, and iş extremely sorry to be under the necessity of troubling Your Majesty on business of so much importance at the present moment. The accounts received from Berlin and the North seem to press for an early decision, and would make Mr. Pitt desirous, if possible, of personally submitting to Your Majesty the ideas which occur to Him and of receiving Your Majesty's commands before any answer is prepared to the Court of Berlin or any other steps proposed, but he is almost afraid to mention the circumstance at present, from the fear that it may be inconvenient before Your Majesty is entirely recovered from the effects of your late indisposition.[52]

In short, the history of the English foreign policy during the years from 1785 to 1788 does not indicate that George III exer-

[51] J. H. Rose, *Life of William Pitt,* I, 389.
[52] Clements Transcripts, II, 916.

cised any less influence than he had earlier in his life. Certainly
the fundamental points in his foreign policy, peace and fiscal
rehabilitation until the country could once more make her influence felt, were successfully carried out during these years.
Splendid as were Pitt's achievements, they were those of a minister carrying out a policy which coincided with the wishes of his
royal master; and if he differed with the King on details he had
either to give way or to win George III to his point of view by
convincing arguments. Certainly so far as foreign policy was
concerned during these years, Pitt was a long way from the age
of Palmerston and Salisbury.

But if the points of view of George III and Pitt were made
the same on the financial and foreign policies during the years
covered by this chapter, they differed materially on the impeachment of Warren Hastings. After his severe defeats in 1785 and
"the signs of friskiness" had vanished, Pitt relied less and less
on the advice of his idealistic friend Wilberforce and more and
more on that of his realistic friend Henry Dundas. Although
the influence of the latter seems not to have been very great on
Pitt's financial measures and foreign policy, it was very considerable indeed on the matter of the impeachment of Warren
Hastings.

Dundas was a much older man and a more experienced politician than Pitt. Born in 1742, the son of the Lord President of
the Scottish Court of Session, he made a great success at the Bar
before entering Parliament in 1774 as a member for Midlothian.
Here he attached himself to Lord North and soon became one
of the outstanding politicians, although not one of the first-class
statesmen or orators, in the House of Commons. His strong will,
courage, perseverance, conviviality, and ability to turn out an
enormous amount of work offset to a considerable degree his
deficiencies as an orator and his lack of political principles. His
real genius lay in the field of control and distribution of patronage
once Scotland and India were turned over to his shrewd and
efficient management. Under Lord North he became Lord Advocate and retained the office under Rockingham. Lord Shelburne
made him Treasurer of the Navy and Keeper of the Scottish
Signet for life.[53] Having survived two violent ministerial changes
within a year, Dundas attempted to make it three by inducing

[53] J. W. Fortescue, *British Statesmen of the Great War* (Oxford: Clarendon Press, 1911), p. 51.

William Pitt to become First Lord of the Treasury in March 1783. He perceived that Pitt had political principles enough for two and he was, probably, equally confident that he had sufficient ability on the more sordid side of politics to make up for Pitt's comparative ignorance in this field. The alliance which he wished to arrange for himself with Pitt had to be delayed until December 1783, but when it came Dundas emerged in a stronger position than even he must have anticipated. Not only was he restored to his position as Treasurer of the Navy, but after the passing of the India Bill in 1784 he was given by "private" arrangement patronage of India.[54] Under "Political Miscellanies" in the *Rolliad* both Pitt and Dundas figure in "This Is the House That George Built":

MR. PITT.—This is the Maiden all forlorn, that coaxed the Bull with the crumpled horn (Lord Thurlow), that roared with the Dog (Pepper Arden), that barked at the Cat (Mr. Fox), that killed the Rat (Lord Nugent), that ate the Malt, that lay in the House that George built.

MR. DUNDAS.—This is the Scot by all forsworn, that wedded (This Gentleman's own term for a Coalition) the Maiden all forlorn, that coaxed the Bull with the crumpled horn, that roared with the Dog, that barked at the Cat, that killed the Rat, that ate the Malt, that lay in the House that George built.[55]

But it would be a mistake to estimate the strength of Dundas's position by the office which he held, and by the fact that until June of 1791 he was not a member of the cabinet. In 1789 he was offered the Presidency of the Court of Sessions by William Grenville, but declined in a letter filled with verbose and guarded utterances. This refusal has been translated by Sir John Fortescue in the following words:

My dear foolish Grenville, at present I have the patronage of Scotland and of India; practically I govern both countries; you cannot get on without me. Of course it is very irksome for me to be besieged with requests and petitions whenever I go to Scotland, but in spite of my advancing years I bear up. Do you think that a pair of recluses, such as Pitt and yourself, with a stilted sense of honour and no knowledge of the world or of men, are a match for the great Whig magnates, with their control of rotten boroughs, their great territorial influence, and their commanding position as Lord-Lieutenant?

[54] J. W. Fortescue, *British Statesmen of the Great War*, p. 51.
[55] *The Rolliad* (London, 1812), 22d edition, pp. 410–11.

No, it needs such a man as Henry Dundas to manage these matters. You cannot do without me, and I see no speedy remedy for it, for I have not the slightest intention of effacing myself.[56]

It was such a man who had the greatest influence over Pitt in the question of the impeachment of Warren Hastings; and it was natural that he should, since he was not only one of Pitt's close advisers but also the one most·familiar with Indian affairs. In 1781 Dundas had been a member of the secret committee on Indian affairs, and on May 28, 1782, had moved the vote of censure on Hastings which had been passed by the House of Commons.

Probably no question in modern English history has aroused more heated controversies than the justice or injustice of the impeachment of Warren Hastings. The white heat of the controversy in the seventeen-eighties and seventeen-nineties has not cooled even in the twentieth century. Probably the reason for the absence of a well-accepted historical verdict is to be found in the explanation offered by J. Holland Rose.

Even to-day, when the justificatory facts of Hastings' career are well known, his actions are wholly condemned by men of a similar bent of mind. On the other hand his policy appears statesmanlike to those who look first at the wealth of benefits conferred on India by the British Raj and pay little heed to miscarriage of justice which they regard as incidental to an alien administration. The Hastings episode will ever range in hostile groups men of strongly marked disposition; while the judicial minority will feel themselves drawn perplexingly first to the sentimental side and then to the practical side as new facts and considerations emerge from the welter of evidence.[57]

When Hastings returned to England in 1785 after an absence of thirteen years he not unnaturally expected to be given some sign of appreciation of his great services. From 1772 to 1774 he had done really magnificent work in reorganizing Bengal. It is true that it was only a beginning of what he had hoped to accomplish, but he had been able to sweep away Clive's dual system, to set up a complete new system of justice, and to carry through a new land assessment or settlement. In his relations with the Indian powers he planned to keep peace by making the British power the pivot of a system of alliances. By the India Act of 1773 the Governor of Bengal became the Governor-Gen-

[56] J. W. Fortescue, *op. cit.*, pp. 58–59.   [57] J. H. Rose, *op. cit.*, I, 226.

eral and with the Council was given authority over the other presidencies. The numbers in the new council were reduced to five, including the Governor-General himself; and all were to have equal votes. This provision, combined with the attitude and personalities of the four appointed members, nearly ruined Hastings' work. The leader of the opposition to Hastings was Philip Francis, a man who has earned a singularly unfortunate record with posterity. It is almost universally admitted that he was egotistical, malicious, deceitful, and ambitious and that his best quality was a brilliant literary style. By winning over two members of the new Council to his point of view he was able to block Hastings' program for two years. After that the Governor-General secured control by the death of one of his opponents and managed to retain it until Francis in 1780 returned to England baffled. Differences between Hastings and Francis, however, were not confined to personal hatred but extended to fundamental principles. Francis believed in a permanent settlement of the Bengal land tax and in avoiding alliances with Indian powers. Hastings opposed a permanent settlement and believed strongly in alliances with native powers which would make the British power in India the pivotal one. Thus when Francis returned to England in 1780 he spent the next five years in poisoning the mind of Burke and other Whigs not only against Hastings' character and personality but against his principles and policies. In the years from 1779 to 1784 most of Hastings' time was occupied in a fight for the existence of British India. A confederation of the Nizam of Hyderabad, Hyder Ali, and the Mahrattas, making up all the first-class powers in India, was formed to sweep the British out of the country. This confederation, when combined with French naval and military forces and the strong possibility of little assistance from the North ministry, made Hastings' position extremely precarious. At the end of five years he emerged triumphant over all these obstacles and maintained British India intact. When his achievements are contrasted with those of other English statesmen and military men during these black years, they stand out still more conspicuously.

When Hastings returned to England in 1785, conscious and proud of his great work, he appears to have had some misgivings but no serious fears. His friends and foes could not be divided as government and opposition. George III was openly and ostentatiously friendly, and Hastings and his wife reciprocated by giving the Queen the famous ivory bed which caused so much merriment at the time. But Pitt had not committed himself, and Dundas had introduced the vote of censure against Hastings which had passed in the House of Commons on May 28, 1782. In addition, Hastings considered the India Bill of 1784 a veiled attack. But if he were uncertain about the friendship of Pitt and Dundas, he could be under no delusions as to the enmity of Burke, Fox, Sheridan, and certain other Whigs. Francis had fraternized with them when he returned from India and had converted them to his point of view.

Influenced no doubt by the attitude of the King and by an appreciation of the amazing achievements of Hastings in India, many members of the Whig Opposition wished to drop the motion of censure, but Burke and Fox were eager to take up the question in the session of 1786. They were assisted by Hastings' accredited agent in the House of Commons, Major Scott, who on the opening day of the session challenged Burke to prosecute the charges against the former Governor-General. As J. Holland Rose has pointed out, it is unlikely that Scott issued this challenge without the consent of Hastings, but it is probable that the latter decided to strike immediately at the motion of May 28, 1782, and attempt to stop the spread of gossip and innuendoes.[58]

If this was truly Hastings' campaign plan, he was guilty of a most costly error in tactics, because he gave his enemies the choice of weapons. He and his spokesman, Major Scott, could no more match the oratory of Pitt, Fox, Burke, and Sheridan than these four could compete with him in knowledge of Indian affairs. Burke answered the challenge of Scott on February 17 by requesting that the Clerk of the House read Dundas's resolutions of May 28, 1782, and then suggesting that since the mover of this motion of censure was still in the House of Commons he was the logical one to take action against Hastings. In the course of a speech defending Dundas, Pitt made clear his own position, stating: "I am neither a determined friend nor foe to Mr. Hastings, but I will support the principles of justice and equity. I recommend a calm dispassionate investigation, leaving every man to follow the impulse of his own mind."[59] On the whole,

[58] J. H. Rose, *op. cit.*, I, 228.
[59] H. B. Wheatley (ed.), *Memoirs of Sir Nathaniel William Wraxall* (London, 1884), IV, 261.

Pitt appears to have adhered to this position until June 13. On at least three occasions he refused demands for papers or the presence of certain witnesses at the Bar of the House and was sustained by a substantial majority; but on sixteen other motions for papers he agreed.[60] Hastings seems not to have appreciated how highly the members of the House of Commons valued a skillful presentation and how little acquainted they were with the affairs of India. As a result, his long and dull defense which he read on May 1 and 2 appears to have done his cause more harm than good. This reply, however, was in no sense the decisive factor in bringing about his impeachment.

On June 1 Burke introduced his charges against Hastings on the Rohilla War. Dundas and Grenville, Pitt's closest associates in the ministry, both spoke against the motion. Despite the oratory of the Whig leaders, the motion was rejected early on the morning of June 3 by a vote of 119 to 67.[61] On this question Pitt, Grenville, Dundas, and Wilberforce were in substantial agreement. Thus Hastings was justified in feeling relieved and Burke in fearing that he was leading another lost cause.

The decisive day in the impeachment of Hastings came on June 13. The charge brought forward on that day concerned the treatment of Cheyt Singh, Zamindar of Benares, during the trying period of the war in 1781. Hastings had requested that Cheyt Singh pay fifty thousand pounds in addition to the annual tribute. Beginning in 1778 this payment had been made annually, but in 1780 the Zamindar showed a certain reluctance as well as signs of what Hastings considered disloyalty. As a result, the Governor-General fined Cheyt Singh five hundred thousand pounds and with arrogant self-confidence visited the latter in Benares with only a small retinue. Only his own coolness and the near proximity of Company forces saved him from the results of what proved to be a rash move, for the troops of the Zamindar resorted to violence and besieged him in his own residence. When the danger was over, Hastings deposed Cheyt Singh and substituted another Zamindar with an increased tribute. When Fox on June 13 moved to impeach Hastings for his conduct in this affair, there seemed to be no reason why the speeches and vote should not follow substantially the same lines as those of June 1 to 3. The difference came in the stand taken by Pitt. Whereas

---

[60] J. H. Rose, *op. cit.*, I, 229.
[61] *Parliamentary History*, XXVI, 91.

on the earlier motion he had spoken very briefly and had voted with his colleagues in the ministry, he now spoke at great length and concluded by condemning Hastings for fining Cheyt Singh too much. Pitt was careful to differentiate himself from Fox and Francis. He repudiated the argument of the former that the Company had no right to exact an "aid" from an independent rajah on the ground that Cheyt Singh was not independent; and he answered the argument of the latter that no extraordinary demands could be legally made on a feudal vassal by quoting Francis' own written opinion to the contrary. Pitt's speech was decisive in insuring the impeachment of Hastings, because in spite of the fact that several members of the ministry spoke in favor of Hastings the House endorsed Fox's motion by 119 to 79.[62]

Why did Pitt take such a stand? That is a most difficult question to answer; but it has not prevented historians from 1786 to the present time from attempting it. The explanations offered by critics hostile to Pitt are: that the Prime Minister was jealous of the favor which the King was showing Hastings; that he was influenced by Dundas, who was afraid that Hastings might supplant him at the Board of Control; and that he was glad to have an able opposition spend its energies on a subject of so little concern to the government.[63] Anyone familiar with Pitt's public speeches and private correspondence during this period would certainly exonerate him from the fear of Hastings as a rival. Pitt had altogether too much of the Chatham and Grenville arrogance and self-confidence to fear anybody as a Parliamentary rival. Hastings himself believed that Dundas, actuated by jealousy, had called on Pitt early in the morning of June 13 and after a three-hour conference had convinced him that he should change his stand on the impeachment charges.[64] Mr. P. E. Roberts points out that the impeachment proceedings would not sap the energy of the opposition, because the trial lasted only 118 days and was spread over a seven-year period. Further, Pitt had no advance knowledge of the time which the trial would occupy.

Within recent years the problem has been approached both by biographers of Pitt and by historians interested primarily in

[62] *Ibid.*, p. 115.

[63] H. H. Dodwell (ed.), *The Cambridge History of the British Empire* (New York: Macmillan, 1922), IV, 307–8.

[64] S. Weitzman, *Warren Hastings and Philip Francis* (Manchester: Manchester University Press, 1929), p. 186; footnote from B.M. Add. MSS, 39880.

India. Naturally those who traced the statesman's career as a whole have a better background upon which to judge his motives, and the historians of India are in a better position to judge the responsibility of Hastings. Lord Rosebery and J. Holland Rose, in their well-known biographies of Pitt, speak in the highest terms of the action taken by the Minister. Lord Rosebery states:

But his amazing authority was not more conspicuous than the purity of his rectitude. He declined to associate himself with those who held that the end could justify the means, even for the construction of an empire or in the atmosphere of the East. He gave his decision as calmly as a judge in chambers; while Britain and India abided meekly by the decree of this young gentleman of twenty-eight.[65]

Dr. Rose is equally eulogistic in his justification of Pitt and stresses the statesman's concern for India:

We may reasonably infer that among the motives which led Pitt to break with many of his friends not the least was a heartfelt desire to safeguard the relations of the feudatories to the Suzerain Power, and to protect the myriads of Hindoos who had no protection save in the dimly known court of appeal at Westminster.[66]

P. E. Roberts is as certain as Lord Rosebery and Dr. Rose that Pitt was not swayed by motives of political expediency, because he feels that such an interpretation would run contrary to the commonly accepted opinion of the lofty, pure, and serene mind of Pitt.[67]

It would appear that a great deal of the differences in opinion and interpretation arises from an attempt to show that Pitt was acting entirely from principle or from political expediency instead of attempting to study his reactions to a changing problem. Pitt, in the words of his friend Wilberforce, "paid as much attention to it as if he were a juryman." Believing as he did that he owed it to himself and the nation to maintain his high reputation for objectivity and lofty disinterestedness, he was certain to weigh the evidence as it was presented. His speeches and remarks to Wilberforce show clearly that he wished to hold the balance between the two extremes and to render his decision as a just and upright judge. Pitt's political principles, his India

[65] Lord Rosebery, *Pitt* (London: Macmillan & Company, Ltd., 1923), p. 88. By permission of the publishers.

[66] J. H. Rose, *op. cit.*, I, 239.

[67] Dodwell, *The Cambridge History of the British Empire,* IV, 309.

Bill, and his attitude toward Hastings gave the latter no real reason to expect active support. Even when he spoke against Hastings on the Cheyt Singh charge, he was careful to differentiate himself from Fox and Francis. It is unbelievable that he expected that his speech and vote on this charge would be decisive; and there is good reason to believe that he experienced some pain when it turned out to be so. Three days after Pitt's speech of June 13, a motion by Burke to postpone further consideration of the impeachment to the next session was carried. When the question was taken up again on February 7, 1787,[68] Sheridan introduced the charge relating to the begams of Oudh in a speech which is often referred to as the most eloquent ever delivered in Parliament. Again Pitt voted against Hastings and with the majority. These two instances, June 13, 1786, and February 8, 1787, in which Pitt voted for impeachment, served completely to destroy in the eyes of his contemporaries and of posterity the "juryman" attitude which he tried so hard to attain. Other motions which were introduced after February 7 did not receive the same support from Pitt. Often "the Ministry sought rather to embarrass and retard the motions than to assist them in their progress through the Committee."[69] Yet this phase of Pitt's "juryman" duty is often ignored. The chief result at that time seems to have been that Burke and other Whig leaders reproached him for attempting to backslide and to withdraw from a crusade to which he was committed. Furthermore, Burke did not confine himself to reproaches of this sort; but he undertook to appeal to the self-interest of Dundas, which was the sort of argument that the canny Scot best understood, by pointing out that the position of the Pitt ministry would be threatened by the triumph of Hastings. In his letter of March 25, 1787, to Dundas, Burke paints these dangers most vividly:

As to the material point of numbers, means are using on our side to call in as many as the lax discipline of opposition can secure. With regard to your side, you will excuse the liberty I take, in suggesting that the idea of wholly separating the man from the minister, if carried substantially into effect, cannot fail of being infinitely mischievous; however, the internal circumstances of administration may make some appearance of that kind, and for some time expedient, but

[68] *Parliamentary History*, XXVI, 274–94.

[69] Weitzman, *op. cit.*, p. 187. Quoted by permission of Manchester University Press, publishers.

it ought not to continue overlong, or be at all over-done; for if Mr. Pitt does not speedily himself understand, and give others to understand, that his personal reputation is committed in this business, as manifestly it is, I am far from being able to answer for the ultimate success, when I consider the constitution of the late minorities, combined with the political description of the absentees. But I think it, in a manner, impossible that all this should not be felt by you and by Mr. Pitt. I shall, therefore, only take leave to add, that if ever there was a common national cause totally separated from party, it is this. A body of men in close connexion of common guilt, and common apprehension of danger, with a strong and just confidence of future power if they escape, with a degree of wealth and influence which, perhaps, even yourself have not calculated at anything like its just rate, is not forming, but actually formed, in this country;—that this body is under Mr. Hastings as an Indian leader, and will have very soon, if it has not already, an English political leader too. This body, if they should now obtain a triumph, will be too strong for your ministry, or for any ministry. I go further, and assert without the least shadow of hesitation, that it will turn out too strong for any description of merely natural interest that exists, or, on any probable speculation, can exist in our times. Nothing can rescue the country out of their hands, but our vigorous use of the present fortunate moment, which, if once lost, is never to be recovered, for breaking up this corrupt combination, by effectually crushing the leader and principal members of the corps. The triumph of that faction will not be over us, who are not the keepers of the parliamentary force, but over you; and it is not you who will govern them, but they who will tyrannize over you, and over the nation along with you. You have vindictive people to deal with, and you have gone too far to be forgiven. I do not know whether, setting aside the justice and honour of the nation, deeply involved in this business, you will think the political hints I have given you to be of importance. You who hold power, and are likely to hold it, are much more concerned in that question than I am, or can be.[70]

In his cautious reply of the next day Dundas is at his vaguest and hence at his best. After stating that he had communicated the contents to Pitt, he assured Burke thus: "The motives which have actuated us in the business which your letter treats of, are of a nature too forcible to allow any competition in our minds between them and any political contingencies which may occur."[71]

[70] Charles William, Earl Fitzwilliam, and Sir Richard Bourke (eds.), *Correspondence of Edmund Burke* (London, 1844), III, 50–52.
[71] *Ibid.*, p. 53.

Although he refused to participate in the management of the prosecution, he promised support "which appears to us consistent with national justice and the credit of the House of Commons."[72] Whether or not Pitt was in any way moved by the fears expressed in Burke's letter is not clear; but in any case he did not give up his juryman point of view.

The impression which Pitt created by his stand on the Cheyt Singh and the begams of Oudh charges was not only strengthened but also given final shape by his speech of May 9, 1787, on the occasion of the second reading of the report of the secret committee appointed to draw up articles of impeachment. The burden of his refrain was that there were so many unexplained crimes and glaring instances of breach of orders that, in his opinion, the "House could no otherwise consult their own honour, the duty which they owed their country, and the ends of public justice, than by sending up the impeachment to the House of Lords."[73] The motion was carried by 175 to 89.[74] The trial of Hastings opened in February 1788 and lasted until April 1795. The final verdict was given on April 23, 1795, and Hastings was acquitted on every count. Not even the pro-Pitt and anti-Hastings historians of the present day attempt to justify the manner in which the trial was conducted, even when they expatiate on the wonderful effect which the impeachment had on all classes in India. Hastings spent £71,000 on his defense, and thus found himself impoverished at the end.

Volumes have been written in justification of the impeachment of Hastings, even though few historians will defend the trial. The most important thing to be determined is what steps should have been taken to stop the practices of which Hastings had been guilty, and at the same time to avoid humiliating him in so unjustifiable a fashion. The superb summary of P. E. Roberts gives the answer:

The impeachment was a calamitous mistake and before it had gone very far it developed into something like a cruel wrong. It was not unreasonable that some inquiry should be held; indeed, after the vote of censure of May, 1782, it was perhaps essential. The fair course would have been to hear Hastings' case and then parliament might have expressed a temperate disapproval of some of the methods he

[72] *Ibid.*
[73] *Parliamentary History*, XXVI, 1143.
[74] *Ibid.*, p. 1147.

had employed in the case of Chait Singh and the begams of Oudh, and might well have commented severely upon the laxity of his ideas of account-keeping. Having ensured that these unhappy features of his period of office should not be allowed to become precedents for British policy in the East, they should have recognized the immense difficulties that confronted Hastings and acknowledged his magnificent services to his country. A grant of some high honour from the crown would naturally have followed, and the energies of the reformers might have been devoted, with Hastings' aid and co-operation, to amending the whole system of the Indian government. The impeachment of Hastings was an anachronism, a cumbrous method of inflicting most unmerited suffering on one of the greatest Englishmen of his time, something very like a travesty of justice.[75]

The question naturally arises where the responsibility lies for so grave a miscarriage of justice. To many writers the state of English law is a sufficient explanation. A very good case, however, can be made for placing the blame squarely on the shoulders of William Pitt; and this can be done without any reflection being cast on his high ideals or good intentions. Pitt can be blamed for not adhering to the very principle which he enunciated in his speech of June 13, 1786, namely, that in fining Cheyt Singh five hundred thousand pounds for a delay in paying an "aid" of fifty thousand, Hastings had not proportioned the punishment to the crime. Pitt was in a position of great responsibility and his judgment proved inferior to his ideals. While he could not push through every measure in which he was interested, as his sad experiences in the session of 1785 had conclusively proved, he was in a position to add a sufficient number of his own followers and of independents to the votes of the Opposition to insure the impeachment of Hastings. Had he proportioned the punishment to the crime in the case of Hastings he would have adopted some such measures as Mr. Roberts suggested. Although Pitt may have taken the stand he did on the Cheyt Singh and the begams of Oudh charges without realizing what the end would be, still that does not relieve him from the responsibility for the results; it merely means that he did not have sufficient foresight to suggest the plan for Parliamentary censure and exoneration of Hastings in time, or that he lacked the moral courage to admit his mistake after he committed himself on June 13, 1786, to

[75] Dodwell, *The Cambridge History of the British Empire* (New York: Macmillan, 1922), IV, 309–10. By permission of the publishers.

impeachment. Thus, while Pitt enjoyed the amazing position
which Lord Rosebery referred to as a judge handing down a
decision which was meekly accepted by England and India, the
results show that his decision was a very bad one. Perhaps
nothing emphasizes the prestige which Pitt enjoyed more than
the fact that his reputation remained unimpaired in spite of the
gross miscarriage of justice. Yet in the light of history there
is no reason to exonerate Pitt merely because his motives were
pure and he meant well. Hastings' road to hell was paved with
Pitt's good intentions.

In view of all the research done on the life of Pitt and on
India during this period it may appear that no new explanations for Pitt's actions can be offered. Nevertheless, the present
writer believes that there are two additional ones which must
be given serious consideration. Both assume that the possibility
of adopting such tactics as Mr. Roberts suggested were given
consideration by Pitt; for it is inconceivable that anyone with his
intellect and grasp of existing conditions would have failed to
consider Parliamentary censure and praise as an alternative to
impeachment. The first of these two explanations is the one
used by Professor Laprade to account for Pitt's action on the
Westminster Scrutiny of 1784–85, namely, that the young Minister wished to be considered as the head of the liberal reforming
element both in and outside Parliament and looked with uneasiness upon the attempts of the Whig leaders to supplant him or
even to share with him this leadership. Thus just as Pitt was
vigorously opposed to seeing Fox chosen for Westminster lest
he be considered the tribune of the people, so he was opposed to
allowing the Whig leaders — Fox, Burke, and Sheridan — to
monopolize the position of defenders of the political morality
and to leave to him that of the defender of Hastings' high-
handed actions in India. At the same time Pitt did not want to
take common action with the Whigs and admit that they were
entirely in the right. This would account for the careful differen-
tiation of his position from theirs in his speech of June 13 on
the Cheyt Singh charge, and for his unwillingness to close with
Burke's eager suggestions in the letters to Dundas. Yet had Pitt
used his unique position to confine the action against Hastings
to a Parliamentary investigation, as he should have done, he
would have been subject to the same abuse by the great Whig
orators as if he had actually voted against impeachment on all

charges. Such an explanation is not only consistent with Pitt's action in this case but also with his attitude toward other reform measures during the years following 1785.

The second explanation for his conduct in the Hastings affair is closely allied to the first and concerns his relationship with the King. The partnership between George III and Pitt, as shown in the preceding chapter, rested on freedom of action for both on policies where the two did not agree. Until the question of the treatment of Hastings arose, the King had all the better of the arrangement. Far more members of the Commons who supported the government agreed with George III than with Pitt on the reform measures over which the Minister had fought and lost. The explanation for the votes of these members may be either fear of the King or genuine agreement with him; but in either case Pitt had yet to oppose the King successfully on any important measure.

The attitude of George III is very clear on the Hastings affair. He was a strong believer in and admirer of the great Governor-General and upon the latter's return from India had shown him great consideration and courtesy. Unfortunately the correspondence between the King and Pitt on the subject of Hastings is very limited; and it was disappointing that no new letters seem to have been found in the papers of George III.[76] Still there can be no doubt as to the sovereign's cordial feeling toward Hastings and the regret which he felt at the persecution of nine years. It is fortunate that the one letter from the King to Pitt should be packed so full of significant statements. This letter, which was written on June 14, 1786, the day after Pitt had voted in favor of impeaching Hastings on the Cheyt Singh charge, stated:

Mr. Pitt would have conducted himself yesterday very unlike what my mind expects of him, if as he thinks Mr. Hastings' conduct towards the Rajah was too severe, he had not taken the part he did, though it made him coincide with adverse party. As to myself, I own I do not think it possible in that country to carry on business with the same moderation that is suitable to an European civilized nation.[77]

The King, in all probability, was, as most historians have interpreted the letter, intending to pay Pitt a high compliment; but to anybody who has read hundreds of the letters of George

[76] The absence of any letters is noteworthy in view of the King's interest in the trial of Hastings.

[77] Pitt MSS, 103, June 14, 1786.

III it seems not impossible that the words "what my mind expects of him" may be open to a different interpretation. The next sentence in the letter gives the moderate pro-Hastings point of view about as succinctly and compactly as could be desired.

Thus when considered simply from the point of view of the relations of the King and the Minister, Pitt scored his first distinct triumph over George III in the game of a free hand on undetermined policies. The King, having profited so considerably by this arrangement, could not offer an open objection on the one occasion in which the rule operated against him. Without doubt he was somewhat chagrined, but he was too fine a tactician to accept the result in any other manner than he did. His real attitude, perhaps, is found in the qualifying clause at the end of the first sentence in his letter: "even though it made him coincide with adverse party." In view of the discomfort he must have experienced when the rule operated against him, Pitt probably felt some gratification over this aspect of the affair.

From all points of view except that of the injustice done to Hastings, Pitt had every reason to feel satisfied with the impeachment. He had maintained his reputation for moral integrity; he had prevented the Whigs from assuming all the credit for seeing that justice was done to the oppressed of India; he had obeyed his conscience in not condoning the offenses of Hastings; and he had won a tactical triumph over George III.

The necessity which Pitt felt of maintaining his position as a spokesman for liberal opinion and movements is unmistakable in his attitude toward the reforms brought up in Parliament during the years covered by this chapter. His point of view, however, was by no means determined entirely or perhaps even mainly by the expediency of preventing the Whig leaders from assuming entire control of liberal and reforming movements and forcing him into the camp of the conservatives and King's Friends. This fact is proved conclusively by the degrees of warmth which he took toward what we may call the three chief reforms advocated from 1785 to 1789: Parliamentary reform, abolition of the slave trade, and repeal of the Test and Corporation acts. Furthermore, his attitude toward these suggested reforms was not determined by that of the Whig leaders. For Parliamentary reform Pitt appears to have felt lapsed enthusiasm, for abolition of the slave trade active and sincere enthusiasm, and for the repeal of the Test and Corporation acts no enthusiasm.

During the years 1785 to 1789 the cause of Parliamentary reform was barely kept alive; and so far as Pitt was concerned it was dead. In 1786 several Scotch counties petitioned for reform; and in that year and again in 1787 motions in the House of Commons to inquire into the state of representation were defeated.[78] It is true that in 1788 Lord Mahon's measure which established electoral registers for the voters in the counties was carried; but in the following session the law was first suspended on the grounds of expense and then repealed.[79] Despite the lethargy of Parliamentary reformers, interest was reviving again because of the centenary of the Revolution of 1688–89; and these celebrations were to fit in aptly with the renewed enthusiasm created by the French Revolution.

It is in the study of Pitt's attitude toward the abuses in the slave trade that we get our best insight into the nature of his reforming zeal during these years. This was a reform upon which Pitt had not been rebuffed as on Parliamentary representation, one which aroused his most sincere concern because of the disgusting abuses connected with the trade, and one in which he had a deep personal interest because his dearest friend Wilberforce had resolved to devote his life to the eradication of the evil. Yet despite these three advantages Pitt did not show that wonderful self-confidence of the years 1783 to 1785. The results of the defeats suffered on the Westminster Scrutiny, Parliamentary reform, the Irish commercial resolutions, and the fortification of Plymouth and Portsmouth were still evident in the cautious tactics which he adopted.

It is impossible in this connection to treat the entire movement which led up to the abolition of the slave trade in 1807. Three distinct threads of opposition to this traffic were joined in 1787. These were the Quakers, whose opposition dates back at least to 1671; Granville Sharp, who had been active since 1772; and the Reverend James Ramsay, Rector of Teston, Kent, who had formed his impressions during a stay on the island of St. Kitt's.[80] The first meeting of the "Committee for Procuring Evidence on the Slave Trade," which was later to become the Abolitionist Society, was held on May 22, 1787. Their methods were based on what was at that time the most effective method of securing

---

[78] G. S. Veitch, *The Genesis of Parliamentary Reform* (London: Constable and Company, Ltd., 1913), p. 103.

[79] *Ibid.*   [80] J. H. Rose, *Life of William Pitt,* I, 457.

consideration for a reform measure, namely, arousing public opinion and petitioning Parliament to act. In the long run much of the success of the agitation was due to the soundness of their methods employed in stirring up public opinions in the large cities and towns. Wilberforce's relationship with the Committee is worth noting because he was to be the outstanding advocate of abolition in the House of Commons. He did not communicate with the Committee until October 30, 1787, and he did not become a member of it until 1794.[81] The reason for remaining outside was not hostility to the Committee but the belief that he could work more effectively by co-operating outside its organization.[82] Wilberforce expected to begin his work in Parliament in the session of 1788, but a serious illness early in the year forced him to leave London.

It was because of his illness that Wilberforce asked Pitt to bring forward a motion on the slave trade. Pitt's answer of April 8, 1788, shows both his real affection for Wilberforce and his sincere interest in the subject:

I have just received your letter of yesterday, and as I can easily imagine how much the subject of it interests you, I will not lose a moment in answering it. As to the Slave Trade, I wish on every account it should come forward in your hands rather than in any other. But that in the present year it is impracticable; and I only hope you will resolve to dismiss it as much as possible from your mind. It is both the rightest and wisest thing you can do. If it will contribute to setting you at ease, that *I* should personally bring it forward (supposing circumstances will admit of its being brought forward this session) your wish will decide. At all events, if it is in such a state that it can be brought on, I will take care that it shall be moved in a respectable way, and I will take my part in it as actively as if I was myself the mover. And if I was to consult entirely my own inclination or opinion, I am not sure whether this may not be best for the business itself; but on this, as I have said already, your wish shall decide me. With regard to the possibility of its being brought on and finished this session, I can hardly yet judge. The inquiry has been constantly going on, and we have made a great progress. But it takes unavoidably more time than I expected. In one word, however, be assured that I will continue to give the business constant attention, and do everything to forward it. Whenever it is in such a state that

[81] *Ibid.*, p. 458.

[82] F. J. Klingberg, *The Anti-Slavery Movement in England* (New Haven: Yale University Press, 1926), p. 84.

you could yourself have brought it on with advantage to the cause, I will do it or undertake for its being done, in whatever way seems most proper. I mean, therefore, to accept it as a trust from you to the whole extent you can wish, and to make myself responsible for it, unless it is necessarily delayed until you are able to resume it yourself.[83]

On April 21 Pitt assured Granville Sharp that he believed heartily in the abolition movement and was anxious to do what he could to help the cause. He pointed out, however, that the examination before the Privy Council which he had started earlier might not be completed in time for the subject to be brought up in the present session of Parliament.[84] Apparently the examination progressed in a manner which satisfied Pitt that it was safe to bring the matter before the House, because on May 9 he moved the following cautious resolution:

That this House will, early in the next session of Parliament, proceed to take into consideration the circumstances of the slave trade, complained of in the petitions presented to the House, and what may be fit to be done thereupon.[85]

Both Fox and Burke, eager to harass Pitt on details of procedure or to court the reforming element, objected to the fact that the petitions had been examined in the House of Commons instead of in the Privy Council. Sir William Dolben, the member for Oxford University, however, was unwilling to permit certain aspects of the slave trade to go unregulated even until the next session of Parliament. Therefore he brought in a bill which limited the number of slaves which could be carried in each ship, according to the tonnage of the vessel, and made other provisions to safeguard their health and comfort on the voyage.[86] Pitt warmly supported this measure, and it passed the Commons with little opposition. When it reached the Lords, Thurlow, the Lord Chancellor, opposed it vigorously and Sydney, the Home Secretary, more mildly. This action angered Pitt and he gave vent to his feelings in a letter to Grenville written at Cambridge on June 29:

I think I see the means still of carrying the present Bill. But if it fails, I have made up my mind, after very full reflection, to bring

---

[83] *Private Papers of William Wilberforce* (London, 1897), pp. 17-19.
[84] J. H. Rose, *op. cit.,* I, 460-61. B.M. Add. MSS 21255.
[85] Gifford, *op. cit.,* I, 489.   [86] *Ibid.,* p. 490.

it again immediately in the House of Commons (which I apprehend there is no difficulty in doing in point of order) and to summon all the strength we can for another trial in the House of Lords. If it fails then, the opposers of it and myself cannot continue members of the same Government, and I mean to state this distinctly to the Cabinet before the House meets tomorrow.[87]

Such drastic steps were not necessary, for the bill passed the House of Lords by a majority of two.

Pitt's handling of the question of the slave trade in the session of 1788 gives a better insight into his attitude toward reform during these years than any other action which he took. He firmly believed in abolition and was bound by his promise to Wilberforce, and yet his actions were most cautious. But when Dolben, acting contrary to the Minister's suggestion, insisted upon introducing a bill to alleviate evils in the traffic, Pitt, far from resenting the action, threatened a cabinet crisis if the measure were beaten in the Lords. According to J. H. Rose: "This declaration does honour to his heart and his judgment. It proves the warmth of his feelings on the subject and his sense of the need of discipline in the Cabinet."[88] It may show the warmth of his feelings, but it does not explain why Pitt did not take any initiative in this and in other reform movements. Even more it seems to show the difficulty Pitt was having in attempting to secure unanimity in a cabinet composed of conservatives, King's Friends, and his own followers. Actually Pitt's threat to Grenville was more of an indication that he was tiring of the opposition and tactics of Sydney and Thurlow; and it foreshadows the resignation of the former the next year and of the latter at the end of 1792. Pitt had neither the King nor the cabinet back of him in wishing to abolish the slave trade, and he had no desire to sacrifice his place at the head of the ministry by attempting to make George III and his fellow ministers accept the measure by a threat that he would resign. Thus while Pitt could secure the reluctant acquiescence of his cabinet on small measures by threatening to make the King choose between him and the dissenting ministers, evidently he felt that he could not secure the King's approval of the major reforms by threatening to resign,

---

[87] Historical Manuscripts Commission, *The Manuscripts of J. B. Fortescue, Esq., Preserved at Dropmore* (London, 1892–1927), I, 342. Hereafter referred to as *Dropmore Papers*.

[88] J. H. Rose, *op. cit.*, I, 461.

or it seems likely that he would have tried it. In short, there was a no-man's land between George III and Pitt. The King might have forced Pitt to resign rather than give way on what he considered a major issue; but at the same time he was very anxious to retain his chief minister and was willing to make such concessions as allowing minor reforms to be passed or as permitting members of the cabinet who became distasteful to Pitt to be ousted. Neither George III nor Pitt seemed anxious to find precisely where the line of demarcation was in this no-man's land.

The third of the three great reforms treated in this chapter, the repeal of the Test and Corporation acts, found the King and Pitt on the same side. Pitt does not appear to have had the antipathy for the suggested change which the King so evidently felt. The Corporation Act had been passed in 1661 by the Cavalier Parliament to exclude from offices in corporations members of dissenting Protestant sects; and the Test Act in 1673 to exclude the Catholics from places in the government and the Army. The important test in both acts was that of receiving the Sacrament according to the rites of the Church of England. The exclusion had been effective so far as Catholics were concerned, because it was impossible for members of the Roman Catholic Church to conform to this requirement and because, in addition, the Test Act demanded a declaration against transubstantiation. Neither of these requirements was sufficient to keep Dissenters from holding office in corporations or in the government. In addition, Nonconformists who held office without taking the trouble of qualifying were further protected for some years before 1787 by acts of indemnity passed annually by Parliament. On March 28, 1787, Mr. Beaufoy, a staunch churchman himself, moved that the sacramental test for both acts should be abolished but that the declaration against transubstantiation and the oath of abjuration and supremacy should be retained. The retention of these would be ample protection against Jews, Catholics, and infidels. This mild reform met with opposition from Lord North and Pitt. It may have been slightly embarrassing to Pitt to find himself substantiating the arguments of the man whom he treated so scornfully from 1781 to 1784. Pitt's argument turned largely upon the answer he gave to his own question: "Whether there was any substantial interest which made it necessary, that one part of the community should be deprived of a

THE BEST YEARS OF GEORGE III 181

participation in its civil officers? The security of the established church was an interest of this nature, and he thought that it would be endangered by the proposed repeal."[89] In conclusion he held that the Toleration Act of 1689 and the annual acts of indemnity left the Dissenters without any reasonable grounds of complaint.[90]

Although Pitt's arguments seem weak and his efforts half-hearted, there is no reason to hold that he acted contrary to his convictions. The truth of the matter seems to be that he was not particularly interested one way or the other. According to Bishop Watson, Pitt was so indifferent that he referred the matter to the Archbishop of Canterbury, who in turn referred it to the bishops. When the latter by a vote of 10 to 2 favored upholding the sacramental test in the two acts, Pitt acted accordingly.[91] It may be regrettable that he did not take a more enlightened stand on this question, but on the whole it is less to his discredit than his failure to act more vigorously on issues in which he believed keenly.

By all odds the most important issue during these years was the one which is usually known as the Regency Crisis. The debates and correspondence over the right of the Prince of Wales to exercise during his father's insanity all the rights of the sovereign without any Parliamentary restrictions bring out with amazing clearness the relations not only between the King and Parliament but also between the ruler and his chief minister. In order to place this Regency Crisis in its proper setting, a study of the relationship between George I and the Prince of Wales, later George II, and that between George II and his son Frederick, Prince of Wales, in the ten years preceding the death of the latter in 1751 is necessary. It is even more important, however, to be certain of the stakes for which the antagonists in this great constitutional battle of 1788–89 were struggling. On the one side were the King and Pitt, and on the other the Whig leaders and the Prince of Wales. While a great constitutional issue concerning the right of Parliament to place limitations on the power of a Regent may have been at stake, the contest was really waged over more tangible spoils than a significant principle.

Each of the four mentioned had something in addition to the principle involved which determined his stand. It may be argued

[89] Gifford, op. cit., I, 388.
[90] Ibid., p. 389.   [91] J. H. Rose, op. cit., I, 215.

that the King could not be considered a party to the struggle because he was out of his mind, and that it was as a result of his condition that the question arose. The Regency question, however, was merely a showdown in the bitter contest of the King and Pitt against the Prince of Wales and the Whig leaders. The King's interests were both national and personal. He wanted to see the finances of his country put on a firm basis in order that England might regain the position which he believed and desired she should hold and because he needed money badly to look after his enormous family. Pitt's interests were likewise national and personal. He took a genuine and patriotic delight in improving the finances and diplomatic position of his country; but at the same time he was extremely ambitious to hold his place at the head of the government. The Prince of Wales, it is comparatively safe to say, had no interests other than personal ones. He was a weak and spoiled young man whose youthful good looks and personal charm did not compensate for his complete selfishness and egocentric point of view. His interests were in wine, women, and gambling; and his perpetual grievance was that his royal father, the ministry, and Parliament were not giving him the money which the Prince of Wales was entitled to expect. Under these circumstances it was only natural that the Prince and Whig leaders should draw together. After their own defeats of 1783–84 and even after those inflicted on Pitt in 1785–86, the Whig leaders had no hope of regaining power under George III. As Fox said on February 27, 1786, in the course of the debate on Pitt's or the Duke of Richmond's proposal to fortify Plymouth and Portsmouth:

Does any man imagine that I or any of my friends shall be advanced one step nearer the acquisition of power whether the Duke of Richmond's fortification plan succeeds or is negatived? If defeating the Minister, even upon points which he has exerted his whole force to carry, could have brought us nearer to office, how happens it that, after the failures he has undergone, he not only remains unshaken, but seems to take deeper root?[92]

And Wraxall added very appropriately:

To such a desperate and almost hopeless situation had Fox's want of prudence reduced him, that scarcely any event except the demise

[92] Henry B. Wheatley (ed.), *Memoirs of Sir Nathaniel William Wraxall* (London, 1884), IV, 273. Hereafter referred to as *Memoirs of Wraxall*.

of the crown seemed to afford him a prospect of seizing again the reins of Government.[93]

It was because of the desperate position of the Whig leaders that they very naturally took up with the Prince of Wales. Temperamentally, as well, Fox and Sheridan made good allies of the Prince, for these two men of genius had much in common with the spoiled youth. Although he had not the slightest part of their outstanding abilities, he was Sheridan's equal with port wine and Fox's at the gaming table. Thus because the Prince offered the Whigs the only chance of returning to power and because certain of their leaders had tastes in common with him, the alliance was almost inevitable. On the other hand, as preceding chapters have shown, the alliance of the King and Pitt was just as natural. On the side of George III additional bitterness was added to the contest, if any were needed, because he considered that the Whigs had aided in the ruin of his son by inciting the latter to unnatural disobedience and by encouraging his dissipation.

Thus the struggle between George III and Pitt on the one side and Prince George and the Whig leaders on the other had been going on for several years before the climax came in the Regency Crisis. The long, sordid story of the Prince's many affairs with various women and his constantly growing debts need not be taken up in this connection. George III appears to have felt that bad as was the conduct of his eldest son on the moral side, it was not so reprehensible as his close connection with Charles James Fox and the Whigs. This point of view is well illustrated by his letter of October 6, 1786, to his second son Frederick, the Duke of York, who was at that time on the Continent. The King wrote:

I take the first leisure minute to answer your letter intimating a very natural wish to make your family a visit; however desirous you may be, it cannot exceed the joy I shall feel when I see you, but I must not let My inclinations decide where good reasons clearly shew Me I would be wrong. The conduct of your brother and the Party in whose hands he has unhappily thrown himself give every reason to expect this winter will be a pretty smart one; I know I can depend on your attachment and rectitude, therefore your conduct would be decided, for now a middle part is impossible; however I may be dissatisfied with your brother, the making of a breach between you is not My

[93] *Ibid.*

wish. Your being absent keeps you with propriety out of the conflict.[94]

In the session of 1787 Pitt arranged a settlement of the financial affairs of the Prince. Ten thousand pounds were added to his yearly allowance, twenty thousand were contributed toward the new works at Carlton House, and one hundred sixty-one thousand toward paying his debts.[95] The question of his acceding to his father's wishes and marrying a Protestant princess was shelved for the time; and the secret marriage which the Prince had contracted with Mrs. Fitzherbert on December 15, 1785, which was illegal both under the Act of 1689 because she was a Catholic and under the Royal Marriage Act of 1772 because the Prince was under twenty-six years of age, was not considered in the settlement. If he had had any intentions of reforming at this time, the Prince soon changed his mind; for when the King's illness set in late in 1788 his eldest son was again living the kind of life which his father abhorred—one of extravagance, of dissipation, and of close friendship with the hated Whig leaders. Letter after letter of the King to Pitt during the years 1787–88 shows approbation of Pitt's conduct in dealing with the Prince of Wales and the Opposition, and an intensified dislike and distrust of Fox and Sheridan. Thus the policy of both Pitt and the Whig leaders during these years made the chasm wider between George III and the Prime Minister on the one side and the Prince of Wales and the Whigs on the other. Fox and the other Whig leaders had decided some time before that they stood no chance of returning to office unless the sovereign changed; and consequently their policy was to draw as close to Prince George as possible. Such an alliance gave them the triple satisfaction of paving the way for their return to office when the Prince of Wales became king, of causing George III a great deal of personal annoyance, and of sniping at Pitt in the House of Commons. The opportunity to make effective use of this alliance came with the serious illness of the King in December 1788.

In spite of the almost uniform success which attended Pitt's efforts along the lines in which the King was most interested, the health of the latter showed signs of breaking earlier in 1788. Considerable disagreement still exists over the cause of George

[94] Clements Transcripts, II, 604.
[95] J. H. Rose, *op. cit.*, I, 402.

III's temporary insanity; but there is no doubt that it was preceded by considerable worry over the conduct of the Prince of Wales and the Duke of York, and by several attacks of indigestion. On June 5 he wrote to Pitt that "a pretty smart bilious attack prevents my coming this day to town."[96] A week later he sent another communication from Kew stating that his doctor, Sir George Baker, although considering that everything was going well, had advised him not to go to London or return to Windsor.[97] The summer spent in Cheltenham left him weaker, although his letter to Pitt of August 14 is cheerful enough:

I am this instant returned from seeing the most beautiful sight I ever beheld, namely, the colliery country near Stroud: above forty thousand people were assembled, and they all confess the trade is now brisker than the oldest person ever remembers.[98]

In October he returned to Kew and attempted to carry on in spite of frequent attacks. As late as October 20 the King was still able to re-state his views of the principles which should govern England's foreign policy. Pitt had written him of the necessity of taking action to prevent Russia and Denmark from dismembering Sweden, and had stated that the ministers believed war should be prevented in the north of Europe by assuring the king of Prussia of these sentiments and of full support as well if it became necessary.[99] In reply George III stated:

All I mean by this is, that we must try to save Sweden from becoming a province of Russia; but I do not think this object can only be obtained by a general war, to run the risk of ruining the finances of this country, which, if our pride will allow us to be quiet for a few years, will be in a situation to hold a language which does not become the having been driven out of America.

To speak openly, it is not the being considerably weakened by illness, but the feeling that never have day or night been at ease since this country took that disgraceful step, that has made me wish what years I have still to reign not to be drawn into a war. I am now within a few days of twenty-eight years, having been not on a bed of roses. I began with a successful war; the people grew tired of that, and called out for peace. Since that the most justifiable war any country ever waged—there in a few campaigns, from being popular again peace was called for. After such woeful examples, I must be

[96] Lord Stanhope, *Life of William Pitt* (London, 1861–62), II, i.
[97] *Ibid.*, II, ii.   [98] *Ibid.*
[99] Clements Transcripts, II, 916–17; see footnote 52.

a second Don Quixote if I did not wish, if possible [to avoid] fall-
ing again into the same situation. The ardour of youth may not admire my calmness, but I think it fairer to speak out thus early than
by silence be supposed to have changed my opinion, if things should
bear a more warlike appearance than I now expect, and if I should
then object to a general war.[100]

Again on October 25 and November 3, the King wrote letters
assuring Pitt of his improved physical condition. After that the
communications stopped abruptly, for from most accounts the
King was seized with so violent an attack on November 5 that
his chief physician, Sir George Baker, feared for the life of the
royal patient.[101]

The Prince of Wales and his Whig friends, not unnaturally,
took advantage of this situation at once. Unfortunately for the
Whigs, Charles James Fox was touring the Continent at this
time, and the leadership fell to or was assumed by Sheridan. One
of the first actions of the Prince was to summon Lord Thurlow
to Windsor on November 6 and sound out the Lord Chancellor
on the possibility of deserting Pitt. Thurlow had been on bad
terms with Pitt for some time. The differences were the result
of a clash in temperaments and on policies. "Thurlow was sullen
and often intractable: Pitt, imperious, inflexible, and dictatorial."[102] They differed on the impeachment of Hastings, on the
slave trade, and on appointments to various offices. Thus the
Lord Chancellor, who was not finding his place under Pitt too
pleasant, readily considered the idea of deserting the Prime Minister if he were allowed to hold his present position under a Whig
ministry. The evidence seems strong that Thurlow did for a
while act as a spy for the Prince in the cabinet meetings. The
story of the alleged discovery of the part he played is well known:
After one of these meetings at Windsor, Thurlow's hat was not
to be found in the room where the discussion had taken place.
After a long search a page came in with the hat saying naïvely
in the presence of the other ministers, "My Lord, I found it in
the closet of his royal highness the Prince of Wales."[103] The
obvious embarrassment of the Lord Chancellor betrayed to Pitt
and the other ministers the danger of this intrigue. The Prince

[100] Lord Stanhope, *op. cit.*, II, iii–iv.   [101] J. H. Rose, *op. cit.*, I, 407.

[102] Wheatley, *Memoirs of Wraxall*, V, 197.

[103] G. H. Jennings, *An Anecdotal History of the British Parliament* (London, 1899), 4th edition, p. 143.

of Wales had also sent word to Fox to return at once. The summons reached the Whig leader in Bologna and his return was so rapid that he injured his health rather badly in the nine-day journey. Fox reached London November 24, too late to stop the bargain between Sheridan and Thurlow.[104]

Thus Pitt's position, which at the beginning of November had appeared to be the strongest since his severe defeats in the session of 1785, was very precarious before the month was over. The Prince of Wales made no secret of the fact that he expected to change the ministry if he became regent. Pitt was well aware of his danger and made preparations to resume practice as a barrister. He made it clear from the start, however, that he intended to fight for his position. It was obvious to all that his only chance lay in delaying the time when the Prince should become regent in the hope that the King would recover; and he played this game so cleverly and successfully that he deserved to win. The Prince of Wales gave his consent to having Parliament adjourned for two weeks when it met at its scheduled time on November 20. On December 3, the day before Parliament met after the adjournment, the Privy Council examined the physicians of the King. The testimony of the doctors showed considerable difference of opinion, as to both the possibility of recovery and the probable length of time required in case a cure was effected. When Parliament assembled on December 4, committees were appointed in both houses to examine the royal physicians. In the Commons Pitt was to select a committee of twenty-one members from two lists: one submitted by the Ministry and the other by the Opposition. He gave an indication of the spirit in which he intended to conduct the campaign by his treatment of Burke. When Pitt read the list of twenty-one names, no comment was made on the first twenty; but instead of reading the last name Pitt paused. Then, according to the account of J. B. Burges:

From the Opposition benches the name of Burke re-echoed. Pitt still remained silent, and Burke's name was repeated yet more loudly. All this time he sat erect with much apparent consequence. When Pitt had kept us all in suspense for a couple of minutes, he very quietly proposed Lord Gower. Burke threw himself back in his seat, crossed his arms violently, and kicked his heels with evident discomposure.[105]

[104] J. H. Rose, *op. cit.,* I, 409.
[105] *The Bland-Burges Papers,* p. 118.

Clearly Pitt intended to maintain an uncompromising attitude in dealing with the Opposition.

The real battle between Pitt and the Whigs was fought in Parliament between December 10 and 16, although the decisive factor in the victory of Pitt was the speedy recovery of the King. On December 10 the medical evidence was presented to the House of Commons. This evidence contained the testimony of the royal physicians and of an outsider, the Reverend Dr. Francis Willis, who during the past twenty-eight years had devoted himself to such cases as the King's. Since his testimony was more favorable to speedy recovery than that of the royal physicians, it was eagerly seized upon by the Ministry and deprecated by the Opposition. Moreover, as the reports of the physicians were not so hopeless as might have been expected, it was only natural that Pitt should spar for time. Consequently, after the evidence was presented, he moved:

That a committee be appointed to examine and report precedents of such proceedings as may have been had, in case of the personal exercise of the royal authority being prevented or interrupted, by infancy, sickness, infirmity, or otherwise, with a view to provide for the same.[106]

Fox, who was enough of a parliamentary tactician to perceive that Pitt was endeavoring to postpone the Regency question as long as possible, declared that the motion was productive of unnecessary delay at a time when action was required. The course of Parliament was simple. The heir to the throne was of age and had as clear a right to exercise sovereign power during "the illness and incapacity with which it had pleased God to afflict his Majesty, as in the case of his Majesty's having undergone a natural and perfect demise."[107] Parliament had only the right to decide when the Prince of Wales should begin to exercise sovereign powers. Fox has been severely criticized for making a bad error in judgment. Still, it is difficult to see how his action can be considered a major error; for if the King's incapacity were permanent, all the delays which Pitt could summon would be futile. Naturally Fox was anxious to prevent his rival from dragging out an investigation too long; but he did not need to oppose restrictions on the powers of the regent unless the limi-

106 *Parliamentary History*, XXVII, 705–6.
107 *Ibid.*, p. 707.

tations prevented the Prince from appointing new ministers. Two points were made by Fox: first, the necessity of taking action to place a regent in charge of the government as soon as possible; and, second, the inherent right of the Prince to assume control without any limitations by Parliament.[108]

With a shrewdness which seldom deserted him in the House of Commons, Pitt singled out the second of these two points for attack. He is alleged to have exclaimed to the minister at his side: "I'll *un-Whig* the gentleman for the rest of his life." The Prime Minister then expressed abhorrence of the doctrine that Parliament did not have even the right to deliberate on the subject of the appointment of a regent and concluded: "that it would appear, from every precedent, and from every page of our history, that to assert such a right in the Prince of Wales, or any one else, independent of the decision of the two Houses of Parliament, was little less than treason to the constitution of the country." Pitt evidently decided on the spur of the moment to make himself the champion of Parliamentary rights and to leave Fox as the defender of royal prerogatives. Apparently he enjoyed asserting this doctrine as often as he could without arousing the King's anger, and undoubtedly there was a real danger that George III would take offense at so decided an expression of Parliamentary supremacy. Nevertheless, Pitt concluded with an appeal to the members of Parliament and to the nation to resist this pernicious doctrine of Fox:

Let every man in that House, and every man in the nation, who might hear any report of what had passed in the house that day, consider, that on their future proceedings depended their own interests, and the interest and honour of a sovereign, deservedly the idol of his people. Let the House not, therefore, rashly annihilate the authority of parliament, in which the existence of the constitution was so intimately involved.[109]

Thus the error which Fox made was apparently merely one of judgment in giving Pitt an opening to deliver such a speech.

It would seem that the Whigs had not given Pitt a sufficient chance to pose as the defender of Parliament; but Burke now gave him still another opportunity. With that amazing power of indiscretion which was the terror of his friends and his party, Burke called Pitt "one of the Prince's competitors." Pitt in reply

[108] *Ibid.*, p. 709.   [109] *Ibid.*, p. 711.

assumed his attitude of lofty superiority which was so effective and, after inferring the bad taste shown, asked:

At that period of our history, when the constitution was settled on that foundation on which it now existed, when Mr. Somers and other great men declared, that no person had a right to the crown independent of the consent of the two Houses, would it have been thought either fair or decent for any member of either House to have pronounced Mr. Somers a personal competitor of William 3?[110]

Pitt had reason to be pleased with the events of the day not only because of the indiscretion of his opponents but also because his motion for a committee to inquire into precedents was passed. When the committee reported on December 12, Pitt moved that the House should on Tuesday, December 16, resolve itself into a committee of the whole House to take into consideration the state of the nation.[111] In the course of the debate on this motion, Sheridan followed in the footsteps of Burke and foolishly "reminded the Right Honourable Gentleman (Mr. Pitt) of the danger of provoking that claim to be asserted [a loud cry of hear! hear!], which, he observed, had not yet been preferred."[112] Once again Pitt availed himself of the opportunity to turn this threat to his own advantage when he answered:

He had now an additional reason for asserting the authority of the House, and defining the boundaries of Right, when the deliberative faculties of Parliament were invaded, and an indecent menace thrown out to awe and influence their proceedings. In the discussion of the question, the House, he trusted, would do their duty, in spite of any threat that might be thrown out. Men, who felt their native freedom, would not submit to a threat, however high the authority from which it might come.[113]

When the House of Commons met on the 16th to take into consideration the state of the nation Pitt delivered a long speech in which all historical precedents were considered and the arguments of his opponents examined. At the end he read his resolutions:

I. That it is the opinion of this committee, That his Majesty is prevented, by his present indisposition, from coming to his parlia-

110 *Parliamentary History*, XXVII, 716.
111 *Ibid.*, pp. 717–18.
112 Thomas Moore, *Memoirs of the Life of Richard Brinsley Sheridan* (London, 1826), II, 42.
113 *Ibid.*, pp. 42–43.

ment, and from attending to public business, and that the personal exercise of the royal authority by his majesty is thereby, for the present, interrupted.

II. That it is the opinion of this committee, That it is the right and duty of the lords spiritual and temporal and commons of Great Britain, now assembled, and lawfully, fully, and freely representing all the estates of the people of this realm, to provide the means of supplying the defect of the personal exercise of the royal authority, arising from his Majesty's said indisposition, in such manner as the exigency of the case may appear to require.

Resolved, That it is the opinion of this committee, that for this purpose, and for maintaining entire the constitutional authority of the king, it is necessary, that the said lords spiritual and temporal and commons of Great Britain, should determine on the means whereby the royal assent may be given in parliament, to such a bill as may be passed by the two Houses of Parliament, respecting the exercise of the powers and authorities of the Crown, in the name, and on the behalf, of the king, during the continuance of his Majesty's present indisposition.[114]

The first resolution was agreed to unanimously; but on the second a long debate ensued, in the course of which Fox and Pitt became very personal in their remarks. The Whig leader taunted the Prime Minister with being unable to bear the idea of losing power, and hence, knowing that he had deservedly lost the confidence of the Prince of Wales, with doing all in his power to place obstructions in the way of those who were to be his successors. Pitt's answer was exactly what might have been expected. He appealed to *the House and to the country* to decide whether his conduct in the situation was dictated by a desire to retain power. Personally, he insisted that he knew of only one way to deserve the favor of the Prince of Wales and that was by doing his duty *to the King and to the country.*[115]

To many observers at the time and to many historians later it has seemed that Pitt was striving to impair the hereditary principle and that the Whigs were attempting to bolster the royal prerogative in the person of the Prince of Wales. Pitt was sneered at as a Republican, and in turn he sneered at Fox and other Whigs for their apparent change since 1783. It is true that much of this apparent inconsistency can be explained by the fact that Pitt was merely playing for time and that the Whigs expected office under

[114] *Parliamentary History,* XXVII, 746–47.
[115] *Ibid.,* pp. 771–72.

the Prince. Yet there is one passage in the speech of Pitt on December 16 which appears to have been overlooked by students of constitutional history; in it he comes out in flat opposition to the Whig view of the selection of ministers. In referring to Fox's hint that he expected to be one of the new ministers, Pitt said:

> The nation had already had experience of that right honourable gentleman, and his principles. Without meaning to use terms of reproach, or to enter into any imputation concerning his motives, it could not be denied, that they were openly and professedly active, on the ground of procuring an advantage, from the strength of party, to nominate the ministers of the crown. It could not be denied, that it was maintained as a fundamental principle, that a minister ought at all times to be so nominated.

The Minister then explained that this very principle made it necessary for Parliament to consider with great care what powers should be exercised by these advisers during the unfortunate interval of the King's indisposition. The Prince of Wales did not seem aware of the danger that men holding the views of the Whig leaders would create a permanent weight and influence which would be used against the just rights of the Crown when the King recovered. Hence Pitt concluded:

> The notice, therefore, which the right honourable gentleman in his triumph had condescended to give to the House, furnished the most irresistible reason for them deliberately to consider, lest in providing for the means of carrying on the administration, during a short and temporary interval, they might sacrifice the permanent interests of the country, in future, by laying the foundation of such measures, as might, for ever afterwards during the continuance of his Majesty's reign, obstruct the just and salutary exercise of the constitutional powers of government, in the hands of its rightful possessor, the sovereign, whom they all revered and loved.[116]

Such a decided statement on the part of Pitt can leave little doubt of his stand on the great constitutional question of responsibility of the ministers to Parliament. His affirmation shows that he believed as strongly as George III in the right of the King to appoint his own ministers and not to be compelled to take those dictated by a majority of the House of Commons. Perhaps he expressed this opinion in so decided a fashion because a long letter which he submitted to the Prince of Wales the day before this

[116] *Parliamentary History*, XXVII, 773.

speech was delivered had remained unanswered. Pitt had certainly written in a restrained and tactful manner, pointing out how often he had attempted to get in touch with the Prince and denying that he intended to go into details on the limitation of the powers of the regent in the House of Commons on the next day. Until Parliament had decided that some restrictions should be placed on these powers, Pitt assured the Prince, the details of the limitations would not be considered. If Parliament decided that some restrictions were necessary, Pitt admitted that he had certain ideas which he would have asked leave to submit to His Royal Highness:

Those ideas were in substance, that it was in my opinion highly desirable that whatever portion of the royal authority might appear necessary to be exercised during the present unhappy interval, should be vested in Y.R.H. That it should be exercised by Y.R.H. unrestrained by any Permanent Council, and with the free choice of the political servants to act under Y.R.H. Precisely what portion of royal authority ought to be given, and what ought to be withheld, I conceived it would be improper then particularly to discuss, but I added in general terms the principle on which in my opinion the distinction ought to be made, with a view to the exigency of the public service during the present interval, and to the situation of the King when His Majesty should be enabled to resume the personal exercise of the government.[117]

When the Prince did not favor him with the courtesy of an answer Pitt evidently felt justified in inserting into his speech the portions quoted above. The amendment to Pitt's second resolution which produced so many speeches was beaten by 268 to 204, after which the second and third resolutions were carried.[118] The majority of 64 against them was greater than the Whigs had expected.[119]

The discussions in the House of Lords did not rank in importance with those in the House of Commons. The debates of December 15, however, produced two declarations worth noting. The Duke of York stated that the Prince of Wales "understood too well the sacred principles which seated the House of Brunswick on the throne of Great Britain ever to assume or exercise

[117] Clements Transcripts, II, 919–22.
[118] Parliamentary History, XXVII, 778.
[119] The Countess of Minto (ed.), Life and Letters of Sir Gilbert Elliot, First Earl of Minto (London, 1874), I, 247.

any power, be his claim what it might, not derived from the will of the people, expressed by their representatives, and their Lordships in Parliament assembled."[120] On the same day Lord Thurlow, influenced by the fact that Fox was unwilling to stand by Sheridan's agreement to permit the Lord Chancellor to retain his office in case the Whigs were asked to form a ministry and by his own belief that the King would recover, made public his decision to stick with the King and Pitt. With effrontery which he alone could carry off, Thurlow, after dwelling on the many reasons why he should feel loyalty and gratitude to the King, concluded with "which whenever I forget, may God forget me."[121] This astonishing statement produced famous rejoinders from three listeners: Pitt, Burke, and Wilkes. Pitt, in exasperation, exclaimed: "Oh! the rascal." Burke, in disgust, declared: "The best thing that could happen to you." Wilkes, with satanic glee, said: "Forget you! He'll see you damned first." It must be admitted that Wilkes' contribution seems most adequate.

The ministerial resolutions having passed both houses of Parliament, Pitt turned his attention to putting the limitations on the powers of the regent into concrete form. In a letter to the Prince dated December 30 he gave a more definite account of the nature of these limitations than in his letter of December 15, which had remained unanswered. The ministers, according to the letter, believed the following four restrictions necessary: first, the Queen should have control of the King and the royal household; second, the Prince should have no right over the real or personal property of the King except in the renewal of leases; third, the Prince should be allowed to make appointments to offices only during the King's pleasure, except in cases where the law made it necessary to grant the place for life or during good behavior; and, fourth, the Prince should be permitted to create no new peers except "his Majesty's issue" who had reached the age of twenty-one.[122] The next day Pitt sent a most courteous letter to the Queen explaining the limitations passed on the power of the regent and suggesting that he wished to consult Her Majesty's pleasure on questions of the management of the royal household.[123]

The reply which the Whig leaders drew up, dated January 2,

---

[120] *Parliamentary History*, XXVII, 678.
[121] *Ibid.*, p. 680.
[122] *The Speeches of William Pitt* (London, 1808), 2d edition, I, 298.
[123] Pitt MSS, 101, December 31, 1788.

1789, for the Prince to send to Pitt through the Lord Chancellor, seems to have been the product of the joint efforts of Burke, Loughborough, and Sheridan.[124] In the main the Prince reserved judgment until the outlines of the proposed plan should be sent for his approbation and preferred to comment only generally on the heads communicated to him. Three objections offered by the authors are worth noting. First, the Prince characterized the plan as

A project for dividing the Royal Family from each other, for separating the court from the state; and therefore, by disjoining government from its natural and accustomed support, a scheme for disconnecting the authority to command service, from the power of animating it by reward; and for alloting to the Prince all the invidious duties of government, without the means of softening them to the public, by any one act of grace, favour, or benignity.[125]

Second, the Prince is made to state that

holding as he does that it is the undoubted and fundamental principle of the constitution, that the powers and prerogatives of the crown are vested there, as a trust for the benefit of the people; and that they are sacred only as they are necessary to the preservation of that poise and balance of the constitution, which experience has proved to be the true security of the liberty of the subject—must be allowed to observe, that the plea of public utility ought to be strong, manifest and urgent, which calls for the extinction or suspension of any one of those essential rights in the supreme power, or its representative; or which can justify the Prince in consenting, that in his person, an experiment shall be made to ascertain with how small a portion of the kingly power the executive government of this country may be carried on [126]

Third, on the matter of alienation of the royal property the Prince was able to take a tone of injured indignation and to make a malicious thrust at Pitt in his concluding sentence:

Upon that part of the plan which regards the King's real and personal property, the Prince feels himself compelled to remark, that it was not necessary for Mr. Pitt, nor proper, to suggest to the Prince the restraint he proposes against the Prince's granting away the King's real and personal property. The Prince does not conceive, that, during the King's life, he is, by law, entitled to make any such grant; and

[124] J. H. Rose, *Life of William Pitt*, I, 421.
[125] *The Speeches of William Pitt*, I, 300.
[126] *Ibid.*, p. 301.

he is sure, that he has never shewn the smallest inclination to possess any such power. But it remains with Mr. Pitt to consider the eventual interests of the Royal Family, and to provide a proper and natural security against the mismanagement of them by others.[127]

It is unnecessary to go into the details of the Parliamentary debates on the restriction of the powers of the regent; for speeches are more or less an amplification of the points brought out in these letters. On January 16 Pitt moved a series of resolutions in which the Prince of Wales was to be made regent with the restrictions mentioned in his letter of December 30. Little new was brought out in the long speeches except Pitt's frank declaration of the reasons why the regent should not be allowed to create new peers. There were, in his opinion, three grounds for entrusting the creation of peers to the Crown, and none of them was applicable to the present case. These were: first, to enable the King to counteract the influence of a factious cabal which might have acquired a predominant position in the House of Lords; second, to enable him to reward eminent merit; and, third, to enable him to make allowances for the fluctuation of property and wealth by raising men of great landed interest to the peerage.[128] The relative strength of the government and opposition was shown by the vote on this resolution to restrain the Prince, as regent, from creating new peers. Pitt's resolution was passed by 216 to 159.[129] After the resolutions had been agreed to by both houses, Pitt on February 5 introduced his Regency Bill in the Commons. Eventually it passed the third reading on February 13, at which time a clause was introduced which limited to three years the restriction on the creation of peers,[130] and was then sent up to the Lords. On February 19, however, after the second reading in the House of Lords, Lord Thurlow announced that the King was far advanced on the road to recovery. The House of Lords immediately adjourned, and all further proceedings on the bill were, naturally, suspended.

The question of course arises what would have been the result had the bill passed and had the Prince of Wales become regent even for a short time? Without doubt Pitt and the other ministers would have been removed and Fox and the Whigs placed

---

127 *The Speeches of William Pitt,* I, 301–2.
128 *Parliamentary History,* XXVII, 942–44.
129 *Ibid.,* p. 1003.
130 *Ibid.,* pp. 1249–58; Tomline, *Memoirs of the Life of William Pitt,* II, 479.

in charge of the government. Both Whigs and other friends of
the Prince had spent some time in attempting to decide on the
division of offices; but since this ministry did not materialize, it is
unnecessary to go into the details of the proposed distribution.
The Prince would have been hobbled to a considerable extent by
the restrictions on creating peers and on making permanent appointments to offices, and by the fact that the Great Seal had been
entrusted to a Commission.[131] But it is doubtful if even the
handicaps of being unable to fill the Lords with his own creations
or of being unable to obstruct legislation, could have prevented
the Prince from controlling the government. The ability of the
Whig leaders combined with his restricted powers would almost
certainly have been enough to insure Pitt's overthrow. The Prime
Minister, himself, did not expect to survive, as his plans to return
to his profession as a barrister clearly indicate.

The practical certainty of this overthrow was not due to the
unpopularity of the King or of Pitt. The amazing joy shown by
the public on the recovery of George III is eloquent proof of the
grip which the ruler had upon the affections of his subjects. The
popularity of Pitt was probably even greater as the reluctant admissions of his opponents prove. Sir Gilbert Elliot in the course
of the December debates wrote to his wife complaining that the
people did not resent the restrictions on the powers of the Prince
as regent.

But I see no reason to suppose the blind will be restored to light by
this, as their eyes have continued shut to so many instances of a
similar kind. Pitt is the only object the nation can perceive, and the
only thing they think valuable in the world; and I rather think they
would be content and pleased to set aside the whole Royal Family,
with the Crown and both Houses of Parliament, if they could keep
him by it.[132]

In addition, the Prince and such Whigs as Fox, Burke, and
Sheridan were as unpopular as the King and Pitt were popular.
The solution of this apparently puzzling situation lies in the English Constitution of the eighteenth century. The position in which
Pitt found himself when with the backing of a majority of the
two houses, the favor of the King at the time of the latter's col-
lapse, and his enormous popularity outside Parliament he would
have been unable to stand against the weak and self-indulgent

[131] J. H. Rose, *op. cit.*, I, 422–23.
[132] The Countess of Minto, *Life and Letters of Sir Gilbert Elliot*, I, 248.

young regent, even with the severe restrictions which the ministry had imposed, is a sufficient answer to historians who attempt to prove that he was a "responsible" Prime Minister of the nineteenth-century model.

The uncertain element in the situation during this crisis of 1788–89 was the recovery of the King. Had the physicians been overwhelming in their verdict that the King would recover, would die, or would remain permanently insane, there could have been no doubt as to the outcome. In case of the first possibility the Prince and Whigs would scarcely have considered it worth while to attempt to take over the government; and in the case of the second and third, it would have been equally futile for Pitt to have delayed as he did in the hope that the King would recover. Thus peers, placemen, and members of Parliament were placed in a dilemma. Many were unwilling to commit themselves, and others were equally reluctant to desert the old King or to be among those who failed to hail the rising sun. Despite the uncertainty involved the number who deserted the King and Pitt was quite astounding. It shows what the exodus would have been if certainty of the permanence of the King's incapacity could have been assured.

The question naturally arises as to why Pitt with his popularity outside Parliament and his control of a majority in both houses, which remained steadfast even during the crisis, did not consider defying the Prince and the Whigs. A coalition of the Rockingham and Shelburne Whigs in 1782 and of the followers of North and Fox in 1783 had forced George III to accept a ministry in each case of which he heartily disapproved. Why did not Pitt keep his majority, even if he were turned out of office, and make it impossible for the government to be carried on as the Fox-North Coalition had done in 1783? The answer is found in a paper dated May 1, 1788, which was discovered in the papers of one of Pitt's private secretaries.[133] According to this paper the House of Commons could be divided into four groups: First, the "party of the Crown," made up of "all those who would probably support His Majesty's Government under any minister not peculiarly unpopular," was estimated at 185 members; second, "the independent or unconnected members of the House," at 108; third, the followers of Fox, at 138; and, fourth, the followers of

[133] Lord Rosebery, *Pitt* (London: The Macmillan Company, Ltd., 1923), p. 78.

Pitt, at 52.[134] How little even these fifty-two could be counted on was shown by the statement in the same paper that "of this party, were there a new Parliament and Mr. P. no longer to continue minister not above twenty would be returned."[135] These figures show the real weakness of the position of Pitt. He relied upon the King's 185 janissaries and on a substantial number of independents to keep his government going. The latter he held by oratory or statesmanship. In case he were turned out of office, how many of the three groups outside of the followers of Fox could Pitt hope to hold? The answer depends upon how many of the 185 would feel that a government of Portland and Fox was "peculiarly unpopular," and upon whether or not Pitt's tactics in opposition would seem to the independents as sound as when he was Prime Minister. Certainly if a general election had been held in the near future, Pitt, despite his great popularity outside Parliament, would have lost heavily as a result. With the enormous influence which the Crown wielded plus the backing of the Whig magnates a comfortable majority could have been secured for the government of the Whigs. Popularity outside Parliament had little influence in the unreformed House of Commons of the eighteenth century, as the careers of Pitt's father before 1756 and of John Wilkes had proved conclusively. In 1784 Pitt had the support of Jenkinson, the King's best "Friend," and of the East India Company. In an election held after Portland and Fox came into office some substitute for Jenkinson would have represented the Prince, and the East India Company would in all probability have been with the new ministry, since they had split with Pitt earlier in 1788 over the responsibility for transporting troops to India. Unquestionably, all these points were perfectly clear to Pitt, and hence it is small wonder that he planned to resume his work as a barrister.

After several adjournments both houses met on March 10. The speech which was read by Lord Thurlow was cautiously worded; and in both houses addresses were voted to the King and Queen. In the addresses and the debates which followed, considerable caution was shown by both the ministry and the Opposition. No such restraint, however, was shown by the people of London. It is a vivid picture which Wraxall paints of the city on the night of March 10:

[134] *Ibid.*, p. 78.
[135] *Ibid.*, pp. 78–79.

These legislative deliberations were followed on the same night by the most brilliant as well as the most universal exhibition of national loyalty and joy ever witnessed in England. It originated not with the police nor with the Government, but with the people, and was the genuine tribute of their affection. No efforts of despotism could indeed have enforced it. London displayed a blaze of light from one extremity to the other; the illuminations extending, without metaphor, from Hampstead and Highgate to Clapham, and even as far as Tooting, while the vast distance between Greenwich and Kensington presented the same dazzling appearance. Even the elements seemed to favour the spectacle, for the weather, though cold, was dry. Nor were the opulent and the middle orders the only classes who came conspicuously forward on this occasion. The poorest mechanics contributed their proportion, and instances were exhibited of cobblers' stalls decorated with one or two farthing candles.[136]

On April 23 a Thanksgiving service was held at St. Paul's Cathedral and the ovation given the King seems to have touched the heart of the not too susceptible monarch. George III had seen the same adulation bestowed on the Earl of Chatham and John Wilkes, but he appears not to have allowed even this memory to interfere with the satisfaction which he enjoyed from the demonstrations of March 10 and April 23. A few days after the service he gave his consent to having the sermon preached on this occasion published; or, as he quaintly worded it: "The proper mode of directing the Bishop of London to print the sermon he preached at St. Paul's on the Thanksgiving seems to be for Lord Sydney to intimate to the Archbishop of Canterbury that it is My desire He should express to the Bishop of London my wish that this Sermon may be published."[137]

The natural conclusion to this chapter is the attitude taken by George III toward the events which occurred during his illness and the action that he took when he recovered. Since the Queen, Pitt, and Thurlow very naturally got the ear of the King first, the actions of the Prince and the Whigs were not placed in any too favorable a light. There appears to have been a tacit agreement all around not to wash any more dirty linen before the King than was absolutely necessary; but the result of washing this irreducible minimum was to widen the breach between the King and the Prince, to give George III an even lower opinion of Fox, and to

[136] Wheatley, *Memoirs of Wraxall,* V, 336.
[137] Clements Transcripts, II, 993.

increase enormously the veiled hostility of Pitt and Thurlow. The
most significant action of the King was his keen interest in the
debates and divisions on the Regency question; for he read carefully the speeches and examined painstakingly the list of members
who voted on each side of every important division.[138] As soon
as George III acted thus, it was clear that he was once more
normal. His attitude toward members of both houses would for
some time in the future be regulated by these speeches and votes.

In some respects the months following the recovery of the
King marked the high-water point in the career of both George III
and Pitt. Certainly it was the point of highest popularity for
both, and it appeared to mark the beginning of a period of even
more satisfactory relations between the Crown and the Prime
Minister than the one which had preceded the Regency Crisis.
For patriotic and personal reasons the King and the Minister felt
the necessity of closer co-operation. Each felt the danger to the
position of the country in case the Prince and Whigs were put in
full charge. The King appreciated the tremendous grip which
Pitt had upon public opinion; and the Minister appreciated how
weak his apparently strong position was without the support of
the Crown. All that was necessary was that George III and Pitt
should not disagree on any fundamental principle which would
cause the Minister to resign or the King to insist upon his retirement. The reason that the years which followed did not measure
up to the expectations of the post-crisis period is found in events
across the channel. On May 4 the Estates General met in Paris,
and the tremendous upheaval which followed this first step in the
French Revolution was to ruin most of the good effects and to
force the abandonment of many of the most worth-while policies
upon which the King and his minister had agreed from 1783 to
1789.

[138] *Memoirs of Wraxall*, V, 328.

VI. THE YEARS OF LOST OPPORTUNITY, 1789 TO 1793

The years covered by this chapter are among the most momentous in the history of modern Europe, yet from the points of view of the relations of George III and Pitt and of the changes in the Constitution they are years of comparative insignificance. So far as Pitt's financial and internal policies are concerned there is no break between 1785 and the outbreak of the war with France in 1793; and his foreign policy was a continuation of that of the years preceding 1789. The Regency Crisis of 1788–89 was really a sharp peak in the midst of the comparatively smooth and placid plain of the years 1785 to 1793.

There are, however, certain decided characteristics which distinguish the relationship of the King and his Minister before and after 1789. From the point of view of the King the change is best expressed in the letter which George III wrote to Pitt on February 23, 1789, at the time of his recovery. The King states that he will be unable to enter into the pressure of business and adds: . . . . "indeed for the rest of my life shall expect others to fulfill the duties of their employments, and only keep that superintending eye which can be effected without labour or fatigue."[1] This sentence is the guide to the relationship between the King and his ministers during the remainder of his active life. After his recovery George III did not take the active part in the government that he had earlier, and that, for two reasons: first, he felt such confidence in Pitt after the Regency Crisis and was so convinced that their views were essentially the same on nearly all important issues that he believed the careful attention which he had given to details in the first twenty-eight years of his reign was no longer required, and, second, he wished to conserve his energy in order to prevent a repetition of the illness of 1788. Such a change in attitude does not necessarily mean a significant constitutional change. George III's view of the Constitution did not alter one iota: he still believed in the right of the King to choose his own ministers and to veto bills passed by both houses. The same change in the attitude of the ruler might have taken place in any other kingdom of Europe at that time or during the

[1] Earl Stanhope, *Life of the Right Honourable William Pitt* (London, 1861–62), III, vii.

reign of any sovereign in England after 1689. A king who found a minister more competent than average and who found himself wearied after years of active participation in the government might well decide to watch over only major policies and leave the detailed work to this trustworthy political servant. Only if the ruler failed to reclaim a right to more active participation or his successor neglected to assume such a role would there be much resulting danger of a significant constitutional change. In such a case an institution might well develop which through prescriptive or traditional right would take over the actual control of the government. George III made it perfectly clear by his actions before 1788 and from 1801 to 1806 that he had no intention of surrendering any prerogative of the Crown. He was as hostile to the novel idea of cabinet solidarity and responsibility in 1806 as he had been at the time the Duke of Portland suggested it to him in 1783. Thus the increased work which the King piled on the backs of his ministers after 1789 should be interpreted as a sign of his confidence in them and of his fears concerning his own health rather than as the beginning of a Tory party which was to introduce the principles of party supremacy acting through a unified ministry and cabinet.

Despite the fact that George III announced and apparently made good his determination to play a supervisory role, it is interesting to note that this role produced no change in any one of Pitt's policies discussed at length in the preceding chapter. This statement applies to his financial policy, to his attitude toward the slave trade, Parliamentary reform, and modification of the Test and Corporation acts, and to his foreign policy. An examination of these topics and of the changes in the cabinet and ministry whereby Pitt was able to secure subordinates more to his liking is the subject of this chapter.

Pitt's financial policy can be dismissed shortly as a successful continuation of the work carried on from 1784 to 1789. Probably in no other sphere of public activity did he maintain so consistently the approval of Parliament, of public opinion, and of the King. Since the main principles of his policy have been discussed already, this phase of his activities as a minister need not be dwelt upon in this chapter.

The most important topic to be considered during these years is the attitude which Pitt took toward the three reform measures listed above; for it is in matters of internal rather than of foreign policy, at least until late in 1792, that the French Revolution most affected England. Generally speaking, during the first two years the English people took a favorable attitude toward the Revolution. Especially did the events of 1789 meet either with the warm approval or with the cautious suspended judgment of the English people. The meeting of the Estates General on May 4, the Oath of the Tennis Court on June 20, the Royal Session of June 23, the storming of the Bastille on July 14, the abolition of the worst of the feudal customs on August 4, and the march on Versailles of the mob on October 5–6, all met with approval or reticence. Little criticism was heard in England at this time; and many members of the nobility, many country gentlemen, and many of the middle class expressed their outright approbation. Since no record has come down of the attitude of the great mass of the lower classes in cities and country, it is impossible to speak of their point of view with certainty. But both prominent and obscure members of the upper and middle classes have left an abundant record in their letters and diaries. Many of the poets and literary men of the period were especially enthusiastic.

The reasons for this approbation varied. Of course, some nationally minded Englishmen were glad to see France embarrassed by this revolution and thus incapacitated, for the time being, as an enemy; and others were glad to see retribution overtake France as a punishment for assisting the American Colonies. It is highly probable that Pitt should be listed among the first group and George III among the second. But the French Revolution was, everything considered, a great encouragement to those who believed in change.[2] Reformers of all kinds were vastly pleased. The prosperity of the seventeen-eighties had deadened the interest in and the enthusiasm for many of the reforms previously advocated. Now the reformers, who were especially encouraged by the example of France, were those interested in the slave trade, in Parliamentary reform, and in modification of the Test and Corporation acts; and they set to work with new enthusiasm.

It is because he failed to take advantage of this renewed zeal for highly desirable changes that Pitt's sincerity as a reformer is open to question. It was his defense at the time and is that of his biographers since that he abandoned reform in 1785 because

[2] Philip Anthony Brown, *The French Revolution in English History* (London: Crosby Lockwood and Son, 1918), p. 29.

of lack of interest in the country. This stand applied particularly
to Parliamentary reform. Beginning in 1793 he argued that
important reforms should not be passed, and under certain conditions not even advocated, while the country was at war. Both
arguments might disgust a fervent reformer, but certainly the
two are mildly defensible and not inconsistent. But neither of
these arguments can apply to Pitt's conduct from 1789 to 1793.
The enthusiasm which he missed in 1785 was now present; and
the war which he feared after 1793 was not threatening. In fact,
France was considered much less of a menace during these four
years than during the six preceding ones, because there was a
general feeling, which Pitt seems to have shared, that internal
dissension would greatly weaken the part which the Bourbon
monarchy could play in European affairs in the immediate future.
Thus every ingredient, except his own willingness, was present
for Pitt to prove his sincerity as a real reformer. But it is often
argued that because the King and the majority of his cabinet and
of both houses of Parliament were opposed to the three great
reforms agitated during these years Pitt was helpless. Such an
argument does not explain why he actually opposed both the
modification of the Test and Corporation acts and any Parliamentary reform during these years, even though he supported the
abolition of the slave trade with great fervor as a private member.
On the other hand, if Pitt were anxious to see reforms other than
the abolition of the slave trade carried through and was held back
by lack of power and influence, nothing could prove more effectively how far from being a modern prime minister he actually
was. His attitude on the slave trade shows him to have been a
sincere reformer without the power to enforce his will and
without the willingness to risk his position by an ultimatum; and
that on Parliamentary reform and modification of the Test and
Corporation acts shows him to have been indifferent.

The question of the abolition of the slave trade was taken up
in Parliament soon after the recovery of the King. On May 12,
1789, Wilberforce, after a very powerful and stirring speech,
moved the adoption of twelve resolutions. During the intervening year, sufficient testimony had been taken by the Privy
Council to render invalid the excuse of inadequate knowledge.
Wilberforce's speech[3] described vividly the way in which the

[3] *Parliamentary History*, XXVIII, 41–67.

slave trade was carried on along the west coast of Africa, the effects on the civilization of the natives, the horrors of the middle passage, the loss of life among both slaves and seamen, and the lack of natural increase in slaves on the islands of the West Indies. He argued that the slave owners would suffer no loss from a discontinuance of the trade and that the merchants could readily turn to transporting other products of the west coast of Africa than human cargo. The arguments offered in answer to Wilberforce were the ones used until abolition passed in 1807: that the City of London would be ruined without this trade; that Parliament had no right to dictate to plantation owners in the West Indies; that the cruelties practiced in Africa were not due to the slave trade; that the slaves in the plantations were not badly treated; and that other countries, notably France, would merely take over the trade in place of England. The argument which proved decisive, however, was one offered by Viscount Maitland that the House of Commons should not give up its historic right of hearing evidence given at their own bar instead of that given before the Privy Council. As a result the House voted to hear the evidence again. After hearing evidence for several days the question was again postponed until the next session. To reassure Wilberforce a motion was passed that the Commons, early in the next session, would consider the circumstances of the slave trade.[4] Thus although Pitt, Fox, and Burke warmly supported the twelve resolutions of Wilberforce, postponement until the next session could not be avoided. It is true that the temporary gain of 1788 was not lost, for the Dolben Act for regulating certain phases of the trade was amended and continued.[5]

The next session was taken up with examining witnesses. The enemies of abolition offered their evidence first and then attempted to induce the House to vote on the question without allowing the friends of the movement to present their evidence. Fortunately such an unfair political trick failed and Wilberforce and the abolitionists were allowed to bring in witnesses on their side. The examination of witnesses progressed so slowly, however, that no debate was held on the question during the session of 1790. After the general election of that year the matter was brought up in the first session of the new Parliament. On April 18, 1791, Wilberforce moved for "leave to bring in a

[4] R. Coupland, *Wilberforce* (Oxford: Clarendon Press, 1923), pp. 133–34.
[5] *Ibid.*, p. 134.

Bill to prevent the further importation of Slaves into the British colonies in the West Indies."[6] The debate which followed had much in common with the one of 1789. Wilberforce, Pitt, and Fox all made long speeches favoring abolition, and Burke contented himself with a much shorter effort. Although the oratory was on one side, the votes were on the other. "Property, precedent, prescription—these were stronger forces than Pitt's justice or Fox's humanity; and the strongest of them was property."[7] Finally early in the morning of April 20 Wilberforce's motion was beaten by 163 to 88.[8]

Before the question of abolition could be brought up again the issue was further complicated by the action of the French. The part which France played in postponing the abolition in England is an interesting one. At first the opponents of the movement argued against abolition on the grounds that France would take over the trade, and hence no improvement would take place on the coast of West Africa, in the middle passage, or in the lot of the slaves in the West Indies. On May 15, 1791, however, the National Assembly in France not only liberated all slaves in French colonies but gave them full rights of citizenship as well. The results in many parts of the French Empire were disastrous. In St. Domingo the freed slaves rose and wrecked the cities and plantations. The news from St. Domingo furnished the opponents of abolition with as effective an argument against the French as the threatened loss of the trade had earlier. Wilberforce was strongly advised not to bring up the question in Parliament during the session of 1792 because of the fact that public opinion was greatly inflamed over the excesses in St. Domingo. Pitt was among those who believed in postponement, for Wilberforce stated that the Prime Minister "threw out against Slave Motion, on St. Domingo account." Here we see Pitt's fundamental weakness as a reformer. The old "this is not the time" argument of a faltering and lukewarm advocate of change seemed likely to bring about a reversal of the Minister's stand on the slave trade as it had already done on Parliamentary reform.

Wilberforce, however, persisted in bringing the motion forward. On April 2, 1792, after 508 petitions had been presented praying for the abolition of the slave trade, he moved: "That it is the opinion of this committee, that the trade carried on by

[6] *Parliamentary History*, XXIX, 278.
[7] Coupland, *op. cit.*, p. 143.   [8] *Parliamentary History*, XXIX, 359.

British subjects, for the purpose of procuring slaves from Africa, ought to be abolished."[9] Wilberforce emphasized the horrors of various practices and his opponents the danger of producing atrocities like those of St. Domingo. An amendment by Dundas insured the defeat of Wilberforce's proposal. Pitt's right-hand man professed to favor gradual rather than immediate total abolition, and for the methods of the abolitionists he would substitute the breeding of Negroes in the West Indies, the gradual ending of hereditary slavery, the improvement in the conditions of slaves, and education for their children.[10] These proposals of Dundas were clever enough from a political point of view, for they salved the consciences of the uneasy and postponed immediate abolition. In fact he appealed to moderate men to follow him; and his call did not remain unanswered, as both the subsequent speeches and division were to show.

The most interesting part of the evening's debate turned on the stand taken by Pitt, who had been opposed to having the subject considered at this time. He found the man who had been his closest personal friend, Wilberforce, and the man who was his closest political associate, Dundas, on opposite sides of the question; and since 1785 the influence of the latter appeared to have increased and that of the former to have decreased. It was near the break of dawn and after listening for hours to the speeches on both sides that Pitt rose to divulge his sentiments. Although exhausted by listening for so many hours he gave what was considered by many who were present the finest speech he ever delivered. If Pitt's weakness as a reformer lay in his unwillingness to take action unless the signs seemed very propitious, his strength lay in his ability to make a magnificent presentation of his case in the House of Commons. With that unwillingness to agree absolutely with a member of the opposition, to which attention has so often been called, Pitt emphasized the fact at the beginning of his speech that he did not agree with all the criticisms which Fox had bestowed upon Dundas and upon Speaker Addington, who had supported the latter's amendment. Next Pitt made it clear that he believed it to be a matter for congratulation that all were now agreed on abolition and that the issue had now narrowed down to one of the time when it should take place. The question to be determined, then, was

9 *Parliamentary History*, XXIX, 1073.
10 Coupland, *op. cit.*, p. 164.

whether immediate or gradual abolition would effect this object in the shortest time and the surest manner. He proposed to treat the subject from the points of view of expediency, of the infringement on legal inheritance, and of the relations of England and Africa.

The test which Pitt proposed to apply for expediency was "that whatever tends most speedily and effectually to meliorate the condition of the slaves, is undoubtedly, on the ground of expediency, leaving justice out of the question, the main object to be pursued."[11] He held that the only effective method of improving the conditions of the slaves already on the islands was to stop importation at once. The slaves already in the islands would then be treated with greater care and the threatened shortage of labor would be solved in two ways: by a natural increase in the population, which was impossible under the existing system, and by increased efficiency on the part of the slaves working under improved conditions. In answer to their warning of inviting a repetition of the atrocities of St. Domingo in the British islands, Pitt was able to point out to the conservatives how much more dangerous were the newly arrived slaves than ones who had been slaves for some time.

Pitt next took up the argument of Dundas that to interfere in the slave trade would be an invasion of the legal heritage of the West Indian planters. In answer he pointed out that the plan which Dundas offered was equally an invasion, since it mattered not whether the change came at once or gradually. He reserved his heavy artillery, however, for the real weakness of this argument. Parliamentary sanction to a commercial measure did not mean that it was forever removed from the jurisdiction of the legislature; for such a position, if made effective, would prevent Parliament from ever passing a new regulation contrary to an existing one. He concluded this argument with:

If the laws respecting the slave-trade imply a contract for its perpetual continuance, I will venture to say, there does not pass a year without some act, equally pledging the faith of parliament to the perpetuating of some other branch of commerce. In short, I repeat my observation, that no new tax can be imposed, much less can any prohibitory duty be ever laid on any branch of trade, that has before been regulated by parliament, if this principle be once admitted.[12]

[11] *Parliamentary History*, XXIX, 1141.
[12] *Ibid.*, p. 1146.

Pitt had now finished with expediency and legal dialectic, and next turned to justice. It is the latter part of his speech dealing with what he called the incurable injustice to Africa which gave his speech such fame. Every sentence from this point is worth quoting, but only a few extracts can be given:

Instead of any fair change of commodities; instead of conveying to them, from this highly favoured land, any means of improvement, you carry with you that noxious plant by which everything is withered and blasted; under whose shade nothing that is useful or profitable to Africa will ever flourish or take root. Long as that continent has been known to navigators, the extreme line and boundaries of its coasts is all with which Europe is yet become acquainted; while other countries in the same parallel of latitude, through a happier system of intercourse, have reaped the benefits of a mutually beneficial commerce. But as to the whole interior of that continent you are, by your own principles of commerce, as yet entirely shut out: Africa is known to you only in its skirts. Yet even there you are able to infuse a poison that spreads its contagious effects from one end of it to the other, which penetrates to its very center, corrupting every part to which it reaches. You there subvert the whole order of nature; you aggravate every natural barbarity, and furnish to every man living on that continent, motives for committing, under the name and pretext of commerce, acts of perpetual violence and perfidy against his neighbour.

Thus, Sir, has the perversion of British commerce carried misery instead of happiness to one whole quarter of the globe. False to the very principles of trade, misguided in our policy, and unmindful of our duty, what astonishing—I had almost said, what *irreparable* mischief, have we brought upon that Continent! I would apply this thought to the present question. How shall we ever repair this mischief? How shall we hope to obtain, if it be possible, forgiveness from Heaven for those enormous evils we have committed, if we refuse to make use of those means which the mercy of Providence hath still reserved to us for wiping away the guilt and shame with which we are now covered? If we refuse even this degree of compensation, if, knowing the miseries we have caused, we refuse even now to put a stop to them, how greatly aggravated will be the guilt of Great Britain! and what a blot will the history of these transactions forever be in the history of this country! Shall we then DELAY to repair these injuries, and to begin rendering this justice to Africa? Shall we not count the days and hours that are suffered to intervene and to delay the accomplishment of such a work? Reflect, what an immense object is before you—what an object for a nation to have in view, and to have a prospect, under the favour of Providence, of being now permitted to attain! I think the house will agree with me in cherishing the ardent wish to enter without delay upon the measures necessary for these great ends: and I am sure that the immediate abolition is the first, the principal, the most indispensable act of policy, of duty, and of justice, that the legislator of this country, has to take, if it is indeed their wish to secure those important objects to which I have alluded, and which we are bound to pursue by the most solemn obligations.[13]

Pitt concluded with an inspired description of the possibilities of civilizing Africa and an appeal to his listeners to take the first step in this direction by immediate abolition of the slave trade.

Despite the tremendous effect which this appeal made to the listeners Dundas's amendment for inserting in the original motion the word "gradually" was passed by 193 to 125; and the amended motion was next carried by 230 to 85.[14] Before the question was again brought up in Parliament the war with France had broken out and this postponed for years any hope of a successful conclusion.

Upon no other issue during these years does Pitt show so strikingly his strength and his weakness. The doubts which were openly expressed as to his sincerity before this speech were certainly dispelled as a result of it. If, then, he felt so deeply on this subject why did he not do something besides making a wonderful appeal? As stated earlier in the chapter, he was opposed by the King, the majority of the cabinet and ministry, and the majority of both houses of Parliament. Yet this opposition is not enough to explain why he opposed Wilberforce's bringing up the question in Parliament. No single explanation seems adequate. One factor contributing to Pitt's apparently contradictory conduct was the enormous amount of work that his office required. This in part prevented him from taking the active part in an agitation which Wilberforce, for example, took in the abolition movement and at the same time did not prevent such a fine individual effort as his great speech. Another question which must be considered, if not answered, is why Pitt was unable to secure the passage of such a measure through Parliament and the subsequent assent of the King, when the Fox-Grenville ministry succeeded in doing so in 1806–1807. In part this difference may be explained by changed conditions in the

---

[13] *The Speeches of the Right Honourable William Pitt in the House of Commons* (London, 1808), I, 385–86.   [14] *Parliamentary History*, XXIX, 1158.

attitude toward the slave trade and a weakening of the opposition of George III. It would seem, however, that the most significant reason for Pitt's obvious inability to put through a reform in which he was so keenly interested lay in his political position. His weakness was twofold: first, in the understanding which he had with George III that each minister was allowed freedom of action on issues in which unanimity was lacking; and, second, in the comparatively small personal following which, despite his great popularity outside Parliament and with the independent members of Parliament, he had in the House of Commons. Thus the position of Pitt was in reality weaker than that of a Whig ministry would have been at this time, because the Whigs would not have permitted the exercise of so much personal freedom by individual members of the government, would not have felt any qualms at bringing pressure to bear on the King, and would have had far more members upon whose votes they could have relied than the meager number which supported Pitt.

Turning to the question of Parliamentary reform during the years 1789 to 1793, we find that Pitt had become a cooled reformer. The effect of the French Revolution on Parliamentary Reform was not unlike that on the slave trade. Exactly as the Rights of Man encouraged abolitionists in England and as the results of emancipation in the French West Indies made their task more difficult, so did the first steps in France toward constitutional government encourage Parliamentary reformers in England and the events, especially beginning in 1791, blight the hopes of reform. Certain phases of the agitation for Parliamentary reform cannot be separated from the movement to modify the Test and Corporation acts. Part of this close relationship was due to the fact that prominent Nonconformists were interested in both reforms. Pitt's attitude toward the two movements differed: he claimed still to believe in Parliamentary reform and alleged that he would himself bring in a reform bill some time in the future; and he was, as before the King's illness, still mildly hostile or indifferent to modification of the Test and Corporations acts.

The organizations which bridged the gap between the suspension of the Society for Promoting Constitutional Information in 1784 and its revival in 1791 were the Revolution societies. These societies sprang up in many parts of England as the centenary of 1688 approached; and permanent organizations appear to have grown out of the practice of groups of people meeting

annually on November 4 or 5 to celebrate the Revolution of 1688
by a public dinner. In many places these annual dinners laid the
foundations for permanent institutions. In both Leicester and
London the societies became linked with the cause of Parliamentary reform; but in many other places they appear to have
merely combined civic pride, political aphorisms, and conviviality.
In the London Revolution Society an important part was played
by prominent Dissenting politicians and distinguished members
of the advanced wing of the Whigs.[15] Thus when the invigor-
ating achievements of the first months of the French Revolution
affected England, it was only natural that they should influence
these Revolution societies. At the annual meeting of the London
Society in November 1789 the events in France received considerable attention; and Dr. Price, the well-known Unitarian
minister who had played an important part in Pitt's sinking
fund scheme, first delivered a sermon and later moved an address,
which was unanimously adopted, congratulating the French
National Assembly on the victory of justice and liberty over
arbitrary power.[16] In the course of his sermon he brought out
that liberty as achieved by the Revolution of 1688 had left two
great deficiencies to be made up: the removal of the Test and
Corporation acts, and the establishment of more equitable representation. Until these two were supplied, toleration and political
liberty would be incomplete. Because Burke in his famous
Reflections on the French Revolution chose to single out the
sermon for the subject of his reply, this particular meeting is the
best known of any event in the history of the various Revolution
societies.

It is unnecessary at this point to go into the details of the
influence which Burke's *Reflections,* published on October 31,
1790, had upon English public opinion.[17] The evidence is fully
as strong that Burke effected no vital change in English opinion
concerning the French Revolution as that he converted the country to his side. It seems likely that Burke became popular when
members of all classes began to react against what they considered
the excesses of the Revolution and found in his *Reflections* their
own opinions vividly phrased. The meeting of November 4
marked the beginning of the friendly intercourse between the

---

[15] P. A. Brown, *op. cit.,* p. 25. [16] *Ibid.,* p. 30.

[17] *Ibid.,* chapter iv; G. S. Veitch, *The Genesis of Parliamentary Reform*
(London, 1913), chapters v–viii.

English democrats and the French revolutionists; and the address which Price moved and which was unanimously adopted by the society was warmly received by the National Assembly in France. In the letters of thanks which were exchanged between representatives of the society and the National Assembly emphasis was placed on "the reverence for constitutional monarchy and the fair dream of universal peace." But the significance of this exchange of good will was later to be much misinterpreted:

The meaning of the name of the Revolution Society was misunderstood, and the society came to be erroneously regarded, both in France and England, as the Society of the French Revolution. Such a mistake may well be excused in the unenlightened, but it had serious consequences. When the tide of opinion in England turned against the Revolution, people tended to saddle the society with all its errors, and to visit the members of the society with the same condemnation as the revolutionists in France. The cause of reform was discredited in England because reformers were thought to approve of violence in France. How misleading this view was can best be realised by examining the correspondence of the Revolution Society and the known opinions of their French correspondents.[18]

The correspondence between the London Revolution Society and popular societies in France seems to have lasted until February 1792. But by that time the vigor of the reform movement had passed to the revived Society for Promoting Constitutional Information and to two new societies, the London Corresponding Society and the Society of the Friends of the People.

The London Corresponding Society was founded on January 25, 1792, by a group of men who had been meeting since the previous autumn for the purpose of agitating for the reform of Parliament. Stress was placed on the fact that the organization was to represent the unrepresented; for throughout its history the society was made up largely of workingmen, and the secretary and treasurer of the society was a Scotsman named Thomas Hardy who had a shoemaker's business at No. 9 Piccadilly.[19] The founders believed that the heavy burden of taxation was imposed by Parliament for the benefit of a few hundred gentlemen and that the remedy lay in equal representation and the right of every individual to share in the government.[20] Each member contributed a penny as a weekly subscription, and the money was

18 Veitch, *op. cit.*, p. 125.
19 P. A. Brown, *op. cit.*, pp. 55–56.   20 *Ibid.*, p. 56.

used largely in corresponding with similar societies which had grown up in London and in other cities.[21] The society was first organized into divisions of thirty members each, and an additional unit was to be created when each old one reached sixty. By the end of July, 1792, twelve divisions were flourishing in London. An estimate of the number in the Corresponding Society varies; for the fall of 1792 it was placed at 3,000 by one writer[22] and at from 5,000 to 10,000 by another.[23]

The Society of the Friends of the People, founded in April 1792, was very different in personnel from that of the London Corresponding Society. The nucleus was the cream of the young Foxite Whigs,[24] although Fox himself did not join. It was made up of such well-known peers as Lauderdale, Buchan, and Kinnaird and of such prominent commoners as Sheridan, Francis, Grey, Lambton, Whitbread, and Erskine.[25] The objects of the new society were to establish a more equal representation in Parliament, a greater freedom in elections, and more frequent elections of representatives.[26] The Friends of the People were careful to stress the moderation of the reforms they suggested, to repudiate the republican doctrines of Tom Paine, and to disavow any desire to imitate France. Thus the society was certain to meet with the disapproval both of the conservative ruling class which wished no change and of the more vigorous reformers among the lower classes.

It has been said that "France, Burke, and Paine were the stimulating forces of this revival" of interest in reform. The influence which Burke's *Reflections* had upon the ruling class has already been noted; and of the many answers Paine's *The Rights of Man* probably had the greatest effect among the working classes. Part I appeared in March 1791 and Part II in February 1792. By this time all the elements were at hand for Pitt to start his policy of repression: France had put its new constitution in operation in 1791; the Society for Promoting Constitutional Information had been revived, and the London Corresponding Society and the Society of the Friends of the People had been organized; the Birmingham riots of July 14, 1791, had shown the attitude of the "Church-and-King mob" toward Dissenters, particularly Unitarians, and reform; and the workingmen, especially in London and the industrial cities of the

---

[21] *Ibid.*, pp. 58–59.   [22] *Ibid.*, p. 59.   [23] Veitch, *op. cit.*, p. 218.
[24] P. A. Brown, *op. cit.*, p. 54.   [25] *Ibid.*   [26] *Ibid.*

Midland and North, had eagerly read the message in *The Rights of Man*.

The point of interest here is, of course, the attitude taken by George III and Pitt on the movement to reform Parliament from the beginning of the French Revolution through the founding of the Society of the Friends of the People in April 1792. Needless to say, the point of view of the King remained the same: he was inexorably opposed to Parliamentary reform. At first his views on the French Revolution were somewhat contradictory because he could not help feeling a certain satisfaction in the obvious difficulties of the French government, a feeling which was partially offset by a brotherly concern for the troubles of a fellow monarch. The long rivalry between the two nations, which culminated in the assistance given the American Colonies in 1778, had left too deep an imprint on the mind of the King to be immediately effaced. Likewise the Revolution seemed to help along the path of foreign policy in which George III was most interested: pacific relations with other countries in order to give England a chance to strengthen further her financial position. Only when he saw that the doctrines of the Revolution were dangerous to his throne as well as to that of Louis XVI did his mixed feelings fade and become replaced by the hard, clear-cut opinions which he held on practically every subject.

Pitt's feelings also were mixed; and it is possible to get a glimpse of the enthusiastic reformer of 1781-1785 alongside the more sophisticated Minister of 1789. As the head of a rival government, Pitt, like the King, could not help feeling a certain satisfaction at the weakening of a dangerous rival; but he also felt the possibilities of the tremendous movement under way in France. It was, however, the cautious politician of 1789 who was to triumph over the enthusiastic reformer of 1781-1785.

Had he been a sincere reformer in 1789 and during the three years which followed, Pitt would have taken advantage of the enthusiasm aroused by the French example to revive his projects for Parliamentary reform. His attitude in the sessions of 1790 and 1791 is especially significant because the influence of Paine and the three great reform societies was negligible before the end of 1791 and the beginning of 1792. As a sincere reformer Pitt stands condemned more for his actions of 1790 than for those either of 1792 or of the years of the war. His conduct at this time bears a close resemblance to that of the short session of May to

August, 1784, when he begged Sawbridge not to bring forward his motion for Parliamentary reform. The difference in his attitude, however, is based on the fact that although he argued in both 1784 and 1790 that the time was not ripe, in the former year he promised to bring in a reform measure of his own in the next session and made good his promise, whereas in 1790 he made no such promise.

On March 4, 1790, Henry Flood, an Irish orator, introduced the subject of Parliamentary reform. He was careful to stress that he was himself a friend of timely reform and not of revolution. The principle which he wished to establish was that, since the nation had to abide by the decisions of the majority of Parliament, the representatives of the nation should be elected by a majority of the people. While friendly to the representative idea, he admitted that it should be tempered by a property qualification; and therefore Flood proposed to add to the House of Commons a hundred new members to be chosen by the resident householders in every county. The chief attack was made by Windham, who denied that the present representation was inadequate and affirmed that the liberty of the country could not be better secured than at present. But the part of his speech best remembered by posterity is his well-known query if Mr. Flood would advise them to repair their house in the hurricane season. Fox supported Flood, but not with one of his inspired speeches.

Our interest of course lies in the stand taken by Pitt. It is significant that he complimented Windham, a well-known Whig, on the arguments used against Flood's motion, and then observed:

that the proposition which he had himself brought forward, some years before, had been successfully opposed, although the times were then much more favourable than they were now. The chief objection then urged, was the danger of innovation, and it was a knowledge of the impression which that argument had made, that had rendered him desirous of waiting till some more favourable moment than the present should offer itself, when he certainly meant again to submit his ideas on the subject to the House. If pressed to a vote on the question, he must give his negative to the proposed plan; and, even if it were his own proposition, he should act in the same manner, feeling that the case of reform might suffer disgrace, and lose ground, from being brought forward at an improper moment.[27]

---

[27] John Gifford, *A History of the Political Life of the Right Honourable William Pitt* (London, 1809), II, 469. This version differs slightly from that given in the *Parliamentary History*.

Flood withdrew his motion, but claimed that he had secured the desired pledges from both Fox and Pitt. The general election of 1790 was approaching, and Flood evidently wished to commit both statesmen to the support of Parliamentary reform.

Perhaps in no other public utterance did Pitt give so clear an idea of the part that he believed a statesman should play in reform movements. It was to wait until the time when the charge of innovation could not be leveled against the proposal and when it would be favorably received. While it does not appear that Pitt would discourage real reformers outside the House of Commons from carrying on a crusade, it does seem quite evident that he did not intend to help on any such movement throughout the country or take notice of it in Parliament until he felt that it would be favorably received. There was little evidence that a reform of the House of Commons was demanded throughout the country at the time of the general election of 1790. An attempt to revive the County Associations of a decade earlier failed; and the reformers were disappointed by the small number of contested elections.[28] Thus from the point of view of a practical politician or that of a busy statesman the movement to reform the House of Commons had so little support in Parliament or throughout the country that the-time-is-not-yet-ripe argument was the logical one.

The question of Parliamentary reform was not brought up in the first session of the Parliament elected in 1790. This session, which lasted from November 1790 to June 1791, did not cover a period of anxiety for the English government as to danger either from France or from the reforming societies. The King's flight to Varennes had not taken place, the Society for Promoting Constitutional Information had not been revived, and the Birmingham riots of July 14, 1791, had not yet occurred. Therefore there was no particular reason why reform should not have been discussed. But it was exactly because there was no marked enthusiasm for reform that the opposition of the government and of the ruling classes had not been more pronounced.

During the second session of this Parliament, which lasted from January 31 to June 15, 1792, the marked hostility to any change, which resulted from events in France and the activities of the three reform societies, became acute. Because of these circumstances the attitude which Pitt took on Grey's motion of

28 Veitch, *op. cit.*, p. 116.

April 30, 1792, is significant. Grey, with the first enthusiasm which came from the organization of the Society of the Friends of the People, gave notice of his intention to submit a motion for Parliamentary reform in the next session. Pitt answered him immediately and, after admitting that he might be out of order in speaking on a mere notice of a motion, denounced in no uncertain terms any consideration of Parliamentary reform at that time. After expressing regret that Mr. Grey had not brought forward some distinct proposition in order that the House might take up the entire matter for consideration early in the next session, Pitt then stated:

But, as this was a general notice, without any specific proposition, he felt no difficulty in asserting, in the most decisive terms, that he objected both to the time and the mode in which the business was brought forward. He felt this subject so deeply, that he must speak on it without any reserve. He would, therefore, confess that, in one respect, he had changed his opinion on the subject, and he was not afraid to own it. He retained his opinion of the propriety of a reform in Parliament, if it could be obtained without danger or mischief, by a general concurrence, pointing, harmlessly, at its object. But he confessed he was afraid, at this moment, that, if agreed on by that House, the security of all the blessings we enjoyed would be shaken to the foundation. He acknowledged he was not sanguine enough to hope that a reform, at this time, could safely be attempted. His object always had been, but now was most particularly so, to give permanence to that which we actually enjoy, rather than seek to remove any subsisting grievances. He conceived, that the beautiful system of our constitution, and the only security for the continuance of it, was in the House of Commons; but he was sorry to say, that security was imperfect, while there were persons who thought that the people were not adequately represented in Parliament. It was essential to the happiness of the people, that they should be convinced, that they, and the members of that House, felt an identity of interest; that the nation at large, and the representatives of the people, held a conformity of sentiment: this was the essence of a proper representative assembly; under this legitimate authority, a people could be said to be really free; and this was a state in which the true spirit of proper democracy could be said to subsist. This was the only mode by which freedom and good order could be well united. If attempts were made to go beyond this, they ended in a wild state of nature, which mocked the name of liberty, and by which the human character was degraded, instead of being free.[29]

[29] Gifford, *op. cit.*, III, 138–40. This version differs slightly from that given in the *Parliamentary History*.

Later in his speech Pitt made a statement which, if sincere, shows that he realized both the numerical weakness of the reform movement and the lack of danger to the community:

But it seemed that there were a great number of persons in this country who wished for a reform in Parliament, and that they were increasing daily. That their number was great he was happy enough to doubt; what their interest or their vigour would be, if called upon to exert themselves, against the good sense and courage of the sober part of the community, did not occasion him much apprehension.[30]

In conclusion he described the British Constitution, in terms which must have delighted his Tory listeners, as "a monument of human wisdom, which had hitherto been the exclusive blessing of the English nation."[31]

Some biographers of Pitt have gone so far as to call his speech of April 30, 1792, the turning point in his career as a reformer; but it is more probable that it was merely a public avowal of a change which had taken place some time earlier. Nevertheless it must have filled the King with elation; for there were passages in Pitt's speech which George III probably felt he could not have expressed better himself. The King and Pitt now held identical opinions on the great issue which had threatened to keep them apart in the early years of the ministry; and the former might justly feel that he had won a great victory when his Minister publicly repudiated Parliamentary reform. George III's answer to Pitt's account of the debates of April 30 showed how extreme his attitude had become on Parliamentary reform:

The most daring outrage to a regular government committed by the new Society, which yesterday published its Manifesto in several of the newspapers, could only be equalled by some of its leaders standing forth the same day to avow their similar sentiments in the House of Commons; and I cannot see any substantial difference in their being joined in debate by Mr. Fox, and his not being a member of that Society.[32]

It is at least questionable whether or not the King, in this state of mind, would have retained Pitt as his chief minister had the latter adhered to the views of Parliamentary reform which he had held as late as April 18, 1785. With the tide of public opinion

---

[30] *Parliamentary History*, XXIX, 1311.
[31] *Ibid.*, p. 1312.
[32] Stanhope, *op. cit.*, II, xiv.

sweeping so relentlessly against reform of any kind, the King could easily have formed a ministry from the Whigs who were soon to desert Fox, from his own "Friends," and from members of the existing government.

Pitt did not stop with denouncing reform. On May 21 the government issued a proclamation for the preventing of tumultuous meetings and seditious writings which appears to have expressed quite clearly the point of view of the law-and-order classes of England. The King's loving subjects were warned against "divers wicked and seditious writings" published to raise groundless discontents respecting the liberties and happy constitution of the country; and against persons corresponding with foreign parts to forward "criminal and wicked purposes." Faithful subjects were strongly advised to guard against all attempts to subvert the Constitution, and to avoid and discourage all proceedings which tended to produce tumults and riots. Magistrates throughout the country were charged to discover the authors and printers of seditious and wicked writings and to suppress riots and disorders.[33] These instructions do not seem to have been carried out with any vigor until autumn, when the system of espionage and terror so characteristic of repression began to play its part.[34] It is true that the extreme limits of repression were not reached until after the outbreak of the war with France on February 1, 1793; but a very good start was made in the late months of 1792. Thus the renewed agitation for Parliamentary reform which grew out of the early achievements of the French Revolution led to no happy results. The reformers did not take vigorous action in the period before the developments in France aroused suspicion; but, unhappily for them, beginning in the latter part of 1791 they did take such action when practically every step taken by the nation across the channel was suspected.

The obvious result of confusing the excesses of the French Revolution with Parliamentary reform in England was to discredit the movement in the eyes of the great mass of both the ruling and the lower classes. As far as Pitt was concerned it meant that he was driven willingly or unwillingly into the arms of the King and the law-and-order element of the population. Had he taken the stand of Fox it is questionable if even his great popularity throughout the country and in Parliament would

[33] Gifford, op. cit., III, 519–21.
[34] P. A. Brown, op. cit., p. 85.

have survived or his previous services to the Crown have been sufficient to insure his retention as First Lord of the Treasury. When the war with France began on February 1, 1793, Pitt was definitely committed to the Conservative point of view on Parliamentary reform.

The third of the three great reforms agitated during these years, modification of the Test and Corporation acts, aroused less interest than either the abolition of the slave trade or Parliamentary reform. The explanation lies in the absence of that fervor which accompanied the abolition movement and of the spawn of such societies as popularized Parliamentary reform, and in the fact that Dissenters interested in reforming the system of representation linked it with modification of the Test and Corporation acts. As far as the relations of the King and Pitt are concerned, the agitation for modification is of little importance, because no change took place in the point of view of either. In this chapter it will be sufficient to examine the attempts made to alleviate the disabilities of the Dissenters and the arguments offered against any change by Pitt.

Four attempts were made by the friends of Dissenters to remove disabilities: the motions to repeal the Test and Corporation acts, in 1789 by Beaufoy and in 1790 by Fox; the motion to repeal these acts as far as they applied to Scotland, by Elliot in 1791; and the motion to extend toleration to Unitarians, by Fox in 1792. All failed.

The first of these four attempts came on May 8, 1789, only a few days after the thanksgiving ceremony celebrating the recovery of George III. Beaufoy's motion for repeal lost by only twenty votes: 122 to 102.[35] Pitt spoke against the motion and argued, as he had done two years earlier, that the Dissenters were allowed religious toleration but that if full civil rights were given them they might use this power to overthrow the Church establishment. Had Pitt supported this measure, it would without doubt have passed the House of Commons; but in all likelihood the House of Lords would have thrown out the bill, had it reached them. The King felt so violently on this subject that had it been necessary it is highly probable he would have resorted to the same tactics which he used in the India Bill of 1783.

Encouraged by the close vote in the session of 1789, Fox brought up the question again on March 2 of the following year.

[35] *Parliamentary History,* XXVIII, 41.

After giving an account of the circumstances which brought these laws into existence, Fox argued that a religious test was entirely unfair for a political office and that a direct monarchial one would be fairer and better. He then went out of his way to strike at the churchmen by stating that the only "Danger was apprehended to the church from the supine indolence of the clergy, and the superior activity and zeal of dissenters in the discharge of the duties of their sacred functions."[36] Pitt, in his answering speech, spoke at much greater length than on previous occasions when similar motions had been made. His attitude is made clear by the statement in his opening paragraph that "he should still continue to pursue the same line of conduct, with this difference only, that he was but the more strengthened and confirmed in his former opinions upon the subject, and should therefore now restate them with greater force and confidence."[37] The greater part of his speech is taken up with a plausible justification of keeping the existing laws on the statute books. In conclusion he took advantage of the opportunity to defend the Church and to praise the Constitution in terms which his royal master might well have used:

So far was he from agreeing with the right honourable gentleman, that no danger whatever was to be apprehended, that he could easily conceive a man, with all the abilities of the right honourable gentle man, but without the integrity of his principle, who, influenced by ambition and corrupt views, might exercise his powerful talents in rousing the disaffected to an attack upon the church. Would there not, in that case, be real danger? Most certainly. To guard against danger to the constitution however distant, was the indispensable duty of every member of that house, but of none more than of a person in the situation he had the honour to hold, with whom the safety of his country ought ever to be his principal object.[38]

The motion was beaten by the enormous majority of 294 to 105.

The fact that Pitt took this stand twice within ten months after the meeting of the Estates General and before many people in England were in the least perturbed by the events in France shows that his carfully considered decision to oppose relief to Dissenters was not due to the French Revolution. That political reasons—unwillingness to offend the King and churchmen upon a matter in which he was comparatively indifferent—were responsible for Pitt's stand seems undeniable, since he offered no

---

[36] *Ibid.*, p. 395.   [37] *Ibid.*, p. 405.   [38] *Ibid.*, pp. 414–15.

opposition in the session of 1791 to the bill relieving protesting Catholic Dissenters from the operations of the penal code or in the session of 1792 to the one abolishing the disabilities of the Episcopalians in Scotland. But when Fox moved on May 11, 1792, to extend toleration to Unitarians, Pitt fell back on his familiar argument of the danger of innovations in times of trouble. Since this was eleven days after his famous speech denouncing Parliamentary reform and ten days before he issued his proclamation for preventing tumultuous meetings and seditious writings, such an argument is perfectly comprehensible. The Birmingham riots beginning July 14, 1791, when a Church-and-King mob destroyed several meetinghouses and homes of the Dissenters, had given dramatic evidence that the fury directed against the Catholics in the Gordon riots could, if aroused, be turned against Dissenters. In Birmingham hatred of the Unitarians was combined with distrust of the principles of the French Revolution; for the immediate cause of the riot was the celebration by a number of leading Dissenters and Parliamentary reformers of the second anniversary of the storming of the Bastille. George III, although an enemy of mob violence, especially since the Wilkes riots and the Gordon riots of 1780, allowed his antipathy in this direction to be overcome by a greater one. His hatred of reformers and Unitarians was so great that in writing to Dundas he declared: "I cannot but feel better pleased that Priestley is the sufferer for the doctrines he and his party have instilled."[39] If the King were in this state of mind in July 1791, it is easy to understand why he would not tolerate any reform after April 1792.

The history of British foreign policy from the time of the King's recovery and the calling of the Estates General in France to the outbreak of war in 1793 is, in the main, overshadowed by the later events of the French Revolutionary wars. At the time of the King's recovery, England was interested in maintaining the status quo in the Baltic, southeastern Europe, and the Austrian Netherlands. If the ambitions of the Prussian ruler could be controlled, the alliance with Prussia and the Dutch Netherlands gave promise of making success possible in all three direc-

---

[39] P. A. Brown, *op. cit.*, p. 81. Dr. Joseph Priestley was a well-known Unitarian minister and a scientist of considerable reputation. For eleven years he occupied the position of literary companion to Lord Shelburne before accepting the position in Birmingham which he held at the time of the riot.

tions. In comparison with that in Belgium, the English interest in the Baltic and the southeast was lukewarm. Pitt and the Duke of Leeds (formerly the Marquis of Carmarthen) had to exercise considerable care in restraining Prussia from using the Triple Alliance for purposes of aggression. The Prussian government was encouraging dissatisfaction in various provinces of the Emperor Joseph, particularly Galicia and Belgium, and hoped to take advantage of the difficulties of Russia and Austria in the Balkans and the Baltic. In August 1789 Pitt made it clear that he preferred to keep Belgium in her present status—belonging to Austria but dependent on Great Britain and Holland—rather than to see her a small independent country or a province of France. In fact he was willing to risk a war rather than allow annexation of Belgium to France. Prussia, on the other hand, was less concerned about the fate of the Austrian Netherlands than with making some territorial gains at the expense of Austria. The acquisitions which she especially yearned to make were Danzig and Thorn from Poland. The Republic would be compensated by recovering Galicia from Austria, and out of gratitude to Prussia would pass from the Russian to the Prussian sphere of influence. The chances for the success of the Prussian plan turned largely on the outcome of the wars in eastern Europe. If the campaigns of Russia and Austria against Turkey continued with the same ill success with which they opened and if the King of Sweden continued the war against Catherine II in the north, Prussian prospects were bright.

In short, the policy of Pitt and the English government was to cling to the Triple Alliance because of the need for Prussian support against France in Belgium, and to hold together this alliance by giving the King of Prussia the minimum support necessary in eastern Europe. Pitt succeeded in guaranteeing this minimum support until April 1791. By the end of 1789 the Russian and Austrian armies had been sufficiently successful against Turkey to make Frederick William believe that the imperial allies would be able to retain much Turkish territory at the end of the war and that, if properly backed by England, he could secure compensation from Austria. The British government continued to cling to its interpretation of the defensive nature of the Triple Alliance and to remain loyal to it. This conservative caution annoyed Frederick William, even though it resulted in England's refusal to suggest terms of peace in eastern Europe

without consulting her ally. On January 9, 1790, the Triple
Alliance declared its intention of upholding Belgian liberties and,
if necessary, recognizing her independence. Being convinced that
the British government would adhere to her program, the Prussian court decided that the Triple Alliance should propose a general peace on status quo ante terms; and since it was probable that
the imperial courts would refuse to accept, Prussia would thus
secure her ally, her war, and her compensations.[40]

The Prussian hopes for success in this direction were somewhat marred by the death of Joseph II in February 1790. His
successor, Leopold, assured the British representatives first in
Florence and then in Vienna of his willingness to make peace if
the conditions were not humiliating. This made it difficult for
Prussia to get her war and resulting compensations. A conference to settle the Austro-Prussian differences was opened at
Reichenbach on June 27, 1790, and on July 27 declarations and
counterdeclarations were exchanged. Austria agreed: that she
would not continue in the Russo-Turkish War; that she was willing to conclude an armistice with Turkey on the status quo basis
or at most with minor frontier adjustments; that the powers of
the Triple Alliance should guarantee both Austrian possession of
Belgium and its present constitution; and that she would give
Prussia some compensation if Turkey freely gave her something.
The settlement was a triumph for the English policy. Frederick
William, although dissatisfied with securing no more tangible
results in the way of compensation, felt that the next step must
be to force the status quo on Russia. He confidently hoped for
British support because he had promised England aid in case
her quarrel with Spain over Nootka Sound led to war.

The handling of the Nootka Sound affair by Pitt and Leeds
is in marked contrast with the methods employed in eastern
Europe. The explanation undoubtedly lies in the keen interest
which the English showed when their maritime or colonial interests were threatened in contrast with their comparative indifference to territorial changes in eastern Europe. The controversy
arose over the seizure by the Spaniards of an English vessel in
the port of Nootka on what is now called Vancouver Island.
Certain merchants of the British East India Company had decided
to open up trade between China and the west coast of America,

---

[40] *The Cambridge History of British Foreign Policy,* I, 193.

and a small settlement had been started at Nootka. By order of the Viceroy of Mexico, one of the vessels engaged in this trade and the settlement itself were taken over by two Spanish vessels. News of the seizure reached the ministry in January 1790, although the seizure had taken place in the previous May. On February 11 the Spanish envoy in London handed a dispatch to the English government claiming absolute sovereignty for Spain as far north as the 60th parallel, and requesting the punishment of future undertakings by British subjects to trade and settle in this territory. In reply the Duke of Leeds stated that no discussion of the pretensions of Spain could be made until the Spanish government offered satisfaction for the injuries inflicted on the English traders. When Spain reiterated her exclusive claim to the west coast of America up to latitude 60°, the English ministry in a dispatch of May 4 again demanded satisfaction and dismissed the Spanish claim of exclusive right to the west coast of North America. As a result the threat of war loomed large and feeling ran high in both countries. The policy adopted by Great Britain was dictated by Pitt. He preferred peace but was willing to go to war rather than make any concession. He was well aware that his efforts of the six preceding years had put the Navy and national finances in good condition for such a contest. George III, although still as eager to maintain peace as he had been since 1783, felt that Great Britain was adopting the correct policy. In his letter to Pitt dated May 5, 1790, he stated: "The proposed draft of the message to Parliament on the depredations and claims of the Court of Spain seems every way calculated for the unpleasant occasion for it is a concise and fair narrative of what has as yet passed between the two courts."[41]

Prussia and Holland, without great enthusiasm, agreed to support England. The question, then, whether or not Spain would back down turned largely upon whether or not she could get support from the other great powers. Her requests for aid from France, Austria, and Russia brought no satisfactory answers. Under the Family Compact Spain was entitled to expect aid from France, but the changes brought about by the Revolution made this unlikely. Eventually, France, at Mirabeau's suggestion, offered to change the Family Compact to a National Compact, but under such conditions that the Spanish court would not

[41] Pitt MSS, 103, May 5, 1790.

consider the change. The crisis dragged on until the end of October, when Spain, finding that it was useless to expect real assistance from any of the three powers, capitulated. On October 28 the Spanish minister signed the convention agreeing to the following terms: Spain was to restore the buildings and lands of the British subjects at Nootka; both countries were to make reparation for the outrages committed on subjects of the other nation since April 1789; both Spaniards and Britons were to be allowed to trade freely north of the Spanish settlements on the west coast of North America; and freedom of navigation and fishery was conceded in the Pacific so long as no attempts were made to trade with the Spanish colonies.[42]

While the British government was concerned with the Nootka Sound crisis, important events had occurred in eastern Europe. The Austro-Prussian agreement at Reichenbach on July 27 had left Catherine II of Russia still at war with Turkey and Sweden. Prussia was anxious to use the Triple Alliance to force the status quo upon Russia. As soon as news of Reichenbach reached her, Catherine II took steps to avoid having to make peace on this basis. The Prussian monarch felt that the threat of his army and of the navies of Holland and England, when added to the wars which Russia was waging with Turkey in the south and with Sweden in the north, would bring Catherine to terms. She speedily managed, however, to detach Sweden from the side of the Triple Alliance. The eccentric Gustavus III of Sweden, who had upset Catherine's plans earlier by suddenly declaring war on her, now upset the plans of Prussia by suddenly making peace. He had promised not to make a separate peace with Russia, and the British fleet was ready to sail for the Baltic at the time. His reasons for making peace in spite of these factors seem to have been: first, that Catherine offered him practically the same terms which the Triple Alliance had; and second, he was anxious to have his hands free to help his fellow monarch, Louis XVI. Hence the peace to which Catherine and Gustavus agreed on August 14 made the task of the Triple Alliance more difficult.

The English ministry gave some consideration to widening the Triple Alliance in order to make up for the defection of Sweden. The British representatives in Berlin and Warsaw were par-

[42] The account in the preceding paragraphs is based largely on J. H. Rose, *Life of William Pitt*, I, 562–88, and *The Cambridge History of British Foreign Policy*, I, 197–201.

ticularly anxious that Poland should be added. Such an arrangement would remove the Republic from the Russian sphere of influence, in addition to securing an eastern power to compensate for the loss of Sweden. Prussia, however, looked askance at such a proposal because she regarded Poland as her own sphere of legitimate aspiration. On account of this feeling, the English proposals for admitting Poland to the alliance were not acted upon when presented to both countries, and the question was still undecided when the action of Pitt in April 1791 wrecked the Triple Alliance.

Late in 1790 and early in 1791 Pitt and Leeds were showered with advice by various British representatives on the Continent on the question of supporting Prussia, to the extent of going to war if necessary, in forcing the status quo on Russia. The chief advocate of the principle of enforcement was Ewart and the chief opponent Lord Auckland. By the beginning of February Ewart had won.

Reluctance to risk the break up of an Alliance which had done much for the peace of Europe and our own prestige; a measure of gratitude to the King of Prussia; fear lest the Austro-Turkish Peace, for whose character Great Britain stood pledged, should miscarry; forebodings of an ultimate clash of interest between Russia and ourselves in the Near East; and perhaps some desire to school a particularly arrogant woman—all contributed to the decision.[43]

On March 27 an ultimatum, of which the original is in Pitt's handwriting, was sent to Catherine in the form of a representation. She was invited to declare that she would accord the Porte reasonable terms, which meant taking no additional territory from Turkey, and was told that if she failed to give a favorable answer within ten days the British and Prussian courts would regard this omission as a refusal.

From March 21 to April 16 in the cabinet and from March 28 to April 15 in Parliament the contest raged over the expediency of the policy adopted. The Duke of Leeds has left a particularly vivid description of the differences in the cabinet.[44] At first only Grenville and the Duke of Richmond opposed coercion; but on March 31 Stafford stated that he agreed with them. At the

[43] *The Cambridge History of British Foreign Policy,* I, 205. Quoted by permission of The Macmillan Company, publishers.

[44] Oscar Browning, *The Political Memoranda of Francis Fifth Duke of Leeds* (Westminister, 1884), pp. 150–68.

cabinet meeting of this date Pitt suggested that a special messenger be dispatched to Berlin to stop the sending of the ultimatum to Catherine, and gave as his reason for advising such action the arrival of a dispatch from the British envoy in Copenhagen containing pacific proposals by the Danish minister, Count Bernstorff. The latter stated that the Russian Empress would be willing to accept a limited status quo if the Triple Alliance would modify their terms so as to permit her to retain a single fortress and a desert region. Catherine thus indicated that she intended to retain the city of Oczakow on the Black Sea and the surrounding territory. J. H. Rose feels that it is not improbable if this dispatch from Copenhagen had arrived before the ultimatum to Catherine was drawn up and agreed to by George III it might not have been sent.[45] Leeds was decidedly opposed to what he considered an unworthy surrender, and in the end the dispatch sent to Berlin merely ordered the ultimatum held up for a few days.

In Parliament the lack of unanimity so evident in the cabinet made itself felt. On March 28 a message from the King suggested the need of further augmenting the naval force because of his failure to effect a reconciliation between Russia and Turkey; and on the next day Pitt moved an address of thanks and a promise of support. This action brought out a vigorous debate on the advisability of the present foreign policy. Fox, in particular, condemned the ministry for failure to form an alliance with Russia. Pitt's argument that the aggrandizement of Russia would affect British political and commercial interests was apparently not very effective. His admirers explained this on the ground that he spoke under considerable restraint in order not to disclose anything except general principles.[46] The address was carried by a majority of 93. The opposition was encouraged by the fact that this majority was less than the usual ministerial one, and on April 12 Grey introduced a set of resolutions expressing disapprobation of the policy pursued by the government. Pitt and other members of the cabinet "observed a profound silence, rather choosing to subject themselves to the effects of misrepresentation, than to betray the duty which they owed to their Sovereign, and to the country."[47] Partly as a result of this attitude the resolutions were beaten by a majority of only 80. Further

[45] J. H. Rose, *op. cit.*, I, 615.
[46] Gifford, *op. cit.*, III, 19.
[47] *Ibid.*, p. 21.

encouraged, a member of the opposition moved on April 15 that it was the right and duty of the House to inquire into the justice and necessity of the object for which additional burdens were being laid on their constituents; and that no information had been given the House to justify the present armament. Pitt explained his own silence by the duty which he owed his sovereign and country, and asked the House to have confidence in the servants of the Crown during the negotiations. In reply Fox managed to conclude with a eulogy of the new constitution of France, an act which may account for the fact that the government's majority increased to 92. It is clear, however, that the debates in Parliament did not bring out the reasons for the about-face of Pitt on the Russian question, even though the divisions may have influenced him considerably.

The explanation which Pitt offered Ewart, the British envoy to Prussia, who was in England at the time, for not insisting on the terms of the original ultimatum was his inability to secure the backing of Parliament. Ewart reported him as saying:

But all my efforts to make a majority of the House of Commons understand the subject have been fruitless; and I know for certain that, tho' they may support me at present, I should not be able to carry the vote of credit. In short, Sir, you have seen that they can be embarked in a war from motives of passion, but they cannot be made to comprehend a case in which the most valuable interests of the country are at stake. What, then, remains to be done? Certainly, to risk my own situation, which my feelings and inclination would induce me to do without any hesitation; but there are unfortunately circumstances in the present state of this country which make it certain that confusion and the worst of consequences might be expected, and it would be abandoning the King.[48]

Pitt, according to Ewart, repeatedly stated with tears in his eyes that it was the greatest mortification he had ever experienced, but that he was determined to keep up a good countenance.[49] J. H. Rose has suggested that, in view of the size of his majorities in the Commons on April 12 and 15, Pitt was merely using Parliamentary opposition as an excuse for his real difficulties: lack of unity in the cabinet. When Pitt drew up the dispatches on April 15 and 16 in which England did not demand that Russia make peace strictly on the status quo, the Duke of Leeds refused

[48] J. H. Rose, *op. cit.*, I, 617.
[49] *Ibid.*

to sign. Dr. Rose has further suggested that Pitt may have hoped that the Duke would consent to remain as Foreign Secretary if Ewart would consent to return to Berlin and attempt to carry out the less vigorous policy. For two reasons it is difficult to accept this interpretation of Pitt's conduct: first, his conversation with Ewart, "on or about April 10th," is not proof that he did not fear the House of Commons would not support him; and, second, there is an abundance of evidence that he wished to get rid of several important members of the cabinet in order to replace them with ministers more to his liking. In regard to his conversation with Ewart it is clear that he could not be certain how divisions several days later in the House of Commons would result.[50] Also

[50] Pitt amplified this April explanation with a long letter to Ewart written on May 24, 1791:

"You are so fully apprised from your own observation, and from our repeated conversation of all which has passed here in relation to affairs abroad, and of every sentiment of mine on the subject, that I can have nothing fresh to add in this letter. I wish however to repeat my earnest and anxious desire that you should find means of informing the King of Prussia as openly and explicitly as possible of the real state of the business and of the true motives of our conduct. He knows I am persuaded too well the effect which opinion and public impression must always have in this country, either to complain of our change of measures or to wonder at it, if the true cause is fully explained to Him. You perfectly know that no man could be more eagerly bent than I was on a steady adherence to the line which we had at first proposed, of going all lengths to enforce the terms of the strict Status Quo; and I am still as much persuaded as ever, that if we could have carried the support of the country with us, the risk and expense of the struggle, (even if Russia had not submitted without a struggle) would not have been more than the object was worth.

"But not withstanding this was my own fixed opinion, I saw with certainty, in a few days after the subject was final discussed in Parliament, that the prospect of obtaining a support sufficient to carry this line thro with vigor and effect was absolutely desperate. We did indeed carry our question in the House of Commons by not an inconsiderable majority, and we shall I am persuaded, continue successful in resisting all the attempts of opposition, as long as the negotiation is depending. But from what I know of the sentiments of the greater part of that majority and of many of the warmest friends of government, I am sure that if in persisting on the line of the Status Quo we were to come to the point of actually calling for supplies to support the war and were to state (as would then have been indispensible) the precise ground on which it arose, that we should either not carry such a question or have carried it only by so weak a division as would nearly amount to a defeat. This opinion I certainly formed neither hastily nor willingly; nor could I easily make a sacrifice more painful to myself than I have done in yielding to it. But feeling the circumstances to be such as I have stated them, the only question that remained was whether we should persist at all hazards in pushing our first determination, tho without a chance of rendering it effectual in its object, or whether we should endeavour to do what appears to be the next best, when what we wished to do, became impracticable.

"To speak plainly, the obvious effect of our persisting would have been to risk the existence of the present government, and with it the whole of our system both at home and abroad. The personal part of this consideration would have been our duty to overlook and I trust we should all have been ready to do so, if by any risk of our own we could have contributed to the attain-

it is highly probable that he was warned by many of his own followers that, although they would not embarrass him by voting with the opposition, he could not count on them to vote supplies to carry on a war. If he did not believe this, why did he repeat several times, with tears in his eyes, that this was the greatest mortification he had ever suffered? J. H. Rose's explanation would place Pitt in a very unfavorable light in his interview with Ewart. Pitt was not anxious to retain Leeds permanently but only through the Russian crisis. The Duke's entry in his Political Memoranda on March 4, 1791, indicates clearly that he knew of a plan to displace him:

On Fryday, March 4th, Burges called upon me in the evening and mention'd a report, which he had heard from Nepean, that besides Dundas being appointed Secretary of State for India it was supposed to be in contemplation to make Lord Auckland Secretary of State for the Home Department; Ld. Grenville to take that for Foreign Affairs; that Mr. Pitt, Lord Grenville, the D. of Montrose and Dundas were daily closetted together for hours at a time. Nothing had transpired respecting the mode in which the foreign department was to be vacated, whether I was to be dismissed, driven to resign, or any arrangement proposed to me.[51]

As will be shown in the next topic treated in this chapter, Pitt was dissatisfied with Leeds's management of foreign affairs and was awaiting an opportunity to get rid of him. As later events were to prove, Pitt was also anxious to eliminate Thurlow and the Duke of Richmond. It would have been embarrassing for Pitt to have Leeds quit at this particular moment; but it was the ideal time for the latter to make his exit, since he could have attributed his resignation to considerations of national honor and have gone out on principle instead of waiting to go the way of Lord Sydney, Lord Thurlow, and the Duke of Richmond. It is difficult to doubt· that the manner of his departure gave Leeds some satisfaction and Pitt some chagrin.

The necessity for modifying the stiff policy which Pitt had

ment of a great and important object for this country and its allies. But the consequence must evidently have been the reverse. The overthrow of our system here, at the same time that it hazarded driving the government at home into a state of absolute confusion, must have shaken the whole of our system abroad; and on these grounds it is not difficult to foresee what must have been the consequence to Prussia of a change effected by an opposition to the very measures taken in concert with that court and resting on the avowed ground of our present system of alliances."—Pitt MSS, 102, May 24, 1791.

[51] Browning, op. cit., p. 148.

first adopted was not the only factor in the success of Catherine II. The Emperor Leopold took advantage of the evident rift in Anglo-Prussian relations to attempt to wriggle out of his agreement at Reichenbach. Furthermore, the great Polish revolution of May 3, 1791, caused Leopold to draw closer to Russia. For a time it seemed that the attitude which Leopold took toward the Turks might result in the renewal of the war, with additional gains for both Russia and Austria at the expense of the Turks. That such was not the case was due largely to the shock which Leopold experienced at the news of the flight of Louis XVI to Varennes, and that which Catherine II felt at the tidings of the Polish revolution. Because Leopold felt the necessity of devoting time to the revolution in France and Catherine to that in Poland, the terms of peace which both countries made with Turkey were moderate. The humiliation of Pitt, then, consisted not so much in his failure to save Turkey from further dismemberment as in the loss of prestige which he suffered by taking a strong stand and not maintaining it.

From the point of view of this study the significance of Pitt's failure with Russia lies in the ruin of the diplomatic structure and prestige which Pitt had, with the approval of George III, built up since 1786; but for Europe in the next generation it had far greater importance. Prussia, despairing of real help from England, allowed the Triple Alliance to lapse, even though the Prussian monarch and his court seem to have been greatly relieved when the threat of war with Russia was lifted. Russia, Prussia, and Austria now turned their attention to dividing up the unfortunate Polish Republic; and the time and resources spent by the three Eastern powers in devouring their neighbor gave the French democracy a chance to organize so effectively that it took the combined efforts of European powers years to overcome it.

Many reasons have been offered for Pitt's failure in 1791, among them the unreliability of Leopold and Gustavus III, the double policy of Prussia, and the factious opposition of the Whigs. Still these are not enough in themselves to explain Pitt's failure. His great successes from 1786 to 1791 had been due, so far as he was concerned, to his ability as a financial minister and to the economic prosperity of the country. He had handled national finances cleverly and had built up a navy that made the British position in foreign affairs important. It was the fact that England's finances and navy were in condition to make war possible—and this was due largely to Pitt—which enabled him to play so successful a role for five years. His successes began with diplomatic victory over France in the Dutch Netherlands and the Triple Alliance which resulted from it. This alliance

rescued Gustavus III from ruin; it prescribed terms to Austria at the Conference of Reichenbach, and thereby saved the Turks from the gravest danger; it served to restore the ancient liberties of the Brabanters and Flemings; it enabled England to overawe Spain and win the coast of the present colony of British Columbia; last, but not least, Pitt, by singular skill, thwarted the dangerous schemes of the Prussian Hertzberg at the expense of Poland.[52]

Yet the events of 1791 broke up this highly successful Triple Alliance in spite of the fact that the British Navy and British finances were in good condition and Pitt had had additional years of experience in the world of diplomacy. Despite the handicaps under which Pitt labored in 1791, not all of the blame rests on the Prussians, the Swedes, the Austrians, and the Whigs. For one thing he was not an experienced or skilled foreign minister, even though his amazing ability did enable him to appear as such during the intervals in which he temporarily dropped his duties as Chancellor of the Exchequer and leader of the House of Commons to take up the writing of dispatches for the Duke of Leeds Pitt, in the opinion of the present writer, failed because he had become primarily an officeholder. His failure in foreign affairs in 1791 is the complement of his failure to put through reforms in the years 1789–1791. His attitude on the abolition of the slave trade, Parliamentary reform, and the modification of the Test and Corporation acts has been fully dealt with earlier in the chapter. Pitt, feeling the necessity of adapting his policies to the views of both the King and the majority in Parliament, moved so cautiously in the field of reform and foreign politics that he lost the knack of striking at the right moment. His attitude on the three reforms and the ultimatum to Russia shows how fearful he was of going against the King's wishes and the majority of Parliament. Clearly Pitt lost a chance to include Poland, Sweden, and Turkey in the Triple Alliance in 1790 as soon as the Nootka Sound controversy with Spain was settled. Pitt's outstanding ability enabled him to see the steps which should be taken in both internal and foreign problems; but either this ability did not ex-

[52] J. H. Rose, *op. cit.,* I, 589.

tend to carrying out these policies or he was so intent upon keeping his measures in line with the views of the King and majority of Parliament that he was unable to strike at the right time.

But when Pitt turned from his unsuccessful conduct of foreign affairs to handling a critical situation which involved the continuation of his ministry, he displayed every evidence of his old-time skill. Probably his hold on King, Parliament, and cabinet was weaker during the year following the diplomatic defeat at the hands of Catherine II than at any time since the series of rebuffs which he experienced in the session of 1785. If he felt that Fortune had frowned on him at the time of the Russian ultimatum, Pitt must have appreciated that she more than smiled on him in the following year, since the opposition took the unpopular side on both of the two big issues of the day, the French Revolution and Parliamentary reform. After the flight of Louis XVI to Varennes in June 1791 public opinion in England became increasingly hostile to the Revolutionary forces in France and tended to associate this hostility with the question of Parliamentary reform at home. Although Pitt did not need to alter his stand on the French Revolution in order to take advantage of the position of the Foxite Whigs until late in 1792, he did find it necessary, as explained earlier in this chapter, to take a more extreme stand against Parliamentary reform in the famous debate of April 30, 1792. Whether his stand at that time was dictated by party interests or by a real change of heart is unimportant from the purely tactical point of view; for by adopting or championing the popular point of view on the French Revolution and Parliamentary reform Pitt was able to make his own stand on the paramount issues of the day identical with those of the King, to strengthen his own position in the cabinet and the ministry by ejecting "non–co-operators" and filling their places with his own nominees, and to take advantage of the split in the ranks of the Whigs.

The second and third points cannot be separated, because Pitt planned to use the places left vacant to tempt the moderate or conservative Whigs to join his ministry. During the years following the King's recovery in 1789 Pitt was clearly dissatisfied with several members of his cabinet, and since he was in so strong a position it seems strange that he should have waited until his prestige was weakened by the Russian fiasco before insisting upon these changes. The men with whom he appears to have been most dissatisfied were Lord Chancellor Thurlow, the Duke of Leeds, Foreign Secretary, and the Duke of Richmond, Master-General of Ordnance. The resignation of the Duke of Leeds in 1791 has been described already, and the Duke of Richmond was not a source of serious worry to Pitt. Thurlow had managed to retain his hold on the affections and confidence of the King in spite of his dubious conduct at the time of the Regency Crisis. Evidently Pitt felt that despite his strengthened position after 1789 it was inexpedient to attempt to rid himself of the Lord Chancellor. Since Pitt seldom made an error in judgment in this sphere, we may safely conclude that the King was not susceptible to any pressure that his chief minister could bring to bear during the three years following the Regency Crisis. Two things made possible Pitt's demand for and George III's reluctant acquiescence in Thurlow's dismissal: first, the Lord Chancellor's unwise arrogance in taking advantage of the apparent strength of his position with the King; and, second, Pitt's stand against Parliamentary reform on April 30 and his vigorous measures for repression in May. It was the combination of the Prime Minister's weakened position since the spring of 1791 and his complete adoption of the royal point of view on the French Revolution and the dangers to the English Constitution which caused the King to choose so readily between Pitt and Thurlow. Although it may appear that the reverse should be true, George III was afraid of Pitt when the ministry was weak and the opposition strong, and not when the government was strong and the opposition weak. It was when Pitt was needed to tip the balance against a possible return of the Whigs that he was worth most to the King. In addition Pitt had started his campaign to induce the Portland Whigs to abandon Fox and join his ministry, and if the attempt were successful George III could feel safe against the return of Fox for a long time to come.

Thus the events from April 30 to May 21 follow one another in a logical fashion. In the debate on Grey's motion Pitt not only took the stand which delighted the King but also obviously went out of his way to court the Portland Whigs. Pitt followed up this initial move by his letter of May 9 to the Duke of Portland:

Having the satisfaction of thinking that your Grace and many persons of weight and consideration with whom you are connected, are disposed to manifest your concurrence in such measures as may on due consideration be thought necessary under the present circumstances for checking any attempts dangerous to Public Order and Tranquillity, I have received His Majesty's permission to state to your Grace the ideas which have occurred to His Majesty's servants, and to request the communication of your sentiments upon them.[53]

Portland answered cautiously, agreeing to listen to Pitt's proposals. On May 15 Thurlow culminated a series of attacks on government measures by scoffing at Pitt's proposals for joining a sinking fund to every new state loan. Pitt struck instantly and, disregarding the King's plea, which had been effective on previous occasions, that the Chancellor's outburst should be overlooked for reasons of state, demanded that George III should choose between Thurlow and him. At the same time Pitt informed Thurlow of the step he had taken.[54] The King, in a letter to Dundas, gave his reasons for deciding in favor of the Prime Minister:

Mr. Dundas is to acquaint the Lord Chancellor that Mr. Pitt had this day stated the impossibility of his sitting any longer in Council with him, it remains therefore for my decision which of the two shall retire from my service. The Chancellor's own penetration must convince him however strong my personal regard nay affection is for him, that I must feel the removal of Mr. Pitt impossible with the good of my service.[55]

Thurlow immediately resigned. Evidently he did not expect the King to allow Pitt to retire, but he did seem to have believed that George III would not part with him so readily. On May 21 Pitt issued his proclamation against seditious writings. The way was now clear for the Prime Minister to make further overtures to Portland and his followers.

When the question of the breakup of the opposition and the strengthening of the government is considered, the make-up of both groups must be clearly kept in mind. The ministry was composed of the King's Friends, of followers of Pitt, and of individuals who did not fall within either division but who gave their support either on principle or for the love of holding office. Neither Pitt nor George III believed in the Whig principle of cabinet solidarity. Pitt, naturally, was anxious to have in key positions as many men as possible who would acknowledge him

---

[53] Pitt MSS, 102, May 9, 1792.

[54] *Ibid.*, May 16, 1792.

[55] "Correspondence of King George III," Transcripts by Sir John Fortescue in William L. Clements Library, IV, 1530.

as leader and who held views closely akin to his own. The King was equally desirous of keeping men in cabinet positions who were acceptable to him personally and who held political principles of which he could approve. Since the King's recovery in the spring of 1789 the changes in the cabinet had been uniformly in favor of Pitt. Within three years the minister had been able to rid himself of the home and foreign secretaries and of the Lord Chancellor. In 1789 he had replaced Lord Sydney in the Home Office and in 1791 the Duke of Leeds in the Foreign Office by his cousin, W. W. Grenville. Upon the resignation of the Duke of Leeds Pitt had moved Grenville to the Foreign Office and had replaced him in the Home Office by Dundas. In forcing the resignation of Thurlow in May 1792 Pitt was able to remove the most powerful friend of the King in the cabinet. Without doubt George III was aware that Pitt was strengthening his own following in the cabinet at the expense of that of his royal master. But he had little cause for alarm; the services rendered by Dundas and Grenville had been satisfactory to the King, and neither had insisted upon any measure extremely distasteful to him. If any such issue did arise, George III could always act as he had earlier in his reign and was to do again in 1801 and 1807, that is, to dismiss the ministry. Further, in the case of Thurlow, the Lord Chancellor had so obviously brought about his own fall by his tactless action that it was difficult for the King to make a logical stand against Pitt's demand, particularly since the latter had so delighted George III by his stern resistance to Parliamentary reform. Thus Pitt's strengthening of the personnel of the cabinet favorable to him was accompanied and to a certain extent made possible by the fact that his own principles and policies tended to coincide with those of the King. When Pitt, with the consent of George III, began overtures to the Portland Whigs, there was nothing in political precedent or in the principles of either side to interfere with such a policy. George III had stated early in his reign that he was willing to take individual Whigs, or even groups, provided they entered the cabinet or ministry as such; and every government during his reign, with the possible exception of the first Rockingham one in 1765–66, had been made up of Whigs, Tories, and King's Friends. Pitt had never accepted the Rockingham-Portland doctrine that a ministry should come in and go out as a body; and the only administrations in which Pitt had served, that of Shelburne in 1782–83 and his own formed in December 1783, were both composed of King's Friends, former followers of Lord North, and Rockingham and Shelburne Whigs. Pitt seems to have considered himself still a Whig in the line of succession from his father and Lord Shelburne as opposed to the magnates or the Newcastle-Rockingham-Portland Whigs. Thus the policy of splitting the Whigs was not so much an ethical question as a political one. Would the accession of the desired strength to his government both in the cabinet and in Parliament offset the discomforts of forming a coalition with these magnates whom Pitt had disliked since Rockingham had refused to find him a seat in the election of 1780 and the negotiations with Portland had broken down early in 1784? Pitt evidently felt that their support was more than worth the discomfort, for he stuck tenaciously to his purpose from May 1792 until he was successful in July 1794.

The Whigs, or the group acknowledging the leadership of the Duke of Portland, were by no means a homogeneous body. Fundamentally they were the men, grown nearly ten years older, who had formed the Fox-North Coalition of 1783. The fact that they were called Whigs merely shows how completely the followers of North had been submerged by the Portland Whigs. In part this was due to the great debating skill and oratorical powers of the great Whig trinity, Fox, Burke, and Sheridan; and to the force of circumstances which kept any major issue from splitting the opposition to the government. Individuals and groups within the ranks of this organized opposition were permitted the same freedom of action on such controversial questions as Parliamentary reform and repeal of the Test and Corporation acts as was granted to the followers of Pitt and the King's Friends within the government. Solidarity, however, was maintained in the ranks of the opposition from 1783 to 1792 by attacking Pitt's fiscal and foreign policies and by the hope that good fortune in the nature of the death or incapacitation of the King or the overthrow of Pitt might enable them to come into power as a body and not as individuals. This solidarity was wrecked by the irreconcilable differences of members of the opposition on the French Revolution and reform.

The rift in the Whig party really began with the publication, on October 31, 1790, of Burke's *Reflections on the French Revolution*. At that time the point of view expressed was widely condemned by followers of both Pitt and Fox; and it is significant that Sir William Windham, who was within eighteen months to adopt Burke's conclusions, wrote in his diary that the author of *Reflections* was "a man descried, persecuted and proscribed; not being much valued, even by his own party, and by half the nation considered as little better than an ingenious madman!"[56] Burke was clearly disappointed by the reception which his friends gave the *Reflections*. He appears to have believed that he was serving the interests of both his party and the Prince of Wales. Instead, he came to the conclusion that Fox and Sheridan had seriously damaged his reputation in the eyes of both the aristocratic Whigs and the Prince.[57] Thus he had the double grievance of seeing principles in which he fervently believed scoffed at and his chances of political advancement severely checked. Consequently his break with Fox in 1791 and his untiring efforts to win over the aristocratic Whigs to his point of view had, seemingly, motives of political principle and personal grievance. The differences in the points of view of Fox and Burke on the French Revolution were brought out with increasing frequency in the course of debates on various measures throughout the month of April 1791. Fox on more than one occasion expressed his great admiration for the Revolution, although he denied that he ever advocated republican principles for England; and Burke never failed to warn his listeners of the dangers in the French Revolution and constitution.

The climax came on May 6, 1791, in the course of a debate on the Quebec Bill. Burke at the end of the speech declared that it was indiscreet at his age to provoke enemies "or give his friends occasion to desert him; yet if his firm and steady adherence to the British constitution placed him in such a dilemma, he would risk all; and, as public duty and public prudence taught him, with his last words exclaim, 'Fly from the French constitution.' "[58] Fox at this point whispered to Burke that there was no loss of friends. Whereupon Burke insisted: "Yes there was a loss of friends—he knew the price of his conduct—he had done his duty at the price of his friend—their friendship was at an end."[59]

This open declaration of war on the part of Burke could not

[56] Mrs. Henry Baring (ed.), *The Diary of the Right Hon. William Windham, 1784 to 1810* (London, 1866), p. 213.

[57] William T. Laprade, *England and the French Revolution* (Baltimore: Johns Hopkins University Press, 1909), p. 33.

[58] *Parliamentary History*, XXIX, 387.

[59] *Ibid.*

but be very welcome to Pitt. Although it was a year before Pitt began to take full advantage of this obvious rift, it clearly pointed the way out of his difficulties which had reached a climax in the Russian fiasco a short time before this debate of May 6. The change in the attitude of Pitt and the government press toward Burke indicates that the value of his contribution had not been missed. Furthermore the events of the French Revolution from June 1791 until the outbreak of the war on February 1, 1793, tended to drive the great mass of the English people more and more to the point of view of Burke. This need not, however, have reacted any more unfavorably on the opposition than on the government because the attitude of Pitt and most of his supporters was not unlike that of the great majority of the followers of Portland. The real reason why Pitt was able to take advantage of the shift in the attitude toward the French Revolution was that Fox and a minority of the Whigs refused to turn violently against the principles of the Revolution and reform, and some of them even went beyond Fox in forming the Society of the Friends of the People in April 1792. Thus although it was not due to Pitt that Fox and a minority of the Whigs chose the unpopular side of the paramount issues of the day, the Minister certainly took every advantage of their choice. As soon as the debate of April 30 revealed publicly the differences in the opposition, Pitt at once went to work.

The detailed story of the negotiations between Pitt and the Portland Whigs from May 1, 1792, to February 1, 1793, can be traced from the *Diaries* of Lord Malmesbury, the *Political Memoranda of the Duke of Leeds,* and the *Life and Letters of Sir Gilbert Elliot.* Practically every member of the government and of the opposition had at least one friend in the other camp and as a result not only were cross communications easy but there was also an abundance of opportunity for discrepancies to crop up during the negotiations. Matters were further complicated by the fact that Lord North (after 1790, Lord Guilford) died on August 5. Whether or not his removal from the political scene had any influence on that section of the opposition which in 1783 had acknowledged him as leader is difficult to say. It did, however, have the result of making available for immediate use the Chancellorship of Oxford University, a "blue ribbon," and the office of Lord Warden of the Cinque Ports. Nearly all of the followers of the former Prime Minister were among the members of the opposition who welcomed the overtures of Pitt. As Lord Holland remarks: with Lord Loughborough, "Lord Stormont, Lord Carlisle, and Sir Gilbert Elliot and other adherents of Lord North's administration, fell off. With the exception of his son, and Mr. Adam, there was scarce a follower of that Minister [then Lord Guilford, and dying] who remained in the Opposition."[60]

In many respects the most amazing feature of this nine months of negotiations is the fact that every important person except the Duke of Portland seems to have had his mind made up at the beginning of the period. Pitt was anxious to strengthen the government by adding the Portland Whigs to his cabinet and ministry and to weaken the opposition by dividing its forces. Fox was anxious to maintain the opposition to Pitt intact and to allow its members freedom of action on issues in which a general agreement could not be reached. These tactics had been used by Pitt and George III and by the followers of Fox and North from 1783 to 1792 on such issues as Parliamentary reform and the repeal of the Test and Corporation acts. Fox counted on the support of the more liberal group in the party composed of the element which made up the Society of the Friends of the People and his own personal followers. The remaining members of the opposition fell into two groups: those who wished to accept office with Pitt, and those who would be content merely to support such government measures as were deemed necessary to preserve the constitution. Both of these groups worked hard on the poor Duke of Portland: the first to induce him to accept office in the Pitt ministry or to give his consent to members of his party doing so; and the second to make him state publicly his willingness and intention to support the government. Fox, on the other hand, still had enough influence with Portland to prevent the Duke from accepting office and to postpone for months any promise to support government measures. After months of relentless conflict between Fox on the one side and the individuals who wished Portland to commit himself in some manner against reform and revolutionary principles on the other, Burke summed up the situation admirably in a conversation with Malmesbury by declaring, "We had killed Patroclus, and were now fighting for the dead body."[61] Yet mem-

[60] Henry Edward Lord Holland (ed.), Henry Richard Lord Holland, *Memoirs of the Whig Party* (London, 1852), I, 24.

[61] The Third Earl of Malmesbury (ed.), *Diaries and Correspondence of James Harris, First Earl of Malmesbury* (London, 1844), II, 495. Hereafter cited as Malmesbury, *Diaries*.

bers of the Whig party were unwilling to accept office or even to offer to support the government without the consent of the Duke. This reluctance on the part of Portland's followers and his own vacillation explain why the negotiations with Pitt were so long and indecisive.

The fullest account of the fight over the dead body of Patroclus is to be found in Malmesbury's diaries. On the evening of June 9 Portland, Lord Fitzwilliam, Lord Loughborough, Burke, and Malmesbury met at Burlington House. There Burke for an hour declaimed against the conduct of Fox.[62] The next day in a conversation with Malmesbury, Portland agreed that a coalition with Pitt was a very necessary measure and that overtures to bring one about should be both listened to and made.[63] Three days later Portland reported to Malmesbury that Fox was in favor of a coalition; but the conditions under which he favored it were so strongly reminiscent of those which he had attempted to impose on Pitt during the early months of 1784 that in reality they amounted to opposition to the position of Portland. Fox expressed the wish that the coalition

be brought about in such a way as it should appear they had not *acceded* to Pitt's Ministry, but went to it on fair and even conditions to share equally with him all the power, patronage, etc.—Duke's idea that Pitt should not keep the Treasury, but some neutral man be put there—the Duke of Leeds—that he himself should not come into office, but support Government *out of employment*. This I was strongly disinclined to, but did not express it that day. I doubted whether the King, or rather the Queen, knew of these proposals; stated the difficulties there, and the still greater at Carlton House.[64]

From this date the important entries in Malmesbury's diary are devoted largely to what Lord Loughborough told either Portland or Malmesbury. Loughborough was one of the most eager advocates of a coalition because he hoped to become Lord Chancellor. According to Malmesbury, Loughborough met Pitt at the home of Dundas on the evening of June 14 and asked if the King was familiar with the negotiations.

Pitt said he did not come with the King's command to propose a coalition, but that he would be responsible that it would please the King *and the Queen,* and that the only difficulty at all likely to arise

[62] Malmesbury, *Diaries,* II, 453.
[63] *Ibid.,* pp. 454–55.   [64] *Ibid.,* p. 459.

was about Fox, and that difficulty entirely owing to Fox's conduct in Parliament during the last four months. That *everything else* was entirely forgotten, and that he himself did not recollect that in all their Parliamentary altercations, a single word had ever dropped from either of them to prevent their acting together without any fair reproach being made of a disavowal of principles, or an inconsistency of character. Pitt said that it *perhaps* would not be quite easy to give Fox the Foreign Department *immediately,* but that in a few months he certainly might have it. Dundas was in this conference very eager for bringing about the Union, and Pitt did not seem less so.[65]

When he took up the question with Fox, Malmesbury found the latter full of misgivings and a little hurt that the first advance had not been made to him. Fox

doubted Pitt's sincerity, and suspected he had no other view than to weaken their party and strengthen his own—that to divide the opposition was his great object . . . . He contended that it was impossible ever to suppose Pitt would admit him to an equal share of power, and that whatever might be his own feelings or readiness to give way, he could not, for the sake of the honour *and pride* of the Party, come in on any other terms.[66]

On June 18 Lord Fitzwilliam gave Malmesbury his views on the proposed coalition. He said he believed that the greatest obstacle was Fox's being entangled with the men who had founded the Society of the Friends of the People. In conclusion Malmesbury declared:

Lord Fitzwilliam and myself agreed on every point; he, however, went beyond me in insisting on the indispensable necessity of Pitt resigning the Treasury for another Cabinet office. He acquiesced in the wisdom of trying to bring Fox to be less attached to these false friends, and said Tom Grenville was the best man to speak to him. Lord Fitzwilliam expressed his dislike to Sheridan, said he might have a lucrative place, but never could be admitted to one of trust and confidence.[67]

On June 21 Lord Bute confided in Malmesbury that on the previous day he had assured the King how happy he was

from being informed that His Majesty had it in his contemplation to add a great strength to his Administration by joining to it some of the most respectable and considerable families in the country. The King was silent, looked down, and for a minute or two said nothing;

---

[65] *Ibid.,* p. 460.   [66] *Ibid.,* pp. 461–62.   [67] *Ibid.,* p. 465.

he then asked Lord Bute, who was the person in that party he was most attached to—Lord Bute replied, the Duke of Portland; and upon this, the King spoke out loudly in praise of the Duke, and spoke of him with expressions of highest regard and esteem.[68]

The next morning Malmesbury had breakfast with Burke and the latter bewailed the fact that the much-needed coalition would fail because of the opposition of Fox. As he phrased it: *"Mr. Fox's coach stops the way."*[69]

The point of view of every interested individual or group concerned in these negotiations is expressed in the preceding paragraph. In some instances the point of view may be somewhat distorted by self-interest and by the ordinary variations which result from conversations repeated by two or three persons before they are put down in writing. Fox was willing to form a coalition on a basis of equality with a new man, presumably a figurehead, as First Lord of the Treasury. Pitt wanted to remain at the head of the government and to offer a certain number of places to Portland's followers. Fox was not to be included until later. This was the "time-is-not-yet-ripe" argument which Pitt used so successfully both before and after 1792. The chances are that the time never would have been ripe so long as both George III and Pitt lived. The Duke of Portland tended to agree with any strong character with whom he conversed; but his first choice, probably, was to have the government reconstituted with the Duke of Leeds as First Lord of the Treasury and to give the new ministry his support without accepting office. The right wing of Portland's forces wished to support either the existing government or a reconstituted one, but differed as to whether or not any member or members of the group should accept office. The King was willing to have Pitt's ministry strengthened by the accession of Portland, but it was clear from his reticence in speaking with Bute that there were members of Portland's party who would not be acceptable. The first phase of these negotiations was definitely over before the end of June. Even the most eager of the Whigs, Loughborough, admitted that Pitt had told him on June 25 that it was useless at this time to go further with the arrangement.[70]

These June negotiations, although disappointing to the right wing of Portland's followers and probably to the Duke himself,

---

[68] Malmesbury, *Diaries,* II, 465–66.
[69] *Ibid.,* p. 466.   [70] *Ibid.,* p. 468.

could not have been entirely unsatisfactory to Pitt and Fox. Even though he did not secure any recruits for the cabinet, the Prime Minister knew that he could count on the support of a majority of the Portland Whigs to back him in opposing the spread of revolutionary doctrines and in resisting reform. Thus Pitt could feel that his position in Parliament was no longer precarious. Fox, on the other hand, must have felt a certain satisfaction in being able to hold together his party, even though he realized that the former unity of spirit was lost. Probably George III was not especially perturbed or elated. He had made up his mind long before not to admit Fox as a minister if he could possibly avoid it. Thus it is likely that he would have welcomed the addition of Portland and some of the Whigs to the ministry as making the necessity of ever having to accept Fox as a minister still more unlikely; but, unquestionably, he realized that practically the same result was secured by the assurance of support from the followers of Portland.

The second phase of the negotiations for a new or revised ministry centered around the efforts of the Duke of Leeds. On July 20, at the request of the Duke of Portland, he met the Whig leader for an interview on the "subject of an administration upon a more extensive plan." After discussing at length the possibility of Pitt and Fox working together, Portland, according to Leeds,

stated a circumstance of difficulty in the arrangement supposing the plan to be adopted, which was Mr. Pitt remaining at the Head of the Treasury, which of course would give him in point of Etiquette a nominal superiority over Mr. Fox in the House; his Grace added he did not believe Mr. Pitt would make any difficulty upon this point, as the Idea was that He and Mr. Fox should be the two Secretarys of State, and therefore some person of character and unexceptionable to the country at large and in whom both parties at their outset (meaning hereafter to form one mass) could have confidence should be appointed First Lord of the Treasury, by which neither of those gentlemen could officially claim a superiority in the Cabinet. To this I made no particular answer, having heard from Sir R. Woodford that the Friends of the D. of P. had thought of me for that situation.[71]

Leeds concluded the entry in his diary with a statement of his willingness to hold the balance between the two parties and thus accomplish an essential service to his King and his country.[72]

[71] Browning, *op. cit.*, pp. 178–79.
[72] *Ibid.*, p. 179.

Portland now took up with Fox the matter of Leeds's communicating directly with the King, and Fox readily gave his consent. We are able to follow the subsequent history of these negotiations in the diaries of Lord Malmesbury and the Duke of Leeds. The difference between the accounts which the two men give of the conversations held during Malmesbury's visit to Leeds, from July 27 to 29, is very enlightening. The entries in his diary show that Leeds was for the plan to reconstruct the ministry; but Malmesbury's plan, on the other hand, clearly shows a defeatist attitude: "The Duke of Portland, although he placed no great faith in the intervention of the Duke of Leeds, in consequence of Fox's promoting it, acquiesced in the Duke of Leeds's seeing the King."[73] Portland's letter to him on the same date justified this pessimistic view, since the Duke declared: "I own, besides, to *you,* that I have no expectation of any effect from the Duke of Leeds's intervention. But I think the bringing about of such a coalition of such importance to this country, that I should be very sorry indeed to omit any means of doing it within my power."[74] Malmesbury seems to have felt some misgivings on the advisability of Leeds's conferring with the King on so delicate a subject. Leeds, however, assured him that "he was on a footing of *perfect confidence* since the Regency, and more particularly since his conduct on the Russian armament."[75] Even this did not convince Malmesbury, for he added: "The Duke of Leeds was in earnest, but, as he always is, carried away more by his imagination and sanguine hopes, in which his string of toadeaters encourage him, than by reason and reflection."[76] On July 31 Malmesbury sent word to Leeds that Fox had expressed great satisfaction over the proposed interview with the King, but that he himself feared that Fox's insistence on an alteration in the Treasury would prove to be an insurmountable objection. It is interesting to note that this is the last entry in Malmesbury's diary until December 11.

How is it possible to reconcile the great enthusiasm which Fox showed for Leeds's negotiations with the halfhearted and reluctant consent which Portland and Malmesbury gave? The explanation clearly lies in Fox's firm conviction that Pitt "was not sincere, and only wished to separate and break up the party."[77] Having Leeds go directly to the King before consulting Pitt

---

[73] Malmesbury, *Diaries,* II, 470.
[74] *Ibid.*   [75] *Ibid.,* p. 471.   [76] *Ibid.*   [77] *Ibid.,* p. 472.

would, Fox was confident, prove his point, since he was certain that the Prime Minister had not taken George III completely into his confidence and that the latter would never consent to the reorganization of the ministry along lines which Fox insisted were necessary. In short, Fox was eager to have Leeds conduct these negotiations, not because he expected success, but because he was anxious for failure. Knowing George III and Pitt as well as he did, Fox could be fairly certain that the proposals of Leeds would seriously cripple and probably completely ruin the coalition contemplated. Whether or not he had heard all the details of the Dundas-Loughborough negotiations, the King would not allow Pitt to resign as First Lord and return merely as Secretary of State on an equality with Fox; and Pitt would not only decline to play the role which Leeds had cast for him but was also certain to be offended by the fact that the negotiations were made with the King instead of with him. Once Fox took this attitude the danger became clear to Portland and it is highly probable that he regretted his initial advance to Leeds. Portland and Malmesbury really wanted a coalition, and once the significance of the negotiations of Leeds with the King became clear they were as much chagrined as Fox was elated over the fact that failure would postpone or ruin the chances of a union with Pitt. In many respects the whole affair was a bit hard on Leeds; but Fox seems to have felt that since the Duke was so very eager to play a part any rebuff which he might suffer was more or less deserved.

An August 14 Leeds succeeded in securing an interview of a half-hour with the King in the library of the Queen's Lodge. The Duke opened the conversation with a summary of events which had led him to seek this interview, and added that he took it for granted that His Majesty was informed of all negotiations down to this time. The answer of the King was undoubtedly a considerable shock to the Duke: "To my great surprise the King answered that he had not heard anything upon the subject for a long time. That Mr. Pitt had indeed some months ago mentioned something like an opening on the part of the Duke of Portland and his friends, to which H.M. had answered, *Anything Complimentary to them, but no Power!!!*"[78] When he came to enter this conversation in his diary a great revelation struck Leeds and he added: "The first part of this brief but pretty copious answer ex-

[78] Browning, *op. cit.*, p. 188.

plains the circumstance of the offer of the Garter to the Duke of Portland and of the Marquisate of Rockingham to Lord Fitzwilliam, and the latter proves but too clearly the great difficulty, if not impossibility, of succeeding in the proposed arrangement."[79]

George III, having listened to the Duke, now took charge of the conversation himself. Leeds, evidently without realizing the humor of the situation and failing to appreciate how remarkably the description applied to him, reported that: "The King very truly observed that it frequently happened that people from eagerly wishing an object to succeed deceived themselves by thinking it much nearer its accomplishment than in truth it was."[80] George III then explained gently to the Duke why the changes he proposed were impossible. In short, by declaring that he could not see how Pitt or his friends would possibly consent to such an arrangement, he took exactly the stand which Fox had expected and had prophesied. Next His Majesty asked the embarrassing question who would be selected to supplant Pitt as First Lord of the Treasury? Leeds did not show up too well in his answer, in which he declared that he could not tell, "but that it was meant that some one should be in that situation who was upon terms of Friendship and Confidence with both Parties."[81] The King then pointed out how awkward it would be for Pitt to take an inferior position after being at the head of the Treasury Board for nearly nine years and added that "whoever was the First Lord must either be a Cypher or Mr. Pitt appear as a *commis*."[82]

The King communicated the results of this interview to Pitt, who, judged by his subsequent treatment of Leeds and his letter of August 18 to George III, was not too pleased. Pitt must have been annoyed for two reasons: first, it placed him in the uncomfortable situation of withholding information from the King; and, second, it meant that he had been ignored in important negotiations which concerned the future personnel of the ministry. To satisfy both George III and himself he took up the matter with Loughborough, with whom through Dundas the June negotiations had been conducted. Pitt appears to have been satisfied with the explanation of Loughborough which he handed on to the King:

Mr. Pitt humbly begs leave to acquaint your Majesty that Mr. Dundas and He yesterday saw Lord Loughborough, and found from Him that the suggestion conveyed by the Duke of Leeds could not

---

[79] Browning, *op. cit.*, p. 188.   [80] *Ibid.*   [81] *Ibid.*, p. 189.   [82] *Ibid.*

have been in any degree founded on Lord Loughborough's representation of what had passed in conversation with His Lordship, and
that it was totally contrary to his sentiments. There seems reason on
the whole to suppose that the step itself is principally to be ascribed
to the sanguiness [sic] of the Duke of Leeds in persuading himself
and representing to others that he would find great facility in accomplishing his scheme, on no other ground than that of his own Wishes.
Lord Loughborough understands the Duke of Portland to have imagined that the Duke of Leeds meant to communicate the proposed
arrangement to all the Parties concerned, and thought it probable
that they would be easily reconciled to it.[83]

It is, however, difficult to reconcile the contents of this letter
with the entries in Leeds's diary. On August 15, the day after his
interview with the King, the Duke sent to Portland an account of
what had taken place; on the 18th he related the details to Malmesbury; and on the 20th he went over them once more in the presence of both Portland and Malmesbury. After this second interview he called on Pitt but found that the latter was at Lord Grenville's home. On the 21st he received a letter from Malmesbury
giving an account of the interview of August 17 between Loughborough on the one side and Pitt and Dundas on the other very
different from that which Pitt had written to the King. Malmesbury in his letter to Leeds stated:

Lord Loughborough to have been perfectly satisfied with what passed
between the King and me, and thought nothing but good could come
from it. That he could not collect from his Lp. that when he saw
Pitt and Dundas together last Friday that from anything they said
they had taken any alarm from my conference; that they indeed expressed a wish that I had spoken to one or both of them about it, and
an expectation that I still would. He then observed how proper my
visit and subsequent note to Mr. Pitt yesterday were, and adds that
the whole business is in as good a train as possible, concludes that,
hoping to see me to-morrow, it was unnecessary to go into further
detail in this letter of what Lord Loughborough had said.[84]

With all these assurances Leeds appears to have looked forward to his interview with Pitt on August 22 with considerable
satisfaction. But after relating in detail the steps in the negotiations since July 20 Pitt fairly staggered him by declaring that
"there had been no thoughts of any alteration in the Government,
that circumstances did not call for it, nor did the people wish it,

[83] Clements Transcripts, IV, 1586.   [84] Browning, op. cit., pp. 193–94.

and that no new arrangement, either by a change or coalition, had ever been in contemplation!!!"[85] Later in the interview Pitt made an admission which convinced Leeds that the Prime Minister was not consistent in saying that no change had ever been contemplated. The Duke went immediately to Malmesbury and told him the results of this conversation. Then follows what is, without doubt, the most delicious passage in Leeds's Memoranda:

We agreed it would be right to soften it to the Duke of Portland and particularly to Mr. Fox, for as he had all along doubted Mr. Pitts being sincerely disposed towards the arrangement in question, what had now passed would be a matter of triumph to his discernment, and he might perhaps not have discretion enough to be silent, and the whole getting wind might be productive of many bad consequences.[86]

The only conclusion which the saddened Duke could reach was that either Pitt's statements were contrary to the truth or that Loughborough had misled his friends; and he expressed the belief that "there must have been some strange mistake somewhere which perhaps time would clear up."[87]

Time has not entirely cleared up this strange mistake. The veracity of Pitt, Leeds, and Loughborough is at stake; for one or more of the three are clearly guilty of falsehood or misrepresentation. On first impression Pitt's categorical denial to Leeds of any contemplated change or coalition appears to convict him of some degree of falsehood. Several lines of defense, however, are possible. Pitt was without doubt exasperated with Leeds for consulting the King without first notifying him, and he may have made the denial in more sweeping terms than he would have done under more normal circumstances. Again Leeds may have misquoted him, although under the conditions in which Pitt's statement was made this is not very probable. But the most effective defense for Pitt is that he was telling the truth and that he did not contemplate a change in government or a coalition but only an accession of strength to his ministry from the Portland Whigs. In short to exonerate Pitt it is necessary to accept the point of view of Fox. Leeds may be accused of falsification or exaggeration, but no one who has read his political memoranda would ever suspect him of playing a deep game. The accounts which he gives of his own activities show him in such a ludicrous light that it is highly probable that any attempt at double dealing would have

[85] Browning, *op. cit.*, p. 194.   [86] *Ibid.*, p. 196.   [87] *Ibid.*, p. 197.

been betrayed in his own writing. Recent historians have been inclined to place most of the blame on the shoulders of Loughborough. This attitude is due partly to his general reputation for shiftiness and partly to the fact that he was the Whig representative in the negotiations with Pitt's representative, Dundas. According to the editor of Leeds's *Political Memoranda* "the mistake appears to have been that Lord Malmesbury and others put too much confidence in Lord Loughborough's reports of interviews at which he was present with one or two others. Lord Loughborough was probably extremely desirous of office for himself, and objected to no steps which were likely to secure that end."[88] This interpretation, however, fails to take into account Pitt's letter to the King in which the Minister takes Loughborough's word that Leeds's conduct could not have been based on anything that took place in the interviews between the two. But Loughborough's denial does not explain away the fact that the Duke of Portland first approached the Duke of Leeds on the question of a change in government. Dundas's reputation for straightforward dealings was little higher than Loughborough's, and it may be that his reports to Pitt were as garbled as those handed on to Malmesbury and Portland.

Regardless of where the blame lies, Leeds's interview with Pitt on August 22 definitely marks the end of the second phase of the negotiations to strengthen the existing ministry. The end marks another triumph for Fox at the expense of Pitt and the Portland followers, notably Malmesbury and Loughborough, who either wished to coalesce with Pitt or to support actively his policies for preserving the constitution. It was to the interest of Pitt and Dundas on the one side and of Portland and his friends on the other to keep negotiations under cover until some working agreement could be reached. The mystery is why Portland sought the original interview with Leeds, which from available evidence he seems to have regretted very soon, and thus started a train of events which vindicated the judgment of Fox. Portland, who on so many occasions blew hot and cold, may have felt a desire to test the truth of some of Loughborough's reports by finding out if the King was actually a party to these negotiations.

Although Fox won his point in exposing the real purpose of Pitt's negotiations, his triumph was largely one of satisfaction

[88] *Ibid.;* note at the bottom of the page.

rather than of tangible results. Pitt was annoyed at the turn taken and the followers of Portland most eager for office were temporarily thwarted; but that was not all. Pitt was still as confident as he had been in June that he could at least count on the support of the majority of the Whigs in opposing the spread of the doctrines of the French Revolution and any reform measures. Also he knew that certain followers of Portland were still anxious to secure office. In addition, Pitt had until Parliament met on November 15 to strengthen his ministry, and there was a good chance that Portland might weaken before that time and consent either to take office or permit some of his eager henchmen to do so. Events were moving rapidly in France, and the September massacres further strengthened the position of the Prime Minister.

Sometime between May and November of 1792 Pitt appears to have widened his plans to include a war with France. It is obvious that no such conflict was in his mind when in his famous budget speech of February 17, 1792, he reduced the appropriations for the Army and Navy. The most likely time for Pitt to have arrived at such a decision was after the French massacres in September, but unfortunately documentary evidence on his opinions and those of George III during these months is very scarce.[89] In his speech of February 17 Pitt had declared: "unquestionably there never was a time in the history of this country, when, from the situation of Europe, we might more reasonably expect fifteen years of peace than at the present moment."[90] Before many months had passed the clear sky of international peace was filled with black war clouds. In September, following the massacres, a republic was established in France and the new government immediately declared war on Austria. It may be argued that Pitt's stand of rigid neutrality as late as the declaration of the republic shows that he had undergone no change by that date.[91] On the other hand, it is just as likely that he had no intention of repeating the misfortune of his Russian failure of 1791 and hence did not make known his policy until confident of success. "He would not interfere in the French troubles without a pretext sufficient to justify such an action to the English people; and he would make sure of his majority in Parliament."[92] In case France became

[89] J. H. Rose, *op. cit.*, II, 60.
[90] *Parliamentary History*, XXIX, 826.
[91] J. H. Rose, *op. cit.*, II, 61.   [92] Laprade, *op. cit.*, p. 100.

embroiled in war with other great powers of Europe, as seemed likely, a glorious opportunity presented itself to Pitt for duplicating his father's triumphs during the Seven Years' War and for avenging England's losses in the War of the American Revolution. Thus both the example of his father, which had always influenced Pitt so profoundly, and the fundamental principles of eighteenth-century diplomacy favored taking advantage of so wonderful an opportunity.

Regardless, then, of when Pitt definitely decided either that the chance was too good to be missed or that a war of defense was certain, he must have given the question of the likelihood of hostilities his careful attention. Thus the probability of war must be studied along with that of opposition to the spread of the doctrines of the French Revolution in England and to reforms, when one considers Pitt's negotiations with the Whigs from August 22 until the declaration of war on February 1. Yet despite the fact that events in France played into Pitt's hands and that the propertied classes throughout the country became increasingly fearful of revolution, the contest which raged "over the dead body of Patroclus" continued without decisive results. The Duke of Portland, although pressed harder and harder by his followers, refused to give his permission to any of them to accept places in the ministry or to guarantee Pitt anything but support on certain measures. So little progress was made in the negotiations that the meeting of Parliament which was fixed for November 15, 1792, was postponed until January 3, 1793. The situation as far as securing any increase in strength from the Portland Whigs was concerned is summed up in Pitt's report to Lord Grenville on November 18:

Lord Loughborough's language was that he was himself indifferent to his situation, but had always stated that he would take it whenever the Duke of Portland and his friends thought it would be useful that he should; and he therefore declined (as we expected) giving his answer till he should have seen the Duke. In the course of the conversation he confirmed the account of the disposition of the party to support without making terms, mentioned Lord Fitzwilliam, the Duke of Devonshire, Lord Egremont, Lord Carlisle, and Lord Portchester as all likely to be so disposed, and stated his own clear opinion that it was the only line for them to adopt.[93]

[93] Historical Manuscripts Commission, *The Manuscripts of J. B. Fortescue, Esq., Preserved at Dropmore* (London, 1892–1927), II, 335–36.

Unfortunately for Pitt, Loughborough's efforts to secure anything more than spontaneous support failed as had his previous attempts.

Although Pitt may have considered for some time the possibility of war with France, the decision to embark on hostilities in the near future seems to have come from the decree of the French Executive Council on November 16 which opened up the Scheldt. News of this decree reached the British government on November 25, and Pitt took immediate action which doubtless he hoped would bring the wavering Whigs into line. The militia was called out on December 1, and Parliament, which under the law had to be assembled within fourteen days, was summoned to meet on December 13. In issuing the proclamation of December 1 the ministry justified calling out the militia on the grounds that definite information had been received that, despite the proclamation of May 21,

the utmost industry is still employed by evil disposed persons within this Kingdom, acting in concert with persons in foreign parts, with a view to subvert the laws and established constitution of this realm, and to destroy all order and government therein; and that a spirit of tumult and disorder, thereby excited, has lately shown itself in acts of riot and insurrection.[94]

The danger in issuing such a proclamation lay in the strong probability that the opposition would ask for evidence of insurrection when Parliament met. To guard against this threat it was necessary for Pitt either to have definite proof of uprisings which would stand the light of an unbiased examination or to arouse public opinion to such a pitch that obvious flaws in the proof would be passed over by the great majority. It is perhaps unnecessary to pass judgment on whether or not Pitt was reduced to the second alternative; but it is obvious that public opinion was so inflamed that practically any charge would have been believed without adequate proof. This state of mind was brought about by means of loyal associations, sermons, and circulars, and was effective because those who spread the alarm were, in the main, actually frightened. Thus all the ministry had to do was to take advantage of and exploit a widespread uneasiness and fear. But it is highly probable that even Pitt was astonished and gratified by the warmth of the reception given his proclamation of December 1.

[94] Laprade, *op. cit.*, p. 80. Quoted from *London Gazette,* 1792, p. 901.

The assembling of Parliament brought about the third and most bitter phase of the struggle within the Whig party to separate Portland from Fox. In view of the stand which the government had taken on law and order and of the practical certainty of war with France, the conservatives were more anxious than ever to get a public avowal from the Duke. The details of this civil war can be followed in the letters of Elliot and Malmesbury. Meetings of Whig lords and other important members of the party were held during the days immediately preceding the meeting of Parliament. Fox insisted that there was no insurrection or danger of invasion and that the action of the ministry was a trick. On the other hand, Fitzwilliam, Portland, and Devonshire were inclined to blame the government for neglect and carelessness.[95] On December 12, the day before Parliament met, "it was agreed in consequence of a proposal from the Duke of Norfolk that no amendment should be proposed to the Address, nor any supported; that it should pass without a division, and be generally approved, although each Lord should reserve to himself the faculty of reasoning on any parts of it he might think exceptionable."[96] When, however, Fox heard of the policy decided upon he declared to Malmesbury with an oath *that there was no address at this moment Pitt could frame, he would not propose an amendment to, and divide the House upon."*[97] The case which Sir Gilbert Elliot made on December 16 in his conversation with Portland expresses perfectly the point of view of the wing which wished to break with Fox, and the attitude taken by the Duke explains why Pitt failed to win the complete victory which he still hoped to secure. Sir Gilbert declared that the principles of Fox were the worst possible, since they were based on those of the French Revolution, and that the personal regard which his friends had for him should not deter them from separating from him. But the heart of the appeal lay in Sir Gilbert's insistence

that if the Duke of Portland delayed or hesitated, he would become partaker of his bad reputation and unpopularity—that besides this, which was the *first consideration,* the party would be broken up, for it was impossible for us or for many others, not publicly and on our legs to express our entire disapprobation of Fox's conduct and principles—that although *we* know he was averse to them, yet his being silent on the subject left the minds of the world at large impressed with the conviction he was favourable to them; . . . . That this

[95] Malmesbury, *Diaries,* II, 474.   [96] *Ibid.,* p. 475.   [97] *Ibid.*

would and did already pronounce him as acting a doubtful and wavering part, unbecoming his high character, and the head of such a party, and us who were amongst the leading members of it, either as having differed with him, and, of course, become *rats* and deserters, or else, which hurt us still more, as having concurred in Fox's doctrines; that therefore we entreated him as friends, sincerely and affectionately loving him, and attentive to his honour and reputation, to come to a fair and short explanation with Fox, and separate from him *amicably,* but decidedly; and not to lend his name and commit our opinions and character by being silent and inactive on this occasion.[98]

The Duke on this occasion as on many others pained and exasperated those who argued with him by refusing to say a word or even answer their questions. All that Sir Gilbert could wring from him was that he was opposed to any action which would widen the breach in the party by forcing Fox into more desperate opposition and making it impossible for the latter to return.

Briefly the policy of the right wing of the Portland Whigs was to force the Duke to break with Fox, to declare his support of the government measures, and to permit members of the party, if they wished, to accept offices in the government. Since Portland refused to break with Fox, his eager followers concentrated on the second point. The poor Duke was hounded to declare his sentiments in the House of Lords, and after a series of false starts he finally expressed himself on the second reading of the Alien Bill; but his speech did not please these followers because he stressed the fact that he was merely supporting the ministry on this one measure and he more than offset the value of this declaration by arraigning the ministers for neglect and by harping back to the circumstances under which the present ministry had come into power. Worst of all he neglected to state that he would support the government.[99] The Duke was equally obdurate as to Lord Loughborough's acceptance of the office of Lord Chancellor.[100] Finally, on December 24 Windham, Elliot, and Malmesbury wrung from him the promise that he would make an immediate declaration of the necessity of supporting the government, and that his son, Lord Titchfield, would do the same in the House of Commons. Yet two days later Portland again disappointed his importunate friends by keeping silent during the debate on the third reading of the Alien Bill. Elliot, Malmesbury, and Windham had an interview with Portland on the 24th which

[98] Malmesbury, *Diaries,* II, 476–77.   [99] *Ibid.,* p. 480.   [100] *Ibid.*

Elliot reduced to writing, and which according to him was "approved by Lord Malmesbury and Windham, shown to the Duke of Portland and assented to by him as a just report of what had passed."[101] Elliot, speaking in the House of Commons on December 28, expressed his entire difference of opinion with Fox and the conviction that it was necessary to support the government in saving the constitution and the country, and he then added that he would take this stand even if he had to do it alone, but that he was fortunate enough to believe that he agreed with the majority of those with whom he had long acted. But the part of his speech which gave great offense to Fox was his declaration:

that those who differed from me, though weighty and respectable, acted only as individuals, and did not express the sense of any party, but that I, and those who agreed with me, stood precisely on the same footing that we had ever done—perfectly unconnected with ministry, but connected amongst ourselves, as formerly, on our ancient principles, and under our ancient chief (the Duke of Portland), who I knew agreed with me, or whose sentiments I knew I had expressed on this occasion.[102]

Fox in the House of Commons and after the debate in Burlington House took vigorous exception to what Sir Gilbert had said. When the two antagonists threshed out these differences in the presence of the Duke, Fox insisted that Elliot had declared Portland meant to separate from him. Elliot, on the other hand, contended that the first part of his speech applied to himself as an individual and that only in the declared intention of supporting the government was he speaking for Portland and the party as a whole. The Duke upheld Sir Gilbert for pledging support to the government in the present crisis, but not for declaring that he intended to separate from Fox. The latter was vehement both in insisting that Elliot conveyed the impression in his speech that the Duke meant to separate, and that Portland had agreed with him on Sunday, December 16, that "he saw no reason why opposition should not be carried on against the present Government, on the same principles and from the same reasons as ever."[103] Despite the fact that the Duke upheld him on the pledge of support, Sir Gilbert did not seem particularly pleased with the out-

---

[101] The Countess of Minto (ed.), *Life and Letters of Sir Gilbert Elliot, First Earl of Minto, from 1751 to 1806* (London, 1874), II, 97.
[102] *Ibid.,* p. 96.
[103] Malmesbury, *Diaries,* II, 492.

come of the interview, because Malmesbury reported that both Elliot and Windham were convinced that Fox had an "invariable ascendency"[104] over Portland.

Thus all the combined pressure of the various Whig lords and commoners failed before the grip which Fox retained on the affections of the Duke of Portland. This right wing had been unable to carry out its program mentioned earlier of inducing the Duke to break with Fox, to support government measures, and to permit members of the party, if they wished, to accept offices in the government. Portland resisted every attempt to separate him from Fox; he would not give general support to the government but only support in the present crisis; and he firmly refused permission to Loughborough or any other member of his party to accept a post in the government.[105] The last hope of the Elliot-

---

104 Malmesbury, *Diaries,* II, 493.

105 It is only fair to Portland to point out that his weakness and vacillation so decried by Elliot, Malmesbury, and Loughborough did not prevent him from being sufficiently firm to refuse their importunate demands. The Duke had a real case, and he presented it rather ably in the following communication to the Prince of Wales (Clements Transcripts, IV [1792–93], 1716–21):

The Duke of Portland to the Prince of Wales.
"SIR,

"I must request Your Royal Highness's permission, most thankfully, to acknowledge the condescension with which You have honoured me, and to offer You the most Respectfull & Grateful tribute of my Admiration of the more important motives you are pleased to assign for opening your Mind to me, upon the present position of Affairs.

"The Declaration which Your Royal Highness judges it proper to make, of your intention to give the most Publick & Active testimony of Your duty & affection to the King, of the lively interest you take in the security of the Government, and of Your Care & Solicitude for the Happiness & Prosperity of the Nation, though expressive only of Sentiments with which I have been always acquainted, can never be repeated without producing that satisfaction and Gratitude, which must attend so wise, so beneficial and so salutary a determination. Although the exalted Sphere in which Your Royal Highness is happily placed, elevates you above those prejudices to which persons of every other description are subject, and disposes you as well as it enables you to disdain the recollection of a series of measures, highly prejudicial to the Interests of the Kingdom, and even of a system not less injurious to Your Royal Highness's feelings and Interests and those of Your Illustrious House, than they were subversive of the Constitution itself. You must allow me, Sir, to admire the generosity and magnanimity which suggest and influence, that conduct. But Sir, as a Subject of this Empire, as a Supporter of its Constitution, as one for whom Your Royal Highness deigns to profess a regard, I must entreat Your Pardon, for saying that it is not in my power to imitate that Liberality which is so conspicuous and so meritorious in Your Royal Highness. I cannot place an implicit confidence in the Persons who compose His Majesty's present Administration,—I am willing and even desirous of giving it to them in all measures which may be necessary for the safety of the State, and for enabling them to act with effect in the present crisis. Your Royal Highness possesses means of information which I cannot and ought not to have. The Indulgence of your natural affections can give vigour and

Malmesbury-Loughborough group faded on December 31, when Lord Titchfield made the eagerly awaited declaration in the House of Commons. High hopes were held because Windham had written the speech; but, Malmesbury sadly remarked, it was evident that Fox added some sentences. Titchfield did pledge support of the government, but his abuse of the ministry more than offset the

energy to the United efforts of the Kingdom, and it is the most earnest and anxious of my wishes, that you should enjoy all the benefits of those sensations in their utmost extent. My situation on the contrary inclines me to think that I can more effectually serve the cause (which Your Royal Highness will give me leave to say You cannot have more at heart than I have) by more circumspect and measured conduct.

"Whatever influence I may be supposed to possess can only be productive of effect by a confidence of others in the prudence and disinterestedness of its possessor, I am persuaded that that influence would be greatly reduced, and perhaps annihilated by a profession of unconditional support to any set of Measures, or for any stipulated time. I avow it to be my wish, that the Measures of Administration may be such as to enable me to give my support to them. Upon all measures respecting the safety of the country, internally and externally, I pray for Unanimity.

"If these considerations should lead me to attempt to modify the regret which Your Royal Highness so effectually expresses for the difference of opinion upon radical Principles which appear to Your Royal Highness to prevail among persons whom you have condescended to distinguish by your good wishes and esteem, I believe I may safely venture to rely upon Your Royal Highness's candour and partiality for forgiveness, and should I prove successful in these endeavours, I should flatter myself that I had rendered an acceptable service to Your Royal Highness. In the very many conversations I have had with the principal person to whom I imagine Your Royal Highness to allude, I have not observed any such difference as should seem to me to preclude a rejunction, or to render it not desirable. I certainly very much lament his conduct at the opening of the Session and the time he chose for recommending a negotiation to be entered into with France, and yet I am sure that that conduct could only be dictated by the purest motives and that in a cooler moment, the expediency of the Measure which in particular gave so much offence, may not only be admitted but approved.

"When I have the misfortune to differ from Your Royal Highness, it would ill become me to contest the point at all, unless I should have reason to think it so essential to your Honour or to your Happiness as to believe that Your Royal Highness would have a pleasure in discovering that your judgment had been formed upon an imperfect view, or state of the case, and conceiving that the difference between Mr. Fox and me consists in the opinions we entertain of the existence and extent of the danger to which the Constitution has been and continues to be exposed.

"I know not how to suffer myself to believe that such a difference only can be thought by Your Royal Highness to require an irreconcilable, or even more at most than a temporary or occasional separation. The liberality of Mr. Fox's Disposition the confidential intercourse in which he has lived with his political as well as his private connexions and his natural habits render him averse from fear, jealousy and suspicion. He had a confidence in the good sense of the people of England, and in their attachment to the Constitution of which I most sincerely congratulate Your Royal Highness on the recent and unequivocal proof you have received by the Associations, etc. which have been formed throughout the Kingdom.

"Mr. Fox further thought that the interests of the ruling power in France evidently and necessarily opposed itself to any interference on their part in the domestic concerns of this Country, and he still contends that France

value of the pledge. Having failed after months of bullying to induce the harassed Duke of Portland to break with Fox or to promise more than the meager and unsatisfactory support offered in Titchfield's speech, the members of the opposition most eager for office decided to sacrifice themselves no longer. This meant accepting offices as individuals, since either a coalition with Pitt or support of the government as a party, minus Fox and his friends, had failed.

Loughborough was the first to succumb. He became Lord Chancellor on January 28, although his decision to accept the place had been made much earlier. The account of the final negotiations which Loughborough gave to Malmesbury emphasizes phases different from the one which Pitt gave the King. According to Loughborough the Prime Minister gave him authority to offer Sir Gilbert Elliot office and to assure Malmesbury that their differences at the time of the Regency were forgotten and that the latter might consider himself "as much connected" as ever. Pitt also assured Loughborough in the course of this same interview on January 20, 1793, that "war was a *decided measure,* that . . . . it was inevitable, and that the sooner it was begun the better. That we might possess ourselves of the French islands; that the nation

---

has been governed by this sense of Her Interest. These then, Sir, are the principal and perhaps the only material points of difference between Mr. Fox and me, in every other question in which the State of France can make a part of the consideration, whether it be peace or war, the prevention of the aggrandisement of France, or of the Propagation of her Principles, the support of our Allies, the observance of Treaties, or the maintenance of the Good Faith and Honour of the Nation, I think I have good reason to believe that Your Royal Highness will not and cannot find any one more explicit and more zealous, or more to be depended upon.

"In times like the present where Passion too often assumes the place of Reason it cannot have escaped Your Royal Highness's Penetration, to what strange misconceptions and misrepresentations the conduct of every public man is exposed. Your Royal Highness cannot but have observed the jealousy with which the best intentions are scrutinised, and the warmth and violence with which opinions are arraigned and condemned.

"Suffer me then, Sir, to appeal to that conciliatory, that indulgent, that parental spirit which has so often and so lately animated Your Royal Highness's exertions for the public good, in behalf of one whose ability I believe to be fully equalled by his Integrity, and whose attachment to Your Royal Highness's person, to His Majesty and to His Government, are fully known to you.

"I most humbly beg Your Royal Highness's pardon for having taken up so much of your time. I shall only presume further to trespass upon it while I add my most earnest intreaties that Your Royal Highness will believe me to be, with every sentiment of attachment, veneration and Gratitude, Sir,

"Your Royal Highness's most dutiful Servant

PORTLAND."

21st January 1793."

now was disposed for war, which might not be the case six weeks hence. That we were in much greater forwardness than the French."[106] But when he described this interview to George III Pitt emphasized the fact that Loughborough had

confirmed to him his entire readiness to accept the Seals; and expressed himself in the most satisfactory manner on all Political Subjects. He seemed however rather to wish that his actually receiving the Seals might be deferred till Friday as he was desirous of previously communicating his determination to the Duke of Portland. This however seemed intended only as a step of propriety, and not at all with the view of consulting the Duke of Portland on the subject.[107]

Since he did not accept a foreign mission until much later in 1793, Sir Gilbert Elliot could in February write rather patronizingly:

Nothing has happened in politics, nor seems likely to happen. One reason of this *calm,* I think is Lord Loughborough's having attained his own point. Lord Malmesbury is now equally still on the subject; we neither meet, nor converse, nor bustle with him as we did a few months ago. The fact is that he has also settled his point, and will accept of the first foreign mission that is offered to him.[108]

Sir William Windham, according to Sir Gilbert, was offered the office of Secretary of State for the Home Department by Pitt[109] shortly before the news of the declaration of war by France reached the English government. At this time, however, Windham was not so susceptible as Loughborough and Malmesbury.

With the declaration of war which the French made on February 1, 1793, and which reached London on February 9, the problems of the ministry and the King changed. It is true that the negotiations with the Portland Whigs continued until Pitt induced both the Duke and Windham to join the government in July 1794; but the conduct of the war became the main problem for the ministry.

In view of the success which both the King and Pitt attained during the years from 1789 to 1793 it may well be asked why they should be termed years of lost opportunity. After 1789 George III had secured the relaxation which he felt he was

[106] Malmesbury, *Diaries,* II, 501–502.
[107] Clements Transcripts, IV, 1714–15.
[108] Minto, *op. cit.,* II, 115.   [109] *Ibid.,* p. 112.

entitled to enjoy, the satisfaction of seeing Pitt come over to his point of view on the question of reform, and the failure to include in the government any members of the Whig party, as a result of the negotiations of May 1792 to February 1793, who would have been distasteful to him. Thus these years were agreeable to George III because he was not looking for opportunities to make revolutionary changes in internal or foreign policies or in the make-up of the cabinet and ministry. Again it may be argued that these years do not represent lost opportunities for Pitt, since he suffered no defeat on any domestic measure, cleverly recovered from the results of his disastrous Russian venture, and ended by taking advantage of the divisions in the ranks of the opposition in such a way as to leave his government in a stronger position even than at the time of the King's recovery in 1789. But these years do represent lost opportunity in the failure to make necessary reforms, or at least to pave the way for them; in an unfortunate foreign policy which first led to the Russian fiasco and then to the far greater error of failing completely to appreciate the forces of the French Revolution; and in neutralization of the promising beginnings of party organization.

Most of these opportunities, however, were neither realized nor appreciated by George III and Pitt. The King felt that the failure to make certain reforms was a victory rather than a defeat and that the breakup of any party organization was a gain rather than a loss. It is true that George III suffered as keenly as Pitt from the diplomatic defeat at the hands of Catherine II and that he was fully as anxious as Pitt to keep out of costly European wars; but he appears to have taken the excesses of the Revolution and the destruction of old French institutions more after the manner of Burke than of Pitt. Still the King probably felt that he could look forward to years of constitutional calm, since his chief minister was young and since after over nine years of decreasing differences of policy they had finally reached substantial agreement.

To Pitt as well the years would scarcely seem those of lost opportunity. The country was not ripe for reform or for a vigorous foreign policy in eastern Europe. He had had as narrow an escape on foreign policy in 1791 as he had had on internal reforms in 1785, but he had managed to weather the second as he had the first storm. Then the excesses of the French Revolution gave him a wonderful opportunity to adopt a policy which appeared to be equally strong in both foreign and domestic spheres. The only sacrifice was in the direction of turning definitely against certain reforms upon which he had already become lukewarm; and in foreign affairs and party politics the prospect was dazzling. France in her weakened and unprepared state, menaced by the English, Dutch, Spaniards, Russians, and Austrians, should offer little resistance to Pitt's completing what his father had started so effectively in the Seven Years' War. On the side of party politics results and not merely brilliant prospects were already evident. He had strengthened his position in the cabinet by ridding himself of Leeds and Thurlow, although very likely he was disappointed because more of the Portland Whigs did not join his ministry or agree to support him more generally than merely in the present crisis, and because Portland himself did not break with Fox. To offset this, the sentiment of the country and of the aristocratic Whigs in particular was strongly back of his policies, and the opposition was actually broken in fact if not in name. As a consolation for the slight disappointments listed above, Pitt could look at the vote on the King's address of December 13, 1792, which had carried in the House of Commons by 290 to 50. "Of these 50, 21 were reformers, 4 Lord Lansdowne's members, and the rest people personally attached to Fox, and who, from this feeling, and *against their sentiments,* voted with him."[110]

Doubtless the future looked brighter to Pitt than at any time since the opening of the session of 1785 and he walked confidently into the worst years of his career.

[110] Malmesbury, *Diaries,* II, 176.

VII. THE WORST YEARS OF WILLIAM PITT, 1793 TO 1801

The years from the outbreak of the war with France in 1793 until the retirement of Pitt in 1801 constitute a unit in the relationship of George III and his chief minister. During these years Pitt had a free hand in both foreign and domestic affairs, because of the overwhelming majority which he enjoyed in Parliament and because of the unfailing support of the propertied classes throughout the country. It is true that February 1, 1793, marks neither the beginning nor the end of the negotiations which broke up the Parliamentary opposition to Pitt. These negotiations from April 30, 1792, until February 1, 1793, were traced in the preceding chapter; and they were not to be crowned with complete success until July 1794. Nevertheless, Pitt was confident at the time France declared war that he could count on the support of the Portland Whigs in carrying on this war and in opposing reform at home. To George III these years, at the beginning, showed every indication of being even more satisfactory than those from 1785 to 1793. Undoubtedly he felt some uneasiness or at least kept on his guard during the preceding eight years because Pitt still professed to believe in certain reforms and because a well-organized opposition was waiting for an opportunity to return to power. But after April 30, 1792, the attitude of Pitt toward all reform measures except the abolition of the slave trade could scarcely have been more satisfactory to his royal master; and the breakup of the resolute opposition in the latter half of 1792 was probably even more gratifying. With the prospects so rosy for both George III and Pitt, the title of this chapter may seem singularly inappropriate; but the early and consistent blighting of these high hopes justifies it. The monotonous series of failures which the policies of Pitt experienced after 1793 cannot be blamed on the activities of the opposition as can the defeat of his reform measures in 1785 and of his Russian policy in 1791. The only explanations possible are: first, that Pitt lacked ability; second, that the odds against him were too great; and, third, that he was unable to maintain solidarity on matters of policy with his ministry and the King. Doubtless all three contributed in some measure to the failures and disappointments of these years.

From the point of view of British party government of the past century, the years covered by this chapter probably represent retrogression rather than advance over the previous thirty years. This generalization is particularly true for the years after 1785. Although the Fox-North Coalition of that year is described in full, and usually unfavorably, in histories of the period, little is ever said of the tenacity it showed until 1792. Despite the loss of numbers in the terrific defeat in the election of 1784, the wings of this "infamous" coalition did remain united under the nominal leadership of the Duke of Portland. This party believed in going out of and coming into office as a group, and in retaining office if it commanded a majority in the House of Commons. The same freedom was allowed members of the party as to favoring or opposing reform which George III and Pitt had agreed to give each other. Despite this similarity, the opposition from 1783 to 1793 had much more in common with the modern parties than did the heterogeneous followers of the government during those years. Pitt made no attempt to weld his own personal followers, the King's Friends, and the great mass of independents into a unified party. His efforts were devoted more to securing unity in the cabinet by replacing the King's Friends with his own closest associates. Consequently the breakup of the opposition after April 30, 1792, marks a decided setback for the evolution of "His Majesty's Opposition."

In many respects the most significant result of the violent realignment of political factions beginning in 1792 was the company in which the King now found himself. Owing to the sharp change in political issues in 1792 George III discovered that his own views of the new and most important questions— the conduct of the war and the repression of reform movements at home—coincided with those of the Portland or, as Burke called them, the Old Whigs. In the years following 1783 the opposition had been able to combine into a fairly coherent body held together by hostility to the coalition of the King and Pitt and manifesting this feeling by opposition, in most instances, to the financial and foreign policies and the reforms advocated by the government. George III and Pitt were held together by common hostility to the opposition and by belief in the same financial and foreign policies. On reform a rather stiff neutrality at the start had become by 1792 a very willowy acquiescence on the part of Pitt. With the coming of the war in 1793 two paramount issues overshadowed all others: the conduct of the war and the preservation of the constitution. Under the second of these two issues were included the attitudes not only toward such live prewar questions as Parliamentary reform, abolition of the slave trade, and repeal of the Test and Corporation acts but also toward such new problems as the suppression of reform societies, the suspension of the writ of habeas corpus, and limitation of the freedom of the press and of public meetings. After 1794 the closely allied problems of governing Ireland and of Catholic Emancipation became a third great issue; but in 1793 they were not so significant as they later became.

Before that occurred, however, a new alignment of political groups had taken place. Instead of the united opposition and the combination of the King's Friends and Pitt's followers we find three new groups: first, those who believed that the doctrines of the French Revolution were a menace and must be suppressed by war with France and by stern measures at home; second, those who believed in using the war as an excuse for seizing the colonies and crippling the commerce of France and for a repressive policy at home to keep the country solidly back of the government and the war; and, third, those who believed in giving the revolutionists in France and the reformers in England a comparatively free hand. Naturally, the divisions were not so clear-cut as this enumeration indicates; but, allowing for a certain amount of overlapping, these groups did include the points of view of the overwhelming mass of the English people and of the men in public life. In the first group were the Portland Whigs and George III, in the second Pitt and many of his followers, and in the third Fox and the Whigs who still remained loyal to him. Despite the fact that the opinions of Burke's Old Whigs and of George III on the two major issues were so much alike, memories of the year 1783 and ten additional years of differences prevented any real warmth at this time in the relations between them.

These memories in part explain why Portland and many of his followers refused office in the government at a time when the French principles and the reform societies in England vexed them more than they did Pitt. It was only after a year and a half that Portland and others succumbed to the point of view which Burke, for more than two years, had urged so vigorously, and consented to take office. In capitulating, they were doubtless influenced also by the lack of success of the war and by the reform societies which appeared to them to threaten the Constitution. These important changes in the cabinet came early in July 1794, at the end of the session of Parliament. Four places in the cabinet were given to the Whigs: Portland himself was made Home Secretary, Earl Fitzwilliam Lord President, Earl Spencer Lord Privy Seal, and Sir William Windham Secretary at War. Although the places given the new ministers were important ones, Pitt, Grenville, and Dundas continued to dominate the government.

The scope of this work makes it unnecessary to go into the details of the causes and events leading to the outbreak of war in 1793 and of the war itself. Here we are concerned with the attitude of George III and Pitt toward the war, reform, and repression. Did George III allow himself merely to register the decisions of Pitt, Dundas, and Grenville in the sphere of war and foreign affairs? Did he continue to allow his royal powers to slip away from him because of his growing infirmities and the cabinet changes of 1791–1794 which brought in friends of Pitt and followers of Portland with views hostile to his ideas of royal prerogatives? The answer given in most histories is that the decline in the power wielded by George III which began with Pitt's ministry in 1783 continued unabated or with increasing velocity during the war with France. Yet an examination of the correspondence of George III shows that his interest in the policies of the government increased during the years covered by this chapter and that, as time went on, he differed more and more from his three principal ministers as to the way in which the war was conducted. Apparently George III followed the policy which he laid down to Pitt at the time of his recovery in 1789, namely, that of supervising only the major policies of the government and making no attempt to continue the detail work of the preceding twenty-eight years. But beginning at the end of 1792 the King took a more active part again, both because of the war and because of the greater interest which he felt in domestic problems. The joy, however, which George III felt when by April 30, 1792, his Prime Minister appeared to have reached the same position as his own on reform was short-lived. The war with France soon brought out differences between the two men, as to both the fundamental purpose of the conflict and details of various campaigns. As the war continued, George III seems to have enjoyed less and less being overruled on military decisions by Pitt and Dundas; and this feeling may have contributed to the overthrow of the ministry in 1801.

There can be little doubt that after the French Convention had passed the Decrees of November 16 and 19 George III became converted to the necessity of war with France. By the former, the navigation of both the Scheldt and the Meuse had been declared open to and from the sea, and by the latter assistance had been offered to all peoples interested in recovering their freedom. But even the intense hatred for the doctrines of the Revolution which the King developed long before these decrees were published did not reconcile him to abandoning the attitude toward war which he had adopted at the end of the American Revolution. The clash of these two strong opinions—aversion to war and loathing of the doctrines and policies of the French Revolution—are well illustrated in the King's letter to Pitt written on February 2, 1793, before news of the French declaration of war had reached the English government: "Indeed my natural sentiments are so strong for peace, that no event of less moment than the present could have made me decidedly of opinion that duty as well as interest calls on us to join against the most savage as well as unprincipled nation."[1] After the war broke out the coldness with which George III regarded the plans of Dundas and Pitt for colonial conquests shows both that he regarded the war as a crusade and that he had no desire to indulge in new colonial ventures.

It is difficult to speak with the same degree of assurance on Pitt's attitude toward the war. His stand on the reduction of the Army and Navy in February 1792 proves beyond a reasonable doubt that he did not contemplate war at that time. Two interpretations of his policies during the months before the beginning of hostilities and in the war itself are possible: (1) that he continued to abhor war as much as the King, that his stand in February 1792 represented his real feeling in the years that followed as much as at the time he made them, and that he concentrated on seizing the French colonies because he believed that method to be the best way to win the war; and (2) that sometime before the end of 1792 he saw a magnificent opportunity to complete the task, which his father had so ably begun in the Seven Years' War, of ruining England's chief colonial and com-

[1] Earl Stanhope, *Life of the Right Honourable William Pitt* (London, 1861–62), II, xvii.

mercial rival. As indicated in the preceding chapter, the present writer holds that the second alternative is far more probable.

In this chapter two main topics will be treated: the conduct of the war, and reforms and repression. In dealing with both, emphasis will be placed on the attitude of the King and that of Pitt toward the problems involved.

Pitt placed the conduct of the war in the hands of Dundas. Even after the Portland Whigs had entered the ministry in July 1794 and he had given up the Home Office to Portland, Dundas was left in charge of military and naval affairs. Upon the outbreak of hostilities the government found itself handicapped by the reductions in both the Army and Navy which Pitt, anticipating fifteen years of peace, had made in the previous year. At the time she declared war against England and Holland on February 1, 1793, France was already fighting Austria and Prussia, and in March added another enemy by a declaration of hostilities against Spain. Following the tradition of his father, Pitt undertook to gather together all the enemies of France in a great coalition. He made treaties with Russia, Prussia, the Holy Roman Empire, Sardinia, Naples, Holland, Portugal, and Spain, and granted subsidies to most of them to carry on war. So lightheartedly did Pitt enter the war that even his great financial ability which was so much in evidence before 1793 appears to have deserted him temporarily and he undertook to finance the war by loans.

Although the detailed administration of the war was placed in the hands of Dundas, Pitt must share the blame for the failure to work out and carry through a consistent plan of campaign. At the beginning of the war England was distinctly interested in three separate spheres: the Low Countries, the French district of La Vendée, and the French West Indies. She was interested in Belgium and Holland because of traditional hostility to having either pass into the hands of a great and hostile power; in La Vendée because the stern opposition of the royalists in that district might be used to assist in the overthrow of the Revolutionary government in Paris; and in the French West Indies because these islands represented the cream of the French colonial empire. Unfortunately the reduction of the previous year in the Army and Navy made it difficult to take decisive actions in any one of the three, and the fact that even the scanty resources were scattered and not concentrated made success even more unlikely.

The French army and navy were so badly disorganized by the desertion of their aristocratic officers that the campaign of 1793 offered an excellent opportunity for England and her allies to overthrow the Revolutionary government in Paris.

The beginning of the campaign of 1793 in the Low Countries seemed to indicate that the new government in France would be one of short duration. Pitt and Dundas sent about five thousand troops to Holland where together with George III's Hanoverian troops and some Hessians they were placed under the command of the King's son, the Duke of York. This heterogeneous body of fighting men was intended to join the Austrian army in the Netherlands in the invasion of France. Pitt, however, consented to this army's being placed under the Austrian Coburg only on condition that the first operation should be the siege of Dunkirk. This change appears to have cut short a very promising advance against the demoralized French troops. As a result before the campaign of 1793 was over the high hopes which the allies entertained of capturing the border fortresses, of following the panic-stricken French army to Paris, and of overthrowing the new regime were completely ruined. The Revolutionary armies were reorganized and the contest in the Austrian Netherlands was renewed. The Duke of York was forced to raise the siege of Dunkirk, and Coburg was compelled to retreat before this new onslaught. As a partial offset to the complete failure in Belgium and especially at Dunkirk, Toulon, the great French naval station in the Mediterranean, was turned over to Lord Hood by some French royalists. Pitt and Dundas failed miserably to take advantage of this undeserved luck, however, and, disregarding the advice of Sir Charles Grey that fifty thousand troops would be necessary to hold the captured port, left it so scantily garrisoned that the French easily recaptured it. Instead of sending troops to Toulon, Pitt and Dundas used them to capture the French sugar islands in the West Indies. Thus the campaign of 1793 ended with a complete failure in Belgium and La Vendée sectors but with every promise of success against the French in the West Indies.

The campaign of 1794 was even more disastrous for the self-confident coalition. In Belgium and Holland the rejuvenated French swept everything before them. Their tremendous successes were due in part to their own enthusiasm, and in part to the failure of the Austrians and Prussians to fulfill their treaty obligations, to the lethargy of the Dutch, and to the poor quality of the British soldiers. The Austrians were driven back across the Rhine, and a British army under the Duke of York first fell back on Holland. The French forces followed, and not only forced the British to retreat into Germany but also in alliance with the Dutch republicans they overran the country and made Holland a subject ally. Only in the West Indies were hopes undimmed. Martinique had been captured in 1793 and in 1794 Guadeloupe, St. Lucia, and Tobago were taken. An army was also sent against the most valuable of the French colonies, St. Domingo. These successes seemed more significant than they actually were because the fearful fevers which were in the end to ruin the military conquests had not yet accomplished their deadly work.

The year 1795 saw the actual dissolution of the coalition. Holland, which had gone over to the French the year before, now declared war on England; Spain made peace and in 1796 also declared war on England; Prussia likewise made peace with France and joined Russia and Austria in the third partition of Poland. Only Austria and Sardinia could be counted on to give Great Britain real assistance. In the West Indies the uprisings of the blacks and the spread of fever among the soldiers made the prospect there much darker than in 1794. The final blow of the year came in the belated expedition to assist the Vendéans. Burke, whose point of view was best represented in the cabinet by Windham, had continually advocated assisting the French royalists as the fundamental policy of the war. Pitt and Dundas were still primarily interested in the West Indies and, after considerable urging by Windham, consented to an expedition being sent to Quiberon Bay. The British government, however, was to furnish only the navy and supplies and the French royalists were to provide the land forces. The expedition failed as miserably as other British projects in 1795. The French forces which the British Navy landed were made up of émigrés and prisoners of war, and the failure of this unusual mixture to co-operate with Vendéan insurgents played into the hands of the Revolutionary forces. In the end thousands of the invaders were captured and many hundreds massacred. The British government now sent a force of four thousand to assist the Vendéans, but this expedition was badly managed and resulted likewise in a disastrous failure. "And all this wicked folly," according to Sir John Fortescue, "was due to the divisions between Windham and Dundas in the Cabinet, which Pitt, apparently, was unable to compose. Had he declared firmly for Windham, the operations on the coast of France might have been conducted on a great scale, and some good might have come of them. Had he supported Dundas against Windham, he might at least have saved the waste and discredit of these petty, futile expeditions, and avoided the lasting disgrace of buoying up the insurgents in the north-west of France with false and misleading hopes."[2]

Such a series of unprecedented disasters made Pitt more than willing to enter into peace negotiations with France. Nevertheless, the statement in the King's speech at the opening of the session on October 29, 1795, which signified a willingness to treat with the enemy must have come as something of a surprise both to friends and foes. Using the recent changes in the government of France as the excuse, this statement read:

Should this crisis terminate in any order of things compatible with the tranquillity of other countries, and affording a reasonable expectation of security and permanence in any treaty which might be concluded, the appearance of a disposition to negotiate for general peace on just and suitable terms will not fail to be met, on my part, with an earnest desire to give it the fullest and speediest effect.[3]

This public acknowledgment of Pitt's willingness to treat is significant not only because it marks the ending of the first phase of the war with France but even more because it differentiates so clearly the attitude toward the struggle of George III and the Old Whigs on the one hand and of the Prime Minister on the other. It has been argued that Pitt's sudden bid for peace was quite logical in view of the fact that the new French constitution did not have the ultrademocratic character of the preceding ones and that there was a prospect in France of returning to normal methods of government.[4] Still this does not explain adequately why Pitt should have opposed peace so eloquently not only in 1793–94 but earlier in 1795 as well. The uncertainty of any real change in attitude on the part of the new government in France

[2] J. W. Fortescue, *British Statesmen of the Great War, 1793–1814* (Oxford: Clarendon Press, 1911), p. 117.

[3] *The Parliamentary History of England, 1066–1803* (London, 1806–1820), XXXII, 143.

[4] *The Cambridge History of British Foreign Policy, 1783–1919* (New York: Macmillan, 1922), I, 261.

was too great to account for so radical a change on the part of the Minister. On the other hand, the explanation for this change seems much more obvious if we consider the fundamental purpose for which Pitt was carrying on this war. He looked upon it either as another phase of the long struggle between England and France for colonial and commercial supremacy or as the best means of forcing the latter to accede to reasonable terms of peace. George III, the Portland Whigs, and the propertied classes in general wished a peace based on restoration of the Bourbons and of the French frontiers of 1789. But regardless of which of the two purposes listed above was Pitt's true one, he had failed. If the first one is accepted, then it had become clear to Pitt that the old formula which had worked so well for his father, a coalition subsidized by England to keep France busy on the Continent while the British Navy seized the French colonies and drove the French merchant marine from the seas, had failed, because of circumstances which he could not foresee. If the second alternative is chosen, it had become equally clear to Pitt that the seizure of the French and Dutch colonies and even the ruin of the merchant marines of the two countries were not sufficient to bring about the restoration of the Bourbons and the return by the French of all their conquests during the preceding years. Under the circumstances Pitt showed excellent tactics in putting out this peace feeler. Doubtless he hoped that it would lead to peace; but in case his olive branch was spurned he had a stronger talking point both in and out of Parliament for continuing the war. It must be remembered that when the speech from the throne was given on October 29 there were riots in the metropolis and demands for both peace and relief from the scarcity of provisions.

If there is considerable doubt as to the fundamental war policy of Pitt, there can be none in the case of his royal master. George III makes it easy for the historical student to study his reactions to foreign affairs from 1783 to 1801, because there is only one really fundamental change in his attitude and that came at the end of 1792. In addition, the point of view of the King is easy to follow because it lacked the shades and nuances which characterize those of most public men during the period. From 1783 to the end of 1792 and the beginning of 1793 George III held that Great Britain should adhere to a peace policy because wars during the first twenty-three years of his reign had proved unsatisfactory and because the country needed peace in order to recover its fiscal health. He became converted to the necessity of war with Revolutionary France with the greatest reluctance, but once convinced he remained inflexible in his belief that no peace should be negotiated until the Revolution was crushed. George III was always a good hater, but his letters during these years seem to breathe a far greater hatred of French Revolutionary leaders and of the opposition at home than do his letters on his foreign and domestic enemies during the years before 1792. From 1793 to 1795 he heartily approved of Pitt's policy of repression and opposition to reform but frequently betrayed misgivings concerning the colonial campaigns of Dundas. He made, however, no attempt to conceal his hostility to Pitt's peace move of October 29. In a way it must have been a great disappointment to him, because his Minister had resisted every peace move of the opposition since the outbreak of war in a manner that was truly gratifying.

As early as June 17, 1793, Fox had moved in the House of Commons that measures be taken to secure peace with France. In opposing this motion Pitt expressed the point of view which appears to have satisfied George III until October 1795; he declared that, in his opinion, security against the system established in France which under the name of the rights of man united the principles of usurpation abroad with tyranny and confusion at home could be obtained in only one of three ways: "1st, That these principles shall no longer predominate; or 2ndly, That those, who are now engaged in them, shall be taught that they are impracticable, and convinced of their own want of power to carry them into execution; or 3dly, That the issue of the present war shall be such as, by weakening their power of attack, shall strengthen your power of resistance."[5] No armed truce or temporary suspension of hostilities would accomplish this end. Instead Pitt insisted the present motion could "only tend to fetter the operations of war, to delude our subjects, to gratify the factious, to inflame the discontented, to discourage our allies, to strengthen our enemies."[6] George III expressed his opinion of the motion of Fox in his letter of the following day: "I cannot help observing that it seems very extraordinary that any one

[5] *The Speeches of the Right Honourable William Pitt in the House of Commons* (London, 1808), II, 6.
[6] *Ibid.*

could advance so strange a proposition, and I trust one so contrary to the good sense of the majority of the whole nation, and such as no one but an advocate for the wicked conduct of the leaders in that unhappy country can subscribe to."[7] At the opening of the next session of Parliament on January 21, 1794, the King's speech again enunciated the view that no peace should be made without security against the French danger. The most significant passage reads:

Although I cannot but regret the necessary continuance of the war, I should ill consult the essential interests of my people, if I were desirous of peace on any grounds but such as may provide for their permanent safety, and for the independence and security of Europe. The attainment of these ends is still obstructed by the prevalence of a system in France, equally incompatible with the happiness of that country, and with the tranquillity of all other nations.[8]

Even after the disasters of the 1794 campaign Pitt still agreed with George III on the necessity of continuing the war until the French menace was removed. In the King's speech at the opening of the session on December 30, 1794, hope was expressed that success was still possible:

I entertain a confident hope that, under the protection of Providence, and with a constancy and perseverance on our part, the principles of social order, morality, and religion, will ultimately be successful; and that my faithful people will find their present exertions and sacrifices rewarded by the secure and permanent enjoyment of tranquillity at home, and by the deliverance of Europe from the greatest danger with which it has been threatened since the establishment of civilized society.[9]

When Wilberforce moved as amendment to the address that the King be advised to negotiate for peace on terms that should be deemed just and reasonable, Pitt stoutly opposed on the grounds that the resources of France were nearer exhaustion than those of England. On January 26 and March 24, 1795, he opposed motions for peace negotiations made, respectively, by Grey and Fox. Finally on May 27 Wilberforce introduced another motion that present circumstances in France should not prevent England from entertaining proposals for a general peace. Pitt in opposing this motion took a line somewhat different from that in his earlier

[7] Stanhope, *op. cit.*, II, xviii.
[8] *Parliamentary History*, XXX, 1046.   [9] *Ibid.*, p. 59.

speeches. One sentence is especially significant: "To look for negociation at the present moment is premature, though I look to it at no remote period."[10] He then proceeded to argue that by prosecuting the war vigorously for a short time longer the nation had every reasonable prospect of securing a solid, permanent and honorable peace.

Evidently the events of the first half of 1795 brought about the increasing difference in the attitude of George III and Pitt toward the war. The declaration of the Prime Minister on March 24 that the war was not being waged to force monarchy on the French people and his admission on May 27 that he favored peace at no remote period must have disturbed the King. Finally came the statement in the King's speech of October 29, already referred to, in which Pitt agreed to listen carefully. to any peace overtures by the enemy. George III and Pitt had come to a definite parting of the ways on the issue of continuing the war. Pitt evidently felt that, in view of the unsatisfactory progress of the war abroad and of conditions at home, it was unwise to refuse blindly any reasonable attempts to stop hostilities. If the French refused to negotiate, he was in a stronger position in dealing with the Parliamentary opposition and with dissatisfaction throughout the country. George III, on the other hand, felt that any suggestion of negotiating for peace would strike at the morale of the English people and their allies. The reluctance with which he permitted that section on peace to be inserted in his speech of October 29 is shown in his letter of the 27th to Lord Grenville. Speaking of a rumor of an Austrian success over the French he added: "No one will more sincerely rejoice than me at such an event, as no one more forcibly feels that unless the French are thoroughly reduced no solid peace can be obtained, and no attempt ought to be encouraged of opening a negotiation, which ever has the effect of destroying all energy in those who ought to look forward to the continuance of war."[11]

Despite this opposition to peace negotiations on the part of the King, Pitt in December induced him to associate his name with an additional peace effort. The pressure for peace both outside Parliament and by the opposition, particularly in the

---

[10] *Parliamentary History,* XXX, 91.

[11] Historical Manuscripts Commission, *The Manuscripts of J. B. Fortescue, Esq., Preserved at Dropmore* (London, 1892–1927), III, 143. Hereafter referred to as *Dropmore Papers.*

House of Commons, convinced Pitt that he must take some step to prove the sincerity of his desire to end the war. In an effort to lessen this pressure he persuaded George III to send a message to both houses of Parliament assuring them that it was his earnest desire to conclude a general peace whenever one could be secured which would be fair both to his allies and to himself. By January 27, 1796, however, the King could restrain himself no longer and he set down his own views in one of those vigorous memoranda which have thrown so much light on his real political and constitutional views. He sent copies to the Chancellor, Pitt, Portland, and Dundas, and retained one himself. It is perhaps the fullest exposition of his views of the war to be found in any of his papers:

The allusion in the Speech at the opening of this Session of Parliament to a desire of making Peace which was renewed in December by the messages to both Houses of Parliament, though both calculated to stave off any evil impression which Opposition might create in the minds of some overtender friends of Government in the House of Commons, were perhaps useful steps at home, though certainly of a nature to cause some uneasiness to our Allies on the continent and to damp the rising in the interior of France. I think myself compelled from the magnitude of the subject to state my sentiments on the supposition that this idea of negociation may again be brought forward without waiting for the issue of the Great Armament which has been sent to the West Indies under the Command of Sir Ralph Abercromby; this I do with greater ease at the present moment when I am persuaded none of my ministers can seriously look on this as the proper time for entering on the consideration of that subject, and consequently that my ideas may be of some use, they having as yet not fully weighed the objections which appear to me well grounded for rendering the present period particularly improper for attempting to set any negotiation on foot.

The great force which has been collected and sent to the West Indies, to which I have already alluded, the additions to it to be sent on the first change of wind and in the month of March ought to have sufficient time allowed for it to be seen what success may be obtained in that part of the globe; I perhaps am too sanguine but I fully expect it may secure the possession of St. Domingo without which acquisition I cannot think our possessions in the Islands secure and that peace can be but of short duration.

The further successes in the East Indies which cannot but be expected is an additional reason not to hamper ourselves with a negociation.

We are trying to persuade both the Courts of Vienna and Petersburg to come forward and commence an early Campaign, how fruitless must be this attempt if we open any negociation from hence, we cannot honourably move without first giving them notice, which will be a solid excuse to them for waiting the issue of the measure prior to making preparations which cannot be effected without expense.

In addition to these weighty reasons, the present state of France points out that no better agent can be employed to effect our purposes than time; the ill success of the proved loan and further discredit of the Assignats must soon overwhelm the new modelled Government; the conduct of the Republican Army within France as well as those employed in Germany and Italy will then appear as well as the increasing discontent in the country; every one of those disasters can alone be averted by our proposing peace, which would give a momentary weight to the Executive Government of France and put a stop to the various engines that seem now to threaten the downfall of that horrid fabric, established on the avowed foundation of the dereliction of all Religious, Moral and Social principles.

I wished to have stated my sentiments in fewer words, but the subject would not admit of it.[12]

Despite this vigorous statement on the part of the King, Pitt and Grenville persevered in their peace efforts. Three days later the ministers sent a despatch to Eden, the British representative in Vienna, asking him to press for a joint declaration by the two powers of their willingness to discuss peace terms. The Austrian government was unwilling to make this joint declaration but indicated a willingness to issue one at a later time, expressing these sentiments. The proposals, partly because the English government held back the subsidies, appear to have aroused no enthusiasm on the part of the Austrians. Whether withholding the subsidy was due to dissatisfaction with the results of earlier campaigns or to a belief that a peace with France would make it unnecessary for England to further subsidize her allies is not clear; but the results of the failure to pay Austria, combined with the obvious eagerness of the English government to make peace, were disastrous. France was encouraged to plan a vigorous campaign for the year and to make such extravagant demands as a basis for peace that acceptance was impossible. Further, the proposal for peace weakened the resistance of both Austria and

[12] "Correspondence of King George III," Transcripts by Sir John Fortescue in William L. Clements Library, VII, 3002–3005. Hereafter referred to as Clements Transcripts.

Sardinia in the coming campaign. Both the lack of necessary supplies for Austria and the fear of Sardinia that the joint peace declaration by Great Britain and Austria would leave her in a perilous position proved costly. The negotiations between England and France, carried on at Berne, were prolonged until late in March. The final French demand which was handed in at Berne on March 26 was so extreme that all hopes of continuing the negotiations were instantly killed. The Directory demanded the restoration of all colonial conquests made by England during the war and implied the retention of the natural frontiers of the Rhine, the Alps, the Pyrenees, and the ocean.[13] Clearly Pitt had been outgeneraled by the so-called corrupt politicians of the Directory. George III had foreseen the outcome of these negotiations in almost uncanny fashion; perhaps it was due to the fact that he had dealt with politicians of this type long before Pitt had entered public life.

Any hopes entertained that the Directory would carry on a less aggressive war than the more revolutionary governments which had preceded it or that France was nearing the end of her material resources were speedily dispelled by the campaigns of 1796. Three large French armies were sent against Austria; two of them struck through southern Germany, and the third, under the command of Napoleon Bonaparte, invaded northern Italy. The young Corsican won a series of brilliant victories over both Sardinians and Austrians. The latter were driven out of Lombardy, the Sardinians and smaller Italian states were forced to make peace with France, and as a result the ports of Italy were closed to the British fleet and in November it was withdrawn from the Mediterranean. These successes influenced Spain, which had made peace with France in the previous year, to form an alliance with her former enemy and in October to declare war on Great Britain.[14] Although the main campaign of 1796 was directed against Austria, England was not forgotten by France. An intensive, and not unsuccessful, campaign by French privateers was carried on against British shipping. In December a French force under the command of Hoche actually evaded the British fleet and landed in Ireland; but bad weather and bad seamanship wrecked the enterprise.

Despite the fact that the negotiations first suggested on Octo-

---

[13] *The Cambridge History of British Foreign Policy*, I, 265.
[14] J. W. Fortescue, *British Statesmen of the Great War*, p. 120.

ber 29, 1795, and finally rejected on March 26, 1796, had not only failed disastrously but had also been ruthlessly exploited by the French government, Pitt, in the midst of the disastrous year, decided to make a second attempt to secure peace. Before making this attempt early in September, Grenville and he attempted to secure the support of Prussia by a typical eighteenth-century proposal. Belgium, which had been annexed to France in 1795, was offered to Prussia; and Austria was to be indemnified for her loss by the acquisition of Bavaria, which she had so long coveted. The project failed because France still held Belgium and because George III, Prussia, and Austria looked on the plan with disfavor. Prussia was embarrassed because a short time before she had signed a secret treaty with France which insured her neutrality. Austria, despite the fact that she had so frequently in the past flirted with the idea of the exchange of Belgium for Bavaria, now declined to risk the effect on the Holy Roman Empire. Pitt justified such a step to the King on the grounds that: "It indeed appears to him to furnish almost the only chance of terminating the contest on the Continent without an accession of power to France which must be considered as essentially injurious to this country; and the necessity of the case hardly appears to his mind to admit of not trying the experiment proposed."[15] The vigorous opposition of George III is admirably expressed in a letter of July 30, 1796, to Grenville. The proposal conflicted with his sense of justice and he inquired as to

what right England has to give away the rights and interests of other Princes, who have either by England or Austria been brought forward into a business their own inclinations did not covet, I cannot either see a shadow of justice or the pretence of interference; and whether the violence of France or the encouragement of Britain effect this, I must look on it as equally hard on the individual and subversive of every idea that ought to actuate the stronger to support not oppress the weaker.

His next paragraph, however, shows that he objected not to the principle of the exchange of territories but merely to the smaller powers being forced against their wills.

If Vienna looks on the Netherlands as a burthen she may, on a peace, yield those Provinces to Prussia, and that Court may accept it; and, should the King of Prussia be wise enough, he might in return give

15 Clements Transcripts, VII, 3116–17.

his new acquired Margraviates of Anspach and Bareuth to Austria,
provided for the county of Sayn, which on the death of the present
Margrave comes to me, I should be indemnified by getting the Bish-
opric of Hildesheim whenever the present possessor shall die or resign; these are reasonable exchanges which the necessity might authorize; and if the two Margraviates do not in value equal the
Netherlands, as the support of them would be less expensive that
ought to be taken into the calculation; but, should that not do, the
King of Prussia might make up the difference by some addition from
his Polish acquisitions being given to Austria.[16]

In short, George III presented the point of view not only of
justice but also of the Elector of Hanover as well.

When this attempt to make use of Prussia failed, Pitt merely
renewed his peace efforts in another direction. The main outlines
of the terms which he was willing to make a basis for negotiations are contained in a Minute by Lord Grenville, a copy of
which was sent to the King. The status quo was to be applied to
Austria, and France and England were to indemnify themselves
at the expense of their allies and the smaller countries involved.
England was to keep as many of the Dutch colonial possessions
as possible, the irreducible minimum being Ceylon, the Cape of
Good Hope, and Cochin. France would keep Savoy and Nice,
all conquests on the left bank of the Rhine not belonging to
Austria, and the Spanish part of St. Domingo, and in addition
would recover her former colonial possessions. Thus France
would gain considerably, Austria would recover what she had
lost, and England would retain the most valuable of her colonial
conquests. The rock upon which negotiations might be wrecked
was, as the Minute stated, the possibility that France would
absolutely refuse to restore Belgium to Austria and that the
latter would be willing to accept compensation elsewere. The
procedure which Great Britain intended to follow in such an
event "would be, the preventing the power of Austria from suffering material diminution, and the placing the Netherlands in
a situation of as little dependence as possible on France. And
in proportion as these points were more or less satisfactorily
obtained, we might agree to yield more or less of the concessions
above stated."[17] George III had little confidence in the success
of these negotiations and expressed to Grenville his opinion that

[16] *Dropmore Papers*, III, 227–28.
[17] *Ibid.*, p. 241.

they lacked both timeliness and dignity. But, he concluded, "as perhaps others think the refusal which most probably will ensue may rouse men's minds and make them more ready to grant supplies of men and money, I do not object to the mode proposed being adopted."[18]

Unfortunately for Pitt and Grenville, their peace plans were coldly received by Austria because the imperial armies were enjoying some successes against the French in the Rhineland and because Catherine II of Russia was contemplating taking an active part in the war against France now that the third partition of Poland had been accomplished. In order to offset the Franco-Spanish control of the Mediterranean which appeared certain after the decision to withdraw the British fleet, the English cabinet decided to offer Corsica to Catherine. The Austrian government appears to have been anxious to prolong the war in view of the likelihood of Russian aid, but the British government preferred to use the threat of this assistance to facilitate peace with France. The Directory may have felt inclined to listen to these overtures because of a growing war weariness on the part of the French people, or they may have used this apparent willingness as a screen for the proposed invasion of Ireland under Hoche. Pitt and Grenville, after failing to convince Austria of the necessity of peace, decided, after giving what they conceived to be sufficient warning, to negotiate with France alone. The death of Catherine II ruined the hopes of both Austria and England and enabled France not only to reject the peace overtures but also to carry on the war with every prospect of success. But it is not clear that the news of the death of Catherine was the decisive cause of the rupture of the Anglo-French peace negotiations. Grenville's proposals of December 11 included the restoration of Belgium to Austria, the evacuation of Italy by France, and the surrender of a comparatively small part of her colonial conquests by England.[19] Although these proposals may have been intended to break off the negotiations with France, they were written before the news of the death of Catherine had reached either country. But before the French answer was formulated this fact was known and without doubt contributed to the stiff attitude adopted by the Directory. Lord Malmesbury, who was conducting the negotiations for the British government, was,

---

[18] *Dropmore Papers,* III, 242.
[19] *The Cambridge History of British Foreign Policy,* I, 272.

on December 19, ordered to leave Paris within forty-eight hours.[20] This ended Pitt's second attempt to secure peace.

In many respects 1797 was a darker year for England than any of the preceding ones. The relations between Great Britain and Austria became steadily worse. The English government was dissatisfied with the wretched morale of the Austrian army and with the failure of the imperial court to co-operate with the December peace efforts. The Austrian government, on the other hand, was equally dissatisfied with the withdrawal of the British fleet from the Mediterranean, with the belated payments of the subsidies due from England, and with the peace negotiations of December. This lack of understanding between the two allies and the low morale of the Austrian forces helped pave the way for the complete victories of the French under Bonaparte; and as a result, on April 18, 1797, the preliminary treaty of Leoben was concluded between Austria and France. Affairs at home were even more disquieting: on February 27, owing to unmistakable evidence of financial stringency, the Bank of England had suspended cash payments; Ireland was on the verge of rebellion; and the last straw was the outbreak on April 15 of the mutiny of British seamen at Spithead. The only ray of hope during these gloomy months was the brilliant victory on February 14 of Jervis over a superior Spanish fleet at St. Vincent. Under the staggering weight of this series of reverses the English cabinet decided to make a third bid for peace.

For Pitt an additional incentive to peace came from the obvious increase in the strength of the Parliamentary opposition. On December 30, when Fox moved a vote of censure on the ministers for the way they had carried on peace negotiations, the motion secured only 37 votes;[21] but on April 4, when Sheridan moved to inquire into the advisability of continuing the subsidy to Austria, the motion received the support of 87 members.[22] To so experienced a Parliamentarian as Pitt the warning was unmistakable. Grenville, who in the previous year had been so warm an advocate of bringing in Prussia even at the cost of ceding her the Belgic provinces of Austria, also had additional reasons for desiring peace. Word reached him at the end of March that France and Prussia had signed a secret treaty the

---

[20] The Third Earl of Malmesbury (ed.), *Diaries and Correspondence of James, First Earl of Malmesbury* (London, 1844), III, 364.
[21] *Parliamentary History*, XXXII, 1493.   [22] *Ibid.*, XXXIII, 251.

previous August. A series of communications dated April 9 shows the state of mind of the important members of the government. In a Minute of the cabinet the view was strongly stated that in the light of the unfavorable events abroad and of finances at home negotiations for peace should be made.[23] Grenville in sending this Minute to George III explained his change in attitude:

As long as the financial resources of the country seemed to be such as to afford the means of making vigorous exertions both for the prosecution of your Majesty's part in this extensive war, and for the support of your Majesty's allies, Lord Grenville allowed himself to hope that, by firmness and perseverance, it would be possible to avert the many evils which must result from the conclusion of a peace on inadequate terms, and that under all the circumstances of the present moment. No man can be more deeply sensible than he is of the extent of those evils, but, without resources of finance, it is impossible to resist them by war, and to prolong the attempt would only be to increase the difficulty of those measures that must now be resorted to.[24]

The Duke of Portland and some of his followers in the cabinet acquiesced in this Minute, but Windham was not present at the meeting. This decision was arrived at, evidently, in spite of the outspoken opposition of the King.[25] Pitt appears to have submitted his thoughts to George III before the cabinet met to make a final decision. The King's protest, which he requested Pitt to show to the other ministers, is interesting not only because it shows that the royal mind was unchanged on the main issue but also for the light which it throws on the immediate problems:

Before I enter upon the serious subject that has been this morning brought before me, one natural reflection occurs—the lamenting the mode, but too often adopted of late years, of acting immediately on the impulse of the minute, consequently not giving that cool examination which, perhaps, in more instances than one, might have been beneficial to the service.

I think this country has taken every humiliating step for seeking peace the warmest advocates for that object could suggest, and they have met with a conduct from the enemy bordering on contempt, that I hoped would have prevented any further attempt of the same nature; from my fear of destroying every remaining spark of vigour in this once firm nation.

[23] *Dropmore Papers*, III, 310–11.   [24] *Ibid.*, p. 310.   [25] *Ibid.*, p. 311.

. . . . Would it not, therefore, be wise to wait for further accounts before we cast a die that, I fear, must for ever close the glory of this country, and reduce Austria to a small state in comparison of her situation before this conflict; besides fixing the present wicked constitution of France on a solid ground of more extent and preponderancy in the scale of Europe than the most exaggerated ideas of Lewis XIV, ever presumed to form?

If the Low Countries remain in the possession of France, and the former United Provinces continue a dependent state on the former, one may talk of balances of power, but they cannot exist; and the same chain of reasoning that will admit the above measures will, I fear, not prevent France from adding all the territory between her and the banks of the Rhine to her possessions.

As to the state of our finances, it is impossible for me to decide how far they will enable us to assist Austria. I flattered myself, after the debate on Tuesday, Mr. Pitt had viewed that measure as not difficult; but should that prove otherwise and reduce Austria to sue for peace, I own I should rather see her make a separate peace, as that would leave us at liberty to make one with less sacrifices than if we are to make a joint negotiation, where our acquisitions must be employed to regain the territories of Austria.[26]

Both Pitt's statement to the King of the reasons why the cabinet disregarded this protest and George III's answer accepting the decision of the ministers are worth noting because of their constitutional significance. Pitt insisted that His Majesty's servants

can now reconcile these sacrifices to their minds on no other ground than the public necessity on which it seems to them to rest; nor could they at any rate bring themselves to be the advisers and instruments of such measures if they did not feel themselves bound, both from public duty and from gratitude and devotion to your Majesty, to submit to any personal difficulty or mortification rather than risk the existence of the present system of administration, as long as your Majesty deigns to consider its continuance as important to your personal ease and satisfaction, or to the general interests of your kingdom.[27]

The King's reply reaffirmed his belief in his own opinion, but added:

I am conscious that if that remains a single one, I cannot but acquiesce in a measure that from the bottom of my heart I deplore; and should

[26] Stanhope, *op. cit.*, III, iii–iv.
[27] *Ibid.*, pp. v–vi.

the evils I foresee not attend the measure, I shall be most happy to avow that I have seen things in a blacker light than the event has proved . . . . The die being now cast, we must look forward, and both must do their best to put this country in as good a state by attention, and not by trying new schemes which mislead, and thus preserve a Constitution which has been the admiration of ages.[28]

Pitt boldly hinted that a continuation of the war might result in the overthrow of the present ministry, a suggestion which he was only too well aware would alarm the King. George III in his answer remained true to his own constitutional principles, which were based fundamentally on the right of the ruler to select his own ministers. Since his ministers were unanimous in taking the opposite point of view from him, he could only acquiesce, as he did, or dismiss them and place others in office, a change which he was unwilling to make at this time. The fact that in the light of subsequent events George III's views showed keener insight into the situation than did those of his ministers does not affect the constitutional aspects.

The acquiescence of the King in Pitt's proposed peace negotiations, however, removed only one of many obstacles to a general pacification. From April until June 15, 1797, the British government was severely handicapped if not paralyzed outright by the mutinies of the fleets at Spithead and the Nore. Fortunately for England these mutinies were settled in time not to interfere seriously with Malmesbury's activities in Lille. During April and May the British government tried without success to secure joint action with Austria in making peace with France. By the end of May Pitt's patience was exhausted and he decided to make peace overtures directly to Paris on the ground that Austria had already come to terms with France and had declined to divulge these conditions to her allies. This decision caused a sharp cabinet crisis, and it was only after a severe struggle that Pitt was able to carry the majority of the members with him in favor of a limited negotiation.[29] When shown a copy of the official note to be sent to Paris George III expressed himself in tones of more bitter exasperation than on any previous occasion:

I should not do justice to my feelings if I did not, in confidence, state to Lord Grenville that the many humiliating steps I have been

28 Stanhope, *op. cit.,* III, vi.
29 *The Cambridge History of British Foreign Policy,* I, 278.

advised to take in the last nine months have taken so deep an impression on my mind that I undoubtedly feel this kingdom lowered in its proper estimation much below what I should have flattered myself could have been the case during the latter part of my reign; that I certainly look on the additional measure now proposed as a confirmation of that opinion; at the same time that Lord Grenville has certainly worded it as little exceptionably as its nature would permit. I cannot add more on this occasion but that if both Houses of Parliament are in as tame a state of mind as it is pretended, I do not see the hopes that either war can be continued with effect or peace obtained but of the most disgraceful and unsolid tenure.[30]

If the King continued in this state of mind and no improvement came in the situation abroad, it is easy to see that he might readily have reconciled himself to a change in ministry. What seems to have consoled George III during these various peace nibbles of 1796 and 1797 was his well-founded confidence that these efforts were almost certain to come to naught.

The attempts of Lord Malmesbury to negotiate a satisfactory peace at Lille failed as miserably as his attempt at Paris in the previous year. The French had the choice of making peace with England and then squeezing Austria, or of making a permanent peace with Austria on the basis of the preliminary treaty in April and continuing the war against England. The decision to take the second of these alternatives was reached after the coup d'état of September 4, usually known as the 18th Fructidor, in which the more extreme members of the Directory ousted their more moderate colleagues. The immediate result was a stiff demand on the part of the French government for a far greater restitution of colonial conquests than England was willing to make, and a consequent rupture of the negotiations at Lille. Having insisted upon this third peace attempt in spite of the strenuous opposition of the King and some of the ministers, Pitt brought upon himself the contemptuous criticism of Windham:

You are of opinion, at least so I should collect, that amidst the endless changes of things in France, some government may be found, willing to listen to our vows for Peace, and grant us terms not utterly destructive, in the first instance, of the independence or commerce of the country. Such an event may certainly happen: and if we go lower and lower in our terms, at least within certain limits, the probability may very likely be increased.

[30] *Dropmore Papers*, III, 327.

Yet you must admit that such an event may not happen, and in fact, unless our terms should fall faster than our means is hardly more likely at any future period than at present. My own idea of the probability is that this will not happen; but that we shall go on and on, in this tiding system, till at last we shall be utterly aground and lye, without resistance, at the mercy of the Enemy, to be disposed of as they shall think fit.[31]

Fortunately for England, Windham's fear expressed in this last sentence did not materialize. Bad as the fortunes of the country were during the next four years of war, they never sank again to quite so low an ebb as during the months from February to October, 1797. The Treaty of Campo Formio, which was signed on October 17 between Austria and France, at least left Great Britain unencumbered by her most costly ally. Austria ceded to France the Belgic provinces and her most important possessions in northern Italy. On the other hand the immediate danger to England which her isolation might bring about was more than offset by the second glorious naval victory of the year. On October 11 Duncan crushed the Dutch fleet off Camperdown and thus considerably decreased the chances for a successful invasion of England or Ireland. In the West Indies two decisions were taken in the course of the years 1797 and 1798 which did much to lighten the burden of the war in that area. In 1797 the policy of garrisoning the West Indian islands by black troops was inaugurated, and the next year the British troops, despite the instructions of Dundas, were withdrawn from St. Domingo by Lieutenant-Colonel Thomas Maitland.[32] The troops and resources which had been lavished so long on St. Domingo were now to be utilized with far greater advantage in Europe.

According to Fortescue the turning point in the war against France came with the decision on the part of the ministry early in 1798 to send a fleet to the Mediterranean. Bonaparte had gathered an army and navy at Toulon, and since the Directors at Paris were only too glad to remove from the country so dangerous a man, they readily consented to his making an Egyptian campaign. Austria, although she had made peace with France in the previous October, was strongly urging England to send a fleet to the Mediterranean. Of the British ministers only Grenville seems to have grasped the significance of the Austrian

---

[31] *The Windham Papers* (London, 1913), II, 61.
[32] J. W. Fortescue, *British Statesmen of the Great War*, pp. 127–29.

advice. If Bonaparte's expedition from Toulon was intended for England it was best to meet it before it reached the Straits of Gibraltar, and if designed for the eastern Mediterranean it was a fundamental blunder upon which the British ministers should capitalize at once.[33]

Bonaparte, as is well known, left Toulon on May 19 for Egypt and stopped on the way to capture Malta. This delay turned out to be a most fortunate one for him, because Nelson, who had been put in charge of the English squadron in the Mediterranean, arrived at Alexandria before the French. Nelson then sailed away in search of the French fleet and did not return until Bonaparte had landed his army. Nelson, however, at once destroyed the fleet of the enemy in Aboukir Bay on August 1, 1798, and thus left the French general and his army isolated. Here was the opportunity for which the English government had been waiting since the opening of hostilities in 1793. Italy and Switzerland were ready to revolt against French oppression; Austria was waiting for such an opportunity to renew the war; Russia was willing to join a coalition because the French seizure of Malta had angered the eccentric Czar Paul; and France herself was demoralized by the events of recent months. The failure to exploit this opportunity in 1799 and 1800 was more inexcusable than the failures of the early years of the war.

The logical plan for Great Britain to follow was to establish a base of operations and land an army in Italy; and to make with Austria, Prussia, and Russia treaties, which would include subsidies, for attacking France on the east. The needed base of operations was established in Sicily through the efforts of one of the ablest officers in the British Army, General Charles Stuart, the son of the well-known Earl of Bute. Nelson on his return from Egypt had induced the King of Naples to attack the French. The result was that the King and his court were forced to flee to Palermo in Sicily. Nelson then appealed to Stuart, who was stationed on the island of Minorca, to come to his assistance. Stuart, without even waiting for instructions from England, set out for Sicily and within a short time had organized the defense of the island in such a way as to supply the British government with the needed base of operations in Italy. But owing to the system of recruiting troops then in existence and to the losses

[33] *Ibid.*, p. 134.

in the West Indies the British ministry was unable to place an army in Italy. The next step, that of forming a second coalition against France, was pursued vigorously and here the delay which in the end meant failure was not the fault of the British ministers. Russia, Turkey, and Naples were speedily won over; but Prussia declined to join. The result was that Austria delayed a decision and did not actually become a member of this second coalition until January 1799; and even then her help was not complete, for to watch Prussia she kept troops which were needed against the French in Italy.

The campaigns of 1799 were great disappointments. The Russians sent armies to both Holland and Italy, the former to co-operate with the British and the latter with the Austrians. In both places mismanagement and national jealousies wrecked favorable opportunities of striking severe blows at the French. Pitt after some delay agreed to send 30,000 men to Holland if the Russians would send 15,000; and he was able to secure this number only by paying members of the militia ten guineas each to enlist for service in Europe only. The attack on Holland failed for several reasons: the Dutch did not rise, the British Army was poorly trained, and the campaign opened in September instead of May.[34] The bad feeling which developed between the British and Russian armies had a disastrous effect in the future on the relationship of the two governments. The same jealousy developed between the Russians and the Austrians in fighting the French in Italy. Here the result was not actual failure, as in Holland, but merely incomplete success. Internal dissension had actually dissolved the second coalition before the return to France of the genius who was to undo the little which the allies had accomplished. On October 9 Bonaparte managed to return safely to France and on November 9 to overthrow the Directory and establish himself as First Consul. The skill which he immediately displayed on all sides gave evidence that the allies could no longer count for success on the mistakes of the French government as they had done under the Directory.

It is clear from policies pursued during the winter of 1799–1800 that the British ministers had no idea of what was in store for them during the next year. Even discounting the loss of Russia and making allowances for the military talents of Bona-

---

[34] J. W. Fortescue, *British Statesmen of the Great War,* p. 145.

parte the British government appeared to look forward to the campaign of 1800 with considerable confidence. On no other ground can the reception given Bonaparte's peace proposals of Christmas 1799 be explained. It is true that the style of the letter which the new head of the French government addressed to George III was a bit flamboyant and from the point of view of the British ruler lacking in good taste, and that in view of his later career some skepticism must be shown of the sincerity of his professions. Even these extenuating circumstances, however, do not justify the action taken by the British ministers. Bonaparte's letter to George III, which was enclosed in a note from Talleyrand, the French minister of foreign affairs, to Lord Grenville, asked:

Must the war, which has, for eight years, ravaged the four quarters of the globe, be eternal? Are there no means of coming to an understanding? How can the two most enlightened nations of Europe, powerful and strong beyond what their inclination requires, sacrifice to ideas of vain grandeur the advantages of commerce, internal prosperity, and the happiness of individuals? How is it that they do not feel that peace is an object of the first necessity, as it is one of the greatest glory?[35]

In sending these letters to the King, Grenville remarked that he did not presume to anticipate the result of the decision of the ministers but he could not refrain from expressing "the strong impression of his mind that this overture should at all events be declined in such a way as may be most likely to satisfy the feelings of the public in this country."[36] The reply of George III on the following day, January 1, 1800, must have fulfilled Grenville's expectations:

The last evening I received Lord Grenville's note forwarding the letter addressed to Me by Bonapart, and that to him from Talleyrand. I trust Lord Grenville is convinced that I am perfectly easy that every one of my Ministers must view this in the same light I and he do, namely that it is impossible to treat with a new impious self created aristocracy, and I have too good an opinion of my subjects at large to doubt that when properly stated, they must see it in the same light. Therefore I am clearly of opinion that the only consideration is how to reject the proposal with that dignity and seriousness which must set this Country in an high light with other European

[35] John Gifford, *A History of the Political Life of the Right Honourable William Pitt* (London, 1809), VI, 394.
[36] Clements Transcripts, IX, 0362-63.

Countries, and make Englishmen look with respect on their own situation; I do not enter on the want of common Civility of the conclusion of the Corsican Tyrant's letter, as it is much below my attention, and no other answer can be given, than by a Communication on Paper, not a letter from Lord Grenville to Tallyrand.[37]

When Grenville sent the King a draft of the reply which the cabinet agreed upon the latter answered jubilantly:

Lord Grenville I can with truth assert that I never read a paper which so exactly contained the sentiments of my heart as the Draft of your Declaration to Tallyrand, and I cannot see the shadow of reason for altering any expression it contains,—when sent I desire may have a Cópy of it, as it is a paper I shall with pleasure refer to. I trust no time will be lost in communicating it to the Courts of Russia, Austria, and Prussia, and indeed to all the other Courts of Europe, and I should wish to have it with a Message laid before both Houses of Parliament on the day of their assembling.[38]

The message which gave both George III and Grenville such complete satisfaction proved in the light of subsequent events to have been a most unfortunate one. It stated brusquely the view of the French Revolution which Burke had popularized and insisted that peace negotiations were useless until the fundamental causes of the war were removed. Professions of a desire for peace such as the letter of Bonaparte expressed were worthless, since similar ones had been made by his predecessors who had controlled France and devastated Europe. Until proof was furnished by France that she had abandoned the principles and projects which endangered the very existence of civil society, it would be the duty of His Majesty to continue the present just and defensive war. The best and most natural pledge on the part of France that she had abandoned these principles and projects would be the restoration of the line of princes who had ruled her so ably for so many centuries. Although it had no intention of prescribing the form of government France should adopt or the individuals in whose hands she should place the conduct of affairs, the English government did insist that security for England and safety for Europe must be assured before a general pacification were possible.[39]

This stiff message to the new French government played straight into the hands of Bonaparte, who used it as a justification

[37] Clements Transcripts, IX, 0378–79.
[38] *Ibid.*, IX, 0381.   [39] Gifford, *op. cit.*, VI, 404.

for continuing the war. Such a blunder on the part of the ministry at the very beginning of 1800 was prophetic of the manner
in which the campaign of the year was to be conducted. The
excuse offered for so many of the mistakes early in the war, lack
of an army and competent leaders, was no longer valid. Stuart,
who had done such effective work the year before, suggested
sending twenty thousand troops to Minorca. This force could be
used to strike at the French under the most advantageous conditions; but Dundas and Windham once more disagreed violently
on the use to be made of the English troops, for the latter was
still convinced that the royalists in La Vendée should be assisted.
The troops were then divided so that six thousand were sent to
capture Belleisle and some five thousand to cruise the Mediterranean. The result was that the six thousand proved inadequate and the five thousand found nothing to do. Meanwhile
Bonaparte began what was in many respects his most brilliant
campaign by defeating the Austrians at Marengo on June 14.
Dundas now ordered the troops from Belleisle to Minorca and
soon augmented the force in the Mediterranean to over twenty
thousand. Had this number been used as Stuart had suggested,
the victory of Bonaparte might have been impossible. In December the Austrians suffered another decisive defeat at Hohenlinden
and immediately sued for peace. The treaty of Luneville on
February 9, 1801, left England without the support of her chief
ally.

Matters went fully as badly elsewhere for Great Britain. The
northern powers, Sweden, Denmark, and Prussia, planned a revival of the Armed Neutrality of 1780; and in December the Czar
Paul agreed to join them. The next month the Russian ruler
made peace with France and even proposed an alliance. Thus
when Pitt resigned on February 3, 1801, and the King accepted
the resignation in his letter of the 5th, the war prospects were
very dreary. With no allies, and faced with the League of Armed
Neutrality and a likely Franco-Russian alliance aimed at the
British control of India, Pitt, when he resigned, might well deplore, as he is alleged to have done on his deathbed, the condition
in which he left his country. Before many months the assassina-
tion of Paul, the bombardment of Copenhagen by Nelson, and
the capture of the French army in Egypt by the English under
Abercromby did something to lighten the deep gloom of February.

When judgment is passed on the achievements of Pitt as a war minister from February 1793 to February 1801, the criticisms must fall under two heads: first, his failure to formulate and to carry out a consistent plan of campaign; and, second, his belated and unsatisfactory efforts to create an army. It is much easier to excuse Pitt's failures in 1793 and 1794 than those from 1795 to 1800. During these two first years he believed with some justification that the war was merely one more phase in the Anglo-French rivalry which began in 1689. The ideal plan to follow was that of his father in the Seven Years' War: finance a Continental coalition to distract the French, and use the English fleet to capture the French colonies and sweep the French merchant marine from the seas. When this failed before the unexpected strength of the French Revolutionary governments, he should have adjusted his fundamental policy to the changed conditions or have adopted that of George III and the Old Whigs. Instead he pursued a purely opportunist policy and both oscillated and vacillated between his original plan and that of the Old Whigs and George III. Having brought Portland's followers into the ministry in 1794 he was obliged to give their fundamental policy of crushing the Revolution some consideration. Sir John Fortescue has condemned this opportunist policy in the following words:

His attack on the West Indies, initiated under the influence of Dundas, was designed to please the public by advertisement of victories, which he thought would be cheap, but proved to be ruinous. But Holland cried out for the aid of British troops, and then it was, "Oh yes, send troops to Holland, and let them besiege Dunkirk, because" (here I quote his real words) "it is so near as to give a good impression of the war in England." But Toulon was offered to the British by the French Royalists. "Oh yes, send troops to Toulon." And Corsica also invited a British garrison. "Oh yes, send troups to Corsica." But, with all these enterprises, could troops be spared for the West Indies? "Oh yes, we cannot give up our expedition to the West Indies." Then the Royalists in Vendeé wanted help. "Oh yes, we will send them troops as soon as we have done with Holland; it will keep the Whigs quiet." But where were all the troops to come from? "Oh, raise men somehow or anyhow, as Lord Chatham did. We'll spend a couple of millions in buying Polish soldiers. Hang the expense; it won't last long." But the French threatened invasion, and the country was alarmed. "Oh, let every man turn out for its defence, as he thinks best and easiest for himself." A menace of invasion was, as we have seen, enough to make him withdraw the fleet from the Mediterranean, without a thought of averting the danger by a counter-offensive movement.[40]

Turning to the second of Pitt's major errors, his failure to create an army, we find that at the outbreak of hostilities Great Britain had a very small army. This can be explained partly by the small amount which Pitt devoted to the Army before 1793 and partly to the fact that the country relied on the Navy as the chief offensive weapon. Once the war broke out recruits were difficult to obtain and hence the government fell back on the policy, derided in the preceding paragraph, of offering commissions to anyone bringing in one or more hundred recruits. Both the soldiers and officers so obtained were inexperienced and undisciplined, because rich speculators purchased the recruits at so much per head and placed immature persons in important positions in the Army. To complicate matters further the ministers failed to utilize the power, which was theirs by law, of passing the manhood of the country by ballot through the militia. Exemption from the ballot was extended to all men who joined companies of volunteers. Advantage was taken of this opportunity with the result that numerous independent companies were created utterly lacking in unity and of comparatively little service to the government. As has been indicated, there was some excuse for these blunders in the first years of the war; but as campaign after campaign was fought and no advantage was taken of the example of the French in utilizing conscription, the same excuse cannot be offered after 1795. In January 1798 an act was passed allowing 10,000 militiamen to enlist in the regular Army, but neither the men nor the Lords Lieutenant, who were in charge of the militia in their respective counties, were enthusiastic, because they feared service in the West Indies. As late as 1799 when they needed 20,000 men to carry on the campaign in Holland Pitt and Dundas secured the number in a short time by offering the militiamen ten guineas each to enlist for service in Europe only. After 1798, when the frightful drain of the West Indies ended, the use of militia as a source of recruiting combined with the new organization furnished by the Duke of York paved the way for better things when the war was renewed in 1803.[41]

[40] J. W. Fortescue, *British Statesmen of the Great War*, pp. 164–65.
[41] *Ibid.*, chapter iv.

We have seen that the point of view of George III on the fundamental purpose of the war coincided with that held by Windham and the Old Whigs rather than with that of Pitt and Dundas. The strenuous opposition of the King to the various peace proposals of Pitt have been fully dealt with earlier in the chapter. To many of the military plans of Pitt and Dundas George III, naturally, was vigorously opposed. As on other questions of fundamental importance, the ministers felt it to be their constitutional duty to advise the King what policy the cabinet had decided on before action was taken. Thus George III frequently threw his weight on the side of the attacks which would hurt the Revolutionary government of France and opposed the West Indian campaigns of Dundas. Yet, when he was assured that the cabinet had agreed on a certain measure, he would give his consent, usually with the same reluctance with which he consented to Pitt's peace proposals. This opposition took the form of vigorous objections to the fatal policy which Dundas and Pitt pursued of scattering their military resources; that is, the King opposed both the major policy and the details of various campaigns. Considering the difficulties which a change in ministry would have caused him, George III was reluctant to take the logical step and dismiss his ministers, although it is obvious that his views on the conduct of the war were those of Windham rather than of Pitt and Dundas. Nevertheless, two sharp clashes between the King and Dundas in 1799 and 1800 must not be overlooked when the dismissal of Pitt on the Catholic question is considered.

The act already referred to which permitted militiamen to enlist in the Army had resulted, with the encouragement of the government, in commanding officers forming complete battalions.[42] Lord Granville Leveson-Gower was prepared to raise such a battalion in Staffordshire out of the county militia; but apparently he wished it to be an independent corps for home service only. When George III gave his consent to the formation of such a battalion under this condition, Dundas protested vigorously on the ground that such a precedent might result in the loss of thousands of recruits for service outside the country. Both the King and Dundas refused to give way, and finally Pitt was forced to delay carrying out the orders of the former until a personal explanation was made. In answer to Pitt, George III, while he approved of the delay, insisted:

[42] Sir John Fortescue, *Historical and Military Essays* (London, 1928), p. 53.

I am thoroughly convinced of the propriety of my conduct and I must say in confidence to Mr. Pitt of the great impropriety at least of that of Mr. Dundas from the beginning of the business. I shall certainly as I feel I am right not object to hearing what Mr. Pitt may have to say on the subject when I see him on Wednesday, and as I am certain he is not fully apprized of the unaccountable steps that have been taken I will have the papers laid before him after that conversation, as I am certain however he may feel for others he would be much more mortified at my acting a part unbecoming to myself and open to real blame.[43]

Evidently neither the King nor Pitt could convince each other and the former appears to have persisted in the steps he had taken to allow Lord Granville Leveson-Gower to organize the battalion as Fencibles for home service. As a result of what he deemed unwarranted interference in his sphere of activity, Dundas on December 8 in a letter to the King expressed in the following terms his intention of resigning:

Mr. Dundas begs leave to take this opportunity of humbly submitting to Your Majesty's goodness, his desire to be relieved from the situation he holds in the War Department. His sentiments on that subject remain the same as they were, when in obedience to Your Majesty's special commands, He reluctantly remained in the Exercise of a Part of the Duties usually performed by the Secretary of State for the Home Department. He has repeatedly stated those Sentiments to Mr. Pitt, and has recently urged him to some arrangement of Your Majesty's Business which might confine Mr. Dundas solely to the functions of the Indian Department. He has not hitherto been successfull in satisfying Mr. Pitt upon that subject, and can therefore at present only state his humble hopes that Your Majesty's Goodness will, when convenient, condescend to take his earnest Wishes under Your Majesty's gracious consideration. Mr. Dundas does not presume to press his own convenience or comfort in any manner which may on due reflexion be judged by others incompatible with the Publick Service; But a Commander in Chief being now established at the head of the Army with authority and confidence adequate to the Situation,—all the important foreign Possessions of Your Majesty's Enemies being now subdued,—Your Majesty's own distant and Colonial Possessions being now in a state of safety and tranquillity, the internal Defence of the Kingdom being amply provided for,— and a large and efficient Army being collected adequate to every Exigency,—there seems to remain very little use, if there ever was any before, for the continuance of a separate War Department in

43 Clements Transcripts, IX, 0328–29.

addition to the ordinary Channels through which that part of the Publick Service had formerly been conducted.[44]

The King appears to have been somewhat taken aback by this abrupt offer to resign, and told Dundas that he could not enter into a discussion on the subject unless Dundas had obtained the full acquiescence of Pitt.[45] Since Dundas did not resign as Secretary of State for War, it may be safely assumed that George III yielded and agreed to avoid interfering in the future.[46]

An even more significant clash between the King and Dundas occurred at the end of July 1800. Dundas's well-established practice of scattering the military resources of the empire on "side shows" was the occasion; and the disastrous failure to utilize these armed forces in Italy has been described. A Minute of cabinet drawn up on July 24 suggested that under the present circumstances the attack which had been planned on Belleisle would be inexpedient and that instead one on the Port of Ferrol would be more appropriate.[47] George III protested, as he had done so often before, against what he considered to be an unsound decision. Dundas answered that he had communicated with Pitt, who wished him not to consult the cabinet further but to convey to His Majesty their joint sentiments of the expedition. This Dundas did at great length, but his main argument may be summed up in a short paragraph:

They feel that if an army collected at so much Expense, and by so unusual Exertions, was to remain inactive during the whole of the remainder of the Season, the Spirit of the Country would be let down, Your Majesty's Government justly censured, and the impatience and clamour for Peace *on any terms* increased every hour.[48]

The King remained obdurate, and Dundas then sent another letter much sharper in tone than his earlier ones. After explaining why the steps which the King suggested were not compatible with the secrecy and promptness which the ministers believed necessary, Dundas proceeded to give his version of how such decisions should be reached:

Mr. Dundas perceives with great concern that his mode of bringing this Business before Your Majesty has met with Your Majesty's disapprobation. His only apology must be that he pursued on this

---

[44] Clements Transcripts, IX, 0351–52.   [45] *Ibid.*, p. 353.
[46] Sir John Fortescue, *Historical and Military Essays*, p. 55.
[47] Clements Transcripts, X, 0562–63.   [48] *Ibid.*, X, 0565–66.

occasion; the same line of conduct He has uniformly done since He had the honour of a share in Your Majestys confidential Councils for matters of smaller detail. He has presumed to act on his own judgment but in matters of such Magnitude as that now in question, He has always conceived himself to be acting in the manner most respectfull to Your Majesty and most beneficial to the Publick Service, when he laid his proposition before Your Majesty matured by the united Wisdom of those to whom Your Majesty has entrusted the conduct of Your Confidential Affairs.

Having stated this much in apology for his own conduct, Mr. Dundas begs leave with the utmost Humility, and the most profound Respect, to state to Your Majesty that in his poor judgement the appropriation of the National Force must in time of War, like every other Resource of the Empire, be subject to the Advice and Responsibility of Your Majestys confidential Servants.[49]

George III succumbed reluctantly to this pressure, and the expedition sailed for Ferrol. There, however, those in command found their task an impossible one and returned home. Thus Dundas had his way, but the King proved that his judgment was better.

But this moral triumph did not assist the King when another clash came on the same principle; for Dundas decided to send a force to Egypt to capture the army which Bonaparte had abandoned. Once more the King opposed, and once more Dundas had his way. Finally the War Minister was justified by a success; but the edge was taken off this triumph for Dundas by two circumstances: the capture of the French army did not take place until after Pitt and he had resigned; and the success was not due to judgment shown in planning the expedition, since the enemy proved to be twice as strong as reported, but to the mistakes of the French general.[50]

Sir John Fortescue considers the victory of Dundas over the King in the Ferrol affair to be of great constitutional significance, and that henceforth he merely registered the decrees of his ministers in military questions.[51] In view of the pledge which George III extracted from Grenville in February 1806, which will be dealt with fully in a later chapter, it is difficult to accept this conclusion.

[49] *Ibid.*, X, 0572-73.
[50] J. W. Fortescue, *British Statesmen of the Great War*, p. 153.
[51] Sir John Fortescue, *Historical and Military Essays*, p. 56.

Turning from this survey of military events and of the differences on peace negotiations between the King on the one hand and Pitt and Dundas on the other to the second important issue during the years 1793 to 1801, that of reform and repression, we come to a sphere of ministerial policy which met with the complete approval of George III. In many respects the most interesting phase of English history during the years covered by this chapter is the attempt to carry on the reform movement in and outside Parliament. During recent years this subject has been admirably treated from many points of view in various monographs. In this chapter the topic can be treated with brevity because there was almost complete unanimity between the King and Pitt on the policy which should be pursued. So far as George III was concerned no change in attitude toward Parliamentary reform and popular agitation was necessary. The views which he had held for years on both subjects did not need an iota of variation to carry him through the years 1793 to 1801. The charge of inconsistency hurled so often against Pitt during these years could not be leveled against the King. This charge, however, so far as the minister was concerned, could not be applied after his speech of April 30, 1792. Pitt's career as a Parliamentary reformer falls into three parts: from 1781 to 1785 he was an enthusiastic advocate; from 1785 to 1792, an indifferent and inactive supporter; and from 1792 on, an active opponent. Thus it was the contrast between the first and third periods which his political enemies loved to stress.

Viewed in retrospect it seems fairly obvious that the reform movement in England had no chance of success after April and May, 1792. The ominous signs, stressed in the preceding chapter, of the rising feeling against Parliamentary reform made it very unlikely that any notable change could be brought about even if war were avoided; but the September massacres in France and the events leading up to war made any changes in the Constitution impossible for many years.

The fundamental object of all three reform societies—the Society for Promoting Constitutional Information, the London Corresponding Society, and the Society of the Friends of the People—was to arouse public opinion in the hope that it would operate on Parliament in such a way as to bring about the reform which each organization desired. The easiest way of carrying on constitutional agitation at this time was to hold mass meetings and to send petitions to one or both houses of Parliament. After the outbreak of the war with France such petitions were coldly received by Parliament, and the London Corresponding Society and the Constitutional Society decided to try different tactics. In October 1793 both sent delegates to a Convention in Edinburgh. Although the delegates arrived to find the Convention disbanded, arrangements were made to call another meeting on November 19. This session of the "British Convention of the Delegates of the Friends of the People Associated to Obtain Universal Suffrage and Annual Parliaments" lasted from November 19 to December 6. The minutes of the meeting omitted resolutions, but there is evidence that an amended one provided that the Convention was to be summoned in case of a Convention Bill, the suspension of Habeas Corpus, an invasion, or the admission of foreign troops into Great Britain or Ireland.[52] In the end the Convention was broken up by the authorities, and three prominent London delegates—Skirving, Margarot, and Gerrard—were, on the charge of sedition, sentenced to fourteen years' transportation. They were tried before and sentenced by Judge Braxfield, who in 1793 had inflicted a similar sentence on a young lawyer named Muir. The conduct of the judge in all four of these trials aroused considerable criticism both at the time and since. In the nineteenth and twentieth centuries those convicted became martyrs to liberty and Braxfield a target for liberal historians.

Despite the misfortunes attending the Convention in Scotland, the London Corresponding Society gave some consideration to calling another in England. Although the Society of the Friends of the People declined to join in such a proposal, the Constitutional Society was willing to send a committee to confer with those of the Corresponding Society. Eventually the joint group appears to have decided on a general meeting or convention. The evidence on definite plans for a convention whether called by that name or some other is conflicting. Letters written by prominent members of both societies may be interpreted in favor of either conclusion.[53] But it seems to have been the news, secured in part by government informers, that the Corresponding Society intended to hold a convention and that the Constitutional Society might act with them, combined with the rumors about prepara-

[52] According to Philip Anthony Brown, *The French Revolution in English History* (London: Crosby Lockwood and Son, 1918), p. 105.
[53] *Ibid.*, p. 113.

tions for armed risings, which made Pitt decide to strike. Beginning on May 12 with Thomas Hardy, the government arrested seven members of the Corresponding Society and six of the Constitutional. On the strength of the papers seized, Pitt asked the House of Commons for a secret committee to investigate the charges of calling a convention for the purpose of subverting the Constitution and introducing French anarchy. As a result of the report of this committee an act suspending the habeas corpus law was hurried through Parliament to make it possible to hold members of the societies without producing evidence. Eventually on October 6 a true bill against twelve of the thirteen was found by the Grand Jury of Middlesex, and preparations for their trials on the charge of treason were soon begun.

The government started with Hardy, since he was considered the most important member of the Corresponding Society. The trial began on October 28 and lasted nine days. John Scott, later Lord Eldon, led for the Crown and Thomas Erskine, the famous barrister, for Hardy. When Scott opened with a speech of nine hours, Thurlow is alleged to have exclaimed, "Nine hours. Then there is no treason, by God!"[54] After being out for three hours the jury returned a verdict of not guilty. Despite this setback, the government persevered and on November 17 placed Horne-Tooke on trial. In the trial and verdict the old radical enjoyed the greatest triumph of his life. A long series of witnesses, including Pitt, were played with and made to look foolish. The jury acquitted him almost immediately. ·The government then released the remaining prisoners who were members of the Constitutional Society but made one more attempt to convict a member of the Corresponding Society. Thelwall was placed on trial and acquitted. Three failures evidently convinced Pitt and the other ministers that repression must come from some other direction than that of convicting of treason prominent members of the reform societies.

By the letters which they exchanged and wrote to third parties, and in addition in the case of Pitt by his speeches in the House of Commons, it is easy to trace the sentiments of both George III and Pitt during the years 1793 and 1794. In neither case was there any significant change in point of view throughout these two years. Pitt had many opportunities during the Parliamentary sessions of 1793–94 to express his opinions because he was sub-

[54] Philip Anthony Brown, *The French Revolution in English History,* p. 127.

jected to a series of constant and effective attacks by the opposition. The extravagance of the praise heaped on Pitt and of the denunciation hurled against the opposition leaders by the King indicates that the monarch was more wrought up than at any time since the trying years 1782–1784. The fight made by the Whig leaders in Parliament for reform and against repression was, in many respects, as significant as the activities of the reform societies and as the treason trials outside.

The first test of the strength of the reform party came in the two-day debate of May 6–7, 1793, when Grey introduced a motion to refer to a committee various petitions praying for a reform of representation in the House of Commons. Grey in the course of his speech emphasized the fact that he expected to encounter difficulties from those gentlemen who always maintained that the present was not the time for reform. If the country was prosperous, it was argued that no improvement was needed; but if conditions were adverse, innovations were deprecated as tending to increase the evils under which all classes were suffering. Pitt, Grey pointed out, had suffered from this argument when he brought forward the question of reform in the years 1782, 1783, and 1785. But the section of his speech which probably annoyed George III most was the reference to the strengthening of the executive power. While it was always argued that the time was not ripe for reform, yet

the encroachments of prerogative were overlooked, and no danger was apprehended from the passing of an alien bill, a traitorous correspondence bill, etc. it was no doubt true, that, in troublesome times, it might be necessary to delegate a larger portion of power to the executive government; but why should innovations in favour of prerogative be watched with less jealousy, than innovations in favour of the popular part of the constitution?[55]

Finally Grey argued that if the country had ever been in danger from the French principles, the danger was now ended, since no men in their proper senses would use the experiences of the French Revolution as a model for the kind of reform which was needed in England.

Pitt, in replying to Grey, made every effort to pin on the proposed reform the stigma of the French Revolution and to prove that his earlier plans for reform were very different from the

[55] *Parliamentary History*, XXX, 801–2.

measure which was being considered. Thus no matter where an argument began it was certain to end either with a denunciation of the principles of the French Revolution or by a direct charge or sly insinuation that the English reformers planned to introduce institutions into England based on these principles. Pitt insisted that his earlier proposals for reform were intended to give stability and vigor to the Constitution and not to introduce individual suffrage and the equal right of every man to a share in the representation. Then, after proving to his own satisfaction that the principles which Grey advocated were the same as those of the French Revolution, Pitt concluded with a theatrical warning in the spirit of Burke:

Those rights which entitle all to an equal share in the government, are rights which only serve to remove them from useful labour, from sober industry, and from domestic connexions, and which abandon them to be the slaves of every idle caprice, and of every destructive passion. The government that adopts such principles, ceases to be a government; it unties the bands which knit together society; it forfeits the reverence and obedience of its subjects; it gives up those whom it ought to protect, to the daggers of the Marseillese, and the assassins of Paris.[56]

The motion was lost by the overwhelming vote of 282 to 41. George III wrote to Pitt stressing the infinite satisfaction which he received at the news of the division and added: "I most devoutly pray to Heaven that this constitution may remain unimpaired to the latest Posterity as a proof of the Wisdom of the Nation and its knowledge of the superior blessings it enjoys."[57]

In the speeches of Grey and Pitt and in the letter of George III we find the point of view of the opposition, of Pitt, and of the King summed up for the years that followed. The opposition strove desperately in session after session to have measures considered on their merits and not in the light of the French Revolution. Pitt, on the other hand, seldom failed to drag in the doctrines of that Revolution and to point out that any measure suggested by Fox or his followers would tend to introduce French anarchy and subvert the Constitution. Thus Pitt's fundamental purpose was to make every effort to link the opposition with the French Revolution and to make his listeners believe that reformers were consciously or unconsciously paving the way for the intro-

---

[56] *Parliamentary History*, XXX, 901.
[57] Pitt MSS, 103, May 8, 1793.

duction into England of these revolutionary doctrines. There was a monotony about the fate of the measures both sponsored and fought by the opposition from the outbreak of the war to the end of the session of 1794. In practically every case the attack of the opposition was very able, the defense offered by Pitt serene and effective, the vote crushing, and the elation of George III unconcealed.

An enumeration of the important debates during this year and a half will bring out the overwhelming nature of the Parliamentary defeats suffered by the followers of Fox. On February 18, 1793, Fox's resolutions against the war with France were beaten by 270 to 44; on the 21st, Grey's motion for bringing up the Nottingham petition for Parliamentary reform, by 109 to 21; on April 25, Sheridan's motion respecting Lord Auckland's memorial to the States General, by 211 to 36; on June 17, Fox's motion for re-establishing peace with France, by 184 to 47; on March 6, 1794, Whitbread's motion for a separate peace with France, by 138 to 26; on the 17th, Grey's motion for leave to bring in a bill to indemnify such persons as have advised His Majesty to order a certain corps of Hessian troops disembarked and stationed in the country, by 170 to 41; and on May 30, 1794, Fox's motion to end the war with France, by 208 to 55. The attempt of the government to put through the Traitorous Correspondence Bill met unexpected opposition, and passed the third reading in Commons on April 9, 1793, by only 154 to 153. But the next year, after the arrests of the members of the reform societies had been made, the government was able to hurry through the suspension of the habeas corpus bill. Its third reading on May 17, 1794, passed by 146 to 28. Thus with the single exception of the Traitorous Correspondence Bill, soon after the declaration of war, Pitt found in Parliament eager approval of his repressive measures.

Since the overwhelming support in Parliament for his policy of opposing reform and of emphasizing the repression of all opposition to the government throughout the country was in such marked contrast to the results of the state trials of 1794, it was only natural that, beginning with December of that year, Pitt should rely on his safe majority to pass repressive measures. The next session of Parliament opened on December 30, 1794, and Sheridan attempted to take advantage of the failure of the government to convict the members of the reform societies by moving, on January 5, 1795, that the Habeas Corpus Suspension Act should be repealed. His motion was beaten by 185 to 41. Undaunted by this setback the opposition continued to oppose bitterly the continuation of the Act. In commenting on what seemed to him to be the sheer perversity of the opposition George III wrote Pitt:

Though I am always sorry for the unprofitable time spent in the debates of Parliament, yet at the present moment it is material that the opposition should be entirely unmasked and the opposing so necessary a measure as the continuation of the partial suspension of the Habeas Corpus must in the opinion of all friends to civil order clearly shew that confusion is no bar to their ambition.[58]

Naturally the King was gratified when a few days later the third reading of the bill continuing the suspension was passed by 62 to 4.

It might have been expected that the reform societies would be encouraged by the outcome of the state trials of 1794 to renew their agitation. Actually only the London Corresponding Society survived. The majority of the Society of the Friends of the People became discouraged and, despite the determination of an aggressive minority, gave up agitating. At a meeting on May 30, 1795, it was declared that the society still believed in Parliamentary reform but that rather than risk public disorders or give the impression that a united front was not being presented to the enemy it would cease political agitation. The Society for Promoting Constitutional Information seems not to have survived the loss of its books and papers, which were seized by the government before the trials. Although individual members continued to agitate for reform, the society did not again play an important role. Only the London Corresponding Society decided to carry on; but before the end of 1795 an incident gave Pitt the opportunity to use his safe Parliamentary majority to curtail its activities.

The year 1795 was a most trying one for the nation. Not only did the military campaigns meet disaster and the peace plans fail, as described earlier in this chapter, but scarcity and high prices of foodstuffs, owing chiefly to a cold winter which had damaged the crops of this year, gave additional grounds for dissatisfaction. As a result the King on his way to open Parliament on Octo-

[58] Pitt MSS, 103, January 24, 1795.

ber 29, 1795, was greeted by a mob with cries of "No Pitt," "No War," "Bread," and the glass window of his carriage was broken by a stone or perhaps by a bullet. This outrage was blamed on the Corresponding Society, which two days before had held a monster meeting at Islington, and gave Pitt an excuse for putting through additional repressive measures. The indignation felt in Parliament over this affair made it comparatively easy for Pitt and Grenville to push through both houses the measures commonly known as the Two Acts: the Treasonable Practices Bill, which provided that anybody who spoke or wrote against the Constitution, even though not following either by an overt act, was subject to the penalties of treason;[59] and the Seditious Meetings Bill, which attempted to prevent meetings and lectures of the reform societies by making it necessary to have notice sent to the magistrates by seven householders if more than fifty persons, not summoned by local authorities, wished to convene, and to have a magistrate present at such a meeting who had the power to stop any speech, to arrest any speaker, and to disperse the audience. The Seditious Meetings Law was to be in operation for three years.[60] Pitt introduced the measure in the Commons on November 10, and the following day George III commended him highly:

The House of Commons having by so handsome a Majority approved of bringing in a bill for more effectually preventing seditious meetings and assemblies cannot but give me the greatest pleasure, as the most convincing proof of attachment to our happy constitution and resolution to continue that blessing to future generations, which cannot be ensured if a stop is not made to the seditious meetings. I have equal satisfaction in finding by Mr. Pitt's note that the small minority was imprudent enough to express Violence on this occasion, as it must still more open the eyes of well intentioned persons as to the designs of those champions.[61]

This new danger brought about renewed action on the part of the London Corresponding Society. Two gigantic public meetings, one before and one after the Two Acts were passed, were held to protest against such infringements on liberty. "The orderliness of these vast throngs, comprising perhaps a quarter of a million of men, affords a strong argument against the Two Acts."[62]

[59] 36 George III, C. 7.   [60] 36 George III, C. 8.

[61] Pitt MSS, 104, November 11, 1795.

[62] J. H. Rose, *Life of William Pitt* (London: G. Bell & Sons, Ltd., 1923), II, 286.

Despite this evidence the ministry and Parliament were too panic-stricken to be turned from their self-imposed task.

Once the bills became laws the Corresponding Society did all within its power to continue the agitation legally. Precautions were taken against admitting undesirable members; each division was, as a rule, to include no more than thirty persons; and order at meetings was to be carefully maintained. For a time the Society appears by such policies to have avoided trouble; but when it attempted to send out missionaries into the provinces to show local organizations how to practice the same formula, this good fortune did not last. Two of their representatives, Jones and Binns, who were sent out to organize local societies within the Two Acts and to preach the doctrine of annual parliaments and manhood suffrage, were eventually arrested at Birmingham. One was acquitted and the other convicted, though never sentenced; but before the trials took place in August 1797 events had occurred which made any sort of agitation unwise. To the lack of success in war and to the high prices of provisions in 1795–96 was added the terror of the naval mutinies of April to June, 1797.

The mutinies of Spithead and the Nore concern us in this connection only in so far as they influenced the reform movement. The fundamental causes for the outbreak at Spithead on April 15 were the system of recruiting, living conditions, inadequate pay, brutal disciplinary measures, and other grievances of this nature. In February Lord Howe received several letters from seamen asking to have their grievances redressed. After a somewhat perfunctory investigation he came to the conclusion that there was little danger of trouble and as a result delayed sending these letters to the First Lord of the Admiralty, Earl Spencer. Thus the mutiny on April 15 came as a shock to both the naval officers and the government. Steps were taken at once to satisfy the demands of the mutineers that grievances should be redressed, both general and those of specific ships, and that an act of indemnity should be passed to protect them against the consequences of their uprising. The negotiations which followed satisfied the seamen, for their major demands were met and they felt assured of indemnity by a royal proclamation.

The fleet, with the exception of three vessels, was now ordered to go from Spithead to St. Helens and all appeared to be satisfactory until the seamen on May 7 refused to obey the orders of the officers to weigh anchors. The men had become convinced that the government had no intention of carrying out the promises of indemnity and redress of grievances because no Parliamentary act had followed the royal proclamation. Four days before this second outbreak, members of the opposition in Parliament had upbraided Pitt for his delay in presenting a bill to Parliament for carrying out these promises. When the second mutiny came, members of the ministry blamed this attack of the opposition for shaking the confidence of the seamen in the promises of the government. The opposition, on the other hand, insisted that the second outbreak was the obvious result of the failure of the ministry to follow the royal proclamation by a bill in Parliament. But regardless where the blame lay, Pitt made no delay in introducing a bill, once the news of the action of May 7 was brought to him. A measure granting both the raise in pay and the increase in food allowance was on May 9 rushed through both houses of Parliament. Lord Howe, in whom the seamen had great confidence, was then sent to the scene of the mutiny with copies of the newly passed act and of the royal pardon. Since George III and Lord Howe were the only men in authority whom the sailors did not distrust, "the mutineers felt that at last their negotiation was based on solid rock, and that they were no longer at the mercy of deceitful men."[63] Within a few days the mutiny at St. Helens was over. In more than one respect the affair had been admirably handled by the representatives of the sailors: the organization was magnificent, the demands were reasonable and of the kind to appeal to public opinion, and the spirit in which the negotiations were carried on was moderate and conciliatory. A just tribute has been paid to this leadership in a recent work:

One is compelled to admire the leaders at Spithead, however much one may deplore their action; and even if one does deplore it, one has to admit it was forced on them. They had made every effort to get their wrongs redressed by the ordinary constitutional means, but their attempts had been ignored. When it came to deeds the Delegates proved themselves first-rate trade union leaders, better perhaps than have ever appeared since . . . . These men throughout have one's sympathy, and increasingly gain one's respect; their names deserve to be regarded with honour in the history of the betterment of the Englishman's lot.[64]

[63] Conrad Gill, *The Naval Mutinies of 1797* (Manchester: Manchester University Press, 1913), p. 73. Quoted by permission of the publishers.

[64] G. E. Manwaring and Bonamy Dobrée, *The Floating Republic* (London: Geoffrey Bles, Ltd., 1935), pp. 251–52.

Unfortunately, despite the concessions which the government made in matters of pay, food, and living conditions, the mutiny spread to the Nore and to other parts of the fleet. The sailors in the vessels stationed at the Nore, which of course commanded the Thames and London, were not satisfied with these concessions but wished to secure a more equitable division of prize money and a less brutal disciplinary code. When they found that it was too late to induce the striking sailors at Spithead to continue their mutiny to secure these more ambitious demands, the seamen at the Nore decided to carry on alone. The details of the manner in which this second mutiny was conducted may be found in two able monographs;[65] but in this connection it is sufficient to say that the affair was handled rather badly by both the mutineers and the authorities. The strikers did not know what they wanted, and they had no carefully laid plans to compare with those of the leaders at Spithead. Further they alienated the sympathies of the country by their threat to blockade the Thames. In short the attempt to secure additional concessions failed because of poor organization, lack of competent leaders, and the absence of a well-planned campaign. Modern authorities differ on the underlying causes for the two mutinies. To one it was caused by a fusion of two movements, one economic and the other political: on the economic side they culminated in a successful strike; and on the political, they marked the climax of the revolutionary movement in Great Britain.[66] The most recent writers, on the other hand, maintain that the mutinies were caused almost entirely by justifiable economic grievances; and while conceding that many of the sailors may have held liberal or radical political views, they decline to believe that such beliefs had any great influence on the course of events.[67]

It is unfortunate that the King did not express himself more frequently in his letters to Pitt on these mutinies. It is clear, however, that the handling of the mutineers by the government cannot be listed as one of the controversial issues between George III and Pitt. From the letter of May 9 the King shows that he felt the economic demands of the seamen should or must be met, but that his reactions to their political ones were that they ought to be treated as revolutionary.

[65] Gill, *op. cit.*, and Manwaring and Dobrée, *op. cit.*
[66] Gill, *op. cit.*, p. 358.
[67] Manwaring and Dobrée, *op. cit.*, p. 249.

When I returned from the play the last night, I found Mr. Pitt's note on my table; but not having read the papers from the Admiralty, I was entirely ignorant of the very outrageous mutiny that has a second time broke out in the Channel fleet. I have since read the papers, and cannot in the least form an opinion as to what measures may be necessary for restoring discipline, or what more can with propriety be done than the increase of pay and provisions that has been now fully granted: I shall, therefore, very willingly concur in such opinion as may be suggested by the Cabinet on the present very distressing occasion.[68]

It is safe to conclude that the point of view of George III and Pitt did not differ materially on the mutiny or in the policies pursued by the government. The King may have been slightly critical of the failure of the ministry to redress the economic grievances of the seamen and hence to prevent the outbreak of April 15; but he felt that the second mutiny of May 7 was not justifiable.

The last serious attempt of the Whig opposition to bring about Parliamentary reform came, strangely enough, in the midst of the mutiny at the Nore. The days from May 20 to June 6 were the ones in which the political and revolutionary demands of the seamen under the leadership of Richard Parker were causing the government the greatest concern. Whether or not Fox in moving for the repeal of the Two Acts and Grey in moving for Parliamentary reform were in any way influenced by the mutinies it is difficult to say. Without doubt plans had been made some time earlier for the introduction of both of these motions, but whether the Whig leaders expected to gain or lose by the events of the mutiny is questionable. The debates in Parliament during April, May, and June bring out clearly that the Whigs in opposition felt that demands of the seamen for better pay and working conditions were, in the main, justifiable; that the government was in part responsible for these grievances; and that the ministers had handled the negotiations with the mutineers in a wretched and incompetent fashion. These Whigs were actuated partly by real humanitarian motives and partly by a natural desire to embarrass their political opponents; but despite the equally natural charge of the members of the government that the Whigs encouraged and abetted the mutineers there seems to be no evidence that it went beyond legitimate constitutional opposition.[69]

[68] Stanhope, *op. cit.*, III, vi-vii.
[69] Gill, *op. cit.*, pp. 353-54.

On May 19 Fox moved for a repeal of the Two Acts. In the debate which followed, no fewer than eight speakers vigorously opposed such action; and the motion was lost by 260 to 52.[70] George III hailed the news with delight and assured Pitt that:

Every friend of the British Constitution must rejoice at the decided majority the last Evening for resisting the Motion of Mr. Fox for the Repeal of the Two Bills respecting Treason and Sedition, and not less to find so many Country Gentlemen zealously step forward on every occasion to give a support that shews they feel the blessings they enjoy.[71]

A week later Grey made what was to be the last serious attempt for many years to have Parliamentary reform considered. In his motion of May 26 he proposed to increase the county members from 92 to 113; to extend the franchise from freeholders to copyholders and leaseholders paying a fixed minimum rent; and to substitute for the existing borough representation a group of districts which should be divided according to the number of householders paying taxes.[72] Grey did not neglect the customary attack on Pitt for his inconsistency. Since it was his last Parliamentary utterance on this much-discussed question, it is worth while noting how Pitt answered Grey's proposals. Because the latter specifically disavowed French Revolutionary doctrines and a belief in universal suffrage, Pitt could not open the attack on the old familiar line of introducing French anarchy and subverting the Constitution. Instead he declared his willingness to place the discussion on the footing of the practical benefit it would produce, as Grey had suggested, and began his speech as though he intended to adhere to this promise. In the third sentence after the one in which he made this pledge, however, he attempted to fasten on the moderate reformers the dangerous nature of their association with extremists who did believe in French anarchy. Arguing at great length Pitt attempted to prove that a reform such as Grey proposed would not propitiate the extremists and was not necessary to hold the support of the moderates, since they would not join the radicals under any circumstances in a national crisis. Then, completely forgetting his earlier assurance about the footing upon which the debates should take place, he attacked Grey in the following manner:

[70] *Parliamentary History*, XXXIII, 639.
[71] Pitt MSS, 104, May 24, 1797.
[72] *Parliamentary History*, XXXIII, 644–53.

The honourable gentleman has talked highly of the blessings which are to result to mankind from the establishment of French liberty; and because new lights have appeared to set off the doctrine of freedom, this House is therefore to alter their principles of government, and to accommodate themselves to the new order of things. The system of French liberty is represented as a new light diffusing itself over all the world, and spreading in every region happiness and improvement. Good God! is the House to be told, after the benefits which have been derived from the Revolution in this country, that other and more essential benefits are to be added by adopting the principles of the French revolution? . . . . The doctrines upon which it is founded, are, false, shallow, and presumptuous, more absurd than the most pestilent theories that were ever engendered by the disordered imagination of man; more hostile to the real interests of mankind, to national prosperity, to individual happiness, to intellectual and moral improvement, than any tyranny by which the human species was ever afflicted. And, for this new luminary, shall we abandon the polar star of the British constitution, by which we have been led to happiness and glory, by which the country has supported every danger, which it has been called upon to encounter, and risen superior to every difficulty by which it has been assailed.[73]

Pitt concluded with the assertion that it was never contended that Yorkshire interests were neglected because it had only two representatives or that Manchester and Birmingham suffered ill consequences from not having members in the House of Commons. Further, the extension of small qualifications for voting under the Grey plan would merely make confusion, debauchery, and abuse greater at election time. For all these reasons Pitt advised that the motion be rejected, and it was negatived by a vote of 256 to 91; but under the circumstances the size of the minority is astonishing.

George III did not receive the news of this division with the satisfaction which he usually registered when a reform measure was defeated. In his letter to Pitt acknowledging the latter's account of the debate he stated:

After what has been repeated for some days, I had supposed that the division against Mr. Fox's motion for a Reform of Parliament would have been as large as stated, but the minority less; but his art has succeeded in keeping his party together; and, of course, some speculative men, as on former occasions, have joined him in this vote, many of whom probably were solely biassed from desire of a little

[73] *Ibid.*, XXXIII, 679.

apparent consequence; but I am certain every freeholder in the kingdom, as well as the inhabitants of boroughs, must feel their consequence hurt by the proposal.[74]

If, however, the King was disappointed in the size of the
minority, he must have been more pleased at the famous secession
of the opposition Whigs following the defeats on the repeal of
the Two Acts and on Parliamentary reform. Fox was convinced
that the battle was lost and the liberties of the country doomed.
According to Lord Holland, Fox's nephew, the secession originated principally with Grey, Lauderdale, and the Duke of Bedford, and Fox acquiesced through indolence rather than conviction.[75] In the course of his speech supporting Grey's motion for
Parliamentary reform Fox had declared that he planned to devote
a larger portion of his time to private pursuits than formerly;[76]
and he appears to have expressed his real opinion of the nature
of the secession in a letter to Lord Holland:

> Pray, if there is any opportunity of talking about the 'secession,'
> say, what is the truth, that there was not agreement enough of opinion
> upon the subject to make it possible to take what one may call a
> *measure* upon the subject, but that most of us thought that, after the
> proposition for Reform, we might fairly enough stay away, consid-
> ering the previous events of the session, and the behaviour of Parlia-
> ment upon them.[77]

The reason the secession was not an unqualified success was due
chiefly to the fact that it was incomplete. Even those who voted
to secede returned occasionally, and Tierney and Sheridan kept
up a fairly regular attendance. Nevertheless, the great depletion
in the ranks of the opposition made both houses of Parliament,
but especially the House of Commons, very different places from
what they had previously been. George III was filled with delight
when his enemies—for so he regarded them—acknowledged
defeat.

On the other hand, the evidence seems to point to the fact that
Pitt did not relish the secession as did the King. Lord Holland
pointed out that

[74] J. H. Rose, *Pitt and Napoleon* (London: G. Bell & Sons, Ltd., 1912),
p. 241.
[75] Henry Edward Lord Holland (ed.), Henry Richard Lord Holland, *Memoirs of the Whig Party* (London, 1852), I, 84.
[76] *Parliamentary History*, XXXIII, 699–734.
[77] Lord Holland, *op. cit.*, I, 91.

Mr. Pitt earnestly laboured to draw his opponents back to Parliament, and that, with that view, he sometimes taunted and attempted to exasperate the absent members, and at others studiously magnified the talents and importance of those who were left behind. He is said to have apprehended that the loss of a theatre in which he could defend his measures, would deprive him of opportunities of ascertaining, as well as of leading the publick opinion; and he is also said to have found, that the want of opposition in Parliament deprived him of the readiest weapon which he could hold up in terrorem to the King, to force his compliance with any unpalatable measure, or to deter him from insisting on unreasonable objects.[78]

These tactics, which Holland describes as magnifying the talents and importance of those who were left behind, were especially used on Tierney and Sheridan. The ministers took advantage of every opportunity to compliment Tierney on his judgment, manner of speaking, and knowledge of finance; and Pitt, whether answering Sheridan's attacks or thanking him for his support, was careful to pay him compliments. But when Fox returned to the House for the first time on January 4, 1798, for the third reading of the Assessed Taxes Bill, Pitt taunted him on the secession.

The right honourable gentleman had asserted his right to secede on his own motives of expediency, and, of course, those who surround him will not object if I take their justification on the same principle; but the right honourable gentleman, it seems retains his opinion of that expediency, and only now appears at the particular injunction of his constituents to defend their local interests. How comes it, then, that he appears so surrounded with friends, who, adopting his principle of secession, have not, in the desire of their constituents, the same motive for his particular exception? Can any thing shew in a stronger light the blind acquiescence of party zeal, when, in defiance of every avowed principle of their public conduct, they now attend to add to the splendor of their leader's entry?[79]

There can be little doubt that Pitt missed Fox's presence, for the reasons enumerated by Lord Holland, and would have welcomed his return. On the other hand, the compliments paid by the ministers to Sheridan and Tierney and the support which the former gave to some of the government measures could not help causing a certain amount of recrimination in the ranks of the Whig opposition. Sheridan was accused of abandoning his old

[78] *Ibid.*, p. 92.   [79] *Parliamentary History*, XXXIII, 1273.

associates and making overtures to the government because he warmly supported the government's policies on such issues as the mutiny and the threatened French invasion of 1798. It was with some exasperation that he defended himself against the charge of intending to separate from Fox by asserting in the Commons that it was difficult for a member in opposition to obtain credit for publicspiritedness or to support a minister without being accused of acting from interested motives.[80] Thus Sheridan was careful to mix virulent opposition with support of Pitt's proposals. The respective points of view of Sheridan, Pitt, and George III are best expressed in the speeches of the two statesmen on the royal message of April 20, 1798, and the King's comment to Pitt on this debate. The nature of the King's speech may be judged by the opening sentence:

His Majesty thinks it proper to acquaint the House of Commons, that from various advices received by his Majesty, it appears that the preparations for the embarkation of troops and warlike stores, are now carried on with considerable and increasing activity in the ports of France, Flanders, and Holland, with the avowed design of attempting the invasion of his Majesty's dominions, and that in this design the enemy is encouraged by the correspondence and communication of traitorous and disaffected persons and societies of these kingdoms.[81]

Sheridan expressed full conviction of the necessity of making every effort to resist the invaders and justified the actions taken by the government to protect the country, but he wished it to be distinctly understood that this approval did not extend to earlier policies of the ministers which he had previously condemned. "The wrongs and sufferings of the people," he was convinced, were due to these mistaken policies. Pitt in reply dwelt on his appreciation of the support which Sheridan had given, on the approbation which this conduct would receive in every quarter of the country, and on his reluctance to mention the parts of the honorable gentleman's speech in which he found it impossible to concur. Having thus performed his duty as a gentleman, Pitt renewed his warfare with Sheridan in effective if somewhat malicious language:

He hoped he should not be considered depreciating the effect of that zeal which the hon. gentleman had manifested; but he begged leave to say, that though by the accession of the hon. gentleman they

---

[80] *Parliamentary History*, XXXIII, 1194–1209.   [81] *Ibid.*, pp. 1421–22.

might gain as much as could be gained by the talents of an individual, still, even such an accession could add but little to the spirit and unanimity which the nation had previously manifested. The nation, long before the hon. gentleman, had displayed the utmost unanimity. In maintaining this arduous conflick, ministers would certainly be happy in the assistance of the hon. gentleman; but they would have been fully able to maintain the contest, even if they had not had the benefit of such assistance. Let us give the hon. gentleman our thanks for the support which he promises;—let us give him every degree of praise for the spirit which he has displayed; but let us not be guilty of that injustice to the rest of the nation, as to suppose that the country was not fully as secure before the hon. gentleman's declaration as it is now.[82]

The King's reaction to Sheridan's support and to Pitt's reply showed that his attitude was unchanged. Because he suspected the sincerity of Sheridan at this crisis, George III was delighted with Pitt's answer.[83]

The action of Sheridan in supporting the government on various points beginning with the naval mutinies, it has been pointed out, coincided with a marked change in public opinion in the country as a whole.[84] It was obvious during the mutinies and at the time of the consideration of Grey's motion that Parliamentary reform was dead so far as the country was concerned. Wyvill, who both in 1797 and 1798 attempted to organize Yorkshire as he had done in 1780 and 1781, recognized the futility of continuing the agitation. The London Corresponding Society, which had been sinking rapidly since the passing of the Two Acts in 1795 because of discouragement, debts, and the resignations of its best members, decided to hold a great public meeting, in defiance of the Sedition Act, on July 31, 1797. The meeting was broken up by the orders of Middlesex magistrates, and the society never recovered from the blow. The Duke of Portland as Home Secretary reported to George III the steps taken to prevent public meetings being held.

The Duke of Portland humbly begs leave to acquaint Your Majesty that an account is this moment received from the meeting of the London Corresponding Society that they were dispersed without resistance by the Magistrates, but that five persons who persisted in

[82] *Ibid.*, pp. 1428–29.   [83] Pitt MSS, 104, April 21, 1798.
[84] Thomas Moore, *Memoirs of the Life of the Right Honourable Richard Brinsley Sheridan* (London, 1826), II, 281–82.

speaking after the orders given by the Magistrates for the dispersion of the meeting were apprehended and were bringing away in custody.

The Duke of Portland begs leave to add for Your Majesty's information that he has reason to believe that no other meeting will take place in any part of the Kingdom except at Nottingham and that he is well assured that cannot consist of more than two or three hundred people at most of the lowest and most contemptible description.[85]

Although the society was not actually suppressed until 1799, its personnel during the remainder of its life was very different from that of its earlier years.

The remaining years of Pitt's first ministry constitute a reign of terror for both constitutional reformers and revolutionists. Any doubt, however, as to the popularity of repression had vanished by 1797. If the results of the state trials in 1794 had indicated that public opinion was not back of the government in its policy, no such question could apply for the years from 1797 to 1801. The misfortunes of the war, the mutiny, and the Irish Rebellion of 1798 made the overwhelming mass of the English people as eager to put down any reform agitation as the government and the ruling class. On the strength of the mutiny and the attempt of the Corresponding Society to meet, two additional laws were added to the repressive measures already on the statute books. By the one act severe penalties could be inflicted on any persons inciting His Majesty's military or naval forces to mutiny;[86] and by the other, administration of unlawful oaths was forbidden.[87]

The last phase of the reform movement in Great Britain is associated with the organizations known as the United Scotsmen and the United Englishmen. They were in fact but feeble imitations of the better-known United Irishmen and, apparently, were made up of the sort of members who believe in an organization based on secret oaths when ordinary constitutional agitation is declared illegal. In 1798 the government seized the leaders of both the United Englishmen and the London Corresponding Society, which in the main were the same men, and put an end to both organizations. After thirteen members of the latter were seized on April 19, 1798, the society seems never to have met again;[88] but, to make perfectly certain that all such reform groups

[85] Clements Transcripts, VIII, 3552.

[86] 37 George III, C. 70.   [87] 37 George III, C. 123.

[88] George S. Veitch, *The Genesis of Parliamentary Reform* (London: Constable and Company, Ltd., 1913), p. 339.

were not only dead but buried, an additional act was passed in 1799 officially suppressing the United Englishmen, the United Scotsmen, the United Britons, the United Irishmen, and the London Corresponding Society.[89] Thus, if the last four years of Pitt's ministry were years of terror, it was a terror in which the great mass of the people not only acquiesced but co-operated vigorously. In the main it was based on genuine fear which resulted from the fearful shocks of the years 1795 to 1801. The government no longer had to take the lead against the reformers and French doctrines or in arousing the nation by acts of questionable honesty. The British people had attained the state of mind which Burke had so strongly urged upon them in the early years of the French Revolution.

In conclusion, what can be said of the policies of George III and Pitt on the two main issues dealt with in this chapter: the conduct of the war, and reform and repression? The point of view of the King as indicated throughout the chapter is simple. He believed in fighting France until the Revolutionary government was overthrown and one based on anti-revolutionary principles was put in its place; this was the main purpose of the war and hence everything should be subordinated to it. Thus he continually and vigorously opposed the "side shows" of Pitt and Dundas; and although he gave way in most cases through the direct or implied threat of resignation by the ministers, it is very likely that he remembered these circumstances when he parted with both men in 1801. George III was equally positive on matters of reform and repression. The views which he held unwaveringly from the beginning of the war to the end were those held by the great mass of the nation after 1797.

Pitt differed from the King on the conduct of the war, and in most instances, as has been shown, he had his own way. The fact that disaster usually followed the military tactics of Pitt and Dundas should not obscure the fact that they had their way rather than the King his. Because of this difference, agreement on the other major issue of reform and repression was doubly important. It is difficult to see how Pitt could have maintained himself at the head of the ministry if his policy on this issue had not in practice exactly coincided with that of the King. The very significant question naturally arises whether Pitt and the King actually

[89] *Ibid.*, p. 340.

and sincerely agreed with one another on repression from April 1792 to February 1801, or Pitt, realizing the fundamental difference on the conduct of the war, made every effort to adapt his own policy to that of George III. In this second alternative, it must be remembered, he had the additional incentive of making it coincide with that of the Portland Whigs and the great mass of the country gentlemen. Because of the importance of this question in the relations of the King and Pitt an attempt to arrive at the basis for the Minister's conduct must be made.

In recent years many historians have made detailed studies of the repressive policies of the Pitt ministry and have endeavored to explain the underlying motives for the actions taken. Most of these works, however, deal in detail only with the years 1791 to 1797 and especially with those through the State Trials of 1794. On one extreme is the verdict that Pitt played a masterful and successful game of party politics; and that in order to assure himself the support of the Portland Whigs, the country gentlemen, and the great mass of the nation in a war of conquest against France, he deliberately exploited the fear of revolutionary principles when he entertained no such fears himself.[90] On the other extreme is a complete justification of Pitt, and an insistence upon the fact that he was dealing with a criminal conspiracy to overthrow the Constitution. Under this interpretation, which almost exactly coincides with the point of view which Burke so stoutly maintained from 1790 to 1797, the Whigs were anti-patriots and very little better than the advocates of violence. Thus, as one of the strongest advocates of this point of view declared, "there can be no doubt that Pitt was amply justified in every step which he took."[91] Neither interpretation, however, has been widely accepted and most of the writers of monographs on reform and repression in the seventeen hundred and nineties have reached conclusions part way between these two extremes. One point of view is that Pitt was really alarmed but misjudged the attitude of the reformers;[92] and another is that these reformers were guilty of seditious practices if not of treason and that the more extreme agitators actually contemplated the use of physical force.[93]

[90] William T. Laprade, *England and the French Revolution* (Baltimore: Johns Hopkins University Press, 1909).

[91] Charles Whibley, *William Pitt* (Edinburgh: Blackwood & Sons, Ltd., 1906), p. 214.   [92] Veitch, *op. cit.*, p. 342.

[93] Walter P. Hall, *British Radicalism, 1791–1797* (New York: Columbia University Press, 1912).

Perhaps it is a mistake to consider Pitt's attitude toward reform and repression during the years from 1792 to 1797 as fixed and unchanging, for practically any of the interpretations cited above would apply to some period during these years or would be justified by some of the available evidence. Since Pitt concealed his real views with greater skill than George III and did not write long memoranda to clarify his own thoughts and help the future historian, it is impossible to arrive at a very accurate conclusion of what these views were. Because of the difference in Pitt's views in 1791 and in 1797 and the startling events which took place between these dates, the following conclusions may be suggested: first, that Pitt was chiefly concerned with carrying on a "traditional" war with a weakened France from 1793 to 1795; second, that because of the disasters of the war, the failure of peace overtures, and the troubles at home he came really to fear the reformers; and, third, that this fear continued to dictate his attitude toward reform from 1797 to the end of his life.

It seems unquestionable that mixed motives decided Pitt's policies toward reform after he became Prime Minister in 1783 and even more after 1792, but the degree to which they were determined by honest conviction and political expediency varied. From 1792 to 1795 Pitt seems to have used opposition to reform and repression chiefly as a means of securing the hearty support of the nation in the French war and of propitiating the King, the Portland Whigs, and the country gentlemen. Probably Pitt was frightened, but not very much frightened, by the activities of the reformers, and it is highly questionable if this fear constituted his major reason for the policy of repression down to 1795. As a result of his failure to end the war in 1795, 1796, and 1797 when his original objectives did not materialize, of the food riots of 1795–96, and of the mutinies of 1797, fear probably became the major factor in this repressive policy. At the same time, increasing hostility of public opinion as well as his own desire to continue to propitiate the King and the Portland Whigs were very strong minor factors. The fear given as Pitt's major reason for his repressive policy after 1795 was not fright over the prospect of the radical reformers overturning the government but rather a state of nerves over the precarious state of the country. Pitt was too well informed as to the numbers and the activities of the few physical-force men and too shrewd a judge of conditions to have any serious fears of a small group of desperate men overturning the government by force. England and, even more, Ireland were continually threatened with invasion by France. There was the danger that certain sections of the community might welcome the invaders, and an even greater one that the Army or Navy might be led astray by political propaganda. Pitt shared the popular attitude of hostility toward a group of reformers who were advocating an unpopular cause, which was greatly accentuated by the fact that the fortunes of the war were going so badly against England and the very national existence seemed to be threatened. Thus it is easier to explain than to justify Pitt's attitude toward reform and repression.

Even without considering the Irish Rebellion and Catholic Emancipation, which will be treated in the next chapter, the years from 1793 to 1801 appear to the present writer to have been the worst of Pitt's entire career. If the interpretation given earlier in the chapter is the correct one, the years should not be treated as a unit. Pitt's plan, which in all probability was evolved in 1792, was to wage an old-fashioned war against France and to secure the support of the King, the Portland Whigs, and public opinion by his repressive policy. Under this interpretation Pitt did not expect the war to last long and did not believe too earnestly in the danger from reformers and revolutionists. That Pitt utterly misjudged the nature of the war should not be so serious a count against him as his failure to adjust his policies to the changed conditions. The campaigns of the three first years of the war, the high price of provisions in 1795, the riots at the opening of Parliament in October, and the failure of peace negotiations showed him only too clearly that his original conceptions of the war were wrong. The events of 1797 and 1798 must have accentuated his views which had grown out of the events of 1795. Pitt's determination to wage a war against France for colonial conquests was much more defensible than his attitude toward reform and repression from 1792 to 1795; but from 1795 to 1801 the reverse became true. With the breakup of the First Coalition and the refusal of France to make peace it became obvious that England must fight for her existence against a most formidable military machine. Pitt should be held responsible, not for the continuation of the war, but for the manner in which he conducted it. His failure to abandon the "side shows" and to reorganize the Army to meet changed conditions was to prove very costly. His policy toward reform and repression seems less reprehensible after than before 1795, because the country was in greater danger after that date, the constitutional reformers had in the main withdrawn from active agitation, and public opinion had become overwhelmingly hostile to any kind of change on account of the seriousness of conditions at home and abroad. Pitt may be blamed for waging war for the purpose of seizing French colonies and for taking so extreme a stand against reform after 1795; but certainly neither of these possible errors seems so open to criticism as his conduct of the war or his policy toward reform from 1792 to 1795.

The years covered by this chapter witnessed important developments in party politics, but they do not mark an advance in the two-party system. In 1794, when to Pitt's followers and the King's Friends were added the Portland Whigs, the government became one of three instead of two groups. The fact that the latter two had practically identical views on both the conduct of the war and repression of reform movements did not make them a unit. The personal differences growing out of the constitutional crisis of 1782–1784 were too great to make that possible. Fully as important from the point of view of nineteenth- and twentieth-century Parliamentary government was the decided decline during these years of *effective* opposition in both houses. This ineffectiveness was due to the small number in opposition and to the set opinions of the vast majority, and not to the lack of well-directed and devastating criticism of the policies and mistakes of the government. Seldom in English history has any government furnished its opponents such wonderful ammunition as Pitt gave the opposition by his conduct of the war and his policy of repression; and seldom has any group availed itself so fully of the opportunity presented as did the Whig remnant from the outbreak of the war in 1793 to the secession of 1797. On reading the speeches of Fox, Sheridan, and others today, it seems impossible that the listeners could have remained unmoved or that Pitt could escape these terrible indictments unscathed. Yet he always gave a serene and confident answer which satisfied the great majority of the House of Commons and left him free to carry on his policies unchecked by constructive or destructive criticism. As Sir John Fortescue wrote:

The most damaging criticism of Fox, Sheridan, and Shelburne—and Shelburne's were the most searching and unanswerable of all—left him unharmed. It was as though a torrent of water had been turned upon a swan: the only effect was to make him float a little higher. For, whatever mistakes he might make, the nation felt vaguely but rightly that he was a fearless and a good man, who would do his best for his country without a thought of himself. Canning aptly expressed the general feeling when, in comment upon Windham's severe criticisms on Pitt, he wrote, "Whether Pitt *will* save us, I do not know, but surely he is the only man that can."[94]

The question naturally arises whether Pitt was not a greater liability than an asset to his country from 1795 to his death in 1806. The supreme confidence which he had in himself and which Parliament had in him made it difficult to improve either the conduct of the war or the internal situation. Thus, since really searching criticism had no effect on either Pitt or Parliament, and no other statesman could hope to carry out an independent policy so long as Pitt maintained his present position, the country had no real hope of improvement. Even when the change did come it was carried out by admiring disciples of Pitt acting in his name. Certainly the years covered by this chapter mark one of the most unusual political situations in English history. Despite the increasing ill success with which he carried on the government, Pitt gained the support of his former political enemies, the Portland Whigs, of a larger proportion of the House of Commons, and of the overwhelming mass of the people outside Parliament. It would seem that this position of Pitt's, particularly from 1797 to 1801, was the result not so much of confidence in a constitutional minister as the blind faith in a savior during a time of danger. The British nation showed the panic of a horse returning to a burning stable.

[94] J. W. Fortescue, *British Statesmen of the Great War*, p. 167.

VIII. THE UNION WITH IRELAND AND THE RESIGNATION OF PITT

Because of the importance of the issue which finally ended the ministry of Pitt after more than seventeen years, this entire chapter will be devoted to the third of the three great fundamental issues which dominated the years from 1793 to 1801. Since both the war with France and the reform movement in Great Britain profoundly influenced the course of events in Ireland, it is impossible to separate the events of this period. But inasmuch as the King and Pitt differed completely on this third issue, the Catholic question in Ireland, and as their disagreement resulted in the fall of Pitt, it is of far greater constitutional interest than either of the other two. Yet in 1793 the Irish problem was not considered of primary importance and certainly is not to be ranked with either war or reform as a primary issue.

Ireland had already come into the story of George III and Pitt on the two important occasions—the granting of legislative independence in 1782 and the commercial resolutions of 1785—but in neither instance did it result in a clash between the two men. In 1782 Pitt was still a new member of Parliament without experience in office, and in 1785 George III agreed substantially with what his minister was attempting to do.

The Irish problem was complicated by the fact that there were three distinct groups in existence: the Anglicans, the Dissenters, and the Catholics. These three divisions were separated by political and economic as well as by religious differences. Generally speaking, the Anglicans were the landlords of the south and west; the Dissenters were largely Presbyterians in Ulster; and the Catholics were peasants throughout the greater part of the country. Naturally the divisions were not so clear-cut as the preceding sentence might indicate, since many Anglicans were not landlords, many Dissenters were to be found outside of Ulster, and many Catholics were not peasants and a considerable number of them were to be found in Ulster. The major grievances of the people living in Ireland were three: religious, political, and economic. Despite the fact that a very small minority of the entire population were members, the Anglican Church was a state or established church. A savage penal code directed against Catholics, which in the main had been put on the statute books during the years following the Revolution of 1688–89, had been somewhat mitigated during the eighteenth century, especially since 1778; but it still left many restrictions on the free practice of religion. In addition the payment of the tithe to the established Church and the cost of maintaining their own priests bore heavily on the great mass of the Catholics. Unless they received the sacrament in the Anglican Church, the Dissenters of Ireland were by an act of the English Parliament in 1704 excluded from public offices and magistracies in municipalities. So far as participation in political life was concerned, both Catholics and Dissenters were in practically the same position in Ireland as in England. The Catholics were absolutely excluded from office, and the Dissenters shared in it only by such evasions as "occasional conformity." But the political grievance which all three religious groups had in common down to 1782 was the subordinate position of the Irish Parliament when legislative independence was granted to Ireland and, after that date, resentment at the interference of the British government. By Poynings' Laws of 1495 no Irish Parliament was to meet until the deputy of the King and the Irish Privy Council had specified the bills which should be enacted, and all laws previously passed in England were to be considered in force in Ireland as well. In 1719[1] the power of the British Parliament had been made more specific by a statute which declared that it "had, hath, and of right ought to have full power and authority to make laws and statutes of sufficient force and validity to bind the kingdom and people of Ireland." Both were repealed by the act which granted legislative independence to Ireland,[2] but the memory lingered and the constant interference of the British government in the transactions of the Irish Parliament marred the value of the concession made in 1782. Thus while the Anglican oligarchy which controlled the Irish House of Commons used its political power to enforce the barbarous Penal Code on the Irish Catholics and the exclusion from local and national offices of both Catholics and Dissenters, all three religious groups shared the resentment against British interference with the Irish Parliament.

Like their religious and political injustices, the economic grievances of the Irish people concerned both Great Britain and their own Anglican oligarchy. The British Parliament used the power

[1] 6 George I, C. 5.
[2] 22 George III, C. 53.

claimed under the Act of 1719 to protect English industries at the expense of the Irish. Since such enactments struck at all classes in Ireland, there was comparative unanimity in the bitterness felt there toward England. The Catholic peasants, however, felt profound dissatisfaction with both the tithe and the conditions of land holding; and these grievances they blamed on their own Anglican oligarchy rather than on the British government.

To sum up the grievances of the three main groups: all resented the interference of the English government in the activities of the Irish Parliament and in enforcing economic discrimination; the Dissenters resented the obstacles placed in the way of their holding office; and the Catholics resented the Penal Code, their exclusion from political life, and the agrarian abuses under which they suffered.

It was probably a great misfortune both for England and for Ireland that a union between the two countries was not made during the reign of Anne. It is true that the Penal Code and the exclusion from political life of the Catholics and Dissenters would not have been abolished, but the Catholics at least would have received better treatment from an imperial Parliament than from the Anglican minority wielding authority through the Irish Parliament. The greatest gain would have come on the economic side. Had Ireland shared in the trade of the British Empire as Scotland did after 1707, a great deal of her economic distress during the eighteenth century might have been avoided. In the end it required a series of agrarian outrages by the miserable peasantry and a vigorous constitutional agitation by the ruling minority to bring about a change in attitude on the part of the British government. The latter movement was based on the platform of securing for Ireland what England had secured by the Revolution of 1689 and the settlement which followed. The Protestant minority were especially anxious to introduce a septennial act, a mutiny act, and a habeas corpus act similar to those in England. Until the American Revolution the only substantial gain made was the Octennial Act of 1768 which limited the life of Irish Parliaments to eight years. The situation was soon complicated, however, by the fact that George III had become interested in breaking the power of the Undertakers, that is, the group of borough owners who controlled the Irish Parliament, as he was breaking that of the Whigs in England. As a result the control of the government in Ireland passed from that of the

Undertakers, who were prominent Irish Protestants, to that of the Lord Lieutenant, who, instead of merely visiting Ireland during Parliamentary sessions, remained in Dublin and assumed control of the distribution of the patronage to build up a party on the order of the King's Friends in England. In order to finance such a party the government was forced to ask for Parliamentary grants; and the differences between the government and the ruling caste in Ireland were accentuated by this new development.

The American Revolution and the first election in 1776 under the Octennial Act brought matters to a head. The fact that another part of the British Empire took up arms because of alleged injustices could not fail to influence that portion of the Irish people who resented their own political subordination and exclusion from the trading rights in Great Britain and the Colonies. The Anglican oligarchy and Ulster appear to have been influenced far more than the Catholics. The members of the Parliament elected in 1776 were in a position to demand reforms. The leadership of these reformers fell to the great Protestant orator Henry Grattan. They concentrated on three main objects: removal of trade restrictions, legislative independence, and Catholic relief. Because the North government in England was faced with the necessity of securing Catholic soldiers, it was the third of these three grievances which first received consideration from Great Britain. In 1778 an act was passed relieving the Catholics of some of the worst features of the Penal Code; but even this timid beginning aroused the English and Scottish Protestants to an opposition which culminated in the Gordon Riots of June 1780. But when North in 1778 attempted to relieve the Irish of the restrictions on their trade, the opposition organized in time to force him to withdraw the measure. This setback was only temporary because the critical state of the war after 1778 forced even greater concessions from the government. When France and Spain entered the war on the side of the American Colonists, the danger was very great that these hostile powers might land a force in Ireland and stir up a rebellion. At this time, however, the loyalty of the Irish people was very different from that shown between 1796 and 1798. Not only did Irishmen remain staunchly loyal, but they also actually organized for their own defense against the possibility of invasion. This organization took the form of groups of volunteers who drilled and applied to the government for arms. Since these companies were commanded by Protestant peers and gentry, and since the country was otherwise undefended, the government, even though recognizing the danger, did not dare to refuse both sanction and arms. Although the organization of these volunteers appears to have had no other motive than defense and loyalty at the start, its members soon began to agitate for freedom of trade and legislative independence. The Irish were able to obtain, merely by assurances of loyalty and threats of non-importation agreements, what the Scotch had acquired only by union with England. At the end of 1779 and the beginning of 1780 Lord North secured the passage in the British Parliament of a series of measures which gave Ireland equality with England and Scotland in the fields of foreign and imperial trade.

Since some alleviation in the Penal Code for the Catholics had been granted before the Volunteers became well organized, and since commercial freedom had been conceded as a result of their first efforts, it was only natural that legislative independence should be the next objective of this victory-flushed group. The leadership in the drive to secure this independence was assumed by two great Ulstermen, Grattan and Charlemont. The drive was opened in the session of 1780; but the only substantial gain then made was a permanent mutiny bill. When the movement lagged in Parliament, the volunteers of Ulster met during February 1782 in a Congress at Dungannon and passed resolutions including a declaration that only an Irish Parliament had the right to legislate for Ireland. Events in England helped the cause of the reformers, since the resignation of Lord North brought in the Rockingham ministry, which was more favorably disposed toward Ireland. The unanimity of opinion in Ireland, combined with the critical state of affairs throughout the Empire, appears to have influenced the new British ministry. The act of 1719 was repealed;[3] and the restrictions imposed by Poynings' acts were swept away. Although the Rockingham ministry would have preferred a change less drastic and abrupt and believed that the relationship between the two kingdoms needed to be defined by an agreement or treaty, no such treaty was made. Nevertheless, from the point of view of good will, the new arrangement started most favorably. The Rockingham Whigs made the desired con-

[3] 22 George III, C. 53.

cessions with evident sincerity and without quibbling; and the Irish appear to have fully appreciated this attitude.

But the hope that the mitigation of the Penal Code, commercial concessions, and legislative independence would mark the dawn of a new era in Ireland failed to materialize; for, despite this very promising beginning, important Irish problems remained unsolved. The mitigation of the Penal Code had not done away with the political disabilities of the Catholics, the commercial concessions had not done away with economic distress among the peasantry, and legislative independence had not done away with the unrepresentative nature of the Irish Parliament. The deep-seated animosity between Catholic and Protestant, which could not be repealed by law, was declining among the upper classes but still could be easily stirred among the peasantry, particularly in Ulster. Even the relationship between the British government and the Irish Parliament had not been settled by the supposedly amicable arrangement of 1782. Since the Crown was the only connecting link between the two countries, the danger that Ireland might pursue a policy inimical to British interests was evident to both the English government and the ruling Irish oligarchy. Not only was this danger self-evident, but the experience of England and Scotland from 1689 to 1707 served as an additional warning.

Since the Irish Parliament was now the sole legislative body for Ireland, all hope of removing Catholic disabilities and alleviating economic distress by legislation lay in the action of its members. But the unrepresentative nature of this Parliament made it difficult to enact reforms which would remove Catholic political disabilities or improve the lot of the peasantry. Catholics could neither vote for members nor be elected; and Ulster Presbyterians could vote but could not be elected. The majority of the three hundred members were chosen from pocket boroughs which were controlled by a small number of borough owners and under these circumstances the influence of the British government was still very strong. The Lord Lieutenant was appointed by the British Crown, was a member of the cabinet, and represented the point of view of the British ministry. Since more than a third of the members of Parliament were placemen or pensioners, he needed to win over only a few of the big borough owners in order to make certain that there would be no divergence in the policies of the two countries. The British government was convinced that it was essential to carry on in this manner in order to avoid a repetition of the Anglo-Scottish difficulties which had preceded the Act of Union in 1707. On the other hand, the ruling Anglican oligarchy of Ireland felt that its only security for maintaining its privileged economic, political, and religious position lay in the maintenance of British supremacy. If the support of the English government were withdrawn, this minority would not be able to maintain its privileges in the face of the demands of the great majority of Irish Catholics and Ulster Dissenters.

Because of the resolute stand by the British government on the one hand and by the Anglican oligarchy on the other, and because of the inability of the Irish reformers to agree upon a common plan of action, practically nothing was accomplished for more than ten years. The sincere efforts which Pitt made in 1785 to improve commercial relations between the two countries failed for the reasons given in an earlier chapter. In Ireland all shades of opinion existed on the all-important questions of the franchise and officeholding. These opinions varied from maintaining the status quo to granting manhood suffrage and the right to hold office to Catholic, Anglican, and Dissenter alike. In the light of history the proposals of Grattan seem the soundest. He favored the granting of equal rights to Catholics and Protestants but the limiting of the franchise on the grounds that it was unsafe to trust political power to lower classes in the present inflamed state of religious differences. Since such a solution was not satisfactory to either the British government or the Anglican oligarchy, it was not adopted.

The settlement in Ireland was eventually decided by the influence of the French Revolution. Conservatives and reformers naturally followed the course of events in France very closely; and the latter were prone to compare their own problems with those of the French people and to argue that similar solutions should be attempted. It was in Ulster that the French Revolution had the greatest influence. The Anglican oligarchy feared the increasing radicalism of French policy even more violently than the propertied classes of Great Britain; and the Catholics hated the anti-religious bias of the revolutionary leaders and the attacks on the Church. Thus the anti-British revolutionary movement not only started in Ulster but also for some years made little progress outside its borders. Smarting under religious, political, and economic discrimination throughout the eighteenth century, she had shown marked sympathy with the American Colonists during the Revolutionary War; she had witnessed the failure of the settlement of 1782 in the years which followed; and she had come to the conclusion that no hope of improvement could be entertained so long as the existing alliance between the British government and the Anglican oligarchy was maintained. The extreme Ulster point of view was presented in 1791 by Wolfe Tone, a young Protestant lawyer of Belfast, who argued that Catholics and Protestants should unite to secure complete freedom from Great Britain, and should make use of French aid, as the Americans had done, to attain this end. Although few Ulstermen appear to have agreed with his extreme views in 1791, the opinion was widely held that Catholics and Protestants should unite to secure the reforms which after 1782 had not materialized. Tone founded a Society of United Irishmen in Belfast for this purpose, and branch organizations spread rapidly in Ulster. Until 1795 this society had little influence in Catholic Ireland, because the wealthy and educated Catholics believed in a solution along the lines advocated by Grattan and the great mass of the peasants were devoting their efforts to the Defender movement.

Defenderism was a product of the long-standing economic grievances of the Catholic peasants, as the United Irish movement was of the political grievances of the Ulster Dissenters. It represented the blind resistance of the peasantry to the misery which they had suffered throughout the eighteenth century. Perhaps the outstanding grievance which they wished redressed was the payment of the tithe to the established Church. When violence was resorted to, it often took the form of destroying the homes and property of Protestants. Since its attitude was so diametrically opposed to that expressed by the Society of United Irishmen, the British government and the Anglican oligarchy felt that there was little danger of the two organizations joining for united action.

When the policy which Pitt followed during the years 1793 to 1801 is considered, all these factors must be kept in mind. In 1785 he had attempted to reconcile, without success, the economic interests of Great Britain and Ireland; but now he had to guard against the effect of the French Revolutionary doctrines on the three main groups of the Irish people and the possibility of a French invasion of Ireland. Even before the outbreak of the war with France, when it was obvious that hostilities would soon commence, Pitt decided to offset the danger from Ulster by bidding for the loyalty of the Irish Catholics. The Langrishe Relief Bill of 1792 was in many respects a forerunner of the more important law of 1793. Since Langrishe, who introduced this first bill, was a private member, it could not be regarded as a government measure. Nevertheless the government supported it cordially. This law repealed the statutes prohibiting Catholics and Protestants from intermarriage, solicitors from having their children educated as Catholics, barristers from marrying Catholics, and Catholic parents from sending their children abroad to be educated; and it removed restrictions on Catholic schools and apprentices. Since Catholics were still excluded from holding most offices and were denied the franchise, these concessions, though generous, fell short of what the Catholics, particularly the wealthy and educated ones, expected. The law of 1793 represented Pitt's attempt to retain the loyalty of all classes of Catholics without making concessions which would be positively unacceptable to the Anglican oligarchy in Ireland and to the King and the strongly Protestant element in England.

In the speech from the throne on January 10, 1793, the Lord Lieutenant recommended that the situation of the Catholics should be given serious consideration by Parliament. Leave to bring in a Catholic relief bill was given on February 4, and after debates lasting many weeks it was passed and became a law in April. The introduction and passage of this bill are astounding because of the radical nature of its provisions and because both the Irish government and the majority of Parliament were really opposed to it. Private correspondence, as well as speeches made during the debates, reveal that it was forced through by the British government. Measures to relieve the Catholics from 1778 to 1792 had been largely confined to repealing laws against their liberty and property, but the Act of 1793 granted them very important political rights. The most significant provisions gave Catholics the franchise in country and town under the same qualifications as Protestants, and with certain exceptions the right to sit on juries, to be magistrates, to bear commissions in the Army and Navy, and to hold civil offices. In the light of history the act was weak in making too extreme concessions to the ignorant Catholic peasantry by granting the franchise on the forty-shilling basis and in excluding the wealthy and educated upper class and gentry from Parliament and the higher offices of government.

But the significance of this law in the history of Anglo-Irish relations in the generation following 1793 is difficult to over-estimate. Having made in a rather precipitous manner a concession of the franchise to the Irish Catholics far more liberal than that enjoyed by the British voters before 1832, Pitt found himself in an embarrassing position. Since he had made these very liberal concessions to the lower classes, the educated and wealthy upper classes naturally expected that complete emancipation would speedily follow. They remembered clearly the manner in which concessions had been secured since 1778, and they felt that loyalty of the kind shown from 1778 to 1782 and opposition to the principles of the French Revolution would bring its reward. That Pitt erred badly in his tactics now seems undeniable. He should either not have forced the law of 1793 through the Irish Parliament, or he should have coupled it with complete emancipation. Events of the next eight years were to prove that Pitt gave either too much or too little at this time.

The Fitzwilliam affair of 1795 which was to blight the fair prospects of complete emancipation is still something of a puzzle; but it is easier to understand the apparent contradictions if the state of affairs in England in 1794 and 1795 and Pitt's tremendous self-confidence are kept in mind. The war was going badly in 1794, but Pitt had not yet come to fear the outcome as he did in October 1795. In July 1794 he had finally induced the Duke of Portland and several of his followers to take office. Among these followers was Earl Fitzwilliam, who was made Lord President with the understanding that he should, in the near future, succeed Lord Westmorland as Lord Lieutenant of Ireland. Pitt evidently felt that he could put through Catholic emancipation or postpone it according to circumstances in and out of Ireland. The ease with which he had obtained the law of 1793 seems to have given him confidence that he could do the same when the time came for giving additional relief to Catholics. Thus Pitt had to consider, in England, his commitments to Portland and the attitude of his own ministers and of the King; and in Ireland, the point of view of the Lord Lieutenant, the other members of the government, of the Catholics, and of the pro- and anti-Catholic Parliamentary groups. From available evidence the most likely interpretation of Pitt's apparently inconsistent conduct in treating Fitzwilliam as he did lies in his belief that when the time was ripe he could win over his own ministers and George III and could force the reluctant acquiescence of the Irish government and the majority in the Irish Parliament. The advantage of sending Fitzwilliam lay in pleasing Portland and his followers and in keeping in a state of pleasant anticipation the Catholics and the party in Parliament which favored emancipation. Under such an arrangement Fitzwilliam would be expected to conciliate Grattan and the Catholics and to avoid offending the members of the government and the anti-Catholic party by any overt act. This plan of campaign failed either because Lord Fitzwilliam did not play the role assigned to him, or because Pitt, on account of the pressure brought to bear on him from both England and Ireland, reversed his policy.

It is clear that even George III was friendly to the plan of sending Fitzwilliam to Ireland. In writing to Lord Mansfield on November 13, 1794, for the purpose of facilitating the substitution of Fitzwilliam for Westmorland as Lord Lieutenant, the King stated:

The Earl of Mansfield has on no occasion accept an office in my Service without first ascertaining that such appointment would be personally agreeable to me, which makes Me choose to address myself to him in writing rather than entrusting any third Person to speak to him in my name. I have reason to imagine that it would be very pleasing to the Earl of Fitzwilliam to be appointed Lord Lieutenant of Ireland, and considering the very handsome manner in which He has come forward in the present unfavourable times, I cannot but with pleasure gratify him in his wish provided I can arrange a suitable and honourable situation for the Earl of Westmorland; it has therefore occurred to Me to propose to place the Earl of Mansfield as President of the Council if he will assist in forming such arrangement by resigning his Scotch Employment.[4]

When this arrangement was carried out with Mansfield, the last step necessary for recalling Westmorland had been made.

Unfortunately for the hopes of Catholic emancipation and for the success of Fitzwilliam in Ireland, a great deal had taken place between July and November. Fitzwilliam, assuming that his appointment as Lord Lieutenant would be announced after the negotiations of the first days in July had been completed, wrote to Grattan and asked his support and that of the latter's friends the Ponsonbys. News of the impending recall of Westmorland

---

[4] Sir John Fortescue, "Correspondence of King George III," Transcripts in William L. Clements Library, V, 2467. Hereafter cited as Clements Transscripts.

and of the prospect of a complete change in system in Ireland leaked out long before November. The unconcealed elation of the friends of emancipation placed the Lord Lieutenant in a very embarrassing position during the second half of 1794, and he complained bitterly to Pitt of the mortification he felt over the turn of events.

Lord Westmorland expressed his point of view, and that of those who feared the consequences of Lord Fitzwilliam's becoming Lord Lieutenant, in a long memorandum of November 17, 1794.[5] He dated the beginning of his woes from the appointment of the Duke of Portland to the Home Office, but insisted that he felt no uneasiness until Fitzwilliam actually wrote official letters regarding their situations to gentlemen of his household. After detailing various slights which he had experienced, Westmorland insisted that

notwithstanding these Indignities and personal Insults so detrimental to the King's Government and so degrading to himself, He never ceased to place the firmest reliance on the assurances, which he had received from Mr. Pitt, that there was no intention whatever to make a change in the government, and on Mr. Pitt's desire that with regard to arrangements he should act as if he were to continue in the Government.[6]

So far as continuing to hold the office of Lord Lieutenant was concerned, Westmorland was willing to act according to Pitt's wishes; but he felt that if he did remain in his present position

a due reparation ought to be made for the Affront which has been put upon him; and that, in order to make his Administration as firm as it was before the Coalition, ostensible assurances should be made that he has the full support of Mr. Pitt and the Cabinet that none of his arrangements are to be interfered with by the Secretary of State after their being transmitted.[7]

But in case a successor were appointed, Westmorland felt that it would be "necessary for his honour and character that a very high Mark of the Royal Favour and Confidence should be conferred upon Him" in order to avoid the appearance that he had been disgracefully superseded. Further, the Lord Lieutenant declared that he would feel great difficulty in accepting a new

---

[5] Clements Transcripts, V, 2474–79. Copy of a Memorandum delivered by Mr. Cooke to Mr. Douglas.

[6] *Ibid.*, V, 2474–75.   [7] *Ibid.*, V, 2475–76.

place in the government unless he could assure the friends of his government that their interests would be protected and that his promises to them would be honored. Then followed a long list of the achievements and successes of Westmorland's administration: he had taken charge at the close of the Regency struggle in 1789 and had tamed an inflamed opposition; he had carried through the act of 1793 in the face of fearful odds; he had taken vigorous measures against those "Factious and Democratic Spirits" in Ireland who had attempted to introduce the principles of the French Revolution into Ireland; he had forced through the Militia Bill, with the result that the country now possessed 14,000 well-drilled militiamen; and he resisted no requisition for regular troops in Ireland by the British government. So long as he remained Lord Lieutenant, Westmorland insisted that the patronage must be entirely at his disposal. But by all odds the most significant part of the memorandum comes in the warning which he gave Pitt on the probable consequences of the policy pursued in Ireland. In view of what took place early in 1795, this section is decidedly prophetic:

The late unprecedented Procedures of the Duke of Portland and Lord Fitzwilliam were either in consequence of Mr. Pitt's approbation, or without his knowledge and concurrence. And the inference in the one case is that Mr. Pitt has abandoned Ireland to their will and pleasure; in the other that they were determined to force him to do so.

That their conduct was a marked public affront to the Lord Lieutenant is acknowledged. That an attempt was in contemplation to sacrifice many of the most valuable supporters of Pitt and Lord Westmorland in Ireland is also acknowledged.

If then Lord Fitzwilliam shall nevertheless succeed whatever stipulations may be made on his appointment, a Persuasion will still remain in the minds of Gentlemen in Ireland that the Duke of Portland's Party in the Cabinet have forced their point, that the Department of Ireland is reluctantly conceded to His Grace by Mr. Pitt, and if such a persuasion continues to be acted upon, it is easy to foresee very unpleasant consequences to Mr. Pitt's government in the event of any future differences.[8]

Thus while Pitt was swamped on the one side with warnings of this sort, on the other he was equally besieged to make good his promises by Portland and Fitzwilliam. The primary reason

[8] *Ibid.*, V, 2478–79.

for the delay was of course the difficulty of finding a suitable place for Westmorland; but both the events and warnings of the months from July 1794 to January 1795 must have made considerable impression on Pitt. By October Portland and Fitzwilliam were threatening to withdraw from the government unless Pitt carried out his earlier promises. During these critical weeks Lord Loughborough seems to have attempted the role of mediator between his old allies, the Portland Whigs, and his more recent chief, William Pitt.[9] In view of the action he was to take early the next year on Catholic Emancipation, his attitude at this time is decidedly interesting. Loughborough attempted to convince Pitt that the new system which the reformers in Ireland demanded and which Fitzwilliam, evidently, was planning to introduce was not really new. Instead it was merely an arrangement which would involve a few changes in personnel at Dublin and in which all persons concerned could be satisfied in some way. Loughborough, however, felt that the new Lord Lieutenant must be given a free hand but that he would act with moderation.[10]

The point of view of the ministry is taken up at great length in a memorandum prepared by Lord Grenville in March 1795.[11] A brief survey of the negotiations with Fitzwilliam between July and December 1794 is given, but the greater part of the memorandum is devoted to a meeting attended by Fitzwilliam, Portland, Spencer, Grenville, Windham, and Pitt. The date of this conference is not given, but at the end of the account Grenville states that Fitzwilliam left immediately for the country and soon went to Ireland. Since Fitzwilliam kissed hands on his appointment on December 10 and arrived in Dublin on January 4, this meeting must have taken place at some time in December. During the negotiations which preceded the conference Fitzwilliam had suggested the removal of Lord Fitzgibbon as Chancellor but had given way before the objections of the ministers; and later he insisted that he told Pitt, who had no recollection of such a statement, he intended to remove Mr. Beresford from his place at the head of the revenue department. Thus, before the meeting was held, "the most explicit assurances were given by Lord Fitzwilliam that he had not in view the establishment of any new

[9] J. H. Rose, *Pitt and Napoleon* (London: G. Bell & Sons, Ltd., 1912), pp. 20–36.

[10] *Ibid.*, pp. 25–26.

[11] Historical Manuscripts Commission, *The Manuscripts of J. B. Fortescue, Esq., Preserved at Dropmore* (London, 1892–1927), III, 35–38.

system in Ireland, but that he was desirous of strengthening his Government by the accession of Mr. Ponsonby and his friends, and the support of Mr. Grattan."[12]

At the meeting itself six points were discussed. The most important ones turned out on the appointment of the Ponsonbys to office, the provision to be made for certain officeholders who were to be supplanted, and the abolition of some offices established by Lord Buckingham. The ministers dissuaded Fitzwilliam from taking any action on the Revenue Board until he reached Ireland and reminded him that "after his explicit disavowal of all intention to introduce a new system, or to countenance imputations on the former Government of Ireland, his colleagues would willingly leave it to him to consider the subject, on such information as he might receive respecting it in Ireland; desiring only that, before any such measure was adopted, they might have the opportunity of deliberating upon it."[13] In view of the sensation created when Fitzwilliam removed Beresford from office, the following statement in the memorandum is noteworthy: "Nothing was intimated in this conversation of any idea of removing Mr. Beresford, nor was even his name mentioned by Lord Fitzwilliam; although the different means which might be adopted for lessening the number of the Commissioners of the Revenue Boards formed part of what he stated on the subject of these Boards." But most important of all matters treated in the memorandum was that of further concession to the Catholics.

The subject was considered as one of much delicacy, and no decided sentiment as to the line which it might ultimately be right to adopt upon it was expressed by any person present. The result of the discussion was an unanimous opinion that Lord Fitz-William should inform himself in Ireland as to the state and disposition of the country in this respect, and should transmit that information, with his opinion, to the King's servants here; that he should, as much as possible, endeavour to prevent the agitation of the question during the present session; and that, in all events, he should do nothing in it which might commit the King's Government here or in Ireland without fresh instructions from hence. With this subject the conversation finished. At the close of it, Lord Fitz-William, who had brought to the meeting a memorandum of matters to be talked of, was repeatedly asked whether there were any other points to be discussed, or any new measures to be proposed. The answer was that he know of none.[14]

---

[12] *Ibid.,* p. 36.   [13] *Ibid.,* p. 38.   [14] *Ibid.*

Such, according to the ministers, was the understanding at the time Fitzwilliam left for Ireland.

It is unnecessary to relate the details of the short rule of Fitzwilliam as Lord Lieutenant. He arrived in Dublin on January 4, 1795, and left at the end of March. Two factors contributed to his failure: patronage and the Catholic question. On January 7 he sent notice to John Beresford, head of the revenue department, of his coming dismissal. Since Beresford and Lord Fitzgibbon, the Chancellor, were the most influential members of the Dublin Castle group, and since the Lord Lieutenant quickly indicated that he had adopted the point of view of the Ponsonbys and Grattan in opposition to that of the existing officeholders, this dismissal was equivalent to a declaration of war. To some historians the action of Fitzwilliam appears to have been actuated by high principles and the desire to sweep away a reactionary clique in Dublin Castle; to others it seems equally clear that it was a rather sordid struggle over patronage.

But it is the question of Catholic Emancipation, with which patronage was closely joined, that is most important. Fitzwilliam did not make emancipation a government measure, but he seems to have done little to dissuade Grattan from introducing such a bill. Thus the disturbing news reached England that he was discharging the old friends of the two previous administrations and was giving dangerous encouragement to further concessions to Catholics. Pitt and Grenville appear to have felt that Fitzwilliam was not sticking loyally to the spirit of the understanding reached in the December conference. George III expressed the same sentiments on January 29 when he wrote to Pitt: "I wish also to mention the great change that seems coming forward in Ireland without the smallest attention to what was understood on the departure of Lord Fitzwilliam."[15] The King had reference to the dismissals, but soon he was to feel even greater agitation over the emancipation proposals.

The reactions of George III to Fitzwilliam's proposals are highly significant because they are the key to the situation which led to Pitt's resignation six years later. The crisis of January–February, 1801, becomes more comprehensible when the King's stand in 1795 is used as a background. On February 5 the Duke of Portland handed the King the dispatches from Fitzwilliam

---

[15] J. H. Rose, *Pitt and Napoleon*, p. 236.

announcing Grattan's proposals for admitting Catholics to the Irish Parliament and his own concurrence in them. The next day George III in a long and important letter to Pitt carefully outlined his stand on Catholic Emancipation which he was to maintain during the remainder of his life:

Having yesterday, after the Drawing Room, seen the Duke of Portland, who mentioned the receipt of letters from the Lord-Lieutenant of Ireland, which, to my greatest astonishment, propose the total change of the principles of government which have been followed by every administration in that kingdom since the abdication of King James the Second, and consequently overturning the fabric that the wisdom of our forefathers esteemed necessary, and which the laws of this country have directed; and thus, after no longer stay than three weeks in Ireland, venturing to condemn the labours of the ages, and wanting an immediate adoption of ideas which every man of property in Ireland and every friend to the Protestant Religion must feel diametrically contrary to those he has imbibed from his earliest youth.

Undoubtedly the Duke of Portland made this communication to sound my sentiments previous to the Cabinet Meeting to be held tomorrow on this weighty subject. I expressed my surprise at the idea of admitting the Roman Catholics to vote in Parliament, but chose to avoid entering into the subject, and only heard the substance of the propositions without giving my sentiments. But the more I reflect on the subject, the more I feel the danger of the proposal, and therefore should not think myself free from blame if I did not put my thoughts on paper even in the present coarse shape, the moment being so pressing, and not sufficient time to arrange them in a more digested shape previous to the Duke of Portland's laying the subject before the Cabinet.

The above proposal is contrary to the conduct of every European Government, and I believe to that of every State on the globe. In the States of Germany, the Lutheran, Calvinist, and Roman Catholic religions are universally permitted, yet each respective State has but one Church establishment, to which the States of the country and those holding any civil employment must be conformists; Court offices and military commissions may be held also by persons of either of the other persuasions, but the number of such is very small. The Dutch provinces admit Lutherans and Roman Catholics in some subsidised regiments, but in civil employments the Calvinists are alone capable of holding them.

Ireland varies from most other countries by property residing almost entirely in the hands of the Protestants, whilst the lower classes of the people are chiefly Roman Catholics. The change proposed, therefore, must disoblige the greater number to benefit a few, the inferior orders not being of rank to gain favourably by the change. That they may also be gainers, it is proposed that an army be kept constantly in Ireland, and a kind of yeomenry which in reality would be Roman Catholic police corps, established, which would keep the Protestant interest under awe.

It is but fair to confess that the whole of this plan is the strongest justification of the Old Servants of the Crown in Ireland, for having objected to the former indulgences that have been granted, as it is now pretended these have availed nothing, unless this total change of political principle be admitted.

English Government ought well to consider before it gives any encouragement to a proposition which cannot fail sooner or later to separate the two kingdoms, or by way of establishing a similar line of conduct in this kingdom adopt measures to prevent which my family was invited to mount the throne of this kingdom in preference to the House of Savoy.

One might suppose the authors of this scheme had not viewed the tendency or extent of the question, but were actuated alone by the peevish inclination of humiliating the old friends of English Government in Ireland, or from the desire of paying implicit obedience to the heated imagination of Mr. Burke.

Besides the discontent and changes which must be occasioned by the direliction of all the principles that have been held so wise by our ancestors, it is impossible to foresee how far it may alienate the minds of this kingdom; for though I fear religion is but little attended to by persons of rank, and that the word *toleration,* or rather *indifference* to that sacred subject, has been too much admitted by them, yet the bulk of the nation has not been spoiled by foreign travel and manners, and still feels the blessing of having a fixed principle from whence the source of every tie to society and government must trace its origin.

I cannot conclude without expressing that the subject is beyond the decision of any Cabinet of Ministers—that, could they form an opinion in favour of such a measure, it would be highly dangerous, without previous concert with the leading men of every order in the State, to send any encouragement to the Lord Lieutenant on this subject; and if received with the same suspicion I do, I am certain it would be safer even to change the new administration in Ireland, if its continuance depends on the success of this proposal, than to prolong its existence on grounds that must sooner or later ruin one if not both kingdoms.[16]

[16] Earl Stanhope, *Life of the Right Honourable William Pitt* (London, 1861–62), II, xxiii–xxv.

So decided a stand on the part of the King undoubtedly played an important part in the recall of Fitzwilliam. Apparently both Pitt and Grenville welcomed such support because they felt that the Lord Lieutenant had broken his agreement on both patronage and concessions to the Catholics. Most interesting of all, however, was the attitude taken by Portland and his followers who had entered the cabinet with him in July 1794. Since they had taken office only on condition that Fitzwilliam receive the Lord Lieutenancy and had threatened to resign later in 1794 when the appointment was delayed, their failure to support him at this point is noteworthy. Pitt reported to the King that in the cabinet meeting of February 7 it had been agreed that no time should be lost in instructing Fitzwilliam not to commit the government to the Grattan proposal.[17] Since he transmitted to Fitzwilliam the decision of the cabinet, he must have concurred in the conclusions reached. As a result of the exchange of correspondence with Portland and Pitt, Fitzwilliam on February 25 announced that he intended to resign within a week. Circumstances, however, prevented him from leaving before the end of March, and his departure was the occasion of a public ovation by the inhabitants of Dublin. Considering the stand taken by the King and the feeling on the part of Pitt and Grenville that Fitzwilliam had not kept the gentlemen's agreement which they considered that he had made with them, the only chance which the Lord Lieutenant had of continuing in office was through threats on the part of the Portland Whigs to retire from the government if he were recalled from Dublin.

The reasons why Portland, Spencer, Windham, and even Loughborough did not support Fitzwilliam with the threat of resignation have never been made entirely clear. Three possible explanations for the stand taken by the Portland group may be offered: a belief that Fitzwilliam had not adhered to the policies agreed upon before he left for Ireland; a change in attitude toward further concessions to Catholics; and a yielding to the arguments of Pitt and others that resignation, in view of the critical condition of the country, would be very disastrous at this time. Probably all three influences played their parts. Certainly the first one was not decisive, as Portland's warm defense of Fitzwilliam on his return was to show.

[17] Clements Transcripts, VI, 2622.

Pitt's strength and weakness are well illustrated by his handling of the Irish situation from the outbreak of the war with France through the recall of Fitzwilliam. His extreme confidence in his own judgment and integrity were so great that he was willing to risk such steps as the Catholic Bill of 1793 or the appointment of a Lord Lieutenant with the views of Fitzwilliam. The weakness of this confidence lay in the fact that, once he had taken a bold action of this sort, he was likely to ignore subsequent events until he was compelled by circumstances to intervene and either to check or to reverse the results of his earlier decision. In the case of Ireland from 1793 to 1795, Pitt first aroused the hopes of the Irish Catholics by the law of 1793 and then failed to carry these concessions to the logical conclusion of admitting them to Parliament. In 1795 he aroused the hopes of the Catholics that this additional concession was to be made by appointing Fitzwilliam Lord Lieutenant, and then dashed them once more by recalling the latter.

But although these qualities and practices of Pitt played an important role in the recall of Fitzwilliam, it seems highly probable that they were no more decisive than the attitude of George III. At the end of the long letter of February 6 he had stated that the subject of admitting Catholics to equal political rights was beyond the decision of any cabinet of ministers and that it would be better to change the administration in Ireland than to continue with such a plan. But the King did not stop at this point. In commenting on Pitt's letter to Fitzwilliam and the answer he expressed the opinion that

Mr. Pitt's letter is direct and highly civil, perhaps had I been called upon for an opinion before it was sent I might have wished it stronger, but the tone in which the answer is drawn makes me glad the former was so mild, as it renders the latter the more inexcusable; indeed I am persuaded the Writer either does not feel the question or is so resolved to view things alone through his own sense that He has drawn up a paper containing many phrases but void of any idea; had he been in a state of mind to be held back by what has been written to Him the temper that dictated his letter would soon have broken forth, and have rendered his removal necessary but then much evil would have first been committed. . . . .[18]

George III, however, was quite willing to co-operate with Pitt in softening the blow for both Portland and Fitzwilliam. The

[18] Pitt MSS, 103, February 20, 1795.

Duke wrote to the King pleading that consideration should be shown "for the sensations of a generous and high spirited mind, suddenly checked in a career in which it had entered from motives and with views solely prompted by a zeal for Your Majesty's service, and for the attainment of those objects which Your Majesty is known to have most at heart."[19] What the Duke wanted was an invitation for Fitzwilliam to remain a member of the cabinet when he returned to England. Pitt favored propitiating Portland in this respect because as he wrote to the King

Mr. Pitt does not think it at all probable that Lord Fitzwilliam would accept the proposal. He sees however no Inconvenience if he should as there is no doubt of Lord Fitzwilliam's Principles on the great Questions now depending here, and as his whole conduct while He was in the Cabinet, was very different from that which he has held under the Guidance of others in Ireland. Mr. Pitt's principal Motive for submitting the Proposal to Your Majesty, arises from seeing how much the Duke of Portland has sacrificed his feelings to an honorable sense of his Duty to Your Majesty's Service. Mr. Pitt has not the least Ground to suppose that either the Duke of Portland or any of those who formerly acted with Him have had any Idea of retiring from their Situations, and he only mentions this suggestion as likely if Your Majesty approves it to afford great relief to their Minds.[20]

The King answered that the "whole conduct of the Duke of Portland in this unpleasant business is so handsome that it is impossible not with satisfaction to gratify his feelings on this occasion. I therefore authorize Mr. Pitt to acquaint him with the suggestion having been laid before me and with my cordial consent though I doubt much whether Earl Fitzwilliam is in a state of mind to accept it."[21] Clearly the King could afford to be magnanimous and Pitt to make such an insignificant concession to avoid the likelihood of the Portland Whigs withdrawing from the ministry.

Thus the Fitzwilliam affair came to an end without further concessions to the Catholics in Ireland and without disrupting the rearranged cabinet of 1794. Doubtless both the Catholic question and patronage contributed to the recall of Fitzwilliam. The officials of Dublin Castle who feared dismissal and the members of the established order in Ireland who feared further con-

---

[19] Clements Transcripts, VI, 2648.
[20] *Ibid.*, VI, 2642–43.   [21] Stanhope, *op. cit.*, II, xxvi.

cessions to Catholics, stirred up sufficient alarm in the minds of the King, Pitt, and the Portland Whigs to make any change at this time impossible.

So far as the King was concerned, however, the recall of Fitzwilliam did not mean a postponement of the question of Catholic Emancipation but a definite closing of it. He had no intention of being caught again as he felt that he had been caught by Portland handing him the dispatches of February 5; and hence decided to fortify himself with the expert opinion of prominent lawyers and churchmen. Thus opinions received from Lord Chancellor Loughborough, Lord Kenyon, and the Archbishop of Canterbury during the first two weeks in March were to be important factors in the failure of emancipation in 1801. Because of their importance the Memorandum of the King and the answers of these three will be given in full. In this Memorandum dated March 7 the King set forth his thoughts and doubts:

The following Queries on the present attempt to abolish all distinctions in Religion in Ireland, with the intention of favouring the Roman Catholics in that Kingdom, are stated from the desire of learning whether this can be done, without affecting the Constitution of this Country; if not there is no occasion to view whether the measure in itself be not highly improper.

The only Laws which now affect the Papists in Ireland are the Acts of Supremacy and Uniformity, the Test Act and the Bill of Rights. It seems to require very serious investigation how far the King can give His Assent to a Repeal of any one of these acts, without a breach of His Coronation Oath, and of the Articles of Union with Scotland.

The Construction put on the Coronation Oath by the Parliament at the Revolution seems strongly marked in the Journals of the House of Commons, when a Clause was proposed by way of Rider to the Bill establishing the Coronation Oath, declaring that nothing contained in it should be construed to bind down the King and Queen their Heirs and Successors not to give the Royal Assent to any Bill for qualifying the Act of Uniformity so far as to render palatable to Protestant Dissenters, and the Clause was negatived upon a Division. This leads to the implication that the Coronation Oath was understood at the Revolution to bind the Crown not to Assent to any Repeal of any of the Existing Laws at the Revolution, or which were then enacted for the Maintenance and Defence of the Protestant Religion as by Law Established.

If the Oath was understood to bind the Crown not to Assent to the Repeal of the Act of Uniformity in favour of Protestant Dissenters, it would seem to bind the Crown full as strongly not to Assent to the Repeal of the Act of Supremacy or the Test Act in favour of Roman Catholics.

Another question arises from the Provisions of the Act limiting the Succession to the Crown, by which a forfeiture of the Crown is expressly enacted, if the King upon the Throne should hold Communication or be reconciled to the Church of Rome. May not the Repeal of the Act of Supremacy and the Establishing the Popish Religion in any of the Hereditary Dominions be construed as amounting to a reconciliation with the Church of Rome.

Would not the Chancellor of England incur some risk in affixing the Great Seal to a Bill for giving to the Pope a concurrent Ecclesiastical Jurisdiction with the King. By the Articles of Union with Scotland it is declared to be an essential and fundamental Article, that the King of Great Britain shall maintain the Church of England as by Law established in England, Ireland, and Berwick upon Tweed. The Bargain made by England in 1782 by Yelverton's Act gives rise to the Question whether the Repeal of any of the English Statutes adopted by that Act would not be a direct Violation of the Compact made by the Parliament of Ireland with Great Britain.[22]

The Archbishop of Canterbury answered that the proposed bill for Catholic Emancipation, which Fitzwilliam had sent to England for the approval of the ministers, appeared to be a direct violation of the act of the 30th of Charles II which forbade a person sitting in Parliament until he had taken the oaths of allegiance and supremacy and had subscribed to a declaration against popery. These terms were extended to Ireland by the Irish act of the 21st and 22d of George III. It further appeared to the Archbishop that the proposed measure would repeal the sections in the Declaration of Rights, the Bill of Rights, and the Act of Settlement which were expressly enacted to remain "the Law of the Realm for ever:" and that it would be a direct violation of the Act of Union with Scotland. In addition the Archbishop felt that by the Coronation Oath an inviolable observation of these laws was made obligatory upon every king and queen of Great Britain.[23]

Lord Kenyon, after consulting with the Attorney General, reached the conclusion that any relief given to "Sectarists" would not be contrary to the Act of Union or the Coronation Oath so long as the King's supremacy and the main features of the Act of Uniformity, the Church of England, and the provision for

[22] Clements Transcripts, VI, 2653–55.   [23] *Ibid.*, VI, 2658–60.

its ministers were maintained. But on the question of giving the Pope concurrent jurisdiction with the King, Kenyon was less reassuring. He expressed the opinion that the Chancellor of Great Britain would incur great risk in affixing the Great Seal to such a bill because "it would be contrary to the Coronation Oath, and subversive of a fundamental part of the Act of Union."[24]

But of far greater interest than the opinions of either the Archbishop or Lord Kenyon were those given by Lord Chancellor Loughborough. On all but the query contained in the final paragraph of the King's Memorandum the advice of Loughborough was more restrained than that of the other two. On three points the Chancellor was especially reassuring: first, that the Coronation Oath imposed no restrictions on the royal assent to any bill passed by both houses of Parliament; second, that the Constitution of Great Britain would not be affected by a law which applied to Ireland alone but every bill passed by the Irish Parliament should be considered in the light of expediency; and, third, that the Test Act and the Acts of Supremacy and Uniformity might be further modified without endangering the royal authority, introducing foreign jurisdiction, or subverting the Constitution of the Church of England, but that every such modification should be examined with great care. From these three opinions George III could extract little comfort; but on the query whether the Chancellor of England might not incur some risk if he affixed the Great Seal to a bill which would give the Pope concurrent ecclesiastical jurisdiction with the ruler he received a more satisfactory answer. Loughborough expressed the opinion that

From the singular Situation of Ireland whose Parliament cannot protect the Office by whom their Bills must be returned, this part of the Chancellor's Office may often expose Him to some risk. If such a Bill could be presented to Your Majesty, it would be the peculiar duty of the Chancellor to implore Your Majesty not to impose a command upon Him to affix the Seal to a Bill which He must know to be so derogatory to the Dignity of the Crown, as well as so prejudicial to the Interests of the Kingdom.[25]

On the whole, the advice given to the King by Loughborough was far more restrained than that of the Archbishop of Canterbury. After all the question at issue was whether Catholics should be given the right to sit in Parliament and to hold certain offices

---

[24] Clements Transcripts, VI, 2672.   [25] *Ibid.*, VI, 2667–68.

and not whether the Pope should have concurrent ecclesiastical jurisdiction. Loughborough was anxious to have Fitzwilliam sent to Ireland, and yet he did not defend the actions and policies of his friend as Lord Lieutenant. Still, there is nothing in the Lord Chancellor's opinions that are actually contrary to the bill proposed by Grattan and endorsed by Fitzwilliam. In this particular episode at least there seems to be little of the duplicity which most historians find in the conduct of Loughborough in 1800 and 1801.

Despite the fact that the opinions rendered by Kenyon and Loughborough were not so satisfactory to George III as that of the Archbishop of Canterbury, the Memorandum which the King drew up on March 7, when considered in the light of his subsequent conduct, makes it perfectly clear that the royal mind was fixed on the matter of further concessions to Catholics in Ireland. Thus, while Loughborough may have acted in a dishonorable manner in 1800, proof is lacking that he had any real influence in fixing the mind of the King on the question of Catholic Emancipation. The question naturally arises why George III should have allowed Pitt to force through the Irish Parliament the act of 1793 without making any serious protest and yet have taken so decisive a stand on the additional concessions in 1795. Perhaps he felt that the liberal franchise of 1793 was not dangerous unless accompanied by the right of Catholics to sit in Parliament; or perhaps the ideas which he phrased so vividly in his Memorandum of March 7 did not crystallize until early in 1795. But to anybody who has read with care this Memorandum the stand of the King, which later led to Pitt's resignation, can occasion no great astonishment.

The concluding phase of the Fitzwilliam affair came after the Lord Lieutenant returned to England. He presented his side of the affair in a personal interview with George III, in a paper which he drew up and left with the King, in his speech in the House of Lords, and in the protest which, along with Lord Ponsonby, he had entered in the journals of that House. Fitzwilliam in describing to Grattan his interview with the King declared that some of the sentiments "which I threw out seemed to be new to him, and to impress him considerably. Upon the whole his attention was gracious, but he gave no opinion whatever, only *as to my intentions*."[26] On the other hand, George III in writing to Pitt

[26] Henry Grattan, *Memoirs of the Life and Times of the Right Honourable Henry Grattan* (London, 1839), IV, 210.

showed that he was not impressed by the paper which Fitzwilliam left with him: "I cannot say much information is to be obtained from it, it seems rather a panegerick on himself than any pointed attack on Ministry, though it shews much disinclination to former Colleagues."[27] A motion was made in the House of Lords by the Duke of Norfolk and in the House of Commons by Mr. Jekyll for all copies of the correspondence between the government and the Lord Lieutenant; but the ministers were successful in resisting this motion in both houses. Pitt refused to make an elaborate defense of the actions of his ministry and contented himself with pleading official secrecy and the right of the King to remove public officers without giving any reasons.[28] George III must have taken considerable satisfaction in having his prerogative defended so stoutly in both houses, and particularly by Pitt in the Commons.

Thus while the Fitzwilliam affair ended in England without breaking up the coalition with the Portland Whigs and without any loss of prestige on the part of the government, the effect in Ireland proved to be much more serious. Regardless of where the blame for the Fitzwilliam fiasco lies, the influence on Anglo-Irish relations was deplorable and tragic. Lord Camden was sent to Ireland to replace Lord Fitzwilliam as Lord Lieutenant and Thomas Pelham was made Chief Secretary. They were expected to reconcile the jarring factions, to soothe the ruffled Protestants, and to propitiate the disappointed Catholics. Grattan's bill, which had contributed so much to the overthrow of Fitzwilliam, was beaten by more than a hundred votes in the House of Commons. Instead, the government sponsored a bill to charter Maynooth College, which was to provide a seminary for the education of Irish priests. Some such arrangement was badly needed, because those seminaries on the Continent where Irish priests had been trained had, in the main, been swept away by the French Revolution, and it was hoped that the establishment of such an institution in Ireland might result in the lessening of anti-British prejudices. But despite the good intentions of Pitt and the British ministers, Maynooth College did not fulfill expectations of reducing friction between the English and the Irish.

Following the recall of Fitzwilliam the United Irishmen began to plan a general rebellion and to count on the support of a French

27 Pitt MSS, 104, April 29, 1795.
28 *The Parliamentary History of England, 1066–1803,* XXXI, 1550–54.

army in Ireland. The way was paved by a most elaborate organization based on numerous local lodges and a hierarchy of committees with a directory at the top. The subordination of everything to the success of the rebellion made the leaders feel that it was necessary to bring in the great mass of the Catholic peasants, whose fundamental interest was not in political democracy but in the abolition of the tithe; therefore they set about capturing the Defender movement. The result was the intensification, especially in Ulster, of the bitterness between Catholics and Protestants. Here the Protestants organized Orange lodges and began to attack Catholics, and all but the more extreme democrats of Ulster withdrew from the United Irishmen. Numerically this loss was more than offset by the rapid increase in United Irish lodges in southern Ireland in 1795 and 1796. The spread of these lodges among the Catholic peasantry was made easier by the fact that the gentry and the priests did not attempt to exercise the restraining influence which they had used before the recall of Fitzwilliam. Yet despite the growing menace, the greater part of the Catholics of southwestern Ireland were still loyal at the end of 1796. This was proved conclusively at the time of the threatened invasion of Hoche in December.

But when the United Irish began to arm and drill they became a real menace to the government. By 1797 the movement had assumed formidable proportions; and had the French been able to land an army in Ireland during the naval mutinies, the British would have experienced great difficulty in retaining their grip on the country. The victory of the British fleet over the Dutch at Camperdown in October 1797, however, ruined any real chance which the United Irish leaders had of securing assistance from France. But despite the loss of this opportunity for French help, various factors brought on a rebellion in May 1798.

Although Camden, the Lord Lieutenant, and Thomas Pelham, the Chief Secretary, had been brought up in the Whig tradition, they found great difficulty in coping with the situation left by Fitzwilliam. Pelham was handicapped by bad health and more than once requested to be relieved of his duties. In fact in March 1798 it was necessary to appoint Camden's nephew, Lord Castlereagh, temporary secretary because Pelham was so ill that he was unable to carry on his work. Circumstances more or less forced the hand of the government in Ireland. Realizing the danger of the increase in the numbers of the United Irishmen during the critical months of 1797, the Lord Lieutenant decided to disarm Ulster. This task was given to General Lake who, finding that the regular troops were inadequate in numbers, made use of the yeomanry. Since this group was made up of wealthy Protestants who were fearful over the threat to both property and religion, the disarming was accompanied by acts of considerable violence. Seeing their organization being broken up and their recruits disarmed, the United Irish leaders decided to precipitate a rebellion before either step was carried further. Before the appointed day, however, the government became acquainted with nearly all the plans for uprisings. The arrest of all except one of the Leinster executives in March 1798 was followed by the extension of martial law to that county. The cruelties of the Ulster disarmament of the previous year were repeated on a larger scale. The flogging and shooting of suspects and the burning of houses produced a veritable reign of terror; but these rigorous measures brought on a rebellion instead of averting one.

The danger from this armed uprising was of comparatively short duration. The signal for opening hostilities was given on May 23, and the rebels in southern Ireland were routed at Vinegar Hill on June 21. The overthrow of the rebels coincided almost exactly with the resignation of Camden and the appointment of Cornwallis as Lord Lieutenant. Camden had long been thoroughly anxious to give up his trying position, and he finally prevailed upon Pitt to combine the offices of Lord Lieutenant and Commander-in-Chief. The new Lord Lieutenant, who is best known for his surrender at Yorktown and his fine record as an administrator in India, inspired confidence in England because of his military reputation and his splendid personal qualities. He was soon working effectively with his temporary Chief Secretary, Lord Castlereagh; but he aroused the hatred of the Dublin Castle clique, particularly the Beresford group, and of the ultra-Protestant group throughout the country by restraining the victorious army and yeomanry. Cornwallis wrote in very unflattering terms of the conduct of the Irish militia and of the ruling oligarchy:

The Irish militia are totally without discipline, contemptible before the enemy when any serious resistance is made to them, but ferocious and cruel in the extreme when any poor wretches either with or without arms come within their power; in short murder appears to be their favorite pastime. . . . .

The principal persons of this country, and the Members of both

Houses of Parliament, are, in general, averse to all acts of clemency, and although they do not express, and perhaps are too much heated to see the ultimate effects which their violence must produce, would pursue measures that could only terminate in the extirpation of the greater number of the inhabitants, and in the utter destruction of the country. The words Papists and Priests are for ever in their mouths, and by their unaccountable policy they would drive four-fifths of the community into irreconcilable rebellion; and in their warmth they lose sight of the real cause of the present mischief, of that deep-laid conspiracy to revolutionize Ireland on the principles of France, which was originally formed, and by wonderful assiduity brought nearly to maturity, by men who had no thought of religion but to destroy it, and who knew how to turn the passions and prejudices of the different sects to the advancement of their horrible plot for the introduction of that most dreadful of all evils, a Jacobin revolution.[29]

In order to prevent this element from ruthlessly annihilating the small bands of scattered rebels who were still capable of doing considerable damage, Cornwallis issued a general pardon to all, with the exception of certain leaders, who would lay down their arms within fourteen days. Castlereagh's announcement of this amnesty in the Irish House of Commons was well received except by the Dublin Castle clique.[30] Within a comparatively short time order was restored in Ireland and the leading rebels were punished. Unfortunately the bitter hatred of Protestant and Catholic, and of the ruling oligarchy and the peasants, which had in a measure abated during the eighteenth century, now returned to the deplorable state of the generation following the Revolution of 1689. Both religious and social grievances must be kept in mind when the passing of the Act of Union is considered.

George III and Pitt did not see eye to eye on all questions of policy and appointments from the recall of Fitzwilliam to the suppression of the rebellion. Despite Pelham's bad health and constant threats to resign, the King had the greatest of confidence in him and showed reluctance at parting with his services late both in 1795 and in March 1798 when Lord Castlereagh was made temporary Chief Secretary. Furthermore, George III seems never to have neglected an opportunity to reiterate his unalterable opposition to Catholic Emancipation. A letter to Pitt written on

---

[29] Charles Ross, *Correspondence of Charles First Marquis Cornwallis* (London, 1859), II, 357–58. Hereafter cited as *Cornwallis Correspondence*.

[30] H. M. Hyde, *The Rise of Castlereagh* (London, 1933), p. 259.

June 13, 1798, at the time of Cornwallis' departure for Ireland to relieve Camden, shows both his regard for Pelham, his antipathy to any additional concessions to Catholics, and his firm belief in the necessity of a union:

Mr. Pitt has in my opinion saved Ireland by engaging Mr. Pelham in the present state of that kingdom to return there as soon as his health will permit, which should be known there at least when the Marquess Cornwallis arrives. That gentleman's knowledge of the country must be of great utility to the new Lord Lieutenant, who must not lose the present moment of terror for frightening the supporters of the Castle into an union with this country; and no further indulgences must be granted to the Roman Catholics, as no country can be governed where there is more than one established religion; the others may be tolerated, but that cannot extend further [than] to leave to perform their religious duties according to the tenets of their Church, for which indulgence they cannot have any share in the government of the State.[31]

The King also violently disapproved the decision to send additional troops to Ireland during this same month. His objection, however, was based on the grounds, treated at length in the preceding chapter, of the foolishness of diverting troops from the "active service" to side shows. But inasmuch as the soldiers were being sent to Ireland he felt that "as the sword is drawn it not be returned to the sheath until the whole country has submitted without condition, the making any compromise would be perfect destruction."[32]

Once quiet, if not order, was restored in Ireland, plans for a union with England were commenced. Pitt had long favored union as a solution for the Anglo-Irish problems and the King, as has been noted above, expressed his approbation on more than one occasion before 1799. The Duke of Portland had become a convert and it seems likely that his refusal to back Fitzwilliam in 1795 was due to his conviction that a union was necessary. In Ireland both Cornwallis and Castlereagh firmly believed in such a policy; and Camden, at the time of his resignation in 1798, had written Pitt a list of suggestions for a proposed union.[33] Thus since the King, Pitt, and the most important ministers in England and officials in Ireland favored union, the problem was how

31 J. H. Rose, *Pitt and Napoleon*, pp. 243–44.

32 Pitt MSS, 104, June 3, 1798.

33 J. H. Rose, *Pitt and Napoleon*, pp. 335–38.

to get such a measure through the Irish Parliament. The support which a bill of this kind would secure depended in no small measure upon whether or not it provided for the admission of Catholics to the imperial Parliament at Westminster. The Protestant oligarchy and its spokesmen were willing to support the union only if Catholics were not admitted; the Catholics would support it only if the reverse were true.

Thus for purposes of this study the methods used in the unsuccessful attempt of 1799 and the successful one of 1800 to put through the Irish Parliament a bill providing for a union with Great Britain are of less importance than the methods used to secure the support of the Catholics in Ireland and the clash between the King and Pitt over following up the union with further concessions to Catholics. Nevertheless, an account of the existing Irish Parliament and the manner in which it was induced to vote its own extinction are necessary for a proper appreciation of the differences between George III and Pitt.

The Irish Parliament at this time was made up of three hundred members: 116 boroughs, 2 cities, and 32 counties each sending two members. Of 116 boroughs, 87 were "close," that is, they were under the control of the government, a corporation, or a local magnate. Since the close boroughs sent a majority of the three hundred members to the House of Commons, it was necessary to indemnify the vested interests for the losses they would incur if the Parliament were extinguished. As soon as news of the proposed union spread through Ireland, it aroused the opposition not only of the threatened borough owners but of the legal profession, the corporation of the city of Dublin, the Orange societies, and the Protestant oligarchy. Even the officials in Dublin Castle were badly divided. Cornwallis, Castlereagh, and Elliot, the Under Secretary, strongly favored the union; Sir John Parnell, Chancellor of the Exchequer, and Foster, the Speaker of the House, strongly opposed it; and Cooke, the other Under Secretary, and Clare, the Chancellor, favored only an ultra-Protestant union.[34] The first and third of these groups immediately made every effort to secure the support of Pitt for their point of view; and evidence points to the conclusion that the group favoring a union only on the ultra-Protestant basis was successful. Clare went to London in October for the purpose of presenting

---

[34] H. M. Hyde, *op. cit.*, p. 281.

this side and his letter of October 16 to Castlereagh shows that he firmly believed that his mission was a success:

I have seen Mr. Pitt, the Chancellor, and the Duke of Portland, who seem to feel very sensibly the critical situation of our damnable country, and that the Union alone can save it. I should have hoped that what has passed would have opened the eyes of every man in England to the insanity of their past conduct, with respect to the Papists of Ireland; but I can very plainly perceive that they were as full of their popish projects as ever. I trust, and I hope I am not deceived, that they are fairly inclined to give them up, and to bring the measure forward unencumbered with the doctrine of Emancipation. Lord Cornwallis has intimated his acquiescence in this point; Mr. Pitt is decided upon it, and I think he will keep his colleagues steady. . . . . .

I hope to be released from my attendance here very soon, and, whenever I can see the King, shall set out for Ireland. If I have been in any manner instrumental in persuading the Ministers here to bring forward this very important measure, unencumbered with a proposition which must have swamped it, I shall rejoice very much in the pilgrimage which I have made.[35]

This letter is significant because of references to the points of view of three important men: Pitt, Cornwallis, and the King. It seems highly probable that Clare convinced Pitt of the impossibility of putting through the union if encumbered by emancipation; that Cornwallis felt obliged to yield to the necessity of postponing consideration of the Catholic claims until a United Parliament came into existence; and that George III heard and welcomed views which so closely coincided with his own.

Cornwallis evidently started with high hopes of making Catholic Emancipation an integral part of the union. The progressive decline in his hopes is shown by three letters from September 30 to November 15. On the first date he wrote:

The great measure from which I looked for so much good, will, if carried, fall far short of my expectations, as all the leading persons here, not excepting the Chancellor, are determined to resist the extension of its operation to the Catholics. I feel the measure of so much importance that it is worth carrying anyhow, but I am determined not to submit to the insertion of any clause, that shall make the exclusion of the Catholics a fundamental part of the Union, as

[35] Charles Vane, Marquess of Londonderry, *Memoirs of Viscount Castlereagh Second Marquess of Londonderry* (London, 1848–49), I, 393–94. Hereafter cited as *Memoirs of Castlereagh*.

I am fully convinced that until the Catholics are admitted into a general participation of rights, (which when incorporated with the British Government they cannot abuse,) there will be no peace or safety in Ireland.[86]

But after conferring with Clare, Cornwallis had less confidence, and in his letter to Pitt of October 8 showed these misgivings:

I certainly wish that England could now make a union with the Irish nation, instead of making it with a party in Ireland; and although I agree with those who assert that the Catholics will not be immediately converted into good subjects, yet I am sanguine enough to hope, after the most plausible and most popular of their grievances is removed (and especially if it could be accompanied by some regulation about tythes) that we should get time to breathe, and at least check the rapid progress of discontent and disaffection.

After what I have said I shall submit the present question entirely to your decision, and shall only press strongly upon you my most earnest recommendation, that, whatever your determination now may be, you will not suffer it to be made irrevocable.[87]

By November 15 Cornwallis had become convinced that the only hope of emancipation lay in action by the United Parliament after the union was passed. He wrote to Ross that

On my pressing the matter strongly, Mr. Pitt has promised that there shall be no clause in the Act of Union which shall prevent the Catholic question from being hereafter taken up, and we must therefore only look forward to the wisdom and liberality of the United Parliament. From what I learn, the present mode is not likely to be opposed by the Catholics: they consider any change better than the present system.[88]

Although some members of the Pitt ministry were lukewarm about passing an act of union at once, Lord Castlereagh, who had been appointed Chief Secretary after the resignation of Pelham, was confident that the measure could be pushed through the Irish Parliament in the next session. On December 21 the cabinet decided to approve of the terms of his general plan for the union. Ireland was to have 100 members in the imperial House of Commons and 32 in the House of Lords. Four spiritual lords were to sit in rotation and the 28 temporal lords were to be selected for life. With respect to the revenue it was planned to have Ireland

[86] Ross, *Cornwallis Correspondence*, II, 415.
[87] *Ibid.*, p. 416.   [88] *Ibid.*, p. 434.

contribute a fixed proportion toward the peace establishment of the empire as well as toward the expenses of war. The procedure as Portland wrote Cornwallis which the cabinet agreed upon was to have the measure recommended on January 22, 1799, to both Parliaments.[39] Castlereagh had only a short time in which to prepare the members of the Irish Parliament for the plan to be presented on that day. On January 5 he published a sketch of a plan for the union and sent a circular letter to the members asking them to be present at the opening of Parliament. The storm of protest which greeted the proposed sketch and the circular showed Castlereagh that the measure was not to have easy sailing.

The King's speech of January 22 recommended consideration and discussion of the question of union. But when Castlereagh admitted that the measure of adjustment alluded to in the speech meant a legislative union, George Ponsonby immediately moved it was the undoubted birthright of the Irish people to have a free and independent legislature as secured by the agreement of 1782. A prolonged debate lasting nearly twenty-four hours then ensued. In all, more than eighty members spoke, and with few exceptions the opposition speakers easily had the better of the contest. Despite this superior oratory Castlereagh is alleged to have declared that the government would carry the division by a majority of 45.[40] He was greatly disappointed when Ponsonby's amendment was beaten by only 106 to 105 and the original motion for a vote of thanks on the King's speech passed by 107 to 105. On the 24th, when the House considered the report of the committee appointed to draw up an address of thanks for the royal speech, an opposition member moved that the paragraph relating to the union should be expunged from the address. In the division which followed the government was defeated by 111 to 106; and thus any hope of passing an act of union during this session of the Irish Parliament was definitely ended.

Both Cornwallis and Castlereagh wrote full accounts to the Duke of Portland explaining the reasons for the failure of the first steps toward union. Castlereagh immediately turned his attention to securing a majority in the next session of Parliament. Cornwallis, on the other hand, gave serious consideration to the policy of the opposition which aimed at securing the support of the Catholics. In letters to Portland of January 26 and 28 he

39 Vane, *Memoirs of Castlereagh*, II, 58–59.
40 H. M. Hyde, *op. cit.*, p. 300.

expressed his misgivings concerning the danger from the opposition. In the first letter declared:

The proposal of Union provoked the enmity principally of the boroughmongers, lawyers, and persons who from local circumstances thought they should be losers, but it certainly has not affected the action at large, nor was it disagreeable either to the Catholics or to the Protestant Dissenters. Very different will be the effect of agitating the question of Emancipation, especially when the Catholics are reminded that it was the intention of the Government to continue to exclude them from a participation of privileges at the Union.[41]

In a second letter written two days later Cornwallis goes into ever greater detail on the dangers of the opposition winning over the Catholics:

The religious question will probably be first taken up. It is plain that upon a mere principle of pursuing power, ambition, and revenge, it is the interest of the Catholics to obtain political equality without an Union; for as the general democratic power of the State is increasing daily by the general wealth and prosperity, and as the Catholics form the greater part of the democracy, their power must proportionably increase whilst the kingdoms are separate and the Irish oligarchy is stationary or declining. The Catholics therefore, if offered Equality without an Union, will probably prefer it to Equality with an Union, for in the latter case they must ever be content with inferiority; in the former, they would probably by degrees gain ascendancy.

In addition to the usual supporters of Emancipation, many of the Anti-Union party will now take up the Catholic cause, the better to defeat the question of Union. They will thus expect to detach the Catholics from Government, and to engage the mob of the whole kingdom against the Union.

Were the Catholic question to be now carried, the great argument for an Union would be lost, at least as far as the Catholics are concerned; it seems therefore incumbent on Government, whatever their inclinations might otherwise be, to prevent its adoption at present. Their resistance may be argued on the grounds that without an Union, the admission of the Catholics must increase rather than diminish religious animosities, by the alarms which it would give to the existing establishments—an evil which would be in a great measure if not altogether avoided, were the concession to take place connected with or after the Union.

[41] Ross, *Cornwallis Correspondence*, III, 52.

I am of opinion that the measure, hereafter to insure its success, must be proposed on a more enlarged principle; but if the immediate object of Government is to resist the Catholic claims rather than to renew the question of Union, I much doubt the policy of at present holding out to them any decided expectations; it might weaken us with the Protestants, and might not strengthen us with the Catholics, whilst they look to carry their question unconnected with Union.[42]

When these various communications from Cornwallis to the English ministers were shown to him, George III expressed himself in unmistakable terms. Fortunately he set down his opinion in the form of a Minute dated January 31:

Approving the Lord Lieut. of Ireland's being directed to use the greatest efforts to prevent an Emancipation of the Roman Catholics and declaring that though a strong friend to the Union of the two Kingdoms, I should become an Enemy to the movement if I thought a change of the Situation of the Roman Catholics would attend this measure.[43]

This Minute furnishes additional proof, if any were needed, of the fixed opposition of the King to further concessions to Catholics either in the Irish Parliament or in the United Parliament if an act of union were passed. Since Pitt and the other ministers could not avoid being familiar with the opinion which George III expressed of the directions being sent to Cornwallis, any argument excusing the later actions of Pitt on the ground that he did not understand how fixed the opposition of the King was to Catholic Emancipation must be dismissed.

Realizing that it was futile to attempt to push through emancipation in this session of Parliament, Cornwallis and Castlereagh turned their attention to making certain of a majority at the opening of the next in January 1800. Castlereagh felt that the reasons for the failure of the bill introduced in 1799 were the opposition of borough owners who would suffer a pecuniary loss and of country gentlemen who feared that the number of members would be reduced from two to one in each county. In addition, he felt that it would be necessary to propitiate the barristers who feared that a union would deprive them of opportunities for advancement, the purchasers of seats in the present Parliament,

42 Ross, *op. cit.*, pp. 54–55. This same letter is published in the *Memoirs of Castlereagh*, II, 139–41, as if it were written by Castlereagh.
43 Clements Transcripts, IX. 021.

and persons in Dublin whose property would depreciate in value if Parliament no longer met in that city.[44] In a memorandum sent to Portland, Castlereagh suggested that effective opposition might be stopped by the following expenditures :[45]

1.	108 Boroughs at £7,000 each..........£	756,000
2.	32 Counties at £7,000 each...........	224,000
3.	50 Barristers at £4,000 each..........	200,000
4.	50 Purchasers at £1,500 each........	75,000
5.	Dublin Influence (say)..............	200,000
		£1,455,000

The history of the passing of the Act of Union through the Irish Parliament is the history of the carrying out of the plan outlined by Castlereagh. Both the Lord Lieutenant and the Chief Secretary worked hard for nearly a year to make certain that the government majority would not fail in 1800 as it had in 1799. Cornwallis' letters show how he writhed under the disagreeable task of solacing the vested interests, but Castlereagh appears to have actually relished his share in the preparedness campaign. When the session of 1800 was opened on January 15, Castlereagh was confident of the outcome. The vote on the address, despite the fact that owing to the operation of the Place Act a considerable number of seats were vacant, was carried in the House of Commons by 138 to 96. Since most of the vacant seats would be filled by government supporters, the outcome of this vote insured the success of the union.

On February 5 Castlereagh introduced to an expectant House of Commons in Dublin the measure which Cornwallis and he had taken up at great length with the British ministers. After dealing with the principle of the union of the two kingdoms, Castlereagh explained the financial, commercial, and Parliamentary aspects. The systems of taxation and the national debts of Great Britain and Ireland were to be kept separate and the latter was to contribute two-seventeenths of the total revenue to the new imperial exchequer. The commercial provisions were to a considerable extent based on Pitt's resolutions of 1785, and with few exceptions the principle of free trade was applied. The earlier arrangement

---

[44] Vane, *Memoirs of Castlereagh*, II, 150.

[45] H. M. Hyde, *op. cit.*, p. 313. Taken from *Memoirs of Castlereagh*, II, 151, where the totals were given erroneously as 1,433,000.

of 32 Irish peers in the House of Lords and 100 Irish members in the House of Commons at Westminster was adhered to in the present plan. The patrons of the 84 boroughs totally disfranchised were to receive £15,000 for each borough. After an acrimonious debate the government triumphed by 158 to 115.[46]

The opposition put up a hard fight for the next few weeks but after March did not trouble on many occasions to divide the House. Whether the attempt of the opposition to match the government bribes was due to a hope that successful bidding was possible or to a desire to make the government pay dearly for the votes of waverers is difficult to say. After months of discussion the third reading passed the Irish House of Lords on June 13 and received the royal assent with appropriate ceremonies on August 1.

When it was obvious that the act would pass in the Irish Parliament, Pitt explained the resolutions accepted in Dublin to the British House of Commons on April 21. The Whig opposition headed by Grey, Sheridan, and Tierney vigorously opposed the proposed measure, but Pitt's majority was sufficient to secure an expression of approval of the union by 236 to 30. Within a few weeks the bill had passed both houses of the British Parliament.

The part which bribery played in securing the passage of the measure through the Irish Parliament has been strongly emphasized by nearly all histories of the period. The unsavory nature of these transactions has been admitted by both friends and enemies of the union. Once the bill had become a law the British and Irish governments were called on to make good the promises given to persons who had rendered services in return for deferred payments. In the main these consisted of peerages for the higher-ups and places within the sphere of Crown patronage for the lower-downs. An attempt on the part of the Duke of Portland to postpone fulfilling the promises for peerages met with a vigorous protest from both Cornwallis and Castlereagh. After an exchange of views the English ministers gave way on most points. Because of services rendered, nineteen men were given Irish peerages and fifteen were promoted in the Irish peerage, while four Irish peers were rewarded with English titles.[47] The same conscientiousness was not shown in honoring the promises made to those of lower rank. Evidently so many commitments had been made in the way

---

46 H. M. Hyde, *op. cit.*, pp. 346–50.   47 *Ibid.*, p. 364.

of government positions that it was impossible to fulfill all claims at once. Some were honored at a later time and some definitely repudiated by the successors of Cornwallis and Castlereagh.[48]

More important from the point of view of this study is the part played by the Irish Catholics in helping to pass the Act of Union. Cornwallis and Castlereagh, even before the first attempt of 1799 failed, had become reconciled, reluctantly it is true, to postponing Catholic Emancipation until the new imperial Parliament could act upon the question. The correspondence which passed between Dublin Castle and Westminster leaves no doubt that the English ministers encouraged the Lord Lieutenant and Chief Secretary to solicit the support of the Catholics on the tacit understanding that Emancipation would receive the support of the English ministry in the imperial Parliament. In no place in the voluminous correspondence over the Irish union is the case more clearly stated than by Castlereagh on January 1, 1801. Writing to Pitt on receipt of the news that the cabinet was divided on the question of emancipation he summed up the history of the negotiations on this subject since 1799. After stating that Cornwallis was unprepared for the resolute opposition which members of the British cabinet were preparing to make, he continued:

As this impression on his Excellency's mind was in a great measure the result of what passed with reference to this subject when I was in England in the autumn of 1799, I think it necessary to recall to your recollection that, after the details of the Union had been completed, I was directed by the Lord-Lieutenant to represent to you the state of parties as they stood at that time in Ireland, and particularly to request that you would ascertain what was likely to be the ultimate decision of his Majesty's Ministers with respect to the Catholics, as his Excellency felt it to be of equal importance to the future quiet of Ireland, to his own feelings, and to the credit of the Administration in both countries, that he should so conduct himself towards that body as to preclude hereafter any well-founded imputation, or even any strong impression on their minds that they had been deceived.

The statement I then made was, as I recollect, nearly to the following effect—that we had a majority in Parliament composed of very doubtful materials; that the Protestant body was divided on the question, with the disadvantage of Dublin and the Orange Societies against us; and that the Catholics were holding back under a doubt whether the Union would facilitate or impede their object. I stated it as the opinion of the Irish Government that, circumstanced as the Parliamentary interests and the Parliamentary feelings then were, the measure could not be carried, if the Catholics were embarked in an active opposition to it, and that their resistance would be unanimous and zealous, if they had reason to suppose that the sentiments of Ministers would remain unchanged in respect to their exclusion; while the measure of Union in itself might give them additional means of disappointing their hopes.

I stated that several attempts had been made by leading Catholics to bring Government to an explanation, which had of course been evaded; and that the body, thus left to their own speculations in respect to future influence of the Union upon their cause, were, with some exceptions, either neutral or actual opponents—the former entertaining hopes, but not inclining to support decidedly without some encouragement from Government; the latter entirely hostile, from a persuasion that it would so strengthen the Protestant interest as to perpetuate their exclusion.

I represented that the friends of Government, by flattering the hopes of the Catholics, had produced a favourable impression in Cork, Tipperary, and Galway; but that, in proportion as his Excellency had felt the advantage of this popular support, he was anxious to be ascertained, in availing himself of the assistance which he knew was alone given in contemplation of its being auxiliary to their own views, that he was not involving Government in future difficulties with that body, by exposing them to a charge of duplicity; and he was peculiarly desirous of being secure against such a risk before he *personally* encouraged the Catholics to come forward, and to afford him that assistance which he felt to be so important to the success of the measure. In consequence of this representation, the Cabinet took the measure into their consideration; and, having been directed to attend the meeting, I was charged to convey to Lord Cornwallis the result, and his Excellency was referred by the Duke of Portland to me for a statement of the opinions of his Majesty's Ministers on this important subject.

Accordingly, I communicated to Lord Cornwallis that the opinion of the Cabinet was favourable to the principle of the measure; that some doubt was entertained as to the possibility of admitting Catholics into some of the *higher offices,* and that ministers apprehended considerable repugnance to the measure in many quarters, and particularly in the *highest;* but, that, as far as the sentiments of the Cabinet were concerned, his Excellency need not hesitate in calling forth the Catholic support, in whatever degree he found it practicable to obtain it.

I trust you will be of opinion that I did not misconceive or misstate what passed in that Cabinet. I certainly did not then hear any direct objection stated against the measure by any of the ministers then present. You will, I have no doubt, recollect, that, so far from any serious hesitation being entertained in respect to the principle, it was even discussed whether an immediate declaration to the Catholics would not be advisable, and whether an assurance should not be given them in the event of the Union being accomplished, of their objects being submitted, with the countenance of Government to the United Parliament upon a peace. This idea was laid aside principally upon the consideration that such a declaration might alienate the Protestants in both countries from the Union, in a greater degree than it was calculated to assist the measure through the Catholics; and, accordingly, the instructions which I was directed to convey to Lord Cornwallis were the following effect: That his Excellency was fully warranted in soliciting every support the Catholics could afford; that he need not apprehend, as far as the sentiments of the Cabinet were concerned, being involved in the difficulty with that body which he seemed to apprehend; that it was not thought expedient at that time to give any direct assurance to the Catholics; but, that, should circumstances so far alter as to induce his Excellency to consider such an explanation necessary, he was at liberty to state the grounds on which his opinion was formed for the consideration of the Cabinet.

In consequence of this communication, the Irish Government omitted no exertion to call forth the Catholics in favour of the Union. Their efforts were very greatly successful, and the advantage derived from them was highly useful, particularly in depriving the Opposition of the means they otherwise would have had in the southern and western counties of making an impression on the county members. His Excellency was enabled to accomplish his purpose without giving the Catholics any direct assurance of being gratified, and, throughout the contest, earnestly avoided being driven to such an expedient; as he considered a gratuitous concession after the measure as infinitely more consistent with the character of Government.[49]

From the contents of this letter and of many other shorter ones in 1799 and 1800 it is clear that the division in the British cabinet after the Acts of Union had passed both Parliaments came as a surprise to both Castlereagh and Cornwallis, that the Catholics through the Lord Lieutenant and Chief Secretary had received assurances of cabinet support for emancipation in the imperial Parliament, and that Dublin Castle as well as the British ministers

[49] *Memoirs of Castlereagh*, IV, 8–11.

were aware of the determined opposition of the King. But in many respects the most significant fact brought out in this long letter is the opinion of Castlereagh that the Act of Union could not have passed the Irish Parliament without the support of the Catholics.

Thus when we come to consider the events of September 1800 to March 1801 we must keep in mind that Pitt, during the months in which the union was being forced through the Irish Parliament, was familiar with the firm opposition of the King and of the commitments of Cornwallis and Castlereagh to the Irish Catholics. Neither Pitt nor the officials of Dublin Castle made an outright promise to the Catholics, because, as Castlereagh's letter stated, it was feared that such an assurance would alienate more Protestants in England and Ireland than it would win over Catholics to active support. Clearly Pitt must have realized that he was dangling the prospect of a reward before the eyes of the Catholics which he was in no position to honor. Consequently he was faced with making a choice of one of the following lines of action: first, he might win over the King; second, he might coerce the King by a threat of resignation; third, he might coolly repudiate his assurances to the Catholics when he found the King obdurate; fourth, he might resign if the King refused to give way and go into a "cordial" retirement; and, fifth, he might resign and carry on a vigorous opposition until the King would be compelled to yield as he had been forced to do to the Whigs in 1782. As is well known, he chose the fourth, but probably only after half-hearted attempts at the first and second. Certainly he did not attempt the third or fifth. His entire conduct from September 1800 until his resignation shows that he was "defeatist" on the prospect of either convincing or coercing the King. Seventeen years of experience with the King in which he had won many skirmishes on policy but never a major battle on a big issue upon which they differed, and the many expressions of opposition to further concessions to Catholics since February 1795, were more than sufficient to make Pitt realize the hopelessness of persuasion or coercion. It is true that he had two arguments which he hoped might move George III: the splendid conduct of the Catholics in Ireland during the debates on the union, and the precarious condition of Great Britain at the end of 1800.[50] Potent as these arguments

50 J. H. Rose, *Life of William Pitt* (London: G. Bell & Sons, Ltd., 1923), II, 434.

were, Pitt evidently sensed that they would prove inadequate to overcome the fixed opinion of the King that if he consented to Catholic Emancipation it would be a violation of his Coronation Oath.

Actually the question of further concessions to Catholics was only one of the three Irish problems that required immediate consideration. In the opinion of Castlereagh some provision for Catholic and Dissenting clergy and a reform of the system of paying tithes were equally important. Pitt appears to have planned to settle all three points with the cabinet and to show the King that his ministers presented a united front on these questions. The plan to reach a decision in the cabinet before consulting the King evidently went back to the cabinet meeting which Pitt called for September 30, 1800. On this occasion Lord Chancellor Loughborough took decided exceptions to the proposal for removing the Oaths of Supremacy and Abjuration as a test for Catholics holding offices, but expressed himself as favorable to a commutation of tithes. It seems unlikely that Loughborough betrayed Pitt's plans to the King either at this time or any time before the end of January 1801, because George III showed no excitement until January 28. The delay in reaching an agreement on the part of the ministry between September and the following January seems to have been due to Pitt's illness during October, to his personal financial worries, and to the attention given to the more pressing problems of the war and the scarcity of provisions. But if he did not betray cabinet secrets to the King, Loughborough did more or less openly oppose any further concessions to Catholics and in December wrote a lengthy Memorandum which stressed the point that "a Protestant government cannot recommend to a Protestant parliament the repeal of all the laws to which both owe their being and their security."[51] On the envelope in which the copy of this Memorandum was found in the Sidmouth papers George III had written: "The Lord Chancellor's reflections on the proposal from Ireland of emancipating the Roman Catholics, received December 13th, 1800."[52] This seems positive evidence that Loughborough was actively opposing further concessions to Catholics and that the King was aware of this fact by December 13; but it does not prove that the Lord Chancellor had in-

[51] George Pellew, *The Life and Correspondence of the Right Honourable Henry Addington, First Viscount Sidmouth* (London, 1847), I, 510.
[52] *Ibid.*, p. 500.

formed George III of Pitt's plans. Of course it is possible that no decision was reached in the cabinet meeting of September 30 or at any subsequent meeting because of the illness of Pitt and more pressing business, and hence that Loughborough had no news which would alarm the King. The only alternatives that will explain the King's sudden excitement at the end of January are: first, that the Lord Chancellor had told him nothing of these cabinet discussions; or, second, that the question was left in such an unsettled state that there was nothing to make George III uneasy even if Loughborough revealed the plans which Pitt placed before his ministers.

In view of the fact that opposition to Catholic Emancipation within the cabinet appears to have greatly increased, if not to have actually originated after September 30, the question arises whether Loughborough's most effective work was not done in winning over converts to the King's point of view rather than in convincing George III himself. Portland, for example, is alleged to have changed his stand on Emancipation after reading Loughborough's Memorandum of December 13. In fact Castlereagh in his long letter of January 1, 1801, quoted earlier, shows more uneasiness over the report that the cabinet was divided than over the anticipated hostility of the King. This growing opposition doubtless explains also why Pitt did not have a definite set of proposals to present to George III before the King's speech for the opening of the first imperial Parliament was prepared. By January Loughborough, Portland, Westmorland, Liverpool, and Chatham appear to have offered various degrees of opposition.

The crisis which brought about Pitt's resignation came with dramatic suddenness on January 28. At his Levee the King walked up to Dundas and eagerly inquired: "What is it that this young Lord has brought over which they are going to throw at my head? . . . . The most Jacobinical thing I ever heard of! I shall reckon any man my personal enemy who proposes any such measure."[53] If Loughborough did any effective betraying it must have been shortly before this date, since any earlier revelations apparently did not disturb the King. Naturally the outburst of George III at the Levee brought about immediate action by the ministers. The next day the majority of the cabinet appear to

---

[53] Stanhope, *op. cit.*, III, 274.

have reached an agreement, since Pitt sent Loughborough a copy of the proposals on the 30th. The King, however, did not await such action. On the same day that the cabinet met, George III sent Addington, at that time Speaker of the House of Commons, to persuade Pitt to abandon his plans for further Catholic relief. The close personal relationship of both Pitt and George III to Addington made him in the eyes of the King an ideal go-between. One section of the letter in which George III requested Addington to undertake this mission is especially significant.

I should be taking up the Speaker's time very uselessly if I said more, as I know we think alike on this great subject. I wish he would, from himself, open Mr. Pitt's eyes on the danger arising from the agitating this improper question, which may prevent his ever speaking to me on a subject on which I can scarcely keep my temper, and also his giving great apprehension to every true member of our church, and, indeed, I should think all those who with temper consider that such a change must inevitably unhinge our excellent and happy constitution, and be most exactly following the steps of the French revolution.[54]

After the interview, Addington appears to have felt that Pitt might yield to his arguments and to the King's will; but his reassuring letter to George III was misleading. Even before he received Pitt's famous letter of January 31 the King seems to have satisfied himself in some way that his Prime Minister would not yield, because he sent for Addington earlier in the day and abruptly asked him to form a new ministry. According to Addington's own version he first begged to be excused, but was unable to answer the dramatic question of George III: "Lay your hand upon your heart, and ask yourself where I am to turn for support if *you* do not stand by me."[55] Addington insisted upon consulting Pitt a second time in an effort to dissuade him from his resolute course on Catholic Emancipation. The Prime Minister, however, refused to give way and advised the Speaker to accept the King's commission.

The agitation which the King felt on January 28 may have been intensified by interviews with Lord Auckland, Lord Clare, the Archbishop of Canterbury, and the Primate of Ireland. Although these gentlemen, individually or collectively, would be unable to strengthen the resolution of George III on the all-

[54] Pellew, *op. cit.*, p. 286.
[55] *Ibid.*, p. 287.

important topic, their fears and warnings may have caused him to act with greater speed and less inflexibility than he might otherwise have done.

Both the differences and the points of view of the King and Pitt are completely brought out in the four letters which they exchanged from January 31 to February 5. In his first long letter of January 31 Pitt attempted to present his case to the King as he should like to have presented it before George III showed himself so highly agitated over the mere mention of the question. Doubtless Pitt realized that his opportunity of having the King study his proposals with an open mind was lost; and this thought may have been back of his later admission that he had erred in not preparing the royal mind for the proposed changes at an earlier time. Pitt, however, persisted in presenting his point of view partly because there was a slight chance for success and partly because he owed it to himself and his colleagues at least to state what their program actually was. Despite the fact that he was laboring under such handicaps as bad health and a depressing situation in foreign and domestic affairs, Pitt's letter to the King[56] presenting the case for Catholic Emancipation is one of his happiest efforts. It falls logically into three parts: the reasons for communicating the plan to the King; the arguments in favor of the proposals; and the action which he proposed to take in case George III remained inexorable. After asserting that in any case he would have presented the results of the deliberations of the cabinet on the Catholic question for the consideration of the King, Pitt declared that the task which would have been a painful one because of "your Majesty's general indisposition to any change of the laws on this subject" had become even more so as a result of the information which had come to him recently of the extent to which "your Majesty entertains, and has declared, that sentiment." Pitt then skillfully elaborated the arguments in favor of the plan which he declared had the approval of the majority of the cabinet:

For himself, he is on full consideration convinced that the measure would be attended with no danger to the Established Church, or to the Protestant Interest in Great Britain or Ireland:—That now the Union has taken place, and with the new provisions which would make part of the plan, it could never give any such weight in office

[56] Pitt MSS, 101, January 31, 1801.

or in Parliament, either to Catholics or Dissenters as could give them
any new means (if they were so disposed) of attacking the Establishment:—That the grounds on which the laws of exclusion now
remaining were founded, have long been narrowed, and are since
the Union removed:—That those principles, formerly held by
Catholics, which made them considered as politically dangerous, have
been for a course of time gradually declining, and, among the
higher orders particularly, have ceased to prevail:—That the obnoxious tenets are disclaimed in the most positive manner by the
oaths which have been required in Great Britain, and still more by
one of those required in Ireland, as the condition of the indulgences
already granted, and which might equally be made the condition of
any new ones:—That if such an oath, containing (among other provisions) a denial of the power of absolution from its obligations,
is not a security from Catholics, the Sacramental test is not more
so:—That the political circumstances under which the exclusive
laws originated, arising either from the conflicting power of hostile
and nearly balanced sects, from the apprehension of a popish Queen,
or Successor, a disputed succession and a foreign pretender, and a
division in Europe between Catholic and Protestant Powers, are no
longer applicable to the present state of things:—That with respect
to those of the Dissenters who it is feared entertain principles dangerous to the Constitution, a distinct political text pointed against
the doctrines of a modern Jacobinism, would be a much more just
and more effectual security than that which now exists, which may
operate to the exclusion of conscientious persons well affected to
the State, and is no guard against those of an opposite description:
That with respect to the Catholics of Ireland, another most important
additional security, and one of which the effect would continually
increase, might be provided by gradually attaching the Popish clergy
to the Government, and, for this purpose, making them dependent
for a part of their provision (under proper regulations) on the
State, and by also subjecting them to superintendence and con-
troll:—That besides these provisions the general interests of the
Established Church, and the security of the Constitution and Government, might be effectually strengthened by requiring the Political
Test, before referred to, from the Preachers of all Catholic and
Dissenting Congregations, and from the teachers of schools of every
denomination.

Both for the circumstances of the time and in the light of history
these arguments appear to be sound. They were adroitly arranged
to appeal to George III's fear of French revolutionary principles,
and place particular emphasis upon the past danger from papists
and the present danger from Jacobins. In short, Pitt presented

his case brilliantly; but he had practically no chance of success, since the jury had already a preconceived opinion.

But by all odds the most important section of the letter is the third part, that concerned with the action which Pitt proposed to take if the King remained unconvinced by his arguments. He pointed out that:

> It would afford him indeed a great relief and satisfaction, if he may be allowed to hope that your Majesty will deign maturely to weigh what he has now humbly submitted, and to call for any explanation which any part may appear to require. In the interval which your Majesty may wish for consideration, he will not on his part importune your Majesty with any unnecessary reference to the subject and will feel it his duty to abstain himself from all agitation of this subject in Parliament, and to prevent it, as far as depends on him, on the part of others. If on the result of such consideration your Majesty's objection to the measure proposed should not be removed, or sufficiently diminished to admit of its being brought forward with your Majesty's full concurrence, and with the whole weight of your Government, it must be personally Mr. Pitt's first wish to be released from a situation which he is conscious that, under such circumstances, he could not continue to fill, but with the greatest disadvantage.

This paragraph decided the resignation of Pitt; but its meaning appears to have been misinterpreted by George III at the time and by many historians since that time. Pitt was acting in perfect consistency with all his political practices and principles in presenting to the King a plan which had the approval of the majority of the cabinet. George III, as Pitt readily agreed, was fully within his rights in completely rejecting the proposals; but so long as he retained the services of his present ministers he must allow them at least to present for his consideration the policies which they had agreed upon in cabinet meetings. In short, all Pitt asked of George III was, first, that he should examine carefully the proposals before giving a decision; and, second, that in return for his minister's promise not to importune him during the interval while he was arriving at a decision the King should effectually discountenance all attempts to use his name, "or to influence the opinion of any individual, or descriptions of men, on any part of this subject." Up to this point Pitt's plan of action seems very clear and to offer no difficulties in interpretation; but it is when we come to his last sentence quoted in the preceding paragraph that uncertainties arise. The usual interpretation is that Pitt meant if the King would not consent to Catholic Emancipation being brought forward as a government measure he would resign as First Lord of the Treasury. In the light of Pitt's attitude on this question during the remainder of his life the present author feels that another interpretation is the more probable one. "It must be personally Mr. Pitt's first wish to be released from a situation" does not mean an unequivocal threat to resign but merely that, from a personal point of view, he would prefer to retire. To a man who continually stressed his disinterestedness and his public spirit it is obvious that service to his country and sovereign took precedence over personal inclination and preference. If there is any reasonable doubt that this unexpressed conclusion was in Pitt's mind it is dispelled by the next paragraph in this letter to the King:

At the same time, after the gracious intimation which has been recently conveyed to him of your Majesty's sentiments on this point, he will be acquitted of presumption in adding, that if the chief difficulties of the present crisis should not then be surmounted, or very materially diminished, and if your Majesty should continue to think that his humble exertions could in any degree contribute to conducting them to a favourable issue, there is no personal difficulty to which he will not rather submit than withdraw himself at such a moment from your Majesty's service. He would even, in such case, continue for such a short further interval as might be necessary to oppose the agitation or discussion of the question, as far as he can consistently with the line, to which he feels bound uniformly to adhere, of reserving himself a full latitude on the principle itself, and objecting only to the time, and to the temper and circumstances of the moment. But he must entreat that, on this supposition it may be distinctly understood that he can remain in office no longer than till the issue (which he trusts on every account will be a speedy one) of the crisis now depending shall admit of your Majesty's more easily forming a new arrangement, and that he will receive your Majesty's permission to carry with him into a private situation that affectionate and grateful attachment which your Majesty's goodness for a long course of years has impressed on his mind,—and that unabated zeal for the ease and honour of your Majesty's Government and for the public service which he trusts will always govern his conduct.

The suggestions which Pitt outlines in this section of his letter adhere closely to the policy which he actually adopted later. So far was he from wishing to embarrass George III that he offered to oppose immediate consideration of the Catholic question on the grounds that the time was not propitious.

Despite the vague and cautious phraseology in sections of Pitt's letter, the present writer feels that the Minister intended to convey to the King his willingness to take any one of three lines of action: first, to resign; second, to remain as First Lord of the Treasury; and, third, to retain office until the King could find a satisfactory person to replace him. The evidence for the first is Pitt's statement that if, after mature consideration, George III was unwilling to have the Catholic measure brought forward with his full concurrence "it must be personally Mr. Pitt's first wish to be released" from his present position; for the second, his statement "that if the chief difficulties of the present crisis should not then be surmounted, or very materially diminished, and if your Majesty should continue to think his humble exertions could in any degree contribute to conducting them to a favourable issue, there is no personal difficulty to which he will not rather submit than withdraw himself at such a moment from your Majesty's service"; and, for the third, his statement that "He would even, in such a case, continue for such a short interval as might be necessary to oppose the agitation or discussion of the question . . . . But . . . . on this supposition it may be distinctly understood that he can remain in office no longer than till the issue . . . . of the crisis now depending shall admit of your Majesty's more easily forming a new arrangement." Stripped of its formal verbiage this declaration says that if the King will not consent to Catholic Emancipation Pitt, from the purely personal point of view, will prefer to resign; but because of the critical state of affairs at home and abroad, the minister, being public spirited, will be willing to sacrifice his personal wishes and to remain at the helm permanently; or he will be willing to make an even greater personal sacrifice, if necessary, and retain office temporarily. Pitt gave the impression that he listed the three choices in the order of his personal preference; but his actions before and after this crisis would indicate that in reality his first choice would have been to remain permanently in office, his second to resign at once, and his third, to retain office until the King could find new ministers.

Thus if this interpretation of his letter to the King is the correct one, Pitt gave George III every chance that a man of his principles and proud nature could offer. In effect he declared that as chief minister he expected the King to give careful consideration to the plan upon which a majority of the cabinet had agreed; that if George III could not accede to his proposals, he was willing to resign or to remain permanently or temporarily at his post; and that he left the door open for a counterproposal from his royal master. Had he handled this situation as skillfully as he had handled every other one in which Pitt was concerned since 1783, the King would not have lost the services of the First Lord of the Treasury. All he needed to do was to keep Pitt's proposals for a few days and then to state earnestly that after careful consideration he had arrived at the conclusion that he could not conscientiously give them his approval. To the reluctant offer to resign he could have countered with the deplorable state of affairs both at home and abroad and an appeal to Pitt's patriotism and vanity. The logical outcome of the exchange of notes and propositions by the two adversaries would have been a promise by Pitt not to bring up Catholic Emancipation again during the life of the King and an understanding that he should in principle remain loyal to his views on the subject but should oppose any such measure introduced into Parliament on the grounds that the time was not yet ripe. This is exactly the policy which Pitt pursued when he gave such a pledge after his resignation. Why, then, did not George III make allowances for Pitt's principles and personal pride and at least go through the motions of considering the proposals on Catholic Emancipation? The answer is to be found in his reply[57] to the long letter of Pitt:

I should not do justice to the warm impulse of my heart if I entered on the subject most unpleasant to my mind without first expressing that the cordial affection I have for Mr. Pitt, as well as high opinion of his talents and integrity, greatly add to my uneasiness on this occasion; but a sense of religious as well as political duty had made me, from the moment I mounted the throne, consider the Oath that the wisdom of our forefathers has enjoined the Kings of this realm to take at their Coronation, and enforced by the obligation of instantly following it in the course of the ceremony with taking the Sacrament, as so binding a religious obligation on me to maintain the fundamental maxims on which our Constitution is placed, namely, the Church of England being the established one, and that those who hold employments in the State must be members of it, and consequently obliged not only to take Oaths against Popery, but to receive the Holy Communion agreeably to the rites of the Church of England.

[57] Stanhope, *op. cit.*, III, xxviii–xxx.

This principle of duty must therefore prevent me from discussing any proposition tending to destroy this ground work of our happy Constitution, and much more so that now mentioned by Mr. Pitt, which is no less than the complete overthrow of the whole fabric.

These arguments of George III may sound feeble indeed when contrasted with the logical ones advanced by Pitt. Nevertheless they represented the firm convictions not only of George III but also of the great mass of Englishmen of that generation. But it was this point-blank refusal to discuss any proposition which dealt with Catholic Emancipation which sounded the death knell of Pitt's hopes. Since the King refused even to consider the propositions of the majority of the cabinet on this question, naturally he could not agree not to influence the opinions of others during the period of consideration; but instead he made a counterproposition:

Mr. Pitt once acquainted with my sentiments, his assuring me that he will stave off the only question whereon I fear from his letter we can never agree—for the advantage and comfort of continuing to have his advice and exertions in public affairs I will certainly abstain from talking on this subject, which is nearest my heart. I cannot help if others pretend to guess at my opinions, which I have never disguised: but if those who unfortunately differ with me will keep this subject at rest, I will on my part, most correctly on my part, be silent also; but this restraint I shall put on myself from affection for Mr. Pitt, but further I cannot go, for I cannot sacrifice my duty to any consideration.

J. H. Rose has found George III guilty of subterfuge in thus answering Pitt's request not to speak against relief to Catholics while giving mature consideration to the measure proposed by the cabinet; and adds: "We may be sure that this sentence clinched Pitt's resolve to resign at the earliest possible moment."[58] Undoubtedly the letter did clinch Pitt's determination to resign because of the King's refusal to give the consideration to his proposals which he firmly believed a chief minister was entitled to expect from his sovereign. Still, it is difficult to see wherein George III was guilty of subterfuge. Pitt made a proposal which the King rejected and in its place suggested another. Thus George III may be accused of bad judgment but scarcely of sub-

---

[58] J. H. Rose, *Life of William Pitt,* II, 439.

terfuge in rejecting point-blank a proposition of which he did not approve. It is absurd to hold that the King needed to influence the opinions of ministers and members of Parliament on the question of Catholic Emancipation; for as he pointed out in his letter to Pitt he had never disguised his opinions on the subject and only a retraction of these views would have affected ministers or placemen. George III actually seems to have hoped that his offer to keep silent on the question and his appeal to Pitt's patriotism and vanity might offset his refusal to consider the propositions of the majority of the cabinet, because he ended his letter with the following plea:

Though I do not pretend to have the power of changing Mr. Pitt's opinion, when thus unfortunately fixed yet I shall hope his sense of duty will prevent his retiring from his present situation to the end of my life; for I can with great truth assert that I shall, from public and private considerations, feel great regret if I shall ever find myself obliged at any time, from a sense of religious and political duty to yield to his entreaties of retiring from his seat at the Board of Treasury.

Pitt did not find the King's counterproposal or his appeal sufficient to offset the point-blank refusal even to consider the advice of his ministers, and hence decided to resign. Yet so little really separated the points of view of the two men. In March Pitt was voluntarily to give his pledge not to agitate the Catholic question again during the life of the King; and if he had received the treatment to which he felt he was entitled at this time, there is no valid reason why he should not have given the same promise early in February. Evidently George III refused to give way either because of the highly emotional state of his mind or because he was too bluntly honest to pretend to be open minded on a measure to which he was in reality so violently opposed. Our sympathies might rest entirely with Pitt on the grounds that he retired from office conscientiously on a fundamental political issue, were it not for the fact that in the following month he not only gave the pledge not to bring up the Catholic question during the lifetime of the King but also was willing to withdraw his resignation. Thus it would appear that it was more a personal blow to his "Grenville" pride than a fundamental constitutional principle which caused Pitt to offer his resignation. Nevertheless, even though it be conceded that personal pique played an important part in his resignation, it must be admitted that Pitt, at this point in the conroversy, had presented a much better case than had the King.

In his letter to the King of February 3[59] Pitt made it clear that the refusal to consider his proposals on Catholic Emancipation left no alternative but resignation because of "his own unalterable sense of the line which public duty requires of him." But in renewing his offer to remain in office until the King could form a new administration he shows the deep resentment which he felt at the unwillingness of George III to consider his proposals and to discountenance the use of the royal name:

But he must frankly confess to your Majesty that the difficulty even of his temporary continuance must necessarily be increased, and may very shortly become insuperable, from what he conceives to be the import of one passage in your Majesty's note, which hardly leaves him room to hope that your Majesty thinks those steps can be taken for effectually discountenancing all attempts to make use of your Majesty's name, or to influence opinions on this subject, which he has ventured to represent as indispensably necessary during any interval in which he might remain in office.[60]

George III in his answer of February 5 accepted Pitt's decision as final. Obviously, as the following passage shows, he was disappointed that his counterproposal was rejected but seems to have felt that any additional appeal at this time would be useless:

I had flattered myself that, on the strong assurance I gave Mr. Pitt of keeping perfectly silent on the subject whereon we entirely differ, provided on his part he kept off from any disquisition on it for the present, which was the main object of the letter I wrote to him on Sunday, we both understood our present line of conduct; but as I unfortunately find Mr. Pitt does not draw the same conclusion. I must come to the unpleasant decision, as it will deprive me of his political service, of acquainting him that, rather than forego what I look on as my duty, I will without unnecessary delay attempt to make the most creditable arrangement, and such as Mr. Pitt will think most to the advantage of my service, as well as to the security of the public; but he must not be surprised if I cannot fix how soon that can·possibly be done, though he may rest assured that it shall be done with as much expedition as so difficult a subject will admit.

On the same day that he wrote this letter to Pitt, George III persuaded Addington to form a ministry. Owing to complica-

59 Stanhope, *op. cit.*, III, xxx–xxxi.
60 *Ibid.*, p. xxxii.

tions, however, Pitt did not actually resign until March 14. Dundas, Grenville, Windham, and Spencer resigned with Pitt, but Portland, Chatham, and Westmorland retained their places. Cornwallis and Castlereagh also handed in their resignations, and Loughborough was not included in the cabinet of Addington.

Thus the King and Pitt severed seventeen years of official relationship with what was, under the circumstances, remarkably good feeling. According to the account of Bishop Tomline, when he saw Pitt at the Levee of February 11 George III greeted his minister in a most gracious manner:

"You have behaved like yourself throughout this business. Nothing could possibly be more honourable. I have a great deal more to say to you."—"Your Majesty has already said much more than the occasion calls for."—"Oh no, I have not; and I do not care who hears me: it was impossible for anyone to behave more honourably." After more conversation of the same kind the King desired to see Mr. Pitt in the closet. . . . . The King went to the closet and Mr. Pitt attended him. Nothing could exceed the kindness of the King towards Mr. Pitt: he was affected very much and more than once. The conversation lasted more than half an hour; and in the course of it the King said that, tho' he could no longer retain Mr. Pitt in his service, he hoped to have him as his friend. Mr. Pitt, with strong expressions both of duty and attachment and love to His Majesty, submitted that any intercourse of that kind might be injurious to His Majesty's Government; for that it was very important that his new Ministers should appear to act by themselves and for themselves, and that if he was frequently with His Majesty, unfavourable conclusions might be drawn concerning his interference or influence. This seemed to satisfy the King, and they parted. At the levee the King spoke in the highest terms of Mr. Pitt's conduct throughout the business of his resignation, and said that it was very different from that of his predecessors.[61]

Again on February 18, after Pitt had presented his budget to the House of Commons, George III wrote him a most cordial note. Contrary to his usual manner in formal communications, the King began the letter with "My dear Pitt." Thus all evidence points to a most friendly feeling on the part of George III. After all he had every reason to feel grateful to Pitt for assisting Addington in the formation of a new administration, even though he had failed to secure a pledge not to bring up again the Catholic question.

[61] J. H. Rose, *Life of William Pitt*, II, 444.

These cordial feelings of the King for his minister, however, were blurred almost immediately by a recurrence of his illness or temporary insanity of 1788–89. This derangement seems to have come on shortly after he wrote the letter to Pitt on February 18; but fortunately the attack did not last so long as the one twelve years earlier. As early as the 23d the Prince of Wales interviewed Pitt on the subject of a regency; and the situation was in one respect more embarrassing than that of 1788–89 because Pitt had resigned but Addington had not taken office. Nevertheless, Pitt took the same stand on the Regency question that he had taken in 1788. In fact he plánned to introduce a bill on March 14 if the King had not recovered by the 12th. No such drastic measure was necessary, because the mind of George III became clear on March 6, and he then sent messages to different persons on the subject of his recovery. Evidence is strong that Dr. Willis delivered the royal message to Pitt at the home of Addington. According to Malmesbury the King instructed Willis to speak or write to Pitt and "Tell him I am now *quite* well, *quite* recovered from my illness; but what has *he* not to answer for, who is the cause of my having been ill at all?"[62] Whether or not these were the exact words delivered by Willis to Pitt cannot be determined, but there can be no reasonable doubt that they represent substantially the spirit of the King's message. Unquestionably Pitt was greatly moved by this reproof, which was so contrary to the sentiments which George III had expressed on February 11 and 18, and evidently he assured Willis verbally, and not in writing, that he would not bring up the Catholic question again during the reign of the King. The testimony of Bishop Tomline and George Rose on the reality of this promise appears to be conclusive. In writing to Rose on August 14, 1801, Tomline stated:

Recollect that when the King was recovering from his illness, Mr. Pitt saw Dr. T. Willis at Mr. Addington's and before Dr. Addington authorized Dr. Willis to tell His Majesty that during his reign he would *never* agitate the Catholic Question; that is, whether *in* office or *out* of office. Mr. Pitt left Dr. Willis and Mr. Addington together. I saw Dr. Willis's letter to Mr. Pitt, and I suspect that the message was not properly and fully delivered.[63]

[62] The Third Earl of Malmesbury (ed.), *Diaries and Correspondence of James, First Earl of Malmesbury* (London, 1844), IV, 32.
[63] Stanhope, *op. cit.,* III, 304.

George Rose stated substantially the same thing in a letter to the King:

It affords me great satisfaction to be able to say to your Majesty that I am authorized by Mr. Pitt to assure your Majesty, that (in whatsoever situation, public or private, he may happen to be) he will not bring forward the question respecting the Catholics of Ireland: and if it should be agitated by others he will supply a proposition for deferring the consideration of it.[64]

When it is considered in the light of the events since January 31, this promise of Pitt is truly amazing. Rather than give such a promise he had resigned his position early in February when he was quite aware of the enormous significance of such an action both to himself and to the country. To him it meant the loss of nearly all of his income and of his position of power, which was his greatest joy in life; and to his country it meant turning over the conduct of affairs to a mediocre successor at a most critical period in both foreign and internal policies. Yet Pitt unhesitatingly sacrificed both private and public interests to what appeared to be a matter of high principle. Hence his action in giving this same promise as a result of receiving a rather spiteful verbal message from the King is, to say the least, very puzzling.

J. H. Rose has explained Pitt's action on the ground that George III took an unfair advantage in his illness to put a pressure on Pitt which exceeded even the immorality of a sickroom.[65] Had a promise been extracted from Pitt when the King was threatened with madness, there might be some force in this argument. Yet George III made no such request either before his illness or when he recovered. He seems merely to have sent a rather peevish message to Pitt which was not accompanied by either a demand or a request for a pledge such as Pitt immediately volunteered to give. Of greater force is the contention that Pitt was justified in giving such a pledge lest the King should again lapse into insanity. Dr. Rose has advanced the additional argument that it was the first desire of all responsible statesmen to prolong the reign of George III; and that a regency would open up "an appalling vista of waste and demoralization."[66] To this it might be answered that the Prince of Wales favored Catholic

[64] Rev. Leveson Vernon Harcourt, *Diaries and Correspondence of the Right Honourable George Rose* (London, 1860), I, 360.

[65] J. H. Rose, *Life of William Pitt*, II, 448.

[66] *Ibid.*, p. 449.

Emancipation at this time, that a new ministry could scarcely make the foreign and internal situation worse than it was early in 1801, that a ministry headed by Fox could be no weaker than the one about to be headed by Addington, that Fox became the King's minister in 1783 and in 1806 without driving him insane, and that the Prince of Wales did not bring demoralization when he became regent in 1810. Thus while it may be admitted that Pitt found himself in an embarrassing position at the time of the King's recovery and that he was justified from his point of view in taking every precaution to prevent a regency, it does not follow that he was justified in offering so sweeping a pledge on the impulse of the moment, when he had refused to give a similar promise to the King in order to remain in office. Perhaps, as Tomline suggested to George Rose, the promise which Willis delivered to the King may have been a more binding one than Pitt instructed the Doctor to give to the royal patient. Pitt, however, adhered to the more sweeping one during the remaining five years of his life.

Conditions both at home and abroad were so dark that Pitt's friends now pressed on him the desirability of remaining in office. They pointed out that the pledge which he had given removed the cause of difference between him and George III. This pressure from Dundas, Tomline, Canning, and Rose seems to have convinced Pitt that he could honorably retain office if some place could be found which would satisfy Addington. According to Tomline such an arrangement was attempted. "Mr. Pitt, Mr. Dundas and myself had a long conversation upon this point at Wimbledon; and I am satisfied that, if Mr. Addington had entered into the idea cordially, Mr. Pitt's resignation might have been prevented."[67] Addington indignantly declined to become Secretary of State in a cabinet in which Pitt should remain as Prime Minister. Evidently Pitt felt in honor bound not to persevere in any attempt to deprive Addington of the position at the head of the government and showed his indignation with his own followers and friends who suggested that the new administration was weak and unworthy of support.

Addington really had a strong personal case for retaining his position as First Lord of the Treasury, for he had given up his Speakership and Sir John Mitford had already succeeded

67 J. H. Rose, *Life of William Pitt*, II, 450.

him in that position. In all probability the only thing that would have induced him to accept another office in lieu of the Speakership which he had abandoned and the Treasury which he expected to take over at once would have been Pitt's outright withdrawal of his resignation and the King's personal appeal to him. Pitt was too proud to take such a step; and, naturally, George III would not take the initiative because he felt that he was better off with Pitt supporting Addington than he was with Pitt in office. Consequently with the King more than satisfied with the new arrangement, with Addington eager to take office, and with Pitt too proud to ask for reinstatement the end was inevitable. On March 14 Pitt retired; but before doing so he made clear his friendliness to the new administration both by his defense of it in the House of Commons and by introducing the new budget. For the first time since 1782, Pitt was neither in office nor in opposition.

IX. THE ADDINGTON INTERLUDE, 1801 TO 1804

The end of Pitt's ministry of seventeen years in March 1801 is the logical time to compare the relationship of monarch and First Lord of the Treasury with that at the beginning of the ministry in December 1783. As the last chapter indicated, George III was almost painfully consistent in insisting upon his fundamental right to choose his own ministers; and this right meant to him the selection of the chief minister and a discussion with that minister on the advisability of the appointment of each member to the cabinet and the ministry, and not merely a formal assent to the appointment of the ministers as a group. Pitt in 1783 and Addington in 1801 conformed perfectly to this ideal, and both had the gracious and almost eager support of the King. In 1801 there was less tension on the part of George III, because he had no occasion to worry about a hostile ministry being forced on him. But the real difference came, not in the formation of the ministries of Pitt and Addington, but in the dismissal of the Portland ministry in 1783 and that of Pitt in 1801. Portland, Fox, and North were dismissed because they had been guilty of what was to George III the greatest of constitutional crimes, that of forcing their way into the cabinet and the ministry contrary to the royal wishes. Pitt had merely been guilty of disagreeing with his sovereign on a fundamental question of policy, and in case of such a deadlock the minister under the constitutional theories of George III had to go. The King's resentment against Pitt for refusing to give way on Catholic Emancipation was almost offset by the conformity which the minister showed to the royal constitutional ideas in matters of opposition. Pitt not only agreed to support the new First Lord of the Treasury, but also declined to join the opposition as Lord North had done in 1793. Consequently the King had every reason to be satisfied. His constitutional position had been maintained, and even the regret at the loss of Pitt, which he had felt at first, was soon offset by the greater satisfaction he found in personal relations with Addington.

In most works on constitutional history it is conceded that George III really abandoned his ambitious plans of ruling as well as reigning during this long ministry of Pitt. The commonly accepted view is that Pitt actually laid the foundations for modern party and cabinet government during the years 1783 to 1801. The account given in the preceding chapters has shown how far this interpretation is from the views of both George III and Pitt. So far as building up a party in the House of Commons was concerned, Pitt followed the tradition of his father rather than that of Walpole, Pelham, Newcastle, and North. His personal following was so small that he recognized in 1788–89 and again in 1801 that a lengthy incapacitation of the King would bring in a new ministry under the Prince of Wales.

Pitt was not interested in building a political machine. He based his position at the head of the government on the confidence of the King and on the support of the majority of both houses of Parliament. The majority in the Commons he expected to secure by the use of placemen, as all ministers had done to a greater or less degree since the passing of the Septennial Act, but even more by the confidence which the independents felt in his character. In the House of Lords he counted on the numerous creations of these seventeen years to offset the hostility of the older Whig lords. Had Pitt been the founder of the modern Tory party and had he paved the way for the two-party system of the last hundred years, he would scarcely have left his "party" in the state he did in 1801. In the first place Pitt was not a Tory, and in the second place he did not consider himself to be the head of a party in the modern sense of the word. In all the many letters which Pitt wrote the present author does not recall a single passage which would justify either assumption. Pitt was a Chatham or Shelburne Whig at the beginning of his career and seems to have felt confidently that his political views never changed. Character was the key to his political career. He believed as did George III that the King had the right to choose his ministers and to dismiss them in case of disagreement on fundamental policy. If the majority in Parliament consistently opposed the King's ministers in such a manner that the government could not be carried on, then the sovereign must give way and take ministers who would be able to carry on His Majesty's government.

In short Pitt was a Revolution Whig, and it is to the period from 1689 to 1785 that one must look in order to understand his political principles and not to the period since 1832. But it was temperament as well as principles which was partly responsible for Pitt's attitude toward party organization. Like his father he had supreme confidence in his own abilities and stressed talent and character on the part of the individual rather than family prestige and group organization. The distribution of the loaves and fishes was left to Dundas during Pitt's long ministry, and in that respect the latter was fortunate in having such essential work in the hands of an expert; but there is no reason to believe that he would have performed it himself with any degree of skill had the task devolved on him. Thus the support of the King and his own confidence in his ability and character with which he managed to imbue the majority of the House of Commons on most questions after 1786 made the organization of a well-controlled government or opposition party appear to Pitt both unnecessary and unworthy of his serious attention. Evidently he did not feel the same objection to giving some attention to insuring a majority in the House of Lords. Here the antipathy for the proud controlling Whig families which he shared with his father made Pitt more willing to combine the task of satisfying influential supporters by peerages with the necessity of securing a majority in the Lords. In this practice there was substantial agreement between George III and Pitt, although the King looked carefully into the social and economic backgrounds of some of the candidates. This policy, however, did not mean that the new peers were brought under a party whip arrangement.

The query naturally arises why Pitt is credited with being a patron saint of the nineteenth-century Tory party in view of the very obvious fact that he was not a Tory himself and did not leave his followers so organized as to be able to carry on as a party. The answer, seemingly, is to be found in the fact that so many of the men who dominated the English government from 1801 to 1827 (1806–7 excepted) were either sincere admirers of Pitt or were quite willing to exploit his reputation by professing to be carrying out his policies. Adherence to the policies of the "immortal" William Pitt became almost as great a platitude from 1807 to 1827 as belief in the principles of the Glorious Revolution was under George I and George II. Many, however, who joined Addington in 1801 or later in his ministry were among those who made up the backbone of the Tory party in the next quarter of a century.

The formation of the new government was conducted along lines very different from those followed when a ministry was overthrown by the efforts of an organized opposition. Addington was selected by the King, not because he was leader of the opposition or because he commanded enough votes in the House of Commons to occupy a key position, but because he was personally and politically acceptable to both George III and Pitt. Addington accepted the appointment of First Lord of the Treasury, not because he was at the head of the party which controlled a majority of the House of Commons, but because he was unable to answer the King's query, "Lay your hand upon your heart, and ask yourself where I am to turn for support if *you* do not stand by me."[1] Addington seemed safe in forming a ministry under these conditions because the opposition was negligible in numbers and because Pitt had urged him to accept the offer of George and had cordially pledged his support.

When Pitt resigned, Grenville, Foreign Secretary; Dundas, Secretary of State for War; Lord Loughborough, Lord Chancellor; Lord Cornwallis, the Lord Lieutenant of Ireland; and Sir William Windham, the Secretary at War, retired from the cabinet with him. All except the Lord Chancellor followed him out of office because they held the same views as he on the Catholic question. The reasons why Loughborough failed to hold his position in the next ministry are somewhat obscure. It is clear that his views on Pitt's proposals for Catholic Emancipation were those of the King and not of the minister; and it is very doubtful if his conduct, no matter how reprehensible, had a real influence on George III. That Pitt should be enraged with Loughborough for spoiling any chance he had to secure a fair consideration of his proposals by the King is quite comprehensible. It is not equally clear why the King should feel harshly toward his Lord Chancellor and in later years speak of him in such terms of scorn. But, regardless of the reasons, Loughborough was not permitted to profit by the overthrow of Pitt to the extent of remaining in office. Addington became First Lord of the Treasury and Chancellor of the Exchequer; Lord Eldon, the Lord Chancellor; Lord Hawkesbury, Foreign Secretary; Lord Hobart, Secretary of War and Colonies; Lord St. Vincent, First Lord of the Admiralty; and Lord Hardwicke, Lord Lieutenant of Ireland. The Duke of Portland retained the office of Home Secretary; Lord Chatham, that of Lord President; and Lord Westmorland, that of Lord Privy Seal. In June Lord Chatham was made Master-General of Ordnance and in

[1] George Pellew, *The Life and Correspondence of the Right Honourable Henry Addington, First Viscount Sidmouth* (London, 1847), I, 287.

July relinquished his position as Lord President to the Duke of Portland. Lord Pelham then succeeded the Duke as Home Secretary.

The new ministry was undeniably weak in everything except lords. In administrative experience and in debating skill its members were far inferior to those in the preceding ministry. Sheridan in a speech in the Commons on February 16 summed up the general opinion by declaring: "When the crew of a vessel was preparing for action, it was usual to clear the decks by throwing overboard the lumber; but he never heard of such a manoeuver as that of throwing their great guns overboard."[2] Yet this obvious weakness of the Addington ministry did not mean its speedy overthrow or termination. Not only was the King satisfied, the opposition weak, and Pitt a decided asset as godfather to the new ministry, but many country gentlemen both in the House of Commons and outside were favorably inclined toward Addington because he, like the King, held ideas so much like their own and because his abilities were more on their own level than those of Pitt and Fox. Lord Holland summed up this attitude many years later when he wrote:

His very mediocrity recommended him to those (and they are not a few) who dread and dislike all superiority of talent. There were more persons than one who felt what an acquaintance of mine expressed on his (Mr. Addington's) Ministry. "He was glad," he said, "that Mr. Pitt and Mr. Fox should know that in spite of their speaking and fine talents, the business of the country could be conducted in a plain way by a man who had no pretensions to genius." Of such men, Lord Sidmouth has always been an idol.[8]

Thus the sincere support of this element in Parliament, of Pitt and his most important followers, and of George III, when combined with a judicious use of patronage, might well insure Addington a long and comparatively quiet ministry. If peace were made with France and the danger of a renewal of the conflict avoided, and if Pitt did not withdraw his support, there seemed little likelihood that either George III or the House of Commons would revolt against Addington's mediocrity. The first year of the new ministry indicated that this optimism might not be misplaced. But even before the war with Napoleon was

---

[2] *Parliamentary History*, XXXV, 969.

[8] Henry Edward Lord Holland (ed.), Henry Richard Lord Holland, *Memoirs of the Whig Party* (London, 1852), II, 212–13.

renewed in 1803 the weakness of the arrangement became clear. A formidable opposition came into existence based on a working agreement between groups hitherto hostile, and Pitt, owing to conditions upon which neither Addington nor he had reckoned, found himself unable to continue his unqualified support. Thus a ministry which George III enjoyed as much as any formed during his reign was to end all too soon for him. But these difficulties of the three years following Pitt's resignation were not obvious at the time to the King, to his retiring minister, or to his new minister. Still there were several of Pitt's friends who predicted dire results from these ministerial changes.

It is difficult to imagine one minister resigning and another accepting office under more trying circumstances than those of the six weeks preceding March 14, 1801. The critical situation produced by the constitutional crisis and the King's insanity have already been described, and in addition the foreign and internal situation added to the gloom. Short crops in 1799 and 1800 combined with the difficulties of importing foreign grain sent the price of wheat to unprecedented heights. It was the misfortune of Addington to assume office during the month that wheat reached the highest monthly price on record.[4] The King's speech at the opening of Parliament on January 22, 1801, had devoted a great deal of time to this problem; but the resignation of Pitt, the King's illness, and disasters on the Continent had driven the question into the background so far as the new and the old ministries were concerned, even though the great mass of the people might still consider it of fundamental importance.

Shortly after Pitt had signified his intention of resigning, the breakup of his Second Coalition against France was completed. On February 9, 1801, France, by the Treaty of Lunéville, secured Belgium from Austria and the Rhine frontier from Switzerland to Holland. Although the independence of the Dutch, the Swiss, and two Italian republics was recognized, all four, along with the kingdom of Etruria, were dominated by Napoleon Bonaparte, now First Consul of France. Not only was Austria lost as an ally, but Russia, owing chiefly to the personal whims of the Tsar Paul, had been transformed in the summer of 1800 from an ally into a dangerous enemy and was now a distinct threat to the British in the Baltic. Paul had been induced to join the Second

---

[4] Donald G. Barnes, *A History of the English Corn Laws* (London, 1930), pp. 77–86.

Coalition largely as a result of Bonaparte's seizure of Malta. When the British fleet was about to capture the island, however, Bonaparte shrewdly made a gift of it to the Tsar, and as a result the latter not only broke away from the Second Coalition but began negotiations with Sweden and Denmark to re-establish the Armed Neutrality of 1780.[5] The three nations reached an agreement on December 16, 1800, the substance of which was that goods of belligerents, except contraband, were free on board neutral vessels, that no port should be considered blockaded unless the blockade were effective, that neutral ships should not be stopped except for adequate cause, and that the mere declaration of a naval officer escorting a convoy that no contraband was carried should be sufficient to guard against search.[6]

Strangely enough the ministry was not so disturbed by the formation of this League of Armed Neutrality as might have been expected. Grenville especially emphasized the necessity of standing firm on the right of search. The British Navy had fully recovered from the effects of the mutinies of 1797 and was quite capable of protecting England and of effectively blockading the French ports. To have recognized the right of the northern powers to ship naval supplies from the Baltic to France unimpeded would have been to throw away the advantages of controlling the seas for which Great Britain had made such tremendous sacrifices and which she hoped to use in such a way as to offset the supremacy of France on the Continent. As Grenville phrased it: "I am every day more and more convinced that nothing will operate on the foolish prejudices of these people but the conviction that they have as much to lose by our shutting them out from the sea as we can lose by their excluding us from the land."[7] On January 14, 1801, before the resignation of Pitt was even considered, an embargo was laid on all Russian, Swedish, and Danish ships in British ports. The attitude of the ministry as expressed by Grenville was: "Our means are ample; the country is in good heart; the distress for provisions is the only real difficulty with which we have to contend, and that these people can neither add to nor diminish."[8] Clearly Grenville did

[5] Sir A. W. Ward and G. P. Gooch (eds.), *The Cambridge History of British Foreign Policy, 1783–1919* (New York: Macmillan, 1922), I, 299–300.

[6] *Ibid.*, p. 301.

[7] Historical Manuscripts Commission, *The Manuscripts of J. B. Fortescue, Esq., Preserved at Dropmore* (London, 1892–1927), VI, 400.

[8] *Ibid.*

not resign along with Pitt because he felt the situation of the country was hopeless and because he wished to have some other minister make an ignominious peace with France.

It was the good fortune of the Addington government to score a decided success in northern Europe a few days after taking office. The secret orders issued to Sir Hyde Parker the day after Pitt resigned were based on the instructions of Dundas. Parker, with Nelson second in command, sailed for the Baltic to deal with the northern powers by negotiations or by force. Late in the month Prussia closed the mouths of the Ems, Weser, and Elbe to British commerce; but Parker's instructions did not include Prussia. This northern danger to Great Britain, however, was dissipated even more rapidly than it had come into existence. On March 24 the Tsar of Russia was assassinated, and on April 2 the Danish fleet in Copenhagen was defeated and captured by Nelson. The conciliatory attitude of the great English seaman prevented more than temporary bitterness on the part of the Danes, the new Russian Tsar, Alexander I, reversed the policy of his father, and Prussia reopened the ports of northern Germany to British commerce. Further, the Addington ministry reached a compromise with Russia on June 17, 1801, whereby it was "agreed that in wartime the neutral flag should exempt from capture all cargoes except contraband of war and enemy property; and that blockade, to be legal, must be effective; contraband was defined, the right of search limited, and the rules of prize-courts were declared subject to the principles of equity."[9] Public opinion gave the credit of the dissipation of this northern danger to the Pitt ministry, where it rightfully belonged. Nevertheless, it was a comfortable achievement for the Addington ministry and seemed a good omen both to members of the government and to many members of Parliament. That the agreement with Russia was not satisfactory to at least one important member of Pitt's ministry and that the new ministers could not count unreservedly on his support was shown by Grenville's letter of July 15, 1801, to Lord Hawkesbury, his successor in the Foreign Office.[10]

The same good fortune which attended the Addington ministry in the Baltic held good in Egypt, although in this instance

[9] *The Cambridge History of British Foreign Policy,* I, 301. Quoted by permission of The Macmillan Company, publishers.
[10] *Dropmore Papers,* VII, 30–33.

Dundas appears to share in the good luck. When Bonaparte had returned to France from Egypt in 1799 he had been forced to leave behind practically all of his army. After failing to use their forces in the Mediterranean to any effect in the campaign of 1800, and influenced by the unsuccessful attempts which Bonaparte made to rescue these troops, the British government decided to send Sir Ralph Abercromby to expel them from Egypt. The idea was Dundas's and despite the opposition of other ministers and the King he succeeded in putting his plan into operation. The Addington ministry, however, thought so little of the plan that it actually sent a messenger to recall the expeditionary forces.[11] In the end, thanks to the skill of the British leaders and the mistakes of the French commander, the campaign proved successful. In June 1801 the French garrison in Cairo surrendered and in August that in Alexandria. The terms of capitulation given the French have been severely criticized on the grounds that they stipulated for the return to France on British and Turkish vessels of some 25,000 veteran troops.[12] Since there was no restriction on the use of these troops in Europe and since peace with France had not been made, these terms really made available for use by Bonaparte many thousand valuable troops which he himself had been unable to rescue. Dundas could now claim one glorious success in this Egyptian campaign to offset his many failures; and he found one of the consolations of his life after he retired to his Scottish estate in regaling his neighbors with the compliments which George III had paid him for carrying through his plan when his sovereign and many of his colleagues, especially Windham, were so much opposed. Modern research has, however, sided almost entirely with the King and the colleagues. Fortescue has gone so far as to say that Windham was correct in maintaining that Abercrombie's force was too small and the information which the cabinet had concerning the number of the French troops in Egypt was quite inadequate. Actually the French were twice as numerous as reported, and only the mistakes of the French general prevented Dundas's Egyptian expedition from being another disaster.[13] Thus Dundas secured undeserved

---

[11] *The Cambridge History of British Foreign Policy*, I, 299. Quoted from the debate of December 8, 1802, reported in *The Parliamentary History*.

[12] *Ibid.*

[13] J. W. Fortescue, *British Statesmen of the Great War, 1793–1814* (Oxford: Clarendon Press, 1911), n. 153.

credit for planning this campaign and the Addington ministry profited from an expedition which they tried unsuccessfully to stop.

The successes in the Baltic and in Egypt were not the only ones enjoyed by Addington. During his first months as Prime Minister the gratitude and affection which George III felt for him appear to have increased. If Pitt should be given great credit for regulating his conduct during the first months of 1801 in such a way as to avoid bringing another period of insanity on the King, Addington should be given even greater credit for restoring George III's peace of mind. If, as has been alleged, it was the first desire of all responsible statesmen to prolong the reign of George III and to prevent a regency,[14] then the greatest service which Addington rendered his country was in accepting the office of First Lord of the Treasury and in his tactful and considerate treatment of the King. An indication of George III's regard is shown by his assigning to Addington on June 13, 1801, the royal lodge in Richmond Park. The King, accompanied by the Queen and Princesses, graciously arranged to meet Mr. and Mrs. Addington on that day and to show them through their new abode. As the admiring biographer of the minister describes the meeting:

Unfortunately, at the time fixed for his departure, Mr. Addington was detained in town by indispensable business; and in consequence, their Majesties were kept waiting, for nearly an hour, in the unfurnished lodge: nothing, however, could exceed the patience with which they awaited the arrival of their expected visitors, unless it was the condescending indulgence with which they received Mr. Addington's excuses.[15]

Even more significant is the exchange of letters between Addington and George III following this generous mark of royal affection and confidence. The night of the bestowal of the possession of the lodge Addington wrote:

Mr. Addington most humbly and earnestly hopes that He shall be forgiven by Your Majesty, if, before He goes to rest, He ventures to indulge the Feelings, with which He is deeply affected in Consequence of the Condescension and Goodness which have been recently manifested towards Himself, and Those most dear to Him.

[14] J. H. Rose, *Life of William Pitt* (London: G. Bell & Sons, Ltd., 1923), II, 449.

[15] Pellew, *op. cit.*, I, 409.

It will be his constant Aim, and anxious Endeavour to prove Himself not altogether unworthy of the Confidence, and Kindness, with which Your Majesty has been invariably pleased to honor Him, and which are perpetually animating the obligations of Duty by the strongest Sentiments of reverential Attachment and Gratitude.[16]

George III in answering this grateful letter at 7:30 the next morning expressed sentiments which he could have used to very few of his prime ministers: "The King is highly gratified at the repeated marks of the sensibility of Mr. Addington's heart, which must greatly add to the comfort of having placed him with so much propriety at the head of the Treasury. He trusts their mutual affection can only cease with their lives."[17] Clearly George III was extremely well pleased with his change of ministers early in the year. Also there seems to have been no abatement of royal interest in the affairs of government, for in July when the Duke of Portland was shifted from his place as Home Secretary to that of Lord President of the Council the King wrote Addington

that it will prevent any difficulties in future if Mr. Addington will now notify to the Lords Hobart and Pelham that the Duke of Portland has made his final determination; that therefore his Majesty thinks they should, in conjunction with Mr. Addington, arrange the division of business between the home and war departments, to prevent any ambiguity in future.[18]

When Parliament was prorogued on July 2 Addington was given a breathing spell. He could look back on the events since March with considerable satisfaction. Obviously he had pleased his sovereign, he had received the benefits of unexpected successes in foreign operations, and he had not yet felt the sting of the strong opposition which he was to experience later. Consequently Addington was able to make plans for the next session of Parliament while his Foreign Minister, Lord Hawkesbury, was carrying on peace negotiations with France.

Steps to end the war, evidently, were commenced by Hawkesbury almost as soon as the Addington ministry took office. These negotiations he carried on in London with M. Otto, who had been sent to England by the French government ostensibly to superintend the exchange of prisoners. The reasons why England

---

[16] "Correspondence of King George III," Transcripts by Sir John Fortescue in William L. Clements Library, X, 264.

[17] Pellew, op. cit., I, 407–8.   [18] Ibid., p. 412.

desired an immediate peace are summed up in a letter of Sir John Macpherson to Addington:

If you get a peace that fixes our supremacy in India, it will of itself consolidate the union with Ireland; and the more France gains near North America, the more she will excite the jealousy of the United States. . . . . An outlet for her commerce and her wild spirits she must have. . . . . Without a speedy peace, the union with Ireland will prove our greatest weakness, and the expenditures of distant war will cultivate the fields of revolution at home. This is our danger.[19]

Bonaparte, however, was equally anxious for peace in order to carry on his conquest of St. Domingo and to make good his promises of an early peace to the French people. Consequently preliminary articles of peace were signed by Hawkesbury and Otto on October 1, 1801.

The satisfaction with which Hawkesbury regarded the agreement is clearly brought out in his communication to Grenville on the very day that the peace preliminaries were signed:

We retain possession of Ceylon and Trinidad, the Cape of Good Hope to be made a free port, Malta to be restored to the Order under the guaranty and protection of a third power, Egypt to be restored to the Turks, the integrity of the Turkish empire and of Portugal to be maintained. The kingdom of Naples and the Roman territory to be evacuated by the French armies.

I am inclined to hope that, under all the circumstances, you will consider this as an honourable peace. I feel as strongly as any man that new difficulties may open upon us in consequence of this event, to what extent and of what nature it is impossible to speculate; but I am confident that nothing could have been reasonably expected from a continuance of the war which would have justified us, under present circumstances, in rejecting these terms.[20]

The hope expressed by Hawkesbury that Grenville would find the terms honorable was doomed to disappointment. From the moment Grenville received the news of the terms he set about resolutely to oppose them. His letters to Pitt and Dundas show his dismay at the extent of the concessions made, and in two short paragraphs to the latter he explained his position:

You can also witness for me how little my mind is disposed to make to the King's kindness to me so ungrateful a return as that of

[19] *Ibid.*, p. 451.
[20] *Dropmore Papers*, VII, 45.

harassing his government, or stirring up or encouraging any factious opposition to his measures.

But is it not too much to expect that I should say, or acquiesce in its being said, contrary to my own conviction of the truth, that the measures in which I bore a share have reduced the country to the desperate necessity of purchasing a short interval of repose by the sacrifice of those points on which our security in a new contest may principally depend?[21]

Grenville's reaction to these peace terms marks the beginning not only of his opposition to the government but of his break with Pitt as well. It is true that the two had differed within the cabinet on points of foreign policy, especially since 1797; but the rift between them was to become a public difference when these peace terms were discussed in Parliament. Because of the opposition to the Addington ministry which developed later, Pitt's reaction to Grenville's objections is interesting. He declared at the beginning of a letter written October 5 that he distrusted his own judgment when it differed from that of Grenville, but confessed that their respective views were far apart on the treaty. Although frankly admitting that the permanence of peace was precarious and that the nation should be prepared for a renewal of the contest, he still felt such considerations should not be made a reason for refusing to make any peace with the present French government. Specifically Pitt regretted the disposal of Malta and the Cape, but since he held that the great object of the peace was that it should not appear to have been dictated and that Great Britain should retain what was most essential for the protection of her East and West Indian possessions, on the whole he felt satisfied. Further he believed that the stipulation in favor of the allies who adhered to Great Britain was most creditable to his country, because, granted that such a stipulation was not to be too much relied upon because of the government on whose good faith it depended, nevertheless, on the face of the treaty it was at least honorable. In conclusion Pitt stated:

On the whole, looking at the terms themselves, and combining them with all the difficulties attending the continuation of war, and the little prospect of being able to make any material impression on the enemy, I cannot but think the conclusion of the treaty fortunate for the country, and see no ground which would justify me in my own mind from withholding the fullest support and general approbation.[22]

[21] *Dropmore Papers*, VII, 48.   [22] *Ibid.*, pp. 49–50.

Thus the preliminary terms were to pave the way for the first attack on the new government by a most important member of Pitt's long ministry.

Most significant of all was the attitude taken toward the peace by George III. Both Addington and Hawkesbury favored peace not only because of the reasons which Pitt gave but because it would give them prestige to succeed where Pitt and Grenville had failed four times and would, on account of the widespread war weariness, give them popularity both in Parliament and in the country. Since George III was so obviously pleased with Addington as a personal minister, it might be expected that he would cordially endorse the treaty which terminated the war. On the contrary, the King's views were very similar to those of Grenville. He had no confidence that the peace would be lasting and was interested principally in seeing that the national defense was not neglected, so that the country might be in a favorable position to renew the inevitable conflict. His two short notes to Hawkesbury of September 30 and October 2 portray most eloquently this state of mind:

The King has received the Minute of the Cabinet on the proposed Peace with France. To repeat His doubts whether any confidence can be placed in any agreement to be made with that Country till it has a settled Government, would be in reality a stop to all Negociation; He will not oppose the concluding Peace, though He cannot place any reliance on its duration but trusts such a Peace Establishement will be kept up as may keep this Country on a respectable footing without which our situation would be most deplorable.[23]

The King has this instant received Lord Hawkesbury's note acquainting him with the Signature of the Preliminaries of Peace. He trusts therefore every attention will be given to put this Country on the most respectable state of Defence; for He can never think any Treaty with France can be depended upon, till it has a settled and regular form of Government.[24]

Naturally the question arises why the King permitted such subservient ministers as Addington and Hawkesbury to conclude a treaty in which he himself had so little confidence. Unfortunately we do not possess one of those memoranda of George III in which he puts his ideas on paper for the clarification of his own mind and to the joy of future historians. The King, however,

[23] Clements Transcripts, XI, 428. [24] Ibid., XI, 429.

was perfectly consistent with both his principles and his practices in permitting the conclusion of peace contrary to his own judgment. He claimed only the right of selecting and dismissing his own ministers, and if he felt satisfied with them there was nothing in his political philosophy which prevented him from deferring to their judgment if he felt so inclined. Further, in yielding to his ministers and the overwhelming majority of the public on this question George III placed himself in a stronger position when the war was renewed. His anxiety for and emphasis on the national defense showed that he considered this to be of fundamental importance. The country was so weary of war and the ministers were so anxious to win popularity by making peace that the King fully realized what bad tactics it would be to disappoint both of them by a vigorous royal opposition. When the war broke out again, as George III was certain it would, then he could count on the more loyal support of the nation as well as continued good relations with his ministers. Lastly, if he were human rather than tactful, he could point out to ministers that he had warned them of the inevitable result of making peace with a country which had no settled form of government.

The popularity of the peace was shown when the discussion of the preliminaries was taken up in Parliament on November 3 and 4, 1801. The attack on the French treaty was led by Windham in the House of Commons and by Grenville in the House of Lords, but neither received much support. Windham did not venture to call for a division, and Grenville, who divided the House of Lords on the address in approval of the treaty, was badly beaten 114 to 10.[25] But many of those who supported the ministry expressed doubts and apprehensions over one or more of the peace conditions. For once Pitt and Fox found themselves on the same side of a question; for both, with certain reservations, spoke in favor of the peace terms.

When, however, the definitive treaty between Great Britain and France and her allies, Spain and the Batavian Republic, was signed on March 27, 1802, the doubts and apprehension expressed in the debates of the previous November were found to have been more than justified. The six months between the signing of the preliminaries and the definitive treaty had been used by Bonaparte to exploit the articles which had been left vague in the

[25] *Parliamentary History*, XXXVI, 190.

former. The Cisalpine Republic was reorganized and became the Italian Republic with Bonaparte as president. By this change the French government was in a position to dominate Italy as a whole. The situation in Switzerland was further altered in favor of France by the detachment of territory from and the imposition of a new constitution on the Helvetic Republic. The commercial treaties which France concluded with other European countries, whereby the French were given special commercial privileges, usually operated to the disadvantage of England. Thus the relative positions of the two countries had changed decidedly between the time of the peace preliminaries and that of the definitive treaty. It was not so much surrender of the colonial possessions in the peace preliminaries as the strengthened position of France in political and commercial spheres on the Continent at the time of the definitive peace which marked the extent of the British humiliation. A comparison of English prestige on the Continent at the beginning of 1793 with that after the Treaty of Amiens on March 27, 1802, gives a true indication of the decline of Great Britain and the rise of France during that decade. Many in England who were unwilling to admit this comparative loss after the peace preliminaries could not deny it after the Treaty of Amiens.

Article Ten, which dealt with the island of Malta, was to cause the greatest difficulty in the next year. By its terms Great Britain was to evacuate the island and its independence was to be guaranteed under the protection of Great Britain, France, Austria, Russia, Spain, and Prussia. Unfortunately no provision was made in case one of the four powers in addition to France and England refused to .guarantee the independence or imposed conditions. Months passed without any serious attempt to secure this guaranty from the four powers. As a result Great Britain did not evacuate the island and France in time came to accuse her of bad faith. To one historian it appears that France purposely left the question involved in order to have available in the future the basis of a dispute which she could successfully exploit.[26] Actions of Bonaparte in the months following the treaty did not make the Addington government anxious to relinquish control of Malta. In August 1802 the French annexed Elba and in September, Piedmont; in October, Switzerland was invaded and a

[26] A. F. Fremantle, *England in the Nineteenth Century, 1801–1805* (New York: Macmillan, 1929), p. 346.

new constitution was forced upon her. When Hawkesbury protested these acts of aggression, Bonaparte maintained that by the terms of the treaty England had no interest in the Continent outside of Naples and Portugal. Bonaparte on this point, as on others, adhered rigidly to the letter of the treaty, and from the strictly legal point of view he was able to offer an effective defense by referring to the actual words of the treaty. Thus England found herself in an embarrassing position as a result of being outgeneraled in the definitive peace.

Since, however, public opinion, which yearned for peace with France at almost any price, was willing to swallow even the Treaty of Amiens in its eagerness to end the war, it is interesting to see what disillusioned the public on this dearly acquired arrangement. War weariness, high prices of food, and a desire to renew normal trade relations had played a large part in the state of mind of the public. Now bountiful harvests in both 1801 and 1802 had brought food prices down to a more reasonable level, but the hoped-for renewal of trade relations with France had not materialized. Again Bonaparte, adhering strictly to the terms of the treaty and to the law of the French Republic, had not only opposed a resumption of normal trade relations between the two countries but still subjected the English to the harsh measures passed during the last war. Thus the failure of the English government to secure in the Treaty of Amiens or later either a commercial treaty or the repeal of the harsh French laws which prevented even ordinary commercial exchange between the two countries was an important factor in disillusioning the trading classes in England. Consequently when war broke out again these business interests were more favorable to a renewal of hostilities than they had been to a continuation of the war in 1801.

The session of 1802 gave Addington his only real opportunity to carry on the government under the conditions which he expected to apply when he assumed control in 1801. In addition to the conclusion of the permanent peace treaty with France, the new Prime Minister found time to readjust national finance and armed forces to what he considered a peace basis. Owing to a variety of factors, Addington enjoyed a peace which he was not to experience in future sessions. He had the advantage of the cordial support of the King and Pitt, of the public approbation which is bestowed on a man who has ended a dreary war and who has just assumed the responsibility of office, and of the fact that the opposition had not yet organized in such a manner as to cause him any real uneasiness. Even though Pitt, owing to illness and an apparent unwillingness to attend the House of Commons regularly, had retired to Walmer Castle, Addington continued to ask his advice and support on all important measures. A good example of this supervision is shown in the corrections which Pitt made to Addington's draft of the speech from the throne on June 28 which closed the session. Pitt wrote:

I lose no time in returning the draft of the speech, which appears to me to be excellent, and to bear no marks either of the lamp or the nightcap. I have ventured, however, to attempt to heighten a little the principle tirade, by a few verbal alterations, but chiefly by inserting, as shortly as possible, two or three leading topics, which seem material enough to deserve particular notice. You will find the sentence, as it would stand according to the suggestion, in a separate paper.[27]

This painstaking care in consulting Pitt was one of the reasons why Addington retained his support for many months in spite of the efforts of Grenville and Canning to draw him into the so-called New Opposition.

The closing of this session was followed on June 29 by the dissolution of Parliament. Surely no general election during the nineteenth century took place under such unusual circumstances. Addington, in the election as in carrying on business in the House of Commons, had the advantage of the support of George III and Pitt and of a weak and scattered opposition. There was really no fundamental issue in the campaign. Pitt and Fox were in semi-retirement, both had endorsed Addington's peace treaty, and there was no outstanding issue in domestic affairs. The memory of the war was so bitter that the public was not yet in a mood to examine the defects in the treaty with a critical eye. Reform, which was so important an issue a decade earlier, was now so universally condemned that even its most energetic supporters in and out of Parliament had no hope in the immediate future. In spite of the fact that he had resigned with Pitt in 1801, Dundas looked after the government interests in Scotland and was able to assure Addington that success north of the Tweed was very complete. Castlereagh's report on Ireland is significant not only because of the information conveyed but also as showing the state of mind

27 Pellew, *op. cit.*, II, 71.

of that gentleman. He wrote "that, fortunately for the tranquillity of the country, the elections had in general been very little contested and that the individuals chosen were perfectly proper persons, both in principles and property."[28] The general results of the election left party strength little changed. In short, Addington, so far as support in the Commons was concerned, was practically in the same situation as when he assumed office.

But if Addington were cheered by the favorable outcome of the general election, by the continued expressions of satisfaction and good will by George III, and by the support and friendship of Pitt, he had occasion to be concerned over the trends in foreign affairs. Although very proud of making peace where Pitt had failed, Addington could not but feel that the aggressive conduct of Bonaparte between the two sessions of Parliament had done much to mar this triumph. Thus if the Prime Minister could face the newly elected House of Commons with considerable confidence in view of his majority and of the support of the King and Pitt, he was fully aware that the New Opposition headed by Grenville and Windham would be certain to demand that the British government do something to stop Bonaparte's aggression in Switzerland and northern Italy.

The speech of the King at the opening of the first session of the newly elected Parliament on November 23, 1802, stressed the internal prosperity of the country and cautiously called attention to the dangerous state of foreign affairs. The fact that the address of thanks was carried without a division gave a misleading impression of the satisfaction which leaders and members of the House of Commons felt. If the general election of this year was a peculiar one, the situation of Parliament at the first meeting was even more unusual. Addington, whose chief assets were the support of the King and Pitt and who before 1801 had not been considered the leader of any substantial group in the House of Commons, had with very little effort or bribery on his part secured a substantial majority. Despite the dark outlook on foreign affairs the First Lord of the Treasury found himself supported by most of the leaders of the Old Opposition, as the followers of Fox were now called to distinguish them from the New Opposition. Pitt was not present on November 23, and although he had begun to weaken in his resolution to support Addington this fact

---

[28] Pellew, *op. cit.*, II, 72.

was not known either to the Prime Minister or to the newly elected members of the House of Commons.

This month of November seems to have marked the turning point in the attitude of Pitt toward Addington. As has been noted earlier, Pitt's friends, notably Canning, Rose, and Grenville, had pressed him to remain in office even during the period in February and March, 1801, when he had tendered his resignation to the King but had not actually given up office. The history of Pitt's relations with Addington from February 1801 to May 1804 falls logically into two divisions: the first, in which he resisted the importunate pleadings of his friends and remained loyal to this successor; and the second, in which he had decided to resume office when the opportunity presented itself. The transition from the first to the second state of mind clearly comes in November of 1802. The length of both periods is both amazing and characteristic of Pitt. It is noteworthy that he should have been able to resist the arguments of his friends for so long a time and even more so that he should delay his return to office by eighteen months. The explanation lies in Pitt's emphasis on character. Above all he was afraid of doing something which both he and others might consider dishonorable. On most questions Pitt was so confident of his own ability and judgment that he could be accused of rashness rather than vacillation or timidity. The difficulty for him lay in the fact that his exalted opinion of his own integrity and nobility of character made it difficult for him to choose between what he owed his country and his friend Addington. On the one hand Pitt was being continually bombarded by his friends with statements that he was allowing his country to suffer because of an ill-advised promise to a personal friend. Canning expresses this point of view in a letter to Windham on April 27, 1802: "Whether P *will* save us I do not know. But surely he is the only man that *can*."[20] Such a declaration is reminiscent of Chatham's famous remark early in the Seven Years' War. It is true that Chatham made the remark about himself and that Canning made it about Pitt; but the latter was sufficiently like his father and had enough confidence in himself to believe in the essential accuracy of both statements.

The biographers of Addington and Pitt agree that the turning point in the relations of the two men came in November 1802.

[20] J. H. Rose, *Life of William Pitt,* II, 471.

On the tenth of the month Pitt, writing from Bath where he had gone for his health, gave Addington his opinion of the foreign situation in a very open and candid manner.[30] The letter was signed "Affectionately your, W. P." Yet on the 21st Rose wrote to Bishop Tomline:

He [Pitt] is positively decided to have no responsibility whatever respecting what has been done or is doing on the subject of foreign politics; he not only adheres to his resolution of not going up for the opening of [Parliament]; but will not attend even on the estimates unless a necessity should arise: he writes today both to Mr. Addington and Lord Hawkesbury in a style that will not only manifest the above, *but will prevent all further attempts to draw him into confidential communication.* He has also made up his mind to take office again whenever the occasion shall arise, when he can come in properly, and has now no reluctance on the subject.[31]

Pellew, the admiring biographer of Addington, feels that Pitt took the first "retrograde" step in not attending the opening of Parliament on November 23, but that the Prime Minister was not aware that his best friend was preparing to desert him until the two exchanged letters on December 30 and 31.

Realizing the increasing dangers from France and the value of Pitt's support, Addington decided to strengthen his position by proposing a coalition with him. The person selected as go-between was Pitt's old colleague, Dundas, now, by grace of Addington, Viscount Melville. The latter gives a most vivid account of the reception of his proposals by Pitt in a letter of March 22 to Addington.[32] The point of view of the former Prime Minister was roughly as follows: he had no desire from the personal point of view to return to office, and if the present ministry adhered to the fundamental principles in foreign and domestic policy which he had stressed for so many years, and proved competent to carry on the government successfully, then he would be willing to give it the same support which he had promised in 1801. As things stood, however, he was profoundly dissatisfied with the conduct of foreign affairs and the financial policy of the government, and considering his long connection with the Treasury doubted whether he was at liberty to refrain much longer from telling the

30 Pellew, *op. cit.*, II, 86–87.

31 J. H. Rose, *Life of William Pitt,* II, 479. Quoted from the Pretyman MSS.

32 Pellew, *op. cit.,* II, 114–16.

public the fatal errors which he was satisfied existed in the statement of the relation of the national revenue and the charges
against it. Under the circumstances he felt that he should not
join the government or take an active part in Parliament. When
Melville, following Addington's suggestion, sounded out Pitt on
the possibility of the formation of a new administration in which
both Pitt and Addington should serve under the Earl of Chatham,
he received a decided negative. Pitt maintained that his health
was so poor that he would not consider taking office except from
an urgent sense of public duty and the knowledge that his services
were in demand both in "the highest quarter" and by the men
with whom he would act in a new arrangement. Further he
stressed the fact that he believed he could be of service to his
country only by returning to the Treasury. In short, Melville took
back to the Prime Minister Pitt's unconditional refusal to take a
share in the government either under Addington himself or under
a nominal leader such as Chatham.

From the point of view of this study, however, the most important feature of these negotiations is the fact that it gives a clear-
cut statement of Pitt's own views of the constitutional position of
the first minister. Unfortunately for the historian, Pitt did not put
down his thoughts in memoranda, as did George III, and when he
expounded his views in the House of Commons it was natural that
he should not allow himself the same freedom as he would in private conversation. Considering the circumstances there is no reason to believe that Melville did not give to Addington an accurate
account of what Pitt stated when he wrote:

Besides this consideration, he stated, not less pointedly and decidedly, his sentiments with regard to the absolute necessity there is,
in the conduct of the affairs of this country, that there should be an
avowed and real minister possessing the chief weight in council and
the principal place in the confidence of the King. In that respect
there can be no rivalry or division of power. That power must rest
in the person generally called the First Minister; and that minister
ought, he thinks, to be the person at the head of finances. He knows,
to his comfortable experience, that notwithstanding the abstract truth
of that general proposition, it is no ways incompatible with the most
cordial concert and mutual exchange of advice and intercourse
amongst the different branches of executive departments; but still, if
it should come unfortunately to such a radical difference of opinion
that no spirit of conciliation or concession can reconcile, the sentiments of the Minister must be allowed and understood to prevail,

leaving the other members of administration to act as they may conceive themselves conscientiously called upon to act under such circumstances. During the last administration such a collision of opinion, I believe, scarcely ever happened, or, at least, was not such as the parties felt themselves obliged to push to extremities; but still it is possible, and the only remedy applicable to it, is in the principle which I have explained.[33]

Although Pitt had stated clearly the position which he held and which he was to adhere to in the months that followed, Addington still had hopes that he could induce Pitt to join his government. Having failed to move Pitt by using Melville, Addington now tried a personal conference. The Prime Minister and Pitt on April 10 and 11 met in the home of their mutual friend, Long, at Bromley Hill. Here Pitt insisted upon a new ministry which would take office by the desire of the King and the specific recommendation of the present ministers. The new government was to include Lord Melville, Lord Spencer, Lord Grenville, and Mr. Windham. Addington, although such proposals were acceptable neither to him nor to the other ministers, agreed to place Pitt's proposals before his cabinet. Quite naturally the ministers declined to make the specific recommendations which Pitt required. They wished to have the ministry strengthened by the accession of Pitt and of his more "acceptable" friends; and they did not desire to resign and to be replaced by those men who had been criticizing their measures so severely. Thus this cabinet Minute of April 14 which Addington sent to Pitt in the form of a letter marked the failure of the negotiations.

The similarity between the point of view adopted by Pitt and that adopted by Portland, Fox, and North in 1784 is very striking. Pitt in that year wished the Portland Whigs to join him as equals in the same sense that Addington wished Pitt and his friends to join in 1803. In 1784 Portland had insisted that Pitt must resign and admit either actually or tacitly that his actions had been unconstitutional; and then the members of the Coalition would admit him into a new ministry. In 1803 Addington was not asked to sign any confession of error but he was requested to resign and pave the way for Pitt, who was to have a free hand in making up a new ministry. If Pitt, however, did not require Addington to admit that his action in becoming First Lord of the Treasury was unconstitutional, he did insist that the proposed changes should be

[33] Pellew, *op. cit.*, II, 116.

by the King's desire and upon the recommendations of the present ministers. In 1784 Pitt had with proud disdain declined to pass under the proposed yoke; yet he now demanded that Addington should pass under one only slightly less humiliating. From the point of view of the King, Pitt's proposal was not so offensive because of the absence of personal hatred which had played so large a part in the royal attitude in 1784; but in 1803 George III was to be required to express his desire that the proposed changes take place, while in the earlier crisis no such demand was made. Here, however, the similarity between the two crises ends: in 1784 the Portland Whigs had a majority of the House of Commons and attempted to use this power to compel George III to accept them as his ministers; and in 1803 Pitt controlled the votes of only a handful of members of the House of Commons and had neither the power nor, apparently, the inclination to compel the King and Addington to yield. Pitt's attitude was simple: his health was bad and his ambition slight, but if the country really needed him in the only post where he could be of real service, let the King indicate that he wished him to assume that office and let Addington make the step possible by vacating the position of First Lord of the Treasury.

Under normal circumstances Addington's letter to Pitt of April 14 stating that the cabinet had rejected the latter's proposals would have ended the matter. Upon considering, however, the interpretation which might be placed on his brief letters to Addington of April 13 and 14, Pitt decided to amplify and clarify his point of view in order that his attitude at this time might not be used against him in the future. He was particularly anxious that his stand should not be misunderstood by the King. To protect himself against future misrepresentation Pitt sent four letters to Addington written on April 15, 21, 22, and 24. Addington replied to the first two on the 18th and 21st.[34] The most significant passage in the exchange of letters came in Pitt's communication of April 15, and it was obviously for royal consumption. Denying that he had ever made any proposition on the subject Pitt insisted that the whole question arose from Addington's suggestion that he return to the King's service:

On this point I stated that the only grounds on which I could think myself called upon to give any positive answer to such a propo-

[34] *Ibid.*, pp. 122–29.

sition, or to say anything that could be in any degree binding with respect to the details of any arrangement connected with it, was, that of receiving some direct previous intimation of his Majesty's wish to that effect, together with full authority to form, for *his Majesty's consideration,* a plan of arrangement in *any* manner I thought best for his service, *as well out of those who were in the former, as those who are in his present government.* I added, that the whole and every part of such plan, when submitted to his Majesty, must of course depend on his approbation or rejection; that nothing could, in any instance, be so adverse to my sense of duty and propriety, as to press, for a moment, any point that might not be consistent with his Majesty's opinion and inclination; but that in case of any such objection, it must be open to me to judge, whether it did not, in my opinion, render it impossible for me to engage in his Majesty's service?[35]

After all, the issue between Pitt and Addington was a simple one. The latter wished to strengthen his ministry by the addition of Pitt, but he had no desire to make way for a new government. Pitt, on the other hand, had no intention of joining Addington's government, but was willing to form a new ministry in which many of the present ministers would be included. At Pitt's expressed desire, Addington showed the entire correspondence to George III. Unfortunately no letter or memorandum giving the King's exact thoughts is available; but the evidence and the attitude taken by the King during the two preceding years leave little doubt that he sympathized with Addington and strongly approved of the manner in which his minister had handled the negotiations.[36]

Although the issue seems almost painfully clear, the whole affair aroused considerable resentment on the part of certain members of the ministry who were friends of Pitt and had consented to serve under Addington. They felt that in so doing they were acting in such a manner as to merit both Pitt's thanks and consideration. Now they could only interpret his conduct as a reflection on them and as an attempt on his part to discredit their conduct of foreign and domestic affairs. This point of view is strongly suggested in the brief entry in Speaker Abbot's diary that "Mr. Pitt left town to go to Walmer. His conduct in the whole transaction is very much disapproved by Lord Melville, Lord Chatham, Lord Castlereagh, Lord Hawkesbury, Steele, etc."[37] This attitude is

---

[35] Pellew, *op. cit.,* II, 123.   [36] *Ibid.,* p. 130.

[37] Charles, Lord Colchester (ed.), *The Diary and Correspondence of Charles Abbot, Lord Colchester* (London, 1861), I, 416. Hereafter cited as *Colchester Diary.*

also brought out in two letters which Lord Redesdale wrote to Pitt on the 16th and 17th of April. Redesdale, now Lord Chancellor of Ireland, who as Sir John Mitford had succeeded Addington as speaker in 1801, was present at the interviews between Pitt and Addington at Bromley. At great length he upbraided Pitt for the injustice he was doing these members of the Addington ministry who had consented to serve because they believed Pitt wished it. Redesdale further emphasized the danger to the country of Pitt returning to office accompanied by those members of his late administration who had resigned because of the Catholic question.[38]

[38] The following two letters (Pitt MSS, 170) written by Lord Redesdale to Pitt during the period of these negotiations indicate the pressure which was brought to bear on the latter while out of office:

"ALBEMARLE ST.
"April 16, 1803

"MY DEAR SIR:

"What passed yesterday and the day before at Bromely Hill has made so strong an impression on my mind, that I have been unable to retrieve myself from the anxiety it has occasioned. However you may flatter yourself to the contrary it seems to me most clear that your return into office, with the impression under which you have appeared to act, must have the effect of driving from their situations every man new in office, and making a greater change than has ever been made on any similar occasion. I think myself as one of those persons, individually entitled to call upon your honour not to pursue the line of conduct which you seem determined to adopt. The present administration so far from having been formed in hostility to you, was avowedly formed of your friends. When you quitted your office you repeatedly declared that you should consider yourself as obliged to those friends who would continue in office, or would accept office, under Mr. Addington. You must recollect that I expressed to you my disapprobation of the change and my wish to retire to my situation at the bar, quitting the office of attorney general—and that you used to me these words—"That you must not do for my sake." The words were too strongly impressed upon my mind at the moment to have escaped my memory. You encouraged me to take the office of Speaker much against my will, and after I had expressly declared that I would not take it without your approbation. If I had not taken that office, nothing should have induced me to take that in which I am now placed, and by which I have been brought into a situation of much anxiety separated from all my old friends. Many, many others are in similar situations; and all are to be sacrificed to those men who were said by yourself, at that time to be acting in contradiction to your wishes in quitting their offices, or those who dragged you out of office with them. You will probably tell me that you have no such intention and particularly with respect to myself. But whatever may be your intentions, such must be the unavoidable consequence of the changes which you have determined upon. I thought when I took a situation under the administration at the head of which you had placed Mr. Addington, that I was doing you service. It was of no such importance to you—whether you looked to a return to office or to retirement from publick life, that the government should not fall into the hands of those who had been engaged in violent opposition to you; and you, yourself stated to me that you apprehended that must be the consequence if Mr. Addington should not be able to form an administration. I understood at the time, indeed, I am very sure that you made the like representations to many others. How then could those who consented to assist in different ways towards forming of that administration, conceive that they were acting in a manner disagreeable to you: and particularly how could they conceive that they were acting so as to warrant you sacrificing

There is no doubt that Pitt was subjected to high pressure from two sides. His old colleagues who had resigned with him in 1801 were urging him once more to assume control of the government as a patriotic measure to save his country from the financial and foreign policies of the incompetent Addington administration; while those who had not resigned but had remained to serve with his successor were accusing him of ingratitude and unethical shifting of position. Still it is doubtful whether these importunate pleas from both groups seriously affected the outcome of the Pitt-Addington negotiations. Pitt had no intention, regardless of the advice and protests of either group, of joining the existing administration under the conditions which Addington suggested. At the

---

them at a future period to men who apparently were acting in contradiction to your wishes, and to those whom they were serving as well as yourself in preventing that violent change which you all dreaded. I must entreat you, therefore, before you consent to proscribe all your old friends who have acted upon your assurances, that you will consider whether those who demand that sacrifice of you are entitled to demand it, and whether your honour will permit you to accede to it, however strongly it may be insisted upon. Some of your last words to me induce me to think that you have not yourself abandoned the plan formed for giving to the Roman Catholic Church, full establishment in Ireland, for such I consider the plan suggested by Lord Castlereagh, with any modification of which it is capable. Indeed if all those who went out of office because that measure was not approved then (such being the ostensible cause of their quitting their stations) are to come into office again, there can be no doubt in the mind of the publick that it is determined to carry that measure. I am so thoroughly convinced that it was a measure formed without sufficient knowledge of the condition either of the established Church or of the Roman Catholics, & above all without sufficient knowledge of the temper and disposition of the Roman Catholics, of their views and hopes that I am persuaded if you followed the judgment of your own mind upon it you would reject it. But there are others who do not consider the plan under the influence of their reason, but under the influence of passion and prejudice, and with a degree of enthusiasm, & almost of fanaticism. If, therefore those who quitted administration with you are to take it also with you, the publick must be persuaded that the measure is decided upon. Fear perhaps may enable you to carry it, tho' I have doubt if in that point. But I am fully persuaded that if the measure should be carried, it will end in the seperation of Ireland from Great Britain, & the extirpation of the protestations or the subjugation of the Catholics by force, after a bloody contest, unless, reconciling Ireland to the church of Rome, you shall make that church (in breach of the articles of union) the established Church of Scotland. I think fit to give you my opinion on the point thus decidedly, because I think it a duty I owe to both countries & to both discriptions of christians in Ireland, protestant and catholics, to endeavour to the utmost of my power to avert a measure which, I think, whatever may be the final result, must deluge the kingdom with blood, and will most probably in the end, compel measures of extreme violence on the part of the conquerors against the conquered & prevent the quiet settlement of the country for many many years—I have now in a considerable degree relieved my mind from a load which has pressed heavily upon me. I have stated to you fairly & openly my sentiments & I trust you will receive them with the openess & candour with which they are given. If they should give you offence I shall be sorry for it, but I should be more sorry if, at a future period, you should have to accuse me of having con-

same time Addington's attitude was, doubtless, that summed up by his biographer:

When it is considered that, as Minister, he was conscious of no error against the public interests; that he retained the perfect confidence of the King and the parliament; that during his administration

cealed them. I am very little disposed to change the feelings of affection & regard which I have once indulged, and should be extremely sorry that you should ever find me otherwise than, with the sincerest friendship & esteem

"My dear Sir,

"your faithful humble servant

"REDESDALE"

"The Rt H^{ble} Wm Pitt."

"ALBEMARLE ST.

"April 17, 1803

"MY DEAR SIR:

"The frankness of your answer to the letter which I took the liberty of addressing to you convinces me that I did not improperly confide in your friendship when I ventured to remonstrate so freely with you. Perhaps I view the result of what you have proposed in too strong a light; & you may think consequences may not follow, which I think unavoidable. On one point I will venture to answer your letter. I believe those who have retained the offices which they held during your administration, & who have since accepted office, or taken other offices instead of those which they before had, will not, in general complain of any measure personally affecting them, if they can consider it as to be for *the purpose of forwarding a play* of arrangement calculated to prove agreement equal to encounter the difficulties suggested in your letter. I have reason to believe that most of them would be disposed to submit cheerfully to such a plan. But the soreness which you have attributed to them arises from their concurring that they are to be removed at the suggestion of others, to gratify a spleen conceived against them because, acting in conformity to what you led them to suppose to be your wishes, they have endeavoured to support a government to which you also gave your support, & which they thought it was your wish to sustain. They feel sore at an attempt to punish them for complying with what they supposed to be your wishes & at the reflexion that this is to be done at the suggestion of those whom they considered as acting against your wishes, in refusing to the administration that support which you gave. With respect to the Catholic question, some things which dropped from you led me to suppose that the plan suggested was not abandoned & when I reflected that *all* those who had quitted office avowedly for no reason but because that measure had been opposed, were to return to office, after a pledge not to do so without a resolution to carry the measure, if in their power, I thought, as I believe the world will think, that in all probability the measure was fully resolved upon; & I consider it as a duty which I owed to you to state to you, explicitly, my sentiments on that subject, that you might act accordingly with respect to me.

"I am sorry that I have taken up so much of your time by engaging you in a correspondence which must be irksome to you. I desire no answer to this letter. I sincerely wish to have the advantage of your publick services and there is no sacrifice which I could not cheerfully make to obtain it. I shall lament for your sake, if they are not to be obtained but upon terms which I think will lessen you in the esteem of the publick & so far will lessen your power to do good.

"With sincere esteem & regard I trust I shall always be

"My dear Sir,

"Your faithful & humble servant

"REDESDALE."

the country had enjoyed unusual prosperity, and the finances been placed in a most satisfactory condition, there were, assuredly, no reasonable grounds for the suspicions so incessantly repeated by a small section of the preceding government, that he would not be found equal to the crisis, and that Mr. Pitt was the only man competent to conduct the impending war.[39]

The Addington ministry expected to carry on as usual. The only question was which of three possible choices Pitt would adopt: support the ministry without taking office; retire to Walmer Castle and remain neutral; or go into active opposition.

Actually within the next few months Pitt adopted all three choices at one time or another. Such an attitude on his part does not necessarily indicate vacillation, but is explained rather by the changed conditions which resulted from the outbreak of war with France. The hopes of Addington and the peace-loving part of the nation had been severely disappointed in the results of the Treaty of Amiens. Bonaparte, who assumed the title of Napoleon in August 1802, had, as had been noted earlier in the chapter, adopted such tactics as to make many people in the country doubt if peace could be of long duration. It is unnecessary at this point to attempt to apportion the relative blame of Great Britain and France. Addington and Foreign Secretary Hawkesbury were delighted at having ended the war, and rather than endanger this new and dearly purchased peace appeared willing for some months after the signing of the Treaty of Amiens to allow Napoleon to continue his encroachments on Switzerland, Italy, and Holland. The growing uneasiness in the country, the warnings of George III who had had little confidence that the Peace of 1802 would last, and the continued aggressiveness of Napoleon, however, caused the ministry, with some reluctance, to abandon its aloof attitude. The publication on January 30 of the famous report of Colonel Sebastiani, one of Napoleon's commercial commissioners, in which the weakness of Turkey was stressed and the ease with which Egypt could be conquered was emphasized, finally goaded Addington and Hawkesbury into action. Steps were taken to strengthen the Army and the Navy, and Parliament readily agreed to an increase of forces. But such warnings had no effect on Napoleon. He had evidently become convinced that the Addington ministry did not deserve serious consideration. The same feeling in England had caused widespread dissatisfaction with the government and was in

[39] Pellew, *op. cit.*, II, 117.

part responsible for Addington's negotiations with Pitt in March and April.

Thus a variety of causes combined to make Addington and Hawkesbury suddenly take a very stiff attitude toward France in place of the cautious hands-off policy which had become so unpopular at home. The ministers felt that it was necessary to adopt an abnormally uncompromising stand in order to convince Napoleon that he was wrong in thinking that they would allow him to continue his aggressive policy unchecked; to prove to the English people that their interests would not be sacrificed through vacillation and indecision; and to revive the drooping spirits of their followers in Parliament. In his communication of April 3, 1803, Hawkesbury notified the French government that his country desired a settlement on the following bases: Great Britain to retain Malta, to acknowledge the kingdom of Etruria and the Ligurian and Italian republics, and to indemnify the Knights of St. John; and France to retain Elba, to evacuate Switzerland and the Dutch Netherlands, and to indemnify the King of Sardinia.[40] Hawkesbury slightly weakened this vigorous action by suggesting that if the French government found these demands impracticable it should offer some alternative or equivalent security for England. When the French government made clear to Whitworth, the British ambassador in France, that the fundamental question at stake was its unwillingness to permit Great Britain to secure a possession in the Mediterranean, the Addington ministry resolved to take vigorous action at once. Urged on by the King, by public opinion, by the criticisms of the New Opposition in Parliament, by the knowledge that if war came it would be more advantageous for Great Britain to strike before the navies of Napoleon and his more or less willing allies should be increased, and by personal resentment against Napoleon, whom they had now come to hate and distrust, the ministers sent what was virtually an ultimatum to France. On April 23 Hawkesbury instructed Whitworth to demand the possession of Malta for ten years and certain other concessions concerning the Netherlands, Switzerland, and Italy. If these terms were not accepted in seven days by the French government, the ambassador was to leave Paris. After various expedients were attempted to delay his departure without specifically answering the ultimatum, Whitworth left Paris on May 12. The decisive factor in Napoleon's refusal may have been his belief that

[40] *The Cambridge History of British Foreign Policy,* I, 320.

the Russian Tsar intended to support France in the Maltese affair. On May 18 Great Britain declared war on France.

Naturally the government was blamed for being too inflexible at the end, for being too naive and trusting since 1801, and for not taking advantage of the Tsar's offer of mediation. Addington, the New and Old Opposition, the King, and the independent members of Parliament were all anxious to find out whether Pitt's political position would be changed by the outbreak of the war with France. They received their answer in part when, on May 23, Pitt returned to his seat in the Commons and made what many of his friends and enemies considered to be the greatest speech of his life.[41] He stressed the necessity of carrying on the war with vigor and the value of national unity; but he omitted to praise the efforts of the ministers in handling the foreign situation or in preparing for the war. According to skilled observers this omission was so obvious that in the minds of the ministers and their followers it more than offset the brilliant plea for a vigorous prosecution of the war. Thus Pitt was careful to distinguish his point of view from that of the ministers and of the Old and New Opposition. Fox still believed that France was essentially in the right and favored peace; while Grenville and his followers firmly believed in the war, but insisted that if it were to be conducted successfully a new and competent ministry must supplant the present incompetent one.

When Addington failed to strengthen his ministry by the addition of Pitt, he induced Tierney to join the government as Treasurer of the Navy. This appointment was bound to be offensive both to Fox and his followers and to Pitt. When the Whigs seceded from Parliament in 1797 Tierney had refused to remain away, and as a result of having little competition he became acknowledged as the leader of an opposition which, as the wits said, could go home in a single coach. In the course of the performance of these duties in 1798 he became involved in a quarrel with Pitt which led to a duel between the two. Addington had been most

[41] J. H. Rose, *op. cit.,* II, 488, cites the testimony of Sir Samuel Romilly and Spencer Stanhope on the excellence of the speech. Sheridan's letter to Lady Bessborough quoted in Walter Sichel, *Sheridan* (London, 1909), II, 440, may refer to this speech. The passage in question states that Grey spoke under a great disadvantage because he rose "immediately after one of the most brilliant and magnificent pieces of declamation that ever fell from that rascal Pitt's lips.—Detesting the Dog, as I do, I cannot withhold this just tribute to the Scoundrel's talents. I could not help often lamenting in the course of his harangue, what a pity it is that he has not a particle of honesty in him." A less flattering version of the speech is given in Pellew, *op. cit.,* II, 135-36.

appreciative both of Tierney's Parliamentary talents and of his speeches in support of the ministry from 1801 to 1803, but he must have realized that this appointment would give offense to both Pitt and Fox.

Whether or not Pitt considered this an overt act and allowed it to influence his attitude toward the ministry is, of course, difficult to decide. On May 23, as already noted, he avoided either criticizing or praising the ministers; on June 1 the government announced the appointment of Tierney; and on June 3 he took an action of direct hostility to the government. Colonel Patten on that day moved a series of resolutions censuring the ministers for the ineffective manner in which they had resisted the aggressions of France. Pitt evidently did not wish to take the identical stand adopted by any other group. Further, he had no desire either to strengthen the position of the government by unqualified opposition to Patten's motion or to break definitely with Addington. The Prime Minister's version of the affair was that Pitt gave Patten his pledge to support the motion and then, regretting his promise, attempted to save his face by a compromise. Using Melville as a messenger, Pitt, following the speech and motion of Patten, offered to move the orders of the day. Addington, according to his own testimony, indignantly refused this offer and declared to Melville: "Nothing shall induce me to remain in power a single day after an indirect censure has been passed on the government."[42] The unwillingness of Addington to consent to this action was twofold: it would have implied that the ministry was dependent for its existence on Pitt; and it would have deprived the government of the opportunity of removing the sting of the indirect censure by a negative vote on the measure. Thus Pitt was faced with a series of unpleasant choices: he could support Patten's motion; he could oppose this motion; he could move the orders of the day; or he could return to Walmer Castle. He decided on the third as the least unsatisfactory of the four. Normally, moving the orders of the day was a harmless procedure and was generally used to sweep aside irrelevant business; but under the circumstances Addington considered this action of Pitt one of hostility.

After Patten had made his motion, Mr. T. Grenville spoke for more than two hours, and was answered by Addington at great length. Pitt then stated that he could neither go so far as Gren-

42 Pellew, op. cit., II, 138.

ville nor accept entirely the explanations offered by the government. Since the Crown still had confidence in the present ministers, he felt that it would be unwise to drive them out of office by a vote of censure because confusion and ineffective conduct of the war would be the natural result; and that under the circumstances the best thing for the House to do would be to take up military and financial problems. Pitt made clear his realization of the fact that the ministers would be mortified by allowing the question to remain undecided, but he was convinced that under existing conditions sacrifices must be made. His solution was to move the orders of the day, but this motion was defeated 335 to 58. Addington, Fox, and Grenville and their followers all voted against the motion, which indicated that the ministry and the Old and New Opposition all insisted on a showdown. Before the vote on Patten's resolution was taken, Pitt and Fox and several of their respective friends departed. Patten's motion was then defeated by 275 to 34.[43]

On the strength of these two divisions an ingenious estimate of the strength of the various groups in Parliament was worked out by a contemporary pamphleteer:[44]

> The Ministers on the last division 275
> Mr. Pitt and his friends who left the House previous to that division 56
> The Grenville party who divided for Mr. Patten's resolutions 34
> Mr. Fox and his friends, to make up the number in the first division 24
> ────
> 389

Had Mr. Pitt and Mr. Fox joined the Grenvilles in the second division, there would have been:

> For the resolutions 114
> Against them 275

Without doubt the outcome of these two divisions was to Addington as satisfactory as any during his entire ministry. To George III the news came as a splendid birthday present and he warmly congratulated Addington in a letter which ended in a strain very reminiscent of his state of mind during the crisis of 1783–84:

[43] *Parliamentary History*, XXXVI, 1570.
[44] Pellew, *op. cit.*, II, 142.

"as these events prove the real sense of the House of Commons, and that parliament truly means support to the executive power, not to faction."[45] The first serious assault on the Addington ministry failed because the three opposition groups did not present a united front and because the great mass of the members of the House of Commons remained loyal to the King's government.

Pitt, true to character, devoted some time during the remainder of the session to a conscientious examination of the measures of the government. For example, he approved of the proposed budget but did not speak in its favor in the House of Commons; and he expressed satisfaction with the principles of the Additional Force Bill and of the Military Service Bill. Despite this façade of cordial support, however, the relations between Pitt and Addington were fundamentally tense and really bitter, as indicated by the clash on July 13 over details of the Property Duty Bill when according to the Speaker "words of considerable asperity, or rather language in a tone of asperity, passed from Mr. Pitt toward Mr. Addington."[46] The session of Parliament came to an end on August 12, and in the interval before the opening of the next one on November 22 the breach between the two men was further widened by a furious pamphlet war in which partisan writers discussed the relative merits of their characters, services, and abilities.

In carrying on the war with France the Addington ministry found its fundamental problems to be those of blockading the French and Dutch fleets and of preparing the army and militia against invasions by Napoleon. When war was declared on May 18 it was discovered that peace economies had affected the efficiency of the British Navy; but, as Addington insisted then and in later years, it was better prepared than the French navy. At the head of the Admiralty, Lord St. Vincent, despite criticisms of his administration and unwise economies, carried out a strict and on the whole effective blockade of the ports of the enemy. This applied to both the French and Dutch fleets and to the Atlantic and Mediterranean spheres. The military problem was a more serious one because of the vast superiority of the French army over the English, and the necessity of providing for some defense against the French forces in case Napoleon succeeded in evading the British Navy and landing troops on the south or east coasts. When the war broke out about 105,000 regular soldiers and some 70,000

45 *Ibid.*, p. 143.   46 *Colchester Diary,* I, 432.

militia were available. The ministry decided to keep part of the
regular army for offensive purposes and to rely on an army of
reserve of 50,000 and volunteers for defense in case of invasion.
The army of reserve as provided for in a measure introduced by
Charles Yorke, Secretary of War, did not prove a success; for by
December of 1803 it numbered only 27,500. It was to the raising
and training of volunteers, however, that the government devoted
its attention, and to these volunteers it pinned its hopes in case of
invasion. Also it was this phase of the activities of the ministry
that came in for the most criticism from the New Opposition. If
Englishmen were reluctant to become members of the army of
reserve, they showed no such diffidence in joining the volunteers.
The ministers were even more embarrassed by the number of
volunteers placed at its disposal than by the failure of the army of
reserve to reach its expected figures. At the end of the year the
340,000 volunteers who were enrolled presented many problems
which the government had not foreseen. It was found impossible
to arm all of them, even though some who could not be provided
with muskets were given pikes. Yet the burst of patriotism which
swept representatives of so many different social classes into
service was not so fervent that reservations such as the rights to
elect their own officers and to resign were not insisted upon.[47] On
the whole, Addington had undertaken a difficult problem which he
and his colleagues did not handle very effectively. When he faced
Parliament again, the Prime Minister was certain to be asked embarrassing questions by the New Opposition headed by Grenville
and Windham and perhaps by Pitt and Fox and their followers.

Despite the fact that the Grenville, Pitt, and Fox factions all
admitted that Addington had handled affairs in a very unsatisfactory manner since Parliament had risen in August, they had
not been able to reach an agreement which would make joint action
possible. The leader in this attempt to secure a united front was
Grenville, who, from early in Addington's ministry, had with his
followers furnished the only consistent and relentless opposition.
His efforts to convince Pitt that they should take joint action
against Addington had been intensified during the interval from
August to November; but they were not successful. Pitt was willing to admit that the ministry had handled affairs badly; but he
could not, for a variety of reasons, bring himself to adopt the

47 A. F. Fremantle, *op. cit.,* pp. 382–83.

point of view which Grenville desired: he was pledged to support
the ministry; he had given Addington and other ministers advice,
which to a certain extent they had followed, on many of the measures which the New Opposition disliked; he was averse to taking
any action which would so alienate George III that it would prevent him from taking office if an opportunity presented itself;
and he was reluctant to acquiesce so late in the game in a policy
which had been inaugurated and carried on for so long a time by
other men. On the other hand, he found it increasingly difficult to
find a satisfactory answer to the pleadings of his friends and a
reasonable explanation for the actions of the ministry. Thus loyalty and pride on one side struggled against personal ambition and
sincere patriotism on the other.

The Old Opposition did not offer so good a target for Grenville as did Pitt, since Fox had supported Addington's peace efforts
because they represented the very policy which he had advocated
for several years. The chief objections which Fox had to the
Addington ministry came with the renewal of the war, and hence
his criticisms were aimed more at the failure of the government to
maintain peace than at its failure to carry on the war vigorously.
The friends of the Prince of Wales, notably Sheridan and Erskine,
had been fairly close to Addington personally and had supported
some of the measures of the ministers; and neither the Prince nor
his friends felt any warm personal regard for Grenville. Thus
both political principles and personal feelings tended to prevent an
immediate understanding between the New Opposition and the
Old Opposition. In the case of Pitt neither of these two obstacles
was present, for it was largely a matter of divided loyalty that
kept him from joining Grenville.

The failure of Grenville to reach an agreement with either Pitt
or Fox made the sittings of Parliament from November 22 until
the Christmas recess, which began on December 20, easier for
Addington than they otherwise would have been. Pitt's reply of
December 9 to Windham's attack on the handling of the volunteers by the government was especially gratifying to the Prime
Minister. The adjournment from December 20, 1803, until February 1, 1804, gave the sorely pressed Addington another breathing spell. Before Parliament assembled, however, another serious
question arose. George III became ill in January, and a recurrence
of his troubles of 1788–89 and 1801 was feared. The incapacitation of the King played an important part in the fall of the Ad-

dington ministry. The unfortunate Prime Minister not only had the additional personal worries that resulted from the serious condition of a sovereign whom he both loved and respected, but he missed the encouragement and advice of his royal master at a time when both were sorely needed.

Immediately before Parliament met on February 1, 1804, Grenville renewed his efforts to secure a working agreement with both Pitt and Fox. Grenville explained to them that he believed two principles of action were necessary if the country were to be saved:

First, that the Government which now exists is manifestly incapable of carrying on the public business in such a manner as the crisis requires; and that persons sincerely entertaining that opinion are bound to avow and actively pursue it. And secondly, that if now, or hereafter, there should arise any question of forming a new Government, the wishes and endeavours of all who mean well to the country should be directed to the establishment of an administration comprehending as large a proportion as possible of the weight, talents, and character to be found in public men of all descriptions, and without any exception. To this was added our decided opinion that it was not necessary, for the purpose of acting on these two principles, to extend the communication to any other matters whatever; or to enter into details of any kind not relating to the Parliamentary business which may from time to time be brought forward. And, above all, that anything leading to compromises of former opinions, or to engagements for future arrangements, was to be carefully avoided, in order that it might be, at all times, and with the strictest truth, distinctly and publicly denied.[48]

Pitt's reaction to this plan is given in a letter written at Walmer Castle on February 4:

I confess that the more I reflect on the subject, the more I regret that the view you form of what is incumbent upon you leads you to embark in a system in which I find it quite impossible to concur, and which, I fear, will not be productive of any increased credit to yourselves, or any advantage to the public. The immediate effect of an active opposition will be to harrass a Government confessedly not very strong nor vigorous in itself, and in a situation of the country most critical, with the constant distraction of Parliamentary warfare. Such a line, though conducted by the first talents and abilities, will I am confident, not be supported by any strength of numbers in Parliament, nor by public opinion. It will therefore have very little chance of accomplishing its object of changing the Administration,

[48] *Dropmore Papers*, VII, 211-12.

and certainly none of doing so in time to afford the country the benefit of abler counsels to meet the difficulties in the present crisis. Those very difficulties it will in the meanwhile certainly aggravate; and even if, sooner or later, it should make a change necessary, I am afraid that instead of leading to the establishment of a comprehensive Administration (such as you describe) it will tend to render the attainment of that object more difficult if not impossible. Whatever unfavourable impression may at any time have existed in the highest quarter towards any of the parties engaged in such a system, will, of course, be strengthened and confirmed; and the natural consequence will be a determination, even in case of a change being found necessary, to put, if possible, a negative on them, in forming a new Government. In the event of such being the state of things, I cannot help foreseeing great mischief to the public, and the source of great uneasiness and embarrassment personally to myself; as nothing is more probable than that a call might then be made upon me which I should feel it impossible to decline, and that I should have no means either of forming that comprehensive Government which I agree with you in thinking most desirable, or of obtaining the assistance of those with whom, from public and private feelings, it has been the greatest happiness to me to act during almost the whole of my political life.[49]

Pitt then concluded that he must continue his old "character" part of giving his opinion on the individual merits of each measure proposed by the government and of avoiding all attempts to embarrass the ministry by systematic opposition.

The reaction of Fox to the proposals for a united opposition was very different from that of Pitt. After relating to his friend General Fitzpatrick the terms suggested by the Grenvilles, he concluded:

My answer was that, I thought with them upon all the subjects discussed, and that I felt no repugnance to agree to the proposal, at least in some degree, but that I must have some days before I could answer. Now what is your advice? If Grey would come to town to stay and engage heartily, (of which, if he would come, I have no doubt,) perhaps it would be right to say *yes*, perhaps it is *right* even now. But the inconvenience is terrible, for to do the thing thoroughly without a stay in London is impossible, and then expense, interruption to history, etc. etc., where after all there is no chance of success; it is very hard to encounter all this. Suppose I were to answer that I will give them all occasional help in my power, but that I cannot alter my plan of life so as to give a regular attendance in Parliament, and that I am afraid Grey can hardly be induced to come up. I must

[49] *Ibid.*, p. 213.

finish now, though I have omitted several circumstances, and among others a very important one, that our old friend sees the possibility, nay the probability, that if we succeed in ousting the Doctor, P. may return to power, and after having proposed terms in vain to some of the *Opposition,* may put himself at the head of the present Administration, or one like it, and this is admitted to be an objection to the plan. I do not feel this so much as he does, but many others will.[50]

In these three quotations is to be found the history of the remaining months of the Addington ministry. All three men run true to form in the expression of opinion. To Grenville the important thing was for all true patriots and statesmen to stand together and rid the country of a government whose weakness was a menace to the nation; and to him the best method was to combine all Parliamentary talent outside the ministry and by every variety of attack to end this menace as soon as it was humanly possible and to substitute a government based on the best individuals available. To Pitt the important thing was to adhere to his own constitutional principles and to avoid acting in such a way that the King would refuse to ask him to form another ministry when the Addington government toppled. To Fox the important thing was to strike a blow to secure the overthrow of the present ministry and the substitution of another made up of the best minds of the country including, perhaps, himself and some of his friends, provided such a procedure did not cut in too seriously on his pleasant life at St. Ann's Hill. Of the three the stand by Grenville appears most admirable both from the point of view of political sagacity and of personal unselfishness. He had certain clear-cut principles in which he believed implicitly and a well-planned campaign to put them into practice.

The triple attack on Addington was slow in getting under way. The explanation, probably, is based on the illness of the King, the attitude of Pitt, and the postponement of the final acquiescence of Fox to the proposals of Grenville. Furthermore, the three-headed opposition did not present a united front on arguments, since in many instances the point of view of Pitt, Grenville, Fox, or one of their respective followers was closer to that of the government than to other members of the "co-operating" group. The issue was really a very simple one: Addington, it was firmly believed, did not have the ability to lead the country in so danger-

[50] Lord John Russell, *Memorials and Correspondence of Charles James Fox* (London, 1853–1857), IV, 18–19.

ous a situation. The three great opposition leaders all agreed that Addington must be forced to resign; but once that was accomplished they all realized that the next step to be taken might find them hopelessly at odds. They were all aware that a "strong" government was needed, but they did not necessarily agree upon what constituted one. During February and March the King's illness and the chance that temporary or permanent insanity might result in a regency had marked influence on both the House of Commons and the Whig friends of the Prince of Wales. Many members of Parliament appear to have continued their support of the Addington ministry because they were unwilling to embarrass a badly harassed ministry during such a period of uncertainty. The chance of the King's incapacitation once more aroused the hopes of the friends of the Prince of Wales that they might come into power if the latter were made regent even under the severe restrictions which Pitt had determined to apply in the crisis of 1788–89. At this time the Earl of Moira, Commander of Forces in Scotland, was the favorite of the Prince of Wales, and a conversation which Mr. Charles Hope, the Lord Advocate, had with Moira and which he related to Lord Melville indicated that the Prince intended to place the Earl at the head of the government in case of a regency.[51] When informed of this matter by Melville, Pitt expressed some skepticism concerning the report that Moira was to head a ministry and pointed out that he had good reasons to believe that Fox expected to have the government placed in his hands by the Prince in case of a regency.[52]

Although the attack on Addington was slow in getting under way during February, the position of the opposition was stronger at the end of the month than at the beginning, because Fox and his friends had accepted the offer of Grenville to "co-operate"; and although Pitt still refused to join the other two groups, he did, during the debate on the Volunteer Consolidation Bill, criticize the ministry on February 27 for lack of vigor. On March 15, however, Pitt himself led the attack on the government by moving for papers on the naval defense of the country. In the course of his speech he severely criticized the Admiralty. The specific criticisms of the ministry during the weeks that followed turned almost entirely on Addington's military, naval, and financial meas-

[51] *Secret Correspondence Connected with Mr. Pitt's Return to Office in 1804* (London, 1852), pp. 5–10.
[52] *Ibid.*, pp. 11–12.

ures. The debates are not worth following in detail, because attacks on minute failures of the government in these three spheres of activity were not the fundamental thing at stake. In the light of history, of the handling of similar situations from 1793 to 1801, and of Pitt's advice to the ministers many of their vigorously criticized measures were quite justifiable; but this is to approach the problem of the opposition to Addington from the wrong angle. The three groups held that the present ministry was not capable of carrying on the war in a satisfactory fashion, and they were reduced to minute and often unjustifiable criticism in order to secure their main objective. Although the Grenvilles and Fox supported Pitt in his motion, the followers of the Prince of Wales, headed by Sheridan, voted with the ministry. The motion was beaten by 201 to 130.[53]

No more concentrated attacks were made on the government until Parliament reassembled, after the Easter recess, on April 5. During this interval Pitt made up his mind definitely, or at least placed his decision on paper, as to the tactics he should pursue in the immediate future. His long letter of March 29 to Lord Melville is one of the most revealing documents which he penned during his entire political life. First he dealt with Melville's query as to the stand he would take if a regency resulted from the King's continued illness and the Prince of Wales carried out the plan to place Moira at the head of a new government. Considering Pitt's professed love of country, Melville may have thought he would be willing to serve in a ministry of the best minds under the conditions laid down by Moira in his conversation with Hope. If Melville held any such views he was speedily disillusioned for Pitt wrote:

> You will not I think wonder at my saying that I do not see how, under any circumstances, I can creditably or usefully consent to take part in any Government without being at the head of it; and I should be very sorry that either Lord Moira, or, through him, the Prince, should suppose that there is any chance of my changing my opinion on this point.[54]

In short, to Pitt a strong government meant one in which he was the head, and patriotism meant willingness to serve only under

---

[53] *Hansard's Parliamentary Debates* (first series, London, 1806–1820), I, 927.

[54] *Secret Correspondence*, p. 12.

these conditions. That Pitt was absolutely sincere there can be no reasonable doubt; but this very fact shows the limitations of his public spirit and the exaggerated value which he placed on his own services. Even more significant is his attitude toward bringing in able men who had incurred the wrath of the King. It is difficult to see how anyone who reads this letter to Lord Melville could be astonished at the weakness of the ministry Pitt formed in May or at his acquiescence in the exclusion of Fox by George III. Obviously Pitt was interested chiefly in his own restoration to the post of First Lord of the Treasury, and he was unwilling to take any action which would not bring him nearer or which would delay his entrance into the promised land. He did not wish to injure his chances even by heading a strong ministry under a regency, because, as he stated:

Much as I wish a strong government, and prepared as I am for that purpose to put aside the recollection of former differences, if a cordial union can be formed on public grounds for the future, I still should feel a great doubt whether it would be right during the King's illness, and while any reasonable chance exists of his recovery, to form any connexion which might preclude him from a fair option in forming an administration, whenever he might resume the exercise of his authority.[55]

This section seems to mean that Pitt did not care to risk his future with George III by forming a "strong" government with the friends of the Prince of Wales. If George III did not recover, Pitt had no future as a prime minister; hence his only chance was to gamble on the survival of his royal master and not to involve himself with the friends of the Prince of Wales in such a manner as to make himself unacceptable when the time came to choose a successor to Addington. Assuming then that the King would recover quickly, and being convinced that the present government could not last much longer and that every week its existence was protracted increased the danger to the country, Pitt declared:

I have therefore satisfied myself that the time is near at hand at which if a change does not originate from the Ministers themselves, or from the King, I can no longer be justified in not publicly declaring my opinion, and endeavouring by Parliamentary measures to give it effect. My present notion therefore is to take the first moment after the present recess, at which the state of the King's health will admit of such a step, to write a letter to His Majesty stating to him

[55] *Ibid.*, pp. 12–13.

the grounds of my opinion, explaining the dangers which I think threaten his Crown and his people from the continuance of his present Government, and representing to him the urgent necessity of a speedy change. From what I have already said in a former part of this letter, you will not be surprised at my saying that the change to which I should point as most beneficial would be one which would introduce precisely the same description of Government as I think desirable in the other event of a Regency. From various considerations, however, and still more from this last illness, I feel that a proposal to take a share in his councils persons against whom he has long entertained such strong and natural objections ought never to be made to him, but in such a manner as to leave him a free option, and to convince him that if he cannot be sincerely convinced of its expediency, there is not a wish to force it upon him. I should, therefore, at the same time, let His Majesty understand distinctly, that if after considering the subject he resolved to exclude the friends both of Mr. Fox and Lord Grenville, but wished to call upon me to form a Government without them, I should be ready to do so as well as I could from amongst my own immediate friends, united with the most capable and unexceptionable persons of the present Government; but of course excluding many of them, and above all, Addington himself, and Lord Vincent.[56]

Pitt then pointed out to Melville that, from what they both knew of the character of the King, the tactics outlined were most likely to succeed in convincing His Majesty of the advantage which he personally and the country would derive from the extinction of parties and the establishment of an able ministry. Pitt added that if the King did not listen to this proposal he would have no hesitation in taking such a stand in Parliament as would bring about the desired end. So far as immediate action in the House of Commons was concerned, Pitt intended to follow up the attack on the Navy by one on public defense in which he expected the support of Fox and his friends. This support Pitt was careful to make clear to Melville did not commit him to do anything for Fox, since he insisted that the latter was "certainly prepared to support a question of the nature I have stated, under the full knowledge that if the result produces the removal of the present Government, I hold myself at full liberty to form a new one without reference to him."[57]

This very revealing letter shows that Pitt had made up his mind on the tactics he should adopt, just as Grenville had deter-

---

[56] *Secret Correspondence,* pp. 13-15.   [57] *Ibid.,* pp. 15-16.

mined his in January and Fox his in February. Further, it takes
the edge off the negotiations between the King and Pitt in May;
for it is obvious that Pitt, for weeks before his interview with
George III, was willing to resume office without either Grenville
or Fox. Thus the details of the Parliamentary attack on Addington by the three wings of the opposition and the steps leading to
Pitt's taking office merely follow the plan outlined to Melville.

But if Pitt's letter to Melville was prophetic of the course of
events in the weeks that followed, the latter's answer was equally
so in pointing out the pitfalls in the plan of the former to take
office without the support of Fox and Grenville. Melville insisted
that a ministry of all talents was necessary not only to suspend
political animosities and to give the country the advantage of its
experience and vigor but also in order to encourage foreign
countries to form alliances with Great Britain. Under these circumstances Melville strongly advised Pitt to make every effort to
include Fox and Grenville and, in case of failure, to make it clear
that such an arrangement was only temporary and that at the first
possible opportunity both would be admitted to the government.
Melville then pointed out with unerring accuracy exactly what the
result would be in case Pitt declined to follow such a plan:

If a Government is formed on the narrow scale without such an
explanation and understanding, I myself feel strongly, and entreat
you to consider with attention, whether the Government formed on
the narrow scale would be much better than the present; and in the
mean time all the jealousies and heartburnings of party spirit would
be lurking, and ready to burst out the first favourable moment, and
would most certainly do so whenever the King's death or return of
illness afforded the opening for it.[58]

Obviously it was apparent to Melville, as it must have been to
many others, that the mere substitution of Pitt for Addington was
not an adequate solution. It was a major error on the part of Pitt
that he conscientiously believed that the fundamental change
needed was his own restoration to the post of First Lord of the
Treasury and that other additions to the government were of only
second-rate importance.

From April 11 to 25 a series of divisions which decided the
fate of the government took place in both houses. The first of
these in the Commons were on Yorke's Irish Militia Augmenta-

[58] *Ibid.*, pp. 20–21.

tion Bill. The motion for committal of the bill on April 11 was carried by 94 to 37;[59] and on the 16th the third reading by 128 to 107.[60] Pitt voted with the minority on the third reading but neither spoke nor voted on the 11th. In the House of Lords the government actually found itself in a minority of one on April 19 as a result of refusing papers in reference to a charge made by Lord Carlisle that it had been tardy in sending intelligence of the war to the admiral in India. The important divisions, however, occurred in the House of Commons on April 23 and 25. Fox's motion relative to the defense of the country, which was practically one of no confidence in the ministry, resulted in a full-dress debate in which Pitt attacked the ministry with ill-concealed sarcasm and asperity. The motion was beaten by 256 to 204.[61] The size of the opposition vote was due to the fact that not only the followers of Grenville, Fox, and Pitt combined but they were joined by those of the Prince of Wales who in earlier divisions had usually supported Addington. Two days later Pitt opposed going into committee to consider the bill for suspending the Army of Reserve Act, and spoke at some length on his own plan for maintaining the reserve army. In the division which followed it was voted by 240 to 203 to go into committee on this bill. When Addington's majority fell to 37 he felt that there was little use in carrying on in face of the opposition of Pitt, Fox, Grenville, and the followers of the Prince of Wales.

Before Pitt joined in the attacks of April 23 and 25 he had taken steps to acquaint the King with his intentions. George III was recovering from his serious illness at this time and Pitt, evidently because he was not aware of the exact state of the King's health and because he did not care to be accused of communicating with his sovereign in a secret fashion while out of office, requested Lord Chancellor Eldon to deliver his message. This letter was written on April 21 and delivered to the King by Lord Eldon on the 27th. Thus in the interval between the writing and delivery of the communication Pitt had taken the action which he stated therein to be, in his opinion, so necessary. In the first part of the letter he took great pains to show that he had supported the present ministers cordially so long as it was honestly possible for him to do so; that when he could no longer approve of the policies and

[59] *Hansard's Parliamentary Debates,* II, 104.
[60] *Ibid.,* p. 139.
[61] *Ibid.,* p. 249.

conduct of the government he had abstained from joining any system of opposition; and that since the commencement of the war, as a private individual, he had attempted to supply what he considered to be important omissions. But, concluded Pitt:

The experience of now nearly twelve months, and the observation of all the different measures which have been suggested or adopted by Government, and of the mode in which they have been executed, have at length impressed me with a full conviction that while the administration remains in its present shape, and particularly under the direction of the person now holding the chief place in it, every attempt to provide adequately and effectually for the public defence, and for meeting the extraordinary and unprecedented efforts of the enemy, will be fruitless.[62]

Having condemned the ministry in such unsparing terms and having indicated that he intended to regulate his conduct in Parliament by these opinions, Pitt might have left George III with the impression that this letter was a declaration of war, had he not added the final sentence:

I trust your Majesty will pardon me if I venture to add the assurance that, whatever may be the course of public affairs, and whatever may be my own personal opinion respecting the system of government which would be most advisable in the present state of the country and of political parties, it will be my determination to avoid committing myself to any engagement the effects of which would be likely to occasion, in any contingency, a sentiment of dissatisfaction or uneasiness in your Majesty's mind.[63]

Even though George III's mind had been still somewhat deranged, it is unlikely that he would have overlooked the significant points in Pitt's letter. Despite the carefully guarded language it made clear that: first, he intended to attack the ministry until Addington resigned; second, he believed a government of all the talents should replace the present one; and, third, he would for the sake of the King form a ministry without Fox and Grenville.

That the Foxites expected such actions from Pitt is clear from the remark which one of them made: "We are the pioneers, digging the foundations; but Mr. Pitt will be the architect to build the House, and to inhabit it."[64] It seems equally clear, however,

[62] Earl Stanhope, *Life of the Right Honourable William Pitt* (London, 1861–62), IV, ii–iii.

[63] *Ibid.*, p. iii.

[64] *Colchester Diary*, I, 496–97.

that Pitt did not inform either the Foxites or the Grenvilles of the communication which he sent to the King.

Before Eldon presented Pitt's letter of April 21 to the King on the 27th, Addington already had made up his mind to resign. It appears that he arrived at this determination after the division of the 25th and that he informed George III of his intention on the 26th. The King was alarmed and dismayed at the news, for he had no desire to part with Addington. His first instincts were to fight vigorously as he had done earlier in his reign with all the resources at his command. Addington summed up this state of mind in conversation on April 29 with Abbot, the Speaker of the House of Commons:

> The King dreads a defeat of his Ministry in Parliament as the forerunner of a Regency. To keep his health safe is the cause of the country. At present, if necessary, he may still change his Ministry without being driven to it by a forced junction of the three opposi- tions. Mr. Pitt is not now pledged to any men; but the King is ready to avert this by the utmost exercise of his authority, if that can, all things considered succeed; and Parliament would be dissolved now, if the state of business and public affairs did not preclude that meas- ure. It is now for consideration whether the battle can be fought with a certainty of success, or else the evil would be aggravated and pas- sions exasperated. The King is earnest to do for Mr. Addington everything and more than he can desire or may choose to accept; but to belong to any new arrangement Mr. Addington is resolved not to consent.[65]

Upon consideration George III saw the dangers of giving battle to Pitt, Grenville, and Fox when his own forces were led by Addington. Discretion, he was forced to admit, would in this case be wiser than the attempt to carry out his first and natural reac- tions to fight for the retention of the First Lord of the Treasury "by the utmost exercise of his authority." In reality the situation of the King was very much like the one he had faced at the time of the fall of the Shelburne ministry in 1783. A combination of Fox and North in 1783 and of Fox and Grenville in 1804 threat- ened what was to George III the greatest of all constitutional crimes, that of "forcing his closet." In both years Pitt was the deciding factor. In March 1783 he had refused to rescue the King, and consequently from April to December the latter suffered the humiliation of having an unwanted ministry in control of the

<hr>

[65] *Colchester Diary*, I, 498.

government. Although Pitt consented to become First Lord of the Treasury in December 1783, for two months he flirted with the idea of combining with Fox and excluding North. Had Pitt joined the Fox-North Coalition in 1783 the combination would for a certain length of time at least have become invincible. The same situation prevailed in April 1804. Pitt could by joining with Fox and Grenville not only overthrow Addington but insure for a period a government as distasteful to the King as the Fox-North ministry of 1783. The King felt greater pain at parting with Addington in 1804 than with Shelburne in 1783 because he was much fonder of the former personally and because his health was more precarious at the later date. Pitt could join the opposition with better grace in 1804 than in 1783, since by his own statement he had given the Addington ministry three years to make good while in 1783 he was Chancellor of the Exchequer in the Shelburne ministry which the Fox-North Coalition overthrew. All these points must have passed through the King's head as he surveyed the situation at the end of April and perused Pitt's letter of the 21st. Reluctant as he was to part with Addington and to take Pitt, the last paragraph in this letter clearly pointed the way out of the difficulties. All this is implicit in Addington's conversation with Abbot on April 30 in which he stated that "there was no want of zeal, attachment, or fidelity in the support of his present ministers, but a want of confidence in the success of the contest, according to the King's view of the state of affairs."[66] Once the King reached this state of mind the only real question concerned the terms upon which Pitt would take office.

On April 30 Eldon called on Pitt and informed him that the King wished to receive in writing his plan for a new administration. Pitt supplied this plan in a letter to the Lord Chancellor, written May 2, which was to be laid before the King. In this communication he expatiated at great length on the advantages to the country in domestic problems and foreign affairs of having no real opposition to the ministry in Parliament and in having the best minds at the head of the different departments of government.[67] Every line of the King's reply is significant:

The King has through the channel of the Lord Chancellor expressed to Mr. Pitt his approbation of that gentleman's sentiments of personal attachment to His Majesty, and his ardent desire to support

[66] *Ibid.*   [67] Stanhope, *op. cit.*, IV, iv–viii.

any measure that may be conducive to the real interest of the King or of his Royal Family; but at the same time it cannot but be lamented that Mr. Pitt should have taken so rooted a dislike to a gentleman who has the greatest claim to approbation from his King and country for his most diligent and able discharge of the duties of Speaker of the House of Commons for twelve years; and of his still more handsomely coming forward (When Mr. Pitt and some of his colleagues resigned their employments) to support his King and country when the most ill-digested and dangerous proposition was brought forward by the enemies of the Established Church. His Majesty has too good an opinion of Mr. Pitt to think he would have given his countenance to such a measure, had he weighed its tendency with that attention which a man of his judgment should call forth when the subject under consideration is of so serious a nature; but the King knows how strongly the then two Secretaries of State who resigned at that period had allied themselves to the Roman Catholics; the former, by his private correspondence with a former Lord Lieutenant of Ireland, showed that he was become the follower of all the wild ideas of Mr. Burke; and the other, from obstinacy, his usual director.

The King can never forget the wound that was intended at the Palladium of our Church Establishment, the Test Act, and the indelicacy, not to call it worse, of wanting His Majesty to forego his solemn Coronation Oath. He therefore here avows that he shall not be satisfied unless Mr. Pitt makes as strong assurances of his determination to support that wise law, as Mr. Pitt in so clear a manner stated in 1796 in the House of Commons, viz., that the smallest alteration of that law would be a death wound to the British Constitution.

The whole tenor of Mr. Fox's conduct since he quitted his seat at the Board of Treasury, when under age, and more particularly at the Whig Club, and other factious meetings, rendered his expulsion from the Privy Council indispensable, and obliges the King to express his astonishment that Mr. Pitt should one moment harbour the thought of bringing such a man before his Royal notice. To prevent the repetition of it, the King declares that if Mr. Pitt persists in such an idea, or in proposing to consult Lord Grenville, His Majesty will have to deplore that he cannot avail himself of the ability of Mr. Pitt with necessary restrictions. These points being understood, His Majesty does not object to Mr. Pitt's forming such a plan for conducting the public business as may under all circumstances appear to be eligible; but should Mr. Pitt, unfortunately, find himself unable to undertake what is here proposed, the King will in that case call for the assistance of such men as are truly attached to our happy Constitution, and not seekers of improvements which to all dispassionate men must appear to tend to the destruction of that noble fabric which is the pride of all thinking minds, and the envy of all foreign nations.

The King thinks it but just to his present servants to express his trust that as far as the public service will permit, he may have the benefit of their further services.[68]

Actually the letter is less belligerent than it sounds. Knowing that he was quite safe in being outspoken and in excluding Fox and even Grenville if he so chose, the King merely took advantage of his opportunity to give some very straightforward opinions of the conduct of Pitt, Dundas, Grenville, and Fox. The last paragraph of Pitt's letter of April 21 made it quite safe for the King to express himself in this fashion; and George III was being merely human and malicious in taking advantage of his chance to put over some rather effective pinpricks. Even his insistence that Pitt pledge himself to support the Test Act was an unnecessary precaution, and it is doubtful if the King felt any real uneasiness about Catholic Emancipation after the promise of 1801. In all probability George III had every intention of accepting Pitt as his chief minister; but he felt that no harm could come from a reiteration of his fundamental sentiments and of gaining as many minor concessions as possible in the no-man's land which lay between them.

On the other hand, Pitt, who was willing to go to the length of excluding Fox and even Grenville, insisted that as chief minister he be received by the King personally. His letter in reply to George III is, in the opinion of the present writer, the greatest he ever wrote. Each of the King's objections or slurs was answered in an adroit and courteous manner, and yet he showed that even his concessions had a limit and that his pride demanded that he be treated as a first minister if he were to accept the post of First Lord of the Treasury. In 1801 he felt that George III, in refusing to allow him even to present the case for Catholic Emancipation, had not treated him as a first minister had a right to expect. If George III attempted to treat him in the same manner at this time he would not accept office. The King, there is every reason to believe, was fully aware of the state of Pitt's mind. This interpretation appears to be substantiated by Pitt's answer of May 6 to the letter of May 5:

I had yesterday the honour of receiving from the Lord Chancellor your Majesty's letter, and am very sensible of your Majesty's condescension and goodness in deigning to renew the assurances of your

[68] Stanhope, *op. cit.*, IV, viii–x.

approbation of the sentiments of duty and attachment which it has been my wish to manifest towards your Majesty. At the same time I cannot refrain from expressing the deep concern with which I observe the manner in which my sentiments appear in some respects to have been misunderstood, and the unfavourable impression which your Majesty seems to entertain respecting parts of my conduct. Your Majesty will, I trust, permit me in the first place to assure you that the opinions I have expressed respecting the person now holding the chief place in your Majesty's Government have not arisen from any sentiments of personal dislike to that gentleman; they have been formed wholly on the view of his public conduct, and rest on grounds which I have already taken the liberty of laying distinctly before your Majesty.

On the subject of the proposal made in 1801 respecting the Catholics, it has been far from my desire to renew any detailed discussion; but I feel it due to two of my former colleagues to express my persuasion that they were guided on that important occasion by very different motives from those which your Majesty has been led to impute to them; and in justice to myself I must beg leave to declare that my opinion on that subject was formed on the fullest deliberation, and that the measure then suggested appeared to me, for the reasons which I have submitted at large to your Majesty, to be as much calculated to confirm the security of the Established Church as to promote the general interest of the Empire. My opinion of the propriety and rectitude of the measure at the time it was proposed remains unaltered; but other considerations, and sentiments of deference to your Majesty, have led me since to feel it both a personal and public duty to abstain from again pressing that measure on your Majesty's consideration. The humble assurance of this determination on my part has been long since conveyed to your Majesty, and recently renewed; and to that assurance, without any addition or alteration, I must humbly beg leave to adhere.

It now remains for me to express the extreme regret with which I learn your Majesty's strong disapprobation of the proposal which, on a view of the present state of affairs and of political parties, I thought it my duty to submit to your Majesty, for forming at the present difficult crisis a strong and comprehensive Government, uniting the principal weight and talents of public men of all descriptions. I have already stated that if, on full consideration, your Majesty should object to any part of that proposal, I am ready to acquiesce in that decision, and submit myself to your Majesty's commands; but I, at the same time, expressed my hope that before your Majesty's final decision, I might be permitted to offer such farther explanation as the case may appear to require. On a point, therefore, of this high importance, I cannot but feel it an indispensable duty again to request that you would condescend personally to hear from me the explanation of those reasons which satisfy me that such a plan of Government is best calculated to promote the only objects which I have at heart on this occasion—the lasting ease and honour of your Majesty's Government, the security and prosperity of the country and the general interest of Europe. Unless your Majesty should so far honour me with your confidence as to admit me into your presence for this purpose, I am grieved to say that I cannot retain any hope that my feeble services can be employed in any manner advantageous to your Majesty's affairs, or satisfactory to my own mind.[69]

After this preliminary jockeying for position, the King consented to see Pitt on May 7. In his letter of March 29 to Melville Pitt had prefaced the tactics they should pursue by the words "From what we both know of the King's character." George III now showed that he was equally familiar with Pitt's character by the manner in which he conducted himself during their long interview on the 7th. The royal illness and the letter of May 5 had prepared Pitt for a painful session with a resentful invalid; but he was pleasantly astonished, for the King was not only in excellent health but in a most gracious state of mind as well. Furthermore, the concessions which George III made were surprisingly liberal. He was willing to allow Pitt to include in his ministry practically anyone except Fox.

The usual interpretation of the results of this interview by historians hostile to the King is that his half-crazy prejudices prevented a strong government being formed. Actually he conceded a great deal to the eloquent pleas of Pitt, since he was willing that Fox should be used as an ambassador and only objected to him as a member of the cabinet. In short, Pitt found that the King met him on the basis which he insisted upon in his letter of May 6. So far from being ungracious, George III answered Pitt's congratulations on looking so much better than on his recovery in 1801 by the courteous statement: "That was not to be wondered at, as he was then on the point of *parting* with an old friend, and he was now about to *regain* one."[70] But despite such gracious remarks, such patient consideration of all explanations, and such wide concessions on the part of George III, Pitt reported that, "Never in any conversation I have had with him

[69] Stanhope, *op. cit.*, IV, x–xii.

[70] Rev. Leveson Vernon Harcourt, *Diaries and Correspondence of the Right Honourable George Rose* (London, 1860), II, 121.

in my life has he so baffled me."[71] At least after this interview he knew exactly where he stood with his royal master and could set about forming a ministry from his friends and those of Addington, Grenville, and Fox. Only Addington, St. Vincent, and Fox were absolutely excluded from any post in the new government.

Evidently Pitt had high hopes that the concessions which the King had made would be sufficient to bring both the Grenvilles and the Foxites into the fold and that he would be faced by no real opposition. He sent Canning to Grenville and Lord Granville Leveson to Fox in order to acquaint them with the results of the interview with the King. Fox, who received the news of his exclusion calmly, has been greatly praised for the nobility of his stand; but in all probability it would have been a greater hardship for him to give up his pleasant life at St. Ann's Hill than it was to be barred from the cabinet. Neither Grenville nor Fox's friends, however, took the decision of the King so calmly. Grenville assembled his followers at Camelford House that night and Grey summoned those of Fox to meet at Carlton House, the residence of the Prince of Wales. The Grenvilles decided to refuse office under Pitt and to continue the fight for the comprehensive principle; and the Whigs at Carlton House voted unanimously not to accept office without Fox. Lord Grenville stated his case in a vigorous letter to Pitt which unfortunately for the future relations of the two men fell into the hands of the press and was widely published. One sentence read:

No consideration of personal ease or comfort, no apprehension of responsibility, or reluctance to meet the real situation to which the country has been brought, have any weight in this decision; nor are we fettered by any engagements on the subject, either expressed or implied; we rest our determination solely on our strong sense of the impropriety of our becoming parties to a system of government which is to be formed, at such a moment as the present, on a principle of exclusion.[72]

When Pitt reported to the King that the Grenvilles and Fox refused to join the new ministry, the answer of George III indicated that he was more aroused by the fact that the opposition had held their meeting in Carlton House than by the loss of these two Parliamentary groups.

[71] Stanhope, op. cit., p. 171.   [72] Dropmore Papers, VII, 222.

Pitt was now faced with the alternative either of announcing to the King that he had failed or of forming a ministry from his own friends and from members of the Addington administration. Considering his self-confidence and his correspondence earlier in the year with Melville it was only natural that he chose the second alternative. Pitt, of course, became First Lord of the Treasury and Chancellor of the Exchequer; and he brought in with him the following new cabinet members: Harrowby, Foreign Secretary; Camden, Secretary at War and for the Colonies; Mulgrave, Duchy of Lancaster; Melville, Admiralty; and the Duke of Montrose, President of the Board of Trade. From the Addington cabinet Pitt retained: Portland, Lord President; Eldon, Lord Chancellor; Westmorland, Privy Seal; Chatham, Master of Ordnance; Castlereagh, President of the India Board; and Hawkesbury, who was transferred from the Foreign to the Home Office. Actually the new ministry was very little stronger than the one it had supplanted, since the chief difference was that between the abilities of Pitt and Addington. The old division into four Parliamentary groups remained. The change merely meant that one of three opposition groups had come into power and that Addington and his followers took the place in opposition vacated by Pitt.

What, then, is the constitutional significance of the events from March to May which resulted in the overthrow of Addington and the coming in of Pitt? To the present writer they represent merely one more phase in the consistent actions of both George III and William Pitt. Each adhered firmly to his constitutional principles and practices. During a reign of nearly forty-four years, the King had resolutely insisted that he had the right to select his own ministers and the experience which he had gained during those years made him dread and resist having "his closet forced" by a group of men who secured control of the majority of the House of Commons. Earlier in his reign he had taken steps to see that a majority of the members of the House of Commons chosen at each general election would support his ministers; but when, as a result of the French Revolution, opinion outside Parliament so nearly coincided with his own and that of his ministers on fundamental issues, and when as a result of the Portland Whigs joining Pitt in 1794 the opposition in Parliament became negligible, he no longer found it necessary to take such active measures. In the general election of 1802, the lack of active participation by the King and the ministers was especially noteworthy. The only remaining danger to George III of having his closet forced was the combination of practically all the Parliamentary talent into a group hostile to him. If such a group could ever unite on a consistent set of principles and secure the adhesion to their organization of all the promising Parliamentary recruits, then even the King's influence at general elections would not save him from having to submit to selecting these men as his ministers and from consenting to the measures which they advised. The methods which the King adopted early in his reign and which he continued to use with marked success were the ones employed in 1804. So long as he was able to secure brilliant individuals to act as his ministers, George III did not have to fear hostile combinations forcing his closet. If his minister were defeated on any important measure or found himself in a minority in the House of Commons, the King felt merely that additional strength must be secured from one of the various groups or clusters acknowledging the leadership of some well-known individual. That is, if a ministry were weakening it must be strengthened either by additional votes and debating skill from some group within the House of Commons or by a general election.

Thus when the Addington ministry began to stagger, the obvious method of strengthening it was by absorbing one of the three opposition groups; but each of the three resisted absorption for different reasons: Grenville because his policies were diametrically opposed to those of the ministry; Pitt because he insisted upon being the first minister himself; and Fox, whose views were in many respects closest to Addington's from 1801 to 1803, because of the King's personal veto. The first thought of George III, when he recovered from his illness in April 1804 and discovered the precarious state of the Addington ministry, was to offer to back his minister to the limit exactly as he had offered his full support to North in 1782 and to Shelburne in 1783. The King was willing to help swell Addington's majority by dissolving Parliament, for he was quite certain that he could by influence and proper expression of his opinion insure a substantial majority for his ministers as he had done earlier. When, however, it became clear that even an increased majority would soon melt away before the combined attacks of Pitt, Grenville, and Fox, the King turned once more to his familiar tactics of dividing the opposition. Although no one of these three groups would join with Addington, Pitt, as we have seen, was ready to do the next best thing by coming in alone and carrying on the government under conditions acceptable to George III. Thus the King's equanimity was disturbed only by his feeling that Addington had been treated in a shabby fashion, as in reality he had; and hence George III endeavored to soften the blow by the offer of a peerage and a pension, and by words of praise which the recipient cherished to the end of his days. The King believed that in time Addington would forget his justifiable grievance against Pitt, but that for the present, as he wrote to Eldon on May 18: "Mr. Addington . . . . seems to require quiet, as his mind is perplexed between returning affection for Mr. Pitt, and great soreness at the contemptuous treatment he met with, the end of last Session, from one he had ever looked upon as his private friend. This makes the King resolve to keep them for some time asunder."[73] But in case Pitt's government were hard pressed in the future, it is obvious that George III would make a personal appeal to Addington to assist the ministry if there were any danger of the royal closet being forced. Such tactics had grown old in the royal service.

Pitt was equally loyal to his constitutional principles and consistent in his practice. As has been pointed out more than once, Pitt, like George III, believed that the King had the exclusive right to appoint the First Lord of the Treasury and other ministers. Once a chief minister was appointed, however, Pitt held that he must have the predominant voice in the councils of the King and be free to place before his royal master any proposals upon which the cabinet had reached an agreement. The King then had the choice of accepting or rejecting such measures and of retaining or ousting his ministers. Pitt made no objection to George III communicating often and at great length with the various secretaries of state and with the Lord Chancellor; but he would have objected strenuously had he perceived what he considered to be undue influence from some person who was not connected with his ministry. If a prime minister were ousted, Pitt would admit that he might go into active opposition, support the new ministry, or retire from Parliament. In actual practice he believed that it was bad policy for a minister to act in such a way that the King would refuse to allow him to hold an important office again. From personal observation he knew that the unforgivable sins from the point of view of George III were abetting the Prince of Wales in private immorality and in political defiance

[73] *Secret Correspondence*, p. 53.

to his father, and in forming part of a "faction" which attempted to force the royal closet. Thus Pitt was always careful not to offend in any of these respects. This constitutional philosophy and practice was adequate for a man like Lord North, who did not care whether or not he remained as First Lord of the Treasury, but for Pitt, whose main interests in life were holding office and serving his country, they did not offer any means of forcing the King to place him in charge of the government.

It should be mentioned further that Pitt's attitude toward the King had much in common with that of the Tories in the reigns of Charles II and James II. These Tories stressed the doctrine of passive obedience, but only so long as the kings issued the kind of orders which they wished to obey. When both Charles II and James II promulgated measures which made Tories believe that the Church of England was in danger, these gentlemen temporarily shelved their high-sounding principles and participated in passing the Test Act of 1673 and in the Revolution Settlement of 1689. Similarly the weakness of Pitt's position was that he had no way, under certain conditions, of compelling the King to make the right choice of ministers. He had no desire to form part of a coalition to force his way into the King's cabinet as the Portland ministry had done in 1783, because he knew that such power had no firm basis and in addition meant exclusion from office in the future. After the Regency Crisis of 1788–89 Pitt felt that he would have no hope of remaining First Lord of the Treasury so long as the Prince of Wales were regent or ruler. Further, if the King found a minister like Addington who was more acceptable personally and who could maintain himself with Pitt's support, active or passive, or even with his neutrality, then the latter found himself in the position of the Tories whose passive obedience proved inadequate when James II issued a declaration of indulgence.

Fortunately for Pitt, his resolute belief in his own patriotism provided the necessary loophole. The best explanation of the manner in which he hoped to escape this dilemma is to be found in his letter to Melville of March 29, 1804, so often referred to in this chapter, in which after stating that he was unwilling during the illness of the King "to form any connection which might preclude him from a fair option in forming an administration, whenever he might resume the exercise of his authority," he qualified by adding:

This doubt rests, as you will perceive, entirely on the feeling of what is due to the King; and strong as that motive is, I am nevertheless aware that there may be cases in which considerations of public safety will perhaps not allow of its being yielded to beyond a certain point.[74]

Thus Pitt's game, once he had decided to break with Addington, was to make himself the only available candidate for the post of First Lord of the Treasury. If Addington would not resign voluntarily and pave the way for the King, by his own volition, to ask Pitt to form a government then the latter through love of his country would be forced to attack the ministry successively on its naval, military, and financial policy. Eventually the Addington ministry would crack, and Pitt, having kept himself uncontaminated by any commitment to Grenville and Fox, would be the "voluntary" choice of George III. Thus would Pitt conscientiously uphold the constitutional right of the King to choose his own ministers, and at the same time in actual practice give George III "Hobson's choice." Consequently when he resumed office in May 1804 Pitt was in the thrice-fortunate position of having acted from patriotic reasons, of having preserved his own and the King's constitutional principles, and of having secured the office he desired.

What judgment can be passed on Pitt's actions from 1801 to 1804? On the whole, it is the opinion of the present writer that, despite the effective manner in which he reconciled patriotism, constitutional principles, and self-interest, they were most pernicious in their influence. The King's actions in January and February of 1801 made his resignation quite justifiable from both the personal and constitutional points of view, but his promises to support Addington and to abstain from agitating the Catholic question left him in so involved a situation that only his own belief in the purity of his motives and actions enabled him to escape this maze of divided loyalties. Apparently Pitt's powers of oratory were as great as they had ever been; for whenever the occasion demanded it during these three years he was, even according to his old enemy, Sheridan, able to show his usual parliamentary skill. The events of the years from 1793 to 1801 had shown that Pitt's value to his country was greatly impaired by his amazing and serene self-confidence. This state of mind prevented him from making fundamental changes in policies which had failed

[74] *Secret Correspondence*, p. 13.

miserably and was an important factor in causing the English people to follow him blindly and loyally through so many failures of the first magnitude. His inherited belief in the name of Pitt, his early successes, the adulation of his friends, and the blind confidence of the people had, evidently, led him to accept as applicable to his own case his father's famous remark that he alone could save England. Thus the fundamental planks in Pitt's platform were: first, that he should be First Lord of the Treasury; second, that he should do nothing contrary to his own principles; and, third, that he should respect the King's constitutional right to choose his own ministers without pressure *unless* national danger made it absolutely necessary to exert influence. A patriot who believed in saving his country at all costs would have been willing to serve in some other position than that of First Lord of the Treasury and also to coerce the King into consenting to the formation of a strong ministry. In his heart Pitt believed that a ministry of which he was the head was adequate to meet all foreign and domestic problems, and that while it would be better to have the Grenvilles and the Foxites with him they were in no sense indispensable. The result was that for more than three years Pitt's conscience would not permit him to overthrow the weak Addington ministry; his constitutional principles would not allow him to exert pressure on the King either personally or combined with other groups; and his tremendous self-confidence would not let him admit that it was as important to have Fox and Grenville in a ministry as to be himself First Lord of the Treasury. Pitt's reactions to the refusal of Grenville were according to Lord Eldon as follows: "I recollect Mr. Pitt saying with some indignation, he would teach that proud man that, in the service and with the confidence of the King, he could do without him though he thought his health such that it might cost him his life."[75] J. H. Rose has questioned whether Pitt ever made such a remark. If the likelihood of the remark is judged by Pitt's character, it is safe to say that the first part of the quotation certainly represented his views, although it is very unlikely that he would have made such a reference to his health. But regardless of what judgment is passed on Pitt's actions from 1801 to 1804, and particularly from March to May, 1804, it must be admitted that he had worked out a plan of action to satisfy his conscience, his constitutional principles, and his personal ambition, and carried it to a successful conclusion.

[75] *Secret Correspondence*, pp. 45–46.

X. THE KING MAINTAINS HIS POSITION, 1804 TO 1806

Unfortunately for Pitt the events of the next twenty months were to prove that his ability and self-confidence were not sufficient in themselves to cope successfully with the problems of the country. If his brain were as good as ever, it was soon evident that his physical powers were not. In retrospect it is obvious that he needed both an abler cabinet and different policies if he hoped to meet the great Napoleon on an equal footing. The problems which confronted Pitt in May 1804 were: first, the formulation of military, naval, and fiscal policies which would escape the criticisms which he had leveled against Addington's; second, the formation of a new coalition of Continental powers to oppose Napoleon; third, the defense of his government in the House of Commons against the combined attacks of the Fox, Grenville, and Addington groups; and, fourth, the resumption with the King of relations sufficiently close and cordial to make possible effective functioning of the executive branch of the government.

Since Addington had endeavored to please Pitt by basing his military, naval, and fiscal policies as much as possible on the advice of the latter, no great change in the fundamental principles of any of the three was to be expected. Pitt immediately devoted himself to correcting what appeared to him to be errors in the existing organization of national defense and to increasing the regular army. His own plan for securing recruits to the regular army was subjected to as severe criticism as he had bestowed on Addington's, and it proved such a failure that in March 1805 it had to be abandoned.[1] The most that can be said for Pitt's military policy is that it did iron out some of the existing flaws; but the changes were in no sense revolutionary, because Addington had followed so many of his suggestions, and in practice they did not prove very successful. The growing hostility of Spain and her increasing friendship with France made clear the danger of naval attack by the combined French and Spanish fleets. The seizure of the Spanish treasure fleet in October 1804 was followed in December by a declaration of war by Spain. This new danger

---

[1] J. W. Fortescue, *British Statesmen of the Great War, 1793–1814* (Oxford: Clarendon Press, 1911), p. 178.

necessitated strengthening the coast defenses during the winter of 1804–5.

The cabinet which Pitt formed in May 1804 contained twelve members; six who had held office under Addington; and six new men, including himself. Addington had urged all members of his ministry who could, "consistently with their own sense of propriety," serve under Pitt to do so, but he refused to commit himself on his own future line of conduct and declared: "I will not even tell the King that I shall support his government."[2] Thus while it was unlikely that Addington would join with Grenville and Fox in any permanent opposition, because the King's appeal to his character and integrity would be sufficient to prevent such action, it was fairly certain that he would oppose measures of the new government which reflected on those which he had sponsored while in office. Addington's state of mind at the time he left office is well described by his biographer:

As regards the conduct of the original Opposition, he had no grounds of complaint. It was manly, open and consistent, whilst that of Mr. Erskine, Mr. Sheridan, and some others of the party, was generous and friendly. But it would be wrong to deny, that, not only at the moment, but to the close of his life, Mr. Addington considered he had been unkindly and unfairly opposed by Mr. Pitt. Nor will the existence of this feeling excite surprise when it is remembered, that Mr. Pitt almost obliged his friend to accept the government after he himself had relinquished it; that, to remove his hesitation, he promised him his assistance and advice whenever he might request it; that, nevertheless, he removed to a distance where it would be impossible to consult him; and, finally overthrew the government by uniting himself with the common opponents of its system and his own, who would have been comparatively powerless but for the assistance he thus afforded them. Mr. Addington felt that his conduct towards Mr. Pitt had not merited such a return.[3]

Since Pitt had taken office before the end of the session of 1804, he was immediately exposed to the attacks of the opposition in Parliament. On the whole, the chief measure taken up during the remainder of the session was Pitt's Additional Force Bill, and its terms were such as to bring down upon it the severe criticisms of both wings of the opposition and of Addington. It was with the

[2] George Pellew, *The Life and Correspondence of the Right Honourable Henry Addington, First Viscount Sidmouth* (London, 1847), II, 284.
[3] *Ibid.*, pp. 298–99.

greatest difficulty that the bill was forced through the House of Commons. The majority on the second reading was only forty, and on one division Pitt actually found himself in a minority of six.

More significant than the criticisms of a measure which was so soon found unsatisfactory is the constitutional doctrine which Pitt enunciated in a speech of June 18 in the course of the debates on this Additional Force Bill. Replying to an accusation that his ministry was not worthy of confidence, Pitt declared:

But whatever opinions some people may entertain of the advantages of an administration formed on a broad basis, I am satisfied that the principle, that it is the prerogative of his Majesty to choose his ministers will not be denied. I am the more convinced of this, when I remember that some weeks ago, the honourable gentleman (Mr. Fox) opposite stated in this house, when it was thrown out as a matter of speculation, who were to be the new ministers, if the late ministry were obliged to retire, that it was not within the province of the house to take any notice of such a circumstance; and if it would have been unconstitutional to agitate such a topic before the removal of that ministry, it is equally unconstitutional to deny the King's prerogative as to selection in every instance; and is it reconcilable with any ideas of constitutional principle and public duty, that, when a ministry has been changed, their successors should be obstructed in their very first operations, by any combination founded upon any circumstances connected with the recent exercise of his Majesty's prerogative?

An honourable gentleman [Mr. Sheridan] has said, I have received a *broad hint* to retire after this recent experiment. I beg leave to say, broad as the hint may be, it is not broad enough for me to take it. I am yet sanguine enough to believe the bill will pass; if it should not, all I have to lament is, that the country will be deprived of the increased means of security which I flattered myself I had provided for it. Should I be disappointed in this respect, let not gentlemen suppose I shall consider it as a defeat. I shall merely treat it as the decision of this house on the dry merits of the bill. If this scheme be rejected, another project, which I trust will be less objectionable, shall be submitted, and the *hint* shall not be taken, until I find my attempts to promote the public security utterly nugatory and ineffectual; then I shall retire, not with mortification but with triumph, confident of having exerted my best endeavors to serve my country. I will not discuss how far a wider basis for the formation of his Majesty's government would have evinced the wisdom of the sovereign; but I should not think the prerogative entire, if we were permitted here to deliberate on its exercise, so far as to examine the propriety or impolicy of inviting a principal person on the opposite bench to participate in the public councils of the state. Thus to interfere would be to alter the constitution of the land, which, although free, is yet monarchical, and for the preservation of its liberties and immunities all its parts should be protected from violation.[4]

In order that nobody in the House of Commons could possibly mistake his meaning, Pitt concluded this speech with a reiteration of these sentiments:

If the present bill should be lost, I shall be sorry for it, because the house and the country will thereby lose a good measure; but the honourable gentlemen opposite will be much mistaken if they think they will thereby be any thing the nearer getting rid of me. It is well known, and has ever been allowed to be one of the first and most established privileges and prerogatives of the crown, that his Majesty has a right to choose and nominate his own ministers.[5]

Since this bill was the only really controversial one which Pitt presented during the session, he was not reduced to the expedients which he threatened to take in this speech. But the time devoted to this measure and to the Corn Bill of 1804 kept Parliament in session until July 31.

In addition to strengthening the Army and Navy and to carrying on negotiations which led eventually to the Third Coalition, Pitt during the period from May 1804 until the new session of Parliament opened on January 15, 1805, found it necessary to devote some time both to the King and to strengthening his government. The private correspondence of both men reveals that each felt he must exercise considerable tact and diplomacy in dealing with the other in order to accomplish what the country needed. Pitt's major worry was that the King's illness might recur if he became too excited over the events which led to the formation of the new ministry and over the attacks which the opposition was bound to make. Only the King's sanity stood between Pitt and exclusion from office and the loss of his services to the country. This perturbation is nowhere better brought out than in the joint letter which Pitt and Eldon sent to the King

---

[4] *The Speeches of the Right Honourable William Pitt in the House of Commons* (London, 1808), III, 377–79. Slightly different phraseology in *Hansard's Parliamentary Debates* (first series, London, 1806–1820), II, 744–48.

[5] *Speeches of Pitt*, III, 381–82. Slightly different phraseology in *Hansard's Parliamentary Debates*, II, 747–48.

on May 16, 1804.[6] Here they stressed how important it was for the happiness of his subjects that the King should continue to exercise his full authority, and they begged him to concentrate on important business and not to dissipate his energies by too frequent and lengthy interviews and audiences. The diaries of Lord Malmesbury and of George Rose are full of gossip and anecdotes to prove that during the month of May the conduct of George III was so erratic as to arouse doubts concerning his mental poise. Typical of the stories circulating was one related by Rose to the effect that the King after being cheered by the Eton boys declared that "he had always been partial to their school; that he had now the additional motive of gratitude for being so; and that in future he should be an Anti-Westminster."[7] On the other hand, the testimony of men who interviewed him personally during the weeks following the change in government indicates that he was composed and improving rapidly in health. Certainly his letters of May and June display the same grasp of events, the same prejudices, and the same confused phraseology as those written during periods when he was conceded to be sane. Evidently George III was willing to follow the advice of Pitt and of Eldon, because he was even more anxious than they were to avoid a regency or the distasteful experience of having his "closet forced."

It was the King's particular task during June and July to resist pressure from Pitt to strengthen the government during the crucial period for the Additional Force Bill. This policy necessitated encouraging Pitt and handling Addington in such a way that he would not unite with Fox and Grenville. If one is to judge George III by the skill with which he accomplished this self-imposed task, he was sane politically, for, as he wrote Eldon, the soreness which Addington still felt at Pitt's treatment made it necessary to keep the two men asunder for some time. When Addington under the stimulus of this soreness attacked Pitt's Additional Force Bill, the King expressed the comforting opinion to his minister that such a line of conduct was neither wise nor dignified. A few days later George III wrote Pitt that: "His Majesty trusts to the goodness of his cause, his own resolution to support the present administration with all his might, and to the

[6] "Correspondence of King George III," Transcripts by Sir John Fortescue in William L. Clements Library, XII, 1218–19.

[7] Rev. Leveson Vernon Harcourt, *Diaries and Correspondence of the Right Honourable George Rose* (London, 1860), II, 147. Hereafter referred to as *Rose Diaries*.

spirit, uprightness, and talents of Mr. Pitt: this combination scarcely can fail of success—at least it will *deserve it.*"[8] Although the King probably felt a certain amount of disgust with Addington for not complying more obediently with his wishes, still it must have been both a satisfaction and a relief to him when the session of Parliament ended on July 31 without his having to yield to Pitt on the matter of strengthening the government and without Addington's forming any alarming connections with the opposition.

The interviews which George Rose had with the King on September 30 at Weymouth and from October 28 to November 2, when the royal family visited Rose in his home at Cuffnells in Hampshire, throw considerable light on the ministerial situation during those months. George III's stand was that he was entirely contented with the personnel of the government and with the manner in which it was being conducted; that he was determined not to admit Fox into his councils *"even at the hazard of a civil war"*; that he had come to realize that Addington was not equal to carrying on the government of the country; and that he was free from all apprehension on the Catholic question.[9] Clearly the King did not feel the same perturbation which Pitt and Rose experienced as to the weakness of the government, and he refused to consider any steps for strengthening it by the admission of Fox. The real reason, however, for the serene confidence of George III in the existing state of affairs seems to lie in his belief that he could reconcile Pitt and Addington before the opposition in Parliament became a menace. All that was necessary was for some of Addington's soreness to disappear. This point of view of the King is brought out admirably in the account given by Rose:

Mr. Addington had expressed a positive resolution not to oppose Government further. The strongest ground of resentment in the mind of the latter gentleman, the King told me, was Mr. Pitt having made him ridiculous in the House of Commons; and that Mrs. Addington was infinitely more inveterate on that account, and more irreconcilable than her husband,—having declaimed against Mr. A. receiving any favour from Mr. Pitt, or through him, till he had made some reparation for that offence. This led his Majesty to speak of an intended provision and reward for Mr. A. but declined by him,—*as to*

[8] Earl Stanhope, *Life of the Right Honourable William Pitt* (London, 1861–62), IV, xvi.

[9] *Rose Diaries,* II, 156–57.

the manner, however, only,—describing him as nibbling at it at the moment he was refusing it . . . . And his Majesty said he would, at a proper season, reconcile Mr. Pitt and Mr. Addington; but that matters were not yet ripe.[10]

Thus, while the judgment of George III may be questioned, it cannot be denied that he had a well-thought-out campaign which fitted in perfectly with his own political ideals and peace of mind. All that remained to be done was to have Pitt approach Addington and reach an agreement before the next session of Parliament opened.

In December Pitt took the initiative and made overtures to Addington to join the ministry. The full details of the negotiations are available in the correspondence of George III, Pitt, Addington, and Hawkesbury. The latter, who acted as contact man for the two estranged statesmen, sounded out Addington on the possibility of closer personal and public relations with Pitt and received a reassuring answer. But although Hawkesbury found it comparatively simple to secure the warm approbation of both men to a renewal of personal relations and from Addington an endorsement of the fundamental policies of the administration, he found greater difficulties when he attempted to work out the details for putting into practice this plan of political co-operation. Pitt was anxious to have Addington accept a post in the cabinet and a peerage, in order to be certain of the votes of the latter's followers without the embarrassment of his presence in the Commons. Addington objected strongly to a peerage on the ground that his family fortune was not adequate to support it, and professed to be willing to support the Pitt ministry without office. When Hawkesbury pressed him to state the office which would be most acceptable to him, he indicated that one of the secretaryships of state would be most satisfactory, although he would be willing to accept the position of Lord President. Next came the question of satisfying relatives and friends to whom Addington felt committed: Bragg, Hiley Addington, Bond, and Vansittart. Pitt's intentions, as expressed by Hawkesbury, satisfied Addington, namely, that two should be provided for at once and two as soon as possible. Two points Addington, however, insisted upon: first, that Lord St. Vincent, who had been offended by the manner in which he had been attacked and then excluded from the ministry

[10] *Ibid.,* pp. 161–62.

by Pitt, must be soothed and conciliated in some way; and, second, that Lord Buckinghamshire, to whom he had become committed since leaving office, must be satisfied by a place in the cabinet or by the promise of one in case of a vacancy.[11]

Hawkesbury then succeeded in bringing Pitt and Addington together at his home, Coombe Wood, for a series of personal interviews in which the difficulties mentioned above were adjusted. An unfortunate accident to Lord Harrowby, the Foreign Secretary, early in December, made possible the readjustment of cabinet posts which satisfied Addington. When Harrowby resigned, Mulgrave was transferred from the post of Chancellor of the Duchy of Lancashire to the Foreign Office and Buckinghamshire was given the vacant place. The Duke of Portland, for reasons of health, resigned as Lord President and remained in the cabinet without office; and Addington received this post and was to be moved to the House of Lords with the title of Viscount Sidmouth.

The King showed even greater elation over the renewal of personal and political relations than did the two principals. In suggesting to George III that the friends of Addington be added to the government, Pitt declared that there was no reasonable doubt in his mind that he had a sufficient majority to put through the ordinary business of the session but that he might require additional assistance to pass such vigorous and decisive measures as might be necessary for successful prosecution of the war.[12] The King compressed into one sentence his reaction to this proposal:

His Majesty has, from the first hour of meeting Mr. Pitt the last spring to engage him again into public life, intimated a desire of being the restorer of two friends to that state of affection which would be most gratifying to his own feelings, as well as advantageous to the ease of carrying on the public business.[13]

Pitt, on the other hand, was too much of a Grenville to go into ecstasies over the renewal of a friendship or the addition of forty votes in the House of Commons. Addington was no doubt gratified because the reconciliation meant both a renewal of friendly relations with Pitt and a recognition of the fact that he and his friends were needed in the ministry, and his followers in the House of Commons, to sustain the government. Addington, like

---

[11] Clements Transcripts, XIII, 1504–7.
[12] Stanhope, *op. cit.*, IV, xix.   [13] *Ibid.*, p. xx.

Pitt, was proud of his character; but where the latter was lofty and serene, the former tended to be smug and self-righteous. To forgive Pitt and to return good for evil gave him, in addition to the gratification mentioned, the triple satisfaction of heaping coals of fire on the head of the present First Lord of the Treasury, of serving his country at a personal sacrifice, and of winning additional marks of affection from his King. Little wonder that as his biographer remarks, "this was the merriest Christmas he had enjoyed for many years."[14]

The joy experienced by the King, Pitt, and Addington did not extend to all of the followers of the two statesmen. Canning and Rose, in particular, spoke and wrote bitterly of the coalition. Friends of Pitt feared that the gain in votes would be offset by the weapons which the union of the two groups would place in the hands of the opposition. Many friends of Addington, on the other hand, expressed doubt whether this reconciliation, for which the King was so largely responsible and which was based on personal grounds and common general principles rather than on agreement on specific issues, could stand the wear and tear of Parliamentary debate. The events of the next session of Parliament were to prove that the gloomy prophecies of the rank and file were more accurate than the high hopes of the King, Pitt, and Addington.

On January 15, 1805, George III opened the new session. It was to be the last, and in many respects the most unhappy one, for Pitt. The debates which followed the King's speech indicated clearly the line of attack which the Fox-Grenville opposition intended to follow. The Additional Force Bill, Catholic Emancipation, and the attack on the Spanish vessels which resulted in Spain's declaring war on England were all handled in a very critical speech by Fox. The shrewdness of the attack in each case is clear. The Additional Force Bill was obviously a failure and had been substituted for one which Addington and Yorke had believed to be superior. Thus the opposition not only had the pleasure of taunting Pitt on his failure but of driving a wedge between Pitt and Sidmouth (as Addington had become on January 11), by praising the latter at the expense of the former, and of recalling the criticisms and wrangles of the previous session. The Catholic question was brought up not because the opposition believed there

---

[14] Pellew, *op. cit.*, II, 342.

was any hope of success but partly from adherence to a measure in which both Grenville and Fox honestly believed and partly because it was embarrassing to Pitt. The Spanish problem was attacked because the opposition believed they had a good case against the government for handling the situation in a bungling manner.

If the divisions on the controversial points are taken as a criterion, Pitt could count the session a successful one; but from the point of view of retaining his cabinet intact, it was a failure. Following a great debate beginning February 11 and lasting until five o'clock the next morning, Pitt triumphed on the Spanish question when Grey's amendment was beaten by 313 to 106.[15] Windham's motion on February 21 that the Additional Force Bill and other acts should be referred to a select committee was defeated by 242 to 96.[16]

On March 6 Sheridan returned to the attack by moving for the repeal of the Additional Force Bill. Here again Pitt won, since the motion was rejected by 267 to 127;[17] but the significance of the debate turned not on the size of the vote but on the clash between Pitt and Sheridan. Like the famous occasion more than twenty years earlier when he provoked Sheridan to make his "angry boy" retort, Pitt invited a sharp rejoinder by digressing from the topic long enough to give some common characteristics of the speeches of his opponent.

The Hon. gentleman seldom condescends to favour us with a display of his extraordinary powers of imagination and of fancy; but when he does, he always thinks proper to pay off all arrears, and, like a bottle uncorked, bursts all at once into an explosion of froth and air. All that his own fancy can suggest or that he has collected from others; all that he can utter in the ebullition of the moment; all that he has slept on and studied, are combined and produced for our entertainment. All his hoarded repartees, all his matured jests; the full contents of his common-place book; all his severe invective, all his bold, hardy assertions, he collects into one mass, which he kindles into a blaze of eloquence; and out it comes altogether, whether or not it has any, even the smallest relation to the subject in debate.[18]

But it was not against this section of Pitt's speech that Sheridan delivered his most crushing counterattack, for he selected as a basis for a bitter comparison Pitt's accusation that the support he had given the Addington ministry was insidious and hollow:

[15] *Hansard's Parliamentary Debates,* III, 468.
[16] *Ibid.,* p. 626. [17] *Ibid.,* p. 785. [18] Stanhope, *op. cit.,* IV, 260.

I gave my support to the late administration with the most perfect good faith; and I know that the noble lord has always been ready to acknowledge it. But supposing I had not supported him with firmness and fidelity; what then? I never had professed to do so, either to that administration or to this house. I supported them because I approved of many of their measures; but principally was I induced to support them because I considered their continuance in office a security against the return to power of the right honourable gentleman opposite me, whichever appeared to me as the greatest national calamity. If, indeed, I had recommended the noble lord to his Majesty—if I had come down to the house and described the noble lord as the fittest man in the country to fill the office of chancellor of the exchequer because it was a convenient step to my own safety, in retiring from a situation which I had grossly abused and which I could no longer fill with honour and security;—if having seduced him into that situation, I had afterwards tapered off from a prominent support, when I saw that the minister of my own choice was acquiring greater stability and popularity than I wished for—if, when I saw an opening to my own return to power, I had entered into a combination with others, whom I meant also to betray, from the sole lust of power and office, in order to remove him;—and if, under the dominion of these base appetites, I had then treated with ridicule and contempt the very man whom I had before held up to the choice of my Sovereign, and the approbation of this house and the public;—then, indeed, I should have merited the contempt and execration of all good men, and should have deserved to be told that I was hollow and insincere in my support, and that I had acted a mean, base and perfidious part.[19]

These bitter innuendoes did not impair Pitt's majority on the division, but they did wound him personally and they did, in all probability, affect his relations with Lord Sidmouth exactly as Sheridan intended.

It was not until May that Fox brought up in the House of Commons the third great issue which he had criticized in the King's speech at the beginning of the session, namely, Catholic Emancipation. The long debates of May 13 and 14 may be passed over at this time because the attitude of Fox and his followers, of George III, and of Pitt is well known. At four o'clock in the morning of May 15 Fox's motion to consider the petition from the Catholics in Ireland was defeated by 336 to 124.[20] The King, after receiving Pitt's report that the speeches were so long during the first night

---

[19] *Hansard's Parliamentary Debates,* III, 784–85.
[20] *Ibid.,* IV, 1060.

that an adjournment was necessary, remarked: "it seems wonderful that the fatigue does not incline gentlemen to compress their ideas in a shorter space, which must ever be more agreeable and useful to the auditors, and not less advantageous to the despatch of business."[21]

The real blow to Pitt in the session of 1805, however, came not from any issue which grew out of the debate on the King's speech at the opening of the session but from the loss to his cabinet of Lord Melville. In 1802 Lord St. Vincent, then First Lord of the Admiralty, had appointed a Commission of Naval Inquiry. Of the ten reports which these commissioners sent in, the first nine were of a technical nature and had aroused little public interest; but the tenth dealt with certain transactions which concerned Lord Melville as Treasurer of the Navy during Pitt's first administration.[22] This tenth report clearly showed that a Mr. Alexander Trotter, whom Melville had appointed paymaster in this department, was guilty of misapplication of public funds. The evidence was clear that Trotter had deposited state revenue in his private account at a bank and had used these sums for personal transactions. Trotter's defense was that the public had not lost anything, because the money was paid back; but the commissioners held that the guilt involved in misapplication of funds was not affected by the fact that the money in question was not lost. Melville's own defense, when the transactions were called to his attention in June 1804 by the commissioners, was that he could not furnish them with the account they requested for two reasons: first, when he resigned the position of Treasurer of the Navy several years earlier he had transferred the existing balance to the account of his successor and had subsequently destroyed papers which he felt were of no value; and, second, at the time the transaction took place he held other confidential offices in the government and sometimes he found it necessary to use funds from the Navy for delicate transactions in other branches of government of such a confidential nature that they could not be revealed to the public.[23] Melville obviously referred to money used for Secret Service. The evidence and Melville's letter were both published in the tenth report, and the opposition to the government and the personal enemies of Melville naturally seized on it with great avidity. Soon

---

[21] Stanhope, *op. cit.*, IV, xxv.

[22] *Hansard's Parliamentary Debates*, III, 865–1212.

[23] Stanhope, *op. cit.*, IV, 274–75.

rumors were in circulation that Melville had profited by the use of and interest on public money.

The opposition in Parliament struck almost at once. Whitbread gave notice that he would on April 8 make a motion based on the tenth report. On this date after a long speech, he moved thirteen resolutions which amplified the phrase in resolution eleven that Melville had been "guilty of a gross violation of the law, and a high breach of duty." Had Pitt been able to hold his own followers together as he had been on the other divisions during this session of Parliament, all would have been well. Before Whitbread's motion of April 8, however, Pitt knew that he could count on neither Wilberforce and his following of country gentlemen nor on Sidmouth and his friends. In fact the result of the tenth report was to drive a wedge between the two groups in the government. Sidmouth probably was actuated by both high public principles and personal pique; for he seems to have resented the fact that Melville, who had been raised to the peerage by him and not by Pitt, had taken so prominent a part in his overthrow in 1804. The danger of a breach between the two ministers became serious when Sidmouth expressed the opinion that it would be impossible for Melville to convince the public of his innocence, and added that, if Pitt persisted in defending Melville, he himself would find it impracticable to remain in the government.[24] Pitt frankly acknowledged that if Sidmouth's friends in the Commons voted for Whitbread's motion of censure it would be carried, and so after careful consideration decided that the only plan which gave any hope of success was to refer the matter to a select committee. Sidmouth favored this procedure as the only one possible under the circumstances and Melville consented when he became convinced that the vote of censure to be proposed by Whitbread could not be defeated. Having reached an agreement in the cabinet on this basis, Pitt could feel certain of the support of Sidmouth's followers in the Commons.

Even this assistance proved inadequate when Wilberforce, early on the morning of April 9, delivered a speech which turned the independents against Melville. On the division for Whitbread's motion on the first of the thirteen resolutions the vote stood 216 to 216. Thus it devolved upon the Speaker to cast the deciding vote; and after several minutes of thought he gave it in favor of the

[24] Charles, Lord Colchester (ed.), *The Diary and Correspondence of Charles Lord Colchester* (London, 1861), I, 546–47.

motion.[25] The diaries of the time are full of accounts of the reactions of Pitt and of the boisterous conduct of the opposition
members. The remaining twelve resolutions were then carried,
and it was voted to adjourn until April 10. When Melville heard
the results of the division he resigned his place as First Lord of
the Admiralty. Whitbread, however, persisted, when Parliament
met, in moving an address to the King to remove Melville from all
offices held under the Crown and from His Majesty's councils
forever. Although Whitbread withdrew the motion at this time,
even the appointment of a select committee to consider certain
aspects of the tenth report did not deter him from announcing that
he would move on May 6 to have Melville's name stricken from
the list of Privy Councillors. In order to avert another debate,
Melville wrote to Pitt on the 5th and suggested that his name be
removed from the list before consideration of the motion. Pitt
acquiesced. The most interesting reaction to this phase of the
affair is contained in George III's letter of May 5:

Though the King is much hurt at the virulence against Lord Melville,
which is unbecoming the character of Englishmen, who naturally
when a man is fallen are too noble to pursue their blows, he must feel
the prudence and good temper of Mr. Pitt's proposing his being
struck out of the Privy Council, and it is hoped that after that the
subject will be buried in oblivion.[26]

This optimistic hope was not to be fulfilled, for in June the Commons voted the impeachment of Melville and a year later, on
June 12, 1806, the peers acquitted him on all ten counts.

The whole affair was a great blow to Pitt. Not only did it
deprive him of the services of Melville in the Admiralty at a time
when they were badly needed, but it resulted in the breaking up of
the January union with Sidmouth. Pitt hoped that his concessions
to the latter in referring the accusations against Melville to a select
committee had solved their differences; but he soon found that the
question of the appointment of a new First Lord of the Admiralty
was to cause an even greater difficulty. Sir Charles Middleton,
partly because he had been working with Melville and would be
able to carry on existing policies at the Admiralty, was Pitt's
choice. Sidmouth objected largely on the grounds that Pitt did
not take advantage of this chance to make good the pledges given

[25] *Hansard's Parliamentary Debates,* IV, 320.
[26] Stanhope, *op. cit.,* IV, xxv.

to him in December of finding places in the government for his
friends. Thus, as he indicated in a letter to Pitt, he was torn between his desires to withdraw from public life on the one hand
and to serve the King on the other. Finally, as he informed his
brother Hiley, Sidmouth consented to make the experiment of retaining office on the strength of Pitt's assurances that for him he
cherished the warmest friendship, that Melville should not be consulted on public affairs, that the appointment of Middleton should
be considered a temporary one, and that every allowance should
be made for the peculiar situation of his "friends on many questions that might arise, and every consideration shown to their just
and admitted pretensions."[27] The last concession was the really
important one. Despite its involved phraseology, apparently Sidmouth meant that his followers were to be free to speak and to
vote as they chose on the Melville question and that his close
friends and relatives were to be given good places as soon as opportunities presented themselves. It was because of friction over
these two points that Sidmouth was to resign in July.

If the King's letter of April 30 is interpreted literally, neither
Sidmouth nor Pitt informed him of these differences which so
nearly caused another break between the two friends. In this case
George III was on the side of Pitt, probably because he did not
approve of the continued attacks on Melville and did not like the
idea of the government losing the support of Sidmouth's followers
on such an issue. Although the differences were adjusted before
news of the impending break reached him, George III wrote to
Pitt: "He thinks it but justice to his own sentiments to declare
that, had any disunion arisen, he should have decidedly taken part
with Mr. Pitt, as he has every reason to be satisfied with his conduct from the hour of his returning to his service."[28] The reasons
for this decision are not difficult to estimate. The King believed
that Pitt at the head of the government could resist the attacks of
the Fox-Grenville opposition and that Sidmouth could not; and
that he himself could in a crisis always make certain that the latter
would support the government, even though out of office, by making the appeal of "place your hand on your heart" which invariably
proved successful.

The threat by Sidmouth to resign in April was actually carried
out in July before the end of the session. Bond and Hiley Adding-

27 Pellew, op. cit., II, 364.
28 Stanhope, op. cit., IV, xxiv–xxv.

ton, who expected some office in the government as soon as the time was ripe, acted, in the opinion of Pitt, in such a manner during the June debates and the votes on the motions to prosecute or impeach Melville that postponement of these appointments was necessary. Sidmouth felt that Pitt's attitude was a repudiation of the terms upon which he had taken office in January and of the agreements reached at the end of April. Pitt, on the other hand, insisted that if he gave Bond and Hiley office at this time his own sincerity would be suspected. The accounts of the interviews which Pitt and Sidmouth had on June 30 and July 4 are most revealing. The Minister wished to let matters drift until the next session and to see how the two factions got along during the interim. The phase which seems to have annoyed and pained Sidmouth most was that Pitt did not express any regret or offer any remonstrance when informed of the impending resignations.[29] The King also accepted Sidmouth's explanations of his resignations and seems to have made no effort to induce him to remain. The logical explanation for the equanimity of the King is that he still believed, as in April, that Sidmouth and his followers were worth as much or more to the government out of office as in; and that Pitt was quite capable of carrying on in the face of the Fox-Grenville opposition. As his conduct after the end of the session was to indicate, even Pitt, with his superb self-confidence, does not appear to have believed that his present government was adequate. Rather he seems to have allowed the Sidmouth group to withdraw its support because he was tired of squabbling and because he would not permit insubordination in his cabinet or ministry. Apparently he held the opinion that he could find the needed additional strength elsewhere rather than that his government, after the loss of Sidmouth and Buckinghamshire, was still adequate.

The last session of Parliament which Pitt was to attend closed on July 12, 1805. During the last six months of his life his activities as First Lord of the Treasury were taken up with the negotiations leading to the Third Coalition, with building up the Army and Navy, and with attempts to strengthen his cabinet. The diplomatic, military, and naval events of these months have been described already. Unfortunately for Pitt it was only in naval affairs that any success was attained; for his attempts to strengthen his government met with the same misfortune as his efforts in

29 Pellew, *op. cit.,* II, 372.

diplomacy and as his allies on the battlefield. The weakness of the government aroused hopes in the opposition even before the session closed on July 12. Rumors of the resignation of Sidmouth and Buckinghamshire before they actually took place and of a renewal of offers to the opposition by Pitt to join the government were widespread. Fox discussed fully with his friends what action should be taken in case an offer or even a nibble came from Pitt;[30] and Grenville exchanged impressions with his relatives and followers.[31] Fox felt that Sidmouth had acted with his customary imbecility in resigning at the very end of the session instead of doing so several weeks earlier or at the beginning of the next session. The correspondence of the opposition reads much like that of the members of the Fox-North Coalition more than twenty years earlier, and of that of the Fox and Grenville groups in 1804. Fox still believed that the present ministry should be compelled to resign and a new one formed of which Pitt should be a member but not the head. Grenville gave what would, unquestionably, have been Pitt's answer when he wrote: "I hear from some good authority that P[itt] distinctly says that *rather than find a middleman for the Treasury like the Duke of Portland he should think it better to resign.*"[32] Pitt and Fox were as far apart as ever. The former wished to strengthen his government by the addition of Grenville, Fox, and some of their friends if he could secure the consent of the King; and the latter wished to have a new ministry formed in which both of them should serve under a "middleman." But after all these two points of view never clashed, because George III was not convinced at the end of 1805 that the government was in a sufficiently serious plight to demand the additional strength which Pitt wished to secure.

In order to be in a position to strengthen the government if the opportunity presented itself, Pitt seemingly had an understanding with several members of his cabinet and the ministry that they would relinquish their posts for the good of the country. To fill the posts left vacant by Sidmouth and Buckinghamshire, Camden was transferred from the War Department to the Presidency of the Council, and Castlereagh was given this vacant post.

[30] Lord John Russell, *Memorials and Correspondence of Charles James Fox* (London, 1853–1857), IV, 79–102. Hereafter referred to as *Memorials of Fox*.

[31] Historical Manuscripts Commission, *The Manuscripts of J. B. Fortescue, Esq., Preserved at Dropmore* (London, 1892–1927), VII, 278–300.

[32] *Ibid.*, p. 299.

The relations of Pitt with the King during the last months of his life and ministry were complicated by the growing blindness of the monarch. As early as October 1804 George III told George Rose that he had practically lost the sight of his right eye and could scarcely read a newspaper by candlelight with any kind of spectacles.[33] He was unable to read the speech at the close of the session on July 12, 1805, and in November he took the significant step of retaining Colonel Herbert Taylor as his secretary. This affliction not only made it more difficult for Pitt to bring pressure on the King to consent to including Fox and Grenville in the ministry but it marked the beginning of George III's loss of contact with the details of government. The next five years of his life showed that while he retained old impressions he acquired very few new ones.

The drive which Pitt made to secure the King's consent to changes in the ministry came in September. The reasons of the July to September delay were, in all probability, a desire on the part of Pitt to allow the King to recuperate at Weymouth and a growing realization of the weakness of his own position. The interviews which Pitt and Rose had with George III at Weymouth in September destroyed the hope that the King might consent to any strengthening of the government along the lines suggested by Pitt. The entry of September 22 in the diary of George Rose tells the story:

His Majesty then told me that Mr. Pitt had made very strong representations to him of the necessity of strengthening his Government by the accession of persons from the parties of Lord Grenville and Mr. Fox, but that he was persuaded there existed no necessity whatever for such a junction; that we did very well in the last session, and he was confident we should not be worse in the ensuing one; . . . . I observed . . . . I was perfectly convinced, if Mr. Pitt should be confined by the gout, or any other complaint, for only two or three weeks, there would be an end of us; . . . . I had not the good fortune, however, to make any impression whatever on his Majesty; on the contrary, I found him infinitely more impracticable on the point than last year when at Cuffnells.[34]

A year earlier the King was even willing to allow Fox to have a foreign mission, but now he expressed an unwillingness to admit into the government a single member of the opposition.

Shortly after this interview Fox wrote to Grey that no over-

[33] *Rose Diaries*, II, 196.   [34] *Ibid.*, pp. 199–200.

tures had come from Pitt since his trip to Weymouth and in his opinion none were likely; and to Lauderdale that, although he expected nothing to come of negotiations, he was fairly well decided on the bent they must take. Eighteen months earlier he admitted he would have been willing to settle on an equitable division of offices between his own friends and the few who remained loyal to Pitt. Now the tide had turned in their favor because Pitt no longer had to look after Sidmouth, Melville, and their friends and therefore the greatest care must be taken to insure that a proper First Lord of the Treasury should be chosen. Fox indicated that: "Grey would be best, Fitzwilliam next, and Moira least good of any that I could propose."[35] Fox, like Pitt and George III, remained inflexible.

So far as the relations of the three men are concerned, the September interview and Fox's letters are the last important phases in the dramatic twenty-three-year constitutional struggle. All three men clung grimly to the positions which they had taken in 1783–84. George III insisted at that time that he would rather abdicate than have his closet forced by Fox and, in 1804, when he was, according to George Rose, more tractable than in 1805, that he would risk civil war to avoid the same disaster. It is safe to say that he would have done neither. He had threatened to abdicate in 1783 rather than accept Fox and North; but he had not done so. The civil-war threat might be interpreted as a figure of speech or as a slap at the Prince of Wales; but it should not be taken literally. After all, what forces were to wage this civil war? Fox was, as in the early months of 1784, again insisting that Pitt should "pass under the yoke" and be admitted to a new ministry in which he should not be First Lord of the Treasury. Pitt in both periods held: that the right of the King to choose his ministers must not be infringed upon; that he himself must be First Lord of the Treasury; and that talented members of the opposition should be invited to strengthen the government. Despite the abuse heaped on all three men by different historians and biographers, the position of each was both logical and consistent. In all three instances the points of view adopted and adhered to were based on a combination of fundamental principles and personal motives: the King wished to retain his right to choose his own ministers, and he hated Charles James Fox. Pitt believed in the right of the monarch

[35] *Memorials of Fox*, IV, 115.

to choose his own ministers and felt that pressure to force unwanted ones on the ruler by Parliament should be used only when danger to the people and country demanded it; and also he was firmly convinced that because of his abilities and character he was the logical person to be First Lord of the Treasury. Charles James Fox honestly believed that the power of the Crown had become too great and that the best way to strike a stout blow at prerogative, as he phrased it, was to combine the best minds in Parliament with their followers into a party or coalition which would control the majority of the House of Commons and force the King to accept these leaders as a group and to consent to their policies being put into operation; also he hated George III.

The results of the Weymouth interviews did not depress Pitt so much as might have been expected, because at this time his interests were largely taken up with the formation of the Third Coalition. On the very day he left to interview the King, George Rose reported that he was extremely optimistic about the chances of success against Napoleon as a result of the treaties with Russia and Austria. In April England had made an alliance with Russia, by the terms of which she was to pay a subsidy and her ally was to put a half million men in the field. Prussia and Austria were invited to join the alliance and, if they accepted, were to receive a subsidy from Great Britain. On August 9 Austria joined, but Prussia disappointed Pitt by remaining aloof. Despite the promise of this coalition, the chances of success were lost largely because of a series of major errors in judgment for which Pitt was, in the opinion of Sir John Fortescue, largely responsible. After Russia joined in the war against France, the British ministers feared that Napoleon would seize Sicily and thus secure an all-important base for controlling the Mediterranean. To prevent this from taking place Pitt decided to reinforce Malta; but instead of sending 25,000 men, which would have made it possible to take the offensive against the French, he sent only 5,000. When the Austrians joined the Anglo-Russian alliance, Napoleon almost immediately transferred to the Danube the troops encamped at Boulogne. This gave Pitt an opportunity to repair his earlier mistake of not sending 25,000 soldiers to the Mediterranean. The Kingdom of Naples had now joined the coalition, and the Russians offered to send troops to join the British in southern Italy. With Napoleon occupied on the Danube, 30,000 British soldiers combined with the Russians and the Neapolitans could in all probability have recovered Italy and thus have threatened the French flank from the south. Instead, Pitt decided to attack the French from the north, where he could count on a certain amount of support from the Russians and the insane King of Sweden; and which he hoped would induce the King of Prussia to join the coalition. The desire to recover Hanover and Holland seems to have been responsible for Pitt's decision to send the troops to the Weser instead of to Italy. Prussia, however, refused to join the allies, and the efforts of the British, Russian, and Swedish troops were of no avail. On the other hand, Napoleon struck hard at the Austrians and ended a decisive campaign by a brilliant victory at Austerlitz on December 2, 1805. Fortescue is of the opinion that had Pitt sent the 26,000 troops to the Mediterranean instead of to the Weser they would have seriously embarrassed Napoleon and might even have wholly wrecked his plans.[36]

Even though Pitt is given the benefit of every doubt and the extreme difficulties in his position are admitted, it cannot be denied that his conduct of the war showed the same defects which had characterized his efforts from 1793 to 1801. Both in securing men for the Army and in utilizing his military resources he showed only too clearly that he was no improvement on the preceding ministry. His own serene self-confidence, which meant so much to the nation, gave him an asset which Addington had lacked. When in the course of the year 1805 Pitt began to lose the confidence of the House of Commons and of the people outside, it was the first time in his life, despite his many actual failures in the past, that he had had to undergo such an experience.

The disasters which the Pitt ministry experienced on the military side were somewhat offset by the fine achievements of the Navy. The fact that a genius of the order of Lord Nelson was available made a great deal of difference. For the presence in the service of that great seaman Pitt was in no way responsible, but he could take considerable credit for the fine work done by Sir Charles Middleton, who was made First Lord of the Admiralty and was raised to the peerage as Lord Barham after the resignation in 1805 of Lord Melville. Since Pitt was able to secure Middleton's appointment only after overcoming the threat of resignation on the part of Sidmouth and Buckinghamshire, and since the new First Lord did effective work during the remainder of the ministry, some of the glory of the naval successes culminating in the great victory at Trafalgar must go to the Prime Minister. The significance in the years that followed of the destruction of the French and Spanish fleets on October 21 was not fully realized at the time. The Pitt ministry failed to gain the prestige which should naturally have accrued from so brilliant a victory, because Trafalgar coincided almost exactly with Napoleon's victory over the Austrians at Ulm and was followed shortly by Austerlitz and because the rejoicing over the destruction of the French fleet was marred by the fact that it had been accomplished only at the expense of the life of Lord Nelson. Thus even Trafalgar could not offset Ulm and Austerlitz.

But Pitt's magnificent self-confidence kept up until the news of Austerlitz was definitely verified. It was on November 9 at the Lord Mayor's banquet, three days after the results of Trafalgar reached him, that Pitt spoke his most famous sentence: "England has saved herself by her exertions, and will, as I trust, save Europe by her example." Confident that, if Prussia could be brought into the coalition, Napoleon would be checked, he sent Lord Harrowby to Berlin to carry on the negotiations with the Russians and Prussians. Pitt's anxiety to save Hanover and to bring in the Prussians probably accounts for his failure to use the British forces in Italy. When Harrowby reached Berlin in the middle of November he found that on the 3d of the month Russia and Prussia had signed the Treaty of Potsdam, whereby the latter would join the Anglo-Russian alliance within four weeks unless Napoleon accepted the Prussian terms which required the French withdrawal from Germany, Holland, Switzerland, and Naples. The fly in the ointment for Great Britain was the secret article, to which Russia had agreed, that Hanover should be ceded to Prussia. Pitt indignantly refused to agree to this secret article on the grounds that even to mention such a proposal to the King would either kill him or drive him mad.[37] Instead, Pitt undertook to keep the question open until after the four weeks expired and Prussia would be fighting on the side of the allies by the vague assurance that an "equivalent" for Hanover would be found for her elsewhere. Thus while Pitt and the King of Prussia sparred over Hanover and equivalents, Napoleon struck. Austerlitz on December 2 was followed by the Franco-Austrian armistice of the 6th, by the Russian Em-

---

[37] J. H. Rose, *Life of William Pitt* (London, 1923), II, 541.

peror giving up the campaign, and by the announcement to Harrowby by the Prussian minister, Hardenberg, that his country must consult her own interests. Pitt, however, did not live to see the terrible fate that Prussia by so doing was to suffer the next year. Although his health for some weeks had been growing more precarious, the news of Trafalgar and the high hopes he entertained of adding Prussia to the alliance made him reluctant to leave Westminster. Finally repeated attacks of gout drove him on December 7 to leave for Bath. It was here where he expected the waters to effect a speedy cure that the bad news of Austerlitz reached him; and it is here that when shown a map of Europe he is supposed to have made his famous defeatist remark: "Roll up that map: it will not be wanted these ten years." Such a comment runs contrary to both Pitt's incurable optimism and to the evidence that for some time after the news of Austerlitz arrived he still had hopes that Prussia would back Austria and Russia and that all would be well. It was not Austerlitz that seems to have killed Pitt but the deadly news that dribbled in showing the disintegration of the great coalition upon which he had built his hopes. On January 9 he left Bath for his home on Putney Heath. Here he spent the last two weeks of his life; and it was in this house that the most appalling news reached him.

Left leaderless by Pitt's illness, his cabinet had to decide on the momentous issue of ordering the return of the British reinforcements sent to Hanover. These ministers did not know definitely that the Prussian ruler had decided to accept Napoleon's offer of Hanover in return for certain rather humiliating concessions, but they feared the worst. George III approved the return of these reinforcements and J. H. Rose is of the opinion that Pitt conceded the point.[38] On January 19 the cabinet went further and ordered the immediate recall of all the British troops.

Thus, England had sent forth some 60,000 troops in order to bring them back again. She had paid a million sterling to Austria, and the results were Ulm and Austerlitz. Nearly as much had gone to Russia, and the outcome was the armistice. A British subsidy had been claimed by Prussia, and in return she was about to take Hanover as a gift from Napoleon.[39]

But by this date it was clear that Pitt's death was only a question of time, and on the morning of the 23d he expired. He was less

---

[38] *Ibid.*, pp. 555–56.   [39] *Ibid.*, p. 556.

than forty-seven years of age at the time and had been a member of the House of Commons for exactly twenty-five years.

Considerable controversy has raged over whether or not Pitt spoke the dying words ascribed to him by James Stanhope: "My country! How I leave my country!" Whether or not actually uttered they are exactly in keeping with Pitt's political life and personal self-confidence. As chief minister he had by his ill-advised conduct of the war brought his country into a most precarious position. Yet so great was his belief in his own powers that his chief concern seems to have been over the fate of his country which would be left at so critical a time, without his leadership. It was a manifestation of that magnificent self-confidence and patriotism which had caused the people of England to retain confidence in him for twenty-three years and which had brought his country to the verge of disaster.

After all, how did Pitt leave his country? The precarious position of England in its relation to Napoleon, Prussia, and the members of the Third Coalition has been made clear, and was clearly recognized both at that time and since. On the other hand, the condition in which he left his own ministry and following in the House of Commons is given less attention in the histories and biographies of the period. The new session of Parliament opened on January 22, but owing to Pitt's illness the opposition did not bring its heavy guns into operation that day. Yet in view of the military and diplomatic disasters there is every reason to believe that the government would have been overthrown early in the session by the combined attacks of the Grenville and Fox groups. In a letter written on the last day of the 1805 session, July 12, Fox made an ingenious estimate of the party divisions in the House of Commons:

Supporters of the Chancellor of the Exchequer for
    the time being 180
Opposition 150
Pitt 60
Addington 60

. . . . The first class, were it not for the very precarious state of the K., would, I fear, be much larger; and the second, for the same reason, and from the slowly increasing, but still increasing weight of Carlton House, will much more likely gain ground than lose any. The third class seems very unlikely to increase at present; and the fourth will either gain or lose,—first, according to the notions that will be entertained of the Doctor's being more or less well regarded at Windsor; next, according to their success in getting themselves up (which they will endeavour to do) as opposers of corruption and guardians of the public purse.[40]

During the interim from July to January it is unlikely that either class three or class four gained many adherents. Pitt's lack of success in the war and Sidmouth's action in quitting the cabinet for what seemed to George III to be inadequate reasons seem to preclude any idea of a considerable addition to the numbers of either group. On the other hand, the management of the Prussian problem and the recall of the troops must have increased the opposition numbers considerably. It is highly significant that Fox should estimate that forty per cent of the 450 votes would follow any Chancellor of the Exchequer and that even this figure was abnormally low because of the state of the King's health. Two conclusions based on Fox's estimates and the state of affairs at the death of Pitt appear reasonably certain: first, that the government would have found great difficulty in maintaining itself in view of the additions to the numbers of the opposition and the likelihood of the hostility or at best lukewarm support of the Sidmouth group; and, second, that Pitt at the end of his life as after the general election of 1784 and at the time of the Regency question in 1788–1789 could count on only fifty or sixty followers and relied for his majority on those members of Parliament who would follow any Chancellor of the Exchequer and those who were influenced by his oratory and policies. In short, Pitt ended his career as First Lord of the Treasury almost exactly as he had begun it by relying on a small group of personal followers, on the support of the Crown, and on his ability to secure the votes of the independents. Thus Pitt made no contribution to the development of what in the nineteenth and twentieth centuries is called party government. He did not believe in parties, but in individual ability and character.

The composition of his cabinet in January 1806, along with his oft-expressed opinion that the chief minister must dominate his fellow ministers, indicates that Pitt had no intention of creating a cabinet based on joint responsibility, professing unanimity in public, and acting as the acknowledged leaders of the majority or minority party in Parliament. He took men of Whig or of

[40] *Memorials of Fox*, IV, 98–99.

Tory principles, provided he thought they would be of any assistance and were willing to work under the conditions which he exacted. Before the session of 1806 opened he had planned to strengthen his cabinet and the debating strength of the government in the Commons by the admission of Canning and Charles Yorke; but he had not put this project into operation at the time of his death. The list of the members who met on January 24 and agreed to the Minute drawn up is significant: Lords Eldon, Camden, Westmorland, Castlereagh, Mulgrave, Barham, Hawkesbury, and Chatham, and the Dukes of Portland and Montrose. Eldon, Westmorland, Castlereagh, and Hawkesbury were members of the Tory ministry which ruled the country from 1807 to 1827; and Portland, Mulgrave, Camden, and Chatham held important offices at times during the years 1807 to 1812. Thus one reason why Pitt has been considered a Tory is that the members of his last ministry after his death laid the foundations of the modern Tory party. But during the first forty-six years of the reign of George III, at least, it is very difficult to say in case of many ministers whether they were Whigs or Tories; and certainly in 1806 it would have been a problem to list certain members of Pitt's last cabinet according to this classification. Eldon and Hawkesbury were acknowledged as the King's friends; Camden's father had been a strong Whig and a close friend of the elder William Pitt; Castlereagh and Barham owed their places partly to their relationship to Camden and Melville, respectively; Chatham was the elder brother of Pitt; and Portland was for some years titular head of the Whigs after the death of Rockingham, but in 1794 he had broken with Fox and joined Pitt's ministry, and his presence in the cabinet from 1804 to 1806 was in part due to these past services. Thus members of this ministry as well as the cabinet were chosen largely for their relationship to some important person, for their ability, and for their availability; and not because they were Whigs or Tories.

The extent to which Pitt's own cabinet regarded him as indispensable is shown by the unusual Minute which eight of the ten members drew up the day after his death and to which the two who were absent—Lord Chatham and the Duke of Portland—gave their assent:

Your Majesty's Confidential Servants have in obedience to Your Majesty's commands most seriously consider'd the two following questions.

First whether it is practicable to form an Administration out of the persons who composed the Administration under Mr. Pitt which would be capable of carrying on Your Majesty's Government under the present circumstances with advantage to the Country.

Secondly whether if an arrangement to this effect is judged impracticable there appears to be any considerable addition of strength within the reach of Your Majesty's Servants which would enable them to suggest to Your Majesty the means of constituting such an Administration.

Your Majesty's Servants having fully discuss'd and maturely weighed all considerations which bear on these important questions humbly represent to Your Majesty that they feel it to be their duty to answer both these questions in the negative.[41]

Such a confession of abject uselessness to His Majesty would seem to indicate that Pitt had been hopelessly handicapped by a group of titled mediocrities and that once his guiding genius was removed they would sink back forever into innocuous desuetude. Yet Eldon and Westmorland resumed their respective offices in less than two years and held them continuously until 1827. In addition, Pitt had some of the finest raw material that any First Lord of the Treasury ever possessed. Within his cabinet he had Castlereagh and Hawkesbury and outside the cabinet, but in the ministry, Canning and Perceval. These four men were to dominate the country for the twenty years from 1807 to 1827. The fact that they carried on the war with far greater effectiveness than Pitt, Grenville, and Dundas from 1793 to 1801, than Addington from 1803 to 1804, than Pitt from 1804 to 1806, and than Grenville and Fox from 1806 to 1807 is usually obscured by their unfortunate policy of repression which followed the Congress of Vienna. In short, Pitt had superb material with which to weld together a powerful ministry. By his outstanding abilities and his serene self-confidence he could win the admiration and the respectful support of these future statesmen; but he did not know how to exploit the resources of their ideas and administrative skill. Thus while there is strong evidence that the people outside Parliament and the independents in Parliament were finally convinced that Pitt's character, patriotism, and serene self-confidence were no longer adequate reasons for allowing him to continue his blundering policies in war and diplomacy, there is no evidence that to the young men who were to bring victory to Great Britain from

[41] Clements Transcripts, XIV, 1936-37.

1807 to 1815 he was not at the time of his death still the Immortal William Pitt. Fortunately for him, for them, and for the country, they did not follow his military plans; instead, they adopted wiser ones and ostentatiously burned incense to his memory.

With Pitt dead and his ministers in the state of mind indicated in the Minute quoted, the necessity for taking action devolved upon the King. To his usual physical ailments had been added blindness. Nevertheless, in spite of the derogatory statements made in so many standard histories and biographies of this period, it is difficult to see in what respects he acted other than he had earlier in his reign when confronted by similar situations. The death of Pitt was a shock to him because it meant the loss of the best political prop of his reign. It is doubtful whether the King felt any deep personal loss, since his relations with his minister during the past year had not been particularly happy ones. The two had clashed over the appointment of a successor to Archbishop Moore of Canterbury in January 1805. Pitt was very anxious to have his old tutor, Pretyman, who had changed his name to Tomline and was now Bishop of Lincoln; while the King favored Dr. Manners Sutton, the Bishop of Norwich. Whether George III's decision was based on antipathy to Tomline, a warm regard for Sutton, a desire to circumvent Pitt, or a feeling, as Wraxall says, that a gentleman must receive the appointment, is from the available evidence not clear. In any case the King had his way and Sidmouth is authority for the statement that such strong language in his opinion "had hardly ever passed between a Sovereign and his Minister."[42] According to the gossip prevalent in contemporary diaries, Pitt on one occasion went a month without seeing the King. Clearly even the formal cordiality which characterized the relations of the two men before 1801 was lacking. Nevertheless the loss of his minister was a real blow to George III, because it removed the chief bulwark against the admission to office of the Grenvilles and the Foxites and, above all, of Charles James Fox. Thus the King was in exactly the same position as in 1763-1765 and in 1782-83: he could insure any minister who was willing to serve him and who had the ability to resist the debating power of the opposition and to gain the support of the independents, a substantial bloc of votes in the House of Commons. Unfortunately, as in attempting to find a

42 Stanhope, op. cit., IV, 252.

successor for George Grenville in 1763–1765, for Lord North in 1782, and for Lord Shelburne in 1783, George III discovered that those who were acceptable to him felt that they did not have the ability to carry on the government, and others would serve only on terms disagreeable to him.

The King's first step was to attempt to induce his ministers to carry on under Hawkesbury. The unanimous refusal of the ten members of the cabinet, however, made it necessary for George III to adopt some other expedient. The Duke of Portland wrote him a long letter which is noteworthy for the involved phraseology used to state a simple piece of advice:

As a sense of Duty has compelled the D. of Portland to undertake the painful task of submitting his sentiments on this momentous crisis to Your Majesty; he cannot forbear consistently with the same feelings from submitting to Your Majesty's better Judgement the necessity of Your Majesty's having recourse to the Influence & Abilities of some *at least* of those Persons who compose the present Opposition in order to enable Your Majesty to form an efficient Administration capable of conducting Your Majesty's affairs. The D. of P. fears that such a step is too obvious to require any argument to enforce it & he will therefore only submit to Your Majesty's Consideration whether the advantages which may arise from its being resorted to as soon as it can be made to suit Your Majesty's Convenience may not outweigh any which can be expected to be derived from any delay which can be obtained at such a moment as the present.[43]

Briefly stated, Portland was advising the King to call in the opposition to form a ministry, whether all factions were included or not, and to do so at once instead of postponing the decision for several weeks. The Duke unquestionably had in mind how many weeks George III had delayed the selection of successors to North in 1782 and to Shelburne in 1783. Hawkesbury, writing to George IV in 1821, took the credit for inducing George III to admit Fox into the new ministry.[44] It is comparatively unimportant, however, whether the King arrived at the decision not to exclude Fox as a result of his own mental processes or by the advice of others. The significant fact is that he decided to swallow the bitter pill at once and, according to Hawkesbury, "to do it in the most dignified manner, and to put the whole on grounds which,

<hr>

[43] Clements Transcripts, XIV, 1939–40.

[44] Charles D. Yonge, *The Life and Administration of Robert Banks, Second Earl of Liverpool* (London, 1868), III, 149.

if they should fail, would secure the good opinion and support of the whole country."[45] Feeling that it would be expecting too much of him to request Fox to form a ministry, the King sent for Grenville and asked him to prepare a plan of government. Although no one was excluded by George III, he followed his customary practice of reserving the right to pass judgment on the list of ministers when it was placed before him.

While Grenville was attempting to form a government, an incident occurred which might have caused the King to renew his exclusion of Fox from the cabinet. On January 27 Mr. Henry Lascelles moved an address to the Crown that Pitt be buried at the public charge and that a monument be erected in the church of St. Peter, Westminster, "to the memory of that excellent statesman," with an inscription stating the great and irreparable loss which the nation had suffered. Although the motion carried by 258 to 89,[46] it was opposed by both Windham and Fox. The latter declared that he was willing to join in any mark of public respect which was consistent with his own political principles, such as remedying the financial difficulties in which Pitt had become involved by the acknowledged disinterestedness of his political life, but that he could not under the circumstances vote that his great rival was an "excellent statesman." Fortunately his stand did not result either in the dissolution of his understanding with Grenville or in a renewal of his exclusion from the cabinet by the King.

When the new ministry was formed it was made up of three of the four parties in the House of Commons: the followers of Grenville, Fox, and Sidmouth. The latter was included because there were forty to sixty members of the House of Commons who looked to him for guidance and because he was supposed to enjoy the favor of the King. By January 31 Grenville was able to submit to George III his selections for the cabinet: Lord Chancellor, Mr. Erskine; Lord President, Earl Fitzwilliam; Lord Privy Seal, Viscount Sidmouth; Secretary of State, Foreign Department, Mr. Fox; Secretary of State, Home Department, Earl Spencer; Secretary of State, War Department, Mr. Windham; First Lord of the Admiralty, Mr. Grey; Lord Lieutenant of Ireland, Earl of Moira; Chancellor of the Exchequer, Lord Henry Petty; First Lord of the Treasury, Lord Grenville.[47] To satisfy

[45] Yonge, *op. cit.*, I, 209.   [46] *Hansard's Parliamentary Debates*, VI, 72.
[47] *Dropmore Papers*, VIII, 1.

Sidmouth, Lord Ellenborough, Chief Justice of the King's Bench, was added to the cabinet. Outside the cabinet, but occupying important posts, were such men as Lord Minto, Sheridan, Lord Auckland, and Romilly. Such well-known Whigs as Whitbread, Tierney, and Thomas Grenville received nothing. So many good places outside the cabinet went to the friends of Sidmouth that a great deal of resentment was aroused among the followers of Grenville and Fox.

In the course of his letter explaining the membership of his proposed administration Grenville devoted a paragraph to the defense of the country and to the administration of the military service which so aroused the suspicions of George III that he demanded a clarification of the offending section:

The King regrets that the paragraph to which he refers together with any explanation he has been able to procure, should be of so general a nature as to render it impossible to pass it by without notice, or to answer it with any precision. His Majesty has no desire to restrain his confidential servants from the most thorough investigation into the various and extensive branches of the military service, and he will be favourably disposed to consider any measures relating to this important subject, which upon a full examination may be laid before him.

The King therefore desires that Lord Grenville will, with as little delay as possible, after conferring with those persons with whom he acts, convey to him specifically on paper, for his consideration, the explanation which his Majesty requires; and the King must be understood as reserving to himself at all times the undoubted right of deciding on the measures which may be proposed to him respecting the military service, or the administration of it, both with reference to the prerogatives of the Crown, and the nature and expediency of the measures themselves.[48]

This last sentence shows clearly that George III held in theory and in practice the same views in 1806 that he had held in 1760 and in 1783. It was not enough that he should be merely consulted: he reserved the undoubted right of *deciding* on measures. Grenville's answer the same day must have been most gratifying to the aged monarch. After explaining that the offending paragraph was vague because the new ministers in charge of military service had felt it impossible to frame in advance their opinions on specific defense measures, Grenville gave the required assurance:

[48] *Ibid.*, p. 8.

From the moment that your Majesty is graciously pleased to declare that your Majesty has no desire to restrain your confidential servants from the thorough investigation of this important subject, and will be favourably disposed to consider any measures relating to it which upon a full examination may be laid before your Majesty, they feel that they can have nothing further to ask upon this point. They trust your Majesty could not for a moment doubt that they know too well the respect they owe to your Majesty and the limits of their duty, not to be fully sensible that upon this, as upon every other branch of administration, it is your Majesty's pleasure that can alone decide on the adoption or rejection of any measures which your Majesty's ministers may at any time submit to your Majesty's consideration.[49]

It is difficult to imagine a clearer statement of the power of the ruler and of his relations to his ministers than in the concluding sentence of Grenville. Such a statement makes an admirable ending to a study of the relations between George III and William Pitt; for, if over twenty-three years after Pitt first became Prime Minister and a few days after his death, the monarch was able to obtain such a statement from his successor, the commonly accepted thesis that 1783 marked the beginning of the decline of the royal power must be dismissed as a myth.

[49] *Dropmore Papers,* VIII, 9.

XI. CONCLUSION

As was pointed out in the Preface, the original object of this study was to bring out in detail the exact steps whereby Pitt during his two ministries, 1783–1801 and 1804–1806, reduced Geeorge III to the position of a modern constitutional ruler and firmly established the cabinet system of government. The present writer at the time he began his research accepted the conclusions of practically all historians that Pitt had triumphed at the expense of the King and that cabinet government really dated from the long ministry of 1783 to 1801; and he merely wished to trace exactly how this change had occurred. As a result of an intensive study of the period he has come to the conclusion that the period from 1760 to 1806 has been misinterpreted largely as a result of reading back into these years the constitutional developments in Great Britain since the Reform Act of 1832. For this reason, and for others, the present writer feels that the following conclusions which have been brought out in the course of the narrative should be emphasized.

I. The proper approach to the study of English government in the period from 1689 to 1832 is not that of one hundred fifty years of growth or of evolution in the period between the Magna Charta and the twentieth century, but rather an attempt to understand what the government meant during this century and a half to those for whom and by whom it was administered. To both rulers and statesmen, whether Whig or Tory, the "fixed" characteristics of the Constitution seemed noteworthy. "Our blessed Constitution in Church and State" meant not only the traditions of the common law and the succession of notable statutes beginning with the Magna Charta, but even more the terms of the Revolution Settlement of 1689. Certainly specific points in this settlement appeared to eighteenth-century rulers and statesmen far more important than the evolutionary and unwritten characteristics so much stressed since 1832. Lord Passfield and Mrs. Webb have shown that the years 1689 to 1835 make a natural unit for the study of local government in England and those from 1689 to 1832 offer a similar opportunity for the study of the national government. During these one hundred forty-three years the organization of the House of Commons remained practically unchanged and the powers of the three branches of government underwent little alteration. The greatest change came in the personnel of the House of Lords after 1776. Between 1689 and 1828, when parts of the Test and Corporation laws were repealed, few constitutional measures of first-class importance, with the possible exception of the acts of union with Scotland and Ireland, were passed. Thus what might be called the structure of the Constitution remained almost unchanged during this period.

II. Although the framework of the Constitution was fairly fixed, there were significant developments both before and after 1760. Since the Settlement of 1689 made annual meetings of Parliament necessary, the rulers had either to submit to dictation, such as William III experienced from 1697 to 1701, or to find some method of securing a majority in Parliament to support their policies. The problem was solved in the reigns of George I and II when the King and his ministers made certain of a majority in both houses by adding to the nucleus of placemen, through a judicious use of patronage, bribery, and oratory, a sufficient number of the remaining members. The system for securing this majority in the House of Commons was brought to a high degree of efficiency under Walpole, Pelham, and Newcastle. A second significant development before 1760 was that of the position of Prime Minister. The growing importance of this office was due in part to the increased significance of the Treasury after the Revolution Settlement; to the necessity of having an individual primarily responsible for securing the required majority in both houses of Parliament; to the desirability of having a chief minister take charge of the cabinet when, after 1714, the rulers ceased to attend the meetings; and to the imprint which the personality and the long ministry of Walpole gave to the position of the First Lord of the Treasury. A third significant development was the tendency of disappointed statesmen and politicians to collect around the heir to the throne and to count on holding office in the next reign. Whether the individual statesmen were Whigs or Tories, this attitude was generally characteristic of the opposition in the reigns of William III, Anne, George I, and George II.

When the part which the King played in the government during the reigns of George I and George II came to be understood and individuals wished to oppose its policies and measures, what lines of action were open to them? In Parliament it was possible to join either the forces which had gathered around the Prince of Wales, or the Tories and independents who professed to be eager to rid the country and the King of undesirable ministers. In the nineteenth century opposition could be expressed legitimately as a member of one of the two major parties; but before 1760 opposition, as a permanent practice, had not been accepted. Outside Parliament, especially among the country gentlemen who had no hope of holding office, Jacobitism before 1747 offered some hope of a change as well as an emotional outlet. Those who were unwilling to be Jacobites could, before George III came to the throne, at least adopt an anti-Hanoverian and anti-court attitude. When Jacobitism faded, it was possible for the discontented elements outside Parliament to seek relief by becoming Wilkites or joining other reform movements.

III. The Whig and Tory parties from 1689 to 1806 were not the well-organized political machines of the last seventy-five years, but groups of persons holding certain views on the Constitution in church and state. When they were members of Parliament, groups of Whigs and Tories often acknowledged the leadership of prominent statesmen. Allegiance to such leaders was, however, often both loose and shifting; and throughout the eighteenth century it was at times difficult to decide under what classification many members of Parliament should be listed. Before 1760 the Tories were in the main the country gentlemen who either remained on their country estates and did not take part in national politics or made up a considerable part of the "independents" in the House of Commons. Between 1760 and 1783 the name Tory was often applied to the forces of the government, particularly in the ministry of Lord North. In the years covered by this work, 1783 to 1806, the Whigs and Tories differed in political theory principally upon the greater emphasis which the latter placed on the phrase "Church and King." Actually the fairly formidable opposition of 1783 to 1792 was composed of members from the Rockingham Whigs and followers of Lord North; and the government forces of King's Friends, Shelburne or Pitt Whigs, and so-called Tories. Although the opposition, in the years following 1783, professed the principles which Portland enunciated to George III in 1783, and which the monarch found so novel, still they came to depend more and more upon the accession to the throne of the Prince of Wales to give them an opportunity to hold office. Thus the situation from 1783 to 1801 was not unlike that of 1734 to 1751 when the dissatisfied elements, regardless of party, had felt that the accession to the throne of Prince Frederick offered them the best chance of coming into power. But from any angle the use of the terms Whig and Tory parties is, in the modern sense, very misleading for the periods of both Walpole and the younger Pitt.

IV. The fundamental constitutional position of George III remained unchanged from 1760 to 1806. Much of the confusion over the constitutional issues of his reign is a result of the failure to distinguish between what George III regarded as fundamental and what he regarded as tactics and temporary policies. As he reiterated so frequently, and as has often been brought out in the narrative, George III believed firmly that he had a right to choose his own ministers and to veto laws. Naturally the choice of ministers included the right to pass on measures and policies introduced in Parliament. Whereas during the last century rulers have claimed the right to be consulted, George III insisted upon the right to prevent the introduction, as a government measure, of any bill of which he disapproved. In cases of flat disagreement between the King and his Prime Minister, two lines of action were open to the sovereign: first, to replace his minister or ministers; and, second, to give way on the ground that the particular measure was not worth so great a sacrifice. George III was willing to admit that an occasion might arise when his subjects would express their disapprobation of a minister or a ministry so clearly through a majority of the House of Commons, or of both houses of Parliament, that it would be necessary for him to make a change of government. But whenever such a new arrangement became necessary he insisted that it was his right to choose the new ministers and that it was unconstitutional for a group of men who happened to control a majority of the House of Commons to force their way into his councils. George III even came to the conclusion that there were certain statutes passed at the time of the Revolution Settlement which were permanent and could not be set aside by ordinary acts of Parliament. When, however, he attempted to apply this theory to prevent concessions to Catholics in 1795, his Lord Chancellor was obliged to tell him that an earlier statute could not limit the future action of Parliament. Thus George III was not able to make the inviolability of certain statutes one of the pillars of his constitutional system. As a result he was compelled to act as he did in 1801 to prevent concessions to Catholics which he had satisfied himself, if not his legal advisers, were unconstitutional.

But it was not merely from the personal point of view of George III that his constitutional position remained unchanged. So long as he furnished his ministers with a nucleus of placemen to make possible a majority in Parliament and so long as he passed judgment on the measures which his ministers proposed in Parliament, the King retained an active part in the government. If this condition is made the supreme test, then it is obvious that the constitutional position of George III was the same in 1760, 1770, 1784, 1801, and 1806. Further, these two conditions—the control of an important group in the House by the King and his share in government measures—were to prevail until they were set aside by the Reform Bill of 1832, by the rise of the two-party system, and by the recognition of "His Majesty's Opposition" and of the "neutral" position of the Crown.

This fundamental feature of the position of the King between 1689 and 1832 is obscured by the personalities of rulers, of statesmen, and of agitators; by the effect which different periods of life had on each of them; and by political issues of a temporary and shifting nature. Thus George III was compelled by circumstances to act very differently in the following periods: 1760 to 1768, when he was serving his apprenticeship; 1768 to 1782, when he was forced to furnish much of the initiative for Grafton and North; 1782 to 1784, when he was fighting to prevent the Crown from being relegated to the "neutral" position which it came to occupy after 1832; 1784 to 1788, when he co-operated with a brilliant young minister; and 1789 to 1806, when because of age and infirmities he contented himself with supervising the main policies and gave less attention to details than in his earlier and more vigorous years. Such a tapering off of actual work does not mean any change in the constitutional position of the ruler. George III or any one of his successors could at any time, until the nucleus of placemen who would follow any minister who had the King's approval were swept aside or until cabinet responsibility took the place of the combination of the King and his ministers, have resumed a more active part in the government. Too much emphasis has been placed on the significance of such things as the failure of personal government in 1782 and the resignation of Lord Thurlow in 1792. Unless laws were passed limiting the powers of the King, there would be nothing illegal in any ruler's attempting to secure greater influence in the government through combining a group of his personal followers with those of independent or party leaders. Seemingly there is nothing from the constitutional point of view today to prevent a ruler from attempting such an experiment if he is willing to risk the snub which William IV received as a result of his experience with Peel in 1834–1835.

It may be worth while to trace briefly the policies and tactics which George III pursued from 1760 to 1806. Soon after he became king, he broke the alliance of the Crown and Whigs which had ruled England from 1714 to 1760 and substituted for the Whigs who controlled the political edifice any individuals or groups who were willing to work with him under the new arrangement. For some time he seems to have believed that his operation of the edifice which he had taken over from the Whigs would be adequate to repel all assaults; but a combination of the attacks outside Parliament, especially the Wilkite movement, and the tendency of majorities secured in the House of Commons at general elections to slip away when governmental policies met with ill success, caused George III to build up the House of Lords as a second line of defense. This "development" of the Lords as a body very different from the old Whig magnates began under Lord North and was carried on splendidly by Pitt. So far as George III was concerned it needed to be used only in the fight against the Portland ministry in 1783 and, when they attempted to force the resignation of Pitt, against the Portland forces in the first months of 1784. Had the occasion demanded it, George III would have called on the House of Lords again; but he was not in danger after 1784. The small loss in the number of seats which he controlled in Parliament as a result of economical reforms of 1782 was more than regained through his increased popularity after the failure of the Coalition in 1783. The estimate of the membership of the House of Commons as of May 1, 1788, gave "the party of the Crown" 185 members, Pitt 52, and Fox 138. This is one of many indications that the contribution of the Crown to the majority necessary for the administration to carry on the government had not materially diminished.

That there was any real difference in the relationship between the King and his ministers before and after 1783 is highly doubtful. The printed correspondence of George III to December 1783 and the unprinted after that date indicate that he wrote freely to his First Lord of the Treasury as well as to other ministers, and that the extent and frequency of these communications depended largely upon such circumstances as the person occupying the position and the importance of events in the field of the particular minister's sphere of influence.

Perhaps nothing would better place the two ministries of Pitt in their proper relationship to the constitutional position of George III than a comparison of the different administrations from 1760 to 1807. In general the ministries of George III fall into one of four classifications: first, those headed by first lords of the Treasury who were personally acceptable to the King but who were unable to maintain themselves in Parliament for more than a short period; second, those headed by first lords who were satisfactory to the King and able to maintain themselves in Parliament for a long period; third, those headed by first lords who were taken by the King to avoid having his "closet forced" or as the lesser of two evils; and, fourth, those headed by first lords who had forced themselves on the King or had become undesirable and who could expect to hold office only until they could with safety be supplanted. Under the first classification come the Bute ministry, 1762–1763, the Grafton, 1767–1770, and the Addington, 1801–1804; under the second, the North, 1770–1782, and the Pitt, 1783–1801; under the third, the Rockingham, 1765–1766, the Shelburne, 1782–1783, and the Pitt, 1804–1806; and under the fourth, the Newcastle, 1760–1762, the Grenville, 1763–1765, the Rockingham, 1782, the Portland, 1783, and the Grenville, 1806–1807. The Chatham ministry of 1766–1767 defies classification because Chatham was not First Lord of the Treasury, because he was personally acceptable to the King when he took office, and because of the manner in which he "ebbed" from the government. Even though all the ministries from 1760 to 1807, with the one exception, can be placed in these four categories, this does not mean that there were no differences of degree in each classification. For example, George III undoubtedly was much more attached on the personal side to Bute, North, and Addington than he was to William Pitt and Grafton. Further the conditions which caused the King to accept Rockingham in 1765, Shelburne in 1782, and Pitt in 1804 were very different; but the fact remains that he preferred them at these dates, respectively, to Grenville, Fox, and Portland. There is even greater difference in the manner in which George III acquired his undesirable first lords: he found Newcastle in office at the time of his accession to the throne; he selected Grenville voluntarily in 1763 and only found him dis-

tasteful as a result of his conduct in office; he accepted Rockingham in 1782 and the Fox-North Coalition headed by Portland in
1783 only after he had tried every possible alternative; and he
called in Grenville in 1806 after his lone attempt to secure Hawkesbury. Thus George III wished to rid himself of Newcastle in
1762, and of Portland in 1783; and he wished to retain Bute in
1763, North in 1782, Shelburne in 1783, Addington in 1804, and
the followers of Pitt in 1806. Evidence on the King's reaction to
the retirement of Grafton in 1770 is scanty. Seemingly he was
reconciled to the Duke's decision because he had at hand a better
man in Lord North, and such was not the case when the latter insisted upon resigning in 1782. The retirement of Chatham in
1767 is too wrapped in mystery to be included in this classification; and that of Pitt in 1801 was due to a difference with the
King and not to the attacks in Parliament which made untenable
the positions of Bute, Grafton, North, Addington, and Pitt's own
followers in 1806.

V. The traditional view that the Whigs were decisively defeated in their struggle with George III is, apparently, the correct
one. They could not be certain that the long partnership of 1714
to 1760 was over until the events of December 1762—the passing
of the peace preliminaries in the House of Commons by 319 to 65
and the "massacre of the Pelhamite innocents"—convinced the
most skeptical of them. Whigs in public life then had the option
of conforming to the rule laid down by George III that as individuals they would be eligible to serve in a ministry but not as a
unit, or of working out a new plan of action which would give
them a greater share in the government. Several groups of the
Whigs did conform to this rule, since the followers of Grenville,
Bedford, and Chatham all shared in at least one of the ministries
of the first ten years of the reign of George III. But the Whigs
who successively acknowledged the leadership of Newcastle, Rockingham, Portland, and Fox did not tamely submit to this subordinate position assigned alike to all Whigs, Tories, and independents. The political philosophy which they evolved during the
twenty years from 1762 to 1782, and to which Burke contributed
so brilliantly, is the one which triumphed after 1832. It is true
that it was not enunciated with the completeness of the late nineteenth century and that these Whigs did not apply it fully when
they assumed office in 1765, 1782, or 1806. None the less this
doctrine did represent an alternative to serving as the King's men.

It required that a group of men should unite on fundamental political principles and should secure a majority of the House of Commons to back them, so that no other group upon whom the King should call would be able to carry on the government. Their recognized leader would present the King with the list of the ministers as a unit and the cabinet would act as the real executive. It is on this issue that the Whigs fought and lost from 1782 to 1784.

Such a doctrine would not work continuously unless it were accepted practically unanimously by the men in public life and by the ruler. After 1835 it was eventually accepted by both parties and by the sovereigns; but such was not the case from 1762 to 1806. George III regarded the doctrine as both novel and unpleasing, and he made no pretense of looking upon it as anything but unconstitutional. When he realized the danger in its application, George III relied upon two lines of defense: first, the House of Lords; and, second, a combination of all men in Parliament who were indifferent to these principles or who would sacrifice them to hold office. By using the Lords he could defeat any measure which he disliked and which the men who had forced their way into his councils could put through the Commons; and he could refuse to create peers and to confer similar favors at the request of his undesired ministers. If, however, he refused to accept these men who controlled the House of Commons, the King ran the risk of having supplies refused and the Mutiny Act defeated. In any case it is clear that George III would tolerate ministers who applied such disagreeable principles only until he could supplant them. If necessary he could fall back on the expedient Charles II used from 1679 to 1681 and continually dissolve Parliament until he secured a majority for ministers of his own choice. Considering the advantages he possessed and the fact that he never lost a general election it seems unlikely that George III would have been troubled with the obnoxious Whigs controlling a majority of the Commons for any length of time.

Since the ruler and the great mass of men in public life did not accept this novel doctrine in the reign of George III, what chance of success did the Whigs have? Seemingly their only chance lay in converting all statesmen of any promise to this point of view and of convincing the politically important part of the public outside Parliament of its desirability. In order to defeat the King they needed to be willing to wage a long and grim war in which endurance and tenacity would be the decisive elements. Instead, the

Whigs almost went out of their way to drive into the King's camp the most promising political recruit in a generation and to hopelessly offend public opinion by the Fox-North Coalition. Thus from the general election of 1784 to 1806, and really until 1830, the Whigs had no chance to apply their political principles. Actually the members of the Fox-North Coalition appear to have been held together after 1784 more by the prospect of securing office when Prince George became king or regent than by any deepseated conviction that their principles of cabinet solidarity would triumph. The failure to reach a working agreement with Pitt in 1783 and 1784 or to organize a machine that would in time be capable of winning a general election from the King meant that the attempt of 1782 to 1784 to apply these new Whig principles was a mere flash in the pan. It is possible that, by convincing Pitt and every other statesman who showed enough ability to make a successful first lord of the Treasury that the principles of a cabinet united by political principles and dependent on the majority of the House of Commons were the correct ones rather than those which gave the King a real choice in the selection of ministers, it would have been possible to overcome George III without the campaign to convert public opinion. Such a conclusion would imply that the King would weary of the struggle before his opponents did, and that even success in general elections would not offset his failure to secure ministers who were adequate to carry on the government. But since no attempt was made to convert Pitt to these principles, speculations on the chances of success or on the subsequent influence upon English constitutional history are futile.

VI. The fundamental political principles of William Pitt are, perhaps, more commonly misunderstood even than those of George III. Pitt is often credited with having established the supremacy both of the cabinet and of the Prime Minister in the cabinet at the expense of the Crown. Because since 1832 the two-party system, the cabinet as the executive, and the "neutral" Crown have been the outstanding constitutional developments, it is assumed that Pitt consciously played his part by building up the Tory party and subordinating the King to a powerful prime minister and a unified cabinet. There is little, however, in his written and spoken words, or in his actions and achievements, to justify the conclusions that he contributed heavily to the development of either.

The real key to Pitt's political career and constitutional principles must be sought in the Revolution Settlement and in the principles and career of his father the Earl of Chatham. The phrase, "Men not Measures," which Chatham hurled at the Rockingham Whigs in the seventeen-sixties represents the point of view of the son as well as of the father. Actually· this constitutional position is not fundamentally different from that held by George III. All three believed that men should be selected for places in the cabinet and ministry because of their peculiar fitness for these posts. Of course, a decided difference of opinion might develop over the question of what qualities constituted fitness: George III would be apt to stress the willingness .of an individual to serve the Crown; while the Pitts would emphasize ability and character. The Newcastle-Rockingham-Portland Whigs believed in party solidarity based on measures, in an important part being played by the great families or magnates, and, until George III took charge of the machine, in the control of Parliament by the methods developed from 1714 to 1760. The Pitts, on the other hand, believed in "Men not Measures" (as already noted), hated and despised the magnates, and disdained to do personally the work necessary to hold together a Parliamentary majority. Chatham escaped the consequences of not organizing Parliament by borrowing the majority of the Duke of Newcastle from 1757 to 1761 and by becoming the King's minister in 1766 to 1767; and Pitt avoided the necessity of specializing in this kind of work through his close association with George III and Dundas. Both Pitts feared neither ruler. nor rival because each held a very exalted opinion of his own ability and character. Just as the elder Pitt was willing to enter the ministry in 1757, despite Newcastle's control of the House of Commons, so the younger Pitt was willing to admit the followers of Fox to a share in the government in 1783 and 1784, in 1792, 1793, and 1794, and in 1804 and 1805. This willingness to share power with other men, even those of outstanding ability, was based on the arrogant confidence of being able to dominate any situation or group of men. When Chatham acquired this state of mind is uncertain, but in the case of Pitt it seems to have come in the first months of 1784. Both Pitts disdained to build up political parties, exactly as they refused to follow the Walpole-Pelham-Newcastle–George III method of securing a majority in the House of Commons. Chatham and Pitt certainly counted on support in Parliament and outside, but they expected it because they believed that it was generally appreciated that they had the character and patriotism to wish to serve their country and the ability to do so effectively. George III, Chatham, and Pitt all believed in the principles of the Revolution Settlement not only because they actually felt that the Constitution so established was justifiably the admiration of the civilized world but also because the rules laid down at the time of the Settlement gave them a better chance to play the game of politics successfully than would the new rules promulgated by the Rockingham Whigs.

If all three men had fundamental constitutional ideas so much in common and if Chatham and Pitt held such identical views on the functions of the chief minister, what explanation can be offered for the fact that Chatham lasted only about a year each time that he held the highest post under George III, while Pitt was able to serve continuously for more than seventeen years? The explanation clearly lies in the personalities of the three men. Chatham was almost unbelievably arrogant and dictatorial both in 1760–61 and in 1766–67; while the King was still inexperienced, suspicious, and sulky. Pitt, on the other hand, was proud and aloof, and outwardly displayed more of the Grenville "starchiness" than of his father's aggressive arrogance; while George III by 1783 had become an astute politician with better control over his emotions. Thus it is doubtful whether the King and Chatham could ever have co-operated for any length of time because of differences in personality and temperament; and it is equally doubtful whether George III could have handled Pitt in the seventeen-sixties as he did in the seventeen-eighties.

There is nothing in Pitt's declarations or actions which gives any indication that he thought of succumbing to the Whig doctrine of "measures" either in the crisis of 1783–84 or in later years when he was willing to arrange a coalition or to admit Fox and his followers to a share of power. Once Pitt had convinced himself in January and February, 1784, that he could hold his own with any speaker in the House of Commons, there was no thought in his mind that he should ever hold any post except that of First Lord of the Treasury. The many proposals made from 1784 to 1805 that Fox and he should serve as secretaries of state under a nominal First Lord of the Treasury held no appeal for him.

The attitude which Pitt adopted in dealing with George III and with his colleagues has been treated by certain historians as establishing a precedent for the all-powerful prime minister and as paving the way for the subordination of both the ruler and of his own fellow ministers. The relations of the King and Pitt have been treated fully in the narrative, and a recapitulation at this point seems unnecessary; but those of the latter with his colleagues in the cabinet may be explained by his personality and constitutional ideas, and in no way create a precedent. Walpole and Chatham dominated their cabinets; but this fact did not, as a precedent, enable Newcastle, Bute, or Grafton to do so. Likewise because Pitt through ability and personality towered over other members of his cabinet than Grenville and Dundas, it does not follow that this precedent enabled Addington, Portland, Liverpool, or Goderich to do so.

When Pitt died in 1806 there was no appreciable difference from those of 1783 in the relative positions of the Crown, of the cabinet, and of the political parties. In many respects the honor of being one of the patron saints of the Tory party is the strangest of all achievements which have been thrust upon Pitt. Because many of the clever and promising young men who served their apprenticeship under him were able to control the government from 1807 to 1830, as the Whigs had done from 1714 to 1760, because the title Tory became not inappropriately fixed on this controlling group, and because many nineteenth-century historians were possessed with a mania for showing continuity in party history, Pitt has been placed as a leader of this party between North and Liverpool. Yet to his dying day Pitt seems to have thought of himself as a Whig; as leader of the government by virtue of the confidence which the King, Parliament, and the people had in his ability and character; and as the head of a cabinet and ministry composed of Whigs, Tories, King's Friends, and independents who had the ability to fill certain positions and who would work under him as a leader.

VII. The events of the years 1782 to 1784 did not mark a sharp break in English constitutional development, because the new ideas and constitutional practices which the Whigs had worked out before 1782 and attempted to put in operation in 1782 and 1783 were defeated by a combination of the forces which still believed in the principles of the Revolution Settlement and in most of the practices that had grown up during the eighteenth century. Thus to George III these years marked a narrow escape from going over the precipice; but the remaining years of his life represented a fairly smooth ride on the old familiar constitutional road.

VIII. If any year is highly significant in English constitutional development it is the year 1785; and that for negative and not positive reasons. Enough has been written in chapters iii and iv and in this chapter to show how remote the Whigs' chances of anything more than temporary success actually were. Pitt evidently felt before his defeats in 1785 that it was possible for him to accept the post of First Lord of the Treasury from the King and at the same time, because of his tremendous popularity both in and outside of Parliament, to put through measures contrary to the royal wishes. The precedent for such a policy was, obviously, the conduct of Chatham as virtual war dictator from 1757 to 1761. Both men, however, found, once the excitement of a crisis had passed, that the ability and character of a great individual were no match for established institutions and practices. Pitt, for reasons fully discussed in chapter iv, remained as First Lord of the Treasury after his disheartening defeats in 1785 and did not follow the tradition of his father, who resigned in 1761 when no longer permitted to have a free hand in the conduct of the war. Actually, then, Pitt joined with George III in preserving the status quo from 1785 to 1806, for his political philosophy held him loyal to the view that the King must be free to choose ministers as individuals, and that only when public interests were being sacrificed was their any justification for opposition to a ministry selected by the sovereign. It was on these grounds that Pitt justified his attacks on North in 1781 and 1782 and on Addington in 1803 and 1804; and in both instances he conscientiously maintained that the King must be free to select the successors of the two ministers.

IX. The constitutional struggle which culminated in the years 1782 to 1785 was a triangular affair. The participants were George III, who stood for the status quo; the Whigs, who wished to introduce cabinet government; and Pitt, who believed in an all-powerful minister responsible to King, Parliament, and people. A union of any two, with the exception of the King and the Whigs, would in all probability have insured victory. Had Pitt accepted the new Whig doctrine in 1783 or 1784, it is possible that George III might have been reduced to the position which his successors occupied after 1835, although the King would have succumbed only after a prolonged and bitter fight or as a result of insanity. Had the Whigs joined Pitt in either 1783 or 1784 and allowed him to keep the predominant position in the cabinet which he expected to hold, the combination, after a terrific struggle, might have forced George III into the background. Since it is inconceivable that the King and the Whigs would have joined against Pitt, the only combination which meant almost certain success for the two partners was of course that of George III and Pitt. Once the common enemy was vanquished, the division of spoils followed. It is the opinion of the present writer that George III rather than Pitt attained his objectives in 1785 and in the years following because even the great ability, popularity, and self-confidence of the latter were not sufficient to overcome the well-established constitutional practices during normal times and because the Crown still retained a more substantial and permanent place in Parliament, through control of placemen in both houses, than did the Minister with his handful of personal followers.

X. If George III and William Pitt were able to read what so many historians of the late nineteenth and early twentieth centuries have written about them it would be difficult to decide which of the two would be the more astonished: the King over the discovery that he had lost so much of his power in the twenty years after 1785; or the Minister at finding that he had been a great Tory prime minister and that he had played so important a part in the establishment of responsible-cabinet-party government based on the principles which Portland had enunciated to George III in 1783, and which the monarch had found so novel and so revolting.

APPENDIX

During the course of the narrative I have often referred to the commonly accepted or conventional interpretation of the political relationship between George III and William Pitt and that of English constitutional development from 1783 to 1806. These interpretations, instead of being quoted at length or even cited in footnotes, are grouped together here. I have divided the works selected for this purpose into three classes: first, eighteenth-century histories and monographs; second, biographies of the principal statesmen and political leaders in the reign of George III; and third, textbooks and general histories of England. I had expected to include quotations from many other important works than those given in the following pages, but I failed to discover in many of them appropriate passages dealing with the constitutional crisis of 1783–84 and its influence on the later careers of the King and Pitt. This, for example, is true of the two recent biographies of Dundas. I considered giving summaries rather than exact quotations, but I abandoned this plan because of the danger of misrepresenting the meaning of the author.

The disadvantage of any exact quotation standing alone is that it often leaves uncertain what subject is being discussed. In the hope that it may somewhat lessen this difficulty, each quotation given below is taken from a section of the particular work which deals with events from the overthrow of the Fox-North Coalition through the general election of 1784. Although the overwhelming majority of the works quoted give substantially the same point of view, I have also attempted to include the significant unorthodox interpretations.

I have found it necessary to eliminate many of the fifty quotations originally planned. I had not expected to encounter such difficulties in securing permission from publishers to quote extracts on the constitutional crisis of 1783–84. Thus in its present shorn form the Appendix is made up of quotations and of references. In the latter the quotation and the name of the publisher have been eliminated, leaving only the author, the title, and the page on which the passage in question is to be found. I cling to the hope that enough quotations remain to give the reader a clear idea of the orthodox and unorthodox interpretations of the crisis of 1783–84; and that the more skeptical readers may be willing to consult also the references after reading the quotations given.

I. EIGHTEENTH-CENTURY HISTORIES AND MONOGRAPHS

R. Coupland, *The American Revolution and the British Empire* (London: Longmans, Green and Company, 1930), p. 42.

"And though, again, George III presently found in Pitt at least a refuge from Fox, though he still asserted at times his royal will, ... none the less, after York Town, his 'system' lay on the scrap heap, and after 1784 it was a Prime Minister, with a steadily consolidating Cabinet, that ruled England."

A. M. Davies, *The Influence of George III on the Development of the Constitution* (London: Oxford University Press, 1921), pp. 44–45.

"The year 1785, when William Pitt came into office and established the Tory party in its long lease of power, which, except for two short intervals, was to last for nearly fifty years, ushered in a period of slow transition. The result of the long conflict with Whigs was a compromise. The party whose principles were most in accord with the royal wishes had obtained a crushing victory over their opponents, but on the other hand the king found himself in the hands of a masterful and strong-willed minister, who was a very different man from either of his predecessors—Bute and North—and who held the whip hand over the king, leaving him no alternative except the obnoxious Whigs."

William Edwards, *Crown, People and Parliament, 1760–1935* (Bristol: J. W. Arrowsmith, Ltd., 1937), p. 27.

"By 1783 it appeared as if the idea of ministerial responsibility had been replaced by that of the King's personal power. But Pitt refused to obey the King's orders, and maintained the right of the Prime Minister to pursue his own policy; he re-asserted the doctrine of ministerial responsibility and checked the real danger of autocratic government which had arisen. . . . . Pitt's resignation in 1801, when the King refused to agree to his scheme of Catholic Emancipation, was an assertion of the doctrine of ministerial responsibility; his subsequent undertaking not to revive the question was not an acknowledgement of the right of the King to direct policy, ..."

C. S. Emden, *The People and the Constitution* (Oxford: Clarendon Press, 1933), pp. 106–7.

"George III did not imagine that he could govern in permanent opposition to a parliamentary majority; but he did all he could to interfere with the development of the party system. The elder Pitt, without realizing that he was so doing, to some extent played into the King's hands by his refusal to countenance party connexions and by his preference of 'measures' to 'men' . . . . It was to a large extent due to the personal efforts and contrivances of George III that the Crown servants and adherents were sufficiently large in numbers in the House of Commons to assist him in turning a working majority in his favour. After some ignominious experiences of Whig domination, he succeeded, by skilful management and by the assistance of the younger Pitt, in freeing himself from the control of the Whig oligarchs and in gaining some measure of the independence for which he had striven."

J. A. Farrer, *The Monarchy in Politics* (London, 1917), pp. 58–62.

William Hunt, *The Political History of England from the Accession of George III to the Close of Pitt's First Administration* (London: Longmans, Green and Company, 1905), p. 229.

"The king was defeated. His system of personal government through ministers supported by his influence in parliament received its death-blow from the ill-success of the American war. Before long he adopted a better system; he found a prime-minister who could command the confidence of the nation, and he yielded himself, not always willingly, to his guidance."

W. E. H. Lecky, *A History of England in the Eighteenth Century* (New York: Longmans, Green and Company, 1918), V, 259–60.

"The spell which Pitt at this time threw over his countrymen continued unbroken to his death. It outlived years of discouragement and disaster, and it was scarcely weakened at a time when sagacious men had discovered that his powers as a legislator and administrator were by no means on a level with his almost unrivalled talent for managing a party, and for conducting a debate. The result of a struggle waged under these conditions could hardly be doubtful. . . . . Fox himself barely succeeded in retaining his seat for Westminster. The united Opposition was utterly shattered. The old lines of party division were, for a time at least, submerged or effaced, and Pitt met the Parliament of 1784 at the head of a majority which made him the most powerful minister ever known in the parliamentary history of England."

Lord Macaulay, in three separate passages (*Works,* IV, 516, 530, 563) states:

"In the midst of such triumphs Pitt completed his twenty-fifth year. He was now the greatest subject that England had seen during many generations. He domineered absolutely over the Cabinet, and was the favorite at once of the Sovereign, of the Parliament, and of the nation. His father had never been so powerful, nor Walpole, nor Marlborough . . . .

"From the day on which Pitt was placed at the head of affairs there was an end of secret influence. His haughty and aspiring spirit was not to be satisfied with the mere show of power. Any attempt to undermine him at Court, any mutinous movement among his followers in the House of Commons was certain to be at once put down. He had only to tender his resignation; and he could dictate his own terms. For he, and he alone, stood between the King and the Coalition. He was therefore little less than Mayor of the Palace . . . .

"The memory of Pitt has been assailed, times innumerable, often justly, often unjustly; but it has suffered much less from his assailants than from his eulogists . . . . This mythical Pitt, who resembles the genuine Pitt as little as the Charlemagne of Ariosto resembles the Charlemagne of Eginhard, has had his day."

Simon Maccoby, *Eighteenth Century England* (London: Longmans, Green and Company, 1931), p. 240.

"Pitt not merely founded the Tory Party of the nineteenth century, but restored to the Prime Ministership the prestige and authority which had been lacking since Walpole's day. For his supremacy in Parliament and the cabinet Pitt was very largely indebted to his own abilities and haughty and commanding temper. But his path was much lightened by the universal knowledge that the King placed in him an almost unqualified trust. George was well satisfied with the resounding defeat of Fox in 1784, and recognized that in Pitt he had, perhaps, the one man capable of keeping the Whigs indefinitely at bay. The royal influence was very freely placed at Pitt's disposal, especially in that most useful department, the creation of peerages . . . . Yet though the King's unwavering support was very necessary to Pitt, George felt instinctively that the proud son of Chatham required very different handling from the easy-going North."

T. E. May, *Constitutional History of England* (London: Longmans, Green and Company, 1891), I, 87–88.

"He had only one other minister of the same lofty pretensions,— Lord Chatham; and now, while trusting that statesman's son,—sharing his councils, and approving his policy,—he yielded to his superior intellect."

R. M. Rayner, *England in Modern Times* (London: Longmans, Green and Company, 1929), p. 125.

"The King's experiment in benevolent despotism had broken down; but Whiggery had failed to re-establish itself in its place. Parliament was never again to be dominated by 'the King's Friends' but neither was it to be dominated by the Whig Aristocracy. The net result was a compromise. Pitt was dependent on the support of the King, who still controlled something like a hundred seats; but the King was even more dependent on Pitt, as his only resource against the return to power of the detested Whigs."

C. G. Robertson, *England under the Hanoverians* (London, 1923), p. 305.

G. R. S. Taylor, *A Modern History of England* (London, 1932), pp. 216–17.

A. S. Turberville, *The House of Lords in the XVIIIth Century* (Oxford: Clarendon Press, 1927), p. 496.

"The King apparently gained a great personal victory, as signal as any he had ever achieved. But its fruits were gathered in by William Pitt, and the career of that amazing statesman meant the strengthening and further development of the Cabinet system, which George III had tried to wreck. There opens a new area in our constitutional history."

Maurice Woods, *A History of the Tory Party* (London: Hodder & Stoughton, Ltd., 1924), p. 306.

"George III was an obstinate man, but he was no fool. Looking backwards he must have perceived that the quarrel with Chatham was the beginning of all the evils which had overtaken him, and that the popular King and the popular Minister might have ridden down all opposition. Now in his middle age a second chance was given him in the form of a son sprung from the loins of the genius he had despised. The immense influence of the popular kingship could once more be his. And, like a sensible man, though no doubt with some inward groans, he resigned himself to an alliance on equal terms· with the man who could manage the Commons and the country while burning on the altar of royalty all the incense which it could claim as its due and deferring to the monarch on many vital points of policy. The Patriot King became in 1784, as he ought to have become in 1760, the adjunct and intimate ally of the popular Premier. Nor could the converted monarch have had any illusions as to the extent to which he could control his new Prime Minister . . . . From 1784 onward the Patriot King falls into the line of advance which marks the development of the British Constitution."

E. M. Wrong, *History of England, 1688–1815* (New York: Henry Holt and Company, 1927), p. 189.

"Had the political situation in the next years resembled that of 1765, George might have found Pitt too strong for his liking, and have worked for his downfall. Pitt kept off the King's strongest prejudices though he was never a royal puppet, but his chief value in the royal eyes was that he was the only man who could stand against Fox, whom George loathed both for his qualities and his defects. The Hanoverian family tradition had revived: there was again an heir at feud with his father, and round him clustered a shadow Whig

Government . . . . Pitt was from the beginning supreme in the Government, though not for some years in Parliament."

II. BIOGRAPHIES

A. GEORGE III

J. D. G. Davies, *George the Third* (London, 1936), pp. 218–19.

Lewis Melville, *Farmer George* (London: Pitman & Sons, Ltd., 1907), II, 258.

"During the seventeen years that the younger Pitt ruled, however, the power fell from George III, who little by little was reluctantly compelled to abandon the system of personal government for which he had fought so long and so strenuously."

C. E. Vulliamy, *Royal George* (London, 1937), pp. 189–90.

B. WILLIAM PITT

E. Keble Chatterton, *England's Greatest Statesman: A Life of William Pitt* (Indianapolis: The Bobbs-Merrill Company, 1930), pp. 154–58. Used by special permission of the publishers.

"Some historians have emphasized that in dissolving Parliament George III was taking a tremendous risk, that the country might have sent Fox and his friends back with huge majorities. I submit that the exact opposite is the true case. It was because the astute, cold and cautious calculator, Pitt, with the mathematical Pretyman by his side, so accurately estimated the position that there could be little chance of defeat . . . . The General Election of 1784, with its sweeping results in favor of Pitt's party, not merely brought to a definite end that long Whig rule, which had been such a characteristic of the Georges, but reflected the new enlightenment."

Sir Charles Petrie, *William Pitt* (London: Duckworth, 1935), p. 37.

"The King had managed to break the hegemony of the Revolution families which had existed during the reigns of his grand-father and great-grandfather, but he had failed to put anything durable in its place . . . . The relative positions of the Crown, Parliament, and the electorate had once more become unsettled, and Pitt had to steer the Ship of State through a largely uncharted sea."

J. Holland Rose, *Life of William Pitt* (London: G. Bell & Sons, Ltd., 1923), I, 150.

"Finally we must remember that Pitt did not take office as a 'King's Friend.' . . . . If in July Pitt refused to bow before the royal behests, surely he might expect to dictate his own terms in December. The King's difficulty was Pitt's opportunity; and, as events were to prove, George III had, at least for a time, to give up his attempts at personal rule and to acquiesce in the rule of a Prime Minister who gave unity and strength to the administration. While freeing himself from the loathed yoke of the Whig oligarchy the King unwittingly accepted the control of a man who personified the nation."

J. Holland Rose, *A Short Life of William Pitt* (London: G. Bell & Sons, Ltd., 1925), p. 28.

"As to the charge that Pitt now deserted the people's cause for that of the King, the ensuing narrative will supply a sufficient answer. But we may hazard the conjecture that George III, after the severe lesson he had lately received, was not likely to recur to 'Asiatic' methods of rule. England, too, had had her lesson as to tricky Coalitions and cried out for a return to straightforward methods. At the crisis of December 1783 Pitt neither deserted the people nor went over to the King: he reconciled them."

Lord Rosebery, *Pitt* (London, 1923), pp. 61–62.

C. CHARLES JAMES FOX

Christopher Hobhouse, *Fox* (Boston: Houghton Mifflin Company, 1935), pp. 189–90.

"Pitt was born to show Fox up. They represented the Idle and the Industrious Apprentice, the eighteenth century *versus* the nineteenth. The country was as tired of Brooks's as it was of Buckingham House: Pitt was the negation of both. He was the symbol of a new era in politics. The old aristocratic parties, the old family cabinets, the pensions, and sinecures, the nepotism, the log-rolling, the wire-pulling, were to be swept away. The Whigs were every bit as effete as the Tories; the country had no more use for a Portland than for a North."

Edward Lascelles, *The Life of Charles James Fox* (London: Oxford University Press, 1936), p. 157.

"When the cheering for Westminster died down, the Whigs had leisure to reflect upon the election and upon their immediate future . . . . Beginning with a majority, which might have insured a long life of security, they had split almost at once on the death of Rockingham, and now, after the adventures of Coalition and India Bill, their disaster and the King's triumph were complete."

Lord John Russell, *The Life and Times of Charles James Fox* (London, 1859), II, 97.

"While such was the position and such the genius of Fox, his adversary derived many advantages from the circumstances which attended his dawning power. He was young, and could neither be reproached by the enemies of the American War nor hated by its abettors, for he had neither caused its disasters nor opposed the King. If he appeared more arrogant than became his years, and more confident than his want of eminent colleagues seemed to justify, such haughtiness might be excused in a son of Chatham. Again, while he enjoyed the support, and was entitled to the gratitude of the Court, he could not be considered, like Lord Bute, as a mere reflexion of royal favour, or, like Lord North, as a Minister defending a policy which his judgment did not approve."

Lord John Russell, *The Life and Times of Charles James Fox* (London, 1866), III, 356–57.

"Pitt, as Lord Harrowby often assured me, professed Whig principles. This I can well believe . . . . but all these enlightened views were blasted; all progress arrested; the slave trade continued to flourish, Parliamentary Reform was rejected, religious disabilities were maintained, because the wise and liberal views of the Minister were thwarted by the Sovereign whom he obeyed but too implicitly, and by the Tory party which professed to follow him, but in reality forced him into the path which Lord North had trod before him.

"The unhappy years 1783 and 1784 destroyed at the same time Fox's prospects of office and Pitt's power of doing good. Shorn of his beams, Pitt's Tory adherents, as Mr. Canning truly said, worshipped him only in his eclipse."

D. EDMUND BURKE

R. H. Murray, *Edmund Burke* (Oxford: Clarendon Press, 1931), p. 310.

"Backed by the Court and a moderate Tory following, supported by the people at large, and assailed only by a baffled and distrusted Opposition, Pitt began his celebrated administration."

E. RICHARD BRINSLEY SHERIDAN

Thomas Moore, *Memoirs of the Life of Richard Brinsley Sheridan* (London, 1826), I, 395.

"Dismissed insultingly by the King on one side, they had to encounter the indignation of the people on the other; and, though the House of Commons, with a fidelity to fallen ministers sufficiently rare, stood by them for a time in a desperate struggle with their successors, the voice of the Royal Prerogative, like the horn of Astolpho, soon scattered the whole body in consternation among their constituents . . . . and the result was a complete and long-enjoyed triumph to the Throne and Mr. Pitt."

Walter Sichel, *Sheridan* (London, 1909), II, 71.

III. TEXTBOOKS AND GENERAL WORKS ON
ENGLISH HISTORY

G. B. Adams, *Constitutional History of England* (New York: Henry Holt and Company, 1934), pp. 410–11.

"Pitt was a tory, but he was a tory of the future rather than of the past. As the tories of 1760 had without qualification accepted the results of the revolution of 1688, so now Pitt, and the party which he may be said to have recreated, accepted as final the whig work of cabinet making and the position into which it had brought the king . . . . In other words, we may date from the formation of Pitt's ministry, at the end of 1783, the full establishment of the compromise of 1660: a king in the nominal possession of almost all power, a cabinet in the real exercise of the king's powers, and a parliament with the power of final decision in every question, because it was the voice of the people in whom the ultimate sovereignty resided."

A. L. Cross, *A Shorter History of England and Greater Britain* (New York, 1929), pp. 574–75.

F. C. Dietz, *A Political and Social History of England* (New York, 1937), pp. 462–63.

S. R. Gardiner, *A Students' History of England* (New York: Longmans, Green and Company, 1900), p. 808.

"George III, delighted as he was with Pitt's victory, found it impossible to make a tool of him, as he had made a tool of Lord North. Pitt owed his success even more to the nation than to the king, and, with the nation and the House of Commons at his back, he was resolved to have his own way."

J. R. Green, *A Short History of the English People* (London, 1894), IV, 1726.

W. P. Hall and R. G. Albion, *A History of England and the British Empire* (Boston: Ginn and Company, 1937), pp. 542–43.

"Then, in spite of the majority in the Commons, George took the unconstitutional step of dismissing the ministry and asked young William Pitt to be prime minister. Probably the king expected to find in the twenty-four-year-old Pitt another docile tool like North; instead he found his master . . . . With the backing of the king, of the Lords, of the Commons, and of the people, Pitt was now in a more powerful position than any prime minister had yet enjoyed."

E. M. Hulme, *A History of the British People* (New York: D. Appleton-Century Company, 1924), p. 425.

"By temperament and by affiliation the new leader was a Tory; and he owed his position, in the first place, to the favor of the King, who had called him to office in the face of a hostile majority of the

Commons. The latter fact, however, had a favorable aspect. It made it easier for the stubborn King to gradually give up in the main his personal government without surrendering it."

L. M. Larson, *A History of England and the British Commonwealth* (New York: Henry Holt and Company, 1932), pp. 544–45.

"In the elections that followed the ministerial party won an overwhelming victory: 160 members of the 'infamous coalition' lost their seats. The young prime minister could now feel sure that he was the choice of the nation as well as of the king, and from that day he was undisputed master of the English government . . . . Though he did not allow the king to dictate the policies of the Cabinet, he showed all due deference to his Majesty and carried out the royal desires as far as he consistently could . . . . In his earlier years he was a Whig and professed the Whig doctrine that the king's ministers should be held responsible to the House of Commons; but the circumstances of his appointment, his belief in a strong central administration, and his conflict with the Whig leaders, notably with Fox and Burke, gradually forced him to take Tory ground."

W. E. Lunt, *History of England* (New York: Harper and Brothers, 1928), p. 612. Reprinted by permission of the publishers.

"The election, held in 1784, returned Pitt with a good working majority. It seemed to be another victory for the king, but it turned out otherwise. The new minister was personally more congenial to the king than the defeated leaders, and his opinions often coincided with those of the king, but when they differed, the minister had his way. Pitt was the master. The attempt of the king to rule was finally defeated. Henceforth the cabinet system was an established part of the British constitution."

F. G. Marcham, *A History of England* (New York, 1937), p. 673.

Ramsay Muir, *A Short History of the British Commonwealth* (New York, 1923), II, 108.

Howard Robinson, *A History of Great Britain* (Boston: Houghton Mifflin Company, 1927), pp. 637–38.

"Henceforth for seventeen years Pitt's ministry was unbroken . . . . During his long rule the foundation was laid for the revived Tory party by the creation of a new set of Tory families to offset the older Whig aristocracy. Like his father he possessed supreme self-confidence and a boundless ambition to win and keep the reins of power. This explains his retention of office when a favorite measure was occasionally defeated, and also his willingness to drop plans that proved unpopular. Yet on the whole he was fairly, if not insistently, liberal during the decade of peace, even if a King's man."

D. C. Somervell, *A History for British People* (London: G. Bell & Sons, Ltd., 1929), p. 611.

"With his accession to power it may be said that George III abandoned his attempt to restore royal power. He may have hoped that Pitt, being young, would prove docile. If so, he was disappointed."

T. P. Taswell-Langmead, *English Constitutional History* (Boston: Houghton Mifflin Company, 1929), p. 668.

"Parliament was now dissolved; and a general election gave to Pitt an overwhelming majority, which maintained him in power for seventeen years. The triumph of the king and the minister was complete; the ascendency of the crown was established, and continued, for nearly fifty years, to prevail over every other power in the state. But the king's will was no longer supreme, as it had been during the administration of Lord North."

T. F. Tout, *An Advanced History of Great Britain* (London: Longmans, Green and Company, 1923), p. 589.

"The king had learnt from the younger Pitt what he would never learn from Chatham. He had at least discovered that the right way to win power was not to strive to fight his people as well as the Whigs, but to put himself at the head of his people against the greedy faction that had so long claimed the sole right of governing the country."

G. M. Trevelyan, *History of England* (London: Longmans, Green and Company, 1937), p. 557.

"On the fall of the Fox-North Ministry, which the King actively helped to bring about, young Pitt took the reins of power as the head of the revived Tory party. He had strongly opposed the King's personal government and American policy, but he was ready to make an alliance on his own terms with the Crown. George, since he could no longer rule in person, greatly preferred Pitt to the Whigs."

J. A. Williamson, *The Evolution of England* (Oxford: Clarendon Press, 1931), pp. 328-29.

"The younger William Pitt is a figure who defies classification. At a time when party labels were growing more meaningless than ever, it was impossible to attach one to him. He would have described himself as a Whig, but that was only because he was not a Tory of the King's Friends type . . . . Pitt, although he had no notion of being a puppet-minister like North, realized in his common-sense way that the King was king and that it was the duty of his statesmen to get on with him, for only so could the course of government run smooth . . . . In 1784, with the boroughmongers won over, he dissolved. The boroughs gave him his majority, the voteless public ratified it with their shouts, the King was happy, and William Pitt the Second entered upon an unbroken reign of eighteen years."

E. Wingfield-Stratford, *The History of British Civilization* (New York: Harcourt, Brace and Company, 1933), p. 782.

"Then the King brought off this second master stroke in the game. He called to the premiership a youth of twenty-five, William Pitt, who, with marvellous self-restraint, had refused the honour a few months before as premature. Obstinate George had at last learnt the wisdom of employing the ablest man among his subjects, who, at the same time, was loyal to himself . . . . So the King had dished his Whigs after all, and his young minister was able to get on with the business of pulling the nation out of the mire."

INDEX